2026 새 교과서에 맞춘 16차 개정판

중학영문법 3800제 2학년

발행 16차 개정판 3쇄(2026년 1월 31일)

교재 개발 책임 서은숙 **교재 개발 진행** 박상우, 이혜빈, 최민정, 최은조, 김현수, 유지원, 도예원, 이윤정

문제편 집필 김석화(수원 수원여고) 선생님, 소피아(김규은 경기 분당) 선생님, 남현정, 서연서, 이윤정, 이옥현, 양진희, 김미경(서울 서초) 선생님, 하은옥, 홍성경, 고미라(서울 상경중) 선생님, 김현, 박혜미, 김다영, 박상우

교재 검토 조현정(서울 중계) 선생님, 김경미(강남 대치) 선생님, 윤미선(서울 가양) 선생님, 문명기(서울 강동) 선생님, 김석화(수원 수원여고) 선생님, 김미경(서울 동작) 선생님, 최민제(서울 강동) 선생님, 이은혜(경기 일산) 선생님, 소피아(김규은 경기 분당) 선생님, 양원석(서울 서초) 선생님

교정 김경미(강남 대치) 선생님, 김현수, 최은조, 박상우, 신소미, 이혜빈, 최민정, 신준기, 정은주, 김다영, 유지원, 홍지민, 신진실, 도예원, 조수성, 서연서, 이윤정, 윤수경, 양진희, 성은혜, 홍성경, 오정훈, 하은옥, 이은영

감수 김진희(서울 목동) 선생님, 김정민(서울 대치) 선생님, 고민정(경기 하남) 선생님, 이태규(서울 대치) 선생님

영문 감수 Kathryn O' Handley   **디자인** 김연실, 양은선   **삽화** 박주혜, 이혜승, 정제욱, 백승헌, 이유진, 이순웅, 정재환

단어장 녹음 손정은, Janet Lee, 최석환   **녹음 편집** 와이알 미디어   **인디자인 편집** 박경아

제작 이주영   **발행인** 문숙영   **발행처** 마더텅(Mother Tongue Co., Ltd.)

주소 서울시 금천구 가마산로 96, 708호(가산동, 대륭테크노타운 8차)

팩스 02-3142-9126 **홈페이지** www.toptutor.co.kr **등록번호** 제 1-2423호

마더텅 교재를 풀면서 궁금한 점이 생기셨나요?

교재 관련 내용 문의나 오류신고 사항이 있으면 아래 문의처로 보내 주세요!
문의하신 내용에 대해 성심성의껏 답변해 드리겠습니다.
또한 교재의 **내용 오류** 또는 **오·탈자, 그 외 수정이 필요한 사항**에 대해
가장 먼저 신고해 주신 분께는 감사의 마음을 담아
네이버페이 포인트 1천 원 을 보내 드립니다!

* 기한: 2026년 10월 31일
* 오류신고 이벤트는 당사 사정에 따라 조기 종료될 수 있습니다.
* 홈페이지에 게시된 정오표 기준으로 최초 신고된 오류에 한하여 상품권을 보내 드립니다.

● 카카오톡 mothertongue   @ 이메일 mothert1004@toptutor.co.kr
🏠 홈페이지 www.toptutor.co.kr   📋 교재Q&A게시판
🎧 고객센터 전화 1661-1064(07:00~22:00)   ✉ 문자 010-6640-1064(문자수신전용)

차례

수동태의 형태

형태 : 주어 + be동사 (not) + 과거분사 + by + 목적격.

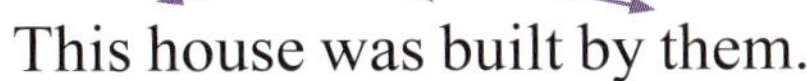

They built this house.

This house was built by them.

	능동태	수동태
현재	Minho plants trees.	Trees **are planted** by Minho.
과거	Minho planted trees.	Trees **were planted** by Minho.
미래	Minho will plant trees.	Trees **will be planted** by Minho.
현재완료	Minho has planted trees.	Trees **have been planted** by Minho.

외워야 할 수동태 표현

be made of	～로 만들어지다	be filled with	～로 가득 차 있다
be interested in	～에 흥미가 있다	be covered with	～로 덮여 있다
be surprised at	～에 놀라다	be known to	～에게 알려져 있다
be pleased with[about]	～에 기뻐하다	be satisfied with	～에 만족하다
be excited about	～에 흥분해 있다	be worried about	～에 대해 걱정하다

명사의 종류

셀 수 있는 명사	a(n)을 붙이거나 복수형으로 쓸 수 있고, many, (a) few, some, any, no처럼 수를 나타내는 형용사와 함께 쓸 수 있다.	
	보통명사	bag, student, book, pencil, computer, tree, dish, animal
	집합명사	class, family, team, audience
셀 수 없는 명사	a(n)을 붙이거나 복수형으로 쓸 수 없고, 물질명사와 추상명사는 much, (a) little, some, any, no처럼 양을 나타내는 형용사와 함께 쓸 수 있다.	
	고유명사	David, Insuk, Korea, Chicago, Monday, Christmas
	물질명사	water, salt, money, juice, air, milk, ice, bread, gold, sugar
	추상명사	love, peace, knowledge, beauty, health, honesty, information, news, happiness, hope, kindness, advice

부정사/동명사를 목적어로 가지는 동사 CHAPTER 7 **PSS 1-2 &** CHAPTER 8 **PSS 2-1~2-3**

1. to부정사를 목적어로 가지는 동사

want, wish, decide, promise, would like, would love,
plan, expect, refuse, hope, need, learn, agree

2. 동명사를 목적어로 가지는 동사

enjoy, mind, finish, stop, give up, practice, put off,
deny, imagine, quit, suggest, dislike

3. 둘 다를 목적어로 가지는 동사

like, love, hate, begin, start, continue, intend, prefer

4. 둘 다를 목적어로 가지지만 뜻이 달라지는 동사

try, remember, forget
- I **tried calling** Bob yesterday. 나는 어제 Bob에게 **전화를 해봤다.**
- I **tried to call** Bob yesterday.   나는 어제 Bob에게 **전화하려고 노력했다.**

외워야 할 주요 접속사, 접속부사 CHAPTER 15

접속사	뜻	예문
and (명령문 + and)	~와, 그리고, ~하고 나서 (~해라, 그러면)	• I went back home **and** (I) studied for the exam. • Wake up now, **and** you'll catch the bus.
or (명령문 + or)	또는, 아니면 (~해라, 그렇지 않으면)	• Have you been to New York **or** Chicago? • Wake up now, **or** you'll miss the bus.
both A and B	A와 B 둘 다	• **Both** Jim **and** Sue like mathematics the best.
not only A but also B	A뿐만 아니라 B도	• Jim is good at **not only** singing **but also** studying.
either A or B	A와 B 중 어느 하나	• **Either** Jim **or** Sue likes mathematics the best.
neither A nor B	A도 B도 ~아닌	• **Neither** Jim **nor** Sue likes mathematics the best.
because	~ 때문에	• Linda often goes to concerts **because** she likes music.
so	그래서	• Linda likes music, **so** she often goes to concerts.

접속사	뜻	예문
if	~한다면	• **If** you read the book, you can do your homework.
so that ~	~하기 위해서, ~할 수 있도록	• I studied hard **so that** I could enter the university.
even though [although/ though]	비록 ~일지라도, 비록 ~에도 불구하고	• **Even though[Although, Though]** it was raining, I went shopping.
시간을 나타내는 접속사		
when	~할 때	• **When** I was a child, my family lived in Busan.
as	~하고 있을 때, ~하면서	• Ann sometimes listens to music **as** she studies.
before	~하기 전에	• I take off my shoes **before** I enter a room.
after	~한 후에	• Let's go for a walk **after** you finish your dinner.
until	~할 때까지	• My sister didn't go to bed **until** I got home.
while	~하는 동안	• **While** I was waiting for the bus, I read a book.
as soon as	~하자마자	• He got a job **as soon as** he finished school.
접속부사		
for example	예를 들면	• Mina does a lot of things for her family. **For example**, she helps her mom cook.
however	그러나	• Everyone agreed with Mark. **However**, I had a different idea.
therefore	그러므로	• I have an English quiz tomorrow, but I haven't studied. **Therefore**, I have to study hard tonight.
in addition [besides]	게다가	• I like the restaurant. The food is very delicious. **In addition[Besides]**, the service is very good.
finally	결국	• Sena was interested in law. **Finally**, she became a lawyer.

불규칙 변화 동사의 과거형 CHAPTER 2 **PSS 2-4**

원형	과거형	과거분사형	원형	과거형	과거분사형
beat	beat	beaten	ring	rang	rung
cut	cut	cut	rise	rose	risen
draw	drew	drawn	run	ran	run
dream	dreamed /dreamt	dreamed /dreamt	see	saw	seen
fly	flew	flown	sink	sank	sunk
hide	hid	hidden	spread	spread	spread
lay	laid	laid	stand	stood	stood
lead	led	led	steal	stole	stolen
lie (눕다/놓여 있다)	lay	lain	sweep	swept	swept
mean	meant	meant	teach	taught	taught
ride	rode	ridden	think	thought	thought

현재완료의 형태와 용법 CHAPTER 2 **PSS 5-1, 2**

형태 : 주어 + **have / has (not)** + 과거분사
예문 : I have lost my puppy.

용법	예문
완료	I **have just planted** 10 trees. 나는 방금 열 그루의 나무를 심었다.
경험	**Have** you **ever tried** potato chips? 감자칩을 먹어본 적이 있니?
결과	She **has lost** her bag. 그녀는 가방을 잃어버렸다.
계속	I **have lived** here **since** March. 나는 3월부터 여기에서 살았다.

중학영문법 3800제 열공 학습진도표 2학년 

CHAPTER 1 문장의 기초

PSS		체크	학습날짜
PSS 1	1-1	☐	/
	1-2	☐	/
	1-3	☐	/
	1-4	☐	/
	1-5	☐	/
	1-6	☐	/
	1-7	☐	/
	1-8	☐	/
PSS 2	2-1	☐	/
	2-2	☐	/
	2-3	☐	/
	2-4	☐	/
	2-5	☐	/
	2-6	☐	/
중간·기말 대비		☐	/

CHAPTER 2 시제

PSS		체크	학습날짜
PSS 1	1-1	☐	/
	1-2	☐	/
	1-3	☐	/
	1-4	☐	/
PSS 2	2-1	☐	/
	2-2	☐	/
	2-3	☐	/
	2-4	☐	/
PSS 3		☐	/
PSS 4	4-1	☐	/
	4-2	☐	/
PSS 5	5-1	☐	/
	5-2	☐	/
	5-3	☐	/
	5-4	☐	/
	5-5	☐	/
중간·기말 대비		☐	/

CHAPTER 3 조동사

PSS		체크	학습날짜
PSS 1		☐	/
PSS 2		☐	/
PSS 3		☐	/
PSS 4	4-1	☐	/
	4-2	☐	/
	4-3	☐	/
	4-4	☐	/
	4-5	☐	/
	4-6	☐	/
	4-7	☐	/
	4-8	☐	/
	4-9	☐	/
중간·기말 대비		☐	/

CHAPTER 4 수동태

PSS		체크	학습날짜
PSS 1		☐	/
PSS 2		☐	/
PSS 3		☐	/
PSS 4		☐	/
PSS 5		☐	/
PSS 6		☐	/
PSS 7		☐	/
중간·기말 대비		☐	/

CHAPTER 5 명사와 관사

PSS		체크	학습날짜
PSS 1	1-1	☐	/
	1-2	☐	/
	1-3	☐	/
PSS 2	2-1	☐	/
	2-2	☐	/
	2-3	☐	/
	2-4	☐	/
	2-5	☐	/
	2-6	☐	/
	2-7	☐	/
PSS 3	3-1	☐	/
	3-2	☐	/
PSS 4	4-1	☐	/
	4-2	☐	/
	4-3	☐	/
PSS 5		☐	/
중간·기말 대비		☐	/

CHAPTER 6 대명사

PSS		체크	학습날짜
PSS 1	1-1	☐	/
	1-2	☐	/
	1-3	☐	/
PSS 2	2-1	☐	/
	2-2	☐	/
	2-3	☐	/
PSS 3	3-1	☐	/
	3-2	☐	/
PSS 4	4-1	☐	/
	4-2	☐	/
	4-3	☐	/
	4-4	☐	/
	4-5	☐	/
	4-6	☐	/
PSS 5	5-1	☐	/
	5-2	☐	/
중간·기말 대비		☐	/

CHAPTER 7 부정사

PSS		체크	학습날짜
PSS 1	1-1	☐	/
	1-2	☐	/
	1-3	☐	/
	1-4	☐	/
PSS 2		☐	/
PSS 3	3-1	☐	/
	3-2	☐	/
PSS 4		☐	/
PSS 5		☐	/
PSS 6		☐	/
중간·기말 대비		☐	/

CHAPTER 8 동명사

PSS		체크	학습날짜
PSS 1		☐	/
PSS 2	2-1	☐	/
	2-2	☐	/
	2-3	☐	/
PSS 3		☐	/
PSS 4		☐	/
중간·기말 대비		☐	/

CHAPTER 9 분사

PSS		체크	학습날짜
PSS 1		☐	/
PSS 2	2-1	☐	/
	2-2	☐	/
PSS 3		☐	/
PSS 4		☐	/
PSS 5	5-1	☐	/
	5-2	☐	/
중간·기말 대비		☐	/

CHAPTER 10 형용사

PSS		체크	학습날짜
PSS 1		☐	/
PSS 2		☐	/
PSS 3		☐	/
PSS 4		☐	/
PSS 5	5-1	☐	/
	5-2	☐	/
	5-3	☐	/
	5-4	☐	/
PSS 6	6-1	☐	/
	6-2	☐	/
	6-3	☐	/
중간·기말 대비		☐	/

CHAPTER 11 부사

PSS		체크	학습날짜
PSS 1	1-1	☐	/
	1-2	☐	/
	1-3	☐	/
	1-4	☐	/
PSS 2	2-1	☐	/
	2-2	☐	/
	2-3	☐	/
	2-4	☐	/
	2-5	☐	/
	2-6	☐	/
	2-7	☐	/
중간·기말 대비		☐	/

CHAPTER 12 가정법

PSS		체크	학습날짜
PSS 1		☐	/
PSS 2	2-1	☐	/
	2-2	☐	/
	2-3	☐	/
PSS 3	3-1	☐	/
	3-2	☐	/
	3-3	☐	/
중간·기말 대비		☐	/

CHAPTER 15 접속사

PSS	체크	학습날짜
PSS 1	☐	/
PSS 2	☐	/
PSS 3	☐	/
PSS 4	☐	/
PSS 5	☐	/
PSS 6	☐	/
PSS 7	☐	/
PSS 8	☐	/
PSS 9	☐	/
PSS 10	☐	/
중간·기말 대비	☐	/

CHAPTER 13 비교구문

PSS		체크	학습날짜
PSS 1	1-1	☐	/
	1-2	☐	/
	1-3	☐	/
	1-4	☐	/
PSS 2	2-1	☐	/
	2-2	☐	/
PSS 3	3-1	☐	/
	3-2	☐	/
	3-3	☐	/
	3-4	☐	/
	3-5	☐	/
	3-6	☐	/
PSS 4	4-1	☐	/
	4-2	☐	/
	4-3	☐	/
중간·기말 대비		☐	/

CHAPTER 14 관계사

PSS		체크	학습날짜
PSS 1	1-1	☐	/
	1-2	☐	/
	1-3	☐	/
	1-4	☐	/
	1-5	☐	/
	1-6	☐	/
PSS 2	2-1	☐	/
	2-2	☐	/
중간·기말 대비		☐	/

CHAPTER 16 전치사

PSS		체크	학습날짜
PSS 1	1-1	☐	/
	1-2	☐	/
	1-3	☐	/
	1-4	☐	/
	1-5	☐	/
	1-6	☐	/
PSS 2	2-1	☐	/
	2-2	☐	/
	2-3	☐	/
	2-4	☐	/
	2-5	☐	/
	2-6	☐	/
	2-7	☐	/
	2-8	☐	/
PSS 3	3-1	☐	/
	3-2	☐	/
	3-3	☐	/
	3-4	☐	/
중간·기말 대비		☐	/

CHAPTER 17 일치·도치·화법&속담

PSS		체크	학습날짜
PSS 1	1-1	☐	/
	1-2	☐	/
PSS 2		☐	/
PSS 3		☐	/
PSS 4		☐	/
PSS 5		☐	/
PSS 6		☐	/
중간·기말 대비		☐	/

PROBLEM SOLVING SKILL

CHAPTER 1
문장의 기초

PSS 1 의문문과 감탄문

PSS 1-1 Yes/No 의문문

Be동사가 있는 의문문	Be동사+주어 ~?
일반동사가 있는 의문문	Do[Does / Did] +주어+동사원형 ~?
조동사가 있는 의문문	조동사+주어+동사원형 ~?

1. 의문사로 시작하지 않는 의문문은 Yes나 No로 대답한다.

   Are you a student? 너는 학생이니?
   – **Yes**, I am. (= Yes, I am a student.) 네, 그렇습니다.
   – **No**, I'm not. (= No, I'm not a student.) 아니오, 그렇지 않습니다.

   Did they finish their homework? 그들은 숙제를 끝냈니?
   – **Yes**, they did. (= Yes, they finished their homework.) 네, 끝냈습니다.
   – **No**, they didn't. (= No, they didn't finish their homework.) 아니오, 끝내지 않았습니다.

   Will you come to my house? 너 우리집에 올래?
   – **Yes**, I will. (= Yes, I'll come to your house.) 네, 가겠습니다.
   – **No**, I won't. (= No, I won't come to your house.) 아니오, 가지 않겠습니다.

2. 부정어로 시작하는 의문문에 대한 대답은 질문과 상관없이 대답의 내용이 긍정이면 Yes,
   부정이면 No로 답한다. 단, 우리말 해석은 반대로 한다.

   Isn't she kind? 그녀는 친절하지 않니?
   – **Yes**, she is. (= Yes, she is kind.) 아니오, 친절합니다.
   – **No**, she isn't. (= No, she isn't kind.) 네, 친절하지 않습니다.

   Didn't you meet Mr. Jones? 너는 Jones 씨를 만나지 않았니?
   – **Yes**, I did. (= Yes, I met him.) 아니오, 만났습니다.
   – **No**, I didn't. (= No, I didn't meet him.) 네, 만나지 않았습니다.

   Can't you play soccer? 넌 축구를 할 수 없니?
   – **Yes**, I can. (= Yes, I can play soccer.) 아니오, 할 수 있습니다.
   – **No**, I can't. (= No, I can't play soccer.) 네, 못합니다.

PRACTICE 1

〈보기〉와 같이 주어진 문장을 의문문으로 바꾸어 쓰세요.

> 보 기 Jack has a nice car.
> ➡ _Does Jack have a nice car?_

1 She can get there on time.
➡ _______________________

2 Those gloves aren't yours.
➡ _______________________

3 He doesn't go to church on Sundays.
➡ _______________________

4 Your mom is angry at you.
➡ _______________________

5 David was drawing a picture.
➡ _______________________

6 This can be true.
➡ _______________________

7 Your classmates study hard.

➡ _______________________

8 Your brother didn't win the race.

➡ _______________________

9 The bus will arrive at 8 p.m.
➡ _______________________

10 The dog likes to play outside.
➡ _______________________

PRACTICE 2

〈보기〉와 같이 주어진 질문에 대한 알맞은 대답을 쓰세요.

> 보 기 You don't have a sister.
> A: Do you have a sister?
> B: _No, I don't._

1 Ted likes swimming in summer.
A: Does Ted like swimming in summer?
B: _______________________

2 They don't have a small car.
A: Don't they have a small car?
B: _______________________

3 You felt cold outside.
A: Didn't you feel cold outside?
B: _______________________

4 He wasn't playing tennis at 5.
A: Was he playing tennis at 5?
B: _______________________

5 You were hungry during the meeting.
A: Weren't you hungry during the meeting?
B: _______________________

6 Cats can see well even in dark places.
A: Can cats see well even in dark places?
B: _______________________

7 He studies hard for the exam.
A: Doesn't he study hard for the exam?
B: _______________________

8 Linda isn't good at sports.
A: Isn't Linda good at sports?
B: _______________________

의문사로 시작하는 의문문은 Yes나 No로 대답하지 않는다.

Who is your English teacher? — **Mr. Kim.**

네 영어 선생님은 누구시니? 김 선생님이셔.

When did she arrive? — **At 9 o'clock.**

그녀는 언제 도착했니? 9시에.

Where does he live? — **He lives in Seoul.**

그는 어디에 사니? 그는 서울에 살아.

What are you watching? — **I'm watching the news.**

넌 무엇을 보고 있니? 난 뉴스를 보고 있어.

How was school today? — **It was good.**

오늘 학교는 어땠니? 좋았어.

Why are you running? — **I'm running because I need to exercise.**

넌 왜 뛰고 있니? 운동을 할 필요가 있기 때문에 나는 뛰고 있어.

When can we meet again? — **Maybe next Tuesday.**

우리 언제 다시 만날 수 있을까? 아마도 다음 주 화요일쯤.

정답 p.2

PRACTICE 3

우리말과 일치하도록 괄호 안에 주어진 말을 바르게 배열하세요.

1 식당에서 누구를 만났니?

→ ____ (you, did, meet, who, at the restaurant)

2 Kelly는 오늘 왜 그렇게 바쁘니?

➡ ______________________________________ (Kelly, so busy, is, why, today)

3 그가 너한테 뭐라고 말했니?

➡ ______________________________________ (he, did, say, to you, what)

4 그 열쇠를 어디에서 찾았니?

➡ ______________________________________ (where, you, did, find, the key)

5 언제 그가 여행에서 돌아올까?

➡ ______________________________________ (return, from the trip, when, he, will)

6 넌 학교에 매일 어떻게 가니?

➡ ______________________________________ (how, you, do, every day, go, to school)

7 넌 어떻게 지내고 있니?

➡ ______________________________________ (everything, how, with, is, you)

정답 p.2

PRACTICE 4

Becky의 대답을 보고, Tony의 질문을 완성하세요.

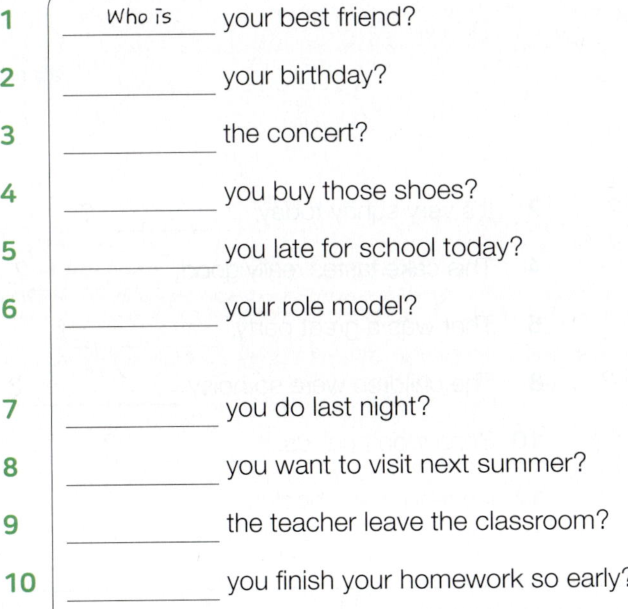

1	_Who is_ your best friend?	My best friend is Carrie.
2	__________ your birthday?	My birthday is August 10th.
3	__________ the concert?	It was great.
4	__________ you buy those shoes?	I bought them at a department store.
5	__________ you late for school today?	I got up late this morning.
6	__________ your role model?	My role model is my grandpa because he's always kind and helpful.
7	__________ you do last night?	I studied English.
8	__________ you want to visit next summer?	I want to visit Hawaii.
9	__________ the teacher leave the classroom?	He left 30 minutes ago.
10	__________ you finish your homework so early?	Because I like to get my work done early so I can relax later.

PSS 1-3 부가의문문 Ⅰ

부가의문문은 문장의 끝에서 우리말의 '그렇지?', '그렇지 않니?'처럼 자신의 말에 확신하며 상대방의 동의를 구하는 표현이다. 평서문이나 명령문 뒤에 「동사＋주어?」의 형태로 쓴다.

1. 주어＋동사의 긍정형 ～, be/do/조동사의 부정 축약형＋인칭대명사?

You **are** the tallest in your class, **aren't you?** 넌 반에서 키가 제일 크지, 그렇지 않니?

Jina **likes** chocolate, **doesn't she?** 지나는 초콜릿을 좋아해, 그렇지 않니?

You **can** go there without me, **can't you?** 너는 나 없이도 그곳에 갈 수 있어, 그렇지 않니?

This movie **was** exciting, **wasn't it?** 이 영화는 흥미진진했어, 그렇지 않았니?

cf. 주어에 this나 that이 포함되어 사물을 가리킬 때, 부가의문문의 인칭대명사는 it을 쓴다.

2. 주어＋동사의 부정형 ～, be/do/조동사의 긍정형＋인칭대명사?

It **isn't** a good idea, **is it?** 그것은 좋은 생각이 아니야, 그렇지?

You **won't** go out now, **will you?** 넌 지금 나가지 않을 거야, 그렇지?

The students **didn't** go on a picnic, **did they?** 그 학생들은 소풍을 가지 않았어, 그렇지?

Those bananas **aren't** fresh, **are they?** 저 바나나들은 신선하지 않아, 그렇지?

cf. 주어에 these나 those가 포함되어 있을 때, 부가의문문의 인칭대명사는 they를 쓴다.

정답 p.2

PRACTICE 5

다음 문장의 빈칸에 알맞은 부가의문문을 쓰세요.

1 You aren't a good swimmer, ____________?

2 It's very sunny today, ____________?

3 Mina didn't like the idea, ____________?

4 This cake tastes really good, ____________?

5 Peter could get the prize, ____________?

6 That was a great party, ____________?

7 Those guys don't work here, ____________?

8 The children were so noisy, ____________?

9 These aren't your notebooks, ____________?

10 Sena won't call us, ____________?

11 She reads many books, ____________?

12 He read many books, ____________?

PSS 1-4 부가의문문 Ⅱ

1. Let's ～, shall we?

Let's have dinner now, **shall we?** 지금 저녁을 먹자, 어때?

Let's not play computer games, **shall we?** 컴퓨터 게임을 하지 말자, 어때?

2. 명령문, will you?

긍정명령문에서는 어조에 따라 'will you?' 또는 'won't you?'를 쓸 수 있다.

즉, 명령조로 말할 때는 will you?, 정중하게 권할 때는 won't you?를 쓴다.

Pass me the sugar, **will you?** 설탕 좀 건네줘, 알겠니? – 명령

Pass me the sugar, **won't you?** 설탕 좀 건네줘, 그렇게 해 주지 않을래? – 권유

Don't be late again, **will you?** 다시는 늦지 마라, 알겠니?

cf. 부정명령문에서는 will you?만 쓰인다.

3. I am ~, am I not[aren't I]?

I'm your friend, **am I not?** 난 너의 친구야, 그렇지 않니?

= **I'm** your friend, **aren't I?**

cf. 구어체에서는 aren't I?가 더 많이 쓰인다.

정답 p.2

PRACTICE 6

다음 문장의 빈칸에 알맞은 부가의문문을 쓰세요.

1 Don't enter the room, ________________?

2 I look so tired, ______________?

3 This movie is famous, ______________?

4 Let's take a break now, ________________?

5 Tom lived there for many years, ________________?

6 Those puppies weren't very healthy, ________________?

7 Let's not go for a movie, ______________?

8 I'm your teacher, ______________?

9 Call me tonight, ______________?

10 Alex and Cathy can't play the flute, ________________?

PSS 1-5 선택의문문

선택의문문은 or를 사용하여 선택의 대상을 묻는 의문문으로, 둘 중 하나를 선택하여 대답해야 하므로 Yes나 No로 대답하지 않는다.

How would you like to pay, **cash or credit card**? – **Cash.**

현금과 신용카드 중 어느 것으로 계산하시겠어요?　　　　현금이요.

Which is longer, **the Nile or the Mississippi**?

나일강과 미시시피강 중 어느 것이 더 깁니까?

– **The Nile is longer than the Mississippi.**

나일강이 미시시피강보다 더 깁니다.

Did you **make them or buy them**?

당신은 그것들을 만들었나요, 아니면 샀나요?

– **I made them.**

나는 그것들을 만들었습니다.

Is it **green or blue**?

그건 초록색인가요, 아니면 파란색인가요?

– **It's blue.**

파란색입니다.

정답 p.2

PRACTICE 7

그림을 보고, 대화의 빈칸에 알맞은 말을 쓰세요.

1 *A*: What would you like to eat, steak or spaghetti?

   B: ________________, please.

2 *A*: Is he playing soccer or baseball?

   B: He is playing ________________.

3 *A*: Which do you wear more often, a skirt or pants?

   B: I wear ________________ more often.

4 *A*: Are they eating hamburgers or noodles?

   B: They are eating ________________.

5 *A*: Who gave the book to you, your father or mother?

   B: ________________ gave me the book.

6 *A*: How would you like to go there, by bus or by train?

   B: I would like to go there ________________.

PSS 1-6 간접의문문 I

한 문장 안에서 의문사가 이끄는 절이 그 문장의 일부로 쓰이는 경우, 의문사가 이끄는 절을 간접의문문이라고 한다.

1. 의문사가 있는 경우 – 의문사 + 주어 + 동사 ~

I don't know. + What is her name?

➡ I don't know **what her name is**. 저는 그녀의 이름이 무엇인지 모릅니다.

Can you tell me? + Why did she cancel the meeting?

➡ Can you tell me **why she cancelled the meeting**?

당신은 왜 그녀가 회의를 취소했는지 나에게 말해줄 수 있나요?

cf. 간접의문문에서 의문사가 주어로 쓰인 경우에는 직접의문문의 어순을 그대로 쓴다.

Do you know? + Who helped her?

➡ Do you know **who helped her**? 당신은 누가 그녀를 도왔는지 아십니까?

Does anyone know? + Who said that?

➡ Does anyone know **who said that**? 누가 그걸 말했는지 누군가 아십니까?

2. 의문사가 없는 경우 – if[whether] + 주어 + 동사 ~

I wonder. + Is she a student?

➡ I wonder **if[whether] she is a student**. 저는 그녀가 학생인지 궁금합니다.

I don't know. + Does she like you?

➡ I don't know **if[whether] she likes you**. 나는 그녀가 당신을 좋아하는지 모릅니다.

정답 p.3

PRACTICE 8 [1-11]

다음 직접의문문을 간접의문문으로 바꾸어 쓰세요.

1 What does that mean? ➡ Do you know ________________________ ?

2 Is it important? ➡ I wonder ________________________ .

3 How can I get to your school? ➡ Can you tell me ________________________ ?

4 Who broke the window? ➡ I don't know ________________________ .

5 Did you pass the exam? ➡ Please tell me ________________________ .

6 Do you love Mike? ➡ I wonder ________________________ .

7 Can she swim? ➡ Could you tell me ________________________ ?

8 Were they playing soccer? ➡ Do you know ________________________ ?

9 Where does she live?　　　　➡ I don't know _______________________________________.

10 Did Max buy a new car?　　　➡ I wonder _______________________________________.

11 How much does this book cost? ➡ Do you know ________________________________?

PSS 1-7 간접의문문 Ⅱ

간접의문문이 포함된 문장에서 think, believe, suppose, guess와 같이 생각이나 추측을
나타내는 동사가 있으면 의문사를 문장 맨 앞에 쓴다.

Do you **think**? + **What** is she doing now?
➡ **What** do you **think** she is doing now? 너는 그녀가 지금 무엇을 하고 있다고 생각하니?

Do you **believe**? + **Who** will win?
➡ **Who** do you **believe** will win? 너는 누가 이길 것이라고 믿니?

Do you **suppose**? + **When** will the copy machine be repaired?
➡ **When** do you **suppose** the copy machine will be repaired?
너는 복사기가 언제 수리될 거라고 생각하니?

Do you **guess**? + **What** was her answer?
➡ **What** do you **guess** her answer was? 너는 그녀의 대답이 뭐였다고 추측하니?

cf. 'Can you guess?'의 경우는 의문사가 문두로 나가지 않는다.

Can you guess? + **What** did I buy? ➡ Can you guess **what** I bought?

정답 p.3

PRACTICE 9

다음 두 문장을 한 문장으로 연결하세요.

1 Do you think? + What is he making?
➡ _______________________________________

2 Do you know? + When did he arrive?
➡ _______________________________________

3 Do you believe? + Who is right?
➡ _______________________________________

4 Do you think? + Why should we learn English?
➡ _______________________________________

5 I don't know. + Does Susan have feelings for me?
➡ _______________________________________

6 Do you believe? + When will he come?

➡ ____

7 Do you guess? + What will happen next?

➡ ____

8 Can you tell me? + Are there bookstores near here?

➡ ____

9 Do you think? + How can we solve this problem?

➡ ____

10 Can you guess? + Which one did I choose?

➡ ____

11 Do you believe? + Where did you lose it?

➡ ____

12 Do you suppose? + Why is he so upset?

➡ ____

PSS 1-8 감탄문

1. What(+a[an])+형용사+명사+주어+동사!

He is a very kind man. ➡ **What** a kind man he is!

그는 매우 친절한 사람이다. 그는 정말 친절한 사람이구나!

They are very good teachers. ➡ **What** good teachers they are!

그들은 매우 좋은 선생님들이다. 그들은 정말 좋은 선생님들이구나!

2. How+형용사[부사]+주어+동사!

You are very creative. ➡ **How** creative you are!

너는 매우 창의적이다. 너는 정말 창의적이구나!

A cheetah runs very fast. ➡ **How** fast a cheetah runs!

치타는 매우 빨리 달린다. 치타는 정말 빨리 달리는구나!

cf. 감탄문에서의 「주어+동사」는 생략할 수도 있다.

정답 p.3

PRACTICE 10 [1-10]

다음 문장을 감탄문으로 바꾸어 쓰세요.

1 You are very patient. ➡ ____

2 It is very hot and humid. ➡ _______________________

3 She is a very smart student. ➡ _______________________

4 That is a very excellent painting. ➡ _______________________

5 They were very angry. ➡ _______________________

6 This journey is very exciting. ➡ _______________________

7 They were very terrible players. ➡ _______________________

8 She is a very friendly teacher. ➡ _______________________

9 He was very polite. ➡ _______________________

10 These are very beautiful songs. ➡ _______________________

PSS 2 문장의 5형식

PSS 2-1 문장의 5형식

1. 목적어를 필요로 하지 않는 동사

① 주어 + 동사 – 1형식

He **walked**. 그는 걸었다.

He **walked** to school. 그는 학교까지 걸었다.

cf. 「주어＋동사」 뒤에는 부사(구)와 같은 수식어가 올 수 있지만 문장의 형식에는 영향을 주지 않는다.

② 주어 + 동사 + 주격 보어 – 2형식

You **look good** today. 너 오늘 좋아 보인다.

cf. 주격 보어로는 형용사나 명사가 온다.

2. 목적어를 필요로 하는 동사

① 주어 + 동사 + 목적어 – 3형식

I **bought a car** last month. 나는 지난달에 차를 샀다.

② 주어 + 동사 + 간접목적어 + 직접목적어 – 4형식

She **gave me some advice**. 그녀는 내게 약간의 충고를 해 주었다.

③ 주어 + 동사 + 목적어 + 목적격 보어 – 5형식

My puppy **makes me happy**. 내 강아지는 날 행복하게 한다.

PRACTICE 11

밑줄 친 단어/구의 문장 성분을 〈보기〉에서 찾아 각각에 해당하는 번호를 쓰세요.

보 기	① 주어	② 동사	③ 목적어	④ 간접목적어	⑤ 직접목적어	⑥ 주격 보어
	⑦ 목적격 보어	⑧ 부사(구)				

1 I like hiphop music very much.

2 I went to school on foot.

3 He gave me a bunch of flowers.

4 The pie tastes good with honey.

5 I found the book very useful.

6 She lives in a great apartment.

7 The people looked active and lively.

8 I made her delicious cookies.

9 We have a computer in our living room.

10 Everyone calls him Mr. Funny.

11 He became a doctor to make a difference.

12 She dances very well.

13 Sunny days make me happy.

14 She asked me a couple of questions.

15 He loves his parents very much.

16 We swam in the sea under the hot sun.

17 This restaurant offers its customers free drinks.

18 These bananas went bad in a very short time.

PSS 2-2 주격 보어를 필요로 하는 동사 I

다음 동사의 보어 자리에는 형용사나 명사가 온다.

1. '〜이다, (〜 상태에) 있다' – be, stay, keep, remain

   This **is** my favorite **book**. 이것은 내가 가장 좋아하는 책이다.
   You should **stay healthy**. 너는 건강을 유지해야 한다.
   They **kept quiet** in the library. 그들은 도서관에서 조용히 있었다.
   cf. stay, keep, remain 등의 동사 다음에는 보어로 주로 형용사가 온다. (학교 내신 빈출 문법사항!)

2. '〜되다' – become, get, go, turn, grow, run

   Bob **became a teacher**. Bob은 선생님이 되었다.
   Suddenly the students **got quiet**. 갑자기 학생들이 조용해졌다.
   The milk will **go bad** in three days. 우유는 3일이 지나면 상할 것이다.
   Her face **turned red**. 그녀의 얼굴이 빨개졌다.
   The players **grew tired**. 그 선수들은 피곤해졌다.
   This well **ran dry**. 이 우물은 말랐다.
   cf. get, go, turn, grow, run 등의 동사 다음에는 보어로 주로 형용사가 온다.

PRACTICE 12

〈보기〉에서 알맞은 단어를 골라 빈칸에 쓰세요.

보 기	popular healthy tired late quiet cold black bored

1 I was ___________ for the meeting this morning.

2 You should stay ___________ for the next match.

3 The weather turned ___________. You have to wear a jacket.

4 Paul became ___________ in his school. Many students wanted to see him.

5 Jinsu felt ___________ during the vacation. He didn't do anything special.

6 You should keep ___________ here. Don't say anything.

7 I got ___________ after the long trip to Australia. I needed a rest.

8 The sky grew ___________ with the clouds.

PSS 2-3 주격 보어를 필요로 하는 동사 Ⅱ

다음 동사의 보어 자리에는 형용사가 온다.

1. 감각을 나타내는 동사 – sound '~하게 들리다', smell '~한 냄새가 나다',
   taste '~한 맛이 나다', feel '~한 느낌이 들다'

   That **sounds strange**. 그것은 이상하게 들린다.
   The food **smells delicious**. 그 음식은 맛있는 냄새가 난다.
   It **tastes great**. 그것은 맛이 좋다.
   I **feel good** today. 나는 오늘 기분이 좋다.

2. '~해 보이다' – look, seem, appear

   You **look tired**. 너 피곤해 보인다.
   The box **seems heavy** to carry. 그 상자는 옮기기에 무거워 보인다.
   Becky **appears rich**. Becky는 부유해 보인다.
   cf. 「감각동사 like＋명사」 '~처럼 …하다'
      The baby **looks like a doll**. 그 아기는 인형처럼 보인다.
      The wind **sounds like a whisper**. 그 바람은 속삭임처럼 들린다.
      The ice cream **tastes like vanilla**. 그 아이스크림은 바닐라 같은 맛이 난다.

PRACTICE 13

괄호 안에 주어진 단어 중 알맞은 것을 고르세요.

1 Sora looks (happy, happily) today.

2 Linda felt (terrible, terribly) about the news.

3 They treated me (nice, nicely).

4 I want to (look, look like) a famous star.

5 I don't speak English (good, well).

6 The mushroom soup tasted (salty, saltily).

7 That sounds (good, well) to me.

8 Jack appeared (sad, sadly).

9 You can solve this math problem (easy, easily).

10 This apple smells so (sweet, sweetly).

11 It seems a little (strange, strangely).

12 That (sounds, sounds like) a good plan.

13 The skin of an elephant (feels, feels like) tough.

14 The lady in white danced (beautiful, beautifully).

PSS 2-4 두 개의 목적어를 필요로 하는 동사

'~에게 …을 주다'라는 의미의 동사를 수여동사라고 하고, 수여동사는 두 개의 목적어가 필요하다. 두 개의 목적어를 필요로 하는 동사를 사용한 4형식 문장은 동사에 따라 to, for, of 의 전치사를 이용하여 3형식 문장으로 바꿀 수 있다.

1.

give lend pay send tell show teach sell write ＋ 간접목적어 ＋ 직접목적어 – 4형식
[~에게] [~을/를]

⬇

give lend pay send tell show teach sell write ＋ 직접목적어 ＋ to ＋ 간접목적어 – 3형식

He **gave** her a blue box. ➡ He **gave** a blue box **to** her. 그는 그녀에게 파란 상자를 주었다.

My sister **sent** me a gift. ➡ My sister **sent** a gift **to** me. 언니가 내게 선물을 보냈다.

I **taught** students history. ➡ I **taught** history **to** students. 나는 학생들에게 역사를 가르쳤다.

2. [buy cook get make find] **+** [간접목적어] **+** [직접목적어] – 4형식

⬇

   [buy cook get make find] **+** [직접목적어] **+** [for] **+** [간접목적어] – 3형식

I **bought** my father a tie. ➡ I **bought** a tie **for** my father. 나는 아버지께 넥타이를 사 드렸다.
My mom **made** me a bag. ➡ My mom **made** a bag **for** me.
우리 엄마는 내게 가방을 만들어 주셨다.

3. [ask] **+** [간접목적어] **+** [직접목적어] – 4형식

⬇

   [ask] **+** [직접목적어] **+** [of] **+** [간접목적어] – 3형식

Can I **ask** you a question? ➡ Can I **ask** a question **of** you?
당신에게 질문을 하나 해도 될까요?

정답 p.4

PRACTICE 14

괄호 안에 주어진 말을 바르게 배열하세요.

1 (me, lent, uncle, the bike, my)
➡ ____

2 (will, Mark, a pretty doll, me, buy)
➡ ____

3 (told, a surprising story, she, me)
➡ ____

4 (I'll, give, a birthday gift, you)
➡ ____

5 (they, us, some food, got)
➡ ____

6 (wooden toys, made, father, us)
➡ ____

7 (asked, him, I, of the house, the price)
➡ ____

8 (me, show, why don't you, the picture)
➡ ____

9 (cooked, mother, a nice dinner, them)

➡ ____

10 (a thank-you note, we, our teacher, sent)

➡ ____

정답 p.4

PRACTICE 15

〈보기〉와 같이 4형식 문장을 3형식 문장으로 바꾸어 쓰세요.

보 기	You should send Mom a camera. ➡ You should send a camera to Mom.

1 I cooked my son some soup. ➡ ____

2 My teacher asked me a difficult question. ➡ _______________________________

3 Jinho bought her a present. ➡ ____

4 She sent her friend a poem. ➡ ____

5 I wrote my cousin an email. ➡ ____

6 They showed me their car. ➡ ____

7 My friend made me a pencil case. ➡ _______________________________________

8 Mr. Smith teaches us English. ➡ ____

9 Can you get me a Coke? ➡ ____

10 I didn't lend her my bicycle. ➡ ____

PSS 2-5 목적격 보어를 필요로 하는 동사 Ⅰ

1. **keep, find, call, make, turn** – 목적격 보어로 명사나 형용사가 온다.

   You should **keep** it **cool**. 너는 그것을 차갑게 유지해야 한다.

   Suji **found** the question **difficult**. 수지는 그 문제가 어렵다는 것을 알게 되었다.

   We **called** her **Jen**. 우리는 그녀를 Jen이라고 불렀다.

   Exercising regularly **makes** you **healthy**. 규칙적으로 운동하는 것은 당신을 건강하게 만든다.

   Time **turned** my dad's hair **gray**. 시간은 나의 아빠의 머리를 희게 했다.

   Living without rest can **make** you **more depressed**.

   휴식 없이 사는 건 당신을 더욱 우울하게 할 수 있다.

2. **want, tell, ask, get, allow, advise – 목적격 보어로 to부정사가 온다.**

I **want** you **to meet** Dave. 나는 네가 Dave를 만나기를 원한다.
Mom **told** me **to stay** home. 엄마는 내게 집에 있으라고 말씀하셨다.
He **asked** me **to write** about Korea. 그는 내게 한국에 대해 쓰라고 요청했다.
You have to **get** her **to wake** up early. 너는 그녀가 일찍 일어나게 해야 한다.
Dad **allowed** me **to go** fishing. 아빠는 내가 낚시하러 가는 걸 허락하셨다.
I **advised** him **to go** home. 나는 그에게 집에 갈 것을 권했다.

정답 p.4

PRACTICE 16

괄호 안에 주어진 말 중 알맞은 것을 고르세요.

1 I made my dad (angry, angrily).

2 The high temperature turned the milk (sour, sourly).

3 They asked her (come, to come) back to work.

4 I want you (leave, to leave) right now.

5 He told me (clean, to clean) the room.

6 I found the bag (heavy, heavily).

7 Her doctor advised her (rest, to rest).

8 Why don't you keep the kids (quiet, quietly)?

9 My mom gets me (have, to have) breakfast every day.

10 Her dimple makes her (more attractive, more attractively).

11 He allowed me (use, to use) his photographs.

PSS 2-6 목적격 보어를 필요로 하는 동사 Ⅱ

사역동사와 지각동사의 목적격 보어 자리에는 동사원형이 온다.

1. **사역동사 – let, make, have**

I'll **let** you **know** how it works. 그것이 어떻게 작동하는지 내가 알려줄게요.
I can't **make** her **stop** crying. 나는 그녀가 우는 것을 멈추게 할 수 없다.
She **had** me **come** home early. 그녀는 내가 집에 일찍 오도록 시켰다.

cf. help는 준사역동사로 목적격 보어 자리에 동사원형 또는 to부정사가 올 수 있다.
These rules will **help** you **(to) study** well. 이 규칙들이 네가 공부를 잘 할 수 있도록 도와줄 것이다.

2. 지각동사 – feel, see, hear, watch

I **felt** the table **shake**. 나는 탁자가 흔들리는 것을 느꼈다.

Did you **see** my son **ride** a bike? 내 아들이 자전거를 타는 것을 보았니?

I **heard** Mary **play** the violin. 나는 Mary가 바이올린을 연주하는 것을 들었다.

Let's **watch** Hana **swim** in the pool. 하나가 수영장에서 수영하는 것을 보자.

cf. 동작이 진행 중인 것을 강조할 때는 지각동사의 목적격 보어로 동사원형 대신 -ing형이 올 수 도 있다.

I **saw** my students **playing** soccer in the playground.

나는 나의 학생들이 운동장에서 축구를 하고 있는 것을 보았다.

Did you **hear** the dog **barking**? 너는 개가 짖고 있는 것을 들었니?

정답 p.4

PRACTICE 17

괄호 안에 주어진 말 중 알맞은 것을 고르세요.

1 Mina saw a man (to bake, baking) delicious cakes.

2 I'll let you (go, to go) when it is finished.

3 I heard the children (sing, to sing) all together.

4 Sarah had me (stay, to stay) with her baby yesterday.

5 James told me (considering, to consider) my options.

6 He always makes me (laugh, to laugh).

7 I heard people (to shout, shouting) in the cafe.

8 It will help you (remembering, remember) the rule.

9 Her parents didn't want her (marry, to marry) him.

10 Did you have them (come, to come) here?

11 How did you get him (pose, to pose) for this picture?

12 She allows the children (choose, to choose) their own books from the library.

13 I felt something (touching, to touch) my arm.

14 The professor advised me (study, to study) abroad.

15 Did you see Mary (plant, to plant) those trees?

16 I watched an ant (carrying, to carry) a little bit of bread.

17 The police officer asked us (tell, to tell) about the accident.

1 다음 빈칸에 알맞은 단어끼리 바르게 짝지어진 것은?

> • He asked me __________ had told me that information.
> • She asked me __________ I was all right.

① what - that
② who - that
③ what - if
④ who - if
⑤ why - that

2 다음 중 대화의 흐름이 어색한 것을 고르세요.

① A: Can't you sit still?
   B: OK, I'll try. Sorry to bother you.
② A: Will you be there, too?
   B: Of course I will.
③ A: Isn't it a lovely day?
   B: Yes. Let's go for a picnic.
④ A: Aren't you pleased to see me?
   B: No, I missed you a lot.
⑤ A: Did you hear him go out?
   B: No, I didn't hear anything at all.

3 밑줄 친 부분의 쓰임이 잘못된 것은?

① Lily is interested in soccer, isn't she?
② John lost his bike yesterday, doesn't he?
③ They don't have any plans, do they?
④ Close the door, will you?
⑤ He can't go there, can he?

4 어법상 틀린 것의 개수를 고르세요.

> There are various types of students in my class. Yunjin is kind and she makes her classmates ⓐ feeling happy. Jiho is ⓑ friendly and nicely. He makes us ⓒ laugh. Subin is picky, and she often makes us ⓓ uncomfortably.

① 1개   ② 2개   ③ 3개   ④ 4개   ⑤ 없음

5 밑줄 친 (A)에 들어갈 말로 적절하지 않은 것은?

> *Leader*: Attention, please. Let's start this week's classroom debate. The topic is "Should schools be required to provide online books for students?"
> __________(A)__________
> *Student 1*: I fully agree. When we purchase a print book, we always have to carry it. In the case of online books, there's no such burden.
> *Student 2*: I beg to differ. When we read online books on our laptop or tablet PC, it can harm our eyesight over time.
> *Leader*: Alright. Since online books have advantages and disadvantages, you two have different opinions.

① What's your take on it?
② I'd like to hear your views on it.
③ Do you have any thoughts on it?
④ What would you like to do with it?
⑤ What are your feelings about it?

6 Which is NOT a correct answer for the blank?

> I __________ her to do the dishes.

① made　② wanted　③ told
④ helped　⑤ asked

7 다음 밑줄 친 부분과 어법상 쓰임이 같은 것은?

> The shop doesn't have <u>what</u> I need.

① I already knew <u>what</u> Jessie said.
② Tell me <u>what</u> her name is.
③ I wonder <u>what</u> the answer is.
④ She asked me <u>what</u> happened to James.
⑤ Do you know <u>what</u> color her bag is?

8 어법상 옳은 문장을 <u>모두</u> 고르세요.

① How many legs do a spider have?
② Who are your favorite singer?
③ When did you came home?
④ What do you do for a living?
⑤ Why didn't you show up yesterday?

9 다음 주어진 문장을 영어로 바르게 옮긴 것은?

> 그들은 정말 친절한 사람들이구나!

① What nice people they are!
② What a nice people they are!
③ What nice people are they!
④ How nice people they are!
⑤ How they are nice people!

10 밑줄 친 우리말과 같은 뜻이 되도록 괄호 안의 주어진 단어를 이용하여 영작하세요.

> My class met an English teacher, Sophia, for the first time. Before she introduced herself, she asked us a question about herself: "<u>너희는 내가 몇 살이라고 생각하니?</u>"
> (how old, think)

➡ ______________________________

11 (a)~(f)에서 어법상 <u>올바른</u> 문장끼리 짝지어진 것은?

> (a) I heard the baby crying in the next room.
> (b) The story writing by Mark was interesting.
> (c) What amazing students they have become!
> (d) The teacher saw the students to cheat on the test.
> (e) The dishes broken last night are on the counter.
> (f) The soup smell delicious is on the stove.

① (a), (b), (c)　② (a), (c), (e)　③ (b), (c), (e)
④ (a), (d), (e)　⑤ (c), (e), (f)

12 다음 글을 읽고, 어법상 올바른 문장의 개수를 고르세요.

> ⓐ I'm worried about my little sister, Lucy. ⓑ She has a bad stomachache because I let her to eat all the candies and chocolates. ⓒ She has been crying all day long. ⓓ I can't make her to stop crying. ⓔ What should I do?

① 없음　② 1개　③ 2개　④ 3개　⑤ 4개

13 다음 빈칸에 들어갈 말로 올바른 것은?

He was a famous American inventor.
He was born in Milan, Ohio, in 1847. He invented a lot of things including a light bulb, a radio, a typewriter, and a phonograph.
He also invented a toaster and an iron.

① Do you know whom is Thomas A. Edison?
② Who do you know is Thomas A. Edison?
③ Who do you know Thomas A. Edison is?
④ Do you know who Thomas A. Edison is?
⑤ Do you know who is Thomas A. Edison?

14 다음 중 어법상 <u>어색한</u> 문장은?

① Did you see the baby smile at me?
② I felt the house shake.
③ I watched them play games.
④ I heard the rain fell on the ground.
⑤ He noticed a bird sitting on the tree.

15 주어진 단어를 활용하여 다음 우리말을 7단어로 영작하세요. (단, 필요한 경우 단어를 추가하거나, 어형을 바꿀 것.)

• 그 영화는 그녀를 웃고 울게 만들었다.
  (laugh, cry, make)

➡ _______________________

16 다음 문장을 감탄문으로 올바르게 바꾼 것은?

The dancer moves very fast.

① How the dancer moves fast!
② How fast does the dancer move!
③ How fast the dancer moves!
④ What a fast the dancer moves!
⑤ What the dancer fast moves!

17 다음 중 어법상 <u>어색한</u> 문장은?

① Everyone seems busy.
② They look like teachers.
③ He seems like tired.
④ Her advice sounded pretty good.
⑤ It sounds like a very interesting idea.

18 다음 글의 밑줄 친 두 문장을 간접의문문이 포함된 형태의 한 문장으로 바꿔 쓰세요.

February 28th
I went shopping today. At the mall, a woman asked me the way to a restaurant in English. I told her the way, but she didn't look like a foreigner. <u>I wonder. Was she practicing English?</u> It was a little strange.

➡ _______________________

19 다음 제시된 〈조건〉을 반드시 지켜 주어진 우리말을 바르게 영작하세요.

> 그 선생님은 학생들에게 교실을 청소하도록 시켰다.

조 건
- make, clean, classroom 단어를 사용할 것
  (필요할 경우 단어의 형태를 바꾸어 쓸 것)
- 7단어로 쓸 것

➡ ____

____

20 다음 중 의도하는 바가 나머지와 <u>다른</u> 것은?

① Let's go to the park.
② Shall we go to the park?
③ How do we go to the park?
④ How about going to the park?
⑤ Why don't we go to the park?

21 밑줄 친 ⓐ~ⓔ에 들어갈 표현이 바르게 짝지어 지지 <u>않은</u> 것은?

(1) Be careful not to make a loud ________ⓐ________ during the ceremony.
(2) He gave me a piece of ________ⓑ________ about making new friends.
(3) How ________ⓒ________ do you clean your room?
(4) He suddenly took off without saying a ________ⓓ________.
(5) Do you have ________ⓔ________ experience with computer programming?

① ⓐ noise   ② ⓑ advise   ③ ⓒ often
④ ⓓ word   ⑤ ⓔ any

22 다음 대화의 빈칸에 들어갈 말로 알맞은 것은?

> *Jinny* : James runs very fast.
> *Minsu*: Yes, we __________ "Bullet Man."

① called he   ② call them   ③ call she
④ call him   ⑤ call to him

23 다음 대화의 빈칸에 들어갈 알맞은 표현은?

> A: I went to my grandparents' house in the country and had to stay there for two months.
> B: For two months? __________, did you?
> A: No, I didn't. But now I miss being there.

① You didn't come back
② You liked the country
③ You didn't like the country
④ You didn't stay there
⑤ You liked your grandparents

24 〈보기〉의 단어들을 전부 사용하여 우리말 문장을 영어로 쓸 때 ★에 올 단어는?

> 나는 내 차를 Lisa에게 800달러에 팔았다.
> → I ________ ________ ________
> ★________ ________ ________ $800.

보 기 car / Lisa / sold / to / my / for

① Lisa   ② my   ③ car
④ for   ⑤ to

25 다음 중 우리말을 바르게 옮긴 것은?

① 너 유럽에 가 본 적 있지, 그렇지 않니?
→ You have been to Europe, have you?
② 넌 누가 우리 선생님이 될 거라고 생각해?
→ Who do you think will be our teacher?
③ 이 초콜릿은 쓴 맛이 나.
→ This chocolate tastes bitterly.
④ Jason이 자기 엄마에게 꽃을 드렸어.
→ Jason gave to his mom flowers.
⑤ 내가 너 숙제 끝내는 걸 도와줄게.
→ I'll help you to finishing your homework.

26 다음 질문에 대한 답으로 알맞지 <u>않은</u> 것은?

> A: Do you know what her favorite color is?
> B: _______________________

① Yes, I do.
② Yes. I think this is her favorite color.
③ No, I didn't know that.
④ No, I don't.
⑤ Yes. Red is.

27 다음 빈칸에 들어갈 말로 올바르지 <u>않은</u> 것은?

> A: James left for the States.
> B: _______________________
> A: Yes. I am sure.

① Really?
② Are you certain about that?
③ Are you all right?
④ Is that true?
⑤ Are you sure?

28 다음 글에서 밑줄 친 ⓐ~ⓔ 중 어법상 <u>잘못된</u> 것은?

> ⓐ Kevin and I are in the magic club. We stay after school ⓑ on Fridays and practice cool magic tricks. Last weekend, we put on a magic show at the school auditorium. ⓒ Many parents came to see it. Our show ⓓ made the audience joyfully. We hope to present ⓔ another one soon. We should learn a couple of new tricks.

① ⓐ   ② ⓑ   ③ ⓒ   ④ ⓓ   ⑤ ⓔ

29 다음 대화의 빈칸에 들어갈 단어로 알맞은 것은?

> A: You look __________. What happened?
> B: I lost the baseball game.

① sadly   ② sadness   ③ to sad
④ sad   ⑤ like sad

30 다음 대화의 빈칸에 들어갈 알맞은 말을 <u>모두</u> 고르세요.

> A: What is Mike doing?
> B: He is helping his father __________ the house.

① cleans   ② cleaned   ③ clean
④ cleaning   ⑤ to clean

31 빈칸에 들어갈 말로 알맞지 <u>않은</u> 것은?

- I don't know what subjects I ______①______ take.
- My mother wants me ______②______ Chinese, physics, and chemistry.
- I want ______③______ Chinese.
- The other two subjects are very difficult, ______④______?
- Mr. Finch will teach physics ______⑤______.

① should ② to take ③ learning
④ aren't they ⑤ to us

32 괄호 안의 우리말과 같은 뜻이 되도록 빈칸에 알맞은 부가의문문을 쓰세요.

A: Why are you laughing, Kate?
B: This book has a lot of funny pictures.
A: Show me one, ______________ ______________?
(하나만 보여 줘, 그럴래?)

33 우리말에 맞게 주어진 단어를 바르게 배열하여 문장을 완성하세요.

(1) 넌 우리의 문제가 뭐라고 생각하니?
(do, think, what, our, is, you, problem)

➡ ________________________________

________________________________?

(2) 넌 누가 이 케이크를 구웠다고 생각하니?
(do, suppose, who, this, baked, cake, you)

➡ ________________________________

________________________________?

34 다음 대화의 빈칸에 들어갈 단어로 알맞은 것은?

A: How do you feel today?
B: I feel very ____________.

① lonely ② sadly ③ happily
④ likely ⑤ terribly

35 다음 빈칸에 공통으로 들어갈 단어는?

- Stop talking, ____________ you?
- Pick me up at 7, ____________ you?

① do ② aren't ③ are
④ will ⑤ shall

36 어법상 옳은 문장을 <u>모두</u> 고른 것은?

ⓐ Can you tell me you want what time to eat dinner?
ⓑ I don't know how the service is at the new restaurant.
ⓒ The detective asked me when I last saw her and where.
ⓓ Do you think what time we'll leave the amusement park?
ⓔ I'd like to figure out what is the key message of this book.
ⓕ I wonder that you sympathize with the character in the movie.
ⓖ You can find out who is living at an address by using this website.

① ⓐⓒⓔ ② ⓑⓒⓖ ③ ⓐⓒⓓⓖ
④ ⓑⓒⓔⓖ ⑤ ⓓⓔⓕⓖ

37 다음 중 대화 내용이 <u>어색한</u> 것은?

① A: Why don't we have pizza for lunch?
  B: Sure, I'd love to.
② A: Where did you see the ad?
  B: I saw it on TV.
③ A: How do you go to school?
  B: I go there by bus.
④ A: Which one is more boring?
  B: The second one.
⑤ A: Is Brian shorter than Tom?
  B: No, he doesn't.

38 (a)~(e) 중 어법상 옳지 <u>않은</u> 문장을 <u>2개</u> 고르세요.

A: Welcome back home. (a) <u>How was the science camp?</u>
B: It was great! I had much fun.
A: (b) <u>What was your favorite?</u>
B: I liked making water rockets the most!
A: Wonderful! (c) <u>Did yours worked well?</u>
B: Yes, it went really high in the air.
A: Awesome! (d) <u>You didn't make it by yourself, were you?</u>
B: No, I worked with some friends I met there.
A: That's nice. Did you exchange numbers?
B: Of course! (e) <u>I can't wait to see them again!!</u>

① (a), (c)   ② (b), (e)   ③ (c), (d)
④ (d), (e)   ⑤ (a), (e)

39 다음 빈칸에 들어갈 말로 알맞은 것은?

I saw my mom _________ delicious cookies.

① baked   ② to bake   ③ is baking
④ baking   ⑤ have baked

40 다음 중 밑줄 친 부분이 <u>잘못</u> 쓰인 것은?

① The girl <u>looks lovely</u>.
② The restaurant's dishes <u>taste bad</u>.
③ I'm sure my dog <u>feels hungry</u> now.
④ The cookies <u>smell good</u>.
⑤ That <u>sounds nicely</u>.

41 다음 주어진 간접의문문을 두 문장으로 나눌 때 빈칸에 들어갈 알맞은 문장을 쓰세요.

(1) I wonder why he chose to come back.
  ➡ I wonder. + _________________

  ____

(2) What do you guess she said?
  ➡ Do you guess? + _________________

  ____

42 다음 글에서 <u>틀린</u> 부분을 <u>두 군데</u> 찾아 고치세요.

Be a Big Dreamer!
What do you want to be when you grow up? Do you know who you want to do in the future?
You may have some ideas, but you may not know whether the ideas are realistic or not. And some people may make fun of your ideas. Don't let them to do that. You can reach your goals if you try hard enough. Believe in yourself, and go for it!

(1) _________________ ➡ _________________
(2) _________________ ➡ _________________

43 다음 밑줄 친 우리말을 영어로 바르게 옮긴 것은?

> *A*: You won't be late again, will you?
> *B*: 네, 안 그럴게요.

① Yes, I will.　② Yes, I won't.
③ Yes, I do.　④ No, I don't.
⑤ No, I won't.

44 빈칸에 들어갈 말끼리 알맞게 짝지어진 것은?

> • I heard a man ___________ last night.
> • She let the bird ___________ free.

① scream – to go
② to scream – going
③ screamed – go
④ screaming – go
⑤ screaming – going

45 다음 대화의 (A)~(C)에 들어갈 말이 바르게 연결된 것은?

> Mom　　　: What are you doing, sweetie?
> Angelina: I'm making some soup for you.
> Mom　　　: Wow, it smells ______(A)______. Do
> 　　　　　 you want me ___(B)___ you?
> Angelina: No, thanks. Do you want to taste it?
> Mom　　　: OK. (*tastes the soup*)
> Angelina: It tastes good, ___(C)___?
> Mom　　　: Well, I think it's too salty.

	(A)	(B)	(C)
①	well	– to help	– does it
②	good	– to help	– doesn't it
③	better	– help	– doesn't it
④	good	– to help	– does it
⑤	best	– helping	– doesn't it

46 다음 빈칸에 들어갈 말로 알맞은 것은?

> • I don't ___________ play computer games.
> 　= 나는 그가 컴퓨터 게임을 하는 것을 원하지 않아.

① want him to　② want to him
③ want him　④ he want to
⑤ to want he

47 다음 대화의 빈칸에 들어갈 말로 알맞은 것을 모두 고르세요.

> *A*: I heard my dog ________________.
> *B*: Really? Are you sure?
> *A*: Yes, I am sure.

① crying　② to cry　③ cried
④ be crying　⑤ cry

48 다음 문장을 How로 시작하는 감탄문으로 고쳐 쓰세요.

> • Her new house is very nice.
> ➡ ________________________________

49 다음 중 밑줄 친 부가의문문의 쓰임이 올바른 것은?

① Jane isn't ready, <u>isn't she</u>?
② He's already finished dinner, <u>didn't he</u>?
③ Mike and Ted are coming to the party, <u>aren't they</u>?
④ Let's not go out, <u>will you</u>?
⑤ You can tell me, <u>can you</u>?

50 다음 빈칸에 들어갈 단어로 알맞은 것은?

> • Dad will get me a book.
> = Dad will get a book __________ me.

① of ② for ③ with
④ to ⑤ by

51 다음 빈칸에 들어갈 수 <u>없는</u> 것은?

> That lady looks very __________.

① happy ② friendly ③ sadly
④ healthy ⑤ lovely

52 다음 대화의 빈칸에 들어갈 말로 알맞은 것은?

> A: Let's go on a picnic this weekend, __________?
> B: I'm sorry, but I can't. I've got to go to my uncle's place.

① will we ② won't we
③ shall we ④ will you
⑤ don't you

53 괄호 안에 주어진 단어들을 알맞게 배열하여 대화를 완성하세요.

> Minho: Do you know who invented Hangeul?
> Jinhee: Yes, I do. King Sejong invented it.
> Minho: Do you know __________
> __________?
> (Hangeul, how, letters, has, many)

54 다음 중 어법상 올바른 문장은?

① The milk went sourly.
② All the students grows tired.
③ He never stays angry for long.
④ Billy becomes a doctor last year.
⑤ The store stays openness until late on Thursdays.

55 다음 질문에 대한 답으로 알맞은 것은?

> A: Which do you like better, pop or jazz?
> B: __________

① Yes, I do. ② It's really good.
③ Do you think so? ④ I like jazz better.
⑤ I don't think so.

56 다음 세 문장의 빈칸에 공통으로 들어갈 수 있는 단어를 쓰세요.

> • We __________ a good time yesterday.
> • I __________ my daughter write a letter.
> • They __________ a nice dinner last night.

57 다음 중 어법상 틀린 문장은?

① She wants you to stay home.
② I will give it to your brother.
③ Jake saw a bus came around the corner.
④ Draw a dog on the paper, will you?
⑤ They live in the cold weather, don't they?

58 그림을 보고, 〈보기〉에서 알맞은 말을 골라 Jamie에 대한 문장을 완성하세요.

(1) 

(2) 

보 기	cutely cute health healthy

(1) Exercising makes Jamie ______________ .

(2) Jamie found the puppy ______________ .

59 ⓐ와 ⓑ를 각각 어법에 맞게 고치세요.

During our mountain hike, I shared my feelings with my friends. I told them ⓐ how fresh was the morning air and ⓑ what an amazing view did we see from the top. They all agreed it was a perfect day.

ⓐ ______________

ⓑ ______________

60 우리말과 같은 뜻이 되도록 괄호 안에 주어진 단어를 올바르게 배열하세요.

- 우리는 때때로 누군가를 기분 좋게 하려고 거짓말을 한다.
  = We sometimes tell a lie to ______________

  ______________ .

  (good, make, feel, someone)

61 다음은 과학 박람회에 다녀온 학생들의 후기이다. 밑줄 친 부분 중 어법상 잘못된 것은?

Seoul Science Fair Review		
	Junho Kim	J Middle School 1st grade
It showed ① the infinite scientific world to me. It was an opportunity to understand what I learned in class more widely.		
	Yujin Lee	Y Middle School 3rd grade
② What a creative fair it is! I'd like to go again with my classmates. So, I wonder ③ if it will be held next year.		
	Jina Choi	W Elementary School 6th grade
There were many different activities and exhibitions. I ④ became interested in science.		
	Woobin Hwang	P Middle School 2nd grade
My teacher ⑤ advised me go to the fair. Thanks to her, I spent valuable time there.		

62 다음 빈칸에 알맞은 단어끼리 바르게 짝지어진 것은?

- Mark found the necklace __________ me.
- Can I ask a favor __________ you?

① for – of   ② for – to   ③ to – of
④ to – for   ⑤ of – to

63 다음 중 4형식 문장의 3형식 전환이 어법상 어색한 것은?

① People gave me a big hand.
= People gave a big hand to me.
② The boy sent his friend a doll.
= The boy sent a doll to his friend.
③ She asked me a question.
= She asked a question to me.
④ Can you find me my bag?
= Can you find my bag for me?
⑤ I lent him my bicycle.
= I lent my bicycle to him.

64 주어진 우리말과 같은 뜻이 되도록 형식에 맞게 영작하세요.

Amy는 나에게 책 한 권을 보냈다.

4형식: __________
3형식: __________

[65-67] 다음 글을 읽고, 물음에 답하세요.

I didn't like Brad at first ⓐ because he always seemed ⓑ anger at everything. However, as time went by, I (A) found him very ⓒ cheerfully. He was also kind to everyone and tried ⓓ to help us with our math homework. (B) 그가 작년에 무슨 상을 탔는지 너는 아니? Don't be ⓔ surprised! First prize in the math contest.

65 다음 중 윗글의 밑줄 친 (A) found와 쓰임이 같은 것은?

① I found gold inside the mine.
② I found no serious problems with your health.
③ I found the most useful information.
④ I found his mother a warm-hearted woman.
⑤ I found it in the newspaper.

66 괄호 안에 주어진 말을 바르게 배열하여 밑줄 친 (B)의 우리말을 영어로 완성하세요.

➡ __________
____

(know, last year, he, do, what, you, won, prize)

67 윗글의 밑줄 친 ⓐ~ⓔ 중 틀린 것을 모두 찾아 기호를 쓰고, 고쳐 쓰세요.

기호	맞게 고친 내용

CHAPTER 2
시제

PSS 1 현재시제

PSS 1-1 동사의 3인칭 현재 단수형

일반적인 경우	동사원형+s	work – works say – says see – sees	leave – leaves grow – grows put – puts
-o, -s, -x, -ch, -sh로 끝나는 경우	동사원형+es	do – does relax – relaxes wash – washes	pass – passes teach – teaches
자음+y로 끝나는 경우	자음+i+es	study – studies try – tries *cf.* 모음+y로 끝나는 경우 ➡ 동사원형+s play – plays	cry – cries copy – copies pay – pays

정답 p.9

PRACTICE 1

다음 동사들의 3인칭 현재 단수형을 쓰세요.

1 depart – ___________

2 reward – ___________

3 bite – ___________

4 answer – ___________

5 use – ___________

6 sing – ___________

7 breathe – ___________

8 open – ___________

9 destroy – ___________

10 close – ___________

11 change – ___________

12 prove – ___________

13 make – ___________

14 cry – ___________

15 draw – ___________

16 reduce – ___________

17 tell – ___________

18 miss – ___________

19 mix – ___________

20 complain – ___________

21 leave – ___________

22 raise – ___________

23 shoot – ___________

24 lift – ___________

25 like – ___________

26 bear – ___________

27	take	– __________	28	elect	– __________
29	recycle	– __________	30	recommend	– __________
31	stop	– __________	32	want	– __________
33	exchange	– __________	34	interview	– __________
35	allow	– __________	36	keep	– __________
37	marry	– __________	38	pray	– __________
39	act	– __________	40	enjoy	– __________
41	rescue	– __________	42	start	– __________
43	vow	– __________	44	mention	– __________
45	imagine	– __________	46	bring	– __________
47	do	– __________	48	lead	– __________
49	find	– __________	50	fight	– __________
51	wrap	– __________	52	flow	– __________
53	argue	– __________	54	travel	– __________
55	produce	– __________	56	seem	– __________
57	serve	– __________	58	give	– __________
59	follow	– __________	60	finish	– __________
61	add	– __________	62	borrow	– __________
63	copy	– __________	64	discover	– __________
65	admire	– __________	66	sink	– __________
67	understand	– __________	68	worry	– __________
69	remember	– __________	70	quit	– __________
71	stretch	– __________	72	knock	– __________
73	hope	– __________	74	wake	– __________
75	report	– __________	76	introduce	– __________
77	appear	– __________	78	save	– __________
79	suppose	– __________	80	agree	– __________
81	beat	– __________	82	hatch	– __________
83	become	– __________	84	describe	– __________
85	wonder	– __________	86	try	– __________

PSS 1-2 동사의 3인칭 현재 단수형의 발음

발음	용례
[s]	[s, ʃ, tʃ]음을 제외한 무성음으로 끝나는 동사 stops, departs, picks, laughs
[z]	[z, dʒ]음을 제외한 유성음으로 끝나는 동사 robs, digs, drives, breathes, becomes, runs, bears, vows
[iz]	[s, z, ʃ, tʃ, dʒ]음으로 끝나는 동사 passes, raises, pushes, reaches, exchanges

정답 p.9

PRACTICE 2

〈보기〉와 같이 주어진 단어의 밑줄 친 부분의 발음으로 알맞은 것을 [s], [z], [iz] 중에서 골라 쓰세요.

원어민 발음 들어보기 ▶

보 기	makes [s]	complains [z]	mixes [iz]

1	shoots	[　]	2	leaves	[　]	3	rewards	[　]
4	answers	[　]	5	cries	[　]	6	bites	[　]
7	lifts	[　]	8	bears	[　]	9	uses	[　]
10	prays	[　]	11	starts	[　]	12	enjoys	[　]
13	brings	[　]	14	hatches	[　]	15	finds	[　]
16	spills	[　]	17	sinks	[　]	18	admires	[　]
19	publishes	[　]	20	selects	[　]	21	understands	[　]
22	supposes	[　]	23	remembers	[　]	24	washes	[　]
25	dictates	[　]	26	seems	[　]	27	consists	[　]
28	sets	[　]	29	loses	[　]	30	runs	[　]
31	relaxes	[　]	32	drops	[　]	33	wishes	[　]
34	walks	[　]	35	carries	[　]	36	waits	[　]
37	studies	[　]	38	fixes	[　]	39	forgets	[　]
40	teases	[　]	41	hurts	[　]	42	teaches	[　]
43	cuts	[　]	44	plans	[　]	45	invents	[　]

PSS 1-3 현재시제의 쓰임 Ⅰ

1. **현재의 사실이나 상태를 나타낼 때 쓴다.**

   I **am** a nurse. 나는 간호사이다.
   My dad **works** at the bank. 우리 아빠는 은행에서 일하신다.

2. **현재의 습관이나 반복적인 동작을 나타낼 때 쓴다.**

   I **eat** lunch at one o'clock every day. 나는 매일 1시에 점심을 먹는다.
   John **reads** books before he **goes** to bed.
   John은 잠자리에 들기 전에 책을 읽는다.

3. **불변의 진리나 격언, 과학적 사실을 나타낼 때 쓴다.**

   The Sun **rises** in the east. 해는 동쪽에서 뜬다.
   A friend in need **is** a friend indeed. 어려울 때 친구가 진정한 친구다.

정답 p.10

PRACTICE 3

그림을 보고, 〈보기〉에 주어진 단어를 골라 알맞은 현재시제 형태로 바꾸어 빈칸에 쓰세요.
(단, 한 번씩만 쓸 수 있습니다.)

보 기	move sleep teach go play be

1 She ___teaches___ music in high school.

2 My father __________ tennis after work.

3 The bear __________ during the winter.

4 Jack __________ a great doctor.

5 The Earth __________ around the Sun.

6 I __________ to bed at 10 o'clock every day.

PSS 1-4 현재시제의 쓰임 Ⅱ

1. 눈앞에서 진행되고 있는 일을 나타낼 때 쓴다.

   Here comes the teacher. 선생님이 오신다.

2. 왕래발착동사(leave, go, depart, start, arrive, come, reach)가 미래를 나타내는 부사구와 함께 쓰일 때는 현재시제로 미래를 나타낼 수 있다.

   He **comes** back home **tomorrow evening**. 그는 내일 저녁에 집에 돌아온다.
   My sister **leaves** Busan **next week**. 나의 여동생은 다음 주에 부산을 떠난다.

3. 시간과 조건의 부사절에서는 현재시제로 미래를 나타낸다.

   Call me **when** you **arrive** home. 집에 도착하면 내게 전화해.
   I will go out **if** the weather **is** fine tomorrow. 내일 날씨가 맑으면, 나는 밖에 나갈 거야.
   I'll call you **as soon as** I **meet** him. 그를 만나자마자 너에게 전화할게.

정답 p.10

PRACTICE 4

괄호 안의 단어를 현재시제의 쓰임에 맞게 바꾸어 빈칸에 쓰세요.

1 There he ___goes___ with his son. (go)

2 My daughter ___________ in London next Monday. (arrive)

3 Come to my house before you ___________ lunch. (have)

4 Sam ___________ for Seoul tomorrow. (leave)

5 Here ___________ Mr. Smith. (come)

6 A bad workman always ___________ his tools. (blame)

7 Mom will be surprised if she ___________ about it. (hear)

8 Hana ___________ her aunt every Sunday. (visit)

9 Tom ___________ until late at night every day. (study)

10 Come back home before it ___________ dark. (get)

11 Our ship ___________ the island next month. (reach)

12 We'll have a quick bite before the train ___________. (depart)

13 He will email you when he ___________ the report. (finish)

PSS 2 과거시제

PSS 2-1 be동사의 과거형

과거시제는 과거에 일어난 동작이나 상태, 역사적 사실과 같이 과거에 이미 끝난 일을 나타낸다.

주어	현재형	과거형
I	am	was
you	are	were
he		
she	is	was
it		
we		
you	are	were
they		

Hangul **was** created by King Sejong. 한글은 세종대왕에 의해 만들어졌다.

We **were** at the library with Jina yesterday. 우리는 어제 지나와 함께 도서관에 있었다.

정답 p.10

PRACTICE 5

다음 문장의 빈칸에 알맞은 be동사를 쓰세요.

1 I _____was_____ a student last year, but I _____am_____ a teacher now.

2 It is sunny today, but it ___________ cloudy yesterday.

3 Tony, where ___________ you now?

4 They ___________ at school two hours ago.

5 Those pants ___________ very expensive. I can't buy them.

6 Susan is my friend. She ___________ also Jenny's friend.

7 My grandfather ___________ 70 years old this year. He is still very healthy.

8 Namsu and I ___________ at home last night. We played cards.

9 John ___________ very sick yesterday, so he couldn't come to school.

10 I know Liz. She ___________ my classmate before.

PRACTICE 6

다음은 Tony와 Becky의 대화입니다. 빈칸에 알맞은 be동사를 쓰세요.

1 Were you tall when you __________ a kid?
   Yes, I __________ very tall.

2 __________ your brother good at football?
   No, he __________ . And he didn't like it.

3 __________ your mom a teacher?
   Yes, she __________ . She teaches math.

4 How __________ your travel last week?
   It __________ wonderful. I'll never forget it.

5 How __________ your new school these days?
   It __________ very exciting. I have a lot of new friends.

PSS 2-2 규칙 변화 동사의 과거형

일반적인 경우	동사원형+ed	open – open**ed** start – start**ed** wash – wash**ed**	look – look**ed** pull – pull**ed** talk – talk**ed**
-e로 끝나는 경우	동사원형+d	decide – decide**d** live – live**d** use – use**d**	promise – promise**d** hate – hate**d** hope – hope**d**
자음+y로 끝나는 경우	자음+i+ed	study – stud**ied** worry – worr**ied** *cf.* 모음+y로 끝나는 경우 ➡ 동사원형+ed enjoy – enjoy**ed** play – play**ed**	reply – repl**ied** try – tr**ied** stay – stay**ed** delay – delay**ed**
단모음+단자음으로 끝나는 1음절과 뒤에 강세가 오는 2음절의 경우	동사원형 +마지막 자음 +ed	drop – drop**ped** pop – pop**ped** *cf.* 강세가 앞에 오는 2음절 동사 ➡ 동사원형+ed visit – visit**ed** enter – enter**ed**	stop – stop**ped** prefer – prefer**red** offer – offer**ed**

PRACTICE 7

다음 동사의 과거형을 쓰세요.

1	stay	–	**2**	rip	–
3	smell	–	**4**	cause	–
5	worry	–	**6**	destroy	–
7	die	–	**8**	bow	–
9	prefer	–	**10**	apply	–
11	judge	–	**12**	waste	–
13	control	–	**14**	play	–
15	watch	–	**16**	delay	–
17	invite	–	**18**	hurry	–
19	copy	–	**20**	hope	–
21	shop	–	**22**	expect	–
23	disappear	–	**24**	observe	–
25	study	–	**26**	fix	–
27	chat	–	**28**	carry	–
29	smile	–	**30**	jog	–
31	pop	–	**32**	notice	–
33	dance	–	**34**	try	–
35	stop	–	**36**	rush	–
37	enjoy	–	**38**	marry	–
39	plan	–	**40**	wait	–
41	reply	–	**42**	practice	–
43	pick	–	**44**	drop	–
45	agree	–	**46**	decide	–
47	fry	–	**48**	grab	–
49	clap	–	**50**	clean	–
51	save	–	**52**	cry	–
53	wrap	–	**54**	dry	–

PSS 2-3 규칙 변화 동사 과거형의 발음

발음	용례
[t]	[t]음을 제외한 무성음으로 끝나는 동사 pick**ed**, ripp**ed**, lik**ed**, rush**ed**, laugh**ed**
[d]	[d]음을 제외한 유성음으로 끝나는 동사 cri**ed**, believ**ed**, pull**ed**, us**ed**, hurri**ed**
[id]	[t, d]음으로 끝나는 동사 paint**ed**, invit**ed**, want**ed**, plant**ed**, need**ed**

PRACTICE 8

정답 p.10

〈보기〉와 같이 주어진 단어의 밑줄 친 부분의 발음으로 알맞은 것을 [t], [d], [id] 중에서 골라 쓰세요.

원어민 발음 들어보기 ▶

보 기	pick<u>ed</u> [t] smil<u>ed</u> [d] hat<u>ed</u> [id]

1	arriv<u>ed</u>	[ ]	2	play<u>ed</u>	[ ]	3	decid<u>ed</u>	[ ]
4	lik<u>ed</u>	[ ]	5	di<u>ed</u>	[ ]	6	us<u>ed</u>	[ ]
7	want<u>ed</u>	[ ]	8	realiz<u>ed</u>	[ ]	9	watch<u>ed</u>	[ ]
10	talk<u>ed</u>	[ ]	11	invit<u>ed</u>	[ ]	12	popp<u>ed</u>	[ ]
13	agre<u>ed</u>	[ ]	14	chang<u>ed</u>	[ ]	15	ripp<u>ed</u>	[ ]
16	plant<u>ed</u>	[ ]	17	delay<u>ed</u>	[ ]	18	look<u>ed</u>	[ ]
19	stay<u>ed</u>	[ ]	20	paint<u>ed</u>	[ ]	21	work<u>ed</u>	[ ]
22	wast<u>ed</u>	[ ]	23	collect<u>ed</u>	[ ]	24	form<u>ed</u>	[ ]
25	bak<u>ed</u>	[ ]	26	hurri<u>ed</u>	[ ]	27	protect<u>ed</u>	[ ]
28	tri<u>ed</u>	[ ]	29	dropp<u>ed</u>	[ ]	30	guid<u>ed</u>	[ ]
31	kick<u>ed</u>	[ ]	32	call<u>ed</u>	[ ]	33	prov<u>ed</u>	[ ]
34	repli<u>ed</u>	[ ]	35	wait<u>ed</u>	[ ]	36	publish<u>ed</u>	[ ]
37	cri<u>ed</u>	[ ]	38	mix<u>ed</u>	[ ]	39	consist<u>ed</u>	[ ]
40	clean<u>ed</u>	[ ]	41	hop<u>ed</u>	[ ]	42	report<u>ed</u>	[ ]
43	wrapp<u>ed</u>	[ ]	44	describ<u>ed</u>	[ ]	45	appreciat<u>ed</u>	[ ]

PSS 2-4 불규칙 변화 동사의 과거형

원형	과거형	과거분사형	원형	과거형	과거분사형
be	was, were	been	bear	bore	borne/born
beat	beat	beaten	become	became	become
begin	began	begun	blow	blew	blown
bring	brought	brought	build	built	built
buy	bought	bought	choose	chose	chosen
come	came	come	cost	cost	cost
cut	cut	cut	do	did	done
draw	drew	drawn	dream	dreamed/ dreamt	dreamed/ dreamt
drink	drank	drunk	drive	drove	driven
eat	ate	eaten	fall	fell	fallen
feel	felt	felt	fight	fought	fought
find	found	found	fly	flew	flown
forget	forgot	forgotten	get	got	got(ten)
give	gave	given	go	went	gone
grow	grew	grown	have	had	had
hear	heard	heard	hide	hid	hidden
hit	hit	hit	hold	held	held
hurt	hurt	hurt	keep	kept	kept
know	knew	known	lay	laid	laid
lead	led	led	leave	left	left
let	let	let	lie (눕다, 놓여 있다)	lay	lain
lose	lost	lost	make	made	made
mean	meant	meant	meet	met	met
overcome	overcame	overcome	pay	paid	paid
put	put	put	read[riːd]	read[red]	read[red]
ride	rode	ridden	ring	rang	rung
rise	rose	risen	run	ran	run
say	said	said	see	saw	seen
sell	sold	sold	send	sent	sent

원형	과거형	과거분사형	원형	과거형	과거분사형
set	set	set	shut	shut	shut
sing	sang	sung	sink	sank	sunk
sit	sat	sat	sleep	slept	slept
smell	smelled/smelt	smelled/smelt	speak	spoke	spoken
spend	spent	spent	spread	spread	spread
stand	stood	stood	steal	stole	stolen
sweep	swept	swept	swim	swam	swum
take	took	taken	teach	taught	taught
tell	told	told	think	thought	thought
throw	threw	thrown	understand	understood	understood
wake	woke	woken	wear	wore	worn
win	won	won	write	wrote	written

PRACTICE 9

정답 p.10

다음 동사의 과거형과 과거분사형을 쓰세요.

원어민 발음 들어보기 ▶ 

1 choose – _________ – _________ **2** lay – _________ – _________

3 meet – _________ – _________ **4** fall – _________ – _________

5 ring – _________ – _________ **6** run – _________ – _________

7 spend – _________ – _________ **8** take – _________ – _________

9 give – _________ – _________ **10** keep – _________ – _________

11 hear – _________ – _________ **12** sit – _________ – _________

13 bear – _________ – _________ **14** teach – _________ – _________

15 sing – _________ – _________ **16** cost – _________ – _________

17 think – _________ – _________ **18** fly – _________ – _________

19 wear – _________ – _________ **20** hurt – _________ – _________

21 read – _________ – _________ **22** tell – _________ – _________

23 make – _________ – _________ **24** fight – _________ – _________

25 see – _________ – _________ **26** go – _________ – _________

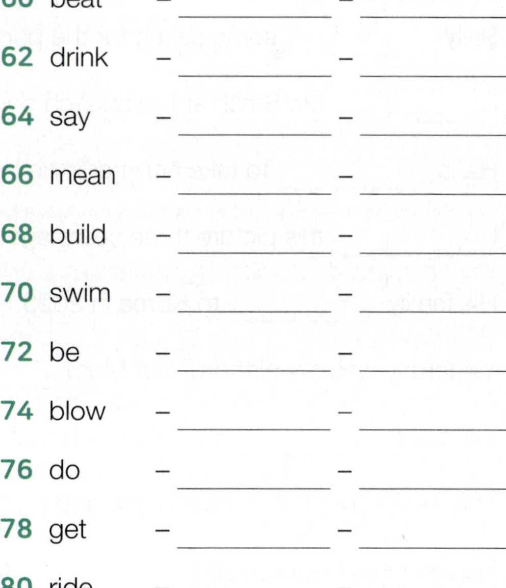

#	동사		
27	bring	– ___________	– ___________
28	pay	– ___________	– ___________
29	draw	– ___________	– ___________
30	find	– ___________	– ___________
31	hit	– ___________	– ___________
32	buy	– ___________	– ___________
33	speak	– ___________	– ___________
34	begin	– ___________	– ___________
35	understand	– ___________	– ___________
36	lie(눕다)	– ___________	– ___________
37	steal	– ___________	– ___________
38	put	– ___________	– ___________
39	hold	– ___________	– ___________
40	sink	– ___________	– ___________
41	wake	– ___________	– ___________
42	write	– ___________	– ___________
43	overcome	– ___________	– ___________
44	lead	– ___________	– ___________
45	know	– ___________	– ___________
46	leave	– ___________	– ___________
47	set	– ___________	– ___________
48	rise	– ___________	– ___________
49	sweep	– ___________	– ___________
50	smell	– ___________	– ___________
51	eat	– ___________	– ___________
52	forget	– ___________	– ___________
53	have	– ___________	– ___________
54	become	– ___________	– ___________
55	sleep	– ___________	– ___________
56	let	– ___________	– ___________
57	spread	– ___________	– ___________
58	dream	– ___________	– ___________
59	send	– ___________	– ___________
60	beat	– ___________	– ___________
61	stand	– ___________	– ___________
62	drink	– ___________	– ___________
63	come	– ___________	– ___________
64	say	– ___________	– ___________
65	feel	– ___________	– ___________
66	mean	– ___________	– ___________
67	grow	– ___________	– ___________
68	build	– ___________	– ___________
69	cut	– ___________	– ___________
70	swim	– ___________	– ___________
71	throw	– ___________	– ___________
72	be	– ___________	– ___________
73	lose	– ___________	– ___________
74	blow	– ___________	– ___________
75	drive	– ___________	– ___________
76	do	– ___________	– ___________
77	hide	– ___________	– ___________
78	get	– ___________	– ___________
79	win	– ___________	– ___________
80	ride	– ___________	– ___________
81	sell	– ___________	– ___________
82	shut	– ___________	– ___________

PRACTICE 10

괄호 안의 단어를 알맞은 형태로 바꾸어 빈칸에 쓰세요.

1 She ___________ me a photo from her vacation in Paris last week. (send)

2 Sujin ___________ born in Gwangju in 2018. (be)

3 I ___________ soccer with my friends these days. (play)

4 The oranges looked very sour, so I ___________ ___________ them. (not, eat)

5 Mark ___________ up late and hurried to school. (wake)

6 Kate ___________ ___________ anything last night. (not, hear)

7 My sister ___________ the window, so my mom was upset. (break)

8 The soccer ball ___________ the goalpost and rebounded into the field. (hit)

9 Tony ___________ down on the street and hurt his arm. (fall)

10 I ___________ ___________ the flute when I was young. (not, play)

11 The bank ___________ at 4 o'clock on weekdays. (close)

12 Yumi ___________ down on her bed and got some rest. (lie)

13 Peter ___________ the newspaper after he finished his lunch. (read)

14 Sally ___________ some cakes for the party yesterday. (bring)

15 I ___________ Mr. Smith at the speech contest last month. (see)

16 Hana ___________ to take her medicine because she was in a hurry to leave. (forget)

17 I ___________ this picture three years ago. (draw)

18 His family ___________ to Korea in 2023. (come)

19 Yesterday was my birthday, but Mom ___________ ___________ me anything. (not, give)

20 My plane ___________ at 8 o'clock tomorrow morning. (leave)

21 The movie ended at 10 last night, and I ___________ straight home. (drive)

22 He went into his room and ___________ the door. (shut)

23 Last night, the choir ___________ hymns at the church service. (sing)

PSS 3 미래시제

will+동사원형	**1.** 미래에 일어날 동작이나 상태를 예측한다. It **will be** very sunny this Friday. 이번 금요일은 매우 화창할 것이다. = It **is going to be** very sunny this Friday. ***cf.*** be going to와 바꾸어 쓸 수 있다. **2.** 미래에 일어날 일에 대해 '〜하겠다'는 의지를 나타낸다. Your bags look very heavy. I **will help** you. 네 가방들이 매우 무거워 보이는구나. 내가 널 도와줄게.
be going to +동사원형	미래에 일어날 일이 미리 계획되거나 예정되어 있음을 나타낸다. Jack **is going to play** tennis with Sam this weekend. Jack은 이번 주말에 Sam과 테니스를 칠 것이다. They **are going to arrive** here at 6 o'clock. 그들은 6시에 여기에 도착할 것이다.

정답 p.11

PRACTICE 11

괄호 안에 주어진 말 중 알맞은 것을 고르세요.

1   My mom (will, is, be) show us some famous paintings.

2   (Will, Are, Be) you going to have a birthday party soon?

3   My team will (go, going, going to go) to the mountain next week.

4   We (will, be, are) going to play basketball this weekend.

5   I'm (going, go, will go) to teach at a middle school.

6   Susan (will join, joins, joining) us for lunch tomorrow.

7   I'm not (go, going, will go) to do the housework.

8   My grandfather (is, is going, will) be here during summer vacation.

9   Tomorrow I (am, will, be) going to leave for Incheon.

10   I (will, am, be) open the door for you.

PRACTICE 12

그림을 보고, 괄호 안의 단어와 be going to를 사용하여 문장을 완성하세요.

1 I _____am going to eat_____ ice cream after dinner. (eat)

2 ___________ you ___________________ those shoes? (buy)

3 My mom ___________________ me a bicycle on my birthday. (give)

4 Yoonhee and Jiho ___________________ until midnight. (study)

5 It ___________________ tomorrow. (rain)

6 Ted ___________________ his house. (paint)

PSS 4 진행시제

PSS 4-1 동사의 -ing형

일반적인 경우	동사원형+ing	watch – watch**ing** hold – hold**ing**	follow – follow**ing** learn – learn**ing**
발음되지 않는 -e로 끝나는 경우	e를 빼고 ing	face – fac**ing** take – tak**ing**	smile – smil**ing** date – dat**ing**
발음되는 -e로 끝나는 경우	동사원형+ing	agree – agree**ing**	see – see**ing**
ie로 끝나는 경우	ie를 y로 고치고 ing	die – dy**ing**	lie – ly**ing**

<table>
<tr><td>단모음+단자음으로
끝나는 1음절과
뒤에 강세가 오는
2음절의 경우</td><td>동사원형
+마지막 자음
+ing</td><td>run – run**ning**   plan – plan**ning**
get – get**ting**   sit – sit**ting**
cf. 강세가 앞에 오는 2음절 동사 ➡ 동사원형+ing
visit – visit**ing**   enter – enter**ing**</td></tr>
</table>

PRACTICE 13 [1-100]

다음 동사의 -ing형을 쓰세요.

1	plant	– ________	2	take	– ________
3	get	– ________	4	play	– ________
5	smile	– ________	6	bow	– ________
7	become	– ________	8	see	– ________
9	lose	– ________	10	breathe	– ________
11	stand	– ________	12	open	– ________
13	argue	– ________	14	tumble	– ________
15	worry	– ________	16	bite	– ________
17	teach	– ________	18	wrap	– ________
19	swim	– ________	20	copy	– ________
21	sing	– ________	22	bake	– ________
23	die	– ________	24	return	– ________
25	plan	– ________	26	operate	– ________
27	serve	– ________	28	join	– ________
29	carry	– ________	30	climb	– ________
31	go	– ________	32	set	– ________
33	study	– ________	34	clean	– ________
35	date	– ________	36	encourage	– ________
37	pull	– ________	38	burn	– ________
39	use	– ________	40	stay	– ________
41	come	– ________	42	act	– ________

43	win	–	44	produce	–
45	celebrate	–	46	write	–
47	deny	–	48	repeat	–
49	enter	–	50	eat	–
51	make	–	52	hit	–
53	run	–	54	marry	–
55	shine	–	56	beat	–
57	enjoy	–	58	cause	–
59	move	–	60	solve	–
61	face	–	62	destroy	–
63	fight	–	64	roll	–
65	wash	–	66	say	–
67	stop	–	68	shake	–
69	introduce	–	70	happen	–
71	fly	–	72	hold	–
73	save	–	74	share	–
75	visit	–	76	put	–
77	lie	–	78	talk	–
79	ride	–	80	collect	–
81	dream	–	82	control	–
83	try	–	84	drive	–
85	hurt	–	86	fill	–
87	pay	–	88	wear	–
89	agree	–	90	cheat	–
91	cut	–	92	sell	–
93	form	–	94	fix	–
95	remove	–	96	turn	–
97	mention	–	98	increase	–
99	wait	–	100	pick	–

PSS 4-2 과거진행시제와 현재진행시제

1. 과거진행 「was/were+-ing」 – 과거의 한 시점에 진행되고 있던 동작을 나타낸다.

   I **was having** lunch **an hour ago**. 나는 1시간 전에 점심을 먹고 있었다.

2. 현재진행 「am/are/is+-ing」 – 말하고 있는 시점에 진행되고 있는 동작을 나타낸다.

   I **am taking** a walk **now**. 나는 지금 산책을 하고 있는 중이다.

3. 가까운 미래에 있을 일이 미리 계획된 일인 경우에는 미래시제 대신 현재진행시제를 쓸 수 있다.

   We **are going** on a picnic **tomorrow**. 우리는 내일 소풍을 갈 것이다.
   What **are** you **doing** this Sunday? 너는 이번 일요일에 무엇을 할 거니?

정답 p.12

PRACTICE 14 [1-15]

괄호 안에 주어진 단어를 이용하여 진행시제의 문장을 완성하세요.

1 The sky was blue and the birds ____were____ ____singing____ . (sing)

2 He is in the kitchen now. He ____________ ____________ a cake. (bake)

3 They ____________ ____________ about the rule a few minutes ago. (argue)

4 When I saw her, she ____________ ____________ a bicycle. (ride)

5 You should be quiet. The baby ____________ ____________ . (sleep)

6 The weather is hot now. He ____________ ____________ his tie and jacket. (remove)

7 What time ____________ you ____________ tomorrow? (leave)

8 Jina can't answer the phone right now. She ____________ ____________ . (cook)

9 I saw you at the police station this morning. What ____________ you ____________ there? (do)

10 Sora and I ____________ ____________ tennis after school. Would you like to join us? (play)

11 Let's go shopping tomorrow. I _____________ _____________ _____________ then. (not, work)

12 I saw Minsu on my way to school. He _____________ _____________ at the bus stop. (stand)

13 At two o'clock yesterday, I _____________ _____________ lunch. (have)

14 Tom _____________ _____________ _____________ his bike this afternoon. You can take it if you need it. (not, use)

15 I can't go out now. I _____________ _____________ cookies for my husband. (make)

정답 p.12

PRACTICE 15

다음은 Mike가 오늘 아침에 한 일입니다. 그림을 보고, 진행시제의 문장을 완성하세요.

1 At 07:40 ➡ He ___*was*___ ___*taking*___ a shower.

2 At 08:25 ➡ He _____________ _____________ breakfast.

3 At 08:55 ➡ He _____________ _____________ his dog.

4 At 09:50 ➡ He _____________ _____________ the living room.

5 At 10:30 ➡ He _____________ _____________ on the phone.

6 At 11:40 ➡ He _____________ _____________ a book.

PSS 5 현재완료

PSS 5-1 현재완료의 형태

현재완료는 「have/has+과거분사」의 형태로 과거에 일어난 사건의 발생 시점을 나타내는 것이 아니라 과거의 그 사건이 현재와 관련이 있음을 나타낼 때 쓰인다.

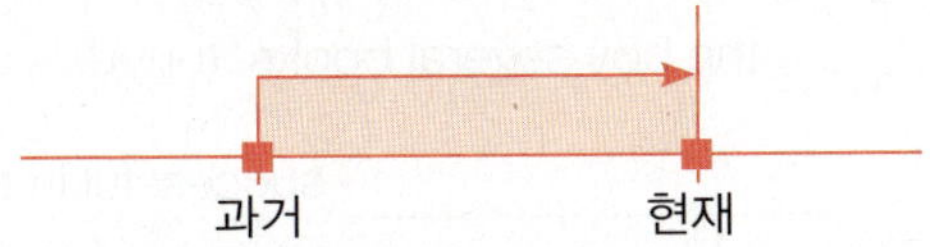

Jerry forgot my name. He still can't remember it.

Jerry는 내 이름을 잊어버렸다. 그는 여전히 그것을 기억할 수 없다.

➡ Jerry **has forgotten** my name. Jerry는 내 이름을 잊어버렸다.

I lost my puppy. I still can't find it. 나는 강아지를 잃어버렸다. 나는 여전히 그것을 찾을 수 없다.

➡ I **have lost** my puppy. 나는 강아지를 잃어버렸다.

주어	have/has	과거분사
I/We/You/They	have (not)	been studied done　～ gone found
He/She/It	has (not)	

현재완료의 의문문은 주어 앞에 Have/Has를 쓰며, 긍정일 때는 「Yes, 주어+have/has」, 부정일 때는 「No, 주어+haven't/hasn't」로 답한다.

Have you finished your homework? 너 숙제 다 끝냈니?

Yes, I have. 응, 다 끝냈어. / **No, I haven't.** 아니, 다 안 끝냈어.

정답 p.12

PRACTICE 16 [1-16]

괄호 안에 주어진 단어를 이용하여 현재완료시제의 문장을 완성하고, 의문문의 경우 대답을 완성하세요.

1 ___Have___ you ever ___heard___ of this actor? (hear) → Yes, I ___have___.

2 My mother's parents ___________ ___________ away. (pass)

3 ___________ you ___________ about your future? (think) → No, I ___________.

4 I ___________ ___________ your cake. (not, touch)

5 The hen's eggs ___________ ___________. (hatch)

6 Mr. Smith ___________ ___________ his job. (lose)

7 ___________ you ever ___________ Korea, Cathy? (visit) → Yes, I ___________.

8 The plants ___________ ___________ no water for a week. (get)

9 They ___________ ___________ up places for them to live in. (set)

10 They ___________ ___________ the boy several books. (buy)

11 The singer's latest song ___________ ___________ successful in the USA. (be)

12 I ___________ ___________ how to use a computer. (not, learn)

13 ___________ you ever ___________ to Singapore? (be) → No, I ___________.

14 Seoul ___________ ___________ my second home. (become)

15 This area ___________ ___________ so much. (change)

16 We ___________ ___________ potatoes since then. (not, eat)

PSS 5-2 현재완료의 용법

용법	예문	주로 함께 쓰이는 단어
완료	He **has already finished** his homework. 그는 이미 그의 숙제를 끝마쳤다. I **have just planted** 10 trees. 나는 방금 10그루의 나무를 심었다. ***cf.*** just는 완료시제와 함께 쓰이지만 just now는 '방금 전에, 조금 전에'의 의미로 과거시제와 함께 쓰인다. She **hasn't arrived** in Seoul **yet**. 그녀는 아직 서울에 도착하지 않았다.	already, yet, just ***cf.*** already와 just는 주로 have와 과거분사 사이에 위치하고 yet은 문장의 끝에 위치한다.
경험	**Have** you **ever tried** tacos? 타코(멕시코 음식)를 먹어본 적이 있니? ***cf.*** ever는 의문문에서 '지금까지, 여태껏'이라는 의미로 have와 과거분사 사이에 위치한다. **I've been** to London **once**. 나는 런던에 가본 적이 한 번 있다. **I've never read** the book **before**. 나는 전에 그 책을 읽어본 적이 없다.	ever, never, before, once, often

결과	She **has lost** her bag. 그녀는 가방을 잃어버렸다. (그래서 지금 가방이 없다.) They **have gone** to New York. 그들은 뉴욕으로 갔다. (그래서 지금 여기에 없다.) ***cf.*** have been to: ~에 가본 적이 있다 (경험) have gone to: ~에 갔다 (그래서 지금 여기에 없다.)	go, come, leave, lose, buy
계속	Rachel **has worked** here **for** 6 years. Rachel은 여기에서 6년 동안 일했다. I **have lived** here **since** March. 나는 3월부터 여기에서 살았다.	for, since

정답 p.12

PRACTICE 17

주어진 단어나 어구를 이용하여 현재완료 문장을 완성하고, 괄호 안에 각 문장의 용법을 쓰세요.

1 _____*She has met*_____ Mr. Kim before. (she, meet) [경험]

2 _______________ to Paris. (my father, go) [ ]

3 _______________ my homework. (I, already, do) [ ]

4 _______________ for two years. (she, stay, in Korea) [ ]

5 _______________ once. (he, be, to India) [ ]

6 _______________ their lunch. (they, just, finish) [ ]

7 _______________ the dog. (Brian, just, walk) [ ]

8 _______________ a pet. (I, never, own) [ ]

9 _______________ since I was ten. (I, play, the guitar) [ ]

10 _______________ his leg. (he, break) [ ]

PSS 5-3 for와 since

for – '~ 동안'의 뜻으로, 사건이 일어나 지속된 시간의 길이를 나타낸다.

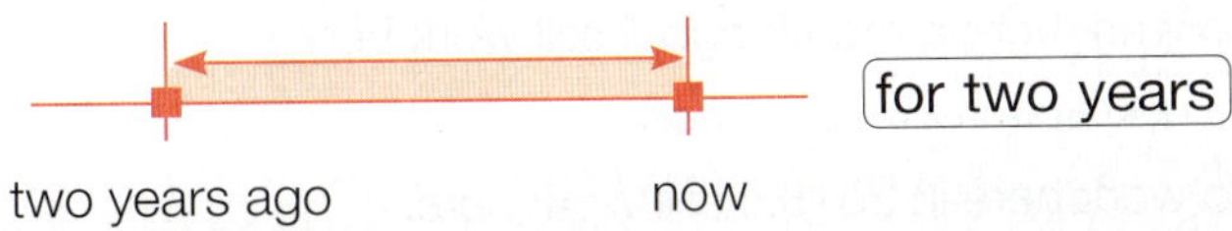

She started to play the violin two years ago. She still plays the violin.

그녀는 2년 전에 바이올린을 연주하기 시작했다. 그녀는 아직도 바이올린을 연주한다.

➡ She **has played** the violin **for** two years. 그녀는 2년 동안 바이올린을 연주해 왔다.

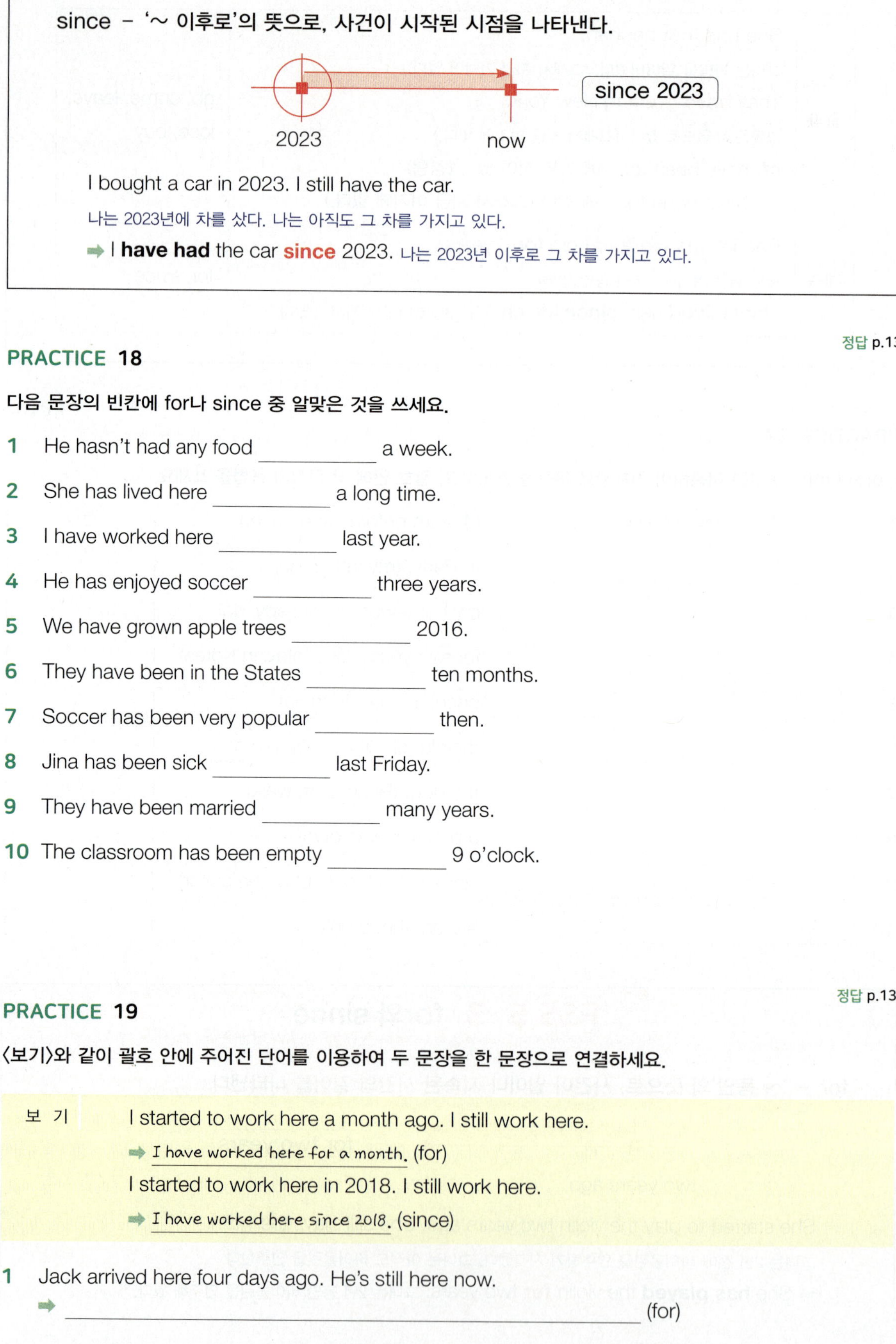

정답 p.13

PRACTICE 18

다음 문장의 빈칸에 for나 since 중 알맞은 것을 쓰세요.

1 He hasn't had any food ___________ a week.

2 She has lived here ___________ a long time.

3 I have worked here ___________ last year.

4 He has enjoyed soccer ___________ three years.

5 We have grown apple trees ___________ 2016.

6 They have been in the States ___________ ten months.

7 Soccer has been very popular ___________ then.

8 Jina has been sick ___________ last Friday.

9 They have been married ___________ many years.

10 The classroom has been empty ___________ 9 o'clock.

정답 p.13

PRACTICE 19

〈보기〉와 같이 괄호 안에 주어진 단어를 이용하여 두 문장을 한 문장으로 연결하세요.

> 보 기
>
> I started to work here a month ago. I still work here.
> ➡ I have worked here for a month. (for)
> I started to work here in 2018. I still work here.
> ➡ I have worked here since 2018. (since)

1 Jack arrived here four days ago. He's still here now.

➡ ____ (for)

2 I began to teach students fifteen years ago. I still teach students.

➡ ____ (for)

3 Liz started to study Japanese two years ago. She still studies it.

➡ ____ (for)

4 My mom bought the house last year. She still has it.

➡ ____ (since)

5 Kate first met Dave last April. She still dates him.

➡ ____ (since)

6 Mark started to play tennis in 2023. He still plays tennis.

➡ ____ (since)

PSS 5-4 현재완료시제와 과거시제

현재완료	과거
1. 과거에 시작되어 현재까지 계속되는 동작이나 상태를 나타낸다. I **have stayed** in London for two weeks. (I'm still in London.) 나는 2주 동안 런던에 머물러왔다. (나는 아직도 런던에 있다.)	1. 과거에 시작되어 과거에 종료된 동작이나 상태를 나타낸다. I **stayed** in London for two weeks. (I'm not in London anymore.) 나는 2주 동안 런던에 머물렀다. (나는 더 이상 런던에 있지 않다.)
2. 과거의 불특정한 시점에 일어난 동작이나 상태를 나타낸다. 과거의 특정한 때를 나타내는 부사(구)와 함께 쓰지 않는다. She **has lost** her purse. 그녀는 지갑을 잃어버렸다.	2. last year, yesterday, four weeks ago와 같이 과거의 특정한 때를 나타내는 부사(구)와 함께 쓰여 그 동작이나 상태가 일어난 구체적인 시점을 나타낸다. She **lost** her purse **last night**. 그녀는 지난 밤에 지갑을 잃어버렸다.

정답 p.13

PRACTICE 20 [1-10]

괄호 안의 단어를 알맞은 형태로 바꾸어 빈칸에 쓰세요.

1 *A*: Have you seen Mary lately?

  B: Yes, I have. I ___________ her last night at a restaurant. (see)

2 *A*: What do you think of the novel *Pride and Prejudice*?

   B: I don't know. I ____________ ____________ ____________ it. (never, read)

3 *A*: How's your sister doing in London?

   B: I'm not sure. I ____________ ____________ with her recently. (not, talk)

4 *A*: Did you pass the exam?

   B: Of course. I ____________ good grades. (get)

5 *A*: How's the weather there?

   B: It ____________ a lot this morning, but it has stopped now. (snow)

6 *A*: Are you nervous?

   B: Yes, I am. I ____________ ____________ ____________ a truck before. (never, drive)

7 *A*: Have you finished your homework?

   B: Yes. I ____________ ____________ ____________ it. (just, finish)

8 *A*: Your kitchen is very clean.

   B: Thank you. I ____________ it yesterday. (clean)

9 *A*: Are you hungry?

   B: Yes. I ____________ ____________ anything since this morning. (not, eat)

10 *A*: Why did you walk home?

   B: I ____________ home because I missed the bus. (walk)

정답 p.13

PRACTICE 21

밑줄 친 부분 중 잘못된 곳이 있으면 올바르게 고치세요.

1 Yesterday we <u>have had</u> our first English class of this year. ____________

2 Doctors <u>have found</u> that this is very useful. ____________

3 It <u>has rained</u> heavily last night. ____________

4 My friend <u>has lost</u> his job lately. ____________

5 Yumi <u>has been</u> born in Gwangju. ____________

6 I <u>have bought</u> this tablet PC last year. ____________

7 She <u>has just gone</u> out to have dinner. ____________

8 I <u>have finished</u> the work two hours ago. ____________

9 He <u>has already seen</u> the movie. ____________

10 My dad <u>has got</u> a new job last month. ____________

PRACTICE 22

괄호 안의 말과 과거시제 또는 현재완료시제 중 알맞은 것을 사용하여 문장을 완성하세요.

1 (I / not / check / my email / yesterday). So, I didn't know what happened in London.

➡ _I didn't[did not] check my email yesterday._

2 (I / solve / ten problems / so far). I feel very confident now.

➡ _______________

3 I don't remember what year they started working at this company.

(they / work / here / since 2020)?

➡ _______________

4 (the train / leave / the station / five minutes ago). I missed it by a second.

➡ _______________

5 Did you say one million dollars? (How / you / earn / so much / last year)?

➡ _______________

6 (Eva / not / see / her sister / for a long time). She is going to the Philippines to meet her.

➡ _______________

PSS 5-5 현재완료 진행시제

현재완료 진행시제는 과거에 시작된 어떤 동작이 현재까지 계속될 때 쓴다. 계속의 의미를 나타내므로 for, since와 함께 쓰이는 경우가 많다.

> have/has+been+-ing

Jake started playing the piano an hour ago. He is still playing the piano now.

Jake는 한 시간 전에 피아노를 치기 시작했다. 그는 지금도 아직 피아노를 치고 있다.

➡ Jake **has been playing** the piano for an hour.

Jake는 한 시간 동안 피아노를 치고 있다.

cf. 현재완료시제는 과거의 한 사건이 현재와 관련이 있을 때 쓰인다. 반면, 현재완료 진행시제는 과거에 시작한 어떤 동작이 현재까지도 계속 진행 중인 것을 강조한다.

I **have taught** her.

나는 그녀를 가르쳤다 (→ 뜻이 분명하지 않음. 현재완료의 '계속', '완료', '경험'으로 해석 가능)

I **have been teaching** her.

나는 그녀를 가르치고 있다. (→ 과거부터 지금까지 계속 가르치고 있는 상황)

PRACTICE 23

괄호 안에 주어진 동사를 이용하여 현재완료 진행시제 문장을 완성하세요.

1 I ___________________ English for ten years. (study)

2 My friends and I ___________________ basketball for three hours. (play)

3 How long ___________ he ___________________ in his room? (sleep)

4 She ___________________ for this company since she was 28 years old. (work)

5 ___________ you ___________________ this magazine for two hours? (read)

6 The engineer ___________________ the air-conditioner in the living room. (repair)

7 They ___________________ for you since 2 o'clock in the afternoon. (wait)

8 Amy ___________________ to her friend on the phone for one hour. (talk)

9 ___________ Daniel ___________________ an apple pie in the kitchen? (bake)

10 She ___________________ TV for two hours. (watch)

PRACTICE 24

주어진 두 문장을 for나 since 중 알맞은 것을 사용하여 현재완료 진행시제 문장으로 바꿔 쓰세요. (단, 밑줄 친 단어를 주어로 사용하세요.)

1 I got my glasses in March. I still wear them.
➡ I have been wearing my glasses since March.

2 Seyeon turned on her laptop two hours ago. She is still using it.
➡ ___________________

3 Two people started playing tennis at 4 o'clock. They are still playing tennis.
➡ ___________________

4 Mike began making lunch at noon. He is still making lunch.
➡ ___________________

5 Jisu and I began building a sand castle an hour ago. We are still building it.
➡ ___________________

6 It began to rain this morning. It is still raining.
➡ ___________________

1 Which one is NOT natural in grammar in the following sentence?

> If you will take that flight now, what time will
> ①　　　　②　　　　　　　　③　　　　④
> you arrive?
> 　⑤

2 다음 밑줄 친 말 중 어색한 것을 고르세요.

> A: Look! ⓐ There's a dog on the bench.
> B: I know that dog. ⓑ I had seen it here since last month.
> A: Have you? Doesn't it have a home?
> B: ⓒ It is, but it waits here for its owner until he ⓓ comes home every day.
> A: The owner must be happy.
> B: You can say that again. I think the dog ⓔ is waiting for its owner now.

① ⓐ, ⓒ　　　② ⓑ, ⓒ　　　③ ⓑ, ⓓ
④ ⓐ, ⓒ, ⓔ　⑤ ⓑ, ⓓ, ⓔ

3 다음 중 주어진 문장과 현재완료의 용법이 같은 것은?

> I have been to Europe before.

① My son has lost his watch.
② Have you finished the homework yet?
③ Have you ever seen this movie?
④ Mother has worked there since last year.
⑤ Has she lived in this house since then?

4 다음 중 어법상 틀린 문장을 고르세요.

① Mina has studied English for two years.
② I have slept for ten hours.
③ My uncle has lived there for last month.
④ I have had this book since 2020.
⑤ She has been sick since last night.

5 다음 단어 중 동사의 3단 변화의 패턴이 〈보기〉와 다른 것을 고르세요.

> 보 기 | buy – bought – bought

① catch　　② teach　　③ think
④ bring　　⑤ speak

6 Which sentence is grammatically correct?

① My brother leaves for Gyeongju tomorrow.
② Ed studies English for the finals yesterday.
③ I was playing the violin next Sunday.
④ Was your parents angry at you?
⑤ You doesn't want to learn Chinese.

7 다음 두 문장을 현재완료를 이용해서 한 문장으로 만드세요.

> • My uncle and aunt moved to Washington D.C. three years ago.
> • They still live there now.

➡ My uncle and aunt ＿＿＿＿＿ ＿＿＿＿＿
＿＿＿＿＿ Washington D.C. for three years.

8 어법상 틀린 부분을 고친 것으로 바르지 <u>않은</u> 것은?

① Lisa and Lily have studied Spanish in 2022.
→ Lisa and Lily have studied Spanish since 2022.
② Someone has break into my car and steal my laptop.
→ Someone has broke into my car and stole my laptop.
③ He has returned my call yet.
→ He hasn't returned my call yet.
④ She has lived in Seoul in five years.
→ She has lived in Seoul for five years.
⑤ Have you ever solve a jigsaw puzzle before?
→ Have you ever solved a jigsaw puzzle before?

9 다음 대화의 밑줄 친 <u>read</u>와 같은 소리로 발음되는 것은?

> B: Mary, how many books did you read last year?
> G: I <u>read</u> only four books. What about you?
> B: I read one book a month.

① He learned to <u>read</u> at the age of five.
② She could <u>read</u> the excitement in his eyes.
③ We will <u>read</u> a play in English class next week.
④ The driver tried to <u>read</u> the road sign that was far away.
⑤ The children gathered around as their teacher <u>read</u> a story aloud.

10 다음 중 밑줄 친 부분의 쓰임이 <u>잘못된</u> 것의 개수를 고르세요.

> Have you ever ⓐ <u>trying</u> *Pho*? *Pho* is one of ⓑ <u>the most popular foods</u> in Vietnam. It is a beef soup with rice noodles. I ⓒ <u>have tried</u> it when I visited Vietnam last year. It ⓓ <u>was</u> one of my favorite dishes ever since. Some people hate it because of the herbs in it, but I ⓔ <u>have been enjoying</u> it since I first tasted it.

① 2개   ② 3개   ③ 4개   ④ 5개   ⑤ 없음

11 우리말과 뜻이 같도록 빈칸에 알맞은 말끼리 바르게 짝지은 것은?

> • 우리 엄마는 전에 인도에 다녀오신 적이 있다.
> ➡ My mom ___________ India before.
> • 내 남동생이 막 숙제를 끝냈다.
> ➡ My brother ___________ his homework.

① has been to – just finishes
② has been to – has just finishing
③ has gone to – has just finishing
④ has been to – has just finished
⑤ has gone to – has just finished

12 다음 중 어법상 올바른 문장의 개수로 알맞은 것은?

> ⓐ I have met my boyfriend in 2020.
> ⓑ We depart from the hotel this evening.
> ⓒ He swum in the river with them last week.
> ⓓ I have worked here since 2022.
> ⓔ They are arriving on the 9 o'clock flight.
> ⓕ My father was reading a newspaper when dinner was ready.

① 1개   ② 2개   ③ 3개   ④ 4개   ⑤ 5개

13 다음 문장의 밑줄 친 부분과 쓰임이 같은 것은?

> She <u>has lived</u> in Australia since last year.

① I <u>have learned</u> Chinese for two years.
② Jenny <u>has read</u> the story twice.
③ She <u>has lost</u> her wallet.
④ I <u>have met</u> her before.
⑤ Kevin <u>has been</u> to America.

14 다음 대화에서 틀린 문장을 찾아 바르게 고치세요.

> A: ⓐ <u>Have you finished packing your bag yesterday?</u>
> B: Yes, I did. ⓑ <u>I have been looking forward to the trip.</u>
> A: How are you feeling?
> B: ⓒ <u>I'm really excited.</u> I don't think I will be able to sleep tonight.
> A: Well, ⓓ <u>if you don't sleep, you'll be tired tomorrow.</u>

➡ ____________________________________

____

15 다음 빈칸에 들어갈 말로 알맞은 것은?

> The captain of the boat checks everything. When something __________, he will take care of it.

① happen ② happens ③ will happen
④ happening ⑤ to happen

16 주어진 문장의 밑줄 친 부분과 용법이 같은 것은?

> <u>Have</u> you ever <u>heard</u> of the yellow bird in this town?

① We <u>have lived</u> here for six months.
② I <u>have</u> never <u>seen</u> a rainbow.
③ Julie <u>has</u> just <u>broken</u> the vase.
④ He <u>has gone</u> to school.
⑤ I <u>have stayed</u> in Korea since 2020.

17 다음 밑줄 친 부분 중 어법상 틀린 것을 고르세요.

① They <u>chose</u> the boy for the team last week.
② The sleeping babies <u>lied</u> on the bed.
③ He <u>hurt</u> his back playing tennis yesterday.
④ We <u>drank</u> a whole bottle of orange juice.
⑤ I <u>read</u> the book to the children last night.

18 그림의 내용과 일치하도록 주어진 단어를 사용하여 알맞은 말을 쓰세요.

A: What is your dad doing in the yard?
B: He __________________________. (wash)

19 다음 괄호 안에 주어진 각각의 단어를 알맞은 형태로 고쳐 쓰세요.

> • I have just __________ the project. (finish)
> • My mom __________ to America last year. (go)

20 다음 우리말을 참고하여 빈칸에 들어갈 알맞은 말을 <u>모두</u> 고르세요.

> • Bob은 매주 일요일마다 축구를 한다.
> = Bob plays soccer _______________ .

① next Sunday　　② last Sunday

③ this Sunday　　④ on Sundays

⑤ every Sunday

21 다음 글에서 <u>틀린</u> 부분을 한 군데 찾아 고치세요.

> A new English teacher came to my school. His name was Paul. He asked us about our plans for the school year. I said, "I've make a special plan. I'm planning to keep a diary in English." Then he said, "That's a great idea." I felt very good about myself.

_______________ ➡ _______________

22 다음 두 문장을 현재완료를 이용하여 한 문장으로 바꿔 쓰세요.

> • They started to serve free meals two years ago.
> • They still do.

➡ _______________

23 밑줄 친 (A)를 대신할 수 있는 표현으로 가장 적절한 것은?

> W: (A) <u>Have you ever tried coding a robot?</u>
> M: Yes, I have. I built a small robot in science class last year.

① Did you ever try coding a robot?

② Have you ever coded a robot before?

③ Why don't you try to code a robot?

④ Are you going to try coding a robot?

⑤ Will you try coding a robot?

24 Alex와 Samantha가 어제 한 일을 적은 표를 보고, 바른 것을 <u>모두</u> 고르세요.

Time	Alex	Samantha
10 a.m.~11 a.m.	cleaned a room	took a shower
12 p.m.~1 p.m.	had lunch	made spaghetti
2 p.m.~3 p.m.	took a nap	took care of her little brother
4 p.m.~5 p.m.	listened to pop music	played the cello
6 p.m.~7 p.m.	played a computer game	had dinner with her family
8 p.m.~9 p.m.	read a novel	talked to her friend on the phone

① Alex was cleaning the kitchen at 10:30 a.m.

② Samantha was taking care of her little brother when Alex was taking a nap.

③ Samantha was taking a shower at 12:20 p.m.

④ Alex was listening to pop music when Samantha was having dinner with her family.

⑤ Alex was reading a novel when Samantha was talking to her friend on the phone.

25 다음 대화의 빈칸에 공통으로 알맞은 것은?

> *Tom*: Where have you _______, Julia?
> *Julia*: I have _______ to China.

① gone　　② were　　③ been

④ went　　⑤ be

26 다음 빈칸에 들어갈 말로 알맞은 것은?

> Your son _______ arrive here next Monday.

① is being　　② is going　　③ was

④ will be　　⑤ is going to

27 다음 주어진 〈조건〉을 <u>반드시</u> 사용하여 아래의 문장과 의미가 같도록 영작하세요.

> I started learning Japanese last summer, and I'm still learning it.

> 조 건
> 1. 7단어로 작성
> 2. 현재완료 시제 사용

➡ _______________________________

28 다음 문장의 현재완료와 용법이 같은 것을 <u>모두</u> 고르세요.

> Karen has never lost her mobile phone.

① I have read the magazine before.
② She has already done her homework.
③ My sister has met him twice.
④ I have just washed my car.
⑤ I have lived in Busan for a year.

29 다음 두 문장을 한 문장으로 바르게 만든 것은?

> She began to wait for the bus twenty minutes ago.
> She's still waiting for it.

① She have been to wait for the bus twenty minutes ago.
② She has been waiting for the bus twenty minutes ago.
③ She has been to wait for the bus since twenty minutes.
④ She have been waiting for the bus for twenty minutes.
⑤ She has been waiting for the bus for twenty minutes.

30 다음 밑줄 친 부분 중 어법상 <u>어색한</u> 것은?

> Many people ① <u>stood</u> around the man. He ② <u>kept</u> ③ <u>saying</u>, "I'm not a thief. I haven't ④ <u>stole</u> ⑤ <u>anything</u>."

31 다음 중 어법상 <u>틀린</u> 문장만 짝지은 것은?

> ⓐ Have you ever emailed your friends?
> ⓑ My sister has visited London last year.
> ⓒ They arrived at the hotel yesterday.
> ⓓ Sam has lived in Seoul in 2018.
> ⓔ I saw the movie six months ago.

① ⓐ, ⓒ   ② ⓐ, ⓔ   ③ ⓑ, ⓒ
④ ⓑ, ⓓ   ⑤ ⓓ, ⓔ

32 (가)에 들어갈 표현으로 가장 알맞은 것은?

> I believe the best way to learn a foreign language is to be exposed to it constantly. So I've decided to expose myself to English as much as possible. I have started to watch English TV shows to adapt to listening to English, and I ___(가)___ speaking English with my language exchange partners regularly.

① have practicing
② have been practiced
③ have been practicing
④ had been practicing
⑤ had practiced

33 다음 중 어법상 옳은 문장을 <u>모두</u> 고른 것은?

ⓐ James has been struggled with the problem lately.
ⓑ My daughter has stayed in Italy for a year.
ⓒ The use of disposable plastics have been falling since the ban was imposed.
ⓓ He has been absent from school since last Thursday.
ⓔ I haven't already read the book.
ⓕ I have met him four days ago.
ⓖ The woman has played many famous roles in several musicals since 2002.

① ⓐ, ⓓ, ⓖ   ② ⓑ, ⓓ, ⓖ   ③ ⓑ, ⓔ, ⓖ
④ ⓒ, ⓓ, ⓕ   ⑤ ⓓ, ⓔ, ⓖ

34 다음 밑줄 친 ⓐ~ⓕ 중 어법상 잘못된 것을 골라 그 기호를 쓰고, 문장을 바르게 고쳐 쓰세요.

Seth: Alice, what are you going to do this weekend?
Alice: I'm going to visit my grandma. ⓐ <u>She lives in the country.</u>
Seth: I thought she lived in your neighborhood.
Alice: She moved. ⓑ <u>She has lived there since last year.</u>
Seth: I see. ⓒ <u>Do you go there often?</u>
Alice: I want to, but ⓓ <u>I have been not there since two months.</u>
Seth: Why is that?
Alice: ⓔ <u>I have been busy studying for the final exam.</u> ⓕ <u>It will be over tomorrow.</u>

➡ _______________________________

____

35 다음 중 어법상 올바른 문장은?

① They have gone to New York last winter.
② When have you taught him?
③ She has met him yesterday.
④ He has worn glasses since he was a kid.
⑤ They have been happy a week ago.

36 다음 밑줄 친 부분 중 will로 바꾸어 쓸 수 <u>없는</u> 것은?

① I <u>am going to</u> ask him about this.
② Jane <u>is going to</u> the library.
③ Matthew <u>is going to</u> go back to Canada.
④ The kids <u>are going to</u> go on a picnic.
⑤ My brothers <u>are going to</u> fly to Japan.

37 다음 두 문장을 한 문장으로 표현하려고 할 때, 가장 올바른 것은?

- He began to work with us two years ago.
- He still works with us.

① He has worked with us for two years.
② He has worked with us for two years ago.
③ He has worked with us two years ago.
④ He has begun to work with us for two years ago.
⑤ He has begun to work with us two years ago.

38 다음 글의 (A), (B), (C)에 알맞은 것끼리 바르게 연결된 것은?

I (A) ⌊was doing / am doing⌋ my homework
in my room when a thief (B) ⌊broke into / has
broken into⌋ our house last week.
I was very surprised but I called 911 calmly.
My parents have been telling me to call
911 in an emergency (C) ⌊since / for⌋ I was
a toddler. Five minutes later, a police officer
came to our house and arrested the thief.

	(A)	(B)	(C)
①	was doing	has broken into	– since
②	was doing	broke into	– since
③	am doing	broke into	– for
④	was doing	broke into	for
⑤	am doing	has broken into	– for

39 다음 중 흐름이 어색한 대화는?

① A: Have you ever thought about making a
　　movie?
　B: No, I haven't. Why?
② A: Has he done his work well?
　B: Yes, he did.
③ A: Who has seen the new movie?
　B: I don't know. Maybe Minho has.
④ A: I have never been to Japan.
　B: Really? I hope you will visit there someday.
⑤ A: Have we met before?
　B: No, we have never met before.

40 다음 그림을 보고, 빈칸에 들어갈 알맞은 말을 쓰세요.

It started snowing at 2 o'clock in the afternoon.

It is still snowing now.

➡ It ＿＿＿＿＿ ＿＿＿＿＿ ＿＿＿＿＿ since
　2 o'clock in the afternoon.

41 〈보기〉에서 가장 적절한 말을 골라 빈칸을 완성하세요.

보 기	win / break / drive / spread / forget

조 건	
	1) 필요시, 〈보기〉의 단어를 적절히 변형할 것. 2) 〈보기〉의 단어 중복 사용 불가.

(1) We saw the window ＿＿＿＿＿ by the storm.
(2) The virus has ＿＿＿＿＿ to many countries.
(3) His father allowed him ＿＿＿＿＿ the car.
(4) I'm sorry, but I've ＿＿＿＿＿＿＿＿＿＿
　your name again.
(5) Our school team has just ＿＿＿＿＿＿＿＿＿
　the championship.

42

다음 대화의 빈칸 (A), (B)에 들어갈 말로 가장 적절한 것은?

A: I'm so excited to try out this recipe!
B: Emily, what are you trying to make?
A: Oh! I'm trying to make a strawberry tart.
B: I love tarts! My mom has made it for me _____(A)_____ I was a little boy.
A: You're so lucky. I've never _____(B)_____ a tart before.
B: Really? Then, this one would be your very first tart.
A: I know! I hope I can make it look as good as the one in this picture.

	(A)	(B)		(A)	(B)
①	since	eat	②	when	eaten
③	since	eaten	④	since	ate
⑤	when	ate			

43

수지와 지호가 경험해 본 것들을 표시한 표를 보고 〈보기〉와 같이 현재완료 문장을 완성하세요.

경험한 내용	Suji	Jiho
• eat Thai food	o	x
(1) visit Brazil once	o	o
(2) win a prize in the piano competition	x	x
(3) read *Anna Karenina*	o	x

보 기
• Suji has eaten Thai food, but Jiho has not eaten Thai food.

(1) Suji and Jiho ___________________________ .

(2) Suji and Jiho ___________________________ .

(3) Suji ___________________________ ,
but Jiho ___________________________ .

44

다음 빈칸에 들어갈 알맞은 말은?

A: I have been in Korea for almost three years now.
B: Wow! That is amazing. Then, have you ever been to Haeundae in Busan?
A: No, ___________________________ .

① I have never been there
② I have been there for a week
③ I went there last Friday
④ I didn't like the place very much
⑤ I have been there since last month

45

다음 여행 계획표 (A)를 참고하여 〈보기〉에서 알맞은 표현을 골라 블로그 게시글 (B)의 빈칸을 완성하세요. (단, 중복하여 사용할 수 있습니다.)

보 기 | will   have been   am

(A) My Travel Plan

Day 1	see the Statue of Liberty
Day 2	go to Times Square
Day 3	go on a picnic in Central Park

(B) My Blog

I __________ going to visit New York this summer. I started to plan the trip a week ago, and I'm still planning it. So I __________ planning the trip for a week. On the first day, I __________ see the Statue of Liberty. On the second day, I __________ go to Times Square and enjoy a famous musical. On the third day, I __________ go on a picnic in Central Park.

CHAPTER 3
조동사

PSS 1 조동사의 쓰임

조동사는 동사 앞에서 의무, 추측, 가능, 요청, 허가, 제안 등의 의미를 더하는 동사로 조동사 뒤에는 동사원형이 온다.

조동사	뜻	예문
must	의무 ~해야 한다	You **must work** together as a team. 너희는 한 팀으로 함께 일해야 한다.
can	능력 ~할 수 있다	I **can swim** in the sea. 나는 바다에서 수영을 할 수 있다.
could	능력(과거형) ~할 수 있었다	We **could plant** more trees. 우리는 더 많은 나무들을 심을 수 있었다.
do	강조의 do 정말로[확실히, 꼭] ~하다	She **does show** a talent in math. 그녀는 정말로 수학에 재능이 있다.
should	의무 ~해야 한다	We **should listen** to what he is saying. 우리는 그가 말하고 있는 것을 들어야 한다.
had better	충고, 권유 ~하는 것이 낫다	You **had better do** your homework. 너는 숙제를 하는 것이 낫다.
will	미래(의지) ~할 것이다	He **will sing** at the school festival. 그는 학교 축제에서 노래를 부를 것이다.
would	미래(의지) 과거형 ~할 것이다	I **would shake** hands with him. 나는 그와 악수를 할 것이다.
may	추측 ~할지도 모른다	Scientists **may discover** a new planet. 과학자들은 새로운 행성을 발견할지도 모른다.
might	추측 ~할지도 모른다	She **might get** caught in the rain. 그녀는 비를 맞을지도 모른다.
used to	과거의 반복적 행위 ~하곤 했다	He **used to play** computer games all night. 그는 밤새도록 컴퓨터 게임을 하곤 했다.

정답 p.17

PRACTICE 1

빈칸에 들어갈 말로 알맞은 것을 고르세요.

1 Your sister must ___________ me for the cakes. ① pay ② pays ③ paying

2 When we go abroad, we can ___________ English. ① to use ② use ③ used

3 You should ___________ off your shoes in the room. ① take ② to take ③ took

4 Jina ___________ to go for a walk in the evening. ① like ② likes ③ liking

5 I used to ___________ in a small house. ① lived ② live ③ living

6 You had better ___________ a doctor right now. ① see ② to see ③ saw

7　She may ＿＿＿＿＿ us the answer.　① gave　② gives　③ give

8　That would ＿＿＿＿＿ very nice.　① is　② being　③ be

9　I ＿＿＿＿＿ watching TV two weeks ago.　① stopped　② stop　③ stops

10　Paul must ＿＿＿＿＿ his homework by eight o'clock.　① finishes　② finish　③ finishing

11　We could ＿＿＿＿＿ hiking next week.　① went　② to go　③ go

12　She might ＿＿＿＿＿ this horror movie.　① hated　② hate　③ hates

13　I will ＿＿＿＿＿ a taxi to the train station.　① took　② taking　③ take

14　My mom does ＿＿＿＿＿ brown hair.　① having　② have　③ has

15　Mark always ＿＿＿＿＿ to tell the truth.　① trying　② tries　③ try

PSS 2 조동사의 부정형

조동사+not	축약형	예문
must not	**mustn't**	You **mustn't** jump into the pond. 너는 연못에 뛰어들면 안 된다.
cannot	**can't**	They **cannot[can't]** buy anything to eat. 그들은 먹을 것을 살 수 없다.
could not	**couldn't**	He **couldn't** take his eyes off her. 그는 그녀에게 눈을 뗄 수가 없었다.
do not	**don't**	I **don't** understand. 나는 이해를 못한다.
should not	**shouldn't**	You **shouldn't** touch the artworks. 당신은 그 예술작품들을 만지면 안 된다.
had better not	**'d better not**	You**'d better not** complain. 너는 불평하지 않는 게 낫다.
will not	**won't**	I **won't** forget you. 나는 너를 잊지 않을 것이다.
would not	**wouldn't**	I **wouldn't** worry about it. 난 그것에 대해 걱정하지 않을 것이다.
may not	-	He **may not** get an invitation. 그는 초대장을 받지 못할지도 모른다.
might not	**mightn't**	She **mightn't** join the speech contest. 그녀는 말하기 대회에 참가하지 않을지도 모른다.
did not use to (used to의 부정)	**didn't use to**	I **didn't use to[used not to]** go camping with my parents. 나는 부모님과 캠핑을 가지 않곤 했다.

PRACTICE 2

다음 문장의 밑줄 친 부분을 부정형으로 바꾸어 쓰세요.

1 My teacher <u>goes</u> to church on Sundays.

➡ *My teacher does not[doesn't] go to church on Sundays.*

2 I <u>can</u> wait to meet them.

➡

3 You <u>may</u> play the computer game now.

➡

4 You <u>must</u> break your promise.

➡

5 You <u>had better</u> go on a diet.

➡

6 It <u>might</u> be safe to do so.

➡

7 I <u>could</u> get to the office early.

➡

8 You'<u>d better</u> bring your kids.

➡

9 I <u>will</u> bring it to you.

➡

10 You <u>should</u> hang it on the wall.

➡

11 I <u>used to</u> play the guitar.

➡

12 She <u>could</u> finish the work on time.

➡

13 I <u>clean</u> my room every Saturday.

➡

14 They <u>should</u> wear their hats.

➡

15 You <u>must</u> cross the street now.

➡

PSS 3 조동사로 시작하는 의문문

조동사로 시작하는 의문문은 「조동사＋주어＋동사원형 ～?」의 어순으로 나타낸다.

조동사	주어	동사원형		
Can	you	**join**	our club?	너 우리 클럽에 가입할 수 있니?
Will	they	**leave**	here?	그들이 이곳을 떠날까?
Should	I	**bring**	an umbrella?	내가 우산을 가져와야 하니?

정답 p.17

PRACTICE 3

다음 문장을 주어진 조동사로 시작하는 의문문으로 바꾸어 쓰세요.

1 You fix the computer. (can)
➡ _Can you fix the computer?_

2 Dave plays basketball. (will)
➡ ______________________________

3 Jihye takes the first train. (should)
➡ ______________________________

4 He drives a car. (can)
➡ ______________________________

5 I give him my notebook. (should)
➡ ______________________________

6 He teaches English at a middle school. (will)
➡ ______________________________

7 Mike speaks five languages. (can)
➡ ______________________________

8 She takes art classes in Italy. (will)
➡ ______________________________

9 I order some food. (can)
➡ ______________________________

10 They make Chinese dishes. (can)
➡ ______________________________

PSS 4 조동사의 종류

PSS 4-1 must I

의무 (~해야 한다)	과거	We **had to** buy boots and gloves yesterday. 우리는 어제 부츠와 장갑을 사야 했다.
	현재	We **must** buy boots and gloves. 우리는 부츠와 장갑을 사야 한다. = We **have to** buy boots and gloves.
	미래	We **will have to** buy boots and gloves when we get there. 우리는 그곳에 도착하면 부츠와 장갑을 사야 할 것이다. = We **must** buy boots and gloves when we get there. = We **have to** buy boots and gloves when we get there. *cf.* 조동사끼리는 나란히 쓰일 수 없다. 　　 We **will must** buy boots and gloves when we get there. (×)

cf. must, have to, should는 모두 '~해야 한다'는 의미를 가지지만 강제성 강도와 뉘앙스가 다르다. 강제성의 강도는 must>have to>should의 순서이며 must는 '반드시 해야 한다'는 의미로 법이나 규제로 정해진 내용을 나타낼 때 쓴다. have to는 일상적인 '~해야 한다'는 의미로 개인적인 책임이나 의무 또는 필요를 나타낸다. should는 '~하는 게 좋을 거야'라는 의미로 추천이나 제안할 때 주로 사용한다.

정답 p.17

PRACTICE 4

괄호 안에 주어진 단어 중 알맞은 것을 고르세요.

1 Did you (must, have, had) to leave the party so early?

2 Mary (must, has, had) go home and get some rest.

3 I (must, have, had) go to the station to meet him.

4 We (must, have, had) to find the exit now.

5 You will (must, have, had) to fix it by tomorrow.

6 You (must, have, had) take off your shoes to enter this room.

7 If Junho wants to be a lawyer, he will (must, have, has) to study hard.

8 The sun is too strong. I (must, have, had) buy sunglasses.

9 You (must, have, had) to wait for me last night.

10 Minji (must, have, has) to go to the airport to pick up her parents.

PRACTICE 5

have to를 알맞은 형태로 바꾸어 빈칸을 채우세요.

1 They are very weak. You ________________ treat them very carefully.

2 Kelly ________________ learn Chinese when she was young.

3 I'll have a test next week. I ________________ study very hard.

4 I want to go shopping with Jane, but I ________________ clean the house now.

5 He ________________ stay there for the next three weeks.

6 Last Friday my dad ________________ work until 10 p.m.

7 Jennifer needs money now. She ________________ go to the bank.

8 My friend Jihoon ________________ move to Chicago in two months.

9 I ________________ buy a dictionary yesterday.

10 You ________________ feed your dog twice a day, and walk him every morning.

PSS 4-2 must Ⅱ

	추측 (~임에 틀림없다)	She **must** be very sick. 그녀는 몹시 아픈 게 틀림없다. ↔ She **can't** be very sick. 그녀는 몹시 아플 리가 없다. *cf.* 「can't+동사원형」은 '~일 리가 없다'의 뜻도 지닌다.
부정	금지 (~해서는 안 된다)	You **must not** park there. 너는 거기에 주차를 해서는 안 된다. You **must not** take a photo here. 너는 여기에서 사진을 찍으면 안 된다.
	불필요 (~할 필요가 없다)	He **doesn't have to** carry those books. 그는 그 책들을 가지고 다닐 필요가 없다. = He **doesn't need to** carry those books. = He **need not** carry those books.

정답 p.17

PRACTICE 6 [1-10]

괄호 안에 주어진 단어 중 알맞은 것을 고르세요.

1 Mark got the highest grade again. He (must, can't) be very smart.

2 I can't believe the news. It (must, can't) be true.

3 Mary watches a movie every weekend. She (must, can't) like movies.

4 Suji was on the plane for 10 hours. She (must, can't) be very tired.

5 All of her friends came to her party. She (must, can't) be sad.

6 Bob has never learned Korean. He (must, can't) speak Korean.

7 She didn't eat anything. She (must, can't) be very hungry now.

8 Mr. Lee is a new teacher. He (must, can't) know all of the students.

9 Andy is always late for school. He (must, can't) be lazy.

10 I just saw Cathy on the street. She (must, can't) be home now.

정답 p.18

PRACTICE 7

그림을 보고, must not 또는 don't/doesn't have to 중 빈칸에 알맞은 것을 쓰세요.

1 *A*: Why don't we sit there?

   B: It's for the elderly. We ________________ sit there.

2 *A*: I'm worried about tomorrow's quiz.

   B: You ________________ worry about that. It won't be difficult.

3 *A*: I'm off today.

   B: Good. You ________________ wake up early then.

4 *A*: You ________________ tell this to anyone.

   B: Of course not. I'll keep it secret.

5 *A*: You ________________ stay late. You can go home.

   B: Thanks. See you tomorrow.

6   *A*: You ___________________ wear shoes here.

    B: Oh, sorry. I'll take them off.

PSS 4-3 can, could I

능력/가능 (~할 수 있다)	과거	She **could** do it without your help. 그녀는 너의 도움 없이 그것을 할 수 있었다. = She **was able to** do it without your help.
	현재	I **can** speak with them in English. 나는 그들과 영어로 이야기할 수 있다. = I **am able to** speak with them in English.
	미래	Daniel **can** go to London next summer. Daniel은 다음 여름에 런던에 갈 수 있다. = Daniel **will be able to** go to London next summer. = Daniel **is able to** go to London next summer.

정답 p.18

PRACTICE 8 [1-10]

be able to를 이용하여 두 문장의 의미가 같도록 빈칸을 채우세요.

1   The players can't win the game if they break the rules.

    = The players ____aren't able to____ win the game if they break the rules.

2   We could watch the concert from the front row.

    = We ___________________ watch the concert from the front row.

3   I don't know if I can do it well.

    = I don't know if I ___________________ do it well.

4   Kevin couldn't meet my sister last night.

    = Kevin ___________________ meet my sister last night.

5   Can't you speak Chinese well?

    = ___________ you ___________ speak Chinese well?

6   Ben can't go to university next year.

    = Ben ___________________________________ go to university next year.

7 I could run faster when I was young.

= I ___________________ run faster when I was young.

8 They couldn't get there by bus.

= They ___________________ get there by bus.

9 We can go on a picnic next month.

= We ___________________ go on a picnic next month.

10 Mom is a great cook. She can make very good Chinese dishes.

= Mom is a great cook. She ___________________ make very good Chinese dishes.

PSS 4-4 can, could Ⅱ

요청	~해 주시겠어요?	**Can you** show me how to make it? 그것을 어떻게 만드는지 보여줄래? **Could you** open the door? 문 좀 열어주시겠어요? *cf.* Could you ~?는 Can you ~?보다 공손한 표현이다.
허가	~해도 될까요?	**Can I** speak to Mr. Kim? 김 선생님과 통화할 수 있을까? **Could I** borrow some money from you? 당신에게 돈 좀 빌려도 될까요? *cf.* Could I ~?는 Can I ~?보다 공손한 표현이다.
추측	~일 리가 없다. ~일 수 있다.	It **can't** be true. 그게 사실일 리가 없다. (강한 의심) I **could** be right. 내가 맞을 수도 있다. (can보다 약한 추측)

정답 p.18

PRACTICE 9

다음 문장에서 밑줄 친 단어가 어떤 의미를 나타내는지 고르세요.

1 Could you do me a favor? (요청 / 허가)

2 That couldn't be my cap. Mine is red, but that one is yellow. (추측 / 요청)

3 I've been playing football since I could walk. (요청 / 능력)

4 I can't find my purse. Where is it? (능력 / 추측)

5 It's unbelievable. She can't do such a bad thing. (허가 / 추측)

6 Could you pass me that bag of chips over there? (허가 / 요청)

7 I <u>couldn't</u> play the violin well before I took the lesson last year.　　　(허가 / 능력)

8 <u>Could</u> you stop by next week?　　　(요청 / 추측)

9 <u>Could</u> I borrow your umbrella? I'll give it back to you tomorrow.　　　(추측 / 허가)

10 There is a box office near the elevator. We <u>can</u> buy tickets there.　　　(요청 / 능력)

11 <u>Can</u> I use your phone to make a quick call?　　　(허가 / 추측)

12 Visitors <u>can't</u> take photographs inside the museum.　　　(능력 / 허가)

PSS 4-5 do

1. 일반동사의 의문문과 부정문에 쓰이는 do

Do you remember his birthday? 넌 그의 생일을 기억하니?
She **did** not go to school yesterday. 그녀는 어제 학교에 가지 않았다.

2. 동사를 강조하는 do

I **do have** good memories about my friends. 나는 내 친구들에 대해 좋은 기억을 정말 가지고 있다.
She **does like** pizza. 그녀는 피자를 정말 좋아한다.
We **did meet** him in the stadium. 우리는 그를 경기장 안에서 정말 만났다.
cf. be동사는 강조할 수 없다.
　　She does be kind. (x)　　　She is really kind. (o)

3. 동사(구)의 반복을 피하는 대동사 do

Who won the game?　　　– She **did**. (= She won the game.)
누가 그 경기를 이겼니?　　　그녀가 이겼어.

정답 p.18

PRACTICE 10 [1-10]

do를 알맞은 형태로 바꾸어 빈칸을 채우세요.

1 ____________ you like baseball? – Yes, I do.

2 She ____________ have blue eyes.

3 Brian plays the piano better than Sue ____________.

4 My mom ____________ live in the city two years ago.

5 I'm certain that my son has a bright future. – Yes, he really ____________.

6 ____________ your brothers go to school in Tokyo? – Yes. They go to Tokyo University.

7 Luke ___________ not speak Spanish very well, so he's taking a Spanish lesson.

8 Kate and I ___________ like to go to the movies. We watch a movie twice a week.

9 Do they find the idea interesting? – No, they ___________.

10 I ___________ clean my room yesterday.

정답 p.18

PRACTICE **11**

우리말과 같은 뜻이 되도록 알맞은 조동사와 괄호 안의 단어를 사용하여 빈칸을 채우세요.

1 그것은 매우 지루한 게 틀림없다. (be)

➡ It ___________________________________ very boring.

2 그녀는 그에게 그 돈을 줄 필요가 없다. (give)

➡ She ___________________________________ him the money.

3 너는 버스를 타야 할 것이다. (take)

➡ You ___________________________________ a bus.

4 내 남동생은 수영하는 것을 정말 좋아한다. (like)

➡ My brother ___________________________________ swimming.

5 그는 똑똑하다. 그가 시험을 망칠 리가 없다. (fail)

➡ He is smart. He ___________________________________ the exam.

PSS 4-6 should, had better

should	의무, 추천, 제안 (~해야 한다/ ~하는 게 좋다)	We **should** wear school uniforms. 우리는 교복을 입어야 한다. **Should** I write it in my notebook? 제가 그것을 공책에 써야 하나요? You **shouldn't** do that again. 넌 다시는 그렇게 해서는 안 된다.
had better	충고, 권유 (~하는 게 낫다)	should보다 더 강한 뜻을 내포하며, 축약형인 'd better의 형태로 주로 쓰인다. You**'d better** go to bed right now. 너는 지금 당장 자러 가는 게 낫다. We**'d better** ask our teacher about the test. 우리는 그 시험에 대해 선생님께 여쭤 보는 게 낫다. You**'d better not** make a noise. 넌 시끄럽게 하지 않는 게 낫다.

PRACTICE 12

우리말과 같은 뜻이 되도록 괄호 안에 주어진 단어를 바르게 배열하세요.

1 너는 너의 부모님께 그렇게 말해서는 안 된다. (to your parents, like that, should, talk, not, you)

➡ ____

2 제가 그곳에 다시 가야 하나요? (I, there, again, should, go)

➡ ____

3 우리는 우리의 선생님들께 공손해야 한다. (we, polite, to our teachers, be, should)

➡ ____

4 Jenny는 그 사실을 잊어서는 안 된다. (Jenny, not, forget, the truth, should)

➡ ____

5 나는 그녀에게 사과해야 한다. (apologize, I, should, to her)

➡ ____

PRACTICE 13

그림을 보고, 괄호 안의 단어와 had better를 이용하여 대화를 완성하세요.

1 A: I have a sore throat.
   B: __________ You'd better see __________ a doctor. (see)

2 A: My brother studied until late last night. He looks very tired.
   B: ___________________________ some rest. (get)

3 A: It's getting dark. We might miss the last bus.
   B: ___________________________ back home now. (go)

4 A: I have midterms next week.
   B: ___________________________ hard. (study)

5 A: I had a cast on my arm yesterday.
   B: ___________________________ if the cast affects your mobility. (not, drive)

PSS 4-7 will, would

Will[Would] you ~?	~해 주시겠습니까?	**Will you** introduce yourself? 자기 소개를 해 주시겠어요? **Would you** introduce yourself? 자기 소개를 해 주시겠습니까? ***cf.*** Would you ~?는 Will you ~?보다 공손한 표현이다.
would like +명사	~을 원하다	**I'd like** some bread. 저는 빵을 좀 원해요. = I **want** some bread.
would like to +동사원형	~을 하고 싶다	**I'd like to** have dinner with you. 나는 너와 함께 저녁식사를 하고 싶어. = I **want to** have dinner with you.

정답 p.19

PRACTICE 14

괄호 안에 주어진 조동사 중 알맞은 것을 고르세요.

1   (Will, Would) you like some oranges?

2   (Will, Should) you do me a favor?

3   (Will, Would) you like to play soccer tomorrow?

4   (Would, Can) I have some juice?

5   (Will, Would) you like to go fishing?

6   (Can, Will) I speak to Mr. Smith?

7   (Will, Must) you pass me the sugar, please?

8   (Will, Would) you like to take a cooking class together?

9   (Could, Do) you bring it to me?

10 (Do, Will) you like your new car?

11 (Will, Would) you like an ice cream?

12 (Will, Could) I get your address, please?

13 (Will, Should) you open the door for me?

14 (Will, Would) you like some sugar in your coffee?

15 (Will, Do) you give it to your sister for me?

추측	~일지도 모른다, 아마 ~일 것이다	Mr. Lee **may** be sick. Lee 씨는 아플지도 모른다. She **may** not know your name yet. 그녀는 아마 아직 네 이름을 알지 못할 것이다. It **might** take more than two weeks. 2주 이상 걸릴지도 모른다. ***cf.*** might는 may보다 불확실한 추측을 나타낸다.
허가	~해도 좋다, ~해도 되다	You **may** go home now. 너는 지금 집에 가도 좋다. **May** I see your ID card? 제가 당신의 신분증을 봐도 될까요? – Yes, you **may**. 네, 그래도 돼요. – No, you **may not**. 아니오, 그럴 수 없어요. – No, you **must not**. 아니오, 그러면 안됩니다. ***cf.*** must not이 may not보다 더 강한 금지의 표현이다.

정답 p.19

PRACTICE 15

〈보기〉에서 알맞은 단어를 골라 may를 포함하는 문장을 완성하세요. (단, 필요한 경우 부정문으로 쓰세요.)

보 기	know come go work feel want

1   A: Where are you going for your holidays?
   B: I'm not sure. I ______may go______ to Busan.

2   A: Why does Sally look so sad these days?
   B: I'm not sure. She ____________ lonely.

3   A: Why doesn't Minsu call my name?
   B: I'm not sure. He ____________ your name.

4   A: When is Jina coming to see us?
   B: I'm not sure. She ____________ on Saturday.

5   A: Why doesn't Tom answer the phone?
   B: I'm not sure. He ____________ to talk to anyone.

6   A: What does Sam do for a living?
   B: I'm not sure. He ____________ at a bank.

PRACTICE 16

괄호 안에 주어진 조동사 중 알맞은 것을 고르세요.

1 (May, Will) I take your order?

2 Jane (might, had better) be sick. I'm worried about her.

3 (Will, May) you turn down the volume?

4 Believe me. He (do, did) solve the problem by himself.

5 May I use your camera? – No, you (must not, might not).

6 (Can, May) you come to my office at 7?

7 You (might, have to) study hard for the next quiz.

8 (Would, Will) you like to have dinner with me?

9 I will (can, be able to) finish it by tomorrow.

10 (May, Will) I speak to June?

11 (Would, Could) you like some tea?

PSS 4-9 used to, would

1. 과거에 반복적으로 일어났던 행위를 나타낼 때는 '～하곤 했다'의 의미를 가진 used to 또는 would를 쓸 수 있다.

   I went swimming every morning before, but I don't go swimming anymore.
   나는 전에는 매일 아침 수영하러 갔지만, 더 이상 수영하러 가지 않는다.
   ➡ I **used to** go swimming every morning. 나는 매일 아침 수영하러 가곤 했다.
   ➡ I **would** go swimming every morning. 나는 매일 아침 수영하러 가곤 했다.

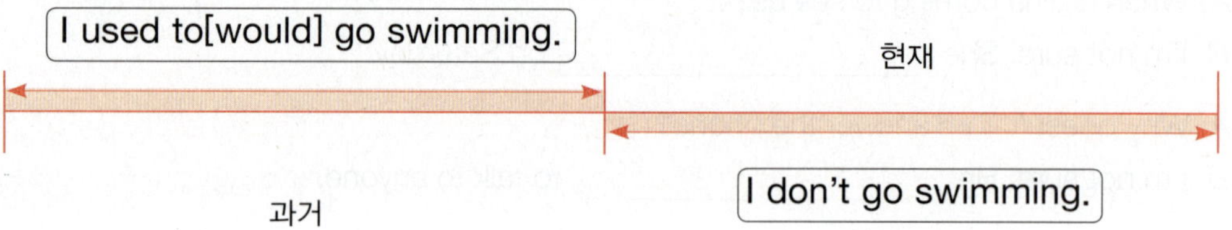

2. 과거에 있었던 행위가 아닌 상태를 나타낼 때는 would를 쓸 수 없다.

   Ben had a car before, but he sold it. Ben은 전에 차가 있었지만 팔았다.
   ➡ Ben **used to** have a car. Ben은 차가 있었다.
   ➡ Ben **would** have a car. (×)

3. used to(~ 하곤 했다)와 형태가 비슷하지만 전혀 다른 의미를 지닌 아래의 표현들을 혼
   동하지 말아야 한다. (학교 내신 시험에 자주 출제되므로 각각의 용법을 확실히 익힐 것.)

used to+동사원형 : (과거에) ~하곤 했다	I **used to play** the piano. 나는 피아노를 연주하곤 했다. (지금은 연주하지 않는다.)
be used to+동사원형 : ~하기 위해 사용되다	Flour **is used to make** a cake. 밀가루는 케이크를 만들기 위해 사용된다.
be used to+~ing : ~에 (이미) 익숙하다	My brother **is used to playing** the piano. 내 남동생은 피아노를 연주하는 데 익숙하다.

정답 p.19

PRACTICE 17 [1-6]

그림을 보고, 괄호 안의 단어와 used to나 would를 이용하여 문장을 완성하세요.

1

BEFORE　　　NOW

There ___used to be___ a tree in the park. (be)

2

BEFORE　　　NOW

He _______________ dark hair. (have)

3

BEFORE　　　NOW

My family _______________ a dog. (own)

4

BEFORE　　　NOW

He _______________ soccer, but now he focuses
on basketball. (play)

5

BEFORE　　　NOW

I _______________ a bike to school. (ride)

6

BEFORE → NOW

Sujin _________________ in a city. (live)

정답 p.19

PRACTICE 18

우리말과 같은 뜻이 되도록 〈주어진 표현〉과 괄호 안의 단어를 사용하여 문장을 완성하세요.

주어진 표현	used to+동사원형 / be used to+동사원형 / be used to+~ing

1 나는 아침에 요가하는 것에 익숙하다. (do)

➡ I _________________________________ in the morning.

2 그 기금은 나무들을 심는 데 사용되었다. (plant)

➡ The funds _________________________________ trees.

3 난 오후 9시에 잠자리에 들곤 했다. (go)

➡ I _________________________________ at 9 p.m.

4 많은 구급차들이 부상자들을 실어 나르기 위해 사용되었다. (carry)

➡ Many ambulances _________________________________ the injured.

5 Mike는 차를 운전하는 데 아직 익숙하지 않다. (drive)

➡ Mike _________________________________ a car yet.

6 우리는 유기견들을 위해 자원봉사를 하는 것에 익숙하다. (volunteer)

➡ We _________________________________ for abandoned dogs.

7 카카오는 초콜릿을 만드는 데 사용된다. (make)

➡ Cacao _________________________________ .

8 Jessica는 어렸을 때 통통했었다. (chubby)

➡ Jessica _________________________________ when she was young.

9 내 딸은 아침에 일찍 일어나는 것에 익숙하다. (wake)

➡ My daughter _________________________________ early in the morning.

10 나의 여동생은 거미를 무서워하곤 했다. (afraid)

➡ My sister _________________________________ spiders.

중간·기말고사 대비문제

1 다음 중 짝지어진 대화가 자연스럽지 <u>않은</u> 것은?

① A: Could I borrow your pen for a minute?
　B: Yes, of course.
② A: May I use the toilet?
　B: No, you may not.
③ A: Will I need my jacket there?
　B: I think you won't need it.
④ A: Shouldn't you be studying for the exam?
　B: Yes, you should. You are out of time.
⑤ A: Can you give me a hand?
　B: Of course, what should I do?

2 다음 우리말과 같은 뜻이 되도록 빈칸에 들어갈 알맞은 말은?

> • 저한테 100달러를 빌려주시겠어요?
> = _______________ me 100 dollars?

① Should you lent
② Would you lend
③ Can you borrow
④ May I lend
⑤ Do you have to borrow

3 다음 문장의 밑줄 친 부분과 뜻이 같은 것은?

> Helping her grandmother every day <u>must</u> be difficult for her, but she always smiles.

① You <u>must</u> turn left here.
② You <u>must</u> clean the window.
③ You stayed up late last night, so you <u>must</u> be tired.
④ You <u>must</u> be careful when you cross the street.
⑤ You <u>must</u> do your best to win the game.

4 밑줄 친 부분 중 어법상 알맞은 것은?

> Here ⓐ <u>are</u> Donna's plan for this Saturday. In the morning, she will clean the house. She will vacuum the floor and ⓑ <u>wipes</u> all the windows. Then, she will go to the community center for her volunteer work. She takes care of kids there, and they always want her ⓒ <u>spending</u> more time with them. If it ⓓ <u>will be</u> sunny, she ⓔ <u>will go</u> on a short picnic with them.

① ⓐ　　② ⓑ　　③ ⓒ　　④ ⓓ　　⑤ ⓔ

5 다음 중 어법상 오류가 있는 문장은 몇 개인가?

> ⓐ I used to living in China when I was little.
> ⓑ She is the actress was on the TV show.
> ⓒ Do you know if your brother came home late last night?
> ⓓ The girl musts be very smart and bright.
> ⓔ Penny hates to see her dentist regularly.
> ⓕ You need to stop making excuses.
> ⓖ Mr. Shang wanted me attend the meeting instead of him.

① 1개　　② 2개　　③ 3개　　④ 4개　　⑤ 5개

6 다음 빈칸에 들어갈 말로 가장 알맞은 것은?

> Matthew can't run fast now, but he _________ run fast before.

① could　　② couldn't　　③ can
④ can't　　⑤ is able to

7 다음 중 어법상 옳은 문장을 <u>모두</u> 고르세요.

① Bricks are used to make the building.
② I used to playing soccer on the weekends.
③ James is used to eat meat, but now he doesn't eat it.
④ Four colors are used to painting the national flag.
⑤ She is not used to speaking in public.

8 다음 밑줄 친 (a)~(e) 중에서 어법상 옳지 <u>않은</u> 것은?

Heather: Hey, Erin! I have this serious problem with my friend, Dana. You know, I always had long hair, but I decided to cut my hair short. All my friends said that it looked (a) <u>good</u> on me. And guess what? Dana cut her hair (b) <u>short</u> the next day. I was kind of angry and I didn't want us to look the same, so I dyed my hair brown. And she also dyed her hair brown the next day. Why is she copying me? I'm so (c) <u>stressed</u> out.

Erin: I know how you feel. I also had this friend who used to (d) <u>copying</u> everything that I did. At first, I was really stressed out and I even told her to stop copying me. The reason why Dana is copying you is because she doesn't know (e) <u>what</u> she likes yet. Just let her copy you until she finds what is right for her. Maybe she will thank you later.

① (a)　　② (b)　　③ (c)　　④ (d)　　⑤ (e)

9 다음 중 어법상 <u>어색한</u> 문장은?

① He doesn't must read it.
② Jane must get there on time.
③ You have to follow the rules.
④ We must not get up late.
⑤ They had to study for the test.

10 다음 문장의 밑줄 친 부분과 그 쓰임이 <u>다른</u> 것은?

Experience really <u>does</u> make you a better man.

① I <u>do</u> like swimming in the river in the summer.
② I <u>did</u> my math homework.
③ He <u>did</u> love his pet, Molly.
④ Jane <u>does</u> hate her cousin, David.
⑤ They <u>do</u> want to learn Japanese in Tokyo, Japan.

11 다음 중 어법상 올바르지 <u>않은</u> 문장은?

① You didn't do well on the test.
② I did nothing for them.
③ She does have your key.
④ He did look tired.
⑤ Mr. Kim does knows the truth.

12 다음 빈칸에 들어갈 말로 알맞은 것은?

You ___________ drink coffee a lot because you can't sleep well at night.

① must　　　② should　　　③ can
④ should not　　⑤ could not

13 우리말과 같은 뜻이 되도록 주어진 단어를 사용하여 9단어로 영작하세요.

이 문제를 해결할 다른 방법이 있는 게 틀림없다. (way, solve, problem)

= _______________________________________

____

14 밑줄 친 (A)에 공통으로 들어갈 단어는?

- _____(A)_____ they close at 10 p.m. on weekdays?
- You _____(A)_____ not need to worry about me.
- I _____(A)_____ enjoy a good cup of coffee every morning.

① be ② am ③ are
④ do ⑤ does

15 대화의 흐름상 가장 어색한 것은?

A: Hey, do you have any plans for the summer vacation?
B: Yes. ⓐI'm going to go on a trip.
A: Really? ⓑWhere are you going to go?
B: ⓒTo Jeju Island.
A: Oh, I've been there before. ⓓYou shouldn't try horse-riding.
B: That sounds like fun. ⓔI will definitely try it.

① ⓐ ② ⓑ ③ ⓒ ④ ⓓ ⑤ ⓔ

16 주어진 문장의 밑줄 친 부분과 그 쓰임이 같은 것은?

I do have a lot of memories about them.

① She doesn't have anything to do.
② I do like her very much.
③ The boy smiles as you do.
④ Do you remember me?
⑤ I do not have to do it.

17 우리말과 같은 뜻이 되도록 괄호 안의 말을 바르게 배열하여 문장을 완성하세요.

- 나는 스무 살 때 우리 집 근처의 식당에서 일하곤 했다.
  = When I was 20 years old, ___________
  _______________________________.
  (used to, my house, at, work, I, near, a restaurant)

18 다음 짝지어진 두 문장의 의미가 서로 다른 것은?

① You don't have to go to school tomorrow.
  = You need not go to school tomorrow.
② I used to go hiking every Sunday.
  = I would go hiking every Sunday.
③ You'd better ask him about the science project.
  = You would like to ask him about the science project.
④ We can solve the problem without your help.
  = We are able to solve the problem without your help.
⑤ Would you open the window for me?
  = Could you open the window for me?

19 다음 대화의 빈칸에 들어갈 말로 알맞지 <u>않은</u> 것은?

> *Mom*: Don't you see the sign? We ________________ sit here.
>
> *Son* : Oh, I see. It is for disabled people.
>
> *Mom*: Right.

① should not　　② must not
③ cannot　　④ are not allowed to
⑤ don't have to

20 밑줄 친 @~@ 중에서 빈칸에 들어갈 조동사가 나머지 넷과 <u>다른</u> 것은?

> If you'd like to ride a bicycle, there are some rules you should follow. First, you ____@____ always wear a safety helmet. Second, you ____ⓑ____ never violate the traffic signs. Third, you ____ⓒ____ turn on the lights at night. Finally, you ____ⓓ____ never use a cellphone while riding a bicycle. Breaking these rules ____ⓔ____ lead you to an accident. Keep these safety rules and be safe!

① @　　② ⓑ　　③ ⓒ　　④ ⓓ　　⑤ ⓔ

21 다음 빈칸에 들어갈 말로 알맞은 것은?

> The mother koala takes good care of her baby. The mother koala holds tight to the tree because the baby koala is on her back. When the baby koala gets lost, it cries as a little kid ________.

① are　　② is　　③ do
④ does　　⑤ did

22 괄호 안에 주어진 말과 had better를 사용해 대화의 빈칸에 알맞은 충고의 문장을 쓰세요.

(1) *A*: I have a headache.

　　B: ________________________

　　________________________

　　(you, take, some medicine)

(2) *A*: I often feel sleepy in class.

　　B: ________________________

　　________________________

　　(you, go to bed, earlier)

(3) *A*: My sister has lost her cell phone on the subway.

　　B: ________________________

　　________________________

　　(she, check, the Lost and Found)

23 다음 밑줄 친 부분 중 어법상 알맞은 것은?

> ① <u>Do you like read books?</u> ② <u>Would you like to having a discussion</u> with your friends about the books you read? Then, come and join the book club. ③ <u>We might looks like a quiet club</u> that only reads books, but we are more than that! This is a place ④ <u>where you can talk about the book and watching the film version of the book as well.</u> Also, we make short films critiquing books. ⑤ <u>So, why don't you join our club where you will be able to indulge in books?</u>

24 우리말과 같은 뜻이 되도록 괄호 안에 주어진 단어를 바르게 배열하세요.

> • 너는 오늘 밤에 밖에 안 나가는 게 좋겠다.
>
> = ________________________
>
> 　(not, had, go, you, tonight, better, out)

25 다음 대화의 빈칸에 들어갈 말로 알맞지 <u>않은</u> 것은?

> A: Pets aren't allowed in the hotel.
> B: But I have my dog with me.
> A: I'm sorry, guests _______________ here.
> B: Understood. I'll find a nearby pet-friendly place.

① can't bring pets
② must not bring pets
③ shouldn't bring pets
④ don't have to bring pets
⑤ are not supposed to bring pets

26 다음 밑줄 친 <u>did</u>를 대신해서 쓸 수 있는 말로 알맞은 것은?

> A: Who finished the work last night?
> B: Mina <u>did</u>.

① has not finished the work yet
② finished the work last night
③ didn't finish the work last night
④ didn't want to finish the work last night
⑤ worked with me last night

27 다음 질문에 대한 대답으로 바르지 <u>않은</u> 것을 <u>모두</u> 고르세요.

> Q: May I take a photo here?
> A: _______________________________

① Yes, you may.
② Yes, you may not.
③ No, you may.
④ Only without flash, please.
⑤ I'm afraid you can't.

28 다음 문장의 밑줄 친 부분과 바꿔 쓸 수 있는 말은?

> I <u>want to</u> thank you for helping me finish the project today.

① like
② would like to
③ would like
④ want
⑤ had like to

29 다음 상황을 고려하여 Emma가 Carl에게 도움을 요청하는 말을 〈조건〉에 맞게 쓰세요.

> Emma is trying to hang a large poster on the classroom wall. She's holding the poster with both hands and can't reach the tape. She wants someone to hand it to her. Then, her classmate Carl walks in and says, "Can I give you a hand?"

조 건
1. Could로 문장을 시작하고 총 6단어로 쓰세요.
2. 필요한 도움의 내용을 구체적으로 언급하며, 글의 마지막에 이어질 Emma의 말을 4형식 한 문장으로 쓰세요.

➡ _______________________________
____

30 다음 빈칸에 들어갈 말로 알맞은 것은?

> I'm very happy because I am _________ hear from you again.

① can
② able
③ able to
④ should
⑤ will

31 대화의 흐름상 빈칸에 들어갈 문장으로 알맞지 <u>않은</u> 것을 <u>모두</u> 고르세요.

> A: Mom, I'm going to Priya's birthday party tomorrow.
> B: Did you choose what to wear?
> A: No, not yet. Could you help me choose my outfit?
> B: _______________________________

① You will buy a dress for her.
② Sure. Let me see your closet.
③ You'd better invite Priya to your party.
④ Why don't you ask your sister for help?
⑤ You should wear the dress you bought last weekend.

32 다음 중 어법상 올바른 문장만 짝지은 것은?

> ⓐ I'd not better go shopping today.
> ⓑ I'd better not eat them.
> ⓒ You'd better to answer him now.
> ⓓ You'd better not to bring the bag.
> ⓔ You'd better wash your clothes.

① ⓐ, ⓑ   ② ⓐ, ⓓ   ③ ⓑ, ⓔ
④ ⓒ, ⓓ   ⑤ ⓓ, ⓔ

33 다음 표를 보고, 세 학생이 어렸을 때 할 수 있었던 것과 할 수 없었던 것에 대한 문장을 완성하세요.

	cook *ramen*	run errands
Amanda at age six	x	o
Travis at age ten	o	o
Jennifer at age ten	x	o

(1) Amanda _________ _________ _________ _________ cook *ramen* at age six.

(2) Travis and Jennifer _________ _________ _________ run errands at age ten.

34 그림을 보고, 주어진 우리말과 같은 뜻이 되도록 빈칸에 알맞은 말을 쓰세요.

> • Jessica wants to win a prize in the violin competition.
> • She practices playing the violin every day.

> • She _________ _________ _________ _________ win a prize in the violin competition.
> = 그녀는 바이올린 경연대회에서 상을 받을 수 있을 것이다.

35 괄호 안의 단어를 이용하여 다음 표지판이 나타내는 주의사항을 완성하세요.

➡ You _________ _________ _________ here. (should, turn)

CHAPTER 4
수동태

PSS 1 수동태에 많이 쓰이는 불규칙 동사

원형	과거형	과거분사형	원형	과거형	과거분사형
be	was, were	been	lend	lent	lent
bear	bore	borne/born	make	made	made
break	broke	broken	pay	paid	paid
bring	brought	brought	put	put	put
build	built	built	read[ri:d]	read[red]	read[red]
buy	bought	bought	say	said	said
catch	caught	caught	see	saw	seen
choose	chose	chosen	send	sent	sent
cut	cut	cut	sing	sang	sung
do	did	done	speak	spoke	spoken
draw	drew	drawn	steal	stole	stolen
eat	ate	eaten	take	took	taken
find	found	found	feed	fed	fed
give	gave	given	teach	taught	taught
grow	grew	grown	think	thought	thought
tell	told	told	throw	threw	thrown
hold	held	held	understand	understood	understood
hurt	hurt	hurt	write	wrote	written
keep	kept	kept	know	knew	known

cf. 수동태로 쓸 수 없는 동사

   1) 타동사 일부: have(가지다), resemble(닮다), fit/become/suit(어울리다), cost(비용이 들다)

   2) 자동사 전체: happen(일어나다), exist(존재하다), disappear(사라지다), occur(발생하다)

정답 p.22

PRACTICE 1

괄호 안의 단어를 알맞은 형태로 바꾸어 빈칸에 쓰세요.

1 Jenny was born___________ on July 2nd, 2020. (bear)

2 The classic novel is ___________ by many people. (read)

3 The picture was ___________ yesterday. (steal)

4 That song was ____________ by a famous singer on TV last night. (sing)

5 These toys are ____________ by Mr. Han. (make)

6 The chair was ____________ by my younger brother. (break)

7 The elephants were ____________ by the people. (catch)

8 I was ____________ how to fish by my grandfather. (teach)

9 This book was ____________ by Thomas Hardy. (write)

10 English is ____________ in New Zealand. (speak)

11 Coffee is ____________ in Brazil. (grow)

12 My dog is ____________ twice a day. (feed)

13 These photos were ____________ at the beach. (take)

14 Eggs are ____________ in the refrigerator. (keep)

PSS 2 수동태 문장 만드는 법

1. 능동태와 수동태의 차이

능동태: 주어가 동사의 동작을 하는 경우에 쓴다. (~가 …한다)

My grandfather built this house. 우리 할아버지께서 이 집을 지으셨다.

수동태: 주어가 동사의 동작을 받을 때 쓴다. (~가 …되어진다)

This house was built by my grandfather. 이 집은 우리 할아버지에 의해 지어졌다.

2. 수동태 문장 만들기

① 능동태 문장의 목적어를 수동태 문장의 주어로 한다.

I made **them**. 내가 그것들을 만들었다.

➡ **They**

② 능동태 문장의 동사를 「be동사＋과거분사」의 형태로 바꾼다.

I **made** them.

➡ They **were made**

③ 능동태 문장의 주어를 「by＋목적격」으로 바꾼다.

I made them.

➡ They were made **by me**. 그것들은 나에 의해 만들어졌다.

PRACTICE 2

다음 문장을 수동태로 바꾸어 쓰세요.

1 Susie cleans the room.

➡ *The room is cleaned by Susie.*

2 My friends love me.

➡

3 Leonardo da Vinci painted the Mona Lisa.

➡

4 They recycle plastic bottles.

➡

5 I bought those black pants.

➡

6 My mom made those cookies.

➡

7 He reads a lot of books.

➡

8 Jason invited all the classmates to the party.

➡

9 The police catch thieves.

➡

10 Harry reported the news.

➡

11 Mrs. Lopez collects stamps and coins.

➡

12 The hunter killed two black bears.

➡

13 The police officer stopped the bus.

➡

14 Mr. Kim held the meeting.

➡

15 The president changed the rules of the meeting.

➡

PSS 3 수동태의 부정문과 의문문

수동태의 부정문은 다음과 같은 어순으로 쓴다.

주어 + be동사 + not + 과거분사 + by + 목적격 .

Jinhee **doesn't clean** the room. 진희는 방을 청소하지 않는다.

→ The room **isn't cleaned** by Jinhee. 방은 진희에 의해 청소되지 않는다.

Jason **didn't draw** this picture. Jason은 이 그림을 그리지 않았다.

→ This picture **wasn't drawn** by Jason. 이 그림은 Jason에 의해 그려지지 않았다.

수동태의 의문문은 다음과 같은 어순으로 쓴다.

Be동사 + 주어 + 과거분사 + by + 목적격 ?

Park Guell **was built by** Gaudi. Guell 공원은 Gaudi에 의해 지어졌다.

→ **Was** Park Guell **built** by Gaudi? Guell 공원은 Gaudi에 의해 지어졌나요?

The trees **were planted by** the volunteers. 그 나무들은 그 자원봉사자들에 의해 심어졌다.

→ **Were** the trees **planted** by the volunteers? 그 나무들은 그 자원봉사자들에 의해 심어졌니?

정답 p.22

PRACTICE 3 [1-10]

괄호 안의 지시에 맞게 주어진 문장을 바꾸어 쓰세요.

1 The homework wasn't done by me.

→ I didn't do the homework. ________________ (능동태)

2 My mother didn't make the cookies.

→ ________________ (수동태)

3 Some people in Japan don't speak English.

→ ________________ (수동태)

4 He was grounded for a week.

→ ________________ (의문문)

5 That book was written by him.

→ ________________ (의문문)

6 That play was not written by Shakespeare.

→ ________________ (능동태)

7 Some students don't respect the elderly.

➡ ____ (수동태)

8 Frank is loved by his classmates.

➡ ____ (의문문)

9 The bill was not paid by Yuri.

➡ ____ (능동태)

10 The stray cat was fed by Jake.

➡ ____ (의문문)

PSS 4 수동태의 시제

시제＼태	능동태	수동태
현재	Minho **plants** trees. 민호는 나무를 심는다.	Trees **are planted** by Minho. 나무들이 민호에 의해 심어진다.
과거	Minho **planted** trees. 민호는 나무를 심었다.	Trees **were planted** by Minho. 나무들이 민호에 의해 심어졌다.
미래	Minho **will plant** trees. 민호는 나무를 심을 것이다.	Trees **will be planted** by Minho. 나무들이 민호에 의해 심어질 것이다.
현재완료	Minho **has planted** trees. 민호는 나무를 심어왔다.	Trees **have been planted** by Minho. 나무들이 민호에 의해 심어져 왔다.

cf. 행위의 주체가 일반인이거나 말하지 않아도 알 수 있는 경우, 또는 나타낼 필요가 없을 때는 「by+목적격」을 생략할 수 있다.

Someone stole my purse. ➡ My purse was stolen **(by someone)**.

누군가가 내 지갑을 훔쳤다.　　　 내 지갑이 (누군가에 의해) 도난당했다.

정답 p.22

PRACTICE 4

다음 능동태 문장을 수동태 문장으로 바꾸어 쓰세요. (경우에 따라, 「by+목적격」의 생략이 가능합니다.)

1 Some people saw the thief.

➡ The thief was seen by some people.

2 The man will deliver the magazine.

➡ ____

3 Somebody will clean the room later.

➡ ____

4 Roger has built a new restaurant.

➡ ____

5 People will cut down more trees in the future.

➡ ____

6 Everyone has believed his lies.

➡ ____

7 Directors make movies or TV programs.

➡ ____

8 Tom fixed the car this morning.

➡ ____

9 The people have built this building for three years.

➡ ____

10 He will use the money to buy a new game character.

➡ ____

정답 p.22

PRACTICE 5

그림을 보고, 괄호 안의 동사를 알맞은 형태로 바꾸어 수동태 문장을 완성하세요.

1 The light bulb _______________________________ by Thomas Edison in 1879. (invent)

2 The chair _______________________________ yesterday. (move)

3 My work _______________________________ by next Friday. (do)

4 This picture _______________________________ by Marie last week. (paint)

5 The river _______________________________ since 2023. (pollute)

PSS 5 조동사가 있는 수동태

조동사가 있는 수동태는 다음과 같은 어순으로 쓴다.

주어 + 조동사 + be동사 원형 + 과거분사 + by + 목적격.

You **can** easily **find** the restaurant. 너는 그 식당을 쉽게 찾을 수 있다.
➡ The restaurant **can be** easily **found**. 그 식당은 쉽게 찾아질 수 있다.

You **must fix** the car right now. 너는 그 차를 지금 당장 수리해야 한다.
➡ The car **must be fixed** right now. 그 차는 지금 당장 수리되어야 한다.

정답 p.23

PRACTICE 6

다음 능동태 문장을 수동태 문장으로 바꾸어 쓰세요.

1 Kelly can finish the work.
➡ The work can be finished by Kelly.

2 Tony may do it tomorrow.
➡

3 He must solve the problem.
➡

4 They should obey the rules for this game.
➡

5 We might change the plans for the summer.
➡

6 I couldn't prepare dinner last night.
➡

7 Suji must use a computer for this task.
➡

8 We should not put them here.
➡

9 Tom may not keep the promise.
➡

10 The people could see the view very well.
➡

PRACTICE 7

그림을 보고, 괄호 안의 단어를 알맞은 형태로 바꾸어 수동태 문장을 완성하세요.

1 Your clothes ___________________ soon. (should, wash)

2 A lot of resources ___________________. (can, save)

3 They ___________________ by Paul. (will, cook)

4 This house ___________________ by tomorrow. (must, paint)

5 My dog ___________________ forever. (will, love)

PSS 6 주의해야 할 수동태

PROBLEM SOLVING SKILL

---

1. **4형식의 수동태 :** 4형식은 간접목적어와 직접목적어 둘 다 수동태 문장의 주어가 될 수 있지만, 주로 사람을 나타내는 간접목적어를 주어로 하는 경우가 많다. 직접목적어가 수동태의 주어가 되는 경우에는 간접목적어 앞에 to, for, of와 같은 전치사가 온다.

   Mom gave me some old pictures. 엄마가 내게 오래된 사진 몇 장을 주셨다.
   ➡ **I** was given some old pictures by Mom. 나는 엄마에 의해 오래된 사진 몇 장을 받았다.
   ➡ **Some old pictures** were given **to me** by Mom. 오래된 사진 몇 장이 엄마에 의해 내게 주어졌다.

   She asked the students their names. 그녀는 학생들에게 그들의 이름을 물었다.
   ➡ **The students** were asked their names by her. 학생들은 그녀에 의해 그들의 이름을 질문 받았다.
   ➡ **Their names** were asked **of the students** by her. 그들의 이름이 그녀에 의해 학생들에게 물어졌다.

   cf. 직접목적어만을 수동태의 주어로 하는 동사로는 buy, write, cook, make가 있다. 이 동사들은 사람(간접목적어)이 주어인 수동태 문장이 될 경우 의미가 어색해지므로(사람은 사지고, 써지고, 요리되고, 만들어질 수 없음) 쓰지 않는다.
   I bought my brother an interesting book. 나는 내 남동생에게 재미있는 책을 사 주었다.
   ➡ **An interesting book** was bought **for my brother** by me. (O)
   재미있는 책이 나에 의해 내 남동생에게 사 주어졌다.
   My brother was bought an interesting book by me. (X)

2. 5형식의 수동태

5형식 문장을 수동태 문장으로 전환할 때, 목적격 보어가 명사나 형용사인 경우에는 「be동사+과거분사」 뒤에 목적격 보어를 이어서 쓴다.

They call her Liz. 그들은 그녀를 Liz라고 부른다.

➡ She is called **Liz** by them. 그녀는 그들에 의해 Liz라고 불린다.

The news made me happy. 그 소식은 나를 행복하게 만들었다.

➡ I was made **happy** by the news. 나는 그 소식에 의해 행복해졌다.

정답 p.23

PRACTICE 8

〈보기〉와 같이 능동태 문장을 수동태 문장으로 바꾸어 쓰세요.

보 기	Sora gave me a book.	➡ I was given a book by Sora.
		➡ A book was given to me by Sora.
	His music makes me sad.	➡ I am made sad by his music.

1 Mr. Kim bought the boy a new bag.

➡ ____

2 I made my brother angry.

➡ ____

3 They elected him the president.

➡ ____

4 They showed Bob their pictures.

➡ ____

➡ ____

5 Nick gave me lovely flowers.

➡ ____

➡ ____

6 Jenny kept the place clean.

➡ ____

7 My daughter named the fish "Wish."

➡ ____

8 People call the restaurant George's.

➡ ____

9 My mom cooked me spaghetti yesterday.

➡ ______________________________________

10 Minho lent me 5,000 won yesterday.

➡ ______________________________________

➡ ______________________________________

PSS 7 수동태의 관용 표현

1. be made of '～로 만들어지다'(재료의 성질이 변하지 않는 경우)
    be made from '～로 만들어지다'(일련의 과정을 거쳐 재료의 성질이 변하는 경우)
    This notebook **is made of** used paper.
    이 공책은 쓰고 난 종이로 만들어진다.
    Wine **is made from** grapes. 와인은 포도로 만들어진다.

2. be filled with '～로 가득 차 있다'
    Her eyes **were filled with** tears. 그녀의 눈은 눈물로 가득 차 있었다.

3. be interested in '～에 흥미가 있다'
    I**'m interested in** English. 나는 영어에 흥미가 있다.

4. be covered with '～로 덮여 있다'
    The mountain **is covered with** snow. 그 산은 눈으로 덮여 있다.

5. be surprised at '～에 놀라다'
    I **was surprised at** the news. 나는 그 소식에 놀랐다.

6. be known to '～에게 알려져 있다'
    be known for '～로[때문에] 알려져 있다(유명하다)'
    be known as '～로서 알려져 있다'

    She **is known to** every student in my class. 그녀는 우리 반 모든 학생에게 알려져 있다.
    He **is known for** the poem. 그는 그 시로 알려져 있다.
    He wants to **be known as** an actor rather than a singer.
    그는 가수보다는 배우로서 알려지기를 원한다.

7. be pleased with[about] '～에 기뻐하다, 좋아하다'
    My dad **was pleased with[about]** the shirt. 우리 아빠는 그 셔츠를 좋아하셨다.

8. be satisfied with '～에 만족하다'
    I **am satisfied with** the result. 나는 그 결과에 만족한다.

9. be excited about '~에 흥분해 있다'

He **was excited about** the trip. 그는 그 여행에 흥분해 있었다.

10. be worried about '~에 대해 걱정하다'

I **am worried about** your health. 나는 너의 건강에 대해 걱정한다.

정답 p.23

PRACTICE 9

다음 문장의 빈칸에 알맞은 전치사를 쓰세요.

1 He was satisfied ___________ my answer.

2 Are you interested ___________ our project?

3 They were really excited ___________ the possibility of adopting a puppy.

4 Mr. White is known ___________ everyone in the town.

5 I am very pleased ___________ your present.

6 My mom was worried ___________ my brother's exam.

7 Plastic is made ___________ oil and natural gas.

8 His heart is filled ___________ joy.

9 Weren't you surprised ___________ his words?

10 The land is covered ___________ grass.

11 Paper is made ___________ wood.

12 This area is known ___________ heavy snow in winter.

정답 p.23

PRACTICE 10

다음 능동태 문장을 수동태 문장으로 바꾸어 쓰세요.

1 The crowd welcomed the president.

➡ ____

2 I could finish the work easily.

➡ ____

3 Mr. Song will teach science.

➡ ____

4 Millions of people watched the movie.

➡ ____

5 My kids clean the living room and the bathroom.

➡ ____

6 Susan has postponed the party.

➡ ____

7 John gave us some information.

➡ ____

➡ ____

8 My grandmother bought me a pretty skirt.

➡ ____

9 Alex calls me Jen.

➡ ____

10 My son asked me some difficult questions.

➡ ____

➡ ____

11 Mike can fix the photocopier.

➡ ____

12 Cathy didn't paint this wall.

➡ ____

13 You must invite Bill to the show.

➡ ____

14 His story made us bored.

➡ ____

15 Seho paid me 30,000 won.

➡ ____

➡ ____

16 We can use the Internet for our homework.

➡ ____

17 He named his cat Rachael.

➡ ____

18 He made me sandwiches.

➡ ____

1 다음 중 어법상 <u>어색한</u> 문장은?

① Japanese is spoken in Japan.
② The window was broken by Sam.
③ The red car is had by our grandmother.
④ The principal was respected by all of the students.
⑤ Our dog has been taken care of by my father.

2 어법상 바르지 <u>않은</u> 문장의 개수는?

(a) We were given extra homework last Friday.
(b) The songs were sing loudly at the concert.
(c) Lunch is being cook by my mom right now.
(d) The packages have been delivered this morning.
(e) All the bikes are repaired before the race.
(f) The dishes were broke by the cat.
(g) A new library will be built next year.
(h) The windows were cleaned yesterday afternoon.
(i) The cake was eat by all the students.
(j) The test papers is graded by the teacher.

① 3개　② 4개　③ 5개　④ 6개　⑤ 7개

3 다음 중 어법상 <u>어색한</u> 문장을 <u>모두</u> 고르세요.

① Computers are used by many people.
② The boy will be teached by her.
③ This fish should not be overcooked.
④ The red dress was worn by Kate.
⑤ The book was wrote by an old woman.

4 다음 대화의 빈칸에 들어갈 알맞은 단어는?

> A: Are you ___________ in music?
> B: Yes, I am. I especially like pop music.

① to interest　② interesting　③ interest
④ interested　⑤ interestingly

5 다음 대화에서 밑줄 친 부분 중 어법상 자연스러운 것은?

> A: What is this article about?
> B: It says that a thief ① <u>was catch</u> by the police.
> A: You mean the one who ② <u>was stolen</u> jewelry a week ago? I heard the store owner ③ <u>was very shocked</u> because of the incident.
> B: Yes. Fortunately, the police ④ <u>was seen</u> him at the mall. The thief ⑤ <u>was arrest</u> by the police.

6 다음 중 밑줄 친 부분이 어법상 올바른 것은?

① The report must <u>be released</u> tomorrow morning.
② Dinner should <u>prepared</u> by five.
③ These shoes <u>made</u> from rubber tires.
④ This novel <u>were written</u> by Tolstoy.
⑤ They <u>have taught</u> math by Ms. Pierce.

7 주어진 문장을 수동태 문장으로 바꿔 쓰세요.

• He cooked his friends rice noodles.

➡ ________________________________

____

8 다음 수동태로의 문장 전환 중 어색한 것은?

① Tom cooked this food.
➡ This food was cooked by Tom.
② Dad made the pencil case.
➡ The pencil case was made by Dad.
③ My friend read a poem to me.
➡ A poem is read to me by my friend.
④ The students cleaned the classroom.
➡ The classroom was cleaned by the students.
⑤ People speak English in Canada.
➡ English is spoken in Canada.

9 다음 빈칸 ⓐ, ⓑ, ⓒ에 들어갈 말로 바르게 짝지어진 것을 고르세요.

• The bag ________ⓐ________ lots of gold coins by the merchant.
• The building ________ⓑ________ since last year by the workers.
• The result of the game ________ⓒ________ the students.

	ⓐ	ⓑ	ⓒ
①	was filled of	– was built	– satisfied
②	was filled with	– has been built	– was satisfied
③	was filled with	– was built	– was satisfied
④	was filled of	– has been built	– was satisfied
⑤	was filled with	– has been built	– satisfied

10 밑줄 친 (A)~(E) 중 어색한 표현이 있는 것은?

Teacher: Everyone, (A) what's something new you've tried recently?
Jisoo: (B) I tried baking cookies with my little brother last weekend. It was a lot of fun!
Hyunwoo: (C) I started learning Spanish. It's a bit hard, but I enjoy the challenge.
Sumin: (D) I'm interested learning about photography. I saw a great photo exhibition last week, and it inspired me.
Teacher: That's great to hear! Try new things and (E) find out what you're passionate about.

① (A)　② (B)　③ (C)　④ (D)　⑤ (E)

11 다음을 수동태 문장으로 바꿀 때, 빈칸에 알맞은 전치사를 쓰세요.

• I asked him many questions about Mr. Stevenson.
➡ Many questions about Mr. Stevenson were asked ________ him by me.

12 주어진 문장을 능동태로 바르게 바꾼 것은?

The ring was kept in the box by Jiho.

① Jiho keeps the ring in the box.
② Jiho kept the ring in the box.
③ Jiho has kept the ring in the box.
④ Jiho had kept the ring in the box.
⑤ Jiho is keeping the ring in the box.

13 우리말 뜻과 통하도록 괄호 안의 단어를 이용하여 문장을 완성하세요.

- The bridge __________ __________
across the river. (construct)
(다리는 강을 가로질러 건설되었다.)
- The World Cup __________ __________
every four years. (hold)
(월드컵은 매 4년마다 개최된다.)

14 다음 중 어법상 <u>어색한</u> 문장만 짝지은 것은?

ⓐ The city was ruined by the war.
ⓑ All the puppies have being washed.
ⓒ She is loved by her neighbors.
ⓓ It is surrounded by beautiful mountains.
ⓔ Many of them were chose by Mary.

① ⓐ, ⓑ   ② ⓐ, ⓔ   ③ ⓑ, ⓒ
④ ⓑ, ⓔ   ⑤ ⓒ, ⓓ

15 다음 우리말과 일치하도록 빈칸을 채우세요.

- 그 해변은 조개 껍데기와 해초로 뒤덮여 있었다.
  ➡ The beach __________ __________
  __________ seashells and seaweed.

16 두 사람의 대화를 읽고 (A), (B)에 들어갈 문장을 바르게 쓴 것은?

수지: 민수야, 뭐하고 있니?
민수: 영어 문제집을 풀고 있는 중인데, 이 문제의
　　　답을 모르겠어.
수지: 'This room is cleaned every day.'의 부정문
　　　은 (A)이고, 의문문은 (B)야.

① (A) This room is not cleaned every day.
　　(B) Does this room cleaned every day?
② (A) This room is not cleaned every day.
　　(B) Is this room cleaned every day?
③ (A) This room does not cleaned every day.
　　(B) Is this room cleaned every day?
④ (A) This room is not clean every day.
　　(B) Is this room clean every day?
⑤ (A) This room not is cleaned every day.
　　(B) Does this room cleaned every day?

17 다음 중 수동태로 만들 수 있는 문장을 <u>모두</u> 고르세요.

① My brother resembles my grandfather.
② Jake found the subject very interesting.
③ They disappeared without a word last year.
④ Joseph gave his wife a bunch of roses.
⑤ The clothes suited me very well.

18 다음 중 어법상 <u>어색한</u> 문장은?

① They will be surprised at the news.
② The school was built not in 2011.
③ My uncle's store was robbed yesterday.
④ Was the decision made by the manager?
⑤ I have been loved by my grandmother since I
　　was born.

19 다음 문장을 수동태 문장으로 바꿔 쓰세요.

(1) I will give you a lot of time.

➡ _______________________________

____

(2) Someone has stolen my car.

➡ _______________________________

(3) They can explain the mystery.

➡ _______________________________

20 다음 중 어법상 어색한 문장은?

① My car was driven by Paul last week.

② Rosa was given a pencil by her brother.

③ A cake was baked for me by my mother.

④ He was made spaghetti with cream sauce by his wife.

⑤ The teacher was asked a lot of personal questions by her students.

21 다음 글의 ①~⑤ 중 어법상 어색한 것은?

There are many interesting things in my room. Look at this photo. It ① was taken last week. The girl in the photo is my best friend, Jimin. She is very good at ② painting. Do you see those paintings on the wall? They ③ were painted by her. You should also ④ check out the table over there. It was made by my father. Don't you think that my room is clean? It is ⑤ cleaning every morning.

22 다음 중 어법상 옳은 대화를 모두 고르면?

① A: When was this house built?

B: It built in 1960.

② A: Was the poem written by Mr. Black?

B: No, it wasn't. It was written by his son.

③ A: What do you call this game in Korean?

B: It calls *Yunnori* in Korean.

④ A: Who caught the bird?

B: It is caught by my cousin.

⑤ A: Did you go to the party yesterday?

B: No, I wasn't invited.

23 다음 중 우리말과 의미가 통하도록 영작한 것 중 문법적으로 옳은 것은?

① 그 고기는 피자를 만들기 위해서 얇은 조각들로 잘린다.

→ The meat is cutted into thin slices to make a pizza.

② 모차르트는 그의 음악적 지능 때문에 천재로 여겨졌다.

→ Mozart is considered a genius because of his musical intelligence.

③ 칼슘은 우유에서 가장 풍부하게 발견된다.

→ Calcium is founded most abundantly in milk.

④ 그 목걸이는 그 신부를 위해 특별히 만들어졌다.

→ The necklace was specially made to the bride.

⑤ 장난감 자동차 한 대가 내 남동생을 위해 할아버지에 의해 구입되었다.

→ A toy car was bought for my brother by my grandfather.

24 밑줄 친 (A), (B)를 각각 알맞은 형태로 바꾸어 쓰세요.

> • The ring (A) <u>steal</u> yesterday.
> • Thanks to the firefighters, more than 20 people's lives (B) <u>save</u> yesterday.

(A) _______________   (B) _______________

25 주어진 말을 활용하여 〈보기〉와 같은 형태의 문장을 만들 때 어법상 잘못된 것은?

> 보 기
>
> the land / discover / Mr. William
>
> ➡ The land was discovered by Mr. William.

① the watch / break / James
 ➡ The watch was broken by James.
② the cookies / bake / I
 ➡ The cookies was baked by me.
③ the pencil / find / she
 ➡ The pencil was found by her.
④ the book / read / my brother
 ➡ The book was read by my brother.
⑤ this garbage / throw out / that boy
 ➡ This garbage was thrown out by that boy.

26 우리말과 같은 뜻이 되도록 빈칸에 알맞은 단어를 쓰세요.

> • 이 의자는 나무로 만들어진다.
> = This chair is _______________ _______________ wood.

27 다음 중 어법상 어색한 문장은?

① Football is played in many countries.
② Many fish have been caught by me.
③ The song will be sung by the choir.
④ They were made be happy by the news.
⑤ The news was reported last week.

28 밑줄 친 부분을 어법에 맞게 고친 것 중 틀린 것을 고르세요.

① This boat <u>is belonged to</u> my grandfather.
  → belongs to
② I was given <u>to an interesting book</u> by Dad.
  → an interesting book
③ Chinese dishes were cooked <u>to me</u> by my sister.   → for me
④ This beautiful house is <u>made by</u> bricks.
  → made of
⑤ A doll was bought <u>her</u> by her father.
  → to her

29 다음 중 수동태로의 전환이 어색한 것은?

① My friend made a wooden box.
  ➡ A wooden box was made by my friend.
② Her boyfriend sent a postcard to her.
  ➡ A postcard is sent her by her boyfriend.
③ Josh calls me Ben.
  ➡ I am called Ben by Josh.
④ The students will clean the playground.
  ➡ The playground will be cleaned by the students.
⑤ People speak Chinese in Hong Kong.
  ➡ Chinese is spoken in Hong Kong.

30 다음 우리말과 같도록 〈보기〉의 단어를 배열할 때, 네 번째에 오는 단어는?

> • 그 준비는 다음 주 금요일까지 완료되어야 한다.

> 보 기
> should, next, preparation, be, the, Friday, completed, by

① should ② be ③ the
④ Friday ⑤ preparation

31 다음 문장을 수동태 문장으로 바꿔 쓰세요.

> • We have watered all the plants.
> ➡ ________________________________

32 우리말과 같은 뜻이 되도록 괄호 안에 주어진 단어를 반드시 포함하여 6단어로 영작하세요. (단, 필요시 형태 변화 가능.)

> • 이 컵은 물로 가득 차 있다. (fill)

➡ ________________________________

33 다음 중 밑줄 친 부분을 생략해도 의미 변화가 없는 것은?

① The question was asked at the conference by James.
② Apple Inc. was founded by Steve Jobs in 1974.
③ Canned food was invented by Appert.
④ German is spoken by people in Germany and Austria.
⑤ The island was discovered by an English explorer, James Cook.

[34~35] 다음 글을 읽고, 물음에 답하세요.

> Korea ⓐ has gone through numerous wars since ancient times. The most tragic one among them ⓑ were the Korean War. ㉠ 그것은 북한과 남한 간에 싸워졌다 from 1950 to 1953, not long after Japan's colonization had ended.
> The war began when North Korea invaded South Korea on 25 June 1950. The South ⓒ was pushed back to Busan in the blink of an eye. Then, when the South was on the verge of defeat, UN forces were dispatched. They successfully ⓓ repelled the North back to positions around the 38th parallel in 1951. The war continued for two more years. Then it ended with the Armistice Agreement that created the Korean Demilitarized Zone (DMZ), permanently ⓔ separating the North and South.

34 윗글의 ㉠을 주어진 〈조건〉에 맞게 영어로 쓰세요.

> 조 건
> • 〈보기〉의 단어들을 한 번씩 사용하세요.
> • 필요시 단어의 형태를 바꾸세요.
> • 수동태 표현을 포함하세요.

> 보 기
> fight, North Korea, be, between, South Korea, it, and

➡ ________________________________

____

35 윗글의 밑줄 친 ⓐ~ⓔ 중 어법이 틀린 것은?

① ⓐ ② ⓑ ③ ⓒ
④ ⓓ ⑤ ⓔ

36 다음 중 밑줄 친 부분이 어법상 바르지 <u>않은</u> 것은?

① We were surprised <u>at</u> the noise.
② The singer is known <u>to</u> everybody.
③ I was pleased <u>with</u> the gift.
④ He was satisfied <u>to</u> the result.
⑤ I am worried <u>about</u> the final test.

37 우리말과 같은 뜻이 되도록 괄호 안의 말을 바르게 배열하여 문장을 완성하세요. (단, 필요시 어형 변화시킬 것.)

- 그녀의 교실은 그녀에 의해 깨끗이 유지되었다.
  = Her classroom ________________________.
    (her, keep, be, by, clean)

38 다음 중 어법상 <u>어색한</u> 문장은?

① I was given some hard work by my boss.
② The room was kept quiet by the old lady.
③ Lots of toys were given to the children.
④ She was elected mayor in 2024.
⑤ Look at our house. It needs to be painting.

39 다음을 읽고, 괄호 안의 동사를 이용하여 빈칸에 알맞은 말을 쓰세요.

In 1950, the Korean War broke out. The Korean War took the lives of 5 million men and women. Most of them were not soldiers but children, women, and old people. The war ended in 1953 but many things were ruined.

➡ Many people __________ __________ during the Korean War. (kill)

40 다음 글을 읽고, 밑줄 친 괄호 ⓐ,ⓑ,ⓒ에 주어진 단어를 알맞은 형태로 바꿔 쓰세요.

Dogs are wonderful pets that many people love. Dogs ⓐ (know) for being loyal and friendly companions. They love to play fetch, go for walks, and cuddle with their owners. Some dogs ⓑ (train) to help people, like guide dogs for the blind or therapy dogs that visit hospitals to cheer up patients. Taking care of a dog involves feeding them, giving them water, and taking them to the vet when they're sick. Dogs bring lots of joy and ⓒ (happy) to people's lives, and they're often considered part of the family.

ⓐ ________________   ⓑ ________________
ⓒ ________________

41 다음 빈칸에 알맞은 단어를 순서대로 쓰세요.

(1) The whole hill is covered __________ tall trees.
(2) The house was made __________ glass, wood, and stone.
(3) I'm worried __________ my math test tomorrow.

42 다음 〈조건〉에 맞게 괄호 안의 말을 활용하여 문장을 완성하세요.

조 건
- 수동태 문장으로 만들 것.
- 시제는 미래형으로 할 것.

➡ Over four million lives ________________
________________.
(save, this medicine)

PSS 1 명사의 복수형

PSS 1-1 명사의 복수형 I

일반적인 경우	명사+s	shoe – shoes month – months custom – customs student – students animal – animals neighbor – neighbors	friend – friends book – books egg – eggs bicycle – bicycles place – places classmate – classmates
-s, -x, -ch, -sh 로 끝나는 경우	명사+es	bus – buses fox – foxes watch – watches brush – brushes	class – classes box – boxes match – matches dish – dishes

정답 p.27

PRACTICE 1

다음 명사의 복수형을 쓰세요.

1 egg ➡ _______	2 watch ➡ _______
3 horse ➡ _______	4 pen ➡ _______
5 shoe ➡ _______	6 glass ➡ _______
7 book ➡ _______	8 dish ➡ _______
9 church ➡ _______	10 classmate ➡ _______
11 bottle ➡ _______	12 class ➡ _______
13 girl ➡ _______	14 camera ➡ _______
15 bus ➡ _______	16 month ➡ _______
17 beach ➡ _______	18 box ➡ _______
19 neighbor ➡ _______	20 brush ➡ _______
21 house ➡ _______	22 place ➡ _______
23 custom ➡ _______	24 friend ➡ _______

25 fox ➡ _______________	**26** match ➡ _______________
27 sandwich ➡ _______________	**28** wish ➡ _______________
29 bicycle ➡ _______________	**30** animal ➡ _______________

PSS 1-2 명사의 복수형 Ⅱ

자음+y로 끝나는 경우	자음+i+es	country – countr**ies** factory – factor**ies** city – cit**ies** party – part**ies** hobby – hobb**ies**	penny – penn**ies** diary – diar**ies** baby – bab**ies** family – famil**ies** activity – activit**ies**
모음+y로 끝나는 경우	명사+s	day – day**s** boy – boy**s** monkey – monkey**s**	donkey – donkey**s** way – way**s** key – key**s**

정답 p.27

PRACTICE 2 [1-30]

다음 명사의 복수형을 쓰세요.

1 lady ➡ _______________	**2** story ➡ _______________
3 key ➡ _______________	**4** party ➡ _______________
5 diary ➡ _______________	**6** song ➡ _______________
7 couch ➡ _______________	**8** monkey ➡ _______________
9 baby ➡ _______________	**10** activity ➡ _______________
11 city ➡ _______________	**12** donkey ➡ _______________
13 student ➡ _______________	**14** culture ➡ _______________
15 day ➡ _______________	**16** family ➡ _______________
17 boy ➡ _______________	**18** habit ➡ _______________
19 way ➡ _______________	**20** factory ➡ _______________
21 hobby ➡ _______________	**22** ferry ➡ _______________
23 candy ➡ _______________	**24** computer ➡ _______________

25	bench	➡ ___________	26	country	➡ ___________
27	memory	➡ ___________	28	doctor	➡ ___________
29	penny	➡ ___________	30	community	➡ ___________

PSS 1-3 명사의 복수형 Ⅲ

-o로 끝나는 경우	명사+es	potato – potato**es** hero – hero**es**	tomato – tomato**es** mosquito – mosquito**(e)s**
	예외	kangaroo – kangaroo**s** radio – radio**s**	zoo – zoo**s** piano – piano**s**
-f, -fe로 끝나는 경우	f, fe → v+es	yourself – yoursel**ves** life – li**ves** knife – kni**ves**	leaf – lea**ves** wolf – wol**ves** calf – cal**ves**
	예외	roof – roof**s** belief – belief**s**	safe – safe**s** chief – chief**s**
불규칙 변화		goose – **geese** tooth – **teeth** woman – **women** sheep – **sheep** mouse – **mice** Chinese – **Chinese**	foot – **feet** man – **men** fish – **fish** deer – **deer** child – **children** ox – **oxen**

정답 p.27

PRACTICE 3

다음 명사의 복수형을 쓰세요.

1	video	➡ ___________	2	child	➡ ___________
3	wolf	➡ ___________	4	belief	➡ ___________
5	life	➡ ___________	6	ox	➡ ___________
7	potato	➡ ___________	8	mouse	➡ ___________
9	sheep	➡ ___________	10	man	➡ ___________
11	photo	➡ ___________	12	goose	➡ ___________
13	roof	➡ ___________	14	tooth	➡ ___________

15	tomato	➡ __________	16	fish	➡ __________
17	knife	➡ __________	18	clock	➡ __________
19	calf	➡ __________	20	yourself	➡ __________
21	mosquito	➡ __________	22	radio	➡ __________
23	wife	➡ __________	24	memo	➡ __________
25	leaf	➡ __________	26	deer	➡ __________
27	hero	➡ __________	28	neighbor	➡ __________
29	blouse	➡ __________	30	safe	➡ __________
31	shelf	➡ __________	32	foot	➡ __________
33	kangaroo	➡ __________	34	thief	➡ __________
35	studio	➡ __________	36	chief	➡ __________
37	woman	➡ __________	38	zoo	➡ __________
39	piano	➡ __________	40	emergency	➡ __________

PSS 2 명사의 쓰임

PSS 2-1 명사의 종류

셀 수 있는 명사	a(n)을 붙이거나 복수형으로 쓸 수 있고, many, (a) few, some, any, no처럼 수를 나타내는 형용사와 함께 쓸 수 있다.	
	보통명사	bag student book pencil computer tree dish animal
	집합명사	class family team audience
셀 수 없는 명사	a(n)을 붙이거나 복수형으로 쓸 수 없고, 물질명사와 추상명사는 much, (a) little, some, any, no처럼 양을 나타내는 형용사와 함께 쓸 수 있다.	
	고유명사	David Chaewon Korea Chicago Monday Christmas
	물질명사	water salt money juice air milk ice bread paper gold sugar flour
	추상명사	love peace knowledge beauty health honesty information news happiness hope kindness advice

PRACTICE 4

밑줄 친 단어 앞에 a나 an을 붙여야 하는 것을 골라 ○표 하세요.

1 I went to <u>restaurant</u> for dinner yesterday. ___________

2 Would you like to drink <u>juice</u>? ___________

3 There is <u>church</u> across the street. ___________

4 <u>Lady</u> came to see you while you were out. ___________

5 We can't live without <u>air</u>. ___________

6 Excuse me. I'm looking for <u>supermarket</u>. ___________

7 A bird was singing on <u>tree</u>. ___________

8 Most artists try to find and express <u>beauty</u>. ___________

9 Have you ever raised <u>animal</u>? ___________

10 She always eats <u>apple</u> in the morning. ___________

11 I go swimming on <u>Monday</u>. ___________

12 They decided to write <u>letter</u> to Mr. Lee. ___________

13 I met <u>student</u> whose name was Inho. ___________

14 Do you have <u>knowledge</u> about this subject? ___________

15 It is very tiring to take <u>exam</u>. ___________

PSS 2-2 셀 수 있는 명사

1. **보통명사** – 사람이나 동물, 사물을 나타내는 명사로, 단·복수형이 모두 가능하다.

   I bought a **computer** last Friday. 나는 지난 금요일에 컴퓨터를 샀다.
   Jenny didn't bring an **umbrella**. Jenny는 우산을 가져오지 않았다.
   The **students** were playing soccer in the **playground**.
   학생들은 운동장에서 축구를 하고 있었다.

2. **집합명사** – 사람이나 사물의 집합체를 나타내는 명사로, 집합체를 하나의 단위로 보아 단수 취급하거나 개별 구성원에 중점을 두어 복수 취급할 수도 있다.

   My **class** consists of 28 boys and girls. 우리 반은 28명의 남녀로 이루어져 있다.
   There are only two **classes** in this school. 이 학교에는 단지 두 개의 반이 있다.

My **family** lives in Incheon. 우리 가족은 인천에 산다.
My **family** **are** all healthy. 우리 가족은 모두 건강하다. (개별 구성원에 중점을 두어 family를 복수 취급함.)
Seven **families** live in this town. 일곱 가구가 이 도시에 산다.

The **team** consists of nine people. 팀은 아홉 명으로 구성되어 있다.
Mr. Lee supports three baseball **teams**. Lee 씨는 세 개의 야구팀을 후원한다.

정답 p.27

PRACTICE 5

괄호 안에 들어갈 단어로 알맞은 것을 고르세요. (복수 정답 가능)

1 Lisa bought two (book, books) for me.

2 The (scientist, scientists) was happy to solve the problem.

3 I think your (dog, dogs) are all very cute.

4 There is a (hospital, hospitals) around the corner.

5 Five (team, teams) will take part in the contest.

6 They invited more than a hundred (person, people) to their wedding.

7 I need a (calendar, calendars) in my room.

8 My family (was, were) very glad to meet Mr. Park.

9 I met three (friend, friends) of Minsu's yesterday.

10 There (is, are) eleven classes in my year at school.

11 The brave (girl, girls) never cries in front of others.

12 The (class, classes) is going to go on a picnic.

13 Many (family, families) in America have pets.

14 My team (is, are) ready to start the game.

15 We found a new (building, buildings) in our town.

정답 p.28

PRACTICE 6 [1-10]

다음 문장에서 밑줄 친 부분을 바르게 고쳐 쓰세요.

1 About ten <u>family</u> joined the tour.　　　　families

2 As a unit, the class always <u>follow</u> the teacher's instructions.

3 I have been to many <u>country</u>.

4 Mary is saving money to buy <u>car</u>. She has always wanted to have one.

5 The class <u>is</u> excited because they are going on a field trip.

6 <u>Leaf</u> fall down to the ground every autumn.

7 Our teeth <u>is</u> very useful and important.

8 Mom gave me <u>bag</u> for my birthday present. I like it so much.

9 My sister works in <u>restaurant</u> downtown. It offers 24-hour service seven days a week.

10 The book written by my teacher <u>were</u> published last month.

PSS 2-3 셀 수 없는 명사

1. **고유명사** – 사람, 장소, 요일 등의 고유한 이름을 나타내는 명사로, 첫 글자는 대문자로 쓴다.

   My friend **Mike** is a good student. 내 친구 Mike는 좋은 학생이다.
   Paris is a beautiful city. 파리는 아름다운 도시이다.
   I'm leaving this city next **Saturday**. 나는 다음 토요일에 이 도시를 떠날 것이다.
   cf. 요일의 경우 '매주 토요일'의 의미로 쓸 때에는 on Saturdays 또는 every Saturday로 쓰인다.

2. **물질명사** – 일정한 형태가 없는 물질을 나타내는 명사로 much, (a) little, some, any, no, all과 같은 양을 나타내는 형용사와 함께 쓸 수 있다.

   We can't live without **water**. 우리는 물 없이 살 수 없다.
   I have **little money** in my purse. 내 지갑에는 돈이 거의 없다.
   Can I have **some juice**? 주스 좀 마실 수 있을까요?

3. **추상명사** – 눈에 보이지 않는 개념을 나타내는 명사로 much, (a) little, some, any, no와 같은 양을 나타내는 형용사와 함께 쓸 수 있다.

   Bill doesn't have **much knowledge** about science.
   Bill은 과학에 대한 많은 지식을 가지고 있지 않다.
   Too much coffee is not good for your **health**. 너무 많은 커피는 너의 건강에 좋지 않다.
   Honesty is the best **policy**. 정직은 최선의 방책이다.

정답 p.28

PRACTICE 7

괄호 안에 주어진 말 중 알맞은 것을 고르세요.

1 I want to drink (a water, water).

2 (A Saturday, Saturday) is my favorite day of the week.

3 Dad promised to buy (a computer, computer) for me.

4 Some people think (a beauty, beauty) inside is important.

5 One of the biggest cities in the world is (a New York, New York).

6 Most people want (happiness, happinesses) in their lives.

7 Both plants and animals need (an air, air).

8 My friend Bill has three cute (dog, dogs).

9 (A death, Death) is the end of life.

10 (A family, Family) moved into our town last week.

11 My friend Robert likes (September, Septembers) the best.

12 Mrs. Jones uses a lot of (salt, salts) when she cooks.

13 I'm looking forward to (a Christmas, Christmas).

14 We need some (paper, papers) to write on.

15 Thank you for your great (advice, advices).

정답 p.28

PRACTICE 8

〈보기〉에서 알맞은 단어를 골라 빈칸에 어법에 맞게 쓰세요.

보 기	Jane	Seoul	class	apple	question
	time	family	information	juice	happiness

1 The Internet gives us lots of ________________.

2 There is little ________________ in the bottle.

3 I really enjoy living in ________________, the largest city in Korea.

4 You can find ________________ in small things.

5 Let me introduce my best friend, ________________.

6 It takes a lot of ________________ to finish this work.

7 We had dinner with those ________________ yesterday.

8 Each ________________ has 30 students in my school.

9 The teacher had to answer a lot of ________________.

10 Can you buy two ________________ on your way home? I need them now.

PSS 2-4 물질명사의 쓰임

물질명사의 수량은 단위명사를 이용하여 「수사＋단위명사＋of＋물질명사」의 어순으로 표현한다.

1. **piece**

    a piece of **paper** 종이 한 장   six pieces of **cloth** 천 여섯 조각

    three pieces of **cheese** 치즈 세 조각   four pieces of **cake** 케이크 네 조각

    seven pieces of **bread** 빵 일곱 조각   two pieces of **furniture** 가구 두 점

    five pieces of **advice** 충고 다섯 마디

    cf. 물질명사는 아니지만 advice(추상명사), furniture(의미상으로는 집합명사)도 수량 표현 시 piece를 사용한다.

2. **slice**

    a slice of **cheese** 치즈 한 장   two slices of **bread** 빵 두 조각

3. **glass**

    a glass of **milk** 우유 한 잔   two glasses of **water** 물 두 잔

    three glasses of **juice** 주스 세 잔   four glasses of **wine** 와인 네 잔

4. **bar**

    a bar of **soap** 비누 한 개   two bars of **chocolate** 초콜릿 두 개

5. **bottle**

    a bottle of **juice** 주스 한 병   two bottles of **beer** 맥주 두 병

6. **cup**

    a cup of **tea** 차 한 잔   two cups of **coffee** 커피 두 잔

7. **sheet**

    a sheet of **paper** 종이 한 장

8. **spoonful[teaspoonful]**

    a spoonful of **sugar** 설탕 한 스푼   two teaspoonfuls of **salt** 소금 두 티스푼

9. **loaf**

    a loaf of **bread** 빵 한 덩어리   two loaves of **bread** 빵 두 덩어리

10. **pound**

    a pound of **meat** 고기 1파운드   three pounds of **pork** 돼지고기 3파운드

11. **bowl**

    a bowl of **rice** 밥 한 공기   two bowls of **soup** 수프 두 그릇

PRACTICE 9

그림을 보고, 〈보기〉와 같이 빈칸에 알맞은 말을 쓰세요.

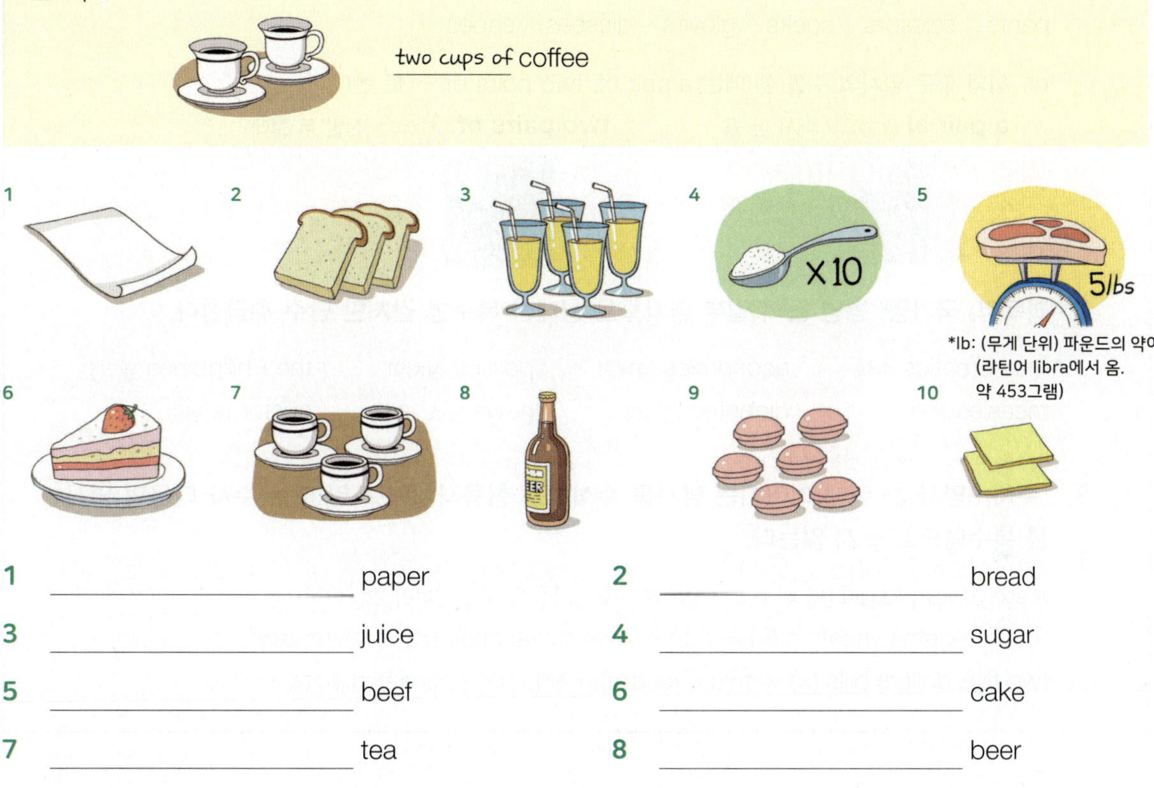

보 기

two cups of coffee

1 ____________________ paper	**2** ____________________ bread	
3 ____________________ juice	**4** ____________________ sugar	
5 ____________________ beef	**6** ____________________ cake	
7 ____________________ tea	**8** ____________________ beer	
9 ____________________ soap	**10** ____________________ cheese	

정답 p.28

PRACTICE 10

괄호 안에 주어진 단어와 알맞은 단위명사를 이용하여 빈칸을 채우세요.

1 I had a _bowl of soup_ ____________________ for breakfast. (soup)

2 Mom baked a ____________________ and cut it into ten pieces. (bread)

3 I'd like to give you a ____________________. (advice)

4 I brought them three ____________________. (water)

5 We need to buy two more ____________________. (furniture)

6 Pass me two ____________________, please. (bread)

7 Can you make a ____________________ for me? (tea)

8 Susie put three ____________________ in the soup. (salt)

9 Mrs. Ford bought four ____________________ for dinner. (meat)

10 Mark drank a ____________________ at my party. (wine)

PSS 2-5 주의해야 할 명사의 수

1. 한 쌍을 이루어야 하나의 물건으로 제 기능을 하는 명사는 복수형으로 쓰고 복수 취급한다.

   pants   scissors   socks   gloves   glasses   shoes

   cf. 이와 같은 명사의 수를 셀 때는 a pair of, two pairs of … 를 쓴다.

   a pair of pants 바지 한 벌   **two pairs of shoes** 신발 두 켤레

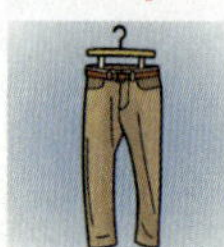

2. 과목명, 국가명, 병명 등의 일부 명사들은 형태상 복수형 같지만 단수 취급한다.

   mathematics 수학   economics 경제학   politics 정치학   the Philippines 필리핀
   measles 홍역   diabetes 당뇨병   news 뉴스, 소식   customs 세관

3. 「수사＋명사」가 뒤에 이어지는 명사를 수식하는 형용사처럼 쓰일 때는 수사 다음의 명사를 복수형으로 쓰지 않는다.

   a six-years-old girl (×) ➡ a **six-year-old** girl (○) 여섯 살짜리 소녀
   a two-months vacation (×) ➡ a **two-month** vacation (○) 두 달간의 휴가
   two five-dollars bills (×) ➡ two **five-dollar** bills (○) 5달러짜리 지폐 2장

정답 p.29

PRACTICE 11

괄호 안에 주어진 말 중 알맞은 것을 고르세요.

1   The news about the earthquake (was, were) very shocking.

2   Customs (is, are) the place where people pay taxes on goods from foreign countries.

3   My mom bought me a pair of (sock, socks).

4   Politics (is, are) the study about countries and governments.

5   Did you see my (glass, glasses)? I can't read without (it, them).

6   I live on the second floor of a (five-story, five-stories) building.

7   Economics (is, are) my favorite subject.

8   Be careful with (that scissor, those scissors).

9   Have you heard about that (two-hour, two-hours) movie?

10   David wants to buy two (pair, pairs) of (shoe, shoes).

11   Mr. Smith loved my (three-month-old, three-months-old) baby.

12 Nayoung got very nice (pant, pants) on her birthday.

13 I need five (ten-dollar, ten-dollars) bills now.

14 Mathematics (make, makes) me really bored.

15 James bought the handmade (glove, gloves) from Italy.

PSS 2-6 명사의 소유격

1. **사람이나 동물을 나타내는 명사는 '(s)를 이용하여 소유격을 만든다.**

   ① 단수 명사+'s

Jenny's book	**the boy's** umbrella	**Dr. Kim's** office
Jenny의 책	그 소년의 우산	김 박사의 사무실
the cat's eyes	**Youngsu's** desk	**my mother's** hand
고양이의 눈	영수의 책상	나의 어머니의 손

   ② 복수 명사+'

kids' toys	a **girls'** high school	**ladies'** shirts
아이들의 장난감	여자 고등학교	여성용 셔츠
parents' day	**farmers'** festival	**teachers'** room
어버이날	농부들의 축제	교무실

   cf. 명사의 복수형이 -s로 끝나지 않으면 명사 뒤에 's를 붙인다.

children's wear	**women's** magazines
아동복	여성 잡지

   ③ 명사의 반복을 피하기 위해서나 가리키는 대상이 명백할 때는 소유격 뒤의 명사를 생략할 수도 있다.

   This is my room and that is **my brother's**. 여기는 내 방이고, 저기는 내 남동생의 방이다.
   (= my brother's room)

   Where are you going to stay? 너는 어디에서 머무를 거니?

   – I'm going to stay at **my uncle's**. 나는 삼촌 댁에서 머무를 거야.
   (= my uncle's house)

2. **무생물의 소유격은 주로 of를 이용한다.**

the title **of the movie**	the top **of the mountain**
영화의 제목	산꼭대기

   cf. 시간, 가격, 거리, 무게를 나타내는 명사는 '(s)를 이용하여 소유격을 만든다.

yesterday's newspaper	**two dollars'** worth of salt	**one hour's** walk
어제 신문	2달러어치의 소금	한 시간의 산책

PRACTICE 12

그림을 보고, 빈칸에 알맞은 말을 쓰세요.

1 Mira (student)

5 Sujin (niece)

Mr. Kim

2 Peter (friend)

4 Minho (son)　　3 Ms. Song (wife)

1　Mira is <u>Mr. Kim's student</u>.

2　Peter is ____________________.

3　Ms. Song is ____________________.

4　Minho is ____________________.

5　Sujin is ____________________.

PRACTICE 13

다음에 주어진 단어나 구를 '(s) 또는 of를 이용하여 하나로 연결하세요.

1　Dave, black cap　➡ <u>Dave's black cap</u>

2　my dog, tail　➡ ____________________

3　the exit, the building　➡ ____________________

4　the owner, this car　➡ ____________________

5　today, TV programs　➡ ____________________

6　the bottom, the bottle　➡ ____________________

7　my students, report cards　➡ ____________________

8　Mr. Brown, blanket　➡ ____________________

9　the result, the test　➡ ____________________

10　my sisters, clothes　➡ ____________________

PSS 2-7 동격

명사나 대명사를 보충 설명하거나 강조하기 위해 그 뒤에 다른 명사(구, 절)를 쓸 수 있는데 이런 관계를 동격이라 한다.

---

1. **콤마(,)를 이용한 동격**

    I like **Mina, the tallest girl in this picture**.

    나는 이 사진에서 가장 키가 큰 소녀인 Mina를 좋아한다.

    This is **my friend, Mariah**.

    이 사람은 내 친구인 Mariah이다.

2. **that을 이용한 동격**

    I know **the fact that he likes you**.

    나는 그가 너를 좋아한다는 사실을 알고 있다.

    It is important to follow **the advice that you should exercise**.

    네가 운동을 해야 한다는 충고를 따르는 것은 중요하다.

3. **of를 이용한 동격**

    The news of his leaving us is very sad.

    그가 우리를 떠난다는 소식이 너무 슬프다.

    I was surprised at **the result of our winning the contest**.

    나는 우리가 그 대회에서 이겼다는 결과에 놀랐다.

정답 p.29

PRACTICE 14

〈보기〉에서 알맞은 것을 골라 빈칸에 넣으세요.

보 기	of / , / that

1   We know the fact _________ the Earth moves around the Sun.

2   Tom _________ the man in a blue shirt, is our English teacher.

3   Jimmy has a dream _________ he wants to be a famous actor.

4   My mom _________ a great cook, makes delicious meals.

5   The news _________ her coming to Seoul made him excited.

6   She has the idea _________ moving to Chicago.

7   He agreed to our opinion _________ he should attend the meeting.

8   There is no hope _________ winning the game.

9   The rumor _________ she stole the money was true.

10 Ms. Scott _________ the ballet teacher, asked her to take ballet classes.

PRACTICE 15

밑줄 친 부분이 동격으로 쓰였으면 ○표, 아닌 경우에는 ×표를 하세요.

1 He likes the song that is easy to sing. [   ]

2 He saw the picture of my little dog. [   ]

3 I heard the surprising news that we would go to an amusement park. [   ]

4 I can't believe the fact of his not coming to the class. [   ]

5 This is a book that I borrowed from my friend. [   ]

6 David, my boss, is a diligent man. [   ]

7 The advice that I should drink more water is very important. [   ]

8 Mary, Kate and Tom are good friends. [   ]

9 I'm sure that he will finish the work. [   ]

10 You are the one that I love most. [   ]

PSS 3 부정관사 a, an

PSS 3-1 a, an의 쓰임

1. a는 첫소리가 자음으로 발음되는 명사의 단수형 앞에, an은 모음으로 발음되는 명사의 단수형 앞에 쓰인다.

a dog	**a** man	**a** bus	**a** cat
a house	**a** nurse	**a** pen	**an** animal
an egg	**an** idea	**an** office	**an** umbrella

2. 명사 앞의 형용사의 첫소리가 자음으로 발음되면 a, 모음으로 발음되면 an을 쓴다.

a large apartment   **a** sweet orange   **an** easy question   **an** old lady

3. 철자는 모음으로 시작하지만 첫소리가 자음으로 발음되는 명사 앞에는 a, 철자는 자음으로 시작하지만 모음으로 발음되는 명사 앞에는 an을 쓴다. 명사 앞에 형용사가 있을 경우에는 그 형용사의 첫 소리 발음에 따라 a와 an을 구별하여 쓴다.

a university   **an** hour   **an** honest man   **a** uniform   **a** unique experience

PRACTICE 16

다음 문장의 빈칸에 a나 an 중 알맞은 것을 쓰세요.

1 I used to live in _________ apartment.

2 That is _________ good idea!

3 During gym class, we played _________ interesting game of dodgeball.

4 He is looking for _________ university student to study with.

5 _________ honest boy brought my lost wallet.

6 We have _________ important meeting tomorrow morning.

7 I have to wear _________ uniform in my school.

8 They saw _________ baby crying in the restaurant.

9 The company needs _________ larger office for the new workers.

10 There is _________ old house on the hill.

11 Did you bring _________ umbrella with you?

12 My little brother drew a picture of _________ cute animal.

13 It will take about _________ hour to finish my homework.

14 Jina took _________ bus to go to Incheon.

15 The customer is looking for _________ unique design for his clothes.

PSS 3-2 a, an의 의미

one 하나의	Susan gave me **an** apple this morning. Susan은 오늘 아침에 내게 사과 한 개를 주었다.
a certain 어떤	Jenny visited **a** Korean family yesterday. Jenny는 어제 어떤 한국 가정을 방문했다.
some 약간의, 어느 정도	I'll tell him the truth in **a** moment. 나는 잠시 후에 그에게 사실을 말할 것이다.
the same 같은, 동일한	Hajun and Minju are of **an** age. 하준이와 민주는 동갑이다.

| per ~당, ~마다 | Mr. Brown goes jogging twice **a** week.
Brown 씨는 일주일에 두 번 조깅을 하러 간다. |
| 대표 단수 | **A** dog is a very cute animal. 개는 매우 귀여운 동물이다. |

정답 p.30

PRACTICE 17

그림을 보고, 〈보기〉에서 알맞은 단어를 골라 a(n)을 이용하여 빈칸에 알맞은 말을 쓰세요.

| 보 기 | glass / tree / elephant / house / egg / monitor / baby / police officer |

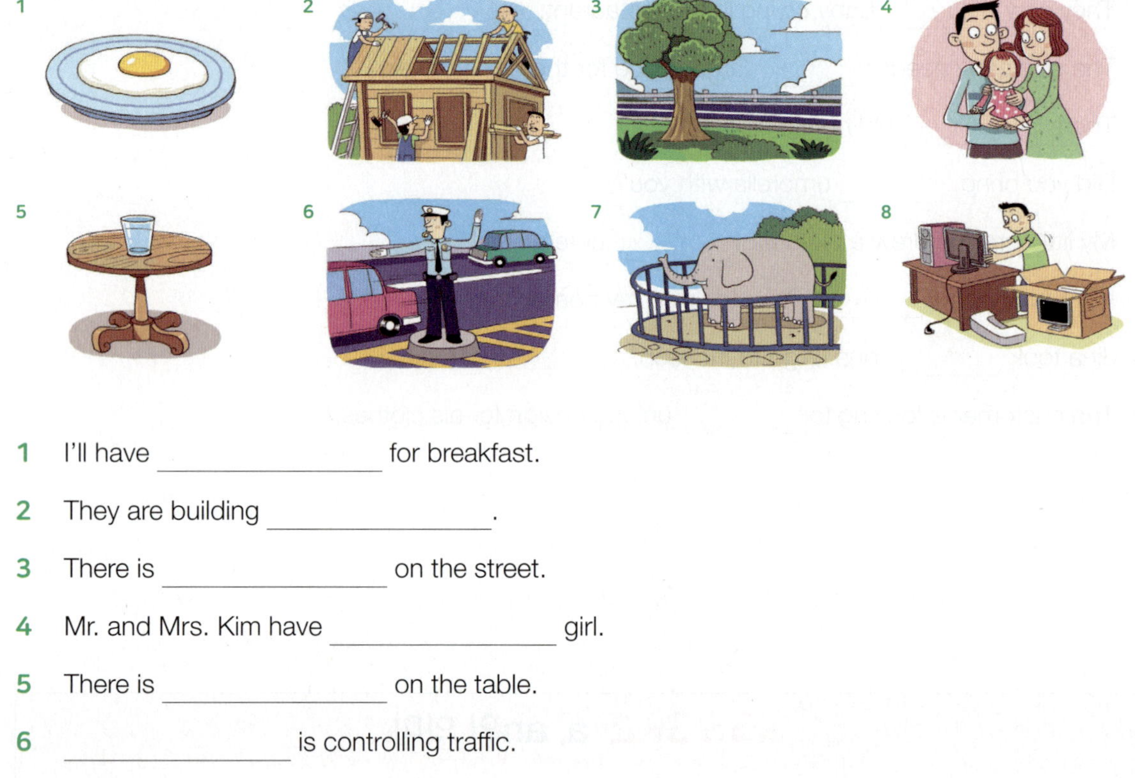

1 I'll have ________________ for breakfast.

2 They are building ________________ .

3 There is ________________ on the street.

4 Mr. and Mrs. Kim have ________________ girl.

5 There is ________________ on the table.

6 ________________ is controlling traffic.

7 There is ________________ in the zoo.

8 Minsu bought ________________ for his computer.

PRACTICE 18

밑줄 친 a(n)의 올바른 의미를 〈보기〉에서 찾아 괄호 안에 번호를 쓰세요.

| 보 기 | ① one ② a certain ③ some ④ the same ⑤ per ⑥ 대표 단수 |

1 He came back after <u>a</u> while. (   )

2 Dad had <u>a</u> sandwich for lunch. (   )

3 Birds of <u>a</u> feather flock together. (   )

4 <u>A</u> child needs parents. (   )

5 This book is about <u>an</u> artist. (   )

6 I have <u>an</u> older sister. (   )

7 I visit my grandparents once <u>a</u> month. (   )

8 How many glasses of water do you drink <u>a</u> day? (   )

9 <u>A</u> girl came to see you yesterday. (   )

10 <u>A</u> whale is one of the heaviest animals. (   )

11 We are of <u>an</u> age. (   )

12 Mark and Sena sat at <u>a</u> distance from each other. (   )

PSS 4 정관사 the

PSS 4-1 the의 쓰임 I

1. 앞에 나온 명사가 반복될 때

There is a book on the desk. **The book** is about science.

책상 위에 책 한 권이 있다. 그 책은 과학에 관한 것이다.

2. 듣는 사람이 무엇을 가리키는지 알 수 있을 때

Could you pass me **the sugar**, please? 설탕 좀 건네주시겠어요?

3. 유일한 것을 나타낼 때

The Sun sets in the west. 해는 서쪽으로 진다.

4. 명사 뒤에 명사를 수식하는 구나 절이 있을 때

Seoul is **the capital of Korea**. 서울은 한국의 수도이다.

정답 p.30

PRACTICE 19

괄호 안에 주어진 단어 중 알맞은 것을 고르세요.

1 People once believed (an, the) Earth was flat.

2 Will you hold (a, the) door for me?

3 It's getting cold. I need to buy (a, the) jacket.

4 I have seen John and Mary's baby. (A, The) baby is so lovely.

5 Today people can go to (a, the) Moon on a spaceship.

6 Jina called you (a, the) while ago.

7 Look at (a, the) bird! It's so beautiful.

8 Insu gave me a pen. (A, The) pen is blue.

9 I had two apples and (a, the) glass of water.

10 We have two long vacations (a, the) year.

11 Did you go to (a, the) concert that you told me about?

12 (A, The) book on my desk is about psychology.

13 Mom bought me a skirt. I'm going to wear (a, the) skirt tomorrow.

14 There is (a, the) restaurant near my house. (A, The) restaurant is really good.

15 Who are they? – (A, The) boy is my brother and (a, the) girl is my sister.

PSS 4-2 the의 쓰임 Ⅱ

1. 서수, 최상급, only, very, same 앞

She was **the first** woman to win the award. 그녀는 그 상을 수상한 첫 번째 여성이었다.

This is **the best** way to solve the problem. 이것이 그 문제를 푸는 가장 좋은 방법이다.

It's **the only** money I have. 그것이 내가 가지고 있는 유일한 돈이다.

These are **the very** pants I wanted. 이것이 내가 원했던 바로 그 바지이다.

Your pen is **the same** as mine. 네 펜은 내 것과 같다.

2. **대표 단수 앞**

   The cat is a smart animal. 고양이는 영리한 동물이다.

3. **악기의 이름 앞**

   Mark can play **the violin** very well.
   Mark는 바이올린을 매우 잘 연주할 수 있다.

정답 p.30

PRACTICE 20

다음 대화의 빈칸에 a(n)나 the 중 알맞은 것을 쓰세요.

1 A: Can I borrow your pencil?
   B: I'm sorry, but this is _________ only pencil I have.

2 A: Where should I sit?
   B: At _________ second seal in _________ first row.

3 A: I'm going shopping. Is there anything you want?
   B: Well, I need _________ notebook.

4 A: Who is Mr. Park?
   B: He is _________ very person who built the house.

5 A: What color do you want?
   B: _________ same color as yours.

6 A: Don't you have _________ older brother?
   B: No. I don't have any.

7 A: Did you like _________ movie?
   B: Yes. It was the most exciting movie I've ever seen.

8 A: What is Linda doing?
   B: She is playing _________ piano.

9 A: I met _________ really handsome boy the other day.
   B: Great! How did you meet him?

10 A: Do you know Mike?
   B: Yes. He is _________ most popular boy in my school.

11 A: What happened last night?
   B: _________ thief broke into my neighbor's house.

PSS 4-3 the의 쓰임 Ⅲ

1. **특정 고유명사 앞**

   the Pacific 태평양　　　**the Alps** 알프스 산맥　　　**the Philippines** 필리핀

   the Netherlands 네덜란드　　　**the Thames** 템즈 강　　　***The New York Times*** 뉴욕타임즈지

2. **the+형용사/분사 '~한 사람들'**

   You should respect **the old**. 당신은 노인들을 공경해야 한다.

3. **어떤 동작을 가하는 신체의 일부를 나타내는 단어 앞**

   He looked me in **the eye**. 그는 내 눈을 똑바로 쳐다보았다.

정답 p.30

PRACTICE 21

밑줄 친 부분이 올바르면 ○, 틀리면 바르게 고쳐 쓰세요.

1　They tried to help <u>a poor</u>.　　　　　＿＿＿＿＿＿＿＿

2　Ben was hit in <u>a face</u> by a stranger.　　　　　＿＿＿＿＿＿＿＿

3　The sailors crossed <u>Pacific</u>.　　　　　＿＿＿＿＿＿＿＿

4　I see Jenny once <u>the week</u>.　　　　　＿＿＿＿＿＿＿＿

5　I have been to <u>Netherlands</u>.　　　　　＿＿＿＿＿＿＿＿

6　<u>A rich</u> tend to spend money carelessly.　　　　　＿＿＿＿＿＿＿＿

7　Peter took me by <u>the hand</u>.　　　　　＿＿＿＿＿＿＿＿

8　Excuse me. Is there <u>the post office</u> around here?　　＿＿＿＿＿＿＿＿

9　<u>The young</u> like to be with friends.　　　　　＿＿＿＿＿＿＿＿

10　We should be quiet for <u>a while</u>.　　　　　＿＿＿＿＿＿＿＿

11　Emily's house is near <u>a Thames</u>.　　　　　＿＿＿＿＿＿＿＿

12　Do you read <u>*a New York Times*</u>?　　　　　＿＿＿＿＿＿＿＿

13　This morning I bought <u>a newspaper</u> on the street.　　＿＿＿＿＿＿＿＿

14　Someone pushed me on <u>a back</u>.　　　　　＿＿＿＿＿＿＿＿

15　<u>The Alps</u> are always covered with snow.　　　　　＿＿＿＿＿＿＿＿

PRACTICE 22

다음 글을 읽고, 괄호 안에 주어진 단어 중 알맞은 것을 고르세요.

(A, An, The) old want to live a comfortable life. (*A*, *An*, *The*) *Korean Times* reported that these days many of them move to Southeast Asian countries after they retire. (A, An, The) Philippines is one of (a, an, the) most popular countries for them to live in. It is in (a, an, the) Pacific Ocean. It has beautiful scenery and warm weather. My family visits the country about once (a, an, the) year because my grandparents live there, too.

PSS 5 관사를 쓰지 않는 경우

1. **식사를 나타내는 명사 앞**

   I didn't have **breakfast** this morning. 나는 오늘 아침에 아침을 먹지 않았다.

2. **운동 경기를 나타내는 명사 앞**

   John usually plays **basketball** on weekends. John은 대개 주말마다 농구를 한다.

3. **by+교통수단**

   My sister and I went to Busan **by train**. 내 여동생과 나는 기차를 타고 부산에 갔다.

4. **장소, 기구를 나타내는 명사가 본래의 목적으로 쓰일 때**

   Jack doesn't go to **school** on Saturday. Jack은 토요일에 학교에 가지 않는다.
   I go to **church** every Sunday. 나는 매주 일요일마다 교회에 간다.
   Sumi went to **bed** late last night. 수미는 지난 밤 늦게 잠자리에 들었다.

5. **가족을 나타내는 명사 앞**

   Mother, Mom, Father, Dad, Uncle, Aunt와 같은 명사 앞에는 관사를 쓰지 않는다.
   (단, brother, sister는 무관사로 쓰지 않는다.)
   Dad and **Mom** are celebrating their anniversary tomorrow.
   아빠와 엄마는 내일 그들의 결혼기념일을 기념할 것이다.

6. **관직, 신분을 나타내는 명사 앞**

   Professor Kim is going to leave for Australia. 김 교수님은 호주로 떠날 것이다.

7. 과목을 나타내는 명사 앞

   My favorite subject is **science**. 내가 가장 좋아하는 과목은 과학이다.

8. 그 외의 경우 – listen to music과 watch TV는 관용적으로 관사 없이 쓴다.

   Mark likes **listening to music**. Mark는 음악을 듣는 것을 좋아한다.
   I usually **watch TV** until late at night. 나는 대개 밤 늦게까지 TV를 본다.

정답 p.31

PRACTICE 23

밑줄 친 부분이 올바르면 ○, 틀리면 바르게 고쳐 쓰세요.

1   My family went to the East Sea by the bus. ➡ ______________

2   She plays tennis very well after the lesson. ➡ ______________

3   I told Dad about the trip. ➡ ______________

4   What do you want to have for the lunch? ➡ ______________

5   The math is the most difficult subject for me. ➡ ______________

6   I am so tired. I will go to bed earlier tonight. ➡ ______________

7   Giho was watching the TV when I called him. ➡ ______________

8   What time did Liz leave home? ➡ ______________

9   Most students really liked Professor Choi's class. ➡ ______________

10 Yumi didn't go to the school today because she was sick. ➡ ______________

11 Tom is listening to a music in his room now. ➡ ______________

12 My brother wants to be an doctor in the future. ➡ ______________

정답 p.31

PRACTICE 24

다음 문장의 빈칸에 a(n)나 the 중 알맞은 것을 쓰고, 필요 없는 곳에는 ×표 하세요.

1   Where did you have ____________ lunch?

2   Jenny used to play ____________ harmonica when she was young.

3   He was ____________ only boy in the group.

4   Would you like to play ____________ baseball together?

5   She looked me in ____________ face.

6 I watched ___________ interesting movie with Nancy yesterday.

7 I think it's ___________ very place that I have lost my book.

8 I usually listen to ___________ music on my way to school.

9 We go to the library twice ___________ month.

10 Koreans tend to respect ___________ old.

11 Junho used to go to ___________ church when he was little.

12 This is not ___________ first time that Julie and I met.

13 She didn't say anything for ___________ while.

14 Ask ___________ Dad what time he comes home.

15 ___________ friend of mine loves swimming.

16 I usually have ___________ breakfast at 7:30.

17 Generally speaking, ___________ dog is friendlier than ___________ cat.

18 Lory plays ___________ cello very well.

19 Every evening I take ___________ walk with my dog.

20 ___________ moon looks really bright tonight.

21 Here is ___________ pencil I borrowed.

22 She works six hours ___________ day, five days ___________ week.

23 Did you come here by ___________ bus or by ___________ subway?

24 The police caught the thief, and now he is in ___________ prison.

25 Have you met ___________ Dr. Choi before?

26 I like ___________ math more than any other subject.

27 My brother watches ___________ TV from morning to night.

28 ___________ children in the room are all of ___________ age.

29 ___________ young have the future in their hands.

30 We are going to play ___________ badminton in the playground.

31 There is a special fish in ___________ East Sea of Korea.

32 Junha is ___________ only man on our team.

33 He didn't go to ___________ bed last night.

34 ___________ hotel we stayed at wasn't very good.

CH
5
명사와 관사

중간·기말고사 대비문제 📝

명사와 관사

1 다음 중 단어의 단수 – 복수의 연결이 올바른 것은?

① piano – pianoes　② wife – wives
③ wolf – wolfes　④ tooth – tooths
⑤ beauty – beautys

2 다음 중 어법상 올바른 문장은?

① I bought five furniture.
② He wants two cheese.
③ I had three cup of coffees yesterday.
④ She needs a piece of paper.
⑤ Nora had two cereal for lunch.

3 다음 중 어법상 올바른 문장을 <u>모두</u> 고르면?

① He toasted two piece of breads.
② I'd like a bar of chocolate, please.
③ Can I offer a piece of advice?
④ Mom put two salt in the soup.
⑤ She bought five meat for dinner.

4 우리말과 같은 뜻이 되도록 빈칸에 알맞은 단어를 쓰세요.

> • 나는 커피 한 잔과 케이크 네 조각을 먹었다.
> = I had ＿＿＿＿＿ ＿＿＿＿＿
> ＿＿＿＿＿ ＿＿＿＿＿ and
> ＿＿＿＿＿ ＿＿＿＿＿ ＿＿＿＿＿
> ＿＿＿＿＿ .

5 다음 문장의 빈칸에 들어갈 말로 알맞은 것은?

> There are ＿＿＿＿＿ in the park.

① three donkeys　② two mouses
③ several benchs　④ some birdes
⑤ five foxs

6 다음 밑줄 친 <u>these</u>와 바꿔 쓸 수 <u>없는</u> 것은?

> I need to buy <u>these</u> at the supermarket.

① two bars of soap
② five pounds of pork
③ some juices
④ many apples
⑤ three loaves of bread

7 다음 중 어법상 <u>틀린</u> 것의 개수를 고르세요.

> ⓐ Do you know the best way to master English?
> ⓑ He was first man to set foot on the Moon.
> ⓒ David is the only person I trust.
> ⓓ The copier and the computer were bought at same year.
> ⓔ I heard Rose playing piano yesterday.

① 0개　② 1개　③ 2개　④ 3개　⑤ 4개

8 우리말과 같은 뜻이 되도록 빈칸에 알맞은 단어를 쓰세요.

• 어머니가 나에게 양말 다섯 켤레를 사주셨다.
= My mother bought __________ __________
__________ __________ for me.

9 다음 빈칸에 공통으로 들어갈 단어로 알맞은 것은?

• I need a glass __________ water.
• I need to know the size __________ the shirt before buying it.
• He has a plan __________ studying for the test.

① at　　② to　　③ of　　④ by　　⑤ in

10 다음 중 어법상 올바른 문장만 짝지은 것은?

ⓐ Would you like some apple?
ⓑ Moon goes round Earth every 27 days.
ⓒ What is the longest river in the world?
ⓓ She works seven hours a day.
ⓔ Seoul is capital of Korea.

① ⓐ, ⓒ　　② ⓐ, ⓔ　　③ ⓑ, ⓓ
④ ⓒ, ⓓ　　⑤ ⓓ, ⓔ

11 다음 중 밑줄 친 부분을 어법상 옳게 고친 것은?

① Suji drinks a cup of <u>milks</u> (→ milkes) every day.
② Jihoon had <u>meats</u> (→ meates) for dinner yesterday.
③ There are two <u>cup</u> (→ cups) of coffee on the table.
④ Could you pass me the <u>sugares</u> (→ sugars), Linda?
⑤ I want to have a bottle of <u>juice</u> (→ juices).

12 다음 대화의 ①∼⑤ 중 어법상 어색한 것은?

A: ① How many ② childrens do you ③ have?
B: I have ④three sons and ⑤two daughters.

13 다음 중 어법상 올바른 문장은?

① Are you student?
② Jiho is a newspaper reporter.
③ Today is a second day of school.
④ My homeroom teacher is math teacher.
⑤ She looks a very honest.

14 다음 글의 밑줄 친 부분 중 어법상 어색한 것은?

When the teacher came into ① the classroom, he got very upset. The students were making a lot of ② noisy. Some were playing music ③ loudly and some were playing ④ games. The teacher tried to stop ⑤ them, but he failed.

15 다음 중 어법상 바른 문장을 <u>모두</u> 고르세요.

① I didn't have the lunch because I was very busy.
② I used to play the violin in my room on weekends.
③ She doesn't go to the school tomorrow.
④ Mary likes the economics.
⑤ I'm the only child in my family.

16 〈보기〉에서 알맞은 단어를 골라 올바른 형태로 바꿔 빈칸을 완성하세요.

> 보 기
>
> glass   piece   bowl   bottle   pair   slice

(1) I'm so hungry. I want __________ __________ __________ __________ right now. (밥 한 그릇)

(2) Bring me __________ __________ __________ __________ , please. (물 두 병)

(3) Last Christmas, my father bought me __________ __________ __________ __________ .
(신발 세 켤레)

(4) I'd like to drink __________ __________ __________ __________ . (오렌지 주스 한 잔)

17 다음 중 어법상 바르지 <u>않은</u> 문장은?

① This is bag of Jenny's.
② I went to a girls' middle school.
③ Hana stayed at her grandparents'.
④ Do you know the owner of this building?
⑤ What's the title of the book?

18 다음 글의 ①~⑤ 중 어법상 <u>어색한</u> 것은?

My friend Mike can't see well, so he ① <u>needs</u> help at school. His ② <u>40-years-old</u> mom comes to school with him every morning and ③ <u>brings</u> him to his classroom. And every ④ <u>student</u> in his class is kind to him and ⑤ <u>helps</u> him a lot.

19 다음 조리법의 ①~⑤ 중 어법상 <u>어색한</u> 것은?

How to Make Cucumber Yogurt Dip

What You Need
① <u>two cup of plain yogurt</u>
② <u>1 cup of sour cream</u>
③ <u>1 spoonful of lemon juice</u>
④ <u>salt and black pepper</u>
⑤ <u>two cucumbers</u>

1. Cut the cucumbers in half, grind them and put them into a bowl.
2. Add yogurt, sour cream, and lemon juice.
3. Stir everything.
4. Season with salt and pepper.
5. Refrigerate for at least 1 hour.

20 다음 빈칸에 들어갈 알맞은 말은?

> You can see many __________ here.

① leaf   ② baby   ③ sheep
④ man   ⑤ child

21 다음 우리말과 같은 뜻이 되도록 괄호 안에 주어진 말을 알맞게 배열하세요.

> · 나는 그가 마라톤에서 우승했다는 소식을 들었다.
> = I heard the news __________________
> __________________________________.
>   (a marathon, he, that, won)

22 다음의 밑줄 친 a와 그 쓰임이 같은 것은?

> Dr. Calvin said, "If you want to be taller, you should drink at least three glasses of milk a day."

① A dog is a very faithful animal.
② We have a difficult problem to solve.
③ I wanted to get paid once a month.
④ Birds of a feather flock together.
⑤ There is a Mr. Johnson on the phone.

23 다음 중 빈칸에 The[the]가 들어가야 할 것은?

① Did you have ________ lunch, Mike?
② I went to Daegu by ________ bus.
③ His favorite subject is ________ Korean.
④ I like to listen to ________ music at night.
⑤ ________ Sun rises in the East.

24 밑줄 친 부분을 바르게 고친 것 중 잘못된 것은?

① The Thames is in the London.
    → in London
② The rich thinks differently about money.
    → think
③ Have you ever been to Netherlands?
    → the Netherlands
④ Then, he began hitting me on arm.
    → on the arm
⑤ Would you look her in an eye?
    → in eye

25 다음 글의 ①~⑤ 중 어법상 어색한 것은?

> Tom is going to have ①a party tonight with ②his friends. There will be ③five men and four women. Tom went to the market to buy some ④food for the party. When he came back home, he found out that he forgot to buy ⑤a bread.

26 다음 빈칸에 들어갈 수 <u>없는</u> 것을 모두 고르세요.

> How many __________ do you want?

① furnitures   ② pencils   ③ informations
④ boxes   ⑤ children

27 다음 밑줄 친 that과 용법이 같은 것은?

> Tom told me the news <u>that</u> he would have a birthday party on Sunday.

① I think <u>that</u> is a wonderful dress.
② Look at <u>that</u> dog over there.
③ Everybody knows the fact <u>that</u> he is innocent.
④ I know <u>that</u> he is kind.
⑤ Jim has a car <u>that</u> is red.

28 다음 중 어법상 <u>어색한</u> 문장은?

① They liked to help a poor.
② Could you do me a favor?
③ I enjoy surfing the Internet on Fridays.
④ They will have a lot of fun.
⑤ He went to the airport by bus.

29 다음 밑줄 친 부분 중 어법상 <u>틀린</u> 것을 두 개 찾아 고치세요.

> (A) He skipped <u>a breakfast</u> this morning.
> (B) Lisa went on a <u>two-week-long</u> vacation.
> (C) That day, she was listening to <u>music</u> on the way home.
> (D) I recently bought two <u>pair</u> of shoes.
> (E) Jude led the old man by <u>the hand</u>.

         〈기호〉   〈고친 표현〉
(1) ________________ ➡ ________________
(2) ________________ ➡ ________________

30 다음 그림의 내용과 일치하도록 빈칸에 알맞은 말을 〈보기〉에서 골라 올바른 형태로 바꿔 쓰세요. (단, 필요시 같은 단어를 한 번 이상 쓸 수 있음.)

보 기	bar bottle loaf slice piece

> There are three ⓐ __________ of cheese, two ⓑ __________ of chocolate, three ⓒ __________ of bread and a ⓓ __________ of juice on the table. There are four ⓔ __________ of paper and three ⓕ __________ of soap under the table.

CHAPTER 6
대명사

PSS 1 인칭대명사

격	단수					복수				
인칭	주격	소유격	목적격	소유대명사	재귀대명사	주격	소유격	목적격	소유대명사	재귀대명사
1	I	my	me	mine	myself	we	our	us	ours	ourselves
2	you	your	you	yours	yourself	you	your	you	yours	yourselves
3	he	his	him	his	himself	they	their	them	theirs	themselves
	she	her	her	hers	herself					
	it	its	it	-	itself					

PSS 1-1 주격, 목적격

1. **주격** – '～은(는), ～이, ～가'로 해석되고, 문장의 주어 자리에 온다.

   I know Mr. Jones. **He** is a lawyer. 나는 Jones 씨를 안다. 그는 변호사이다.

   I ate an apple. **It** was so sweet. 나는 사과를 먹었다. 그것은 매우 달았다.

2. **목적격** – '～을(를), ～에게'로 해석되고, 동사나 전치사의 목적어 자리에 온다.

   Jane and Paul are kind. People **like them**. Jane과 Paul은 친절하다. 사람들은 그들을 좋아한다.

   Susan and I are going shopping. Would you like to come **with us**?

   Susan과 나는 쇼핑을 갈 거야. 너도 우리와 함께 갈래?

정답 p.34

PRACTICE 1

괄호 안에 주어진 단어 중 알맞은 것을 고르세요.

1 Mr. Kim is one of the most popular teachers at my school. I like (he, him).

2 John and I went to the movies. (We, Us) had fun.

3 Thank you for helping me. (You, Your) are very kind.

4 The cat looked at (I, me) through the window, meowing for attention.

5 Did (they, them) visit you last week?

6 Mrs. Park wanted to see my family, so she invited (we, us) to dinner.

7 Susie is my brother's friend. I don't know (she, her) very well.

8 This book is very interesting. I've read (it, them) twice already.

9 Mom bought a new pair of shoes and gave (they, them) to me.

10 Yoonji likes playing musical instruments. (She, Her) likes singing, too.

PSS 1-2 소유격, 소유대명사

1. 소유격 – '~의'로 해석되고, 명사가 뒤따른다.

I am wearing a hat. **My hat** is blue. 나는 모자를 쓰고 있다. 나의 모자는 파란색이다.

Is this **his bag** or **your bag**? 이것은 그의 가방이니, 아니면 너의 가방이니?

cf. its와 it's의 구분: its는 소유격으로 '그것의'라는 뜻을 가지며 it's는 'it is' 혹은 'it has'의 줄임말이다.

My dog was wagging **its** tail. 나의 개는 꼬리를 흔들고 있었다.

It's(= It is) not mine. 그것은 나의 것이 아니다.

2. 소유대명사 – '~의 것'으로 해석되고, 명사가 뒤따르지 않는다.

I have her pencil. This is <u>**hers**</u>. 나는 그녀의 연필을 가지고 있다. 이것은 그녀의 것이다.
(= her pencil)

Are these pants <u>**yours**</u>? 이 바지는 너의 것이니?
(= your pants)

cf. 대명사 it은 소유대명사의 형태를 가지지 않는다.

정답 p.34

PRACTICE 2 [1-6]

다음 문장의 빈칸에 알맞은 대명사를 쓰세요.

1 
Sora has a bicycle.
This is _her_ bicycle.
This is _hers_ .

2 
Tom has a cap.
This is __________ cap.
This is __________ .

3

Mr. and Mrs. Choi have a house.

This is ___________ house.

This is ___________.

4

I have a dog.

It is ___________ dog.

It is ___________.

5

Your name is on the cover.

It's ___________ book.

It's ___________.

6

We study in this classroom.

This is ___________ classroom.

This is ___________.

정답 p.34

PRACTICE 3

괄호 안에 주어진 대명사 중 알맞은 것을 고르세요.

1 I met Jinho yesterday. (He, His) is leaving for London tomorrow.

2 Yumi is (my, mine) friend. I like (she, her) a lot.

3 Have you met Tina and Bob? (They, Them) are my cousins.

4 They brought (our, us) some sandwiches.

5 I've eaten Miyoung's cake. I didn't know it was (her, hers).

6 Do you know the gentleman over there? What is (his, him) name?

7 Did you see the dogs in the picture? Those are (our, ours).

8 Jenny will tell (he, him) the truth.

9 I hope (your, yours) dream will come true in the future.

10 I heard the news but I didn't realize (it's, its) importance.

1. 재귀 용법 – 문장의 주어와 목적어의 대상이 같을 때는 인칭대명사의 목적격 대신 재귀
   대명사를 쓴다. 재귀 용법으로 쓰인 재귀대명사는 생략할 수 없다.

   I saw **myself** in the mirror. 나는 거울 속에 있는 나 자신을 보았다.
   cf. I saw **me** in the mirror. (×)

   Jina is very proud of **herself**. 지나는 자신을 매우 자랑스러워한다.
   cf. Jina is very proud of **her**. (×)
   Jina 자신일 때

2. 강조 용법 – 주어, 목적어, 보어를 강조하기 위해 쓰이는 재귀대명사는 강조하고자 하는
   (대)명사 바로 뒤에 오거나 문장의 끝에 올 수 있고, 생략할 수 있다. 강조 용법의 재귀대
   명사를 생략하면 강조의 의미도 사라진다.

   I **(myself)** fixed the computer. 내가 (직접) 컴퓨터를 고쳤다.
   = I fixed the computer **(myself)**.
   I've seen **the singer (himself)**. 나는 그 가수를 (직접) 본 적이 있다.
   It was **Tom (himself)**. 그것은 Tom (그 자신)이었다.

3. 전치사＋재귀대명사

   ① by oneself '혼자, 다른 사람 없이'
      I couldn't go there **by myself**. 나는 혼자서 그곳에 갈 수 없었다.

   ② for oneself '혼자 힘으로, 스스로'
      Peter did his homework **for himself**. Peter는 혼자 힘으로 숙제를 했다.

정답 p.34

PRACTICE 4

다음 문장의 빈칸에 알맞은 재귀대명사를 쓰고, 어떤 용법으로 쓰였는지 고르세요.

1 James could fix the car ___________. [재귀 / 강조]

2 Sujin wants to stay here by ___________. [재귀 / 강조]

3 I ___________ promised to come back soon. [재귀 / 강조]

4 Take good care of ___________, will you? [재귀 / 강조]

5 History repeats ___________. [재귀 / 강조]

6 We had to solve the problem for ___________. [재귀 / 강조]

7 He is proud of ___________ for not giving up. [재귀 / 강조]

8 The guests made ___________ at home there. [재귀 / 강조]

PRACTICE 5

괄호 안에 주어진 단어 중 알맞은 것을 고르세요.

1 Tony lent (me, myself) the book yesterday.

2 Frank prepared the meeting by (him, himself).

3 He introduced (them, themselves) to his mom.

4 They gave (us, ourselves) something to drink.

5 She cannot live by (her, herself).

6 I have something to tell (you, yourself).

7 The little bird learned to fly by (it, itself).

8 I looked at (me, myself) in the mirror.

9 I will be proud of (me, myself).

10 Peter asked (her, herself) to marry him.

PSS 2 it의 쓰임

PSS 2-1 비인칭주어 it

문장의 주어로 쓰이지만 특별한 의미를 가지지 않기 때문에 '그것은, 그것이'로 굳이 해석하지 않는다.

날씨	**It** will be rainy and windy tomorrow. 내일은 비가 오고 바람이 불 것이다.
거리	**It** is two kilometers to the office. 그 사무실까지는 2km이다.
시간	**It** is five o'clock now. 지금은 5시이다.
요일	**It** is Monday today. 오늘은 월요일이다.
날짜	**It** is April 6. 4월 6일이다.
온도	**It** is 17 degrees Celsius in this room. 이 방은 섭씨 17도이다.
계절	**It** is winter in Korea now. 지금 한국은 겨울이다.

PRACTICE 6

다음 문장의 밑줄 친 부분이 대명사이면 '대', 비인칭주어이면 '비'를 쓰세요.

1 It was dark in the room. [   ]

2 Let's go inside. It is freezing out here. [   ]

3 Look at the cat. It is so cute. [   ]

4 It is hot and humid in summer. [   ]

5 How far is it to the station? [   ]

6 I love autumn. It is a beautiful season. [   ]

7 It is already eight o'clock. We should hurry. [   ]

8 Don't blame yourself. It was not your fault. [   ]

1. **It seems that ~** '~ 인 것 같다'

   It seems that you are a little tired. 너 약간 피곤한 것 같다. = You **seem to** be a little tired.
   It seemed that she had a cold. 그녀는 감기에 걸린 것 같았다. = She **seemed to** have a cold.

2. 「It is[was] ~ that …」 강조구문 – 강조하고자 하는 말을 It is[was]와 that 사이에 쓴다. 단, 동사와 형용사는 It is[was]와 that 사이에 쓸 수 없다.

   Jane bought a new coat last weekend. Jane은 지난 주말에 새 코트를 샀다.
   It was Jane that bought a new coat last weekend. (주어 Jane을 강조)
   지난 주말에 새 코트를 산 사람은 바로 Jane이었다.
   It was a new coat that Jane bought last weekend. (목적어 a new coat를 강조)
   지난 주말에 Jane이 샀던 것은 바로 새 코트였다.
   It was last weekend that Jane bought a new coat. (부사구 last weekend를 강조)
   Jane이 새 코트를 샀던 것은 바로 지난 주말이었다.

정답 p.34

PRACTICE 7

〈보기〉와 같이 주어진 문장을 같은 뜻의 다른 문장으로 바꾸어 쓰세요.

보 기	It seems that you are upset about what happened.
	➡ You seem to be upset about what happened.

1 It seemed that you were very confident when you made the speech.

➡ ____

2 My sister seems to have a plan to stay at Sumi's for a while.

➡ ____

3 It seems that she is nervous about her job interview.

➡ ____

4 You seemed to be satisfied with your test result.

➡ ____

5 It seems that he knows what he is doing now.

➡ ____

PRACTICE 8

다음 문장을 It ~ that 강조구문으로 바꿔 쓰세요.

1 I saw Minji's brother at the theater yesterday. (Minji's brother 강조)

➡ ____

2 I met Sumin at the amusement park a week ago. (a week ago 강조)

➡ ____

3 My uncle was seriously injured in the car accident. (my uncle 강조)

➡ ____

4 I'm going to meet the children at the bus stop this Sunday. (at the bus stop 강조)

➡ ____

5 We were supposed to meet in front of the statue at five. (at five 강조)

➡ ____

PSS 2-3 가주어 it / 가목적어 it

1. 가주어 it – 문장에서 주어로 쓰인 부정사(구), 명사절의 길이가 길 때는, 이들을 뒤로 보내고 원래의 주어 자리에는 가주어 it을 쓴다. 이때 원래의 주어인 부정사(구), 명사절은 진주어라고 한다.

   It is very important **to have breakfast**. 아침식사를 하는 것은 매우 중요하다.
   가주어 　　　　　　　　　　　　 진주어

   It is surprising **that Mina left Korea**. 미나가 한국을 떠났다는 것은 놀랍다.
   가주어 　　　　　　　　 진주어

2. 가목적어 it – 문장에서 목적어로 쓰인 부정사(구), 명사절의 길이가 길 때는, 이들을 뒤로 보내고 원래의 목적어 자리에는 가목적어 it을 쓴다. 이때 원래의 목적어는 진목적어라고 한다.

   I found **it** exciting **to ride a roller coaster**. 나는 롤러코스터를 타는 것이 신난다는 것을 알았다.
   　　　　 가목적어 　　　　　　 진목적어

PRACTICE 9

우리말과 일치하도록 주어진 말을 바르게 배열하세요.

1 병을 재활용하는 것은 중요하다. (the bottles, it, to, recycle, important, is)

➡ ____

2 공상 과학 소설을 읽는 것은 매우 흥미롭다. (very, science fiction, it, exciting, read, to, is)

➡ ____

3 나는 네가 그렇게 말하는 것이 이상하다고 생각했다. (that, so, I, it, strange, you, thought, said)

➡ ____

4 네가 또 거짓말을 했다는 것은 실망스럽다. (you, again, is, that, disappointing, it, lied)

➡ ____

5 나는 매일 새로운 단어를 외우는 것이 어렵다는 것을 알았다.
(it, memorize, every day, I, difficult, found, new words, to)

➡ ____

6 우리 팀이 경기를 이겼다는 것이 나를 행복하게 했다. (won, that, made, it, happy, me, the game, our team)

➡ ____

7 팀을 위해 경기하는 것이 중요하다. (to, the team, important, it, for, is, play)

➡ ____

8 그가 위기 상황에서도 평정을 유지하다니 놀랍다. (a crisis, he, keep, amazing, it, cool, that, in, can, is)

➡ ____

PSS 3 지시대명사

PSS 3-1 this, that

this/these	that/those
가까이에 있는 사람이나 사물을 나타낸다.	멀리 떨어져 있는 사람이나 사물을 나타낸다.
This is my friend, Paul. 이 아이는 내 친구인 Paul이야. **These** are my friends, Paul and Jane. 이 아이들은 내 친구들인 Paul과 Jane이야. *cf.* 지시형용사로서 명사를 수식할 수도 있다. **This book** is my brother's. 이 책은 내 형의 것이다. **These pants** are my brother's. 이 바지는 내 형의 것이다.	**That** is my friend, Paul. 저 아이는 내 친구인 Paul이야. **Those** are my friends, Paul and Jane. 저 아이들은 내 친구들인 Paul과 Jane이야. *cf.* 지시형용사로서 명사를 수식할 수도 있다. **That book** is my brother's. 저 책은 내 형의 것이다. **Those pants** are my brother's. 저 바지는 내 형의 것이다.

<table>
<tr><th>this</th><th>that</th></tr>
<tr><td>전화상에서 전화를 건 사람과 받는 사람을 가리킨다.

Hello, **this** is Minsu.
여보세요, 저는 민수예요.
Is **this** Sujin?
수진이니?</td><td>전화상에서 전화를 받는 사람을 가리킨다.

Is **that** Mr. Jones? Jones 씨이십니까?</td></tr>
</table>

정답 p.35

PRACTICE 10

그림을 보고, this나 these, that이나 those를 이용하여 빈칸에 알맞은 말을 쓰세요.

PSS 3-2 that/those의 특별 용법

1. 앞에 나오는 명사의 반복을 피하기 위해 쓴다. 앞에 나오는 명사가 단수면 that, 복수면 those를 쓴다.

   The temperature of Jejudo is higher than **that** of Incheon.
   제주도의 기온은 인천의 그것보다 더 높다.　　(= the temperature)
   Chinese **customs** are very different from **those** of Australia.
   중국의 관습은 호주의 그것과 매우 다르다.　　(= customs)

2. those는 who와 함께 쓰여 '~하는 사람들'의 의미를 갖는다.

   Heaven helps **those who** help themselves. 하늘은 스스로를 돕는 자를 돕는다.
   Those who want to meet Dr. Park usually wait for 30 minutes.
   박 박사님을 만나기를 원하는 사람들은 보통 30분을 기다린다.

정답 p.35

PRACTICE 11 [1-10]

다음 문장의 빈칸에 that이나 those 중 알맞은 것을 쓰세요.

1　The population of Japan is larger than ____________ of Korea.

2　I love ____________ who love me, and ____________ who seek me diligently will find me.

3　Giho's shoes are bigger than ____________ of Minsu.

4　My classroom is smaller than ____________ of Yumi.

5　The buildings of this city are older than ____________ of Seoul.

6　____________ who work hard often succeed in life.

7　The price of your jacket is twice as high as ____________ of my jacket.

8 The employees of this year work better than ___________ of last year.

9 My brother is one of __________ who love peace.

10 My vacation is shorter than __________ of my sister.

PSS 4 부정대명사

PSS 4-1 one

1. 앞에 나온 명사와 종류는 같지만 대상이 다른 경우에 명사의 반복을 피하기 위해 one을 쓴다.

   cf. it은 특정한 것을 가리킬 때 쓴다.

A: Would you like to have a hamburger?

햄버거 먹을래?

B: No, thanks. I already had **one**.

고맙지만, 괜찮아. 난 이미 하나 먹었어.

햄버거를 의미하지만, 앞에서 A가 권한 햄버거를 가리키는 것은 아니므로 one을 쓴다.

A: Where did you find the ring?

너는 그 반지를 어디서 찾았니?

B: I found **it** under the bed.

나는 그것을 침대 밑에서 찾았어.

앞에서 A가 언급한 바로 그 반지(the ring)를 가리키므로 one이 아닌 it을 쓴다.

2. 명사가 복수형일 때는 ones를 쓴다.

   Are these your shoes? – No, the brown **ones** are mine.

   이것들은 네 신발이니?   아니, 갈색 신발이 내 거야.

   cf. 명사가 복수형이고 앞에서 언급한 명사와 동일한 대상을 지칭할 때는 they[them]를 쓴다.

   Were the groceries delivered on time? – Yes, **they** arrived yesterday.

   식료품들이 제때 배달되었니?   응, 그것들은 어제 도착했어.

3. 일반적인 사람을 나타낸다.

   One should follow the traffic rules. 사람은 교통규칙을 따라야 한다.

PRACTICE 12

〈보기〉에서 알맞은 단어를 골라 빈칸에 쓰세요.

보 기	one ones it them

1 Did you see my cell phone? – No, I didn't see _____________. Sorry.

2 They have only yellow flowers. I need pink _____________.

3 Katie gave me a small balloon, but I wanted a big _____________.

4 My mom made three dolls. Would you like to see _____________?

5 _____________ usually finds that friendship is very important.

6 I need an eraser. Do you have _____________?

7 Alice bought a book and gave _____________ to me.

8 Jane really likes those blue jeans. She will buy _____________.

9 Ted has a nice bicycle. I have _____________, too.

10 Are these pens yours? – No, mine are the _____________ on the desk.

11 We have a dog and a cat. I wash _____________ twice a week.

12 _____________ should save energy for the future.

13 Robert took the papers and threw _____________ away.

14 Here is your cap. – Where did you find _____________?

15 Who are Denny's children? – The smiling _____________ in the front row.

16 Those sneakers don't look very nice. – How about buying these white _____________ instead?

17 We stayed at a famous hotel on Jeju Island, but _____________ wasn't worth the money.

PSS 4-2 other, another

1. others '(불특정한) 다른 사람[것]들'

Ann always tries to help **others**. Ann은 항상 다른 사람들을 도와주려고 한다.

2. the other '(둘 중) 다른 하나'

Mom gave my brother this one, but he wanted **the other**.
엄마는 형에게 (둘 중) 이것을 주었지만, 그는 (남은) 다른 것을 원했다.

3. the others '(나머지) 다른 사람[것]들'

I don't like these. Can I have **the others**?

저는 이것들이 마음에 들지 않아요. (남은) 다른 것들을 가져도 될까요?

4. another '또 하나'

This apple tastes good. Can I have **another**? 이 사과는 맛이 좋군요. 하나 더 먹어도 될까요?

cf. other는 「other+복수 명사」의 형태로 쓰이며, 이 때의 other는 '다른, 그 밖의'라는 뜻이다.
반면 another는 「another+단수 명사」의 형태로 쓰이며, 이 때의 another는 '또 하나의, 또 다른'이라는 뜻이다.
Can I ask you **other** questions? 다른 질문들을 해도 될까요?
Can I ask you **another** question? 또 다른 질문을 해도 될까요?

정답 p.35

PRACTICE 13

괄호 안에 주어진 말 중 알맞은 것을 고르세요.

1 Please, show me (another, other).

2 One of the twins is my friend. (The other, Others) is a friend of my brother's.

3 They gave me (other, another) chance.

4 Do you have any (other, another) books?

5 We should be kind to (another, others).

6 Here are two cats. One is mine and (the other, another) is his.

7 I saw only Alex and Becky. Where are (the other, the others)?

8 I bought four bottles. Two of them are red. (The others, Others) are yellow.

9 Don't care too much about what (others, the other) say about it.

10 Sally entered the room, and (other, another) girls followed her.

11 Some (other, the other) people already took good seats.

12 I've still got a headache. I need (other, another) aspirin.

13 You should keep quiet in the library for (others, another).

14 The bakery is on (another, the other) side of the street.

15 This is my favorite kind of cookie. Can I have (other, another)?

16 You shouldn't talk like that to (the other, others).

one ~ the other …
(둘 중에) 하나는 ~, 다른 하나는 …

There are **two boys** here. **One** is from Korea, and **the other** is from Canada.

여기에 두 명의 소년이 있다. 한 명은 한국 출신이고, 다른 한 명은 캐나다 출신이다.

one ~ another … the other −
(셋 중에) 하나는 ~, 다른 하나는 …,
나머지 하나는 −

There are **three boys** here. **One** is from Korea, **another** is from Canada and **the other** is from Japan.

여기에 세 명의 소년이 있다. 한 명은 한국 출신이고, 다른 한 명은 캐나다 출신이고, 나머지 한 명은 일본 출신이다.

some ~ others …
(불특정한 수의 사람[것]들 중에서)
몇몇은 ~, 다른 사람[것]들은 …

There are **a lot of students** in this room. **Some** are wearing glasses, and **others** aren't.

이 방에는 많은 학생들이 있다. 몇몇은 안경을 쓰고 있고, 다른 학생들은 쓰고 있지 않다.

some ~ the others …
(특정한 수의 사람[것]들 중에서)
몇몇은 ~, 나머지는 …

There are **ten students** in this room. **Some** are wearing glasses, and **the others** aren't.

이 방에는 10명의 학생들이 있다. 몇몇은 안경을 쓰고 있고, 나머지는 쓰고 있지 않다.

cf. the가 붙으면 '나머지, 전부'의 의미가 더해진다.

PRACTICE 14

<보기>에서 알맞은 말을 골라 빈칸에 쓰세요.

보 기	one some the other others the others another

1 Mary has two cups. One is big, and ________________ is small.

2 Some like pets, but ________________ don't like them.

3 I invited ten people to my birthday party. Some came, but ________________ didn't.

4 There are three tables. One is white, another is brown, and ________________ is black.

5 Look at the two birds. ________________ is small, and ________________ is big.

6 John has five sons. ________________ like baseball, and ________________ like soccer.

7 Do you see the three men there? One is tall. ________________ is short. ________________ is thin.

8 Some believe in God while ________________ don't believe at all.

9 I have two sweaters. ________________ is blue, and ________________ is red.

10 Some people go jogging in the morning, and ________________ go jogging at night.

11 Mr. Hong has three children. ________________ is Gildong, another is Sumi, and ________________ is Bora.

12 There are a lot of people in the airport. ________________ are Koreans, and ________________ are Americans.

13 I got three flowers. ________________ was a rose, ________________ was a lily, and the other was a sunflower.

14 Helen has two brothers. ________________ is 10 years old, and ________________ is 8 years old.

15 There are a dozen pens. ________________ are black, and ________________ are red.

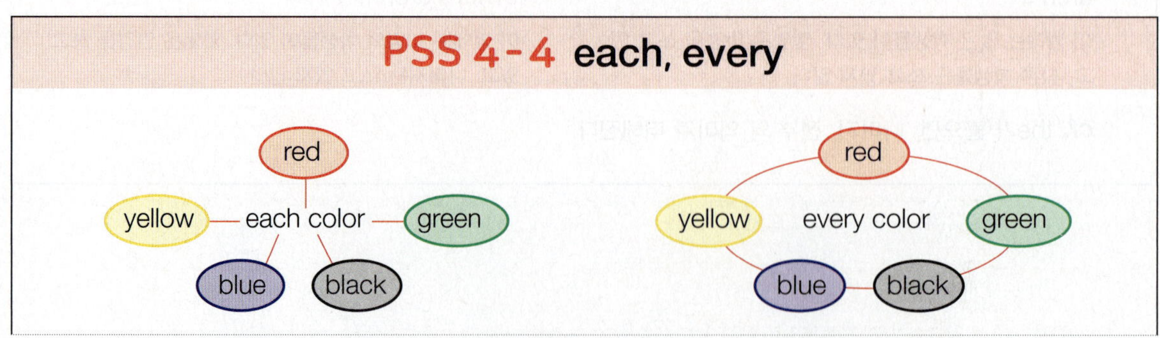

PSS 4-4 each, every

> ### 1. each – '각자, 각기, 각각의'의 뜻으로 명사를 수식하고 단수 취급한다.
>
> ① each+단수 명사+단수 동사
> **Each student has** to tell one story. 각각의 학생은 한 가지의 이야기를 말해야 한다.
>
> ② each of+복수 명사+단수 동사 – each 뒤에 of가 올 때는 명사 앞에 관사나 소유격 등의 수식어가 붙는다.
> **Each of the girls is** from a different country. 그 소녀들 각각은 다른 나라 출신이다.
>
> ### 2. every – '모든'의 뜻으로 명사를 수식하고 단수 취급한다.
>
> ① every+단수 명사+단수 동사
> **Every kid was** excited to go on the field trip. 모든 어린이들은 현장학습을 가게 되어 흥분했다.
>
> ② '～마다, 매 ～'
> My brother and I go to the beach **every summer**. 나의 형과 나는 여름마다 그 해변에 간다.
>
> ***cf.*** every는 not과 같은 부정어와 함께 쓰이면 일부를 부정하는 부분 부정이 된다.
> **Not every** boy likes playing soccer. 모든 소년들이 축구하는 것을 좋아하는 것은 아니다.

정답 p.36

PRACTICE 15

우리말과 일치하도록 괄호 안에 주어진 말을 바르게 배열하세요.

1 각각의 그 꽃들은 다른 색을 가지고 있다.
(each, a, different color, of the flowers, has)

➡ ____

2 김 선생님은 지난 밤 모든 학생들에게 전화를 했다.
(every student, Mr. Kim, called, last night)

➡ ____

3 각각의 테이블은 녹색 천으로 덮여 있다.
(each table, covered, is, green cloth, with)

➡ ____

4 나는 매주 일요일마다 할머니 댁에 가곤 했다.
(every Sunday, I, go to my grandmother's house, used to)

➡ ____

5 각각의 선수들은 빨간색 바지를 입고 있다.
(each player, is, red pants, wearing)

➡ ____

6 이 방에 있는 모든 책들이 다 정치학에 관한 것은 아니다.
(every book, is, about politics, in this room, not)

➡ ____

PSS 4-5 all, both, rest

1. all – '모든, ~ 모두'의 뜻으로, all 뒤에 of가 올 때는 명사 앞에 관사나 소유격 등의 수식어가 붙는다.

   ① all+셀 수 있는 명사의 복수형+복수 동사

   All passengers are sleeping in the bus. 모든 승객들이 버스에서 잠을 자고 있다.

   ② all (of)+셀 수 있는 명사의 복수형+복수 동사

   All (of) the passengers are sleeping in the bus. 승객들 모두가 버스에서 잠을 자고 있다.

   ③ all (of)+셀 수 없는 명사+단수 동사

   All (of) her money is stolen. 그녀의 돈 모두가 도난 당했다.

2. both – '양쪽, ~ 둘 다'의 뜻으로 both 뒤에 of가 올 때는 명사 앞에 관사나 소유격 등의 수식어가 붙는다.

   ① both+셀 수 있는 명사의 복수형+복수 동사

   Both dictionaries are very old. 양쪽 사전 다 매우 낡았다.

   ② both (of)+셀 수 있는 명사의 복수형+복수 동사

   Both (of) the dictionaries are very old. 그 사전들 둘 다 매우 낡았다.

   cf. all과 both는 not과 같은 부정어와 함께 쓰이면 일부를 부정하는 부분 부정이 된다.

   Not all the information is useful. 모든 정보가 유용한 것은 아니다.

   I **don't** know **both** of them. 나는 두 사람 다 아는 것은 아니다.

3. rest – '나머지'의 뜻으로 정관사 the와 함께 쓰이며, 뒤에 of가 올 때는 명사 앞에 관사나 소유격 등의 수식어가 붙는다.

   ① the rest of+셀 수 있는 명사의 복수형+복수 동사

   The rest of the actors are working through the whole night.

   나머지 배우들이 밤새 작업을 하고 있다.

   ② the rest of+셀 수 없는 명사+단수 동사

   The rest of my life is going to be terrible if you don't love me.

   네가 날 사랑하지 않는다면 내 나머지 인생은 비참할 것이다.

   cf. the rest 단독으로 '나머지 것들, 나머지 사람들'의 복수의 의미로 쓰인다.

   The first two questions were difficult, but **the rest were** pretty easy.

   처음 두 문제는 어려웠지만 나머지는 꽤 쉬웠다.

PRACTICE 16

우리말과 일치하도록 괄호 안에 주어진 말을 바르게 배열하세요.

1 너는 이 방에 있는 책 모두를 읽어야 한다.
(all the books, in this room, you, should, read)
➡ ____

2 Ford 부인이 내 생일 선물로 그 접시들 모두를 내게 주었다.
(all of those dishes, Ms. Ford, for my birthday present, gave, me)
➡ ____

3 그녀는 네게 모든 정보를 말해줄 것이다.
(all of the information, she, you, is going to, tell)
➡ ____

4 나는 두 소년 모두를 내 공연에 초대할 거야.
(both boys, will, I, to my performance, invite)
➡ ____

5 그 시험 둘 다 내게 매우 어려웠다.
(both of the tests, for me, were, very difficult)
➡ ____

6 그는 그 규칙들을 둘 다 지키지는 않았다.
(both of the rules, didn't, he, follow)
➡ ____

7 그녀는 식탁 위에 있던 나머지 케이크를 먹었다.
(ate, on the table, she, the cake, the rest of)
➡ ____

8 너희들 나머지는 지금 집에 가도 좋다.
(may, home, the rest, go, you, of, now)
➡ ____

9 나머지 승무원들이 불타는 배에서 구조되었다.
(rescued, from, the crew, the rest of, were, the burning ship)
➡ ____

10 모든 참가자들은 종이 울렸을 때 피곤해 보였다.
(looked, rang, when, the participants, tired, all of, the bell)
➡ ____

11 모든 사람들이 그 변화에 만족하는 것은 아니다.
(the changes, are, not, all people, happy with)
➡ ____

PRACTICE 17

괄호 안에 주어진 말 중 알맞은 것을 고르세요.

1   Each (student, students) has his own diary.

2   All of (the taxis, taxis) were taken.

3   Both (kid, kids) were playing in the kitchen.

4   Jack studies for the next day's classes every (night, nights).

5   (Do, Does) each girl know the truth?

6   All of my cheese (was, were) gone all of a sudden.

7   I drink a cup of milk every (morning, mornings).

8   Both of (the restaurants, restaurants) are very nice.

9   You should say each of (the word, those words) correctly.

10   Mr. Lee talked to every (parent, parents) in the room.

11   All the guests (is, are) waiting for you.

12   Each of them (has, have) a different answer.

13   The rest of the students (have to, has to) study in their classrooms.

14   Here (is, are) the rest of your change.

15   (The rest of, Both of) your money was used to buy eggs at the grocery.

16   Both of us (is, are) quite shy.

17   You should always look both (way, ways) before crossing.

18   All of the furniture there (was, were) made in China.

19   Every (minute, minutes) feels like an hour.

20   Only two of the hats are my brother's, and the rest (is, are) mine.

PSS 4-6 some-, any-

somebody, someone, something

1.   긍정문에 쓰인다.

I want to ask **somebody** about it. 나는 그것에 대해 누군가에게 물어보고 싶다.

2. 권유나 요구를 나타내는 의문문에 쓰인다.

Can you do **something** for me? 날 위해 무언가를 해줄 수 있니?

3. 긍정의 대답을 예상하는 의문문에 쓰인다.

Did **someone** call my name? 누구 내 이름 불렀어?

anybody, anyone, anything

1. 부정문에 쓰인다.

Jenny didn't eat **anything**. Jenny는 아무것도 먹지 않았다.

2. 의문문에 쓰인다.

Can **anybody** help me with this box? 이 상자 드는 걸 도와줄 사람 있니?

3. '어떠한 ~라도'의 뜻일 때는 긍정문에도 쓸 수 있다.

I can do **anything** for you. 난 널 위해 어떠한 것이라도 할 수 있어.

4. 조건을 나타내는 if절에 쓸 수 있다.

If you know **anyone** to help them, please let me know.
만약 당신이 그들을 도와줄 누군가를 안다면, 제게 알려주세요.

정답 p.37

PRACTICE 18 [1-12]

주어진 우리말에 유의하여 밑줄 친 부분을 올바르게 고치세요. (단, 틀린 부분이 없다면 ○표를 쓸 것.)

1 당신이 나가 있던 동안에 누군가 전화했어요.
Anyone called while you were out.　　➡ ________________

2 저를 도와줄 누군가가 필요해요.
I need anyone to help me.　　➡ ________________

3 어떤 것이라도 말할 것이 있다면, 어서 하세요.
If you have anything to say, go ahead.　　➡ ________________

4 그녀는 그 밖의 다른 것을 사길 원한다.
She wants to buy anything else.　　➡ ________________

5 제 제안에 관심 있으신 분이 계신가요?
Is anyone interested in my suggestion?　　➡ ________________

6 경찰은 그녀에게서 아무런 혐의점도 찾을 수 없었다.

The police couldn't find <u>something</u> suspicious about her. ➡ _______________

7 어떤 사람이라도 우리 파티에 와서 참여할 수 있다.

<u>Someone</u> can come and join our party. ➡ _______________

8 뭔가 마실 것을 원하세요?

Would you like <u>something</u> to drink? ➡ _______________

9 Eddie는 돈이 거의 없었기 때문에 아무것도 살 수 없었다.

Eddie couldn't buy <u>something</u> because he had little money. ➡ _______________

10 어젯밤 무슨 일이 발생했고, 당신은 그것에 대해 알아야 한다.

<u>Anything</u> happened last night and you should know about it. ➡ _______________

11 오늘 아침에 누군가 당신을 만나러 왔어요.

<u>Anybody</u> came to see you this morning. ➡ _______________

12 당신은 시장에서 뭔가를 구입했나요?

Did you buy <u>anything</u> at the market? ➡ _______________

PSS 5 의문대명사

PSS 5-1 who

who는 사람을 가리킬 때 쓴다.

who	주격	**Who** broke the window? – Minho did. 누가 창문을 깨뜨렸니?　　민호가 그랬어.
whose	소유격	**Whose** bag is this? – It's Ann's. 이것은 누구의 가방이니?　Ann의 것이야. = **Whose** is this bag? 이 가방은 누구의 것이니?
who(m)	목적격	**Who(m)** did you write to? 누구에게 편지를 썼니? = **To whom** did you write? *cf.* 전치사를 의문대명사 앞으로 보낼 경우에는 who를 쓸 수 없다.

PRACTICE 19

괄호 안에 주어진 단어 중 알맞은 것을 고르세요.

1 (Who, Whom) will come with me?

2 (Who, Whose) pens are these?

3 To (whose, whom) are you talking?

4 (Who, Whom) dropped by your house last night?

5 For (who, whom) does he work?

6 (Whose, Whom) name did you forget?

7 (Who, Whom) does not agree with this decision?

8 (Who, Whose) is that car over there?

9 (Whose, Whom) bag did you carry?

10 With (whom, who) are you going there?

CH
6
대명사

PSS 5-2 which, what

which	사람이나 동물, 사물을 가리킬 때 쓴다. 주로 A or B와 같이 구체적인 선택의 범위가 주어진다. **Which** is bigger, Busan **or** Seoul? 부산과 서울 중 어디가 더 크니? **Which** do you like better, coffee **or** tea? 너는 커피와 차 중 어떤 것을 더 좋아하니? *cf.* 명사를 수식하는 의문형용사로도 쓰인다. 　　**Which bag** is yours? 어느 가방이 너의 것이니?
what	동물이나 사물, 그리고 사람의 직업이나 신분을 나타낼 때 쓴다. **What** will you buy? – I'll buy a pair of jeans. 너는 무엇을 살 거니?　　나는 청바지 한 벌을 살 거야. **What** is his name? – His name is Dan. 그의 이름은 무엇이니?　　그의 이름은 Dan이야. *cf.* 명사를 수식하는 의문형용사로도 쓰인다. 　　**What color** do you like best? 너는 어떤 색깔을 가장 좋아하니?

PRACTICE 20

괄호 안에 주어진 단어 중 알맞은 것을 고르세요.

1 (What, Which) does your father do?

2 (What, Which) book of these two did you borrow?

3 (What, Whom) did the teacher try to talk to?

4 (Which, What) kind of movies are popular in Korea?

5 (What, Which) is special about January 26th?

6 (What, Which) is your brother among these boys?

7 (Whose, Which) is this jacket? I found it under the table.

8 (What, Which) are cheaper, the apples or the oranges?

9 (What, Which) part do you mean, Part 1 or Part 2?

10 (What, Which) did the man say to you?

PRACTICE 21

우리말과 일치하도록 괄호 안에 주어진 말을 바르게 배열하세요.

1 너는 어느 좌석을 원하니?
(seat, you, which, want, do)?
➡ ____

2 너는 내일 어떤 수업이 있니?
(do, what, you, classes, have, tomorrow)?
➡ ____

3 Cathy는 어느 음식을 좋아하니?
(food, Cathy, does, which, like)?
➡ ____

4 그는 어떤 나라를 방문하길 원하니?
(to visit, does, want, what, countries, he)?
➡ ____

5 네 방에 어느 벽지가 좋을까?
(is, your room, for, wallpaper, which, good)?
➡ ____

1 (A)~(C)에 알맞은 말끼리 바르게 연결된 것은?

> The ocean is a vast body of (A) [water / waters] that covers much of the Earth's surface. It is home to many creatures, from tiny fish to enormous whales. The ocean provides food and habitats for many animals, including dolphins, sharks, and sea turtles. (B) [It / They] also plays a crucial role in regulating the Earth's climate and weather patterns. Unfortunately, the ocean is facing many challenges, such as pollution, overfishing, and climate change. These threats are harming marine life and ecosystems. It's important for everyone to take action to protect the ocean and ensure (C) [it's / its] health for future generations.

	(A)		(B)		(C)
①	water	–	It	–	it's
②	waters	–	It	–	its
③	water	–	It	–	its
④	waters	–	They	–	it's
⑤	water	–	They	–	its

2 다음 밑줄 친 himself와 용법이 같은 것은?

> He introduced himself in English.

① Why don't we try it ourselves?
② She painted the wall herself.
③ My father himself designed this house.
④ I looked at myself for a long time.
⑤ The members of this club made the logo themselves.

3 다음 밑줄 친 It과 쓰임이 같은 것은?

> It is still cold out there.

① It is in the closet.
② It is summer now.
③ She wanted to buy it.
④ It was full of treasures.
⑤ I'll check it for you.

4 다음 중 바르게 영작된 것은?

① 그 대학교는 외국어에 특화된 것으로 유명하다.
➡ The university is known as its specialization in foreign languages.
② 그 어려운 퍼즐을 푼 것은 바로 Laura이다.
➡ It is the difficult puzzle that Laura solved.
③ 주차장에 있는 각각의 차들은 눈으로 덮여 있었다.
➡ Each of the cars in the parking lot was covered in snow.
④ 그 개는 기쁘게 그것의 꼬리를 흔들었다.
➡ The dog wagged it's tail happily.
⑤ 나머지 물품들은 뒤쪽 방에 저장되어 있다.
➡ The rest of the supplies is stored in the back room.

5 다음 중 밑줄 친 부분을 생략할 수 있는 것은?

① You have to do that yourself.
② She always thinks of herself.
③ He said to himself, "Shall I try?"
④ I prepared breakfast by myself.
⑤ I solved the problem for myself.

6 〈보기〉와 같은 의미가 되도록 어법에 맞게 쓴 것은?

보 기
She doesn't have any brothers.

① She have no brothers.
② She has no brothers.
③ She doesn't has no brothers.
④ She doesn't no have brothers.
⑤ She has not brothers.

7 다음 중 어법상 <u>잘못된</u> 문장은?

① Every game lasts approximately 40 minutes.
② We arrived in Busan around 3 p.m.
③ I am going to go to France.
④ Each of the girls have her own desk.
⑤ All the seats are taken.

8 다음 밑줄 친 <u>alone</u>과 바꿔 쓸 수 있는 것은?

A: Can I help you?
B: No, thanks. I prefer to do everything <u>alone</u>.

① by myself   ② of itself
③ in itself   ④ beside myself
⑤ to myself

9 어법상 <u>잘못</u> 쓰인 부분을 <u>2개</u> 찾아 바르게 고쳐 쓰세요.

Laura and I has umbrellas. This yellow one is mine and that red one is her. However, I like the red one better than the yellow one.

(1) _______________ ➡ _______________
(2) _______________ ➡ _______________

10 다음 대화의 밑줄 친 우리말을 영어로 쓰세요.

A: Do you have any special plans for summer vacation?
B: Yes, I visit my grandfather in Paris <u>여름마다</u>.
A: Wow, sounds nice.

➡ _______________________________________

11 다음 빈칸에 알맞은 말끼리 짝지어진 것은?

Look at _________ pictures over there.
_________ are my drawings.

① those – That
② this – That
③ that – This
④ those – Those
⑤ this – Those

12 다음 중 밑줄 친 It[it]의 용법이 나머지와 다른 하나는?

① Is <u>it</u> really spicy?
② <u>It</u> is Friday.
③ Is <u>it</u> snowing now?
④ What time is <u>it</u> in Seoul?
⑤ <u>It</u> takes five minutes by bus.

13 밑줄 친 곳에 들어갈 단어를 옳게 배열한 것은?

> My cat lost her toy, but I found ____ⓐ____ under the sofa. Then she ruined her toy, so I gave her a new ____ⓑ____. Now she's tired of it. I'd better get her ____ⓒ____.

	ⓐ		ⓑ		ⓒ
①	it	–	one	–	another
②	it	–	another	–	one
③	it	–	one	–	one
④	one	–	it	–	another
⑤	one	–	another	–	it

14 다음 대화의 빈칸에 들어갈 알맞은 의문사는?

> A: With __________ should I talk about this?
> B: I think you should talk with Dr. Kim.

① who　　② whom　　③ what
④ which　　⑤ whose

15 다음 중 밑줄 친 부분이 바르게 쓰인 것은?

① He came back to <u>his'</u> house.
② How do astronauts wash <u>himself</u> in space?
③ As the month ended, <u>her</u> got a bill for her credit card expenses.
④ All the teachers liked <u>herself</u> a lot.
⑤ Please take good care of <u>yourself</u>.

16 다음 대화의 빈칸에 들어갈 말로 알맞은 것은?

> A: We're going shopping now. Do you want to join us?
> B: Sorry, but I have __________ else to do now. I'll go with you next time.

① something　　② anything
③ everything　　④ thing
⑤ things

17 다음 빈칸에 들어갈 말이 알맞게 짝지어진 것은?

> I made three sandwiches. One has cheese, __________ has chicken, and __________ has salmon.

① other　　–　　the other
② other　　–　　another
③ the other　　–　　the third
④ another　　–　　the other
⑤ another　　–　　the others

18 다음 중 대화의 흐름이 <u>어색한</u> 것은?

① A: Did you get a tea set he sent from Paris?
　 B: Yes! It was so pretty and unique.
② A: Who made these beautiful dishes?
　 B: My mom made them herself.
③ A: Anyone came to see you this afternoon.
　 B: Really? Who was it?
④ A: How far is it to your school?
　 B: It's about half a kilometer from here.
⑤ A: Is this bottle yours?
　 B: No, the black one on the table is mine.

19 다음 빈칸에 알맞은 말끼리 짝지어진 것은?

> • ____________ food do you like better,
>   Korean or Chinese?
>   – I like Chinese food better.
> • ____________ do you think of Mr. Lee?
>   – I think he's very nice.

① Which – When　　② What – Why
③ Which – What　　④ What – What
⑤ Which – Why

20 다음 밑줄 친 <u>It</u>과 쓰임이 같은 것은?

> <u>It</u> is interesting to learn about new cultures.

① <u>It</u> is going to rain tonight.
② <u>It</u> is very hot today.
③ <u>It</u> is on the table in the kitchen.
④ <u>It</u> is one kilometer to the office.
⑤ <u>It</u> is not easy to speak English fluently.

21 다음 글의 빈칸에 들어갈 알맞은 말은?

> Today's topic was school uniforms. Our
> class was divided up into two groups.
> One group was for wearing a uniform.
> ____________________ group was against
> wearing a uniform.

① One　　　② Some　　　③ The other
④ The others　⑤ Others

22 다음 중 밑줄 친 부분의 쓰임이 <u>다른</u> 하나는?

① <u>Who's</u> calling, please?
② He asked me <u>who</u> bought the book.
③ Do you know <u>who</u> the woman is?
④ There were many people <u>who</u> were sleeping.
⑤ <u>Who</u> will be our homeroom teacher?

23 밑줄 친 부분을 바르게 고친 것 중 <u>잘못된</u> 것을 고르시오.

① I lost my bag but I found <u>one</u> (→ it) yesterday.
② <u>These who</u> (→ Those who) are sitting there
　 are waiting for the bus.
③ The climate of the U.S. is milder than <u>this of</u>
　 (→ these of) Canada.
④ There are three girls. One is Susan, <u>other</u>
　 (→ another) is Margaret and the other is
　 Kate.
⑤ We have a lot of pollution in the city <u>those
　 days</u> (→ these days).

24 다음 빈칸 (A)~(C)에 들어갈 말로 알맞은 것은?

Many students have different tastes in music. ______(A)______ prefer hip-hop music, but ______(B)______ enjoy classical music. Their choices often depend on their mood or personality. What one person finds exciting, ______(C)______ might find distracting. It's important to respect those with different preferences.

	(A)		(B)		(C)
①	One	–	the other	–	other
②	Some	–	others	–	another
③	Some	–	the other	–	another
④	One	–	others	–	other
⑤	Some	–	others	–	other

25 주어진 문장의 밑줄 친 (A)와 어법상 쓰임이 같은 것은?

(A) <u>That</u> sounds like a great plan.

① Where's the package <u>that</u> came yesterday?
② Which will you have, this or <u>that</u>?
③ I've got a feeling <u>that</u> Mike likes me.
④ Look at <u>that</u> woman over there.
⑤ It is the book <u>that</u> changed my life.

26 다음 빈칸에 공통으로 들어갈 한 단어를 쓰세요.

My family doesn't spend much time talking to each __________. In the evening, my brother and I usually do our homework or play computer games. On the __________ hand, my parents read the newspaper or watch TV.

27 다음 밑줄 친 It[it]에 대한 설명으로 옳은 것은?

① <u>It</u> is June 19th. (인칭대명사)
② What a beautiful rock <u>it</u> is! (비인칭주어)
③ <u>It</u> is difficult to make a home page. (가주어)
④ How far is <u>it</u> from here to the station? (강조구문)
⑤ <u>It</u> is a new camera that I need to buy. (인칭대명사)

28 다음 밑줄 친 It과 쓰임이 같지 <u>않은</u> 것을 <u>모두</u> 고르세요.

<u>It</u>'s very important to exercise every day.

① A: Where did you put the notebook?
　 B: I put <u>it</u> on my desk.
② A: Hey, <u>it</u>'s rude to stare at people.
　 B: Oh, sorry.
③ A: Is <u>it</u> true that the boy is smart?
　 B: No, it isn't.
④ A: How's the weather today?
　 B: <u>It</u>'s sunny. Let's go on a picnic.
⑤ A: What time is it?
　 B: <u>It</u>'s three o'clock.

29 다음 빈칸에 들어갈 수 <u>없는</u> 말은?

__________ girls in the class are worried about the next week's test.

① All the　　② Every　　③ Both of the
④ Some　　⑤ The rest of the

30 다음 밑줄 친 one의 쓰임이 나머지 넷과 다른 것은?

① I'd like an apple. Would you like <u>one</u>, too?
② My car broke down, so I got a new <u>one</u>.
③ She was wearing her new dress, the purple <u>one</u>.
④ He asked me where a pencil was. I told him there wasn't <u>one</u>.
⑤ He is the <u>one</u> person I can really trust.

31 다음 중 밑줄 친 부분의 쓰임이 어색한 것은?

① He bought a big car and I bought a small <u>one</u>.
② There were ten students in the gym. But now I can see only two. Where are <u>others</u>?
③ I saw a lot of entertainers. Some were kind. <u>Others</u> were not.
④ He has three shirts. One is red, another is blue, and <u>the other</u> is green.
⑤ I don't want this one. Show me <u>another</u>, please.

32 다음 빈칸에 들어갈 말끼리 바르게 짝지어진 것은?

____________ think keeping a pet teaches us many things, but ____________ think having a pet gives us a lot of hard work.

① Some – other
② Some – others
③ Some – the other
④ Other – others
⑤ Other – the other

33 다음 글에서 밑줄 친 that이 가리키는 두 단어를 찾아 쓰세요.

Yesterday, we had the lowest temperature of this year. Many people were surprised by the sudden drop in temperature. It was so cold that even the ponds froze over. The winter of this year is much colder than <u>that</u> of last year.

➡ ______________________________

34 다음 중 어법상 틀린 문장은?

① Not all of them are enjoying the party.
② Both of us were very tired after school.
③ I want to be with you for the rest of my life.
④ Both my sisters lived in Paris ten years ago.
⑤ All of my money were stolen last night.

35 다음 빈칸에 공통으로 들어갈 단어는?

• The cookies are pretty big, not tiny ________.
• Fix the blinds or buy new ________.
• I want some gloves, some warm ________.

① them
② it
③ ones
④ others
⑤ the others

36 〈보기〉의 단어를 한 번씩 써서 빈칸을 채우세요.

| 보 기 | this   that   these   those |

(1) All the buildings built in __________ days were destroyed.

(2) We have mid-term exams __________ Friday.

(3) __________ are not mine. Those are mine.

(4) The population of China is much larger than __________ of Korea.

37 Choose one that CANNOT be placed in any blanks.

- He burned __________.
  (그는 화상을 입었다.)
- My little sister can't look after __________.
  (내 여동생은 자기 자신을 돌볼 수 없다.)
- They set up their tents by __________.
  (그들은 스스로 텐트를 설치했다.)
- You should be proud of __________.
  (너는 너 자신을 자랑스럽게 생각해야 한다.)

① himself   ② yourself   ③ themselves
④ herself   ⑤ itself

38 다음 밑줄 친 부분을 주어로 하여 문장을 다시 쓰세요.

It seems that everyone is thinking the same thing now.

➡ __________________________________

____

39 Write down a common word for the blanks.

- I don't live with my parents. I live by __________.
- I picked up a boiling teapot and burned __________.
- I was invited to the Halloween party and I enjoyed __________.

40 밑줄 친 우리말과 같은 의미가 되도록 괄호 안에 주어진 말을 배열하세요.

A: Have you ever read *Snow White*?
B: Yes. 여왕이 거울로 자기 자신을 보곤 했잖아.
A: She also asked the mirror who the most beautiful person in the world was.
B: Right. I remember it.

➡ __________________________________

____

(herself, in the mirror, the queen, look at, used to)

41 다음 괄호 안에 들어갈 말로 바르게 짝지어진 것은?

- There are two girls in the room. One is from Korea and (ⓐ) is from Taiwan.
- I bought some books but I lost (ⓑ).
- This is (ⓒ) reason why I study very hard.

	ⓐ	ⓑ	ⓒ
①	the other	— them	— another
②	the other	— them	— other
③	the other	— it	— other
④	another	— it	— other
⑤	another	— them	— another

42 다음 대화의 빈칸에 들어갈 알맞은 단어는?

> *A*: ___________ violin is this?
> *B*: It used to be mine, but it's my sister's
> now.

① Who   ② How   ③ Why
④ Whose   ⑤ Whom

43 다음 문장을 영어로 바르게 옮긴 것은?

> Ted는 혼자서 자기 숙제를 마칠 수가 없었다.

① Ted couldn't finished his homework by him.
② Ted was able to finish his homework by him.
③ Ted wasn't able to finish his homework by
   himself.
④ Ted cannot able to finish his homework by
   himself.
⑤ Ted could finished his homework by himself.

44 다음 우리말과 뜻이 같도록 괄호 안에 주어진 말을 바르게 배열하세요.

> • 내가 어떤 동아리에 가입해야 할지 결정하는 것
> 은 쉽지 않다.

➡ ___________________________________

____

(which club, to decide, easy, it, should, join,
not, is, I)

[45-46] 다음 글을 읽고, 물음에 답하세요.

> Most of the students did their best to get
> good grades on the final exam. More than
> half of the students started study groups.
> However, the ⓐ rest of them didn't even
> plan to study for the exam. I was one of
> ⓑ those who wanted to get good grades
> but didn't do their best.

45 윗글의 ⓐ와 같은 뜻으로 쓰인 것은?

① The doctor told me to rest.
② We wanted to stop for a rest.
③ Rest your head on my shoulder.
④ How would you like to spend the rest of the
   day?
⑤ The matter cannot rest there.

46 윗글의 ⓑ를 바르게 해석한 것은?

① 저 사람들   ② ~한 사람들
③ 저것들   ④ ~한 것들
⑤ 해석할 필요 없음

47 〈보기〉에서 알맞은 단어를 골라 빈칸에 한 번씩 쓰세요.

보 기	whose what which

(1) ___________ jacket is cheaper?

(2) ___________ happened to Paul?

(3) I like the story. ___________ idea is it?

CHAPTER 7
부정사

PSS 1 명사적 용법

PSS 1-1 주어와 주격 보어로 쓰이는 to부정사

1. 「to+동사원형」의 형태로 문장에서 명사, 형용사, 부사의 역할을 하는 것을 to부정사라고
   한다.

    A: It's very difficult **to get** a good grade in English.
       영어에서 좋은 성적을 받기는 매우 어려워.
    B: I know. My goal is **to get** 90 points.
       알아. 내 목표는 90점을 받는 거야.

  cf. to부정사가 명사로 쓰일 때는 주어(~하는 것은), 목적어(~하는 것을), 보어(~하는 것이다)의
   역할을 할 수 있다.

2. to부정사가 문장의 맨 앞에서 주어의 역할을 할 때는 it을 주어의 자리에 두고, to부정사
   는 문장의 뒤로 보낸 형태를 주로 쓴다. 이때의 it을 가주어, to부정사가 이끄는 구를 진
   주어라고 한다.

   To study **foreign languages** is not easy. 외국어를 공부하는 것은 쉽지 않다.
   = **It** is not easy **to study** **foreign languages**.
      가주어   진주어

3. to부정사는 주어에 대한 설명을 보충하는 보어의 역할로도 쓰인다.

   The easiest way is **to take** the subway. 가장 쉬운 방법은 지하철을 타는 것이다.
   My dream is **to be** a lawyer. 내 꿈은 변호사가 되는 것이다.

정답 p.40

PRACTICE 1

주어진 문장과 같은 의미가 되도록 빈칸을 채우세요.

1   It is best to treat the disease early.
   ➡ To treat the disease early is best.

2   To read a lot of books is important.
   ➡ _______________________________________

3   It is exciting to go to a concert.
   ➡ _______________________________________

4 To make my dream come true was not easy.

➡ ____

5 To visit foreign countries is a lot of fun.

➡ ____

6 It is helpful to watch English TV programs.

➡ ____

7 To spend so much time playing computer games is not good.

➡ ____

정답 p.40

PRACTICE 2

〈보기〉에서 알맞은 표현을 골라 to부정사의 형태로 바꾸어 빈칸에 쓰세요.

보 기	jog every day	go to Europe	be a famous singer
	take care of patients	watch movies	see things clearly

1 I love singing. My dream is _______________________________.

2 Mike has bad eyesight. His wish is _______________________________.

3 Jiyeon is a nurse. Her job is _______________________________.

4 Jenny likes movies. Her hobby is _______________________________.

5 Minho travels a lot. His plan for the next vacation is _______________________________.

6 I know a lot of good ways to exercise. One of the best ways is _______________________________.

PSS 1-2 목적어로 쓰이는 to부정사

1. 다음 동사들 뒤에 다른 동사가 목적어로 올 때, 목적어는 「to＋동사원형」의 형태로 쓴다.

want	wish	decide	promise	would like	would love
plan	expect	refuse	hope	need	learn	agree
		afford	choose	offer	fail	

We **decided to take** a picture of him. 우리는 그의 사진을 찍기로 결정했다.

I**'d like to be** a musician. 나는 음악가가 되기를 원한다.

I'm **planning to visit** my grandparents next week. 다음주에 조부모님을 방문할 계획이다.

2. to부정사의 부정형은 「not to＋동사원형」의 어순으로 쓴다.

We plan **not to travel** during the busy holiday season.

우리는 연휴 성수기 동안은 여행을 하지 않으려고 계획한다.

cf. We **don't** plan **to travel** during the busy holiday season.

우리는 연휴 성수기 동안은 여행하기로 계획하지 않는다.

정답 p.40

PRACTICE 3

괄호 안의 단어를 알맞은 형태로 바꾸어 빈칸에 쓰세요.

1 I wish _______*to lose*_______ weight. (lose)

2 I'd love ________________ the artist now. (meet)

3 Yumi is planning ________________ a diary in English. (keep)

4 He wants ________________ the exam. (not, fail)

5 She failed ________________ for what she said. (apologize)

6 You need ________________ something. (eat)

7 They decided ________________ a garage sale. (not, have)

8 I learned ________________ two years ago. (swim)

9 Mom expected ________________ Ms. Smith at the party. (see)

10 I agree ________________ about it again. (not, talk)

11 I'd like ________________ a shower. (take)

12 He promised ________________ my birthday. (not, forget)

13 Insu refused ________________ Jina in the hospital. (visit)

14 He chose ________________ abroad after graduation. (study)

15 I hope ________________ my vacation at home. (not, spend)

PSS 1-3 목적격 보어로 쓰이는 to부정사

다음은 「동사＋목적어＋to부정사」의 형태로 자주 쓰이는 동사들이다.

want   ask   tell   allow   would like   expect   order

warn   advise   cause   enable   get

They **want me to become** a doctor. 그들은 내가 의사가 되기를 원한다.

> Dad **told** me **to stay** home and study more.
> 아빠는 내게 집에 머물면서 좀 더 공부하라고 말씀하셨다.
> **I'd like** you **to meet** my friend, Judy. 나는 네가 내 친구 Judy를 만났으면 해.

PRACTICE 4

Tony

Becky

Tony와 Becky의 대화를 참고하여 문장을 완성하세요.

	Tony	Becky
1	I have a bad cold now.	Why don't you go and see a doctor?
2	Could you open the door?	Sure.
3	Do you have time to meet my parents?	No. I'm very busy.
4	Can you come to my place?	Sure. I'll be right there.
5	Could you clean the room?	No problem.
6	Did you call me yesterday?	Yes. Can you repair my car?
7	I finished my homework.	Good. You can go out to play.
8	Shut the door.	OK, I will.
9	Don't touch anything.	All right.
10	What should I do?	You'd better say sorry to your brother first.

1 Becky told _Tony to go and see a doctor_ .

2 Tony asked _____________________________________ .

3 Tony would like _____________________________________ .

4 Tony expects _____________________________________ .

5 Tony wants _____________________________________ .

6 Becky asks _____________________________________ .

7 Becky allowed _____________________________________ .

8 Tony ordered _____________________________________ .

9 Tony warned _____________________________________ .

10 Becky advised _____________________________________ .

「의문사(how, what, where, when)+to부정사」는 문장에서 주어, 보어, 목적어로 사용될 수 있는데 주로 목적어로 많이 쓰인다. 의문사 why는 '의문사+to부정사' 형태로 잘 쓰이지 않음에 유의한다.

1. how to+동사원형 '어떻게 ~할지'

   I **learned how to make** a cake. 나는 케이크를 어떻게 만드는지를 배웠다.

2. what to+동사원형 '무엇을 ~할지'

   I don't **know what to do** for him. 나는 그를 위해 무엇을 해야 할지 모른다.

3. where to+동사원형 '어디서 ~할지'

   Bill didn't **tell** us **where to stay**. Bill은 우리에게 어디에서 머물지 말하지 않았다.

4. when to+동사원형 '언제 ~할지'

   The teacher **explained when to begin** the test. 선생님은 언제 그 시험을 시작할지 설명하셨다.

   cf. 「의문사+to부정사」는 「의문사+주어+should[can]+동사원형」으로 바꾸어 쓸 수 있다.

   She **showed** me **how to grow** vegetables.

   그녀는 내게 어떻게 채소를 재배하는지 보여주었다.

   = She **showed** me **how I should[could] grow** vegetables.

정답 p.41

PRACTICE 5

〈보기〉에서 알맞은 단어를 골라 빈칸에 「how/what+to부정사」 구문을 쓰세요.

보 기	help grow say read wear use solve buy

1 I learned ____how to read____ French.

2 We talked about ____________ the problem.

3 I explained ____________ the elderly.

4 Did you choose ____________ for the family photo?

5 She showed me ____________ the machine.

6 I don't know ____________ to her. She looks so sad.

7 He taught the students ____________ crops.

8 I can't decide ____________ for my mother's birthday.

PSS 2 형용사적 용법

1. to부정사는 '~할'의 뜻으로 명사 또는 대명사를 뒤에서 꾸며주는 형용사의 역할을 한다.

    I have so many **friends to help** me. 나에게는 나를 도와줄 아주 많은 친구들이 있다.

2. something, anything, everything, nothing과 같은 대명사 뒤에 이들을 수식하는 형용사가 나오면 to부정사는 형용사 뒤에 위치한다.

    Do you have **something interesting to read**? 너에게는 읽을 흥미로운 어떤 것이 있니?

3. 「It's (about) time ~」은 '~할 시간이다'의 뜻으로 time 뒤에 동사가 올 때는 to부정사의 형태로 쓴다.

    It's time to go to bed. 잠자리에 들 시간이다.

4. to부정사가 수식하는 명사가 전치사의 목적어일 경우 꼭 전치사를 써야 함에 유의한다. (학교 내신 빈출 문법 사항!)

    We found **a flat rock to sit on**. (O) 우리는 앉을 만한 평평한 바위를 찾았다.
    We found **a flat rock to sit**. (X)

정답 p.41

PRACTICE 6 [1-10]

우리말과 일치하도록 괄호 안에 주어진 단어를 바르게 배열하세요.

1   Bob에게는 그를 이해해줄 사람이 아무도 없다. (understand, no, one, to, him)

    ➡ Bob has ____ .

2   먹을 것 좀 줄까? (eat, to, something)

    ➡ Do you want ____ ?

3   나는 그에게 줄 돈이 하나도 없다. (give, money, no, to, him)

    ➡ I have ____ .

4   이제 회의를 시작할 시간이다. (the, start, meeting, to)

    ➡ It's about time ____ .

5   Kevin은 차가운 마실 것을 원한다. (something, drink, to, cold)

    ➡ Kevin wants ____ .

6   그녀는 같이 놀 친구를 찾고 있다. (friend, with, to, a, play)

    ➡ She is looking for ____ .

7 살 것들이 많이 있다. (a lot of, buy, to, things)

➡ There are ____.

8 그녀는 생각할 충분한 시간을 가지고 있지 않다. (time, to, enough, think)

➡ She doesn't have ______________________________________.

9 이것이 그곳에 도착할 최선의 방법이다. (there, the, way, to, best, get)

➡ This is ____.

10 그는 살기 좋은 집을 찾았다. (house, live, a, in, nice, to)

➡ He found ____.

정답 p.41

PRACTICE 7

다음 밑줄 친 부분이 맞으면 ○, 틀리면 어법에 맞게 고쳐 쓰세요.

1 We still have a problem to <u>deal</u> as a team.   ➡ ____________

2 He finally chose a topic to <u>talk about</u> after much consideration.   ➡ ____________

3 There is no one to <u>rely</u> in this strange place.   ➡ ____________

4 I have a friend to <u>wait</u> at the station.   ➡ ____________

5 There are many tourist attractions to <u>visit</u> in this city.   ➡ ____________

6 With my working conditions, there's nothing to <u>complain</u>.   ➡ ____________

PSS 3 부사적 용법

PSS 3-1 목적을 나타내는 to부정사

1. to부정사가 '~하기 위해서'의 뜻으로 목적이나 의도를 나타낼 때는 in order to나 so as to로 바꾸어 쓸 수 있다.

   She went to Tokyo **to visit** her grandparents.

   그녀는 그녀의 조부모님을 방문하기 위해 도쿄에 갔다.

   = She went to Tokyo **in order to visit** her grandparents.

   = She went to Tokyo **so as to visit** her grandparents.

I got up early **to get** ready for the game. 나는 그 경기 준비를 하기 위해 일찍 일어났다.

= I got up early **in order to get** ready for the game.

= I got up early **so as to get** ready for the game.

cf. 「in order to(so as to)+동사원형」이 「to+동사원형」보다 좀 더 격식을 차린 표현이다.

2. '~하지 않기 위해서'는 「(in order/so as) not to+동사원형」으로 표현한다.

They always spoke quietly **(in order/so as) not to be** overheard by anyone.

그들은 아무도 엿듣지 못하도록 항상 조용히 말했다.

Watch your step **(in order/so as) not to slip**. 미끄러지지 않게 조심히 걸어라.

3. to부정사 대신 「for+명사」를 써서 목적과 의도를 나타낼 수 있다.

You can spend money **to help poor people**. 너는 가난한 사람들을 돕기 위해 돈을 쓸 수 있다.

= You can spend money **for poor people**.

I'm going to study much harder **to get better grades**.

나는 더 좋은 점수를 얻기 위해 훨씬 더 열심히 공부할 것이다.

= I'm going to study much harder **for better grades**.

정답 p.41

PRACTICE 8

〈보기〉에서 알맞은 표현을 골라 to부정사의 형태로 바꾸어 빈칸에 쓰세요.

보 기	buy a present for his mom	take care of the sick	check her email
	ask about the test	pass the exam	protect your eyes
	say hello to me	stay healthy and slim	

1 He put his hand on his hat ________________________________.

2 Becky turned on the computer ________________________________.

3 You'd better wear sunglasses ________________________________.

4 Dr. Park went to Africa ________________________________.

5 Mike went downtown ________________________________.

6 Ann visited the professor's office ________________________________.

7 He studied harder ________________________________.

8 She exercises regularly ________________________________.

PRACTICE 9

〈보기〉와 같이 다음 두 문장을 괄호 안에 주어진 표현을 사용해 한 문장으로 합치세요.

> 보 기　　　I met Peter. I wanted to give him the information. (in order to)
> = I met Peter in order to give him the information   .

1 Hana went to the library. She wanted to study for the final exam. (in order to)
➡ ____

2 I called Minho. I wanted to ask him if he could go shopping with me. (so as to)
➡ ____

3 Mom stopped the car. She wanted to pick up Kelly. (so as to)
➡ ____

4 Tony opened the door. He wanted to watch the birds in the tree. (in order to)
➡ ____

5 I turned on the computer. I wanted to send an email. (in order to)
➡ ____

6 Jenny bought some vegetables. She wanted to make a salad. (so as to)
➡ ____

PRACTICE 10

빈칸에 to나 for 중 알맞은 것을 쓰세요.

1 I'm calling to thank you ___________ helping me the other day.

2 We should keep some money ___________ a rainy day.

3 He does his best ___________ solve the problem.

4 A kind old man came ___________ help them.

5 I went to the store ___________ some cookies.

6 He studied hard ___________ become a doctor.

7 I got out of the car ___________ clean the windshield.

8 Let's go out ___________ lunch next Friday.

9 People nod their heads ___________ mean 'yes'.

10 I have to buy some milk ___________ carbonara pasta.

1. to부정사가 형용사를 뒤에서 수식할 때는 '~하기에(형용사 수식)', '~하다니(판단의 근거)'의 의미를 가진다.

   Hangeul is not **easy to learn**. 한글은 배우기에 쉽지 않다.

   I'm so **lucky to have** such great friends. 그런 멋진 친구들이 있다니 나는 매우 운이 좋다.

2. to부정사가 다음과 같은 감정을 나타내는 형용사를 수식할 때는 '~해서, ~하게 되어'의 뜻으로 감정의 원인을 나타낸다.

sorry	happy	pleased	surprised
glad	disappointed	sad	excited

   Everybody was **surprised to see** him. 모든 사람들이 그를 보고 놀랐다.

   I'm **sorry to hear** the bad news. 그 나쁜 소식을 듣게 되어 유감이다.

3. to부정사는 '~해서 (결국) …되다'의 뜻으로 결과를 나타내기도 한다.

   Jenny **grew up to be** a pianist. Jenny는 자라서 피아니스트가 되었다.

   My grandmother **lived to be** ninety. 나의 할머니는 90세까지 사셨다.

   He studied hard for the exam **only to fail**.

   그는 시험을 위해 열심히 공부했지만 결국 시험에 떨어졌다.

정답 p.42

PRACTICE 11

〈보기〉와 같이 to부정사를 이용하여 두 문장을 한 문장으로 연결하세요.

보 기	I met Mr. Park. I was happy.
	➡ <u>I was happy to meet Mr. Park.</u>

1 I went back to my hometown. I was really excited.

➡ ______________________________

2 I saw Nancy on the street. I was surprised.

➡ ______________________________

3 I got a new computer. I was so happy.

➡ ______________________________

4 Jason was stupid. He showed the answer to his classmate.

➡ ______________________________

5 I introduced my family to you. I was glad.

➡ ______________________________

6 Sora was lucky. She passed such a difficult test.

➡ ______________________________

PRACTICE 12

다음 문장을 밑줄 친 부분에 유의하여 바르게 해석하세요.

1 Sora was glad <u>to see</u> Sujin again.

➡ _______________________________________

2 My daughter grew up <u>to be</u> a police officer.

➡ _______________________________________

3 The river is very dangerous <u>to swim</u> in.

➡ _______________________________________

4 He must like her a lot <u>to wait</u> for her every day.

➡ _______________________________________

5 I reached the station <u>only to find</u> that my train had already left.

➡ _______________________________________

PSS 4 to부정사의 의미상의 주어

1. to부정사의 의미상의 주어는 to부정사가 나타내는 동작의 주체를 의미하고, to부정사 앞에 「for+목적격」으로 쓴다.

   It was too important **for us** **to forget**. 그것은 우리가 잊기에는 너무 중요했다.
   Was it difficult **for you** **to find** a job? 네가 직업을 찾는 것은 어려웠니?

2. to부정사가 사람의 성격을 묘사하는 형용사를 꾸며줄 때는 의미상의 주어를 「of+목적격」으로 나타낸다.

kind	nice	foolish	wise	silly	stupid	generous

   It is very **kind of you** **to say** so. 네가 그렇게 말하는 것을 보니 참 친절하구나.
   It was **foolish of him** **to make** the same mistake again.
   그가 또 다시 똑같은 실수를 저지르다니 어리석었다.

정답 p.42

PRACTICE 13

괄호 안에 주어진 단어 중 알맞은 것을 고르세요.

1 It's important (to, for, of) me to exercise regularly.

2 This skirt is too small (to, for, of) me to wear.

3 It is very good (to, for, of) see you again.

4 It was very nice (to, for, of) you to help the old man.

5 It's hard (to, for, of) me to wake up early.

6 It's so stupid (to, for, of) him to talk like that.

7 I'm too tired (to, for, of) go hiking with you.

8 It's very kind (to, for, of) you to take me home.

9 His questions were too confusing (to, for, of) me to answer.

10 It is very wise (to, for, of) her to act like that.

11 It was generous (to, for, of) him to donate a million dollars.

12 This soup is too hot (to, for, of) me to eat.

PSS 5 too ~ to, enough to

---

1. 「too＋형용사/부사＋to부정사」는 '～하기에는 너무 …한'의 의미를 가지고, 「so＋형용사/부사＋that＋주어＋can't」로 바꾸어 쓸 수 있다.

   I'm **too nervous to sleep**. 나는 잠을 자기에는 너무 불안하다.

   = I'm **so nervous that I can't** sleep. 나는 매우 불안해서 잠을 잘 수 없다.

   cf. 「too＋형용사/부사＋to부정사」를 「so＋형용사/부사＋that＋주어＋can't」로 바꿀 때에는 시제에 유의한다.

   She was **too busy to give** it much thought. 그녀는 많은 생각을 하기에는 너무 바빴다.

   = She was **so busy that she couldn't** give it much thought.

   그녀는 너무 바빠서 많은 생각을 할 수 없었다.

2. 「형용사/부사＋enough＋to부정사」는 '～할 정도로 충분히 …한'의 의미를 가지고, 「so＋형용사/부사＋that＋주어＋can」으로 바꾸어 쓸 수 있다.

   This room is **large enough to hold** ten people.

   이 방은 10명의 사람들을 수용할 정도로 충분히 넓다.

   = This room is **so large that it can** hold ten people.

   이 방은 매우 넓어서 10명의 사람들을 수용할 수 있다.

   cf. 「so that＋주어＋can」은 '～하기 위해서'의 뜻으로 (in order/so as) to와 바꾸어 쓸 수 있다.

   I study hard **so that I can** go to college. 나는 대학에 가기 위해서 열심히 공부한다.

   = I study hard **(in order/so as) to** go to college.

3. 「so ~ that」 표현을 「too ~ to / enough to」 구문으로 전환할 때 to부정사의 목적어
가 주어와 일치하는 경우 to부정사 뒤에는 목적어를 쓰지 않음에 유의해야 한다. (학교
내신 빈출 문법사항!)

The cellphone is **so small that you can put** it in your pocket.

그 휴대폰은 매우 작아서 주머니 안에 넣을 수 있다.

= The cellphone is **small enough to put** in your pocket. (O)

그 휴대폰은 주머니에 넣을 만큼 충분히 작다.

= The cellphone is **small enough to put** it in your pocket. (X)

The water is **so salty that you can't drink** it. 그 물은 너무 짜서 마실 수 없다.

= The water is **too salty to drink**. (O) 그 물은 마시기에 너무 짜다.

= The water is **too salty to drink** it. (X)

정답 p.42

PRACTICE 14

주어진 문장과 의미가 같도록 빈칸에 알맞은 문장을 쓰세요. (단, 밑줄 친 부분에 절이 포함되어 있으면 구로, 구가
포함되어 있으면 절로 바꾸어 쓸 것.)

1 The box is so heavy that I can't lift it.

= The box is too heavy for me to lift.

2 The book was interesting enough for me to read twice.

= ____

3 I studied very hard so that I could be the top student.

= ____

4 The curry was too spicy for me to eat.

= ____

5 The dress was too expensive for her to buy.

= ____

6 Mina went to Canada so that she could study English.

= ____

7 The movie was too scary for children to watch.

= ____

8 The blue shirt is too big for me to wear.

= ____

9 The stadium was big enough for ten thousand people to fit into.

= ____

10 The box is light enough for me to carry.

= ____

PSS 6 원형부정사

사역동사 또는 지각동사가 동사 자리에 있을 때는 목적격 보어 자리에 to부정사를 쓸 수 없고 원형부정사(동사원형)를 쓴다.

1. **사역동사(let, make, have)의 목적격 보어**

   Mary **made** her son **go** to the university. Mary는 그녀의 아들이 그 대학에 가게 했다.

   I **helped** her **(to) do** her homework. 나는 그녀가 그녀의 숙제를 하는 것을 도왔다.

   cf. help는 준사역동사로 목적격 보어 자리에 원형부정사 대신 to부정사를 쓰기도 한다.

2. **지각동사(see, watch, hear, feel, notice 등)의 목적격 보어**

   We **saw** the dog **run** after him. 우리는 그 개가 그를 쫓아 달리는 것을 보았다.

   She **heard** James **play** the violin. 그녀는 James가 바이올린을 켜는 것을 들었다.

   cf. 지각동사의 목적어의 동작이 진행 중임을 강조할 때는 원형부정사 대신 현재분사를 쓰기도 한다.

   She **heard** James **playing** the violin. 그녀는 James가 바이올린을 켜고 있는 것을 들었다.

정답 p.42

PRACTICE 15

괄호 안에 주어진 단어를 이용하여 문장을 완성하세요.

1 My sister doesn't let me ________________ her jacket. (wear)

2 I felt the house ________________ heavily. (shake)

3 I helped my son ________________ his desk upstairs. (carry)

4 Peter heard Susan ________________ the bell. (ring)

5 The teacher had his students ________________ their homework. (do)

6 The songs made me ________________ comfortable. (feel)

7 I saw the policeman ________________ the building. (enter)

8 The old lady helped the boy ________________ his parents. (find)

9 I watched my daughter ________________ the flowers. (plant)

10 Mom made me ________________ writing in English. (practice)

PRACTICE 16

각각의 대화를 보고, 빈칸에 알맞은 말을 써서 문장을 완성하세요.

1   Liz saw Tom _play[playing] tennis_ .

2   She made her son ___________________ .

3   Brian heard Jane ___________________ .

4   Sarah won't let her little brother ___________________ .

5   Jack had his daughter ___________________ .

6   Shelly feels ___________________ .

1 주어진 문장의 밑줄 친 부분과 용법이 같은 것은?

> I study English <u>to talk</u> with foreigners.

① I want <u>to be</u> a teacher.
② Jihye is going to the library <u>to study</u>.
③ Minho likes <u>to take</u> care of sick people.
④ I need something <u>to eat</u>.
⑤ It is exciting <u>to play</u> tennis.

2 다음 밑줄 친 부분과 쓰임이 같은 것을 <u>모두</u> 고르세요.

> She needed someone <u>to talk</u> to.

① It is fun <u>to play</u> in the snow.
② <u>To exercise</u> every day is good for you.
③ He found a book <u>to read</u> on the train.
④ We were surprised <u>to hear</u> the news.
⑤ This is the best time <u>to visit</u> Jeju.

3 주어진 단어들을 우리말과 같은 뜻이 되도록 배열할 때 다섯 번째에 오는 단어는?

> • 나는 버스를 타고 학교에 가는 데 한 시간이 걸린다.
> = _________________________________
> _________________________________
> (go, by, to, hour, school, it, me, bus, to, takes, an)

① go   ② me   ③ to
④ school   ⑤ hour

4 우리말과 같은 의미가 되도록 빈칸에 알맞은 말을 넣을 때 ⓑ에 들어갈 말은?

> • 제가 물리를 공부하는 것이 필요한가요?
> = Is it ___ⓐ___ ___ⓑ___ ___ⓒ___
> ___ⓓ___ ___ⓔ___ physics?

① necessary   ② me   ③ for
④ study   ⑤ to

5 ⓐ~ⓕ 중 어법상 **틀린** 부분이 포함된 문장을 골라 기호를 쓰고, 바르게 고쳐 완전한 문장으로 쓰세요.

> ⓐ I have some emails to reply to before lunch.
> ⓑ She got her computer fixed this morning.
> ⓒ The question was too difficult to answer it.
> ⓓ They made their son clean the kitchen.
> ⓔ He had his car washed at the service center.
> ⓕ I noticed someone entering the classroom quietly.

➡ (   ) _________________________________

6 주어진 문장의 밑줄 친 부분과 용법이 같은 것은?

> There is an easy way <u>to protect</u> the river.

① My hobby is <u>to read</u> comic books.
② A clerk came <u>to clean</u> the floor.
③ He was surprised <u>to hear</u> the news.
④ She decided <u>to study</u> hard.
⑤ I have a pet <u>to play</u> with.

7 두 문장이 같은 뜻이 되도록 빈칸을 채우세요.

> • Mina wanted to buy some snacks, so she
> went to the market.
> = Mina went to the market __________
> __________ some snacks.

8 다음 빈칸에 들어갈 단어로 알맞은 것은?

> *A*: I don't know __________ to do now.
> *B*: You have to finish your homework.

① that ② why ③ what
④ when ⑤ where

9 우리말과 같은 뜻이 되도록 괄호 안의 단어를 알맞게 배열하여 문장을 완성하세요.

> • 그 영화는 끝까지 보기에 너무 지루했다.
> = The movie was __________
> __________ .
> (too, watch, boring, end, the, to, until)

10 문장의 의미가 <u>다른</u> 하나는?

① It was such a strong wind that we couldn't
go out to play.
② Because the wind was strong, we couldn't
go out to play.
③ The wind was so strong that we couldn't go
out to play.
④ The wind was strong, so we couldn't go out
to play.
⑤ The wind was strong enough to go out to
play.

11 다음 중 어법이 <u>틀린</u> 것은?

① He had his son do the laundry himself.
② He was having his passport picture taken.
③ I let my dog run around freely in the park.
④ Ms. Thompson helped me to find my wallet.
⑤ The job fair made me thinking about my
future.

12 다음 ⓐ~ⓕ 중 어법상 <u>틀린</u> 문장의 개수로 알맞은 것은?

> ⓐ I enjoy talking with my grandmother.
> ⓑ Do you mind if I borrow your pen?
> ⓒ Let's decide meeting up and discuss this
> in person.
> ⓓ He has many books to read for two days.
> ⓔ My dad made me to take out the trash.
> ⓕ I want you bring me my car key.

① 1개 ② 2개 ③ 3개
④ 4개 ⑤ 5개

13 다음 중 빈칸에 들어갈 단어가 나머지 넷과 <u>다른</u> 것은?

① It's important ______ me to do my best.
② It's very nice ______ you to take care of the
baby.
③ It's too sensitive ______ us to discuss openly.
④ It's hard ______ her to tell him the truth.
⑤ It's not easy ______ him to live by himself.

14 다음 우리말을 영어로 바르게 옮긴 것은?

I was very happy <u>나의 학급 친구들을 다시 봐서</u>.

① see my classmates again
② seeing my classmates again
③ to be seen my classmates again
④ to see my classmates again
⑤ have seen my classmates again

15 다음 중 밑줄 친 부분의 용법이 같은 것끼리 바르게 짝지어진 것은?

ⓐ It is difficult <u>to explain</u> exactly why.
ⓑ Jiyoung went to America <u>to study</u> English.
ⓒ Why did you agree <u>to do</u> this project?
ⓓ The fastest way <u>to get</u> there is by bus.
ⓔ He studied hard <u>to pass</u> the exam.

① ⓐ, ⓑ   ② ⓐ, ⓔ   ③ ⓑ, ⓒ
④ ⓑ, ⓔ   ⑤ ⓒ, ⓓ

16 다음 중 밑줄 친 부분을 어법상 옳게 고친 것은?

① Would you bring <u>something warm</u> to wear?
(→ warm something)
② I hope to see you soon and <u>heard</u> your travel
stories. (→ hearing)
③ Dad told my sister <u>coming</u> home before it
got too late. (→ come)
④ She stopped <u>to buy</u> lunch, as she was very
hungry. (→ buying)
⑤ To <u>studying</u> ten hours a day is very tiring.
(→ study)

17 〈보기〉의 우리말을 주어진 단어를 활용하여 영작할 때 ⓐ~ⓒ에 들어갈 표현이 바르게 짝지어진 것은?

listen / talk / understand

보 기

당신은 누군가가 말하는 것을 들을 수 있지만 그가 말하는 것을 이해하기 위해서는 그가 말하는 것에 귀 기울여야 합니다.

➡ You can hear somebody ___ⓐ___ but you need ___ⓑ___ to him ___ⓒ___ what he is saying.

	ⓐ	ⓑ	ⓒ
①	to talk	to listen	to understand
②	talking	listening	understand
③	talk	to listen	understand
④	talking	to listen	to understand
⑤	to talk	listening	understand

18 다음 문장의 밑줄 친 부분과 용법이 같은 것은?

I have some books <u>to buy</u>.

① I wish <u>to travel</u> around the world.
② We have a list of tasks <u>to finish</u> before leaving.
③ I went to the cafe <u>to meet</u> him.
④ I'd love <u>to see</u> you at the party.
⑤ It's fun <u>to teach</u> the students.

19 다음 중 어법상 <u>어색한</u> 문장을 <u>모두</u> 고르세요.

① Dad wanted me to clean his car.
② There are a lot of places visit in Korea.
③ I'm planning to take a business course.
④ Would you like to have dinner with us?
⑤ What should I do sing well?

20 다음 중 밑줄 친 부분이 어색한 것은?

① I want to learn <u>how to fly</u> a kite.

② They had trouble deciding <u>which to buy</u>.

③ Let me know <u>where to turn</u> right in advance.

④ My friend and I talked about <u>when to meet</u> tomorrow.

⑤ I taught my grandmother <u>what to use</u> the computer.

21 다음 대화의 (A)~(E) 중 빈칸에 들어갈 말이 나머지 넷과 다른 것은?

> Kevin: I don't know ____(A)____ to solve these math problems. Giho, please help me with my math homework.
> Giho : Sure. I can help you.
> Kevin: Wow, I don't know ____(B)____ to thank you.
> Giho : What are friends for?
> Kevin: Then can you come to my house tomorrow?
> Giho : I'm sorry, but I can't. I'm busy. I'm learning ____(C)____ to bake cookies tomorrow. ____(D)____ are you going to do this Saturday?
> Kevin: My cousin is going to teach me ____(E)____ to swim. Is Sunday OK for you, then?
> Giho : Yes, it is. Let's meet on Sunday.

① (A)　　　② (B)　　　③ (C)

④ (D)　　　⑤ (E)

22 다음 대화의 밑줄 친 부분과 어법상 쓰임이 같은 것은?

① I want <u>to volunteer</u> at the local community center.

② His ambition is <u>to start</u> his own business someday.

③ She went to the beach <u>to enjoy</u> the warm weather and relax.

④ She came over <u>to say</u> hello to me.

⑤ He had no money <u>to buy</u> a new laptop for his college classes.

23 주어진 문장의 밑줄 친 It과 쓰임이 같은 것은?

> <u>It</u> is good to get up early in the morning.

① <u>It</u>'s raining now.

② What is <u>it</u>?

③ I saw <u>it</u> yesterday.

④ <u>It</u>'s March 18th.

⑤ <u>It</u>'s fun to play table tennis.

24 주어진 말을 활용하여 〈보기〉와 같이 문장을 완성하세요.

> 보 기 | (dangerous, swim, in the deep sea)
> ➡ It is dangerous to swim in the deep sea.

(useful, learn, a second language)

➡ ______________________________

25 다음 중 어법상 <u>어색한</u> 문장은?

① Is she well enough to travel?
② It isn't easy to follow that rule.
③ Let's order something to eat cold.
④ I can't wait to go skiing during the winter vacation.
⑤ How about going shopping on Saturday?

26 다음 〈조건〉을 활용하여 주어진 우리말에 맞도록 문장을 완성하세요.

조 건
• 동사 say를 활용할 것.
• to부정사를 진주어로 포힘힐 것.
• how many를 사용할 것.

• 얼마나 많은 사람들이 그것을 사용하는지를 말하는 것은 어렵다.
= It is difficult ___________________
___________________ .

27 주어진 우리말에 맞게 빈칸을 완성하세요. (단어 첨가 및 변형 가능)

(1) 나는 함께 공부할 파트너를 찾고 있다.
(*look, study, to 사용할 것)
➡ I am __________ for a partner
__________ __________ __________ .

(2) 나의 소원은 도움이 필요한 사람들을 돕는 데 참여하는 것이다. (*participate, to 사용할 것)
➡ My wish is __________ __________
__________ helping those in need.

28 다음 빈칸에 들어갈 단어가 나머지 넷과 <u>다른</u> 하나는?

① It was necessary _______ him to get the answer.
② It is very kind _______ you to say so.
③ It is not difficult _______ her to win the prize.
④ It is helpful _______ me to wear a mask.
⑤ It was exciting _______ them to reach the top of the mountain.

29 어법상 <u>틀린</u> 것을 바르게 고친 것 중 <u>잘못된</u> 것은?

① I told him <u>take</u> a break and get some sleep.
→ to take
② He made his son <u>to keep</u> a promise.
→ keep
③ Mom didn't allow me <u>going</u> to the movies.
→ go
④ I helped him <u>moved</u> the desk.
→ to move
⑤ Jenny saw them <u>to hide</u> in the closet.
→ hiding

30 다음 대화의 밑줄 친 부분과 바꾸어 쓸 수 있는 것은?

A: Are you going to the concert this Friday?
B: Of course. <u>I'm dying to see it.</u>

① I don't like music.
② I don't know.
③ I really hate to see it.
④ I can't go there.
⑤ I really want to see it.

31 다음 ⓐ~ⓔ 중 〈보기〉의 밑줄 친 부분과 같은 to부정사의 용법으로 쓰인 것을 <u>모두</u> 고르고, 그 용법을 쓰세요.

보 기
He woke up early <u>to catch</u> the first train.

From: Paul Hugh Emmet <paulhemmet@ outlook.com>
To: Albert Dewey <aldewey@harrington. com>
CC:
Subject: Book Recommendation
Dear Mr. Dewey,

I'm Paul, one of the students in your English class. I'm writing this email ⓐ <u>to ask</u> for your advice. I'm planning ⓑ <u>to do</u> a lot of reading. ⓒ <u>To make</u> a list of good books, could you recommend a few? I'm sure you can think of lots of interesting books ⓓ <u>to recommend</u>. I'd love ⓔ <u>to know</u> what books inspired you during your teenage years.

Thank you for your time.

Sincerely,
Paul

➡ (　　　　), (　　　　) ___________

32 두 문장이 같은 뜻이 되도록 빈칸에 알맞은 말을 쓰세요.

• He doesn't know what he should do.
= He doesn't know ___________

___________ ___________ .

33 다음 밑줄 친 부분을 동명사로 바꾸어 쓸 수 있는 것을 <u>모두</u> 고르세요.

① I advise you <u>to be</u> kind to others.
② Dad helped me <u>fix</u> the bicycle yesterday.
③ <u>To keep</u> a diary in English every day is not easy.
④ I'm sorry <u>to hear</u> that you are sick.
⑤ Jenny started <u>to practice</u> an hour ago.

34 주어진 문장의 밑줄 친 부분과 용법이 같은 것은?

Mrs. Lee has a special way <u>to cook</u> rice.

① There is a lot <u>to learn</u> from this book.
② Do you promise <u>to return</u> the book?
③ I have to take the course <u>to graduate</u>.
④ You should exercise <u>to stay</u> healthy.
⑤ We went to the pool <u>to swim</u>.

35 다음 두 문장이 같은 뜻이 되도록 빈칸에 들어갈 알맞은 말은?

• Adam was too proud to apologize.
= Adam was ___________ proud that he couldn't apologize.

① such
② so as
③ to
④ enough
⑤ so

36 다음 중 어법상 <u>어색한</u> 문장은?

① It's time for dinner.
② It's time for have a meeting.
③ It's time for the yoga class to start.
④ It is about time to go out.
⑤ It is about time to play basketball.

37 다음 중 〈보기〉의 문장을 바르게 영작한 것을 고르세요.

> 보 기 | 나를 용서해 주다니 그녀는 정말 관대하지 않니?

① Is it very generous of her to forgiving me?
② Is it very generous of her to forgive me?
③ Isn't it very generous for her forgiving me?
④ Isn't it very generous for her to forgive me?
⑤ Isn't it very generous of her to forgive me?

38 다음 중 밑줄 친 부분의 쓰임이 같은 것끼리 짝지어진 것을 <u>모두</u> 고르세요.

> (A) My grandmother agreed <u>to visit</u> her hometown with me.
> (B) I bought a digital camera <u>to take</u> pictures on our trip.
> (C) He studied very hard <u>to become</u> a physicist.
> (D) Amanda would be the last person <u>to tell</u> a lie.
> (E) Why did she decide <u>to end</u> it all?

① (A), (E)　　② (A), (C)　　③ (B), (C)
④ (C), (E)　　⑤ (C), (D)

39 다음 중 밑줄 친 부분이 바르게 쓰인 것은?

① What is she <u>do</u> there?
② Mihye <u>studies</u> with us last night.
③ The <u>30-years-old</u> woman is my sister.
④ We need <u>to helps</u> him at school.
⑤ I would love <u>to give</u> him a hand.

40 우리말과 같은 뜻이 되도록 주어진 단어를 알맞게 배열하세요.

> • 그 물은 너무 더러워서 나는 마실 수가 없었다.
>
> = ________________________________
>
> ________________________________
>
> (I, water, the, it, could, so, was, dirty, not, drink, that)

41 다음은 Minji네 가족이 어제 주고 받은 메시지 내용입니다. ask를 활용하여 Mom이 Minji에게 요청한 것을 영어로 완성하세요. (단, 8단어로 쓸 것.)

➡ Mom ________________________________

________________________________.

42 다음 중 어법상 <u>어색한</u> 문장은?

① The orange smells good.
② My bag is as heavy as Denny's.
③ He refused taking my advice.
④ Tom will try to read a book every day.
⑤ The teacher told the students to line up quietly.

43 다음 두 문장이 같은 뜻이 되도록 괄호 안의 말을 이용하여 문장을 완성하세요.

> • I ran so fast that I could catch him in a minute.
> = I ________________________
>   in a minute. (enough, to)

44 주어진 우리말과 같은 뜻이 되도록 괄호 안의 말을 바르게 배열하세요.

> • 네 친구의 생일을 기억하는 것은 중요하다.
> ➡ ________________________
>   ________________________
>   (important, your friend's, birthday, is, to, it, remember)

45 다음 중 어법상 <u>어색한</u> 문장은?

① It's hard for him to get a driver's license.
② It's important for me to practice English.
③ It's generous of you to visit him every week.
④ It's easy for her to pass the exam.
⑤ It's impossible of me to find her house.

46 주어진 말을 알맞게 배열하여 문장을 완성하세요.

> Do you want ________________ ?
> (to, how, a cake, learn, to, make)

47 다음 빈칸에 들어갈 말로 알맞은 것은?

> He promised __________ a diary in English.

① keep ② kept ③ keeps
④ keeping ⑤ to keep

48 다음 글의 빈칸 (A)~(C)에 들어갈 표현이 바르게 연결된 것은?

> How do you usually celebrate your mother's birthday? To be honest, I ___(A)___ my mother birthday presents. When I realized that, I felt very ashamed. So I decided ___(B)___ her a birthday present this year. Yesterday was her birthday. I used my savings to buy a blouse for my mother at the department store. She was very happy ___(C)___ my present. I was pleased that she liked my present.

   (A)   (B)   (C)
① have never given – to buy – to get
② never have given – buying – to get
③ have never given – to buy – gets
④ never have given – to buy – get
⑤ have never given – buying – getting

49 다음 빈칸에 들어갈 단어로 알맞은 것은?

> • When I see the stars in the sky, I feel happy.
> ➡ The stars in the sky __________ me feel happy.

① want ② ask ③ tell
④ make ⑤ allow

50 주어진 문장의 밑줄 친 부분과 쓰임이 다른 것은?

> You need a key <u>to get</u> out of here.

① John went to the library <u>to borrow</u> books.
② He flew to America <u>to visit</u> his grandmother.
③ I called her <u>to ask</u> about the homework.
④ She came to me <u>to pick</u> up her umbrella.
⑤ I am so happy <u>to hear</u> that.

51 다음 대화의 밑줄 친 우리말을 괄호 안의 표현을 이용하여 〈조건〉에 맞게 영어로 쓰세요.

조 건
1. 필요시 괄호 안의 단어를 변형시킬 것.
2. to부정사 표현을 반드시 포함시킬 것.

Mom : You don't look good. What's wrong?
Taeho: Mom, I really did my best. But I got a bad grade. (A) <u>저는 깨어 있기 위해 커피를 마셨어요.</u> (drink coffee, stay awake)
(B) <u>그리고 전 공부를 더 하기 위해 식사를 거르기도 했어요.</u> (also, skip meals, study more)
Mom : Oh, Taeho. You shouldn't have done those things.

(A) ____________________________________

(B) ____________________________________

52 다음 글의 ⓐ~ⓔ를 바꾸어 쓸 때, 어법상 어색한 것은?

> Hola! My name is Diego. I'm from Spain and ⓐ <u>my job is cutting hams!</u> In Spain, people love hams and every famous restaurant has professional ham cutters. While I was working in a restaurant, I learned ⓑ <u>how to slice hams thinly.</u> Last year, I practiced ⓒ <u>so hard that I could win</u> the ham cutting contest and I won first prize. I was ⓓ <u>happy to win the contest.</u> My next goal is traveling the world and ⓔ <u>helping people enjoy</u> the Spanish ham.

① ⓐ: my job is to cut hams
② ⓑ: how I should slice hams thinly
③ ⓒ: too hard to win
④ ⓓ: happy because I won the contest
⑤ ⓔ: helping people to enjoy

53 〈보기〉의 단어들 중 5개를 사용하여 우리말 문장을 영어로 쓸 때 ★에 올 단어는?

> 의사는 그녀에게 설탕이 많이 든 음식을 먹지 말라고 충고했다.
> → The doctor ________ ________ ________
> ________ ★ ________ sugary foods.

보 기
her, not, she, advised, don't, eat, eating, to

① to　　　　② she　　　　③ eat
④ don't　　　⑤ eating

54 다음 그림을 보고 〈보기〉에 주어진 표현을 골라 각 그림의 상황에 알맞은 문장을 완성하세요.

보 기

what　how　to wear　to play the cello

(1) I don't know ＿＿＿＿＿＿＿＿＿＿＿＿ .

(2) I can't decide ＿＿＿＿＿＿＿＿＿＿＿ .

55 다음 그림과 〈조건〉을 참고하여 문장을 완성하세요.

조 건

1. 주어진 가주어 문장을 완성할 것.
2. help, go up을 사용할 것.

➡ It's very kind ＿＿＿＿ them ＿＿＿＿ ＿＿＿＿
the old lady ＿＿＿＿ ＿＿＿＿ ＿＿＿＿ ＿＿＿＿ .

56 주어진 그림을 묘사하는 대화를 만들 때 빈칸 ⓐ, ⓑ에 들어갈 말로 가장 알맞은 것은?

Mom	: I want you ＿＿ⓐ＿＿ food to sick grandma. Also, I order you ＿＿ⓑ＿＿ to strangers!
Red Riding Hood	: Okay, Mom. I'll keep it in mind.

	ⓐ	ⓑ
①	to deliver	to not talk
②	delivering	to not talk
③	to deliver	not talk
④	delivering	not to talk
⑤	to deliver	not to talk

57 다음 우리말 문장을 괄호 안의 말을 이용하여 [조건]에 맞게 영어로 쓰세요.

• 그는 너무 졸려서 늦게까지 깨어있을 수 없었다.
(sleepy, stay up, late)

(1) ＿＿＿＿＿＿＿＿＿＿＿＿＿＿＿＿＿
＿＿＿＿＿＿＿＿＿＿＿＿＿＿＿＿＿

[too, to를 이용할 것]

(2) ＿＿＿＿＿＿＿＿＿＿＿＿＿＿＿＿＿
＿＿＿＿＿＿＿＿＿＿＿＿＿＿＿＿＿

[so, that을 이용할 것]

PSS 1 주어와 보어로 쓰이는 동명사

「동사원형＋-ing」의 형태로 문장에서 주어, 보어, 목적어의 역할을 하는 것을 동명사라고 한다.

1. 주어로 쓰이는 동명사

Listening to music is a lot of fun. 음악을 듣는 것은 아주 재미있다.

cf. 동명사(구)가 문장의 맨 앞에서 주어 역할을 할 때 to부정사(구)의 경우처럼 가주어 it을 주어의 자리에 두고 동명사(구)를 문장의 뒤로 보내는 형태로 쓰기도 한다. 그러나 to부정사(구)가 주어일 때 가주어 it을 내세우는 것이 통상적인 것과 달리, 동명사(구)가 주어일 때는 가주어 it을 내세워 쓰는 경우는 제한적이다.

It is no use **arguing with him**. He never listens to anyone's opinion.

가주어　　　　　　　　진주어

그와 말다툼해 봐야 소용없다. 그는 누구의 의견에도 절대 귀 기울이지 않는다.

2. 보어로 쓰이는 동명사

My plan for this weekend is **going** fishing. 이번 주말 동안의 내 계획은 낚시하러 가는 것이다.
= My plan for this weekend is **to go** fishing.

정답 p.47

PRACTICE 1

우리말과 일치하도록 우리말 주어에 유의하여 괄호 안에 주어진 말을 바르게 배열하세요.

1 일주일에 7일을 일하는 것은 피곤하다. (is, seven days, a week, working, exhausting)
➡ ____

2 그녀의 직업은 신발을 디자인하는 것이다. (her job, shoes, is, designing)
➡ ____

3 샤워를 하는 것은 당신에게 상쾌한 기분이 들도록 한다. (you, taking, refreshed, a shower, feel, makes)
➡ ____

4 영어를 배우는 것은 많은 시간과 노력이 든다. (English, takes, time and effort, learning, a lot of)
➡ ____

5 내 취미는 야외에서 사진을 찍는 것이다. (my hobby, taking, is, photos, outside)
➡ ____

6 너의 실수는 너무 빠르게 말한 것이었다. (speaking, too fast, your mistake, was)
➡ ____

PRACTICE 2

두 문장의 의미가 같도록 동명사를 이용하여 빈칸에 알맞은 말을 쓰세요.

1 It is not easy to practice the violin. = ________________________________ is not easy.

2 It is sometimes necessary to be honest. = __________________ is sometimes necessary.

3 My wish is to travel around the world. = My wish is ________________________________ .

4 It would be nice to make new friends. = ________________________________ would be nice.

5 My job is to teach English to kids. = My job is ________________________________ .

6 It is interesting to live in the countryside. = ________________________ is interesting.

PSS 2 동사의 목적어로 쓰이는 동명사

PROBLEM
SOLVING
S KILL

PSS 2-1 동명사만 목적어로 취하는 동사

1. 다음 동사들 뒤에 다른 동사가 목적어로 올 때, 목적어는 동명사의 형태로 쓴다.

> enjoy   mind   finish   stop   give up   practice
> put off   deny   imagine   quit   suggest   dislike   avoid

Susan **enjoys talking** with her grandmother. Susan은 그녀의 할머니와 이야기하는 것을 즐긴다.
When did you **finish reading** that book? 너는 언제 그 책을 읽는 것을 끝냈니?
Do you **mind turning** down the volume? 볼륨을 줄여도 괜찮겠니?

2. 동명사의 부정형은 동명사 앞에 not을 붙여 만든다.

I imagined **not moving** to Suwon. 나는 수원으로 이사가지 않는 것을 상상했다.
cf. I **didn't** imagine **moving** to Suwon. 나는 수원으로 이사가는 것을 상상하지 않았다.

PRACTICE 3 [1-10]

괄호 안의 동사를 알맞은 형태로 바꾸어 빈칸에 쓰세요.

1 I'll call you when I finish ____________ . (work)

2 I decided ____________ the fireworks show. (watch)

3 She stopped ____________ to me for a week. (talk)

4 Mr. Han put off ____________ a meeting. (have)

5 They promised ____________ him there. (send)

6 Jane enjoys ____________ for her family. (cook)

7 My grandmother finally quit ____________ at age 73. (work)

8 We didn't plan ____________ there tonight. (go)

9 I'll keep ____________ this paper until I finish it. (write)

10 Sujin hopes ____________ us again soon. (see)

PRACTICE 4

Tony와 Becky의 대화를 보고, 괄호 안의 단어를 알맞은 형태로 바꾸어 빈칸에 쓰세요.

1 Becky doesn't mind _____lending_____ her umbrella. (lend)

2 Becky suggests ______________ lunch. (have)

3 Becky denies ______________ to the library. (go)

4 Becky stops ______________ dinner. (eat)

5 Becky doesn't enjoy ______________ late at school this Friday. (stay)

PSS 2-2 동사 + 동명사/to부정사 I

다음은 동명사와 to부정사를 모두 목적어로 취하고, 그 중 어느 것을 목적어로 취하든지 뜻이 달라지지 않는 동사들이다.

| like   love   prefer   hate   begin   start   continue   intend |

Do you **like playing** baseball? = Do you **like to play** baseball?

너는 야구 하는 것을 좋아하니?

It **began raining**. = It **began to rain**. 비가 내리기 시작했다.

When did you **start exercising**? = When did you **start to exercise**?

넌 언제 운동하는 것을 시작했니?

PRACTICE 5

괄호 안에 주어진 말 중 알맞은 것을 <u>모두</u> 고르세요.

1 I don't like (to eat, eating) late at night.

2 I should quit (to waste, wasting) my time.

3 John finished (to read, reading) the book.

4 We decided (to move, moving) to Busan.

5 Tony loves (to paint, painting) in the park.

6 It began (to snow, snowing) this morning.

7 Bill refused (to be, being) the chairman of the club.

8 I intended (to go, going) on a picnic, but I couldn't.

9 I'd like (to drink, drinking) some wine.

10 Did you practice (to play, playing) the cello?

11 Mom dislikes (to make, making) the same mistakes.

12 Sujin hates (to spend, spending) much money buying clothes.

13 They continued (to throw, throwing) away their trash on the street.

14 I wish (to get, getting) the perfect score on the test.

15 Peter started (to run, running) an hour ago.

PSS 2-3 동사 + 동명사/to부정사 Ⅱ

다음은 동명사와 to부정사를 모두 목적어로 취하고, 그 중 어느 것을 목적어로 취하느냐에 따라 뜻이 달라지는 동사들이다.

> try regret remember forget

1. try+동명사 '(시험 삼아) ～ 해보다' / try+to부정사 '～하려고 노력하다, 애쓰다'

   I **tried calling** Bob yesterday. 나는 어제 Bob에게 전화를 해봤다.
   I **tried to call** Bob yesterday. 나는 어제 Bob에게 전화하려고 노력했다.

2. regret+동명사 '～한 것을 후회하다' / regret+to부정사 '～하게 되어 유감이다'

   I **regret telling** her that you failed the exam. 네가 시험에 떨어졌다고 그녀에게 말한 것을 후회한다.
   I **regret to tell** her that you failed the exam. 네가 시험에 떨어졌다고 그녀에게 말하게 되어 유감이다.

3. remember+동명사 '~한 것을 기억하다' / remember+to부정사 '~할[하는] 것을 기억하다'

You should **remember telling** this to Sam. 넌 Sam에게 이걸 말했다는 것을 기억해야 해.
You should **remember to tell** this to Sam. 넌 Sam에게 이걸 말할 것을 기억해야 해.

4. forget+동명사 '~한 것을 잊다' / forget+to부정사 '~할[하는] 것을 잊다'

Did you **forget calling** me this morning? 넌 오늘 아침에 내게 전화한 것을 잊었니?
Did you **forget to call** me this morning? 넌 오늘 아침에 내게 전화하는 것을 잊었니?

cf. stop 뒤에는 동명사와 to부정사가 모두 올 수 있지만, 이때 to부정사는 목적어가 아닌 부사구이다.
stop+동명사 '~하는 것을 멈추다' / stop+to부정사 '~하기 위해 멈추다'
The man **stopped talking** to the woman. 남자는 여자에게 말하는 것을 멈추었다.
The man **stopped to talk** to the woman. 남자는 여자에게 말하기 위해 (가던 길을) 멈추었다.

정답 p.47

PRACTICE 6

괄호 안의 단어를 알맞은 형태로 바꾸어 빈칸에 쓰세요.

1 Ann tried ________________ the answer, but she couldn't get it. (find)

2 Everyone stopped ________________ and left the room. (talk)

3 I regret ________________ my smartphone because it was too expensive for me. (buy)

4 Mom suggested ________________ during peak season. (not, travel)

5 Jason forgot ________________ the alarm, so he got up late this morning. (set)

6 Do you mind ________________ the window for a while? (open)

7 When you make potato chips, try ________________ salt to your potatoes. (add)

8 I stopped ________________ up the gas tank, but the gas station was closed. (fill)

9 Linda dislikes ________________ lies to people. (tell)

10 I won't forget ________________ the famous movie star last night. (see)

11 I decided ________________ the summer vacation on Jejudo. (not, spend)

12 Do you remember ________________ Hana at the beach last Saturday? (meet)

13 I promised ________________ late for school again. (not, be)

14 The boy didn't finish ________________ his room. (clean)

15 Nari didn't come in the end. She must have forgotten ________________ my office. (visit)

PSS 3 전치사의 목적어로 쓰이는 동명사

전치사의 목적어로 동사가 올 때는 동명사의 형태로 써야 한다.

1. thank A for -ing '~에 대해 A에게 감사하다'

   Thank you **for listening** to my speech. 저의 연설을 들어주셔서 감사합니다.

2. be interested in -ing '~에 관심 있다'

   Are you **interested in dancing** with people? 사람들과 춤추는 것에 관심이 있어요?

3. be good at -ing '~을 잘하다'

   Sangmin **is good at playing** the violin. 상민은 바이올린 연주를 잘한다.

4. be responsible for -ing '~에 책임이 있다'

   You **are responsible for caring** for the baby. 너는 그 아기를 돌보는 데 책임이 있다.

5. be worried about -ing '~에 대해 걱정하다'

   She **is worried about taking** an exam tomorrow. 그녀는 내일 시험을 치를 것에 대해 걱정한다.

6. dream of[about] -ing '~을 꿈꾸다'

   Jeff always **dreams of[about] buying** a nice car. Jeff는 항상 멋진 차를 사는 것을 꿈꾼다.

7. think of[about] -ing '~하는 것에 대해 생각하다'

   He **thought of[about] having** a meeting with them.
   그는 그들과 회의를 하는 것에 대해 생각했다.

8. talk about -ing '~에 대해 말하다'

   We **talked about moving** to a smaller city. 우리는 더 작은 도시로 이사가는 것에 대해 말했다.

9. be excited about -ing '~에 대해 흥분되다'

   Are you **excited about meeting** Mr. Smith? 너는 Smith 씨를 만나는 것에 대해 흥분되니?

10. be tired of -ing '~에 지겨워하다'

    I'm tired of taking care of the kids. 나는 아이들을 돌보는 것이 지겹다.

11. look forward to -ing '~을 고대하다'

    I'm **looking forward to visiting** the place some day.
    나는 언젠가 그곳을 방문하기를 고대하고 있다.

12. **feel like -ing** '～하고 싶다'

Jason doesn't **feel like talking** about her. Jason은 그녀에 대해서 말하고 싶지 않다.

13. **on[upon] -ing** '～하자마자'

On[Upon] arriving home, I went to sleep. 집에 도착하자마자 나는 잠을 잤다.

14. **be used to -ing** '～에 익숙하다'

Mr. Smith **is used to getting** up early in the morning.

Smith 씨는 아침에 일찍 일어나는 것에 익숙하다.

15. **prevent A from -ing** 'A가 ～하는 것을 못하게 하다'

The rain **prevented** them **from playing** the game.

그 비는 그들이 그 게임을 치르는 것을 못하게 했다.

정답 p.48

PRACTICE 7

괄호 안의 단어를 알맞은 형태로 바꿔서 빈칸을 완성하세요.

1 Jinho is very interested ______________ ___________ computer games. (play)

2 Mr. Kim thought ___________ ___________ to Busan. (move)

3 I feel ___________ ___________ noodles today. (have)

4 Sujin is worried ___________ ___________ the test next week. (take)

5 I dream ___________ ___________ back to my hometown. (go)

6 I'm tired ___________ ___________ TV these days. (watch)

7 She's responsible ___________ ___________ the house. (clean)

8 Jenny was good ___________ ___________ when she was a kid. (sing)

9 David and I were talking ___________ ___________ our old car. (fix)

10 You are excited ___________ ___________ Europe, aren't you? (visit)

11 Thank you ___________ ___________ so kind to me. (be)

12 I'm looking forward ___________ ___________ wonderful food at the Christmas party. (have)

13 Her illness prevented her ___________ ___________ here. (come)

14 On ___________ the news, she began to cry. (hear)

15 Bill is used ___________ ___________ in the city. (live)

PSS 4 동명사의 관용 표현

1. How[What] about+-ing? = What do you say to+-ing? '~하는 게 어때?'

   How[What] about going on a picnic tomorrow? 내일 소풍을 가는 게 어때?
   = **What do you say to going** on a picnic tomorrow?

2. be busy+-ing '~하느라 바쁘다'

   Mom **was busy cleaning** the house. 엄마는 집을 청소하느라 바빴다.

3. go+-ing '~하러 가다'

   I'm planning to **go camping** with my parents. 나는 부모님과 함께 캠핑을 갈 계획이다.

4. spend+시간[돈]+-ing '~하느라 시간[돈]을 쓰다'

   I **spend** too much **time sleeping**. 나는 잠을 자느라 너무 많은 시간을 쓴다.

5. need+-ing '~되어야 할 필요가 있다'

   The car **needs repairing** after the accident. 그 차는 사고 이후 수리할 필요가 있다.
   = The car **needs to be repaired** after the accident.

6. It's no use+-ing '~해봐야 소용없다'

   It's no use crying over spilt milk. 엎질러진 우유 때문에 울어봐야 소용없다.

7. cannot help+-ing '~하지 않을 수 없다'

   I **cannot help laughing** when I see that funny video.
   그 웃긴 동영상을 볼 때 나는 웃지 않을 수 없다.
   She **couldn't help worrying** about her loved one's safety.
   그녀는 그녀의 사랑하는 이의 안전에 대해 걱정하지 않을 수 없었다.

8. have trouble[difficulty, a hard time]+-ing '~하는 데 어려움을 겪다'

   Jane **had trouble choosing** her major. Jane은 전공을 선택하는 데 어려움을 겪었다.

9. There is no+-ing = It is impossible+to부정사 '~할 수 없다'

   There is no denying the fact that he told a lie to us.
   그가 우리에게 거짓말을 했다는 그 사실을 부인할 수가 없다.
   = **It is impossible to deny** the fact that he told a lie to us.

10. be worth+-ing '~할 만한 가치가 있다'

   It **is worth trying** new things. 새로운 것들을 시도할 만한 가치가 있다.

PRACTICE 8

우리말과 일치하도록 괄호 안의 단어를 이용하여 빈칸에 알맞은 말을 쓰세요.

1 나는 겨울에 종종 언니와 함께 스케이트를 타러 간다.
➡ I often ________________ with my sister in winter. (skate)

2 나는 새 옷을 사느라 돈을 너무 많이 소비했다.
➡ I ________________ too much money ________________ new clothes. (buy)

3 네 컴퓨터는 고칠 필요가 있다.
➡ Your computer needs ________________. (fix)

4 잠시 산책하는 게 어때?
➡ ________________________________ a walk for a while? (take)
➡ ________________________________ a walk for a while?

5 Shelly는 시험 공부를 하느라 바빴다.
➡ Shelly has been ________________________ for the exam. (study)

6 그를 말리려 해봐야 소용없다.
➡ It's ________________________ to stop him. (try)

7 나는 그 순간 웃지 않을 수 없었다.
➡ I ________________________ at that moment. (laugh)

8 Bill은 새 직장을 구하는 데 어려움을 겪고 있다.
➡ Bill is ________________________ a new job. (get)

9 우리는 새 정책에 대해 생각하느라 한 시간을 소비했다.
➡ We ________________ an hour ________________ about the new policy. (think)

10 내 딸은 다음 주말에 스키를 타러 갈 것이다.
➡ My daughter is going to ________________________ next weekend. (ski)

11 논쟁에서는 무식한 사람을 이길 수가 없다.
➡ ________________________ an ignorant man in an argument. (defeat)

12 Sam은 대부분의 시간을 책을 읽으며 보낸다.
➡ Sam ________________ most of his time ________________ books. (read)

13 나는 지난 주말에 캠핑을 갔고, 좋은 시간을 보냈다.
➡ I ________________________ last weekend and had a good time. (camp)

14 우리는 그의 언어를 이해하는 데 어려움을 겪었다.
➡ We ________________________ his language. (understand)

15 이 박물관은 최소한 한 번쯤 방문할 만한 가치가 있다.
➡ This museum ________________________ at least once. (visit)

중간·기말고사 대비문제　📝

1 다음 중 어법상 <u>어색한</u> 문장의 개수는?

> (A) Milk is used to making cheese.
> (B) Jane couldn't help to buy the book.
> (C) We need to practice writing an essay.
> (D) The snow prevented us to cross the bridge.
> (E) He is responsible for prepare the food.

① 1개　　　　② 2개　　　　③ 3개
④ 4개　　　　⑤ 5개

2 ⓐ~ⓔ 중에서 우리말을 영작한 것 중 옳은 것만을 고른 것은?

> ⓐ 몇 주 동안 비가 오지 않았기 때문에 정원에 물을 주어야 한다.
> → The garden needs to be watering because it hasn't rained for weeks.
> ⓑ 그는 마침내 불평하는 것을 그만두고 해결책을 찾기 시작했다.
> → He finally quit complaining and started looking for solutions.
> ⓒ 우리는 함께 별똥별을 봤던 것을 절대 잊지 못할 거야.
> → We'll never forget seeing the shooting star together.
> ⓓ 해외여행을 갈 때 너의 여권을 가져올 것을 기억해라.
> → Remember bringing your passport when you travel abroad.
> ⓔ 그는 기말고사 공부를 하느라 바쁘다.
> → He is busy studying for the final exam.

① ⓐⓑⓒ　　② ⓐⓒⓔ　　③ ⓑⓒⓓ
④ ⓑⓒⓔ　　⑤ ⓒⓓⓔ

3 다음 중 밑줄 친 부분의 쓰임이 나머지와 <u>다른</u> 하나는?

① My battery is <u>running</u> out.
② His goal is <u>finishing</u> the given tasks.
③ Her recent hope is <u>traveling</u> across Europe.
④ His bad habit is <u>biting</u> his nails.
⑤ The key point is <u>keeping</u> your word.

4 다음 중 우리말 해석이 잘못된 것은?

① I tried moving the piano by myself.
　→ 난 혼자서 그 피아노를 옮겨봤다.
② Daniel stopped to talk to his friend.
　→ Daniel은 친구랑 이야기하려고 멈춰섰다.
③ Do you remember watching the sunrise together?
　→ 너는 함께 일출 보기로 한 것을 기억하니?
④ She forgot to visit her grandparents.
　→ 그녀는 조부모님 찾아 뵙는 것을 잊어버렸다.
⑤ My father stopped drinking.
　→ 우리 아버지는 술 마시는 걸 끊으셨다.

5 다음 두 문장의 뜻이 같을 때 빈칸에 들어가기에 알맞은 것은?

> She remembers that she submitted her homework.
> = She remembers ______________ her homework.

① submit　　　　　② to submit
③ submitted　　　　④ submitting
⑤ being submitted

6 다음 두 문장에서 <u>틀린</u> 부분을 고쳐 문장을 다시 쓰세요.

(1) I really dislike be interrupted by people.

➡ _______________________________________

____

(2) Don't forget feeding our dog after school tomorrow.

➡ _______________________________________

____

7 다음 (A)~(E) 중 어법상 올바른 문장의 개수는?

(A) He is running a business.
(B) My dad advises me taking Japanese, Chinese and art this semester.
(C) Do you mind taking a picture with me?
(D) She grew up to be a famous scientist.
(E) He is used to study for hours before exams.

① 0개 ② 2개 ③ 3개
④ 4개 ⑤ 5개

8 다음 대화의 빈칸에 들어갈 말로 알맞은 것은?

Tom : Hi, Diana. Are you going to come to my concert?
Diana: Oh, Tom! I am looking forward __________ you perform.

① see ② seeing ③ saw
④ to see ⑤ to seeing

9 다음 글을 읽고, 〈보기〉에 주어진 단어를 이용하여 빈칸에 알맞은 말을 쓰세요.

보 기 | plant   wash   do   give

My dad promised _______________ me some pocket money if I did some work for him. For _______________ the car, he'll give me 3,000 won. For _______________ the trees, I'll get 5,000 won. I'll get more pocket money by _______________ some chores around the house.

10 다음 빈칸에 들어갈 말들이 알맞은 순서대로 연결된 것은?

• Miranda was very busy _____(A)_____ Oliver's birthday party.
• They kept _____(B)_____ together at the park.
• We wished _____(C)_____ each other to make a happy home.

	(A)	(B)	(C)
①	prepare	– jogging	– to understand
②	preparing	– to jog	– understand
③	preparing	– jogging	– to understand
④	to prepare	– jog	– understanding
⑤	to prepare	– to jog	– understanding

11 다음 중 어법상 알맞은 문장은?

① I don't feel like to talk to you.
② I decided taking a bus to school.
③ He denied stealing my money.
④ Would you mind to hold the door for a second?
⑤ I agreed changing the schedule.

12 다음 중 어법상 어색한 문장은?

① I couldn't help falling in love with Jessie because she was very lovely.
② This computer needs upgrading now.
③ Let's go shopping to buy your jacket after school.
④ What do you say to go for a walk?
⑤ It's no use telling him that because he won't listen.

13 ⓐ, ⓑ, ⓒ에 들어갈 말로 바르게 짝지어진 것은?

> • They agreed ______ⓐ______ at the park tomorrow.
> • Do you mind ______ⓑ______ me with my homework?
> • Don't forget ______ⓒ______ your alarm for tomorrow.

	ⓐ		ⓑ		ⓒ
①	to meet	–	helping	–	setting
②	to meet	–	to help	–	to set
③	to meet	–	helping	–	to set
④	meeting	–	to help	–	setting
⑤	meeting	–	helping	–	to set

14 다음 빈칸에 들어갈 말로 알맞은 것은?

> When I see weak people, I always try ______________ them.

① help   ② to help   ③ to helping
④ helped   ⑤ being help

15 다음 문장에서 틀린 곳을 한 군데 찾아 고치세요.

> Exercise every day is good for your health.

______________ ➡ ______________

16 빈칸 ⓐ, ⓑ, ⓒ에 들어갈 말이 바르게 연결된 것은?

> Are you worried ______ⓐ______ an exam?
> Here are some tips for studying for an exam.
> 1. Use charts and diagrams ______ⓑ______ your notes.
> 2. Try to explain your answers ______ⓒ______ your friends.
> 3. Do not stay up all night to study, and have a good sleep!

	ⓐ		ⓑ		ⓒ
①	about taking	–	organize	–	to
②	for taking	–	organizing	–	from
③	about taking	–	to organize	–	to
④	for taking	–	organizing	–	about
⑤	about taking	–	to organize	–	from

17 다음 중 밑줄 친 부분의 쓰임이 나머지와 다른 하나는?

① I imagined flying in the sky.
② She quit working for the company.
③ Ben is watching TV now.
④ Minhee likes taking pictures.
⑤ My hobby is playing soccer.

18 다음 대화의 빈칸에 들어갈 알맞은 말은?

> *Susan*: I'm leaving for France for my
>   summer vacation next Wednesday.
> *Ted* : Wow, ___________________.
> *Susan*: Don't worry. I won't forget.

① don't forget sending me some photos
② remember to send me some photos
③ forget to send me some photos
④ remember sending me some photos
⑤ don't remember to send me some photos

19 다음 중 밑줄 친 부분의 쓰임이 잘못된 것은?

① I hope to be a social worker.
② I love hiking in the mountains.
③ Jihoon and I practiced to play the guitar.
④ She began to learn how to cook.
⑤ They gave up fixing the computer.

20 다음 우리말과 같은 뜻이 되도록 빈칸에 들어갈 알맞은 말은?

> • 너는 그에게 내일 전화할 것을 기억해야 한다.
>   = You should ________________ him
>   tomorrow.

① remember to call
② remember calling
③ to remember to call
④ to remember calling
⑤ remembering calling

21 다음 우리말과 뜻이 같도록 괄호 안의 단어를 배열하세요.

> • 그들은 이 문제를 해결하는 데 어려움을 겪고 있다.
>
> = ________________________________
>
>   ________________________________

(solving, they, difficulty, this, are, having, problem)

22 다음 대화의 빈칸에 공통으로 들어갈 말로 알맞은 것은?

> *A*: What's your hobby?
> *B*: I like __________ movies. I'm interested
>   in __________ romantic movies.

① watch   ② to watch   ③ watching
④ watched   ⑤ to be watching

23 다음 중 밑줄 친 부분의 쓰임이 다른 것을 바르게 짝지은 것은?

> ⓐ How about meeting at the bus stop?
> ⓑ She is studying science now.
> ⓒ My hobby is riding a bicycle.
> ⓓ They heard him singing in the bathroom.
> ⓔ The sleeping baby is my nephew.
> ⓕ I'm interested in baking cookies.

① ⓐ, ⓑ   ② ⓐ, ⓕ   ③ ⓑ, ⓓ
④ ⓒ, ⓕ   ⑤ ⓓ, ⓔ

24

@, ⓑ의 문장에서 밑줄 친 부분의 쓰임이 서로 다른 것은?

① @ <u>Taking</u> a nap is one of the most efficient ways to rest.
　ⓑ <u>Eating</u> vegetables is good for our health.
② @ My mom always tells me to watch the <u>boring</u> news.
　ⓑ The girl <u>sleeping</u> on the couch is my daughter.
③ @ Tom enjoys <u>swimming</u> in the sea.
　ⓑ When did you finish <u>writing</u> the report?
④ @ My job is <u>teaching</u> English to middle school students.
　ⓑ My plan for this summer vacation is <u>going</u> to Canada.
⑤ @ I didn't recognize that he was <u>doing</u> his homework.
　ⓑ I'm tired of <u>answering</u> your questions.

25

다음 문장에서 틀린 부분을 찾아 올바른 형태로 바꿔 쓰세요.

It was very sunny this morning. I thought of take a walk with my dog.

→ _______________

26

괄호 안에 주어진 단어를 빈칸에 알맞은 형태로 바꾸어 쓰세요.

- They denied (A) _______________ on the exam, despite evidence of identical wrong answers on their papers. (cheat)
- They can't afford (B) _______________ a long vacation this year. (take)

27

다음 헬스클럽의 설문 내용을 바탕으로 대화를 완성할 때, @～ⓔ 중 어법상 옳은 것은? (정답 2개)

> **Muscle Magic's Survey**
> 1. How long have you been exercising?
> *Five years*
> 2. How often do you come to the gym to exercise? *Twice a week*
> 3. What's the purpose of exercising?
> *To maintain a healthy body weight*
> 4. What kind of exercise equipment do you like the most? *Stair Climber*

> Q. Let me know how long you have been exercising.
> A. @ <u>I've been exercising for five years.</u>
> Q. Can you tell me how often you come to the gym to exercise?
> A. ⓑ <u>I go there about two time a week.</u>
> Q. ⓒ <u>Would you mind tell me what the purpose of exercising is?</u>
> A. As you know, exercise has a number of benefits. ⓓ <u>I keep exercising in order to maintain a healthy body weight.</u>
> Q. ⓔ <u>I'm curious about what kind of exercise equipment do you like the most.</u>
> A. My favorite is the Stair Climber.

① @　　② ⓑ　　③ ⓒ　　④ ⓓ　　⑤ ⓔ

28

우리말과 같은 뜻이 되도록 빈칸에 들어갈 알맞은 말을 세 단어로 쓰세요.

- 아침에 일찍 일어나는 것은 나에게 때때로 도전이다.
  = _______________ in the morning is sometimes a challenge for me.

29

다음 중 어법상 **틀린** 문장을 <u>2개</u> 고르고, 틀린 부분을 바르게 고쳐 쓰세요.

ⓐ I don't mind to give you some advice.
ⓑ You should not violate the traffic regulations.
ⓒ I used to finish to wash the dishes before my mom came home.
ⓓ What about going swimming with me this weekend?
ⓔ Eating balanced food is important for your health.

(1) 틀린 문장: _______

　　고쳐 쓰기: _____________ ➡ _____________

(2) 틀린 문장: _______

　　고쳐 쓰기: _____________ ➡ _____________

30

다음 빈칸에 들어갈 단어가 어법상 알맞게 연결된 것은?

- I want ____(가)____ to Busan.
- I like ____(나)____ my bicycle at night.
- I'd like ____(다)____ soda instead of water.
- ____(라)____ at home may upset your neighbors.
- He is not used to ____(마)____ in front of many people.

① (가): going　　② (나): riding　　③ (다): drink
④ (라): Yell　　⑤ (마): perform

31

다음 빈칸에 알맞지 <u>않은</u> 것은?

I ___________ reading the book last Saturday.

① finished　　② enjoyed　　③ decided
④ gave up　　⑤ kept

32

〈보기〉의 말들을 알맞게 배열하여 문장을 완성하세요.

보 기 |
in, using, the classroom, smartphones

In Nina's class today students had a debate. The topic was ___________________
___________. The class was divided up into two groups.

33

다음 빈칸에 들어갈 말이 알맞게 짝지어진 것은?

Mr. Han had a habit of ___________ in thought. He often just walked silently without ___________ anything.

① be lost　　– say
② be lost　　– saying
③ being lost – to say
④ being lost – saying
⑤ being lost – say

34

다음 문장의 빈칸에 들어갈 알맞은 말은?

- It is impossible to replace your best friend.
  = There is no ___________ your best friend.

① replace　　　　② replacing
③ replaced　　　　④ to have replaced
⑤ replaces

35 다음 (A)~(C)에 들어갈 말끼리 바르게 연결된 것은?

> *Eric* : Dad, I stopped (A) playing/to play
>   with my friend to wash your car.
> *Dad*: I'm glad (B) to hear/hearing that.
> *Eric* : I thought washing your car would be
>   an easy way to earn pocket money.
> *Dad*: All right. I want you to keep
>   (C) to wash/washing it until it gets
>   shiny.
> *Eric* : Okay, I will.

	(A)	(B)	(C)
①	to play	– to hear	– to wash
②	playing	– hearing	– washing
③	playing	– to hear	– washing
④	to play	– hearing	– washing
⑤	playing	– to hear	– to wash

36 다음 글에서 어법상 **틀린** 부분 **세 군데**를 찾아 틀린 부분을 바르게 고쳐 쓰세요.

> There is four types of friends: listeners,
> advisors, cheerleaders, and opposites.
> Listeners listen to what you say. Advisors
> don't just listen to you but also give you
> advice. Cheerleaders enjoy to talk and
> spending time with you. Opposites have
> different interests, but you can still get along
> with theirs.

(1) ____________ ➡ ____________

(2) ____________ ➡ ____________

(3) ____________ ➡ ____________

37 다음 밑줄 친 ⓐ~ⓔ 중 어법상 적절하지 **않은** 것은?

> *W*: Are you excited about your camping
>   trip?
> *M*: Yes, but I'm worried about ⓐ going
>   outside at night.
> *W*: Why?
> *M*: I'm not ⓑ used to walk in the dark.
> *W*: There will be ⓒ other people with you,
>   so you won't be alone.
> *M*: That makes me ⓓ feel better.
> *W*: Just ⓔ stay close to the group and you'll
>   be fine.

① ⓐ ② ⓑ ③ ⓒ ④ ⓓ ⑤ ⓔ

38 다음 대화의 밑줄 친 우리말과 뜻이 같도록 〈보기〉의 말을 배열하여 문장을 완성하세요.

> *Dad* : Hey, Sarah. It's three in the morning.
>   What are you still doing up?
> *Sarah*: I'm studying because I have a history
>   test this morning.
> *Dad* : It's not good for your health to study
>   all night long.
> *Sarah*: Actually, I spent too much time
>   playing video games so I didn't have
>   enough time to study.
> *Dad* : 다음 번에는 시험 공부할 계획을 세우는 걸
>   잊지 마라.
> *Sarah*: I won't, Dad.

> 보 기 | forget, to plan, next time, for the
> exam, to study

➡ Don't ________________________

________________________________ .

39 다음 빈칸에 알맞은 말을 <u>모두</u> 고르세요.

Early in the morning, he rushed to his office. He sat down and began __________ the reports on his desk.

① read   ② reads   ③ to read
④ reading   ⑤ to reading

40 다음 중 어법상 <u>잘못된</u> 문장은?

① I suggested moving to a bigger city.
② She hates cleaning the bathroom.
③ My uncle imagined to meet his favorite singer.
④ He came here to fix my computer.
⑤ She still refuses to accept that there is a problem.

41 다음 중 어법상 올바른 문장을 <u>모두</u> 고르세요.

① What do you expect me doing for the party?
② Mike decided support the child.
③ Remember to send him the package tomorrow.
④ I was very tired, but I tried to keep my eyes open.
⑤ He dislikes to work late at night.

42 다음 글에서 어법상 <u>틀린</u> 부분을 <u>2개</u> 찾아 바르게 고쳐 쓰세요.

Do you usually drink lots of water? Doctors say that drinking at least eight glasses water a day is good for our health. I tried to drink lots of water but I couldn't enjoy to do that. I finally gave up my plan.

(1) __________
   ➡ __________

(2) __________
   ➡ __________

43 주어진 문장을 바르게 영작한 것을 고르세요.

만약 사람들이 자기 전에 그들의 휴대폰을 쳐다보는 데 많은 시간을 쓴다면, 그들은 밤잠을 잘 자지 못할 것이다.

① If people will spend a lot of time staring at their cellphones before going to bed, they'll get a poor night's sleep.
② If people spend a lot of time to stare at their cellphones before going to bed, they'll get a poor night's sleep.
③ If people spend a lot of time staring at their cellphones before go to bed, they'll get a poor night's sleep.
④ If people will spend a lot of time staring at their cellphones before going to bed, they get a poor night's sleep.
⑤ If people spend a lot of time staring at their cellphones before going to bed, they'll get a poor night's sleep.

CHAPTER 9
분사

PSS 1 분사의 종류

분사는 「동사원형＋-ing」 / 「동사원형＋-ed」 형태로 형용사처럼 명사를 수식하거나 주어 또는 목적어를 보충 설명하는 보어 역할을 한다.

	현재분사	과거분사
형태	동사원형＋-ing	동사원형＋-ed (동사의 과거분사형)
의미 — 진행 (~하고 있는)	I saw **falling** leaves. 나는 떨어지는 나뭇잎들을 보았다. All the leaves were **falling**. 모든 나뭇잎들이 떨어지고 있었다.	완료 (~한) We collected **fallen** leaves. 우리는 떨어진 나뭇잎들을 모았다. The leaves have **fallen**. 나뭇잎들이 떨어졌다.
능동 (~하게 하는)	Jack told me a **boring** story. Jack은 내게 지루한 이야기를 했다. The story was **boring**. 그 이야기는 지루했다.	수동 (~된, ~해진) **Bored** people don't ask questions. 지루해 하는 사람들은 질문을 하지 않는다. People were **bored** by the speech. 사람들은 그 연설에 지루해 했다.

정답 p.51

PRACTICE 1

괄호 안에 주어진 단어 중 알맞은 것을 고르세요.

1 Gidong has just (repairing, repaired) the computer.

2 He brought some (surprising, surprised) news.

3 She moved the (sleeping, slept) puppy carefully.

4 Today's weather is quite (depressing, depressed).

5 I like to eat (boiling, boiled) eggs in the train.

6 They were (eating, eaten) their lunch.

7 His (giving, given) name is Smith.

8 I was (inviting, invited) to his birthday party.

9 Those pictures were (taking, taken) by him.

10 I think the story is (amazed, amazing).

11 Henry is planning to buy a (using, used) car.

12 She asked whether it was a (rising, risen) sun or a setting sun.

PSS 2 분사의 역할

PSS 2-1 명사를 수식하는 분사

1. 분사가 단독으로 쓰일 때는 명사의 앞에서 명사를 수식한다.

   The **crying boy** is my son. 울고 있는 소년이 내 아들이다.

   Look at the **broken window**. 깨진 창문을 보아라.

2. 분사가 구를 이루어 명사를 수식할 때는 명사의 뒤에서 명사를 수식한다.

   The **girl sitting on the chair** is Ann. 의자에 앉아 있는 소녀는 Ann이다.

   Mom swept the **leaves scattered on the ground**. 엄마는 땅에 흩어진 나뭇잎을 쓸었다.

정답 p.51

PRACTICE 2

〈보기〉에서 알맞은 동사를 골라 분사의 형태로 바꾸어 빈칸에 쓰세요.

| 보 기 | write | shock | speak | talk | burn |
| | paint | interest | use | bark | break |

1 That word isn't used in ________spoken________ English.

2 I'm afraid of dogs ________________ at people.

3 Be careful with the ________________ glasses.

4 I like the wall ________________ in red.

5 ________________ cars are cheaper than new ones.

6 I saw a ________________ accident on the road.

7 Have you read a book ________________ by James Joyce?

8 That boy ________________ with the old lady looks very happy.

9 Andy asked some ________________ questions about the movie.

10 A ________________ child dreads fire.

PRACTICE 3

〈보기〉와 같이 분사를 이용하여 두 문장을 한 문장으로 연결하세요.

> 보 기　　The boy is sleeping under the tree. He is my brother.
> ➡ The boy <u>sleeping under the tree</u> is my brother.

1 I lost my wallet. It was found by my sister.

➡ My _________________________ was found by my sister.

2 The students were dancing. They were happy.

➡ The _________________________ were happy.

3 The leaves have fallen on the ground. Let's pick them up.

➡ Let's pick up the leaves _________________________.

4 The girl is reading a book. She is Kate.

➡ The girl _________________________ is Kate.

5 I ate those cookies. They were burned.

➡ I ate those _________________________.

6 I saw her eyes. They were filled with tears.

➡ I saw her eyes _________________________.

7 The children are exercising in the gym. They are Sena and Minsu.

➡ The children _________________________ are Sena and Minsu.

8 The top of the mountain is covered with snow. It looks great.

➡ The top of the mountain _________________________ looks great.

9 We couldn't look at the sun. It was shining.

➡ We couldn't look at the _________________________.

10 I know the boy. He is singing on the stage.

➡ I know the boy _________________________.

PSS 2-2 보어로 쓰이는 분사

1. **주격 보어 – 주어의 상태나 행위를 설명한다.**

   The news sounded **surprising** to us. 그 소식은 우리에게 놀랍게 들렸다.

   주어와 주격 보어가 능동의 관계일 때는 현재분사를 쓴다. 주로 '～하게 하는', '～하면서'로 해석된다.

Dad looked **surprised** to see his brother. 아빠는 그의 형을 보고 놀란 것처럼 보였다.

주어와 주격 보어가 수동의 관계일 때는 과거분사를 쓴다. 주로 '～한, ～된, ～해진'으로 해석된다.

2. 목적격 보어 – 목적어의 상태나 행위를 설명한다.

I heard **the teacher calling** my name. 나는 선생님이 내 이름을 부르는 것을 들었다.

목적어와 목적격 보어가 능동의 관계일 때는 현재분사를 쓴다. '(목적어가) ～하는 것을'로 해석된다.

I heard **my name called** in the classroom. 나는 교실에서 내 이름이 불리는 것을 들었다.

목적어와 목적격 보어가 수동의 관계일 때는 과거분사를 쓴다. '(목적어가) ～ 되는 것을'로 해석된다.

정답 p.52

PRACTICE 4

괄호 안의 동사를 분사의 형태로 바꾸어 빈칸에 쓰고, 문장 안에서 어떤 역할(명사 수식, 주격 보어, 목적격 보어)을 하는지 쓰세요.

1 We were ___watching___ TV. (watch)   (주격 보어   )

2 I watched Mary __________ at the camp. (cook)   (   )

3 I want my car __________ by tomorrow. (fix)   (   )

4 She felt __________ because of the weather. (depress)   (   )

5 He kept me __________ in that room. (wait)   (   )

6 I know the boy __________ with the old man. (dance)   (   )

7 The people were __________ to watch the game. (excite)   (   )

8 Mr. Kim found the students __________ away. (run)   (   )

9 Let's frame the recently __________ photos. (take)   (   )

10 Jenny wanted her room __________. (clean)   (   )

11 The boy is __________. (smile)   (   )

12 John was __________ to music in his room. (listen)   (   )

13 What an __________ book this is! (interest)   (   )

14 The cookies __________ by Mr. Kim were really good. (bake)   (   )

15 I saw your daughter __________ toward the station. (walk)   (   )

16 I felt my shoulder __________ and turned around. (touch)   (   )

PSS 3 현재분사와 동명사

현재분사와 동명사는 형태는 같지만 현재분사는 형용사, 동명사는 명사의 역할을 한다.

	현재분사	동명사
명사 앞	'~하는, ~인' (명사의 동작, 상태) Look at the **crying** baby. 울고 있는 아기를 보아라.	'~을 하기 위한, ~로 쓰는' (용도) I bought a **sleeping** bag. 나는 침낭을 샀다. *cf.* sleeping bag: a warm, long bag that is used for sleeping outdoors or in a tent
Be동사 뒤	'~중인' (진행시제) I'm **baking** a cheese cake. 나는 치즈 케이크를 굽고 있어.	'~하는 것' (주격 보어 역할의 명사) My dream is **studying** in Germany. 내 꿈은 독일에서 공부하는 것이다.
타동사, 전치사 뒤	명사를 꾸며주는 형용사 역할로, 앞에 정관사나 소유격이 올 수 있다. I like **the dancing** girl. 난 저 춤추는 소녀가 좋아.	타동사, 전치사의 목적어로 명사 역할 I **enjoy listening** to classical music. 난 클래식 음악 듣는 걸 즐겨.

정답 p.52

PRACTICE 5

다음 문장의 밑줄 친 부분의 용법이 〈보기〉의 A와 같으면 A, B와 같으면 B를 쓰세요.

보기	A. They are <u>playing</u> soccer.	B. She gave me a pair of <u>running</u> shoes.

1 She is <u>holding</u> a car key. (　　)

2 I need to buy a <u>frying</u> pan. (　　)

3 My job is <u>driving</u> a taxi. (　　)

4 He was <u>writing</u> an email at his computer. (　　)

5 Let's buy some <u>drinking</u> water. (　　)

6 The <u>boring</u> class made us sleepy. (　　)

7 Their decision was <u>leaving</u> the country. (　　)

8 The boy liked her <u>smiling</u> face. (　　)

9 It's <u>exciting</u> to live in the big city. (　　)

10 There's a TV in the <u>living</u> room. (　　)

PSS 4 감정을 나타내는 분사

This game is very **exciting**.

이 게임은 매우 흥미진진하다.

I am very **excited** about this game.

나는 이 게임에 대해 매우 흥분된다.

-ing (~한 감정을 느끼게 하는) / -ed (~한 감정을 느끼는)

The class is **boring**.

그 수업은 지루하다.

Walking to school is **tiring**.

학교에 걸어가는 것은 피곤하다.

Your question is **confusing**.

네 질문은 혼란스럽다.

Today's weather is very **depressing**.

오늘의 날씨는 매우 우울하다.

The news was **disappointing**.

그 소식은 실망스러웠다.

Playing baseball is **exciting**.

야구를 하는 것은 흥미진진하다.

The service was **satisfying**.

서비스는 만족스러웠다.

That novel is **interesting**.

그 소설은 흥미롭다.

The story was very **surprising**.

그 이야기는 매우 놀라웠다.

His speech was very **embarrassing**.

그의 연설은 매우 당황스러웠다.

The movie was **moving**.

그 영화는 감동적이었다.

The accident was **shocking**.

그 사고는 충격적이었다.

The performance was **amazing**.

그 공연은 놀라웠다.

The weather is very **pleasing**.

날씨가 아주 흡족하다.

All of the questions were **puzzling**.

그 질문들 모두가 곤혹스러웠다.

I'm **bored** with the class.

나는 그 수업에 지루함을 느낀다.

Walking to school makes me **tired**.

학교에 걸어가는 것은 나를 피곤하게 만든다.

I'm **confused** by your question.

나는 네 질문에 혼란스러움을 느낀다.

Today's weather makes me **depressed**.

오늘이 날씨는 나를 우울하게 만든다.

I was **disappointed** with the news.

나는 그 소식에 실망했다.

I'm **excited** about playing baseball.

나는 야구를 하는 것에 흥분된다.

The customer was **satisfied** with the service.

그 고객은 서비스에 만족했다.

I am **interested** in that novel.

나는 그 소설에 흥미를 느낀다.

I was very **surprised** at the story.

나는 그 이야기에 매우 놀랐다.

I was very **embarrassed** by his speech.

나는 그의 연설에 매우 당황했다.

I was **moved** by the movie.

나는 그 영화에 감동 받았다.

I was **shocked** by the accident.

나는 그 사고에 충격을 받았다.

I was **amazed** at the performance.

나는 그 공연을 보고 놀랐다.

I am very **pleased** with the weather.

나는 날씨에 매우 흡족함을 느낀다.

I was **puzzled** by all of the questions.

나는 그 질문들 모두에 곤혹함을 느꼈다.

PRACTICE 6

〈보기〉와 같이 주어진 단어의 알맞은 분사 형태를 쓰세요.

> 보 기　　(interest)　➡ Your story was <u>interesting</u>.
> ➡ I was <u>interested</u> in your story.

1 (bore)
➡ This book is ______________.
➡ I am ______________ with this book.

2 (depress)
➡ He was ______________ by the weather.
➡ The weather was ______________.

3 (confuse)
➡ I was ______________ by the movie plot.
➡ The movie plot was ______________.

4 (disappoint)
➡ Ben's grades were ______________.
➡ Ben was ______________ with his grades.

5 (move)
➡ All the audiences were ______________ by the play.
➡ The play was ______________.

6 (worry)
➡ The exam results are ______________.
➡ He feels ______________ about his exam results.

7 (surprise)
➡ My family felt ______________ at the news.
➡ The news was ______________ to my family.

8 (satisfy)
➡ They were ______________ with my idea.
➡ My idea was ______________.

9 (tire)
➡ Too much exercise is ______________.
➡ Too much exercise makes me ______________.

10 (puzzle)
➡ Ann's essay is ______________.
➡ I am ______________ by Ann's essay.

11 (excite)
➡ Everyone was ______________ about the party.
➡ Everyone found the party ______________.

12 (shock)
➡ The public was ______________ by the picture.
➡ The picture was ______________.

13 (amaze)
➡ The food festival was ______________.
➡ People were ______________ at the food festival.

14 (please)
➡ Mina was ______________ with the pop music.
➡ The pop music was ______________.

15 (embarrass)

➡ His questions were ____________.

➡ The teacher was ____________ by his questions.

정답 p.53

PRACTICE 7

다음은 민지의 일기입니다. 괄호 안의 동사를 알맞은 형태로 바꾸어 빈칸에 쓰세요.

I'm on summer vacation. I was so happy at first, but after a while, I started to feel ____________ (bore). I wanted to go somewhere or do something ____________ (interest). Yesterday, my friend Yumi called and suggested going to a concert. She said, "They are great singers. You won't be ____________ (disappoint)." We went to the art center for the concert today. It was a little ____________ (tire) to go there by bus, but the concert was very ____________ (excite). Both of us had a lot of fun and were ____________ (satisfy).

PSS 5 분사구문

PROBLEM
SOLVING
SKILL

PSS 5-1 분사구문 만드는 법

분사를 이용하여 부사절을 부사구로 바꾼 형태를 분사구문이라고 한다.

After Maria arrived home, she went to bed. Maria는 집에 도착한 후, 잠자리에 들었다.

부사절   주절

① After Maria arrived home, she went to bed.

부사절의 접속사(After)를 뺀다.

② Maria arrived home, she went to bed.

주절의 주어(she)와 같으면 부사절의 주어(Maria)를 뺀다.

③ arrived home, she went to bed.

부사절의 동사(arrived)를 -ing 형태로 바꾼다.

➡ **Arriving home**, she went to bed.

1. 시간

When I saw him at the station, I felt very happy.

그를 역에서 봤을 때, 나는 매우 행복하다고 느꼈다.

➡ **Seeing him at the station**, I felt very happy.

2. 원인, 이유

Because she is young, she can't go there.

그녀는 어리기 때문에 그곳에 갈 수 없다.
➡ **Being** young, she can't go there.

3. 동시동작

While Andy passed my house, he called me. Andy는 우리 집을 지나가면서 나를 불렀다.
➡ **Passing** my house, Andy called me.

4. 연속동작

Sena turned off the light, **and listened to the music.**

세나는 불을 끄고 그 음악을 들었다.
➡ Sena turned off the light, **listening** to the music.

5. 양보

Although I know nothing about you, I want to meet you.

너에 대해 아무것도 모르지만 난 너를 만나고 싶다.
➡ **Knowing** nothing about you, I want to meet you.

정답 p.53

PRACTICE 8

짝지어진 두 문장의 의미가 같도록 분사구문을 이용하여 빈칸을 채우세요.

1 I entered my room, and turned on the TV.

= I entered my room, _turning on the TV_________________.

2 As he studied hard, he passed the exam.

= _____________________________, he passed the exam.

3 As Kelly cooked in the kitchen, she sang some pop songs.

= _____________________________, Kelly sang some pop songs.

4 After I met Hana at the bookstore, I went back home.

= ____, I went back home.

5 While they took a walk, they talked about Bob's birthday.

= _____________________________, they talked about Bob's birthday.

6 This train leaves Daejeon at 9:00, and arrives in Busan at 11:10.

= This train leaves Daejeon at 9:00, ____.

7 While Tom listened to pop music, he looked at the pictures.

= ___________________________, Tom looked at the pictures.

8 After I pushed a boy by mistake, I said, "I'm sorry."

= ___________________________, I said, "I'm sorry."

9 Because they planned to stay at home, they didn't go out.

= ___________________________, they didn't go out.

10 Because I knew him well, I couldn't believe his story.

= ___________________________, I couldn't believe his story.

PSS 5-2 with＋명사＋분사

「with＋명사＋분사」는 '～이(가) …한 채로'의 뜻으로 동시동작을 나타내고, 명사와 분사의 관계가 능동이면 현재분사를, 수동이면 과거분사를 쓴다.

I was having dinner while my dog was sitting beside me.

나의 개가 내 옆에 앉아 있는 동안 나는 저녁을 먹고 있었다.

➡ I was having dinner, **with my dog sitting** beside me.
　　　　　　　　　　　　　└─능동─┘

　나는 나의 개가 내 옆에 앉은 채로 저녁을 먹고 있었다.

Nick was listening to music, and his eyes were closed.

Nick은 음악을 듣고 있었고, 그의 눈은 감겨 있었다.
　　　　　　　　　　　　　　　　┌─수동─┐
➡ Nick was listening to music, **with his eyes closed**. Nick은 눈이 감긴 채로 음악을 듣고 있었다.

정답 p.53

PRACTICE 9 [1-6]

〈보기〉와 같이 짝지어진 두 문장의 의미가 같도록 빈칸을 채우세요.

보 기	Mr. Kim was sitting on the sofa and he was crossing his legs. = Mr. Kim was sitting on the sofa, with his legs crossed.

1

I was walking, and my sister was following me.

= I was walking, ___________________________.

2

Ted is reading the book, and his lamp is turned on.

= Ted is reading the book, ____.

3

They left the place and the trash was cleaned up.

= They left the place, ____.

4

We ran together and our legs were tied.

= We ran together, ____.

5

He is singing a song while his friends are dancing.

= He is singing a song, ____.

6

I kept sleeping while my alarm clock was ringing.

= I kept sleeping, ____.

중간·기말고사 대비문제

1 다음 빈칸에 들어갈 말로 알맞은 것은?

> He listened to Hannah's story very carefully. She told him everything, from beginning to end. "That's a very __________ story," he said and smiled.

① boring
② excited
③ confused
④ interesting
⑤ moved

2 〈보기〉의 문장 중 밑줄 친 부분이 **틀린** 것을 **두 개** 찾아 바르게 고쳐 쓰세요.

> 보 기
> ⓐ The clothes sold at that shop are cheap.
> ⓑ Those pictures were taking by my mom.
> ⓒ They might get burned if they play with fire.
> ⓓ I noticed my name mentioning in the meeting.

〈기호〉　　　　　〈고친 표현〉

__________ ➡ __________

__________ ➡ __________

3 주어진 문장의 밑줄 친 부분과 쓰임이 같은 것은?

> He was planting some flowers.

① Reading helps expand your vocabulary.
② How about going to the beach?
③ I stopped thinking about Jane.
④ She is making some cookies for her parents.
⑤ His hobby is watching movies.

4 다음 중 밑줄 친 부분이 어법상 **틀린** 것은?

① The audience was bored with the new movie.
② The students are interested in English.
③ The manager was satisfying with Jane's report.
④ The speech was so moving that I shed tears.
⑤ All the people in the hall were surprised at the news.

5 다음 빈칸에 들어갈 말로 알맞은 것은?

> Jane heard her name __________ outside.

① calling
② to call
③ called
④ to calling
⑤ have called

6 다음 문장의 밑줄 친 부분과 쓰임이 **다른** 것을 2개 고르세요.

> I'm interested in learning German.

① I like the girl dancing on the stage.
② She is drawing pictures in the field.
③ He gave up talking to his Canadian friend in English.
④ I was waiting for my mother in the waiting room.
⑤ Keeping your body warm in winter is important.

7 (A)~(E)의 괄호 안에 주어진 단어를 활용하여 각 문장을 완성할 때, 빈칸에 들어갈 단어들로 바르게 짝지어진 것은?

(A) Does this shirt need ___________ ? (iron)
(B) I ran towards him with arms ___________ . (outstretch)
(C) It was a ___________ story that moved many of us to tears. (touch)
(D) The doctor is an expert in dealing with patients ___________ from stress. (suffer)
(E) They need to follow the guidelines ___________ . (provide)

(A)	ⓐ ironing	ⓑ ironed
(B)	ⓒ outstretching	ⓓ outstretched
(C)	ⓔ touching	ⓕ touched
(D)	ⓖ suffering	ⓗ suffered
(E)	ⓘ providing	ⓙ provided

① ⓐⓒⓔⓖⓙ
② ⓐⓓⓕⓗⓘ
③ ⓐⓓⓔⓖⓙ
④ ⓑⓒⓕⓗⓘ
⑤ ⓑⓓⓔⓖⓙ

8 다음 밑줄 친 부분과 바꾸어 쓸 수 있는 것은?

Bill talked to Cathy on the phone <u>while he cleaned</u> the room.

① he cleaning
② cleaning
③ clean
④ cleaned
⑤ to clean

9 다음 중 밑줄 친 부분을 어법상 옳게 고친 것은?

① Ben's grades were <u>disappointing</u> (→ disappointed).
② Too much exercise makes me <u>tiring</u> (→ tired).
③ I was <u>shocked</u> (→ shocking) by the accident.
④ This movie was very <u>touching</u> (→ touched).
⑤ Jenny wanted her room <u>cleaned</u> (→ cleaning).

10 〈보기〉의 우리말을 주어진 단어를 활용하여 영작할 때 ⓐ~ⓓ에 들어갈 단어가 바르게 짝지어진 것은?

please / provide / kind / overwhelm

보 기

나는 전자제품 매장에 갔을 때 그곳의 엄청난 크기에 굉장히 압도당한 기분이었다. 하지만 그때, 한 직원이 내게 다가와서 친절하게 도움을 주었다. 난 그가 제공한 훌륭한 서비스에 흡족함을 느꼈다.

→ I felt incredibly ___ⓐ___ by the huge size of the electronics store when I visited. But then, a staff member came to me and ___ⓑ___ offered a helping hand. I was ___ⓒ___ with the excellent service he ___ⓓ___ .

	ⓐ	ⓑ	ⓒ	ⓓ
①	overwhelming	kindly	pleasing	providing
②	overwhelmed	kindly	pleased	providing
③	overwhelming	kind	pleased	providing
④	overwhelmed	kindly	pleased	provided
⑤	overwhelmed	kind	pleasing	provided

11 다음 빈칸에 들어갈 단어로 알맞은 것은?

> Jason went to the park with his 5-year-old sister. But he couldn't find her after he came back from the restroom. He was very __________.

① worries ② to worry ③ worried
④ worry ⑤ worrying

12 다음 중 밑줄 친 부분의 쓰임이 나머지 넷과 다른 것은?

① Nari couldn't help <u>crying</u>.
② I heard some <u>surprising</u> news.
③ I enjoy <u>spending</u> time with my parents.
④ My hobby is <u>playing</u> baseball.
⑤ Ted likes <u>going</u> hiking on weekends.

13 다음의 두 문장을 하나의 문장으로 연결할 때 빈칸에 들어갈 말로 적절한 것은?

> • Jane was lying on the grass. I saw her.
>   = I saw Jane __________ on the grass.

① lied ② lay ③ lying
④ to lie ⑤ to have lay

14 밑줄 친 @~@ 중 어법상 **틀린** 것을 있는 대로 고른 것은?

> A: The movie was ⓐ <u>fantastic</u>.
> B: I don't think so. The actors were ⓑ <u>terrible</u>.
> A: But the story was really ⓒ <u>move</u>.
> B: No, it was very ⓓ <u>boring</u>. I almost fell ⓔ <u>sleeping</u>.

① ⓐ, ⓑ ② ⓑ, ⓒ ③ ⓒ, ⓔ
④ ⓐ, ⓑ, ⓒ ⑤ ⓑ, ⓒ, ⓓ, ⓔ

15 쓰임이 어색한 것을 있는 대로 고른 것은?

> Manjanggul Cave in Jeju Island is one of the longest lava ⓐ <u>tubes</u> in the world. It is famous for its unique lava formations and stable temperature. The cave maintains about 11℃ all year round, ⓑ <u>making</u> it comfortable to explore even in summer. Its ecological value and geological features ⓒ <u>attracts</u> researchers and tourists alike. Some sections of the cave are ⓓ <u>restricted</u> to prevent damage to sensitive areas. Efforts continue to preserve its natural beauty and ⓔ <u>promoting</u> sustainable tourism.   *lava: 용암

① ⓐ ② ⓑ, ⓔ ③ ⓒ, ⓔ
④ ⓐ, ⓑ, ⓓ ⑤ ⓑ, ⓒ, ⓔ

16 다음 중 밑줄 친 부분이 어법상 어색한 것을 모두 고르세요.

① All the people were <u>excited</u>.
② You should recycle <u>using</u> paper.
③ This book was <u>written</u> by Thomas Hardy.
④ I think the book is so <u>confused</u>.
⑤ The flowers in my garden have been <u>watered</u>.

17 다음 빈칸에 들어갈 말이 알맞게 짝지어진 것은?

A: Were you ___________ at the news?
B: Yes, the news was very ___________ .

① surprised – surprising
② surprised – surprised
③ surprising – surprised
④ surprising – surprising
⑤ surprise – surprised

18 다음 중 밑줄 친 부분의 쓰임이 옳지 <u>않은</u> 것은?

① Her speech was <u>shocked</u> to me.
② I was <u>excited</u> when I played the game.
③ My brother is an <u>amazing</u> person.
④ I was <u>tired</u> when I arrived home.
⑤ <u>Drinking</u> a lot of water is good for your
  health.

19 빈칸에 들어갈 말을 〈조건〉에 맞게 영어로 쓰세요.

Pete: Hey, Kate. Look over there!
Kate: There are so many people. What's all
   the fuss about?
Pete: It looks like they're filming something.
Kate: Wow! I've never seen filming taking
   place before.
Pete: Let's take a look! There might be
   famous actors on set.
Kate: Wow! That woman ___________ a blue
   muffler is beautiful.
Pete: Oh my God! That's Lee Ga-Eun! I'm a
   big fan of hers! We're so lucky to be
   here!

조 건
단어 'wear'를 활용하여 한 단어로 쓰세요.

➡ ___________________________

20 다음 글의 (A)~(E) 중 어법상 <u>어색한</u> 것끼리 바르게 짝지은 것은?

I was at a pet store when I was a puppy.
(A) There were a lot of animals waited for
their new owners. One day, a cute girl came
into the store with her mother. She took me
home. (B) At first, she took good care of
me. However, after a few months, (C) she
seemed busy and even forgot feeding
me. (D) Her schedule was filled with her
homework. I was sent to this house after all.
Fortunately, my new owner takes good care
of me. When I was in the park yesterday,
some kids came near me. (E) I thought of
the little girl. I hope she's doing well.

① (A), (E) ② (B), (C) ③ (B), (D)
④ (A), (C) ⑤ (A), (D)

21 밑줄 친 단어가 문맥에 맞게 쓰인 것은?

① *A*: Are you going to the gym?
 B: No, too much exercise is <u>tired</u>.
② *A*: The chocolate cake was <u>amazing</u>!
 B: I know! I want to have it again.
③ *A*: Did you hear what happened to Tom?
 B: Yes, we were <u>shocking</u> to hear that.
④ *A*: Did you find the documentary <u>fascinated</u>?
 B: Are you talking about the one on blue
   whales?
⑤ *A*: Did you show your mom your grades?
 B: Yes. She was <u>disappointing</u> with my
   grades.

22 우리말과 같은 뜻이 되도록 밑줄 친 부분을 부사절로 바꿔 쓰세요.

> • 우리는 일을 마친 후에 저녁을 먹으러 나갔다.
> ➡ <u>Finishing the work</u>, we went out for dinner.

= ________________________________,
we went out for dinner.

23 다음 두 문장을 분사를 이용하여 한 문장으로 쓰세요.

> • The woman is my mother.
> • The woman is waving to my father.

➡ ________________________________
____

24 다음 대화의 빈칸에 알맞지 <u>않은</u> 말은?

> A: What did you do last holiday?
> B: I went to the amusement park with my family.
> A: How was it?
> B: It was ________________.

① exciting　　② great　　③ awesome
④ surprised　　⑤ disappointing

25 우리말과 같은 뜻이 되도록 빈칸에 알맞은 단어를 쓰세요.

> • 그는 그의 눈을 감은 채 소파에 누워 있었다.
> = He was lying on the sofa __________
> __________ __________ __________.

26 다음 대화의 밑줄 친 (A)~(E) 중 어법상 올바른 표현으로만 짝지어진 것은?

> *Sam*: Kate, where are you going?
> *Kate*: (A) <u>I'm going to a concert held in Seoul.</u>
> *Sam*: (B) <u>Whom concert is it?</u>
> *Kate*: Mike Liu. He's a singer from China.
> *Sam*: (C) <u>I'm surprising that you are a fan of a Chinese singer.</u> Will there be an interpreter at the concert?
> *Kate*: No, but (D) <u>I used to live in China for several years</u>, (E) <u>so it's not difficult for me understand Chinese.</u>
> *Sam*: Wow, I didn't know that. Then can you teach me some Chinese later?
> *Kate*: Sure! I'd be happy to.

① (A), (C)　　② (B), (D)　　③ (A), (D)
④ (C), (E)　　⑤ (C), (D)

27 밑줄 친 ⓐ～ⓔ에 각각 들어갈 단어로 어색한 것은?

- Jay usually __________ ⓐ basketball after lunch.
- With her arms __________ ⓑ , my mom was deep in thought.
- My son reads only __________ ⓒ books a year.
- She was __________ ⓓ to see her favorite singer.
- Yesterday I fell down and __________ ⓔ my arm.

① ⓐ: plays   ② ⓑ: folded   ③ ⓒ: a few
④ ⓓ: excited   ⑤ ⓔ: broken

28 다음 대화의 빈칸에 가장 알맞은 말은?

Sora : Look! There are some dolls over there. Which one do you like?
Jenny: Well, I like the one __________ a hat.

① wearing   ② wear   ③ to wear
④ wears   ⑤ wore

29 주어진 우리말과 같은 뜻이 되도록 괄호 안의 단어를 바르게 바꾸어 쓰세요.

- 우리는 그 꽃병이 깨진 것을 발견하고 모두 놀랐다.
  = We were all __________ (surprise) to find the vase __________. (break)

30 다음 중 밑줄 친 부분의 쓰임이 나머지와 다른 하나는?

① Going to the beach is exciting.
② The man kept looking at me.
③ I watched Linda crossing the street.
④ I just finished washing the dishes.
⑤ I love eating cookies.

31 다음 중 어법상 옳은 문장의 개수는?

ⓐ Looked after his sister, the boy was getting tired.
ⓑ With her legs crossing, Sara was sitting in front of them.
ⓒ The man wearing a red necktie is my boss, Mr. Lim.
ⓓ She found the guys talking behind her back.
ⓔ The door painting white looks bright and pretty.
ⓕ When Son finally scored a goal, the crowd got so excited.

① 0개   ② 1개   ③ 2개   ④ 3개   ⑤ 4개

32 다음 우리말을 영어로 바르게 옮긴 문장을 모두 고르세요.

Sally는 청구서를 보면서 앉아 있었다.

① Sally was sitting looked at the bill.
② Sally was sitting while look at the bill.
③ Sally was sitting while she looks at the bill.
④ Sally was sitting looking at the bill.
⑤ Sally was sitting while she was looking at the bill.

33 다음 빈칸에 들어갈 말끼리 바르게 짝지어진 것은?

M: What did you think of the movie?

W: It was very ____(A)____ . I was really looking forward to this movie's release because the original novel was really good. But it didn't meet my expectations at all.

M: I agree that the plot was changed a little. But, I didn't think it was that bad.

W: Come on! Sophie was not supposed to be that active.

M: But that made the movie more lively. It wasn't that ____(B)____ .

	(A)		(B)
①	annoyed	–	confusing
②	disappointed	–	confused
③	disappointing	–	disturbing
④	pleasing	–	confusing
⑤	annoying	–	disturbed

34 〈보기〉의 밑줄 친 단어 ⓐ~ⓒ를 문맥에 맞도록 바르게 활용한 것끼리 짝지은 것은?

The hikers followed the trail to the ⓐ <u>abandon</u> cabin in the woods. They were ⓑ <u>amaze</u> by the changed scenery after the storm. Scattered branches covered the path, ⓒ <u>make</u> their walk more difficult.

	ⓐ		ⓑ		ⓒ
①	abandoned	–	amazed	–	making
②	abandoned	–	amazed	–	made
③	abandon	–	amazing	–	make
④	abandoning	–	amazed	–	making
⑤	abandoned	–	amazing	–	made

35 〈보기〉에서 어법상 옳은 문장의 개수는?

보 기

(a) The pictures painted by my sister look amazing.

(b) The boy who wearing glasses is my cousin.

(c) Hearing the alarm, I jumped out of bed.

(d) I have a friend which loves science-fiction movies.

(e) The homework finished last night was quite difficult.

(f) The city where located the famous temple attracts many tourists.

(g) Students studying in the library must keep quiet.

(h) The cat that it sleeps on the roof every afternoon.

① 3개   ② 4개   ③ 5개   ④ 6개   ⑤ 7개

36 다음 글의 밑줄 친 (A)~(D) 중 어법상 <u>어색한</u> 것을 <u>2개</u> 골라 그 기호와 오류 부분을 쓰고, 바르게 고치세요.

Igloo

(A) <u>An igloo is a type of house building of snow, originally by the Inuit.</u> (B) <u>The name is from the Inuit word, *iglu*.</u> (C) <u>Igloo means snowhouse in English.</u> Have you ever imagined living in an igloo? (D) <u>It would be very excited.</u>

(1) • 기호: ___________

　　• 오류 부분: ___________

　　• 오류 수정: ___________

(2) • 기호: ___________

　　• 오류 부분: ___________

　　• 오류 수정: ___________

37 우리말과 같은 뜻이 되도록 밑줄 친 부분을 부사절로 바꿔 쓰세요.

> • 버스를 놓쳐서 나는 학교에 늦었다.
> ➡ <u>Missing the bus</u>, I was late for school.

= ________________________________,
I was late for school.

38 다음 대화의 ⓐ~ⓔ 중에서 그 쓰임이 같은 것끼리 짝지어진 것은?

> Mina: Jake, what are you doing?
> Jake: I am ⓐ <u>drawing</u> cartoons. My hobby is ⓑ <u>drawing</u> cartoons.
> Mina: Well, what are you ⓒ <u>drawing</u>?
> Jake: I am ⓓ <u>drawing</u> a rabbit.
> Mina: Wow. It's very cute. ⓔ <u>Drawing</u> cartoons is really hard, isn't it?
> Jake: No, it isn't.

① ⓐ,ⓒ,ⓔ   ② ⓑ,ⓒ,ⓓ   ③ ⓐ,ⓑ,ⓒ
④ ⓒ,ⓔ   ⑤ ⓑ,ⓔ

39 다음 우리말을 영어로 바르게 옮긴 것은?

> Michael은 눈을 감은 채 거기 서 있었다.

① Michael was standing there with his eyes closed.
② Michael was standing there his closed eyes.
③ Michael stood there with his eyes closing.
④ Michael was standing there with his eyes closing.
⑤ Michael was standing there with his eye closed.

40 〈보기〉에서 어법상 틀린 것을 있는 대로 고른 것은?

> 보 기
> ⓐ She leaned against the car <u>chat</u> with a friend.
> ⓑ I can express my emotions by <u>writing</u> them down.
> ⓒ I know the man <u>picking</u> up the garbage.
> ⓓ We were standing by the bed <u>watched</u> the baby sleeping.
> ⓔ James looked at me <u>sang</u> a song.

① ⓐ, ⓑ   ② ⓑ, ⓔ   ③ ⓐ, ⓑ, ⓒ
④ ⓐ, ⓓ, ⓔ   ⑤ ⓑ, ⓒ, ⓓ, ⓔ

41 다음 두 문장의 뜻이 같도록 빈칸에 들어갈 알맞은 말은?

> Studying diligently, he still struggled to pass the difficult exam.
> = ________________, he still struggled to pass the difficult exam.

① After he studied diligently
② Though he studied diligently
③ Because he studied diligently
④ When he studied diligently
⑤ And he studied diligently

42 두 문장의 빈칸에 공통으로 들어갈 단어로 가장 적절한 것은?

> • I ________ to the countryside last month because of my work.
> • He was ________ by her speech about loving one another.

① found   ② moved   ③ made
④ touched   ⑤ ran

CHAPTER 10
형용사

PSS 1 형용사의 쓰임

한정적 용법	명사의 앞에서 명사를 수식한다. Mr. Kim is a **great teacher**. 김 선생님은 훌륭한 선생님이다. I went to a **fancy restaurant** yesterday. 나는 어제 근사한 음식점에 갔다.
서술적 용법	주격 보어나 목적격 보어로 쓰여 주어나 목적어에 대한 설명을 한다. **The boy** over there is very **tall**. 저기 있는 소년은 키가 매우 크다. 　　　　　　　　　　　　　주격 보어 We think **the garden beautiful**. 우리는 그 정원이 아름답다고 생각한다. 　　　　　　　　　　　목적격 보어 *cf.* afraid, alike, alive, alone, ashamed, asleep, glad, sorry와 같은 형용사는 서술적 용법에만 사용된다. This ant is **alive**. (○) 이 개미는 살아있다. This is an **alive** ant. (×) My sister is **asleep**. (○) 내 여동생은 잠들었다. The **asleep** girl is my sister. (×)

정답 p.57

PRACTICE 1

괄호 안에 주어진 형용사를 알맞은 곳에 넣어 문장을 다시 쓰세요.

1 Becky has a car. (old)
➡ *Becky has an old car.*

2 Ms. Song is a doctor. (famous)
➡ _______________________________________

3 Mary is wearing a necklace. (beautiful)
➡ _______________________________________

4 I'd like to have coffee. (hot)
➡ _______________________________________

5 Paul watched a movie yesterday. (exciting)
➡ _______________________________________

6 Look at the bird over there. (small)
➡ _______________________________________

7 Inho used to live in an apartment. (large)

➡ ___________________________________

8 Could you pass me the ball? (blue)

➡ ___________________________________

9 Put them on the table. (plastic)

➡ ___________________________________

10 I drank tea last night. (Irish)

➡ ___________________________________

정답 p.57

PRACTICE 2

〈보기〉와 같이 주어진 문장을 바꾸어 쓰세요.

> 보 기　This is a long story.
> ➡ This _story is long_.

1 She is an intelligent woman.

➡ The ___________________________ .

2 It was an impressive movie.

➡ The ___________________________ .

3 This is an empty house.

➡ This ___________________________ .

4 That is a broken computer.

➡ That ___________________________ .

5 She is a diligent student.

➡ That ___________________________ .

6 These are famous artists.

➡ These ___________________________ .

정답 p.57

PRACTICE 3

괄호 안에 주어진 단어 중 알맞은 것을 고르세요.

1 The kids are (sleep, asleep) on the sofa.

2 The (sleeping, asleep) boy is my son.

3 What's she (like, alike)?

4 Did you see the (live, alive) starfish?

5 The boys look (like, alike).

6 The bird is still (live, alive).

7 I'm (glad, gladly) to hear the news.

8 Look at that (glad, cheerful) girl.

9 That (scared, afraid) boy is Minho.

10 I'm (scaring, afraid) of birds.

PSS 2 -thing, -one, -body + 형용사

-thing, -one, -body로 끝나는 대명사는 **형용사가 뒤에서 수식한다.**

Don't you have **anything special**? 너는 특별한 무언가를 가지고 있지 않니?
Jenny met **someone handsome** yesterday. Jenny는 어제 잘생긴 누군가를 만났다.
Do you know **anybody funny**? 너는 재미있는 누군가를 아니?
There was **nothing important** to see. 볼 만한 중요한 것이 없었다.

cf. 한 단어인 명사 thing은 형용사가 앞에서 수식한다.
I don't want to eat **sweet things**. 나는 달콤한 것들을 먹고 싶지 않다.

정답 p.57

PRACTICE 4

괄호 안에 주어진 단어를 바르게 배열하여 빈칸에 쓰세요.

1 I'd like to ___________________________ . (something, eat, spicy)

2 Was there ___________________________ ? (familiar, you, anybody, to)

3 I'm looking for ___________________________ . (for, the, diligent, someone, job)

4 Don't you ___________________________ ? (else, need, anything)

5 Would you like ___________________________ ? (something, drink, to, hot)

6 Have you ___________________________ in the police office? (friendly, met, anyone)

7 She ___________________________ when she needs help. (somebody, to, close, her, calls)

8 I couldn't ___________________________ . (expensive, yesterday, buy, anything)

9 I ___________________________ to tell you. (nothing, have, new)

10 I have ___________________________ near my home. (famous, seen, nobody)

PSS 3 주의해야 할 형용사의 용법

1. 「**the+형용사**」는 '~한 사람들'의 뜻으로, 복수 명사처럼 쓰인다.

He has helped **the poor** for three years. 그는 3년 동안 불쌍한 사람들을 도왔다.
(= poor people)

This seat is for **the old**. 이 자리는 노인들을 위한 것이다.
       (= old people)
The young are interested in foreign languages. 젊은 사람들은 외국어에 흥미가 있다.
(= Young people)

2. 국가와 관련된 형용사는 주로 국가명에 -n, -sh, -ch, -s, -ese를 붙여 만든다. 이 형태는 형용사뿐 아니라 해당 국가의 언어, 그 국가의 사람을 나타내는 명사로도 쓰인다.

England 영국(명사)
English 영국(인)의, 영어의(형용사), 영국인, 영어(명사)
They don't enjoy **English** breakfast. 그들은 영국식 아침식사를 즐기지 않는다.

주요 국가명과 형용사형

국가명	형용사형	국가명	형용사형
Korea 한국	Korean 한국의	Spain 스페인	Spanish 스페인의
America 미국	American 미국의	China 중국	Chinese 중국의
Canada 캐나다	Canadian 캐니디의	Japan 일본	Japanese 일본의
Poland 폴란드	Polish 폴란드의	France 프랑스	French 프랑스의
Denmark 덴마크	Danish 덴마크의	Germany 독일	German 독일의
Switzerland 스위스	Swiss 스위스의	the Netherlands 네덜란드	Dutch 네덜란드의

cf. 「the+국가명의 형용사」는 '국민 전체'를 의미한다.
   the Chinese 중국인 전체   **the French** 프랑스인 전체

단, 형용사 형태가 -sh, -ch, -s, -ese로 끝나지 않는 경우는 -s를 붙인 복수 형태로 국민 전체를 나타낸다.
   the Koreans 한국인들   **the Americans** 미국인들

정답 p.58

PRACTICE 5 [1-6]

〈보기〉와 같이 주어진 문장을 바꾸어 쓰세요.

> 보 기   You should respect old people.
> ➡ You should respect the old.

1 Rich people have their own problems.
   ➡ ____

2 He did a lot of good things for poor people.
   ➡ ____

3 These days blind people keep dogs to help themselves.

➡ ____

4 There are some special schools for deaf people.

➡ ____

5 Mr. Park encourages young people to be brave.

➡ ____

6 I took care of sick people in the hospital yesterday.

➡ ____

정답 p.58

PRACTICE 6

괄호 안에 주어진 단어 중 어법상 알맞은 것을 고르세요.

1 The old (has / have) to exercise regularly.

2 Do (a / the) sick take a lot of medicine?

3 Are the (rich / richly) getting richer?

4 The blind (learn / learns) a special way of reading.

5 The hospital for the elderly (was / were) built last year.

6 The young sometimes (needs / need) guidance from the older generation.

정답 p.58

PRACTICE 7

다음 밑줄 친 단어가 문장에서 어떤 의미로 쓰였는지 빈칸에 쓰세요.

1 Mike has always wanted to learn Korean.   ____________

2 Sarah is an American but she doesn't like traditional American food.   ________ , ________

3 The Polish feel proud of their country.   ____________

4 French women are known for their elegant fashion sense.   ____________

5 My sister has studied German for five years.   ____________

6 Danish dairy products are world-famous.   ____________

7 Have you ever eaten Japanese food?   ____________

8 Chinese is hard to learn because of four intonations.   ____________

9 She found Korean culture similar to Canadian culture.   ____________

10 Spanish is the language spoken by the Argentine people.   ____________

PSS 4 형용사의 어순

1. 2개 이상의 형용사가 함께 쓰일 때는 주로 다음과 같은 어순을 원칙으로 한다.

서수	기수	성질	크기	신구	색깔	국적	재료
first	two	nice	big	new	blue	Korean	wooden
third	four	pretty	small	old	green	English	plastic
tenth	seven	delicious	large	young	red	French	metal

2. 다음은 형용사 앞에 다른 수식어가 올 때의 어순이다.

all both
double half

+

정관사	the
지시형용사	this that these those
소유격	my your his her its our their

정답 p.58

PRACTICE 8

괄호 안에 주어진 단어를 바르게 배열하여 빈칸에 쓰세요.

1 ______________________ dogs (big, white)

2 ______________________ girls (four, all, Korean)

3 ______________________ gardens (green, large)

4 ______________________ vases (metal, small, seven)

5 ______________________ shirts (nice, blue, those)

6 ______________________ roses (red, the, beautiful)

7 ______________________ friend (French, young, my)

8 ______________________ sentences (first, the, two)

9 ______________________ chairs (wooden, comfortable)

10 ______________________ people (million, a, half)

11 ______________________ buildings (beautiful, both, these)

12 ______________________ matches (her, three, all)

PRACTICE 9

다음 문장의 밑줄 친 부분을 바르게 고쳐 쓰세요.

1 I met tall a Japanese woman yesterday. *a tall Japanese*

2 He knows the both pretty girls.

3 She loved her new nice friends.

4 Would you like small this piece of cake?

5 Look at high three those buildings!

6 I like the American exciting movies.

7 They threw black ugly the plastic boxes away.

8 Dain bought these all lovely dolls.

9 My older wise brother told me what to do.

10 Put the book on that white big table.

11 The restaurant is famous for Chinese its nice food.

12 Samuel is the English fifth happy traveler that we've met.

13 I have seen her all three pink sweaters.

14 We were watching young healthy four lions.

15 Abby had red two fresh apples for breakfast.

PSS 5 수나 양을 나타내는 형용사

PSS 5-1 many, much

many – '많은'의 뜻으로 셀 수 있는 명사의 수를 나타낸다.

many trees 많은 나무들

= **a lot of** trees

= **lots of** trees

= **plenty of** trees

= **a number of** trees

Many people use computers.

많은 사람들이 컴퓨터를 사용한다.

How **many students** are there?

얼마나 많은 학생들이 있니?

much – '많은'의 뜻으로 셀 수 없는 명사의 양을 나타낸다.

much money 많은 돈

= **a lot of** money

= **lots of** money

= **plenty of** money

I have so **much work** to do.

나는 아주 많은 할 일이 있다.

How **much food** did you buy?

얼마나 많은 음식을 샀니?

정답 p.59

PRACTICE 10

다음 문장의 빈칸에 many나 much 중 알맞은 것을 쓰세요.

1 Were there __________ kids in the park?

2 There isn't __________ time to waste.

3 There were __________ cars on the road.

4 How __________ water do you drink a day?

5 Ava has __________ kinds of toys in her room.

6 Did he make __________ money through the business?

7 __________ old people live alone in this town.

8 He made so __________ mistakes.

9 How __________ children does he have?

10 Make sure you don't drink too __________ coffee at night.

정답 p.59

PRACTICE 11 [1-10]

밑줄 친 부분을 many나 much로 바꾸어 문장을 다시 쓰세요.

1 Does Minho have a lot of friends?

➡ ____

2 Does it take lots of time to get there on foot?

➡ ____

3 Are there <u>plenty of</u> flowers in the vase?

➡ ____

4 <u>Lots of</u> drivers drive very fast.

➡ ____

5 Should I give the plants <u>a lot of</u> water?

➡ ____

6 <u>Plenty of</u> students stayed in the classroom after school.

➡ ____

7 I don't have <u>a lot of</u> homework today.

➡ ____

8 Did they spend <u>plenty of</u> money on this house?

➡ ____

9 We didn't have <u>lots of</u> fun.

➡ ____

10 Did you borrow <u>a lot of</u> books from the library?

➡ ____

PSS 5-2 few, little

few＋셀 수 있는 명사의 복수형

little＋셀 수 없는 명사

few – '거의 ~없는'의 뜻으로 셀 수 있는 명사의 수를 나타낸다.

There are **few people** on the street.

거리에 사람들이 거의 없다.

Peter has **few friends**.

Peter는 친구들이 거의 없다.

little – '거의 ~없는'의 뜻으로 셀 수 없는 명사의 양을 나타낸다.

There is **little water** in the bottle.

병에 물이 거의 없다.

I had **little time** to prepare dinner.

나는 저녁을 준비할 시간이 거의 없었다.

PRACTICE 12

다음 문장의 빈칸에 few나 little 중 알맞은 것을 쓰세요.

1 I'm not busy today. I have ___________ things to do.

2 She couldn't buy the clothes because she had ___________ money then.

3 We have ___________ milk in the refrigerator. Let's buy some.

4 I like to go jogging, but there are ___________ parks in this city.

5 Nami did the job very well. She made ___________ mistakes.

6 It's hotter today because there is ___________ wind.

7 I met ___________ foreigners in this small village.

8 There is ___________ space left in the car.

9 Help yourself to these cookies. I put ___________ sugar in them.

10 There were ___________ people in the gallery.

PSS 5-3 a few, a little

a few + 셀 수 있는 명사의 복수형

a little + 셀 수 없는 명사

a few – '조금의, 몇 개의'의 뜻으로 셀 수 있는 명사의 수를 나타낸다.

a little – '약간의'의 뜻으로 셀 수 없는 명사의 양을 나타낸다.

There are **a few pens** on the desk.

책상에 몇 개의 펜들이 있다.

I borrowed **a few books** yesterday.

나는 어제 몇 권의 책을 빌렸다.

There is **a little sugar** left.

약간의 설탕이 남아 있다.

Andy had **a little bread** for lunch.

Andy는 점심으로 약간의 빵을 먹었다.

PRACTICE 13

다음 문장의 빈칸에 a few나 a little 중 알맞은 것을 쓰세요.

1 I bought this bag ___________ days ago.

2 You need ___________ water to take this medicine.

3 ___________ girls were talking about the movie.

4 Tom has ___________ trouble doing his math homework.

5 It will take ___________ time to solve the problem.

6 My neighbor has ___________ dogs and cats.

7 I melted ___________ butter on the pan.

8 Sangmin met ___________ friends on the way to school.

9 Do you have ___________ knowledge about computers?

10 She came home ___________ hours later.

PRACTICE 14

다음 밑줄 친 부분을 바르게 고쳐 쓰세요. (단, 문장에서 원래 의도한 의미를 그대로 살리세요.)

1 I don't have <u>many</u> hope for that. ___________

2 He has been reading this book for <u>a little</u> days. ___________

3 I have <u>a few</u> money. Shall I buy you an ice cream? ___________

4 Alex used to exercise for <u>much</u> hours. ___________

5 My brother has <u>little</u> bad teeth. ___________

6 There is <u>few</u> ice in the refrigerator. ___________

7 Insu has been there <u>a little</u> times. ___________

8 There was <u>few</u> light in the dark street. ___________

9 There aren't <u>much</u> restaurants in this town. ___________

10 They bought <u>a few</u> meat for dinner. ___________

11 There's not <u>many</u> traffic now. ___________

12 <u>Little</u> members voted for him. ___________

A: Would you like **some sandwiches**? 샌드위치 좀 먹겠니?

B: No, thanks. I don't have **any time**. I have to go out now.

감사하지만 사양할게요. 저는 시간이 없어요. 저는 지금 나가야 해요.

some과 any는 '얼마간의, 약간의'의 뜻으로 셀 수 있는 명사나 셀 수 없는 명사 모두와 함께 쓸 수 있다.

some	any
1. 일반적으로 긍정문에 쓰인다. Junho gave me **some** eggs. 준호는 내게 약간의 달걀을 주었다. 2. 권유, 요구를 나타내는 의문문에 쓰인다. Would you like **some** salad? 샐러드 좀 드실래요? Can I have **some** water? 물 좀 마실 수 있을까요? 3. 긍정의 대답을 예상하는 의문문에 쓰인다. Were there **some** phone calls for me? 내게 온 전화가 좀 있었나요? 4. some이 불특정한 일부를 나타낼 때는 부정문에 쓸 수 있다. **Some** students don't obey the school's policy. 몇몇 학생들은 학교의 방침을 준수하지 않는다.	1. 일반적으로 부정문과 의문문에 쓰인다. I don't have **any** classes this Saturday. 나는 이번 토요일에 수업이 하나도 없다. Do you have **any** ideas about how to help her? 넌 그녀를 어떻게 도울지에 대한 생각이 좀 있니? 2. '어떠한 ~라도'의 뜻으로 긍정문에 쓰인다. You can take **any** bus here. 넌 여기에서 어떠한 버스라도 탈 수 있다. 3. 조건을 나타내는 if절에 쓰인다. If you have **any** questions, call me anytime. 질문이 있으면, 내게 언제든 전화해요.

PRACTICE 15

우리말과 일치하도록 다음 문장의 빈칸에 some이나 any 중 알맞은 것을 쓰세요.

1 그녀는 아침에 약간의 과일을 먹었다.

➡ She had _________________ fruit in the morning.

2 그는 필기할 펜이 하나도 없었다.

➡ He didn't have _________________ pens to write with.

3 도서관에서 약간의 책을 빌릴 수 있나요?

➡ Can I borrow _________________ books from the library?

4 이 챕터에 대해 어떠한 질문이라도 있나요?

➡ Are there _________________ questions about this chapter?

5 어떤 기차라도 당신을 그곳에 데려다 줄 거예요.

➡ _________________ train will take you there.

6 밥을 좀 더 (드시길) 원하세요?

➡ Do you want _________________ more rice?

7 Mary는 그들로부터 어떠한 충고도 얻지 못했다.

➡ Mary didn't get _________________ advice from them.

8 Jina와 나는 오늘 밤 약간의 계획이 있다.

➡ Jina and I have _________________ plans for tonight.

9 만약 내게 어떤 문제라도 생긴다면, 당신에게 전화할게요.

➡ If I have _________________ trouble, I'll call you.

10 저는 당신으로부터 어떠한 도움도 필요하지 않아요.

➡ I don't need _________________ help from you.

PRACTICE 16

〈보기〉에서 알맞은 단어를 골라 some이나 any를 이용하여 문장을 완성하세요.

보 기	people medicine friends money problems flowers time cake homework place food

1 Mr. Kim gave the students ___some homework___ for today.

2 I'm very hungry, but I don't have _________________ to eat.

3 The news said _________________ died in the accident last night.

4 If you have _________________, let me know. I can help you.

5 I bought _________________ from the drugstore.

6 We can go to _________________ except that unpleasant restaurant.

7 Giho gave me _________________________________ for my birthday.

8 Do you have _________________________________ living around here?

9 I don't have _________________ to take care of it. I have to go out.

10 Would you like _________________ and juice for dessert?

11 Would you mind lending me _________________________________? I'll pay you back soon.

PSS 6 수사

PSS 6 - 1 분수와 소수

1. 분수 – 분자는 기수로, 분모는 서수로 읽고, 분자가 2 이상이면 분모에 '-s'를 붙여 읽는다.

1/5 ➡ a fifth 또는 one-fifth   3/8 ➡ three-eighths

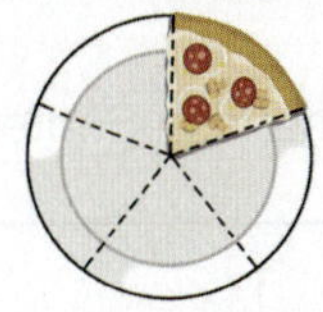
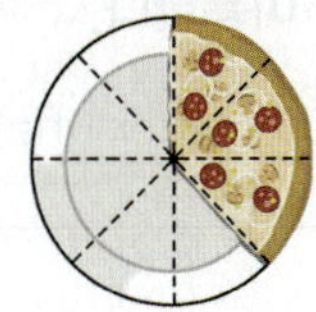

5 3/4 ➡ five and three-fourths [three-quarters]

cf. 1/2 ➡ a half 또는 one-half   1/4 ➡ a fourth 또는 one-fourth

a quarter 또는 one-quarter

2. 소수 – 소수점까지는 기수로, 소수점은 point, 소수점 이하는 한 자리씩 읽는다.

4.25 ➡ four point two five   13.87 ➡ thirteen point eight seven

정답 p.60

PRACTICE 17 [1-15]

다음 분수와 소수를 영어로 읽을 때의 표기법을 쓰세요.

1 1/3   ➡ _________________________

2 2/5   ➡ _________________________

3 2 7/11 ➡ _________________________

4 5/6   ➡ _________________________

5 1/2   ➡ _________________________

6 9/13   ➡ _________________________

7 1/4   ➡ _________________________

8 4 3/7 ➡ _________________________

9 3.14   ➡ _________________________

10 5.56   ➡ _________________________

11 16.29   ➡ _________________________   **12** 50.15 ➡ _________________________

13 127.93 ➡ _________________________

14 612.49 ➡ _________________________

15 2,105.89 ➡ _________________________

PSS 6-2 연도와 날짜

1. **연도 – 두 자리씩 끊어 읽는다.**

   1785년 ➡ seventeen eighty-five   1998년 ➡ nineteen ninety-eight
   cf. 2002년 ➡ two thousand (and) two   2019년 ➡ two thousand (and) nineteen
                                                    twenty nineteen

2. **날짜 – 서수를 이용한다.**

   9월 22일 ➡ September (the) twenty-second 또는 the twenty-second of September

정답 p.60

PRACTICE 18

다음 연도와 날짜를 영어로 읽을 때의 표기법을 쓰세요.

1 1826년   ➡ _________________________

2 1983년   ➡ _________________________

3 2004년   ➡ _________________________

4 2020년   ➡ _________________________

5 5월 1일   ➡ _________________________

6 7월 12일 ➡ _________________________

7 2월 18일 ➡ _________________________

8 11월 24일 ➡ _________________________

9 4월 23일 ➡ _________________________

10 12월 9일 ➡ _________________________

배수사는 once(1배), twice(2배), 그 이후부터는 「기수＋times」(~배)로 나타낸다.

My bag is **three times** as heavy as yours. 내 가방은 네 것보다 3배 무겁다.

= My bag is **three times** heavier than yours.

Insu has **four times** as many clothes as I have.

인수는 내가 가지고 있는 것보다 4배 많은 옷을 가지고 있다.

cf. 배수사를 이용하여 횟수를 나타낼 수 있으며, 횟수를 물어볼 때는 How often ~?을 쓴다.

once a week 일주일에 한 번　　**twice** a month 한 달에 두 번

I have been to Europe **once**. 나는 유럽에 한 번 가본 적이 있다.

정답 p.60

PRACTICE 19

우리말과 같은 뜻이 되도록 빈칸에 알맞은 말을 쓰세요.

1 나는 그녀를 딱 한 번 만났다.

➡ I have met her only ________________.

2 글루텐을 함유하지 않은 빵은 일반 빵보다 거의 3배만큼 비싸다.

➡ Gluten-free bread is nearly ________________ as expensive as regular bread.

3 나는 일주일에 6번 수영하러 가곤 했다.

➡ I used to go swimming ________________ a week.

4 이 연필은 저 연필보다 4배 길다.

➡ This pencil is ________________ as long as that one.

5 저 나무들은 이 나무들보다 5배 크다.

➡ Those trees are ________________ taller than these ones.

6 그들은 부산에 두 번 가본 적이 있다.

➡ They have been to Busan ________________.

7 노란 상자는 빨간 상자보다 10배 무겁다.

➡ The yellow box is ________________ as heavy as the red box.

8 우리 부모님은 한 달에 한 번 등산을 하신다.

➡ My parents go hiking ________________ a month.

9 그녀의 개는 너의 개보다 세 배 크다.

➡ Her dog is ________________ bigger than yours.

10 나는 1년에 8번 제주도에 간다.

➡ I go to Jejudo ________________ a year.

CH
10
형용사

1 다음 글의 빈칸 (A)~(C)에 들어갈 말이 바르게 나열된 것은?

> People in the world greet each other in different ways. When ____(A)____ meet their neighbors or friends, they say *Annyeonghaseyo*. Indian people say *Namaste* when they meet somebody. It means "I respect you." They usually put their hands together at their chest and bow a little when saying this. In ____(B)____, the weather changes quickly. For example, the sun shines strongly in the morning, but later it rains. Then the rain suddenly stops. So, ____(C)____ people are happy when the weather is fine. They always wish for good weather when they say hello.

	(A)	(B)	(C)
①	Korea	– English	– English
②	Korean	– England	– England
③	Koreans	– England	– English
④	Korea	– England	– English
⑤	Koreans	– English	– England

2 다음 중 어법상 잘못된 것은?

① There's nothing wrong with the machine.
② Is there anyone left in the bus?
③ Two thirds of the boys in our class like soccer.
④ Amanda's suitcase is twice as heavy as her brother's.
⑤ She said that she didn't enjoy things sweet.

3 밑줄 친 우리말과 같은 뜻이 되도록 괄호 안에 주어진 단어를 배열하여 문장을 만들 때, 네 번째로 오는 단어는?

> G: Ted, 게시판에 뭐 흥미로운 것이라도 있니? (the, interesting, there, on, is, anything, board)
> B: Hey, Lisa. Look at this poster. It's about the school dance contest this year.
> G: Oh, are you thinking of entering it?
> B: Yeah, you know I like to dance. The contest will be on September 30th. So I have two months to practice.

① the　　② interesting　　③ on
④ anything　　⑤ board

4 다음 중 어법상 올바른 문장은?

① He wore a long black jacket and a red nice tie.
② He wore a black long jacket and a nice red tie.
③ He wore a black long jacket and a red nice tie.
④ He wore a long black jacket and a nice red tie.
⑤ He weared a black long jacket and a nice red tie.

5 다음 문장에서 틀린 부분을 찾아 바르게 고치세요.

> Some people think it is more important to be health than to have a lot of money.

__________________ ➡ __________________

6 다음 빈칸에 들어갈 말로 알맞은 것은?

_____________ minutes later, a stranger came up to me and asked me for some money.

① Much   ② A few   ③ Little
④ A little   ⑤ Any

7 그림을 보고, 밑줄 친 우리말에 맞도록 괄호 안의 말을 바르게 배열하세요.

A: Are you hungry?
B: Yes. 뭐 먹을 만한 맛있는 것 좀 있니?
  ➡ _____________________________________
  _________________________ (something, to eat, you, do, have, delicious)

8 다음 대화 중 흐름상 어색한 것은?

① A: How much money do you have now?
   B: About 5 dollars.
② A: How old is your grandmother?
   B: She is 89 years old.
③ A: How long does it take to get to the airport?
   B: It takes about 30 minutes.
④ A: How often do you take a shower?
   B: I took a shower yesterday.
⑤ A: How many eggs do you have?
   B: I don't have any.

9 다음 중 올바른 표현은 몇 개인가?

ⓐ A few years ago, Jina gave piano lessons.
ⓑ I'd like to have a few soup.
ⓒ The chef added a little hot sauce to the dish.
ⓓ Very few students understood her speech.
ⓔ He's on a diet and eats little sugar.

① 1개   ② 2개   ③ 3개   ④ 4개   ⑤ 5개

10 다음 빈칸에 들어갈 말이 바르게 연결된 것은?

- I borrowed _____________ books from the library.
- Does she have _____________ friends?
- Do you drink _____________ water?
- There is _____________ money left.

① a few – much – a few – a little
② a few – many – much – a little
③ a few – many – a little – few
④ much – a little – many – a few
⑤ much – few   – a few – a little

11 수미가 테니스를 치는 날을 색칠해둔 달력을 보고 질문에 대한 답을 완성하세요.

Sun	Mon	Tue	Wed	Thu	Fri	Sat
		1	2	3	4	5
6	7	8	9	10	11	12
13	14	15	16	17	18	19
20	21	22	23	24	25	26
27	28	29	30			

Q: How often a week does Sumi play tennis?
A: She plays tennis __________ __________ __________.

12 우리말 뜻과 일치하도록 괄호 안의 말을 바르게 배열하여 문장을 완성하세요.

> • 셰익스피어는 보통 사람의 3배만큼 많은 어휘를 알았다.
>
> = Shakespeare knew ＿＿＿＿＿＿＿＿＿
>
> ＿＿＿＿＿＿＿＿＿＿＿＿＿＿＿.
>
> (average, three times, as, person, words, an, many, as)

13 그림을 보고 주어진 단어를 사용하여 다음 대화를 완성하세요.

> A: How much food is left in the refrigerator?
>
> B: ＿＿＿＿＿＿＿＿＿＿＿＿＿＿
>
> ＿＿＿＿＿＿＿＿＿ (there, little, food)

14 다음 대화의 밑줄 친 부분 중 어법상 어색한 것은?

> Ted　　 : ① This Friday is Minji's birthday.
>
> Jiyeon: I know. ② What should we get her?
>
> Ted　　 : Well, ③ how about a really interesting book?
>
> Jiyeon: That sounds good. ④ Did you hear that she's going to invite her all friends?
>
> Ted　　 : No, I didn't know that. ⑤ It'll be very fun.

15 다음 중 밑줄 친 부분이 어법상 <u>어색한</u> 것은?

① Would you like <u>some</u> coffee?

② He put <u>some</u> food in his bag.

③ He doesn't have <u>any</u> friends.

④ Do you have <u>any</u> special plans?

⑤ I bought <u>any</u> oranges at the market.

16 다음 문장의 빈칸 중 어떤 위치에도 들어갈 수 <u>없는</u> 단어는?

> ⓐ I apply sunscreen in order to ＿＿＿＿ sunburn.
>
> ⓑ You have to be ＿＿＿＿ when you take important tests.
>
> ⓒ I don't know what I should wear for the ＿＿＿＿ ceremony.
>
> ⓓ He can't walk ＿＿＿＿ after the injury.
>
> ⓔ The subway was ＿＿＿＿ with people during rush hour.

① graduation　　② crowded　　③ prevent

④ confidence　　⑤ properly

17 다음 문장의 밑줄 친 부분과 동일한 의미의 <u>다른</u> 표현 <u>2개</u>를 영어로 쓰세요.

> Is there <u>a lot of</u> paper on the desk?

➡ ＿＿＿＿＿＿＿＿＿＿＿＿＿＿

＿＿＿＿＿＿＿＿＿＿＿＿＿＿

18 다음 글의 밑줄 친 (A)~(E) 중 어법상 어색한 것 <u>2개</u>를 골라 그 기호를 쓰고 바르게 고치세요.

(A) <u>Have you ever seen</u> this painting?
(B) <u>Its</u> title is *Portrait of Doctor Gachet* and it is one of the most famous paintings by Vincent van Gogh. The subject of the painting is Paul Gachet, a doctor (C) <u>who</u> took care of Van Gogh during the last months of his life. In May 1990, the portrait was sold at auction for $82.5 million to a (D) <u>Japan</u> businessman. This surprised (E) <u>much</u> people at the auction, since no one expected that the painting would sell for so much. It continues to be one of the highest prices ever paid for a painting at auction.

➡ __________________ , __________________

19 다음 빈칸 (A), (B)에 들어갈 말이 바르게 짝지어진 것은?

- You look _____ (A) _____ .
- I can't see _____ (B) _____ with the final report.

	(A)		(B)
①	sad	–	anything wrong
②	sadly	–	anything wrong
③	sad	–	wrong anything
④	sadly	–	wrong anything
⑤	sadly	–	something wrong

20 〈보기〉의 밑줄 친 light와 뜻이 같은 문장끼리 짝지어진 것은?

> 보 기
> Many hands make <u>light</u> work.

> ⓐ Kevin left a <u>light</u> on in the kitchen.
> ⓑ A smile <u>lights</u> up his whole face.
> ⓒ Our guide used a candle to <u>light</u> the way.
> ⓓ My son started to do a little <u>light</u> housework.
> ⓔ The windows let fresh air and <u>light</u> into the room.
> ⓕ The doctor advised me to take regular <u>light</u> exercise.

① ⓐ,ⓕ   ② ⓑ,ⓔ   ③ ⓑ,ⓕ
④ ⓒ,ⓔ   ⑤ ⓓ,ⓕ

21 다음 밑줄 친 (A)~(E) 중 어법상 어색한 것을 모두 고르세요.

> People from different cultures get together for (A) <u>various</u> purposes. For example, your job may make you (B) <u>to attend</u> a meeting with a foreign client. Or you may travel to a country with a language you don't speak at all. The first thing you can do is (C) <u>to make</u> a small effort. You can learn (D) <u>a little</u> basic expressions such as "Thank you," and "It's nice to meet you." It is a great way to show your respect for (E) <u>other</u> cultures.

① (A)   ② (B)   ③ (C)
④ (D)   ⑤ (E)

22 다음 대화의 밑줄 친 (A)~(E) 중 어법상 어색한 것은?

Insu : Would you like (A) some chocolate?

Yunji: No, thank you. I've gained too (B) much weight, so I'm on a diet.

Insu : Really? My mother gets stressed when she is on a diet.

Yunji: Why?

Insu : She likes eating (C) something sweet such as chocolate.

Yunji: Actually, I'm under (D) a number of stress, too.

Insu : Well, do you exercise to lose weight?

Yunji: No, I dislike (E) exercising.

① (A)　　② (B)　　③ (C)　　④ (D)　　⑤ (E)

23 다음 중 우리말 해석과 일치하지 <u>않는</u> 문장을 <u>모두</u> 고르세요.

① 내 여동생은 그녀를 도와줄 친구들이 거의 없다.
→ My sister has a few friends to help her.

② 지난 여름에 비가 많이 내리지 않았다.
→ We didn't have much rain last summer.

③ 나는 약간의 오렌지를 샀다.
→ I bought some oranges.

④ 소수의 사람들이 나를 비웃고 있었다.
→ A number of people were laughing at me.

⑤ 놀이터에 많은 어린이들이 있다.
→ There are many children in the playground.

24 다음을 영어로 바르게 읽은 것을 <u>모두</u> 고르세요.

① 3/5: three-fifth

② 2013년: two thousand (and) thirteen

③ 5월 15일: the fifteen of May

④ 25.43: twenty-five point four three

⑤ 1974년: one thousand nine hundred and seventy four

25 다음 중 밑줄 친 부분의 쓰임이 <u>올바른</u> 것은?

① I have <u>a white small</u> cat.

② <u>My all</u> neighbors are very kind.

③ <u>Her big brown</u> eyes are beautiful.

④ <u>These both</u> sweaters are mine.

⑤ I need <u>a wooden new</u> box.

26 밑줄 친 (a)~(e) 중 어법상 <u>틀린</u> 것을 고르시오.

The new Green Garden behind our school (a) <u>is cared for</u> by students. Every morning, the automatic sprinkler waters the plants (b) <u>for</u> ten minutes. The gardening club members pride (c) <u>themselves</u> on keeping the soil healthy. Last week, fresh compost was delivered to the garden by the city's recycling team. (d) <u>To grow</u> fresh vegetables for lunch is our long-term goal. Unfortunately, we have (e) <u>few</u> sunshine during the rainy season.　　*compost: 퇴비, 비료

① (a)　　　② (b)　　　③ (c)

④ (d)　　　⑤ (e)

27 다음 두 문장이 같은 뜻이 되도록 빈칸에 알맞은 단어를 쓰세요.

- People who are old have a lot of experiences.
  = The ___________ ___________ a lot of experiences.

28 괄호 안의 단어들을 알맞게 배열하여 대화를 완성하세요.

Danny: Hey, guess what? It's almost my birthday!

Sunny: Really? That's great! What do you want as a gift?

Danny: Not sure.

Sunny: Here's ___________________________.
(you, special, for, something)
How about a weekend getaway to a nearby resort?

Danny: Wow, that sounds amazing! I'd love that!

29 ⓐ~ⓔ 중 어법상 올바른 것끼리 묶인 것은?

ⓐ Her song makes me sadly.
ⓑ The injured need to be moved to the hospital quickly.
ⓒ Could you give me warm something to drink?
ⓓ My mother planted some white big flowers in the garden.
ⓔ A little bread is left on the table.

① ⓑ, ⓓ   ② ⓑ, ⓔ   ③ ⓐ, ⓓ, ⓔ
④ ⓐ, ⓑ, ⓓ   ⑤ ⓒ, ⓓ, ⓔ

30 다음 중 어법상 어색한 문장은?

① If you have any questions, feel free to ask me.
② Any child could sing better than those people.
③ Would you like some dessert?
④ I don't have some money.
⑤ Some people don't like the idea.

31 다음 중 밑줄 친 부분의 뜻이 틀린 것은?

① Koreans want to master foreign languages in a short time. (한국인들)
② It's difficult to learn French. (프랑스어)
③ He fell in love with a German. (독일인)
④ The Chinese drink tea at any time of day. (중국인 한 명)
⑤ American restaurants often serve iced water with meals. (미국의)

32 다음 대화에서 틀린 부분을 2개 찾아 바르게 고치세요.

Tutor : I won't give you some homework today.

Student: Wow, thank you. I have few time to do homework today.

Tutor : Why?

Student: I have to take care of my three little brothers this evening.

(1) ___________________ ➡ ___________________

(2) ___________________ ➡ ___________________

33 다음 밑줄 친 말과 바꾸어 쓸 수 있는 것은?

> There are a number of monkeys in this zoo.

① much ② many ③ a lot
④ huge ⑤ few

34 ⓐ~ⓔ 중 어법이 틀린 것은?

> Short-form content is currently trending. As the name suggests, it refers to any type of media that is designed ⓐ to be consumed quickly. It can be as short as ⓑ a little seconds to minutes. It's become more and more prominent with the growth of social media platforms. Then, how come short-form content is popular? These days, people are ⓒ distracted more easily. So, it's easier for short and highly stimulating content ⓓ to grab consumers' attention. However, short-form content can prevent you from ⓔ thinking critically, so be mindful not to consume too much of it.

① ⓐ ② ⓑ ③ ⓒ ④ ⓓ ⑤ ⓔ

35 다음 밑줄 친 부분을 틀리게 고친 것은?

① The ten-years-old(→ ten-year-old) building was finally demolished.
② She gave me an advice(→ a piece of advice) about studying.
③ Mom wore a silk beautiful scarf(→ a scarf beautiful silk).
④ I met a very interestingly(→ interesting) person yesterday.
⑤ She looked happily(→ happy) when she saw the puppy.

36 다음 중 영어로 바르게 표기한 것을 모두 고르세요.

> a. 12월 13일 → The thirteenth of December
> b. ¾ → three-quarters
> c. 1689년 → one six hundred eighty-nine
> d. ⅛ → an eighths
> e. 15.76 → one five point seven six
> f. 2020년 → twenty twenty

① a, c ② a, b, f ③ a, b, c, d
④ b, d, e ⑤ b, e, f

37 다음 중 어법상 올바르지 않은 것을 모두 고르세요.

① Giho went on a picnic yesterday.
② I made some money during the last vacation.
③ Do good something for your mother.
④ Finish your homework by 7 o'clock.
⑤ The wounded was rescued by emergency workers.

38 다음 빈칸에 공통으로 들어갈 말로 알맞은 것은?

> • I didn't eat __________ meat today.
> • She isn't feeling __________ better.

① some ② any ③ many
④ few ⑤ little

CHAPTER 11
부사

PSS 1 부사의 형태

PSS 1-1 형용사를 부사로 만드는 법 I

일반적인 경우	형용사+ly	polite – polite**ly** 예의 바른 예의 바르게 real – real**ly** 진짜의 정말로 final – final**ly** 마지막의 마지막으로 sincere – sincere**ly** 진실의 진정으로	sudden – sudden**ly** 갑작스러운 갑자기 certain – certain**ly** 확실한 확실히 quick – quick**ly** 빠른 빨리 slight – slight**ly** 약간의 약간
자음+y로 끝나는 경우	자음+i+ly	lucky – luck**ily** 운 좋은 운 좋게도 angry – angr**ily** 화난 노하여 busy – bus**ily** 바쁜 바쁘게	happy – happ**ily** 행복한 행복하게 easy – eas**ily** 쉬운 쉽게 heavy – heav**ily** 무거운 무겁게

정답 p.64

PRACTICE 1

다음 형용사의 부사형을 쓰세요.

1	wide ➡ __________	2	sincere ➡ __________
3	happy ➡ __________	4	polite ➡ __________
5	slow ➡ __________	6	slight ➡ __________
7	final ➡ __________	8	easy ➡ __________
9	lucky ➡ __________	10	quiet ➡ __________
11	careful ➡ __________	12	certain ➡ __________
13	sudden ➡ __________	14	sad ➡ __________
15	busy ➡ __________	16	beautiful ➡ __________
17	real ➡ __________	18	angry ➡ __________
19	quick ➡ __________	20	soft ➡ __________

-le로 끝나는 경우	-le → -ly	gentle – gent**ly** 온화한 온화하게	simple – simp**ly** 간단한 간단히
		terrible – terrib**ly** 무서운 무섭게	reasonable – reasonab**ly** 합리적인 합리적으로
		visible – visib**ly** 눈에 보이는 눈에 보이게	comfortable – comfortab**ly** 편안한 편안하게
-ue로 끝나는 경우	-ue → -uly	true – tru**ly** 진실의 진실로	
-ll로 끝나는 경우	-ll → -lly	full – ful**ly** 충분한 충분히	dull – dul**ly** 우둔한 우둔하게

정답 p.64

PRACTICE 2

다음 형용사의 부사형을 쓰세요.

1 visible ➡ _______________
2 simple ➡ _______________

3 dull ➡ _______________
4 true ➡ _______________

5 loud ➡ _______________
6 gentle ➡ _______________

7 nice ➡ _______________
8 serious ➡ _______________

9 heavy ➡ _______________
10 clear ➡ _______________

11 safe ➡ _______________
12 full ➡ _______________

13 pretty ➡ _______________
14 anxious ➡ _______________

15 main ➡ _______________
16 foolish ➡ _______________

17 terrible ➡ _______________
18 reasonable ➡ _______________

19 comfortable ➡ _______________
20 rude ➡ _______________

21 personal ➡ _______________
22 possible ➡ _______________

23 probable ➡ _______________
24 casual ➡ _______________

25 rare ➡ _______________
26 responsible ➡ _______________

27 proper ➡ _______________
28 sensitive ➡ _______________

CH 11 부사

PSS 1-3 형용사와 형태가 같은 부사

fast	빠른	Shelly is a **fast** runner. Shelly는 빠른 주자이다.
	빨리	Time flies very **fast**. 시간은 아주 빨리 흘러간다.
late	늦은	I'm usually **late** for school. 나는 대개 학교에 지각한다.
	늦게	Inho came home **late** at night. 인호는 밤늦게 집에 왔다.
hard	열심인, 단단한	My dad is a **hard** worker. 나의 아빠는 열심히 일하는 사람이다.
	열심히, 단단히	I studied **hard** to pass the exam. 나는 그 시험에 합격하기 위해 열심히 공부했다.
last	마지막인	Today is the **last** day of December. 오늘은 12월의 마지막 날이다.
	마지막으로	When did you see him **last**? 너는 언제 마지막으로 그를 보았니?
long	오래된	They are proud of their **long** history. 그들은 그들의 오랜 역사를 자랑스러워한다.
	오래	My grandmother lived **long**. 나의 할머니는 오래 사셨다.
early	이른	Six o'clock is too **early** to get up. 6시는 일어나기에 너무 이르다.
	일찍	Why did you go home so **early**? 왜 너는 집에 그렇게 일찍 갔니?
enough	충분한	I don't have **enough** money. 나는 충분한 돈을 가지고 있지 않다.
	충분히	The room is large **enough** for me. 그 방은 나에게 충분히 크다. ***cf.*** enough가 부사로서 형용사 또는 부사를 수식할 때에는 뒤에서 수식한다.

정답 p.64

PRACTICE 3

밑줄 친 부분의 역할이 〈보기〉의 (A)와 같으면 A, (B)와 같으면 B라고 쓰세요.

보 기	My (A)<u>good</u> friend, John, speaks Korean (B)<u>well</u>.

1   We walked for a <u>long</u> time.   _______

2   I have to go to school quite <u>early</u> tomorrow.   _______

3   The cold weather will last <u>long</u>.   _______

4   My mom doesn't like <u>fast</u> food.   _______

5   I'm sorry to call you so <u>late</u>.   _______

6 I usually catch a cold in <u>early</u> spring. ___________

7 Alex tried <u>hard</u> to lose weight. ___________

8 Don't be <u>late</u> next time. ___________

9 Sumin came out of the room <u>last</u>. ___________

10 She walked <u>fast</u> to be on time. ___________

11 It was the <u>last</u> train for Seoul. ___________

12 There aren't <u>enough</u> chairs for everyone. ___________

13 I hit my head on the <u>hard</u> floor. ___________

14 Is the water warm <u>enough</u> for you? ___________

정답 p.64

PRACTICE 4

다음 문장의 밑줄 친 부분이 맞으면 O표, 틀리면 바르게 고쳐 쓰세요.

1 Jason arrived home <u>lately</u>. ___________

2 You have to think about it <u>careful</u>. ___________

3 I didn't stay there <u>long</u>. ___________

4 Who arrived <u>lastly</u> at the party? ___________

5 He is a <u>fast</u> speaker. ___________

6 You should talk <u>polite</u> to the elderly. ___________

7 I have breakfast <u>early</u> in the morning. ___________

8 You don't need to run so <u>fastly</u>. ___________

9 They practiced <u>hardly</u> for the contest. ___________

10 I <u>finally</u> finished reading this book. ___________

11 We couldn't solve the problem <u>easy</u>. ___________

12 He smiled <u>sad</u> and shook his head. ___________

13 Ben visited me <u>sudden</u> yesterday. ___________

14 They were waiting for the doctor <u>anxiously</u>. ___________

15 She is <u>certain</u> honest. ___________

16 He got on the plane <u>last</u>. ___________

17 Giraffes are <u>main</u> found in East Africa. ___________

18 Cathy told them the story <u>quiet</u>. ___________

close	가까이	She came **close** to me. 그녀는 나에게 가까이 다가왔다.
closely	주의 깊게, 면밀히	You should look at it **closely**. 너는 주의 깊게 그것을 봐야 한다.
hard	열심히	I worked very **hard** in a restaurant. 나는 식당에서 매우 열심히 일했다.
hardly	거의 ~않는	Mike could **hardly** read the letters. Mike는 글자를 거의 읽을 수 없었다.
high	높이	The kite was flying **high**. 연이 높이 날고 있었다.
highly	크게, 매우(=very)	He is a **highly** creative artist. 그는 매우 창의적인 예술가이다.
late	늦게	We had dinner **late**. 우리는 늦게 저녁을 먹었다.
lately	최근에	Have you seen Becky **lately**? 너는 최근에 Becky를 본 적이 있니?
near	가까이	Insu lives **near** to the park. 인수는 그 공원 가까이에 산다.
nearly	거의	**Nearly** 1,000 people died from the earthquake. 거의 1,000명의 사람들이 그 지진으로 죽었다.

정답 p.65

PRACTICE 5

괄호 안에 주어진 단어 중 알맞은 것을 고르세요.

1 I haven't seen any movies (late, lately).

2 This apple tastes (sweet, sweetly).

3 Christmas is coming (near, nearly).

4 I read the paper (close, closely).

5 The temperature goes up (high, highly) in summer.

6 She (hard, hardly) speaks during meetings.

7 Mrs. Smith talked to me (gentle, gently).

8 She runs a (high, highly) successful business in our town.

9 Dad came home (late, lately) all this week.

10 I like sweets very much, but I (rare, rarely) eat them.

11 She sang (beautiful, beautifully) in front of her classmates.

12 Jane lives (close, closely) to my house.

13 Did you study (hard, hardly) for the exam?

14 (Near, Nearly) 150 countries joined the Olympics.

15 You look (happy, happily) today.

정답 p.65

PRACTICE 6

〈보기〉와 같이 주어진 단어를 이용하여 빈칸을 채우세요.

보 기	polite

① Yumi is a very _polite_ girl.
② Yumi speaks very _politely_.

1 easy
① That was an ___________ question.
② I solved the question very ___________.

2 clear
① Could you speak ___________?
② The sky is very ___________.

3 late
① I had lunch ___________, so I'm not hungry.
② Bill was ___________ for school again.

4 careful
① Be ___________ while crossing the road to avoid accidents.
② Peter drives a car ___________.

5 last
① This is the ___________ chance to get the key.
② Jinho finished the test ___________.

6 early
① Mom woke up ___________ this morning.
② They visited me at an ___________ hour.

7 lucky
① You are such a ___________ guy.
② ___________, she was safe.

8 certain
① She eats only ___________ kinds of food.
② She'll ___________ win the first prize.

9 hard
① I've never seen him working so ___________.
② I could ___________ breathe at the top of the mountain.

10 close
① The cat came ___________ to the box.
② Read the text ___________ to grasp its underlying meaning.

PSS 2 여러 가지 부사의 용법

PSS 2-1 빈도부사의 위치

always – usually – often – sometimes – seldom – rarely – never
항상　　보통, 대개　　종종　　　때때로　　　드물게　좀처럼 ~ 않는　결코 ~ 않는

← 100%　　　　　　　　　　　　　　　　　　　　　　　　0% →

1. 일반동사 앞

| Mary
I
Minho | **often**
never
seldom | **goes**
eat
reads | to the beach in summer.
fast food.
the newspaper. |

주어　＋　빈도부사　＋　일반동사 ~

Mary는 여름에 종종 해변에 간다. | 나는 결코 패스트푸드를 먹지 않는다. | 민호는 드물게 신문을 읽는다.

2. be동사나 조동사 뒤

| They
My room
You
I
She | **are**
is
will
can
has | **usually**
always
sometimes
rarely
never | at home on weekends.
very cold.
face challenges.
see Jack nowadays.
been late for school. |

주어　＋　be/조동사　＋　빈도부사 ~

그들은 주말에 대개 집에 있다. | 내 방은 항상 매우 춥다. | 너는 때때로 도전에 직면할 것이다.

나는 요즘 좀처럼 Jack을 보지 못한다. | 그녀는 절대 학교에 늦은 적이 없다.

cf. 현재완료 「have+p.p.」에서 have는 조동사로 취급하기 때문에 빈도부사는 have 뒤에 쓴다.

cf. sometimes / often / usually와 같은 빈도부사는 문장의 맨 앞이나 뒤에도 올 수 있지만,
많은 경우 일반동사 앞 또는 be동사나 조동사 뒤에 쓴다.

정답 p.65

PRACTICE 7

괄호 안에 주어진 부사를 알맞은 곳에 넣어 문장을 다시 쓰세요. (단, 빈도부사를 문장 맨 앞, 뒤에는 오게 하지 말 것.)

1　I go to Incheon to visit my grandparents. (sometimes)

➡ ______________________________________

2 He leaves the house without his phone. (never)

➡ ____

3 Sangmin could come to our club meetings. (rarely)

➡ ____

4 I have wanted to travel around the world. (always)

➡ ____

5 We will go to the movies together. (sometimes)

➡ ____

6 They shake hands to greet each other. (usually)

➡ ____

7 I should help my mom with the housework. (often)

➡ ____

8 He is excited about the trip. (seldom)

➡ ____

9 She has learned Chinese. (never)

➡ ____

10 You don't clean your room, do you? (often)

➡ ____

정답 p.66

PRACTICE 8 [1-10]

다음 괄호 안에 주어진 말을 바르게 배열하세요. (단, 빈도부사를 문장 맨 앞, 뒤에는 오게 하지 말 것.)

1 (I, go jogging, in the morning, usually)

➡ ____

2 (they, listen to, sometimes, must, others)

➡ ____

3 (often, swimming, we, practice, will)

➡ ____

4 (Hana, brightly, smiles, always)

➡ ____

5 (can, understand, seldom, Nick, Korean)

➡ ____

6 (dangerous, sometimes, is, climbing mountains)

➡ ____

7 (Giho, watches, comic dramas, never)

➡ ____

8 (take care of, younger, I, my, sisters, usually)

➡ _______________________________________

9 (buys, she, expensive clothes, rarely)

➡ _______________________________________

10 (depressed, often, by, I, bad weather, am)

➡ _______________________________________

PSS 2-2 already, yet, still

already	이미, 벌써	already는 긍정문과 놀람을 나타내는 의문문에 쓰인다. Have you **already** forgotten what happened yesterday? 어제 무슨 일이 있었는지 벌써 잊은 거니? I've **already** read the book twice. 나는 벌써 그 책을 두 번 읽었다.
yet	이미, 벌써, 이제, 아직	yet은 의문문과 부정문에 쓰이는데, 의문문에서는 '이미, 벌써, 이제'의 뜻으로, 부정문에서는 '아직'의 뜻으로 해석되고 주로 문장의 끝에 위치한다. Have you seen the movie **yet**? 너는 벌써 그 영화를 봤니? I haven't finished it **yet**. 나는 아직 그것을 끝내지 못했다.

still	여전히, 아직도	still은 긍정문과 의문문에 쓰이고, 계속되는 행위를 강조하고자 할 때는 부정문에도 쓰인다.
		
		Sujin **still** enjoys hiking on weekends.
		수진은 여전히 주말마다 하이킹을 즐긴다.
		Do you **still** have the picture? 너는 아직도 그 그림을 가지고 있니?
		I **still** haven't called my teacher. 나는 아직도 선생님께 전화하지 않았다.
		cf. still이 부정문에 쓰일 때는 부정어보다 앞에 온다.
		cf. 형용사 still은 '가만히 있는, 고요한'의 뜻을 지닌다.
		    My little son finds it difficult to sit **still** for very long.
		    나의 어린 아들은 오랫동안 가만히 앉아 있는 것을 어렵게 여긴다.

정답 p.66

PRACTICE 9

〈보기〉와 같이 빈칸에 already, yet, still 중 알맞은 것을 쓰세요.

> 보 기
> ① I've *already* quit working there.
> ② I'm *still* working there.
> ③ I haven't quit working there *yet*.

1 ① I've __________ talked to David.

② I haven't talked to David __________.

③ I'm __________ talking to David.

2 ① Are you __________ reading the newspaper?

② Have you __________ read the newspaper?

③ Have you read the newspaper __________? – No, I haven't.

3 ① Junho hasn't cooked dinner __________.

② Junho is __________ cooking dinner.

③ Junho has __________ cooked dinner.

4 ① They are __________ doing their homework.

② They haven't finished doing their homework __________.

③ They have __________ finished doing their homework.

5 ① Has she cleaned the room __________? If not, I'll do it now.

② Has she __________ cleaned the room?

③ She is __________ cleaning the room.

정답 p.66

PRACTICE 10

괄호 안에 주어진 단어 중 알맞은 것을 고르세요.

1 I haven't finished my homework (yet, still).

2 I've (already, still) had my lunch.

3 Jenny is (yet, still) doing the dishes.

4 Have you met Mr. Smith (yet, still)?

5 Do you (yet, still) go to church?

6 Kevin has (yet, already) graduated from high school.

7 They haven't sent the email (yet, already).

8 Is he (already, still) nineteen years old? Time flies!

9 Mina (yet, still) wants to go to Europe.

10 Are you (yet, still) working on that report?

11 Have you (still, already) visited that museum?

12 There is (already, still) no news about the accident.

13 She has (already, still) gone somewhere.

14 We haven't decided what to buy (yet, already).

15 Are my clothes dry (already, still)? I washed them just an hour ago.

PSS 2 - 3 too, either

too	~ 또한	**too는 긍정문에 쓰인다.** Jiyeon can play the piano. I can play the piano, **too**. (= Me, too.) 지연이는 피아노를 칠 수 있다. 나도 역시 피아노를 칠 수 있다.
either		**either는 부정문에 쓰인다.** She doesn't like baseball. I don't like baseball, **either**. (= Me, neither.) 그녀는 야구를 좋아하지 않는다. 나도 역시 야구를 좋아하지 않는다. ***cf.*** I don't like baseball neither.은 비문임에 유의한다.

정답 p.66

PRACTICE 11

Tony

Becky

빈칸에 too, either, neither 중 알맞은 것을 넣어 대화를 완성하세요.

1	I miss Mr. Smith.	I miss Mr. Smith, ___________.
2	I'm not going out now.	Me, ___________.
3	She likes movies.	Me, ___________.
4	I don't live here.	I don't live here, ___________.
5	Seho will buy some books.	I will buy some books, ___________.
6	I can't speak French.	Me, ___________.
7	They won't study tonight.	I won't study tonight, ___________.
8	Tom can cook well.	Me, ___________.
9	I don't like those noisy dogs.	I don't like those noisy dogs, ___________.
10	Nami doesn't get up early.	Me, ___________.
11	I am not watching TV.	Me, ___________.
12	I can't attend the meeting.	I can't attend the meeting, ___________.
13	He wants to see the movie.	I want to see the movie, ___________.
14	Semin is not tall.	I'm not tall, ___________.
15	I didn't break this glass.	Me, ___________.

PSS 2-4 very, much

very	매우	1. 형용사의 원급을 수식한다. Your question is **very difficult**. 너의 질문은 매우 어렵다. 2. 부사의 원급을 수식한다. David speaks Korean **very well**. David는 한국어를 매우 잘 말한다.
much	훨씬	1. 형용사의 비교급을 수식한다. Bill is **much taller** than Alex. Bill은 Alex보다 훨씬 더 키가 크다. 2. 부사의 비교급을 수식한다. Kelly runs **much faster** than Hana. Kelly는 하나보다 훨씬 더 빨리 달린다.

정답 p.66

PRACTICE 12 [1-10]

〈보기〉와 같이 빈칸에 very나 much 중 알맞은 것을 쓰세요.

> 보 기
> ① Jane studies _very_ hard.
> ② Jane studies _much_ harder than anyone else.

1 ① My laptop boots up ___________ fast.
　② My friend's new laptop starts up ___________ faster than mine.

2 ① My mom gets up ___________ earlier than any one of us.
　② My mom gets up ___________ early in the morning.

3 ① Jina has a ___________ nice voice.
　② Jina has a ___________ nicer voice than Mary.

4 ① The airplane was flying ___________ high.
　② The airplane was flying ___________ higher than we had thought.

5 ① Today is ___________ cold.
　② Today is ___________ colder than yesterday.

6 ① I found the house ___________ smaller than I had imagined.
　② I found the house ___________ small.

7 ① Lydia plays the piano __________ well.

　② Lydia plays the piano __________ better than I do.

8 ① He arrived here __________ later than the other people.

　② He arrived here __________ late.

9 ① Those cookies are __________ more delicious than the other cookies.

　② Those cookies are __________ delicious.

10 ① Eunchan finished the work __________ quickly.

　② Eunchan finished the work __________ more quickly than I had expected.

정답 p.66

PRACTICE 13

괄호 안에 주어진 단어 중 알맞은 것을 고르세요.

1 The traffic was (very, much) heavy.

2 The gentleman was (very, much) older than he looked.

3 You have to listen to them (very, much) carefully.

4 After the rain, the weather became (very, much) cooler.

5 The task took me (very, much) longer than I had thought.

6 The book was (very, much) useful.

7 Things are (very, much) cheaper to buy here.

8 That is a (very, much) good idea.

9 She speaks English (very, much) better than Siwoo.

10 I tried (very, much) hard to keep the promise.

11 This game is (very, much) more exciting than that game.

12 The blue whale is a (very, much) large mammal.

PSS 2-5 else, even

else	그 밖에	else는 수식하고자 하는 말 뒤에 온다. Have you worked **anywhere else**? 넌 그 밖의 다른 곳에서 일했었니? **What else** should we buy? 그 밖에 어떤 것을 우리가 사야 하니? ***cf.*** else가 의문대명사나 부정대명사 뒤에 올 때의 품사는 형용사이다.

<table>
<tr><td rowspan="2">even</td><td rowspan="2">~조차</td><td>even은 수식하고자 하는 말 앞에 온다.</td></tr>
<tr><td>I didn't **even know** it was his birthday.
나는 그의 생일이었다는 것조차 알지 못했다.
Even when you go for a walk, you should tell your mom.
산책을 갈 때조차도 너는 엄마에게 말씀드려야 한다.
Inho is **even mean** to his sister. 인호는 그의 누나에게조차 짓궂다.
You are not quiet **even in the library**.
너는 도서관에서조차 조용하지 않구나.
Even children can do it. 어린이들조차도 그것을 할 수 있다.</td></tr>
</table>

정답 p.67

PRACTICE 14 [1-15]

괄호 안에 주어진 단어가 밑줄 친 부분을 수식하도록 문장을 다시 쓰세요.

1 <u>What</u> can I do for you? (else)
➡ _______________________________________

2 I didn't <u>imagine</u> it was possible. (even)
➡ _______________________________________

3 It was <u>sad</u> to say goodbye to everyone. (even)
➡ _______________________________________

4 <u>Where</u> did you visit in London? (else)
➡ _______________________________________

5 He <u>took</u> some medicine to fall asleep. (even)
➡ _______________________________________

6 They kept practicing soccer <u>when it rained heavily</u>. (even)
➡ _______________________________________

7 The child brings his toy <u>to the bathroom</u>. (even)
➡ _______________________________________

8 <u>A small pet</u> can give you a lot of trouble. (even)
➡ _______________________________________

9 Jessica <u>gets angry</u> if I don't call her often. (even)
➡ _______________________________________

10 David can run faster than <u>anyone</u> in his class. (else)
➡ _______________________________________

11 Dad sometimes works <u>on Sunday</u>. (even)

➜ ____

12 You can <u>order</u> a pizza on the Internet. (even)

➜ ____

13 Babies need to be watched <u>while they are sleeping</u>. (even)

➜ ____

14 You'd better write these rules <u>somewhere</u>. (else)

➜ ____

15 He speaks English, Chinese, French, and <u>Spanish</u>. (even)

➜ ____

정답 p.67

PRACTICE 15

괄호 안에 주어진 단어 중 알맞은 것을 고르세요.

1 You should not (else, even) look at him like that.

2 I like this place more than anywhere (else, even).

3 The little child couldn't (else, even) hold a spoon.

4 Did you meet anyone (else, even) on your way home?

5 I (else, even) had to dance to make her laugh.

6 What (else, even) do I need to remember?

7 Why should we study (else, even) during the vacation?

8 My friend Susan (else, even) knows where my grandparents are now.

9 This store is too crowded. Let's go somewhere (else, even).

10 Where (else, even) can I get information about the city?

PSS 2-6 「타동사＋부사」의 어순

1. **목적어가 명사**일 때, 목적어는 부사의 뒤에 오거나 동사와 부사의 사이에 온다.
   즉, 「**동사＋부사＋목적어**」나 「**동사＋목적어＋부사**」의 어순 둘 다 가능하다.

   Insu **took off his coat** in the room. 인수는 방에서 그의 코트를 벗었다.

   = Insu **took his coat off** in the room.

2. **목적어가 대명사**일 때, 목적어는 반드시 동사와 부사의 사이에 온다.
즉, 「**동사＋목적어＋부사**」의 어순만 가능하다.

Insu **took it off** in the room. 인수는 방에서 그것을 벗었다.

Insu took off it in the room. (×)

cf. 자동사 뒤에 전치사가 올 때, 전치사의 목적어는 반드시 전치사 뒤에 온다. 즉, 「동사＋전치사＋목적어」의 어순만 가능하다.

I'm **looking for Jack and Cathy**. (○) 나는 Jack과 Cathy를 찾고 있다.

I'm looking Jack and Cathy for. (×)

I'm **looking for them**. (○) 나는 그들을 찾고 있다.

I'm looking them for. (×)

정답 p.67

PRACTICE 16

괄호 안에 주어진 말 중 알맞은 것을 고르세요.

1 I'd like to try (them on, on them).

2 She doesn't care (money about, about money).

3 Could you turn (on the light, on it)?

4 Never give (up it, it up). Try hard.

5 Look (at the picture, the picture at) on the wall.

6 Did she hand (in the homework, in it) to the teacher?

7 I listened (an audio book to, to an audio book) last night.

8 Would you mind turning (off it, it off)?

9 The manager called (the show off, off it).

10 The cat was sitting (the chair on, on the chair).

11 I don't know the answer. Did you find (out it, it out)?

12 You should not throw (away it, it away) here.

13 Will you pick (up the paper, up it) for me?

14 I checked (them out, out them) at the Central Library.

15 I have your key. Were you looking (it for, for it)?

16 Let's talk (it about, about it) this evening.

PRACTICE 17

〈보기〉에서 알맞은 부사를 골라 빈칸에 쓰세요.

보 기	on off in out up away

1 We have to find ___________ who the thief is by tomorrow.

2 Did you throw ___________ the paper on the floor?

3 Do you mind if I turn the TV ___________? I need to watch the 9 o'clock news.

4 Would you like to try the blue shirt ___________?

5 Sora picked ___________ the coins and gave them to the boy.

6 You need to hand ___________ the paper by this Friday.

7 Will you turn the light ___________? I have to sleep now.

8 Could you check ___________ the books about Korea for me?

9 My dad called ___________ our plan, so I was very disappointed.

10 It rained heavily. We had to give ___________ the soccer game.

PSS 2-7 의문부사

when	언제	**When** did you visit Jeff? 넌 언제 Jeff를 방문했니? – I visited him **last Friday**. 난 지난 금요일에 그를 방문했어.
where	어디에	**Where** did you buy those pants? 넌 어디에서 그 바지를 샀니? – I bought them **at a department store**. 난 백화점에서 그것들을 샀어.
how	어떻게	**How** do you go to school? 넌 학교에 어떻게 가니? – I go to school **by bus**. 난 버스로 학교에 가.
	얼마나 ~한	**How long** does it take to get there? 그곳에 도착하는 데 얼마나 걸리니? – It takes **5 minutes**. 5분 걸려. **How many** pencils do you have? 넌 얼마나 많은 연필을 가지고 있니? – I have **five pencils**. 난 5자루의 연필을 가지고 있어. **How old** is your mother? 너의 어머니는 연세가 어떻게 되시니? – She's **43 years old**. 그녀는 43세이셔.

how	얼마나 ～한	**How far** is it from here to the police office? 여기서 경찰서까지 얼마나 머니? – It's **about three kilometers**. 약 3km 정도야. **How much** is this candy? 이 사탕은 얼마야? – It's **five hundred won**. 500원이야. **How often** do you go to the library? 너는 얼마나 자주 도서관에 가니? – I go there about **twice a week**. 나는 약 일주일에 두 번 정도 그곳에 가.
why	왜	**Why** didn't you buy it? 넌 왜 그것을 사지 않았니? – **Because it was too expensive**. 그것은 너무 비쌌기 때문이야.

PRACTICE 18

Becky의 대답을 보고, Tony의 질문을 완성하세요.

정답 p.68

Becky

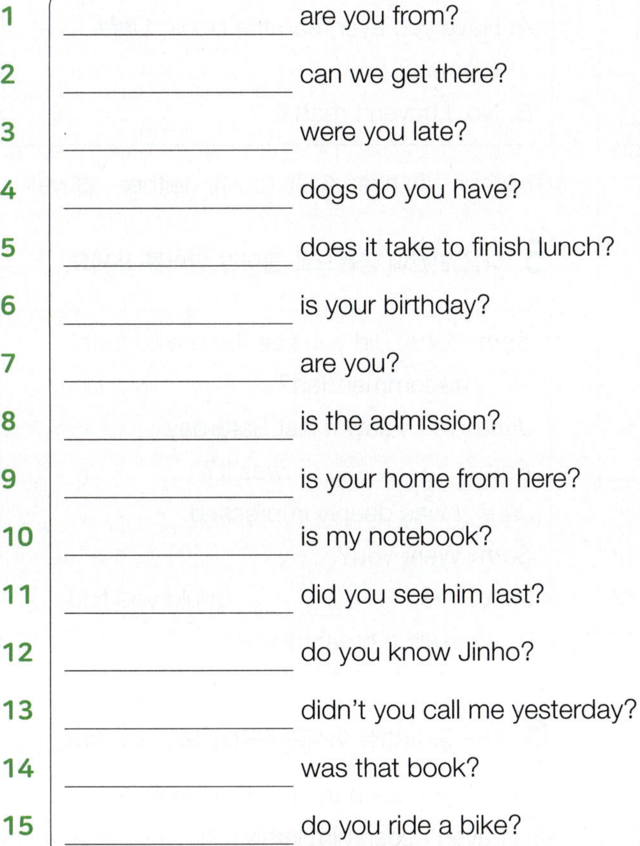

1. ______________ are you from? — I'm from Toronto, Canada.
2. ______________ can we get there? — We can take the 502 bus.
3. ______________ were you late? — Because I got up late this morning.
4. ______________ dogs do you have? — I have three dogs.
5. ______________ does it take to finish lunch? — It takes almost 30 minutes.
6. ______________ is your birthday? — It's April 30th.
7. ______________ are you? — I'm sixteen.
8. ______________ is the admission? — It's 5,000 won.
9. ______________ is your home from here? — It's about a ten-minute walk from here.
10. ______________ is my notebook? — It's on the desk.
11. ______________ did you see him last? — Last Wednesday.
12. ______________ do you know Jinho? — He was my classmate last year.
13. ______________ didn't you call me yesterday? — Because my phone's battery died.
14. ______________ was that book? — It was 18,000 won.
15. ______________ do you ride a bike? — About 3 times a month.

Tony

1
다음 단어를 어법에 맞게 빈칸에 넣었을 때, ⓐ와 ⓑ의 관계가 나머지 넷과 <u>다른</u> 하나는?

①	quiet	• The class suddenly became ⓐ __________ . • She ⓑ __________ went out of the door.
②	careful	• He is a ⓐ __________ man. • She ⓑ __________ cut the paper.
③	right	• She's the ⓐ __________ person for this job. • I didn't feel quite ⓑ __________ today.
④	near	• They will announce their decision in the ⓐ __________ future. • He's ⓑ __________ as tall as his father.
⑤	late	• We are ⓐ __________ for the meeting. • John has been acting strange ⓑ __________ .

2
〈보기〉의 문장 중 어법상 옳은 것의 개수는?

> 보 기
> ⓐ He took them out and looked them at.
> ⓑ Inho came home lately at night.
> ⓒ The airplane was flying highly.
> ⓓ I don't have money enough.
> ⓔ I usually catch a cold in early spring.

① 1개　② 2개　③ 3개　④ 4개　⑤ 5개

3
다음의 우리말을 영어로 바르게 옮긴 것은?

> 그 또한 형제가 없었다.

① He didn't have few brothers, too.
② He didn't have few brothers, either.
③ He didn't have any brothers, too.
④ He didn't have any brothers, either.
⑤ He didn't have some brothers, either.

4
다음 대화의 빈칸에 들어갈 단어로 알맞은 것은?

> A: Have you ever read the book, *Little Women*?
> B: No, I haven't read it __________ .

① either　② already ③ too ④ neither　⑤ yet

5
다음 빈칸에 공통으로 들어갈 단어를 쓰세요.

> *Sam* : Jane, did you see the movie that I recommended?
> *Jane*: Yes. I saw it last Saturday.
> *Sam* : __________ was it?
> *Jane*: I was deeply impressed.
> *Sam* : Were you?
> *Jane*: Yes. __________ could you find such a great movie?

6
다음 중 어법상 <u>어색한</u> 문장을 <u>모두</u> 고르세요.

① Have you seen the new movie yet?
② I haven't seen him lately.
③ You should cross the street careful.
④ Kate is always diligent.
⑤ I studied hardly for the exam.

7 다음 대화의 빈칸에 들어갈 단어로 알맞은 것은?

> *A*: How was your weekend?
> *B*: It was not good. I was very sad.
> *A*: ___________ were you so sad?
> *B*: One of my best friends left for Canada.

① Why ② How ③ What
④ Which ⑤ Where

8 다음 ⓐ～ⓔ 중 어법상 틀린 것을 있는 대로 고른 것은?

> ⓐ They haven't finished it already.
> ⓑ I couldn't visit her, too.
> ⓒ It's more important than anything else.
> ⓓ Please make her stopping crying.
> ⓔ This is very more expensive than that.

① ⓐ, ⓑ ② ⓑ, ⓒ ③ ⓑ, ⓒ, ⓓ
④ ⓐ, ⓓ, ⓔ ⑤ ⓐ, ⓑ, ⓓ, ⓔ

9 다음 대화의 (A)～(E) 중 어법상 어색한 것은?

> *Andy* : (A)Why are you still reading the book?
> *Brenda*: Well, I don't know (B)what the author's intention is.
> *Andy* : (C)Actually, me, too.
> *Brenda*: By the way, (D)why are you still here?
> *Andy* : (E)I'm waiting for my mom to pick me up.
> *Brenda*: I see.

① (A) ② (B) ③ (C) ④ (D) ⑤ (E)

10 다음 빈칸에 알맞은 단어를 넣어 대화를 완성하세요.

> *Mom*: Who broke the vase?
> *Mina* : I didn't break it.
> *Jinho*: I didn't break it, ___________.

11 다음 중 어법상 어색한 문장을 모두 고르세요.

① The company always has provided excellent customer service.
② How long do the journey usually take?
③ Nami is often late for school.
④ Ted sometimes goes swimming.
⑤ He usually eats his lunch at home.

12 다음 문장의 빈칸에 알맞은 단어끼리 바르게 나열된 것은?

> • Don't come too ___(A)___ !
> • Have you seen Helen ___(B)___ ?
> • I've worked here for ___(C)___ two years.

	(A)	(B)	(C)
①	closely	– lately	– near
②	close	– lately	– nearly
③	close	– late	– near
④	closely	– late	– nearly
⑤	close	– lately	– near

13 다음 중 어법상 어색한 문장은?

① I got a bad grade, too.
② He's very better now.
③ Eating regularly is good for your health.
④ I always meet my friends on Saturday night.
⑤ Sudong sometimes goes to the park near his house.

ⓐ She packed necessary everything for the trip.
ⓑ The movie was so boring that I fell asleep in the middle of it.
ⓒ He has been knowing her since they were in middle school.
ⓓ He spoke gentley to calm the frightened dog.
ⓔ Even though it's her first competition, she looks confidently.

① 1개　　② 2개　　③ 3개　　④ 4개　　⑤ 5개

15 다음 중 〈보기〉의 답들에 대한 질문이 될 수 없는 것은?

보 기
(A) Once a week.
(B) It takes about two hours to get there.
(C) It's three hundred dollars.
(D) It's 8 miles from here.

① How far is it from here?
② How long does it take to get to Daegu?
③ How often do you play the piano?
④ How come you measured the distance?
⑤ How much is it?

16 다음 문장의 밑줄 친 much와 의미가 다른 것은?

Lisa is much kinder than Jeff.

① Inho is much taller than Giho.
② She is much healthier than before.
③ I enjoyed the movie very much.
④ Sally can run much faster than her sister.
⑤ I feel much better today.

17 다음 밑줄 친 부분 중 어법상 어색한 것은?

① It was not ② hard ③ to find the station. We could ④ easy find ⑤ it.

18 다음 대화 중 가장 어색한 것을 고르세요.

① A: How often do you exercise?
　 B: I swim at least twice a week.
② A: What made you hurt so much?
　 B: I slipped and fell hardly on the floor.
③ A: How long does it take to take a shower?
　 B: In my case, it takes about 40 minutes.
④ A: It is quite difficult for me to enjoy chess.
　 B: As you know, chess is a highly strategic game requiring deep thought and concentration.
⑤ A: Why didn't he tell you about the due date?
　 B: Because he thought I already knew it.

19 다음 빈칸에 들어갈 말로 알맞은 것은?

A: Do you speak Chinese?
B: No, I don't. How about you?
A: ＿＿＿＿＿＿＿＿＿ But I'm going to take a Chinese class this vacation.

① I do, too.　　　　② Me, too.
③ Me, neither.　　　④ I do, either.
⑤ I don't, neither.

20 밑줄 친 ⓐ~ⓔ 중 어법상 틀린 것을 있는 대로 고른 것은?

In Korea, people take off their shoes when they enter a house, but ⓐ Americans don't take off them. ⓑ So they used to make mistakes. However, these days most of them know that ⓒ they should take their shoes off before entering a house in Korea. ⓓ Some of them even think that ⓔ taking off shoes are good for their feet.

① ⓐ, ⓑ   ② ⓐ, ⓔ   ③ ⓒ, ⓓ
④ ⓑ, ⓓ, ⓔ   ⑤ ⓑ, ⓒ, ⓔ

21 다음 밑줄 친 부분 중 어법상 어색한 것은?

Sumi ① must feel very ② hungry. She ③ only drank ④ a cup of water and had ⑤ else nothing today.

22 다음 글에서 어법상 올바른 것을 모두 고르세요.

Hi, I'm Gina and I live in Los Angeles, often known as L.A. I want to tell you about it. (A) Los Angeles means "the angels" in Spanish. In the central region, there is Hollywood, (B) which visited by many movie fans. Every year, (C) near 3.5 million tourists come to see the famous Hollywood sign. Oh, (D) when the weather gets hot in summer, people go to the Santa Monica Beach to enjoy swimming and water sports. (E) I want you come to L.A. someday.

① (A)   ② (B)   ③ (C)   ④ (D)   ⑤ (E)

23 다음 글에서 빈칸 ⓐ~ⓒ에 들어갈 말로 가장 알맞은 것은?

Welcome back to Daily Reminders. Today we will talk about public transportation etiquette. First, and most ______ⓐ______, we need to be respectful of fellow passengers. Second, avoid using the phone as much as possible. If you need to talk on the phone, try to keep the conversation ______ⓑ______ and do not speak with a loud voice. Third, offer your seat to ______ⓒ______ or disabled passengers. Last, do not use multiple seats and be considerate of others. If everyone follows this etiquette, we can make public transportation a more enjoyable experience for everyone. So, let's keep these in mind when you take the bus or subway.

	ⓐ	ⓑ	ⓒ
①	important	short	elder
②	important	shortly	elderly
③	importantly	short	elder
④	importantly	short	elderly
⑤	importantly	shortly	elder

24 다음 빈칸에 들어갈 수 <u>없는</u> 말은?

Jinho : Who is the best player on your team?
Minsu: I think Bill is the best.
Jinho : ________________________
Minsu: Because he always does his best.

① How come?
② What makes you think so?
③ Why do you say that?
④ What do you think about it?
⑤ What is your reason for saying so?

25 다음 중 밑줄 친 단어의 쓰임이 <u>올바른</u> 것은?

① I sat and watched everyone very <u>close</u>.
② Michelle <u>hard</u> ever calls her parents.
③ His desk was piled <u>high</u> with books.
④ My grandfather hasn't been sleeping well
<u>late</u>.
⑤ A bomb exploded somewhere <u>nearly</u> here.

26 다음 빈칸에 알맞도록 괄호 안의 단어를 바르게 배열한 것은?

> Nari ________________ to school on time.
> (not, come, does, always)

① does not always come
② does not come always
③ always come does not
④ come always does not
⑤ does always not come

27 다음 빈칸에 들어갈 말이 바르게 짝지어진 것은?

> • W: ________(A)________ is your pet adjusting
>   to the new home?
>   M: He's adapting surprisingly quickly.
> --
> • W: ________(B)________ is her new novel
>   coming out?
>   M: It hasn't been decided yet.
> --
> • W: ________(C)________ would you like to sit?
>   M: I want to sit in the middle row.

	(A)		(B)		(C)
①	How	–	When	–	What
②	What	–	Where	–	What
③	How	–	Where	–	What
④	What	–	How	–	Where
⑤	How	–	When	–	Where

28 빈칸에 들어갈 문장으로 가장 알맞은 것은?

> *Boy* : Hey, Yujin! Where are you going?
> *Girl* : Hi, Jun. I'm on my way to the book
>   club meeting.
> *Boy* : Oh, I didn't know that you joined the
>   book club.
> *Girl* : It has only been a few weeks since I
>   joined. You know that I'm a bookworm.
> *Boy* : Right. ________________
> *Girl* : It's really exciting! It offers me the
>   chance to listen to different comments
>   on the book.

① How often do you read?
② What are you reading?
③ How have you been?
④ What do you like it?
⑤ How do you like it?

29 다음 중 밑줄 친 부분이 어법상 <u>어색한</u> 것은?

① John had a seat on the bus, but he offered
to <u>give it up</u> to an elderly lady.
② As soon as Jack saw me watching TV, I
<u>turned it off</u>.
③ He stays in the playground alone until his
mom <u>picks up him</u>.
④ I heard you had sent me a picture, but I
don't have time to <u>look at it</u>.
⑤ She usually listens to pop songs every night,
but she won't <u>listen to them</u> tonight.

30 다음 중 밑줄 친 부분을 어법상 <u>옳게</u> 고친 것은?

① Today is much (→ very) colder than yesterday.
② I can't attend the meeting, either (→ too).
③ Kevin yet (→ already) graduated from high school.
④ Do you still (→ yet) have the picture?
⑤ We will often (→ often will) practice swimming.

31 괄호 안에 주어진 우리말과 일치하도록 빈칸에 알맞은 단어를 쓰세요. (단, 한 단어로 쓸 것.)

A: Wow, your skin looks _____(A)_____ better than before.
(와, 네 피부가 전보다 훨씬 더 좋아 보여.)
B: I started putting some _____(B)_____ good cream on it a few days ago.
(며칠 전에 아주 좋은 크림을 피부에 바르기 시작했거든.)
A: _____(C)_____ can I get it?
(그거 어디서 구할 수 있니?)
B: My mom gave it _____(D)_____ me. I'll let you know later.
(엄마가 내게 그걸 주셨어. 나중에 알려줄게.)

(A) _________________ (B) _________________
(C) _________________ (D) _________________

32 다음 중 밑줄 친 단어의 위치가 <u>잘못된</u> 것은?

① My sister <u>never</u> cleans her room.
② He gets <u>often</u> angry at her.
③ My mother and I will <u>rarely</u> go to the market together.
④ Our boss is <u>always</u> kind to us.
⑤ I <u>usually</u> walk to school.

33 다음 밑줄 친 부분 중 <u>어색한</u> 것끼리 바르게 짝 지어진 것은?

Mom: It's so cold today. ⓐ <u>Put on your coat</u> and ⓑ <u>turn the light off</u> when you leave home.
Son : I see.
Mom: Oh, can you ⓒ <u>take out the garbage</u>?
Son : My friend is ⓓ <u>waiting me for</u> now! Can I ⓔ <u>take it out</u> later? And please ⓕ <u>pick up me</u> after school.
Mom: Okay. See you then.

① ⓐ, ⓓ　　② ⓐ, ⓕ　　③ ⓑ, ⓓ
④ ⓒ, ⓔ　　⑤ ⓓ, ⓕ

34 다음 중 어법상 <u>어색한</u> 문장을 <u>모두</u> 고르세요.

① I feel quite well.
② It is very cold outside.
③ He spends usually a lot of money.
④ She often forget to bring her umbrella.
⑤ I sometimes go to church alone.

35 다음 글의 밑줄 친 ①~⑤ 중 어법상 <u>어색한</u> 문장은?

① <u>The garage sale was hard work.</u> There were many things to do. ② <u>First, we collected plenty of old things.</u> ③ <u>Then, we cleaned everything carefully.</u> ④ <u>Next, early on Sunday morning, we brought everything out and set up it.</u> ⑤ <u>A lot of people came to the sale and we sold so many things.</u>

36 다음 (A)의 말에 어울리는 말을 (B)에서 골라 그 기호를 쓰세요.

(A)

① Jane has already done her homework.

② Did you eat lunch?

③ I remember that you lived in Seattle.

④ Will you show me your homework?

(B)

ⓐ Of course I did. It's already three o'clock.

ⓑ I still live there.

ⓒ I think her mother helped her do that.

ⓓ I haven't finished it yet.

① - _______ ② - _______ ③ - _______ ④ - _______

37 괄호 안의 우리말과 뜻이 같도록 빈칸에 들어갈 질문을 조건에 맞게 영어로 쓰세요.

조 건

• 의문부사 how로 시작할 것.

• 동사 get을 사용할 것.

• 조동사 can을 쓸 것.

• 9 단어로 만들 것.

Molly : ___________________________________

____

(내가 여기서 공항까지 어떻게 갈 수 있어?)

Sophia: You can take a taxi. It will take about 20 minutes.

Molly : Thank you.

38 다음 중 밑줄 친 부분이 <u>어색한</u> 것을 <u>모두</u> 고르세요.

① Nick carried it very <u>carefully</u>.

② Why do you walk so <u>fastly</u>?

③ Have you seen any movies <u>late</u>?

④ You can get there <u>quickly</u>.

⑤ They look so much <u>different</u>.

39 (A)~(C)의 빈칸에 알맞은 말끼리 바르게 짝지어진 것은?

The interview was over. Suddenly, the lights came upon the set, and I could not believe my eyes. My favorite actor was there! He was rehearsing with the other actors. Then the director said, "Ready, action!" My dad and the other camera operators were looking through their cameras ____(A)____. The director asked the actors to do the same scene many times. A lot of people worked ____(B)____ to make the one-hour drama, and my dad was one of them. My dad looked really ____(C)____. I felt proud of him.

	(A)	(B)	(C)
①	careful	– hardly	– wonderfully
②	careful	– hard	– wonderful
③	careful	– hardly	– wonderful
④	carefully	– hard	– wonderful
⑤	carefully	– hard	– wonderfully

CHAPTER 12
가정법

PSS 1 조건을 나타내는 if

1. if는 '~한다면, ~라면'의 뜻으로 현재나 미래에 실제로 일어날 수 있는 상황에 대한 조건을 나타낸다.

   If it's 10 a.m. in New York, it's 8 p.m. in Seoul. 뉴욕이 오전 10시이면, 서울은 오후 8시이다.

   If it doesn't rain tomorrow, I will go out. 내일 비가 오지 않으면, 나는 밖에 나갈 거야.

   cf. 미래의 일을 나타낸다고 하더라도 조건을 나타내는 if절의 동사는 항상 현재형으로 쓴다.

      If it **won't rain** tomorrow, I will go out. (×)

   cf. 「명령문＋and ~」는 If 조건문으로, 「명령문＋or ~」는 If 조건문의 부정형으로 나타낼 수 있다.

      Study hard, **and** you will pass the exam.

      = **If** you study hard, you will pass the exam.

        네가 열심히 공부하면 너는 시험에 합격할 것이다.

      Help him right now, **or** he will be in danger.

      = **If** you **don't** help him right now, he will be in danger.

        네가 당장 그를 도와주지 않는다면 그는 위험에 처하게 될 것이다.

2. if와 when

   A: Are you going to buy the book? 너는 그 책을 살 거니?

   B: I'm not sure. **If** I buy mine, I will buy yours, too. 확실하지 않아. 내 것을 산다면, 네 것도 살게.

     (책을 살 것인지 말 것인지가 확실하지 않은 경우를 나타낸다.)

   A: Are you going to buy the book? 너는 그 책을 살 거니?

   B: Yes, I am. **When** I buy mine, I will buy yours, too. 응, 살 거야. 내 것을 살 때, 네 것도 살게.

     (분명히 책을 살 경우를 나타낸다.)

정답 p.71

PRACTICE 1

〈보기〉에 주어진 단어를 알맞은 형태로 바꾸어 빈칸에 쓰세요.

| 보기 | study finish rain find be hurry leave change meet come |

1 If I ___________ your notebook, I'll call you.

2 Can I go out if I ____________ my homework?

3 If he ____________ here within two hours, we can see him.

4 Let's stay home if it ____________ tomorrow.

5 I will say hello to Jack for you if I ____________ him.

6 If your mom ____________ her mind, let me know.

7 If she ____________ for the office, call me please.

8 Sumi can pass the exam if she ____________ hard.

9 Jina can catch the bus if she ____________.

10 If you ____________ busy now, I will visit you later.

PSS 2 가정법 과거

PSS 2-1 if + 가정법 과거

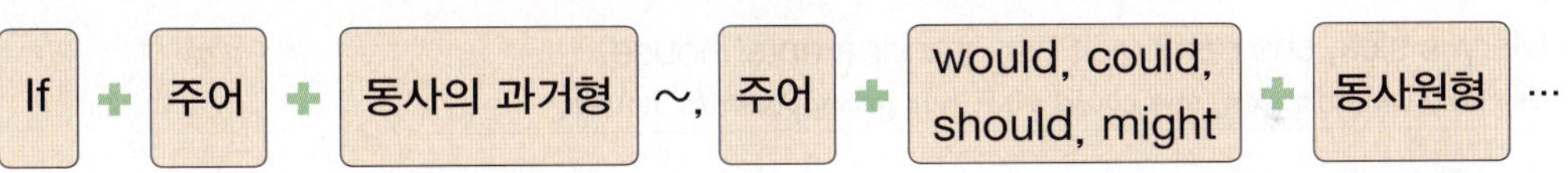

1. 가정법 과거는 '만약 ~한다면 …할 텐데'의 뜻으로 현재 사실에 반대되는 일을 가정할 때 쓴다.

   If we **were** on vacation, we **would be** in Hawaii.
   우리가 휴가 중이라면, 우리는 하와이에 있을 텐데.
   ➡ As we are not on vacation, we are not in Hawaii.
   　 우리는 휴가 중이 아니므로, 우리는 하와이에 있지 않다.

2. if절의 be동사는 인칭에 상관없이 were를 쓴다.

   My son could take care of me if **he were** here.
   내 아들이 여기에 있다면, 나를 돌봐줄 수 있을 텐데.
   ➡ My son can't take care of me because he is not here.
   　 내 아들이 여기에 있지 않기 때문에, 그는 나를 돌봐줄 수 없다.
   cf. 구어체에서는 was를 쓰기도 한다.
   　 If I **was** in New York, I would travel with Linda. 내가 뉴욕에 있다면, Linda와 여행을 할 텐데.

PRACTICE 2

괄호 안의 단어를 알맞은 형태로 바꾸어 빈칸에 쓰세요. (단, 축약형으로 쓸 수 있는 경우에는 축약형으로 쓸 것.)

1 If she _________________ the answer, she could win a prize. (know)

2 If we _________________ enough time, we would discuss the rule. (have)

3 If I were busy, I _________________ so much. (not, travel)

4 If it _________________ a little cheaper, I could buy it. (be)

5 If he were richer, he _________________ a nice car. (get)

6 If she liked the boy, she _________________ him to the party. (invite)

7 If I had an oven, I _________________ some pies. (bake)

8 If he _________________ the recipe carefully, he could bake a delicious cake. (follow)

9 If it _________________ sunny, we couldn't take a walk. (not, be)

10 If I knew her phone number, I _________________ to her right now. (talk)

PRACTICE 3

다음 문장을 if를 이용한 가정법 문장으로 바꾸어 쓰세요. (단, 축약형으로 쓸 수 있는 경우에는 축약형으로 쓸 것.)

1 As Mary is sick, she can't visit her grandparents' house.
➡ *If Mary weren't sick, she could visit her grandparents' house.*

2 As Steve doesn't know the reason, he isn't angry.
➡ ____

3 As this movie isn't fun, I am bored.
➡ ____

4 As you aren't honest, you don't have many friends.
➡ ____

5 As I don't have enough money, I can't buy you a piano.
➡ ____

6 As you aren't old enough, you can't understand this better.
➡ ____

7 As my brother is not hungry, he won't go out for dinner.
➡ ____

8 As I am tired, I can't go swimming now.
➡ ____

9 As she doesn't agree with the writer, she doesn't like his book.

➡ ____

10 As I have other plans, I can't go shopping with you.

➡ ____

PSS 2-2 I wish+가정법 과거

「I wish+가정법 과거」는 '~라면 좋을 텐데'의 뜻으로 현재의 사실과 반대되거나 미래에 이룰 수 없는 일을 소망할 때 쓴다.

> I wish + 주어 + 동사의 과거형 ~

I wish I **had** a sister. 여동생이 한 명 있으면 좋을 텐데.
➡ I'm sorry that I don't have a sister.
　나는 여동생이 없어서 유감이다.

I wish Dave **would come** to see me.
Dave가 날 보러 온다면 좋을 텐데.
➡ I'm sorry that Dave will not come to see me.
　Dave가 날 보러 오지 않을 것이라서 유감이다.

정답 p.71

PRACTICE 4

괄호 안의 단어를 알맞은 형태로 바꾸어 빈칸에 써서 가정법 과거 문장을 완성하세요. (단, 축약형으로 쓸 수 있는 경우에는 축약형으로 쓸 것.)

1 I wish I _______________ taller. (be)

2 I wish I _______________ a cell phone. (have)

3 I wish it _______________ so much. (not, snow)

4 I wish I _______________ Chinese. (can, speak)

5 I wish she _______________ me more often. (will, call)

6 I wish I _______________ him a hand. (can, give)

7 I wish they _______________ here with us now. (be)

8 I wish Mark _______________ Korea. (will, not, leave)

9 I wish I _______________ well. (can, sing)

10 I wish my dad _______________ a bigger car. (have)

PRACTICE 5

다음 문장을 I wish로 시작하는 가정법 문장으로 바꾸어 쓰세요. (단, 축약형으로 쓸 수 있는 경우에는 축약형으로 쓸 것.)

1 I'm sorry that I don't live in the country.
➡ _I wish I lived in the country._

2 I'm sorry that it is cold here.
➡ _______________________

3 I'm sorry that I am not diligent.
➡ _______________________

4 I'm sorry that I don't know how to drive.
➡ _______________________

5 I'm sorry that Angela can't join our club.
➡ _______________________

6 I'm sorry that there aren't trees around here.
➡ _______________________

7 I'm sorry that the class won't finish soon.
➡ _______________________

8 I'm sorry that I can't play the violin.
➡ _______________________

9 I'm sorry that Mark will move to another city.
➡ _______________________

10 I'm sorry that I'm not good at sports.
➡ _______________________

PSS 2-3 동사의 현재형 + as if + 가정법 과거

「as if + 가정법 과거」는 '마치 ~인 것처럼'의 뜻으로 현재의 사실과 반대되는 일을 나타낸다.

동사의 현재형 ✚ as if ✚ 주어 ✚ 동사의 과거형 ～

He **talks** to me **as if** I **were** his son. 그는 마치 내가 그의 아들인 것처럼 내게 말한다.
➡ In fact, I'm not his son. 사실, 나는 그의 아들이 아니다.

Ann **acts as if** she **were** a doctor. Ann은 마치 그녀가 의사인 것처럼 행동한다.
➡ In fact, Ann is not a doctor. 사실, Ann은 의사가 아니다.

PRACTICE 6

〈보기〉와 같이 주어진 문장을 as if를 이용한 가정법 문장으로 바꾸어 쓰세요.

> 보 기 In fact, Matt is not Italian.
> ➡ Matt talks _as if he were Italian._

1 In fact, you are not his friend.
➡ You talk about him _______________________.

2 In fact, she doesn't live here.
➡ It seems _______________________.

3 In fact, Akiko is not Korean.
➡ Akiko appears ________________________.

4 In fact, he is not a king.
➡ He acts ________________________.

5 In fact, the play isn't exciting.
➡ It sounds ________________________.

6 In fact, today is not Saturday.
➡ It feels ________________________.

7 In fact, David doesn't know everybody in my family.
➡ David speaks ________________________.

8 In fact, Kelly isn't very smart.
➡ Kelly talks ________________________.

9 In fact, you are not a child.
➡ You act ________________________.

10 In fact, they aren't sick.
➡ It seems ________________________.

PSS 3 가정법 과거완료

PSS 3-1 if+가정법 과거완료

| If | + | 주어 | + | had+
과거분사 | ~, | 주어 | + | would, could,
should, might | + | have+
과거분사 | ... |

가정법 과거완료는 '만약 ~했다면 …했을 텐데'의 뜻으로 과거 사실에 반대되는 일을 가정할 때 쓴다.

If I **had had** a car, I **could have given** him a ride.
만약 내게 차가 있었다면, 나는 그를 태워줬을 텐데.
➡ As I didn't have a car, I couldn't give him a ride.
나는 차가 없었기 때문에, 그를 태워줄 수 없었다.

> **If** Mom **had not been** in the hospital, she **could have come** to my soccer game.
> 만약 엄마가 병원에 계시지 않았다면, 내 축구 경기에 오실 수 있었을 텐데.
> ➡ Because Mom was in the hospital, she couldn't come to my soccer game.
> 엄마는 병원에 계셨기 때문에, 내 축구 경기에 오실 수 없었다.

정답 p.72

PRACTICE 7

괄호 안의 단어를 알맞은 형태로 바꾸어 빈칸에 쓰세요. (단, 축약형으로 쓸 수 있는 경우에는 축약형으로 쓸 것.)

1 If I ___________________________ the book, I would have lent it to him. (finish)

2 If I ___________________________ her then, I could have helped her. (know)

3 If I ___________________________ you, I would listen to his advice. (be)

4 If they had heard the news, they ___________________________ you. (call)

5 If Ben had any free time, he ___________________________ to see the movie. (go)

6 If she ___________________________ about our party, she could have come. (not, forget)

7 If we had taken the subway, we ___________________________ there on time. (arrive)

8 If you ___________________________ the book, I would give it to you. (like)

9 If Jihoon had been more careful, he ___________________________ the accident. (prevent)

10 If she had slept enough, she ___________________________ so tired. (not, feel)

PSS 3-2 I wish + 가정법 과거완료

「I wish + 가정법 과거완료」는 '~했더라면 좋았을 텐데'의 뜻으로, 과거의 사실과 반대되는 일을 소망할 때 쓴다.

I wish **+** 주어 **+** had + 과거분사 ~

I wish I **had had** breakfast. 내가 아침을 먹었더라면 좋았을 텐데.
➡ I'm sorry that I didn't have breakfast.
나는 아침을 먹지 않아서 유감이다.

I wish he **had not broken** my favorite mug.
그가 내가 가장 좋아하는 머그컵을 깨뜨리지 않았더라면 좋았을 텐데.
➡ I'm sorry that he broke my favorite mug.
그가 내가 가장 좋아하는 머그컵을 깨뜨려서 유감이다.

PRACTICE 8

다음 문장을 I wish로 시작하는 가정법 문장으로 바꾸어 쓰세요. (단, 축약형으로 쓸 수 있는 경우에는 축약형으로 쓸 것.)

1 I didn't do my best. I'm sorry about that.
➡ *I wish I had done my best.*

2 She didn't keep her promise. I'm sorry about that.
➡ ____

3 Jinsu didn't come to my house. I miss him.
➡ ____

4 I'm not in Europe now, but I'd like to be there.
➡ ____

5 They didn't finish cleaning the room. I'm sorry about that.
➡ ____

6 Mina was late for the meeting. I'm sorry about that.
➡ ____

7 My brother doesn't read books, but I want him to.
➡ ____

8 She didn't water the plants. I'm sorry about that.
➡ ____

9 We didn't visit him in the hospital. I'm sorry about that.
➡ ____

10 I studied even on holidays, but I didn't want to.
➡ ____

PSS 3-3 동사의 현재형 + as if + 가정법 과거완료

「as if+가정법 과거완료」는 '마치 ~이었던 것처럼'의 뜻으로 과거의 사실과 반대되는 일을 나타낸다.

동사의 현재형 **+** as if **+** 주어 **+** had+과거분사 ~

It **sounds as if** he **had not studied** last night.
마치 그가 지난밤에 공부를 하지 않았다는 것처럼 들린다.
➡ In fact, he studied last night. 사실, 그는 지난밤에 공부를 했다.

They **talk as if** they **had graduated** from high school.

그들은 마치 고등학교를 졸업한 것처럼 말한다.

➡ In fact, they didn't graduate from high school. 사실, 그들은 고등학교를 졸업하지 않았다.

정답 p.72

PRACTICE 9

〈보기〉와 같이 as if를 이용한 가정법 문장으로 바꾸어 쓰세요. (단, 축약형으로 쓸 수 있는 경우에는 축약형으로 쓸 것.)

보 기	In fact, it was not his car.
	➡ He talks <u>as if it had been his car.</u>

1 In fact, she slept well last night.

➡ She looks ____.

2 In fact, Jennifer is not married.

➡ Jennifer looks ____.

3 In fact, I didn't break the glass.

➡ He speaks ____.

4 In fact, they weren't rich in their youth.

➡ It seems ____.

5 In fact, I didn't lose my watch.

➡ I feel ____.

6 In fact, you were not right all the time.

➡ You talk ____.

7 In fact, Mr. Park doesn't know those students.

➡ Mr. Park acts ____.

8 In fact, Paul isn't popular among his classmates.

➡ Paul talks ____.

9 In fact, they were bored by the lecture.

➡ They look ____.

10 In fact, it wasn't your idea.

➡ You sound ____.

중간·기말고사 대비문제 📝

1 다음 우리말을 영작한 것으로 옳은 것은?

> 운동하지 않는다면, 너는 건강을 잃게 될 거야.

① If you didn't exercise, you will lose your health.
② If you exercised, you wouldn't lose your health.
③ If you don't exercise, you will lose your health.
④ Unless you won't exercise, you will lose your health.
⑤ Unless you will exercise, you will lose your health.

2 다음 두 문장의 뜻이 같아지도록 각각의 빈칸에 알맞은 단어를 쓰세요.

> • Get up early, and you won't miss the bus.
> = ___________ you get up early, you
>   ___________ miss the bus.

3 다음 중 어법상 어색한 문장은?

① If you work hard, you'll succeed.
② If she passes the test, she'll be so happy.
③ If it will snow tomorrow, I will stay at home.
④ If you come to my party, we'll have a good time.
⑤ If you lose weight, you'll be healthy.

4 다음 밑줄 친 부분 중 어법상 잘못된 것은?

> If she ① went there ② by car, ③ she won't ④ arrive ⑤ on time.

5 다음의 직설법 문장을 가정법 문장으로 알맞게 고친 것은?

> As he doesn't know her phone number, he won't call her.

① If he knows her phone number, he will call her.
② If he knew her phone number, he will call her.
③ If he had known her phone number, he would have called her.
④ If he knew her phone number, he would call her.
⑤ If he knew her phone number, he would called her.

6 다음 빈칸에 들어갈 알맞은 말은?

> If she doesn't take a taxi, she ___________ late.

① is   ② was   ③ be
④ does   ⑤ will be

7 다음 중 어법상 어색한 문장은?

① I wish you could spend Christmas with me.
② This book is three times as expensive as that one.
③ If you didn't tell me about the problem, I couldn't have helped.
④ I wish there were no pollution in the world.
⑤ I hope that I can meet many good friends and teachers.

8 다음 중 어법상 <u>어색한</u> 문장은?

① I wish you could come with me.
② You talk as if you are my father.
③ I wish you were here with us.
④ If I were you, I would marry her.
⑤ If I don't get it, I will try it again.

9 다음 중 어법상 올바른 문장을 <u>두 개</u> 고르세요.

① If you eat a snack, you might feel less hungry.
② If you want to stay healthy, exercise regularly.
③ If you turn the music app on, you can listen to music.
④ If you got up early, you might have caught the first train.
⑤ If you study hard, you may passed the test.

10 주어진 문장을 가정법으로 올바르게 바꾼 것은?

> As I am busy, I can't go to the concert with you.

① If I am busy, I can go to the concert with you.
② If I am not busy, I could go to the concert with you.
③ If I weren't busy, I could go to the concert with you.
④ If I were busy, I could go to the concert with you.
⑤ If I were busy, I can't go to the concert with you.

11 다음 문장에서 어법상 <u>틀린</u> 부분을 한 군데 찾아 바르게 고쳐 쓰세요.

> My sister went to America to study music last month. I always think of her and miss her a lot. If I am a bird, I could fly to her. I wish I could go to America this summer.

___________ ➡ ___________

12 다음 ⓐ~ⓔ 중, 어법상 <u>어색한</u> 문장의 개수를 고르시오.

> ⓐ If she were not sick, she could have come to the party.
> ⓑ If she had not been at work, she could have come here.
> ⓒ If I had known the truth, I would have told them.
> ⓓ If we had the key, we could have entered now.
> ⓔ If I had lived there, I would have visited him often.

① 0개　② 1개　③ 2개　④ 3개　⑤ 4개

13 다음 빈칸에 알맞은 단어를 넣어 문장을 완성하세요.

> • I didn't finish it by myself. I'm sorry about that.
> ➡ I ___________ I ___________ it by myself.

14 다음 중 앞뒤 문장의 연결이 의미상 <u>어색한</u> 것은?

① I don't have a lot of free time. I wish I had a lot of free time.

② I am not good at running. I wish I were good at running.

③ I can't swim in the sea. I wish I could swim like a fish.

④ I don't know Chinese. I wish I didn't know Chinese.

⑤ I can't sleep well at night. I wish I could sleep well at night.

15 우리말과 같은 뜻이 되도록 주어진 동사를 활용하여 빈칸에 알맞은 말을 쓰세요.

- 내가 작년에 세계 여행을 했더라면 좋았을 텐데.
  = I wish I ______________ ______________ around the world last year. (travel)

16 주어진 표현을 사용하여 영작하세요. (총 9단어, 축약표현은 쓰지 말 것)

- 내가 그녀였다면, 나는 그 제안을 거절했을 거야.
  (refused / were / offer)

  ➡ ______________________________________

  ____

17 우리말과 같은 뜻이 되도록 빈칸에 알맞은 단어를 쓰세요.

- 그녀는 마치 자신이 여왕인 것처럼 행동한다.
  (실제로는 여왕이 아님.)
  = She acts as if she __________ a queen.

18 빈칸에 알맞은 단어를 써서 주어진 문장을 as if 가정법 문장으로 바꾸세요.

- In fact, Mary is not my close friend.
  ➡ Mary speaks as if she __________

  __________ __________ __________.

19 다음 주어진 문장과 의미가 같은 것은?

If I had enough money, I could buy all the items I want.

① Because I didn't have enough money, I couldn't buy all the items I wanted.

② Although I don't have enough money, I can buy all the items I want.

③ Because I don't have enough money, I can't buy all the items I want.

④ As I have enough money, I can buy all the items I want.

⑤ Though I have enough money, I can't buy all the items I want.

20 다음을 가정법 문장으로 바꿀 때 빈칸에 알맞은 단어를 쓰세요.

- In fact, he didn't meet Ms. Kim.
  ➡ He talks as if __________

  __________ Ms. Kim.

21 주어진 우리말과 같은 뜻이 되도록 다음 각 빈칸에 알맞은 한 단어를 쓰세요.

> A: I wish I ______________ music traveling all over the world.
> (내가 전 세계를 여행하며 음악을 연주한다면 좋을 텐데.)
> B: I wish I ______________ English as well as you.
> (난 너만큼 영어를 잘 말한다면 좋을 텐데.)

22 주어진 문장과 같은 뜻이 되도록 if로 시작하는 가정법 문장을 쓰세요.

> • As I don't know the password, I can't log into the website.

➡ ____

____

23 다음 빈칸에 들어갈 말을 바르게 짝지은 것을 고르세요.

> A: I think Vincent van Gogh is one of the greatest artists of all time.
> B: I'm with you on that. If I ________ talent for art, I ________ a famous artist like him.

① will have – can be
② have – were
③ had – could be
④ will have – could be
⑤ had – could have been

24 다음 우리말을 영어로 바르게 옮긴 것은?

> • 내가 설거지하는 걸 네가 도와주지 않으면, 난 너 한테 쿠키를 구워주지 않을 거야.

① If you help me do the dishes, I won't bake you cookies.
② If you don't help me do the dishes, I won't bake you cookies.
③ If you help me do the dishes, I will bake you cookies.
④ If you didn't help me do the dishes, I bake you cookies.
⑤ If you helped me do the dishes, I will bake you cookies.

25 다음 빈칸에 들어갈 말을 〈보기〉에서 골라 순서대로 바르게 나열한 것은?

> • If I were born as the son of a king, ________
> • If I knew all the answers to the test, ______
> • If I won the lottery, ________________
> • If I were a movie director, ________________
> • If I had a driver's license, ________________

> 보 기
> ⓐ I could drive to the country to relax.
> ⓑ I could get a good grade.
> ⓒ I would be a prince.
> ⓓ I could help the poor in our neighborhood.
> ⓔ I could make movies with famous actors.

① ⓒ – ⓑ – ⓓ – ⓔ – ⓐ
② ⓒ – ⓐ – ⓓ – ⓔ – ⓑ
③ ⓓ – ⓐ – ⓒ – ⓔ – ⓑ
④ ⓒ – ⓑ – ⓐ – ⓔ – ⓓ
⑤ ⓐ – ⓒ – ⓓ – ⓔ – ⓑ

CHAPTER 13
비교구문

PSS 1 비교급과 최상급 만드는 법

PSS 1-1 규칙 변화 I

일반적인 경우	형용사/부사의 원급+er, est	old – old**er** – old**est** tall – tall**er** – tall**est** kind – kind**er** – kind**est**	small – small**er** – small**est** hard – hard**er** – hard**est** high – high**er** – high**est**
-e로 끝나는 경우	형용사/부사의 원급+r, st	close – close**r** – close**st** nice – nice**r** – nice**st**	large – large**r** – large**st** strange – strange**r** – strange**st**

정답 p.74

PRACTICE 1

다음 형용사나 부사의 비교급과 최상급을 쓰세요.

1 cold – ___________ – ___________

2 young – ___________ – ___________

3 nice – ___________ – ___________

4 high – ___________ – ___________

5 fresh – ___________ – ___________

6 small – ___________ – ___________

7 strange – ___________ – ___________

8 fast – ___________ – ___________

9 low – ___________ – ___________

10 new – ___________ – ___________

11 hard – ___________ – ___________

12 close – ___________ – ___________

13 long – ___________ – ___________

14 slow – ___________ – ___________

15 tall – ___________ – ___________

16 old – ___________ – ___________

17 kind – ___________ – ___________

18 warm – ___________ – ___________

19 large – ___________ – ___________

20 smart – ___________ – ___________

PSS 1-2 규칙 변화 II

자음+y로 끝나는 경우	자음+ i+er, est	early – earl**ier** – earl**iest** happy – happ**ier** – happ**iest** pretty – prett**ier** – prett**iest** healthy – health**ier** – health**iest**	heavy – heav**ier** – heav**iest** easy – eas**ier** – eas**iest** busy – bus**ier** – bus**iest**

<table>
<tr><td rowspan="2">단모음+단자음
으로 끝나는 경우</td><td rowspan="2">원급+마지막
자음+er, est</td><td>hot – hot**ter** – hot**test**</td><td>big – big**ger** – big**gest**</td></tr>
<tr><td>thin – thin**ner** – thin**nest**</td><td>fat – fat**ter** – fat**test**</td></tr>
</table>

정답 p.74

PRACTICE 2

다음 형용사나 부사의 비교급과 최상급을 쓰세요.

1 happy – __________ – __________　　2 healthy – __________ – __________

3 hot – __________ – __________　　4 easy – __________ – __________

5 heavy – __________ – __________　　6 early – __________ – __________

7 wise – __________ – __________　　8 thin – __________ – __________

9 funny – __________ – __________　　10 pretty – __________ – __________

11 dirty – __________ – __________　　12 lucky – __________ – __________

13 friendly – __________ – __________　　14 tasty – __________ – __________

15 sweet – __________ – __________　　16 lazy – __________ – __________

17 noisy – __________ – __________　　18 big – __________ – __________

19 busy – __________ – __________　　20 dry – __________ – __________

21 wet – __________ – __________　　22 ugly – __________ – __________

23 hungry – __________ – __________　　24 strict – __________ – __________

PSS 1-3 규칙 변화 Ⅲ

-y, -er로 끝나는 형용사를 제외한 대부분의 2음절 이상의 형용사	more+원급, most+원급	helpful – **more** helpful – **most** helpful useless – **more** useless – **most** useless beautiful – **more** beautiful – **most** beautiful expensive – **more** expensive – **most** expensive
분사 형태의 형용사	more+원급, most+원급	tired – **more** tired – **most** tired surprised – **more** surprised – **most** surprised boring – **more** boring – **most** boring shocking – **more** shocking – **most** shocking

<table>
<tr><td rowspan="4">'형용사+ly'
형태의 부사</td><td rowspan="4">more+원급,
most+원급</td><td>exactly – **more** exactly – **most** exactly</td></tr>
<tr><td>slowly – **more** slowly – **most** slowly</td></tr>
<tr><td>easily – **more** easily – **most** easily</td></tr>
<tr><td>fluently – **more** fluently – **most** fluently</td></tr>
</table>

정답 p.74

PRACTICE 3

다음 형용사나 부사의 비교급과 최상급을 쓰세요.

1 useful   – _____________ – _____________

2 serious   – _____________ – _____________

3 cheap   – _____________ – _____________

4 afraid   – _____________ – _____________

5 excited   – _____________ – _____________

6 hard   – _____________ – _____________

7 tired   – _____________ – _____________

8 scary   – _____________ – _____________

9 curious   – _____________ – _____________

10 popular   – _____________ – _____________

11 handsome   – _____________ – _____________

12 large   – _____________ – _____________

13 slowly   – _____________ – _____________

14 famous   – _____________ – _____________

15 helpful   – _____________ – _____________

16 surprised   – _____________ – _____________

17 expensive   – _____________ – _____________

18 poor   – _____________ – _____________

19 boring   – _____________ – _____________

20 anxious   – _____________ – _____________

21 convenient   – _____________ – _____________

22 wide   – _____________ – _____________

23 lonely   – _____________   – _____________

24 foolish   – _____________   – _____________

25 patient   – _____________   – _____________

26 strong   – _____________   – _____________

27 useless   – _____________   – _____________

28 deep   – _____________   – _____________

29 beautiful   – _____________   – _____________

30 creative   – _____________   – _____________

31 exactly   – _____________   – _____________

32 mild   – _____________   – _____________

33 easily   – _____________   – _____________

34 important   – _____________   – _____________

35 fluently   – _____________   – _____________

36 great   – _____________   – _____________

37 quickly   – _____________   – _____________

38 difficult   – _____________   – _____________

39 interesting   – _____________   – _____________

40 nervous   – _____________   – _____________

CH
13
비교구문

PSS 1-4 불규칙 변화

good – better – best	좋은	This car is **better** than that one. 이 차가 저 차보다 더 좋다.
well – better – best	건강한, 잘	Kelly speaks French **better** than Nick. Kelly가 Nick보다 프랑스어를 더 잘 말한다.
bad – worse – worst	나쁜	The movie is **worse** than I thought. 그 영화는 내가 생각했던 것보다 더 나쁘다.
ill – worse – worst	병든, 건강이 나쁜	Jim is **worse** than yesterday. Jim은 어제보다 상태가 더 나쁘다.

old – older – oldest	나이든, 오래된	My purse is **older** than yours. 내 지갑은 네 것보다 더 오래되었다.
old – elder – eldest	연상의, 손위의	Jason is my **elder** brother. Jason은 내 형이다.
late – later – latest	〈시간〉 늦은	Sujin arrived in Korea **later** than I had expected. 수진은 내가 기대했던 것보다 한국에 더 늦게 도착했다.
late – latter – last	〈순서〉 늦은	The **latter** part of this book is very interesting. 이 책의 후반부는 매우 흥미롭다.
far – farther – farthest	〈거리〉 먼	I can't go **farther** because I'm very tired. 나는 매우 피곤하기 때문에 더 멀리 갈 수 없다. ***cf.*** 시간, 공간상으로 먼 것을 나타낼 때 further, furthest를 쓰는 경우도 있다.
far – further – furthest	〈정도〉 더욱, 한층	We'd better discuss this problem **further**. 우리는 이 문제에 대해 더 논의해 보는 게 좋겠어요.
many – more – most	〈수〉 많은	Susan has **more** friends than Jeff has. Susan은 Jeff보다 더 많은 친구가 있다.
much – more – most	〈양〉 많은	Give me some **more** water. 내게 물을 좀 더 주세요.
few – fewer – fewest	〈수〉 적은	**Fewer** students attended the class today. 더 적은 학생들이 오늘 수업에 참석했다.
little – less – least	〈양〉 적은	You have to eat **less** meat. 너는 고기를 덜 먹어야 한다.

정답 p.75

PRACTICE 4

다음 형용사나 부사의 비교급과 최상급을 쓰세요.

1 good   – __________ – __________
2 late(시간) – __________ – __________
3 old(나이든) – __________ – __________
4 bad   – __________ – __________
5 many   – __________ – __________
6 far(거리)   – __________ – __________
7 well   – __________ – __________
8 few   – __________ – __________
9 old(손위의) – __________ – __________
10 late(순서) – __________ – __________
11 little   – __________ – __________
12 ill   – __________ – __________
13 far(정도)   – __________ – __________
14 much   – __________ – __________

PSS 2 원급을 이용한 비교

PSS 2-1 as+원급+as

1. 「as+원급+as」 '~만큼 …한'

   Sumi is **as tall as** Mira.

   수미는 미라만큼 키가 크다.

   Today is **as cold as** yesterday.

   오늘은 어제만큼 춥다.

   John speaks Korean **as well as** Kelly.

   John은 Kelly만큼 한국어를 잘 말한다.

   I go shopping **as often as** you.

   나는 너만큼 자주 쇼핑하러 간다.

   cf. 「배수+as+원급+as」 '~배 더 …한'

   The train is **three times as fast as** the car. 그 기차는 그 차보다 3배 빠르다.

2. 「not as[so]+원급+as」 '~만큼 …하지 않은'

   The bread **is not as[so] heavy as** the banana.

   빵은 바나나만큼 무겁지 않다.

   = The banana is **heavier than** the bread.

   바나나가 빵보다 더 무겁다.

   I **didn't** get up **as[so] early as** you.

   나는 너만큼 일찍 일어나지 않았다.

   = You got up **earlier than** I did.

   너는 나보다 더 일찍 일어났다.

   = You got up **earlier than** me.

   cf. than 뒤의 「주어+동사」는 목적격으로 바꾸어 쓸 수 있다.

정답 p.75

PRACTICE 5 [1-10]

〈보기〉와 같이 짝지어진 두 문장의 의미가 같도록 「as ~ as」 구문을 사용하여 빈칸을 채우세요. (단, 축약형으로 쓸 수 있는 경우에는 축약형으로 쓸 것.)

> 보 기
>
> Insu studies harder than Giho.
>
> = Giho _doesn't study as[so] hard as_ Insu.

1 Tony is more polite than Jack.

= Jack ________________________________ Tony.

2 Jieun is taller than Minyoung.

= Minyoung ____ Jieun.

3 My dog is cuter than my cat.

= My cat ____ my dog.

4 The train to Busan is faster than the bus.

= The bus to Busan ____ the train.

5 My shirt is whiter than his shirt.

= His shirt ____ my shirt.

6 We bought more books than they did.

= They ____ we did.

7 I speak English better than Sumi does.

= Sumi ____ I do.

8 This sofa is more comfortable than that sofa.

= That sofa ____ this sofa.

9 I like baseball more than basketball.

= I ____ baseball.

10 Math is more difficult than science for me.

= Science ____ math for me.

PRACTICE 6

정답 p.75

다음 대화를 읽고, 괄호 안의 단어를 알맞은 형태로 바꾸어 as ~ as 구문을 완성하세요.

#	Tony	Becky
1	I'm 15 years old.	I'm 15 years old, too.
2	My bag was 30,000 won.	My bag was 40,000 won.
3	I go to bed at eleven o'clock.	I go to bed at eleven o'clock, too.
4	I have two brothers.	I have two brothers, too.
5	I'm so tired. I can't play any longer. How about you?	I'm OK. I think I can play longer.
6	It took me 2 hours to do my homework.	My homework took me 2 hours, too.

1   Tony is ____ Becky. (old)

2   Tony's bag was ____ Becky's. (expensive)

3   Tony goes to bed ____ Becky. (late)

4   Tony has ____ Becky does. (many)

5   Becky is ____ Tony. (tired)

6   Becky's homework took ____ Tony's. (long)

PSS 2-2 as+원급+as+주어+can[could]

「as+원급+as+주어+can[could]」은 '~가 할 수 있는 한 …하게'의 뜻으로 「as+원급 +as possible」로 바꾸어 쓸 수 있다.

I'll finish it **as quickly as I can**. 나는 내가 할 수 있는 한 빨리 그것을 끝낼 것이다.
= I'll finish it **as quickly as possible**.

Jim ran **as fast as he could**. Jim은 그가 할 수 있는 한 빨리 달렸다.
= Jim ran **as fast as possible**.

정답 p.76

PRACTICE 7

괄호 안에 주어진 말을 바르게 배열하세요.

1   Jane always ____. (she, can, studies, hard, as, as)

2   I tried to ____. (possible, clearly, as, as, speak)

3   Frank ____. (early, could, got, up, as, he, as)

4   She threw the ball ____. (as, she, high, could, as)

5   Can you ____? (me, possible, soon, as, as, call)

6   Yuri ____. (as, as, helped, possible, us, much)

7   I ____. (counted, as, I, exactly, could, as, the number)

8   Ben ____. (goes, swimming, as, can, often, as, he)

9   They'll ____. (the questions, as, possible, as, make, easy)

10 Sujin wants to ____. (look, possible, as, young, as)

PRACTICE 8

짝지어진 두 문장의 의미가 같도록 문장을 완성하세요.

1 I spoke to her as slowly as possible.

= I spoke to her *as slowly as I could* .

2 Carrie sang as loud as she could.

= Carrie sang _______________________ .

3 Speak up in class as much as possible.

= Speak up in class _______________________ .

4 Ingyu wrote back to me as quickly as he could.

= Ingyu wrote back to me _______________________ .

5 Let's work as hard as possible.

= Let's work _______________________ .

6 I usually have breakfast as fast as I can.

= I usually have breakfast _______________________ .

7 Ann talked to him as kindly as possible.

= Ann talked to him _______________________ .

8 I'll wait for you as long as I can.

= I'll wait for you _______________________ .

9 She tries to eat food as little as possible.

= She tries to eat food _______________________ .

10 They read the report as closely as they could.

= They read the report _______________________ .

11 Try to experience as many things as possible.

= Try to experience _______________________ .

12 He walked as quietly as possible not to get caught.

= He walked _______________________ not to get caught.

13 We woke up as early as we could to take the first train.

= We woke up _______________________ to take the first train.

14 I wanted to see deep sea animals, so I dived as deep as I could.

= I wanted to see deep sea animals, so I dived _______________________ .

PSS 3 비교급을 이용한 비교

PSS 3-1 비교급+than

「비교급+than」 '~보다 더 …한'

My sister is **smarter than** I am.
나의 언니는 나보다 더 똑똑하다.
= My sister is **smarter than** me.

I can cook **better than** he can.
나는 그보다 요리를 더 잘할 수 있다.
= I can cook **better than** him.

I have **more** books **than** she does.
나는 그녀보다 더 많은 책들을 갖고 있다.
= I have **more** books **than** her.

cf. 비교급 문장에서 비교의 대상은 대등해야 하며, 이때, '주어+동사'는 목적격, '소유격+명사'는 소유대명사로 바꿔 나타낼 수 있다.

My bag is heavier than **you**. (X)
→ My bag is heavier than **your bag**. (O) 내 가방이 네 가방보다 더 무겁다.
　= My bag is heavier than **yours**.
Her hair is longer than **me**. (X)
→ Her hair is longer than **my hair**. (O) 그녀의 머리카락은 내 머리카락보다 더 길다.
　= Her hair is longer than **mine**.

정답 p.76

PRACTICE 9

괄호 안의 단어를 비교급 형태로 바꾸어 빈칸에 쓰세요.

1　Ann made ＿＿＿＿＿＿＿＿＿＿ money than I did. (much)

2　This flower is ＿＿＿＿＿＿＿＿＿＿ than that one. (beautiful)

3　Tom looks ＿＿＿＿＿＿＿＿＿＿ than Brad. (short)

4　I was ＿＿＿＿＿＿＿＿＿＿ than he was. (nervous)

5　He arrived at the airport ＿＿＿＿＿＿＿＿＿＿ than us. (late)

6　Jenny came to school ＿＿＿＿＿＿＿＿＿＿ than I did. (early)

PRACTICE 10

짝지어진 두 문장의 의미가 같도록 빈칸에 알맞은 말을 쓰세요.

1 I studied harder than him.

= I studied harder than __________ __________ . *he did*

2 Your cake looks larger than my cake.

= Your cake looks larger than __________________ .

3 My elder brother is more patient than me.

= My elder brother is more patient than __________ __________ .

4 Lisa was happier than we were.

= Lisa was happier than __________________ .

5 He can type more quickly than she can.

= He can type more quickly than __________________ .

6 My dog is smarter than your dog.

= My dog is smarter than __________________ .

PRACTICE 11

다음 대화를 읽고, 비교급을 사용하여 빈칸에 알맞은 말을 쓰세요.

	Tony	Becky
1	I'm 16 years old.	I'm 14 years old.
2	I'm 158cm tall.	I'm 160cm tall.
3	I can't play the guitar well.	I can play the guitar well.
4	I'm very diligent.	I'm not very diligent.
5	I weigh 48kg.	I weigh 59kg.
6	I'm very excited about the vacation.	I'm not so excited about the vacation.
7	I'm not so popular.	I'm very popular.
8	I run 7 meters per second.	I run 5 meters per second.
9	I study very hard.	I don't study very hard.
10	I'm not so active.	I'm very active.

1   Tony is <u> *older than* </u> Becky.

2   Becky is <u>   </u> Tony.

3   Becky can play the guitar <u>   </u> Tony.

4   Tony is <u>   </u> Becky.

5   Becky is <u>   </u> Tony.

6   Tony is <u>   </u> about the vacation <u>   </u> Becky.

7   Becky is <u>   </u> Tony.

8   Tony runs <u>   </u> Becky.

9   Tony studies <u>   </u> Becky.

10   Becky is <u>   </u> Tony.

PSS 3-2 비교급 강조

much, still, even, far, a lot은 비교급 앞에서 '훨씬'의 뜻으로 비교급을 강조한다.

I feel **much happier** now than before. 나는 전보다 지금 훨씬 더 행복하다고 느낀다.

Nami is **still busier** than Yuri. 나미는 유리보다 훨씬 더 바쁘다.

This bag is **even smaller** than I thought. 이 가방은 내가 생각했던 것보다 훨씬 더 작다.

It's **far colder** here than in Korea. 여기가 한국에서보다 훨씬 더 춥다.

Jinho speaks English **a lot better** than I expected.

진호는 내가 기대했던 것보다 훨씬 더 영어를 잘 말한다.

cf. very는 '매우'의 뜻으로 원급을 강조한다.

Your tie looks **very nice**. 네 넥타이는 매우 멋져 보인다.

Minsu was walking **very slowly**. 민수는 매우 천천히 걷고 있었다.

정답 p.76

PRACTICE 12 [1-10]

다음 중 밑줄 친 부분의 쓰임이 바른 것은 ○표, 바르지 않은 것은 ×표 하세요.

1   Mike is <u>even</u> lazier than Suji.   <u>   </u>

2   Helen is <u>very</u> shorter than my sister.   <u>   </u>

3   This computer is <u>far</u> expensive.   <u>   </u>

4   Minji is <u>much</u> kinder than other students.   <u>   </u>

5   You look <u>very</u> sleepy.   _____________

6   Jeff dances <u>very</u> better than anyone else.   _____________

7   I can swim <u>still</u> faster than he can.   _____________

8   You are <u>very</u> smarter than I am.   _____________

9   Peter sang the song <u>very</u> well.   _____________

10   This information is <u>a lot</u> important for the test.   _____________

정답 p.77

PRACTICE 13

다음 문장의 빈칸에 주어진 철자로 시작하는 비교급 강조어를 쓰세요.

1   His score is s____________ higher than mine.

2   The patient felt a____________ better than a week ago.

3   Steve was e____________ funnier than Daniel.

4   The car is f____________ more expensive than I expected.

5   She made the work m____________ easier for us.

6   They invited e____________ more people than we had wanted.

7   Her idea was f____________ more creative than yours.

8   Miss Ford looks m____________ younger than she is.

9   The cost of digital books is s____________ lower than that of print versions.

10   The movie star has become a____________ more famous since her last movie.

PSS 3-3 less + 원급 + than

「less+원급+than」은 '~보다 덜 …한'을 의미하고, 「not as[so]+원급+as」로 바꾸어 쓸 수 있다.

Brian watches the news **less often than** Kate. Brian은 Kate보다 뉴스를 덜 자주 본다.
= Brian **doesn't** watch the news **as[so] often as** Kate.

Driving in the country is **less hard than** driving in the city.
시골에서 운전하는 것은 도시에서 운전하는 것보다 덜 힘들다.
= Driving in the country is **not as[so] hard as** driving in the city.

cf. Driving in the country is less <u>harder</u> than driving in the city. (X)

PRACTICE 14

〈보기〉와 같이 짝지어진 두 문장의 의미가 같도록 as ~ as 구문을 사용하여 빈칸을 채우세요.

> **보 기**
> This bed is less comfortable than that bed.
> = This bed isn't as[so] comfortable as that bed.

1 Fishing is less exciting than hiking.
  = Fishing ____ .

2 This bag is less expensive than that one.
  = This bag ____ .

3 I met Insu less often than you did.
  = I ____ .

4 Money is less important than friendship.
  = Money ____ .

5 Your article is less interesting than mine.
  = Your article ____ .

6 Nami speaks Japanese less fluently than Seho.
  = Nami ____ .

7 The movie version was less boring than the book itself.
  = The movie version ____ .

8 Swimming in a pool is less dangerous than swimming in the ocean.
  = Swimming in a pool ____ .

CH
13
비교구문

PSS 3-4 the+비교급, the+비교급

「the+비교급, the+비교급」 '~하면 할수록 더 …하다'

The more you practice, **the better** you will become.
더 많이 연습할수록 너는 더 잘하게 될 것이다.
The harder you study, **the smarter** you will become.
더 열심히 공부하면 할수록 너는 더 똑똑해질 것이다.
The heavier it is, **the more expensive** it is.
더 무거우면 무거울수록 더 비싸다.
The earlier you arrive, **the better** seats you'll get for the concert.
더 일찍 당신이 도착할수록 당신은 콘서트에서 더 좋은 자리들을 얻을 것이다.

PRACTICE 15

〈보기〉와 같이 「the+비교급, the+비교급」을 이용하여 주어진 문장을 바꾸어 쓰세요.

> 보 기   If the weather is worse, I feel more depressed.
> ➡ The worse the weather is, the more depressed I feel.

1 When you give more, you feel happier.
➡ _______________________________________

2 As I walked faster, the building became closer.
➡ _______________________________________

3 If you want more, you will be more disappointed.
➡ _______________________________________

4 If you get to know him more, you will like him more.
➡ _______________________________________

5 As I listened to the music longer, I became more cheerful.
➡ _______________________________________

6 As he went farther, he looked smaller.
➡ _______________________________________

7 If you practice more, you will play better.
➡ _______________________________________

8 When it grew darker, we felt more scared.
➡ _______________________________________

9 If you stay longer, it will be harder to leave.
➡ _______________________________________

10 As it gets colder, people drink more hot chocolate.
➡ _______________________________________

PSS 3-5 There is nothing ~ 비교급+than …

「There is nothing ~ 비교급+than …」은 '…보다 더 ~한 것은 없다'의 뜻으로 최상급의 의미를 나타낸다.

1. 「There is nothing + 비교급 + than …」

There is nothing more interesting than reading books.
책을 읽는 것보다 더 흥미로운 것은 없다.

= Reading books is **the most interesting**. 책을 읽는 것이 가장 흥미롭다.

There is nothing more boring than waiting for somebody on the street.

길에서 누군가를 기다리는 것보다 더 지루한 것은 없다.

= Waiting for somebody on the street is **the most boring** thing to do.

길에서 누군가를 기다리는 것이 하기에 가장 지루한 일이다.

2. 「There is nothing + 주어 + 동사 + 비교급 + than …」

There is nothing I do **better than** drawing. 그림을 그리는 것보다 내가 더 잘하는 것은 없다.

= I draw **(the) best**. 나는 그림 그리는 것을 가장 잘한다.

There is nothing I enjoy **more than** teaching kids.

아이들을 가르치는 것보다 내가 더 즐기는 것은 없다.

= I enjoy teaching kids **(the) most**. 나는 아이들을 가르치는 것을 가장 즐긴다.

정답 p.77

PRACTICE 16

괄호 안의 말을 어법에 맞게 배열하여 문장을 완성하세요.

1 내가 가장 잘하는 것은 요리하는 것이다. (nothing, I, than, there is, do, better)

➡ ____ cooking.

2 수학이 나에게 가장 어렵다. (there is, than, more, difficult, nothing)

➡ ____ math for me.

3 그가 가장 관심이 있는 것은 축구이다. (there is, he, interested in, nothing, is, than, more)

➡ ____ soccer.

4 내 엄마의 쿠키는 가장 맛있다. (there is, more, delicious, nothing, than)

➡ ____ my mom's cookies.

5 액션 영화는 가장 흥분된다. (there is, than, exciting, nothing, more)

➡ ____ action movies.

6 나는 내 아이들을 가장 걱정한다. (than, I, nothing, more, there is, worry about)

➡ ____ my children.

7 John은 영어를 가장 잘 말한다. (than, there is, better, John, nothing, speaks)

➡ ____ English.

8 내가 가장 좋아하는 것은 사진을 찍는 것이다. (like, than, there is, nothing, better, I)

➡ ____ taking pictures.

PSS 3-6 비교급+and+비교급

「-er+and+-er」 또는 「more and more ~」 '점점 더 ~한'

Mark is becoming **thinner and thinner**. Mark는 점점 더 야위어가고 있다.
The man ran **more and more slowly**. 그 남자는 점점 더 천천히 달렸다.
The sky is getting **darker and darker**.
하늘은 점점 더 어두워지고 있다.

정답 p.77

PRACTICE 17

〈보기〉와 같이 괄호 안의 단어와 「비교급+and+비교급」 구문을 이용하여 빈칸을 채우세요.

보 기	Her voice was getting *louder and louder*. (loud)

1 The weather is getting ________________. (cold)

2 Sue will become ________________. (pretty)

3 The tree is growing ________________. (tall)

4 We are getting ________________. (old)

5 The man was getting ________________. (well)

6 The child was growing ________________. (tired)

7 Jerry is becoming ________________. (popular)

8 The bird was flying ________________. (high)

9 I started walking ________________. (fast)

10 The houses became ________________. (expensive)

PSS 4 최상급을 이용한 비교

PSS 4-1 the+최상급

「the+최상급」은 '가장 ~한'의 뜻으로, 비교의 대상을 한정할 때는 주로 최상급 뒤에 in, of 가 이끄는 전치사구나 절이 나온다. in 뒤에는 장소나 집단을 나타내는 단수 명사가 오며, of 뒤에는 주로 복수 명사 및 복수의 의미를 나타내는 명사가 온다.

What's **the longest** river **in the world**? 세계에서 가장 긴 강은 무엇이니?

Bob is **the tallest** of the students. Bob은 그 학생들 중에서 가장 키가 크다.

That's **the most boring** book **I've ever read**.

그것은 내가 지금껏 읽은 것 중 가장 지루한 책이다.

정답 p.77

PRACTICE 18

괄호 안의 단어를 최상급의 형태로 바꾸어 빈칸에 쓰세요.

1 This is ________________________________ restaurant in the city. (cheap)

2 Jim is ________________________________ of my friends. (young)

3 It was ________________________________ thing I've done. (foolish)

4 Angela is ________________________________ friend of mine. (close)

5 That is ________________________________ story I've ever heard. (strange)

6 Seho is ________________________________ swimmer in my school. (good)

7 This is ________________________________ problem I've ever had. (serious)

8 This is ________________________________ car in our company. (new)

9 I had ________________________________ birthday in my life. (bad)

10 The computer is ________________________________ invention I've ever used. (convenient)

정답 p.78

PRACTICE 19 [1-5]

그림을 보고, 주어진 단어를 이용하여 빈칸에 비교하는 말을 바르게 쓰세요.

1 

(hot)

① July is ________________ June.

② August is ________________ .

2

(tall)

① The elephant is ________________ the lion.

② The giraffe is ________________ .

3

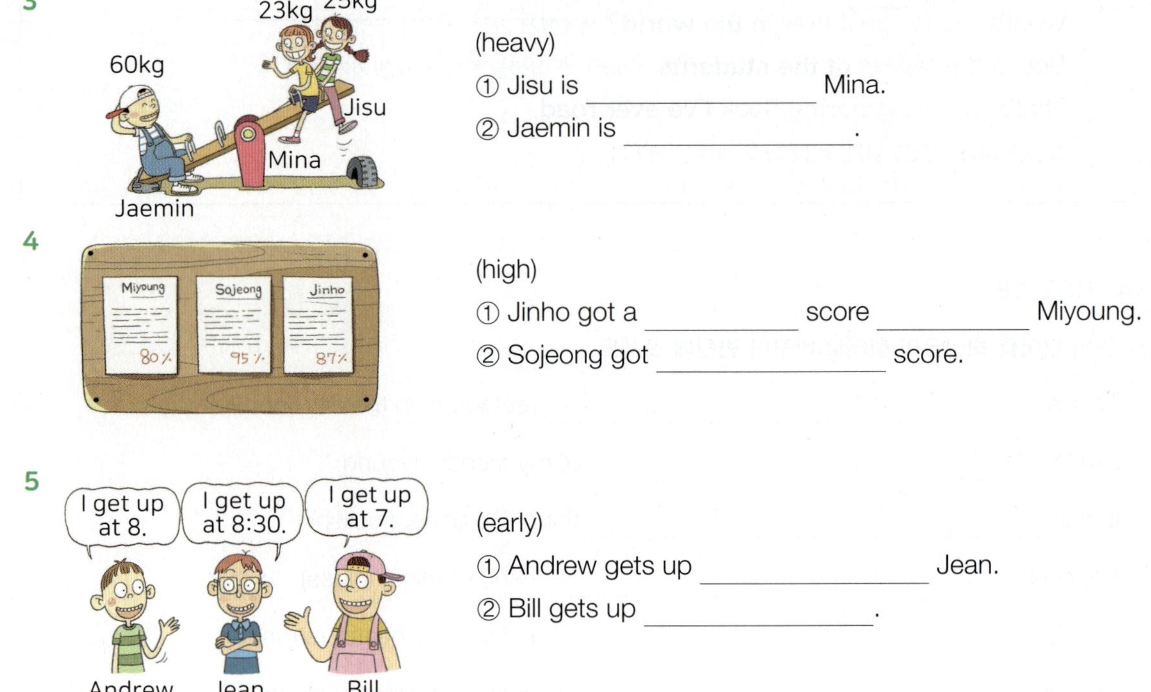

(heavy)

① Jisu is ___________________ Mina.

② Jaemin is ___________________ .

4

(high)

① Jinho got a ____________ score ____________ Miyoung.

② Sojeong got ___________________ score.

5

(early)

① Andrew gets up ___________________ Jean.

② Bill gets up ___________________ .

PSS 4-2 one of + the + 최상급 + 복수 명사

「one of + the + 최상급 + 복수 명사」는 '가장 ~한 것 중의 하나'라고 해석하고, 주어 자리에 올 경우 단수 취급함에 유의한다.

Shakespeare **is one of the greatest writers**. 셰익스피어는 가장 위대한 작가들 중 한 명이다.

One of the easiest ways is to use public transportation.

가장 쉬운 방법들 중 하나는 대중교통을 이용하는 것이다.

This is **one of the most expensive rings** I have. 이것은 내가 가진 가장 비싼 반지들 중 하나이다.

정답 p.78

PRACTICE 20

〈보기〉와 같이 최상급 표현을 이용하여 빈칸에 알맞은 말을 쓰세요.

보 기   It is a very large city. It is _one of the largest cities_ in the world.

1 The Han River is a very long river. It is ___________________________ in Korea.

2 Gandhi is a very famous man. He is ___________________________ in the world.

3 Sumi is a very diligent student. She is ___________________________ in her class.

4 Mt. Halla is a very high mountain. It is ______________________ in Korea.

5 China is a very big country. It is ______________________ in the world.

6 Ralph is a very happy boy. He is ______________________ in the town.

7 This is a very boring movie. It is ______________________ I've ever seen.

8 Mr. Kim is a very kind teacher. He is ______________________ I've ever met.

9 Mira is a very beautiful girl. She is ______________________ I know.

10 This is a very popular restaurant. It is ______________________ in Seoul.

PSS 4-3 최상급의 다른 표현

다음과 같은 표현을 사용하여 최상급의 의미를 나타낼 수 있다.

「No (other) ~ as[so]＋원급＋as」 ~만큼 …한 것은 없다
= 「No (other) ~ 비교급＋than」 ~보다 …한 것은 없다
= 「비교급＋than any other＋단수 명사」 ~는 다른 어떤 −보다도 더 …하다
= 「비교급＋than all the other＋복수 명사」 ~는 다른 모든 −보다도 더 …하다

Alex is **the strongest boy** in his class. Alex는 그의 반에서 가장 힘이 센 소년이다.

= **No (other) boy** in his class is **as[so] strong as** Alex.

그의 반에서 Alex만큼 힘이 센 소년은 없다.

= **No (other) boy** in his class is **stronger than** Alex.

그의 반에서 Alex보다 힘이 센 소년은 없다.

= Alex is **stronger than any other boy** in his class.

Alex는 그의 반에서 다른 어떤 소년보다도 더 힘이 세다.

= Alex is **stronger than all the other boys** in his class.

Alex는 그의 반에서 다른 모든 소년들보다도 더 힘이 세다.

This is **the most interesting** book of all. 이것은 모든 책 중에서 가장 재미있는 책이다.

= **No (other) book** is **as[so] interesting as** this book.

이 책만큼 재미있는 책은 없다.

= **No (other) book** is **more interesting than** this book.

이 책보다 더 재미있는 책은 없다.

= This is **more interesting than any other book**.

이것은 다른 어떤 책보다도 더 재미있다.

= This is **more interesting than all the other books**.

이것은 다른 모든 책들보다도 더 재미있다.

PRACTICE 21

다음 문장들이 같은 뜻이 되도록 빈칸에 알맞은 말을 쓰세요.

1 This is the most expensive bag in the shop.

= ________________________ in the shop is ________________________ this bag.

= ________________________ in the shop is ________________________ this bag.

= This is ________________________ in the shop.

= This is ________________________ in the shop.

2 Sarah is the tallest girl in my school.

= ________________________ in my school is ________________________ Sarah.

= ________________________ in my school is ________________________ Sarah.

= Sarah is ________________________ in my school.

= Sarah is ________________________ in my school.

3 He was the most popular singer in the 1990s.

= ________________________ in the 1990s was ________________________ him.

= ________________________ in the 1990s was ________________________ him.

= He was ________________________ in the 1990s.

= He was ________________________ in the 1990s.

4 This is the most difficult question of all.

= ________________________ is ________________________ this.

= ________________________ is ________________________ this.

= This is ________________________ .

= This is ________________________ .

5 My childhood pet, Daisy was the cutest dog in my town.

= ________________________ in my town was ________________________ my childhood pet, Daisy.

= ________________________ in my town was ________________________ my childhood pet, Daisy.

= My childhood pet, Daisy was ________________________ in my town.

= My childhood pet, Daisy was ________________________ in my town.

6 The Red Sea is the saltiest sea in the world.

= ________________________ in the world is ________________________ the Red Sea.

= ________________________ in the world is ________________________ the Red Sea.

= The Red Sea is ________________________ in the world.

= The Red Sea is ________________________ in the world.

중간·기말고사 대비문제

1 다음 괄호 안에 주어진 단어의 형태가 바르게 짝지어진 것은?

> • I consider time (important) than money.
> • Water is the (important) thing in the desert.
> • Saving money is as (important) as making money.

① important – important – important
② important – most important – more important
③ most important – important – more important
④ more important – most important – important
⑤ more important – more important – important

2 다음 각 빈칸에 알맞은 말로 바르게 짝지어진 것은?

> • This product is __________ better than that one.
> • This cake tastes __________ good. I'd like to have another piece.

① much – much
② even – much
③ even – very
④ very – still
⑤ very – very

3 다음 주어진 문장과 의미가 같은 것은?

> This room is not so dark as that room.

① That room is not dark at all.
② This room is as dark as that room.
③ This room is darker than that room.
④ That room is darker than this room.
⑤ That room is not so dark as this room.

4 다음 문장의 밑줄 친 much와 쓰임이 같은 것은?

> They found out that she had a much better sense of humor than others in the room.

① She did not use much butter.
② How much money do you have now?
③ I don't like classical music that much.
④ You should not spend too much time watching TV.
⑤ It will be much more expensive than you imagined.

[5 - 6] 괄호 안에 주어진 조건대로 다음 우리말을 영작하세요.

5

> 그가 더 열심히 노력할수록, 그는 춤을 더 잘 출 수 있다. (hard를 활용하여 9단어로)

➡ ______________________________

6

> 우리가 더 많은 시간을 함께 보낼수록, 우리는 더 가까워진다. (become을 활용하여 10단어로)

➡ ______________________________

7 Which sentence has an error in grammar?

① I need to get up earlier.
② Sujin is even more beautiful than her sister.
③ His hands are bigger than his brother.
④ My grandfather really wants to look better than now.
⑤ He arrived in Japan later than I had expected.

8 우리말 해석에 맞게 빈칸을 완성하세요.

• __________ we save, __________ we become.
= 더 많이 절약할수록, 우리는 더 부유해진다.

➡ __________________, __________________

9 다음 글의 밑줄 친 ⓐ~ⓔ를 바르게 고친 것은?

I went to the zoo with my daughter last week. The zoo was ⓐ the large. She was ⓑ much happy to see a lot of animals. She especially liked the elephants, bears, lions, and kangaroos. The elephants were ⓒ very bigger than the kangaroos. The bears were as ⓓ bigger as the lions. My daughter said that the kangaroo was ⓔ much cutest animal.

① ⓐ the → much
② ⓑ much → very
③ ⓒ very → the
④ ⓓ bigger as → bigger than
⑤ ⓔ much cutest → more cutest

10 주어진 단어들을 반드시 사용하여 다음 우리말을 바르게 영작하세요.

• 그녀의 이구아나는 나의 이구아나만큼 빠르지 않다.
(iguana, fast, mine, as)

➡ __________________________________

11 다음 중 주어진 도표와 내용이 <u>다른</u> 것은?

	Lions	Elephants	Bears	Giraffes
Height (m)	1	3.1	1.8	5.3
Weight (kg)	200	1,600	1,000	1,400

① Lions are the shortest of the four animals.
② Giraffes are the tallest among the four animals.
③ Elephants are taller than lions and bears.
④ Lions are as heavy as giraffes.
⑤ Bears are heavier than lions.

12 다음 빈칸에 들어갈 알맞은 표현은?

Junho: Hey, Sunmi. I heard you caught a bad cold.
Sunmi: I did. That's why I couldn't come to school yesterday.
Junho: Are you okay?
Sunmi: Yeah, __________________. Thanks for asking.
Junho: That's good to hear.

① I'm feeling much good yesterday than
② I'm feeling very good than yesterday
③ I'm feeling much better than yesterday
④ I'm feeling much better yesterday than
⑤ I'm feeling very well than yesterday

13 다음 대화의 빈칸에 들어갈 말로 알맞은 것은?

A: How old are you?
B: I am 20 years old. How about you?
A: I am 18 years old.
B: You are not __________________ I am.

① as older as
② younger than
③ old than
④ as old as
⑤ as the old as

14 괄호 안에 주어진 단어를 알맞게 배열하여 문장을 완성하세요.

> Minsu hit the ball ________________________ .
> (he, as, could, as, hard)

15 다음 중 어법상 <u>잘못된</u> 문장 2개는?

① She is singing as loudly as she can.
② Can cats jump twice so high as dogs?
③ Sehwa is the most pretty girl in our school.
④ The whale is the biggest mammal in the world.
⑤ This stamp is one of the most expensive stamps in the country.

16 다음 중 어법상 <u>어색한</u> 것을 <u>모두</u> 고르세요.

① Suji is as kind as Jiyeon.
② My brother speaks Japanese as better as you.
③ I ran as fastly as I could.
④ Today is as hot as yesterday.
⑤ Paul spoke as slowly as he could.

17 우리말과 같은 뜻이 되도록 빈칸에 알맞은 한 단어를 쓰세요.

> • 너는 가능한 한 집에 빨리 와야 한다.
>   = You should get home as quickly as
>   ________________ .

18 다음의 빈칸에 공통으로 들어갈 단어는?

> • 잠을 적게 잘수록 너는 더 피곤하게 느낀다.
>   = The __________ you sleep, the more tired you feel.
> • Alex는 Jim보다 덜 먹는다.
>   = Alex eats __________ than Jim.

① little　　② less　　③ few
④ fewer　　⑤ more

19 다음 ⓐ~ⓔ 중 어법상 <u>틀린</u> 것을 있는 대로 고른 것은?

> ⓐ I can't run as faster as you.
> ⓑ Turtles live longer than wolves.
> ⓒ Chimpanzees are one of the smartest animal on earth.
> ⓓ The harder the wind blows, the colder we feel.
> ⓔ A cheetah is a very fastest of all land animals.

① ⓐ, ⓑ　　② ⓑ, ⓒ　　③ ⓐ, ⓒ, ⓔ
④ ⓐ, ⓓ, ⓔ　　⑤ ⓑ, ⓒ, ⓓ, ⓔ

20 다음 표의 내용과 일치하지 <u>않는</u> 것은?

Name	Weight	Height
Michelle	48kg	165cm
Tina	53kg	170cm
Ronnie	60kg	155cm
Hannah	45kg	150cm

① Michelle is taller than Hannah.
② Ronnie is lighter than all the other girls.
③ Ronnie is shorter than Tina.
④ Tina is the tallest of all the girls.
⑤ No other girl is lighter than Hannah.

21 다음 밑줄 친 far를 문맥에 맞게 바르게 고치세요.

Jason ran <u>far</u> than anyone else.

➡ ______________________________

22 다음 중 어법상 <u>틀린</u> 문장의 개수로 알맞은 것은?

ⓐ I'm not as smartest as my sister.

ⓑ I studied for the exam as hard as I could.

ⓒ If I were an English teacher, I would make my student speak English more fluently.

ⓓ The well you eat, the healthier you become.

ⓔ Vostok Station is the coldest area in the world.

ⓕ There is nothing difficulter than math.

ⓖ No other country is large than Russia.

ⓗ I didn't forget to call my grandparents.

① 3개　　　② 4개　　　③ 5개
④ 6개　　　⑤ 8개

23 다음 주어진 문장과 같은 뜻으로 쓰인 것은?

Jiyeon is not as funny as Inho.

① Inho is as funny as Jiyeon.
② Inho is funnier than Jiyeon.
③ Jiyeon is very funny.
④ Jiyeon is the funniest.
⑤ Inho is not funnier than Jiyeon.

24 다음 그림에 대한 설명 중 옳지 <u>않은</u> 것은?

A　B　C　D

① A is bigger than B.
② B is as big as D.
③ C is smaller than A.
④ C isn't as big as D.
⑤ D is the biggest of all.

25 두 문장이 같은 뜻이 되도록 할 때 빈칸에 들어갈 말이 순서대로 짝지어진 것은?

• Which do you __________, apples or bananas?
= Which do you like __________, apples or bananas?

① better – a lot　　② like　 – prefer
③ better – better　　④ prefer – better
⑤ prefer – prefer

26 다음 문장과 의미가 같도록 조건에 맞게 문장을 완성하세요.

Others' problems were worse than mine.

조 건
• as ~ as 비교구문을 사용할 것.
• 단어의 수는 제시된 빈칸의 수에 일치시킬 것.

➡ My problems were __________ __________

__________ __________ __________.

27 우리말 해석에 맞게 주어진 단어를 활용하여 빈칸을 완성하세요.

> Who's ____________ (handsome) ____________ in Italy?
> (누가 이탈리아에서 가장 잘생긴 가수인가?)

➡ ____

____

28 다음 밑줄 친 단어의 올바른 형태끼리 짝지어진 것은?

> • Reading is often <u>easy</u> than writing.
> • The question was the <u>hard</u> of all.

① easy – hard
② easy – harder
③ easier – harder
④ easier – hardest
⑤ easiest – hardest

29 두 문장이 같은 뜻이 되도록 할 때 빈칸에 들어갈 말로 알맞은 것은?

> • I like spaghetti more than any other food.
>   = I like ____________________.

① only spaghetti
② spaghetti most
③ spaghetti more
④ spaghetti very much
⑤ spaghetti better

30 다음 대화에서 <u>틀린</u> 부분을 찾아 바르게 고치세요.

> A: Paris is one of the most famous city in the world.
> B: I know. I'm going there this summer.

________________ ➡ ________________

31 다음 빈칸에 알맞은 말끼리 바르게 짝지어진 것은?

> • Money and fame are not as important as health.
>   = Money and fame are ____________ important ____________ health.

① less – than
② more – than
③ so – as
④ either – or
⑤ the – of

32 다음 중 어법상 <u>올바른</u> 문장은?

① I ran as fast as possibly.
② The least we have, the happiest we become.
③ It was getting darkest and darkest.
④ This question is very easier than that one.
⑤ There is nothing greater than the mother's love for her child.

33 다음 표를 보고, 괄호 안의 조건에 맞게 두 사람씩 비교하는 긍정문을 완성하세요.

	Calvin	Jason	Brad
Age	15	14	15
Height	175cm	170cm	165cm
50-meter race record	8.1 sec	7.5 sec	6.9 sec

(1) Calvin is ____________________ Brad.
   (Age)
(2) Jason is ____________________ Calvin.
   (Height)
(3) Brad is ____________________ Jason.
   (50-meter race record)

34 (가)~(마) 중 오류 없이 쓰인 것은?

Tea is one of the world's most popular drinks. (가) Green tea do contain caffeine. (나) Drinking too many tea before bed can make it hard to sleep. (다) Black tea is stronger than herbal tea. (라) India is one of the largest tea producer in the world. (마) Many people drinks tea every morning.

① (가)　② (나)　③ (다)　④ (라)　⑤ (마)

35 다음 빈칸에 들어갈 수 없는 것은?

- __________ of the fastest growing sports __________ China is baseball.
- It's not easy to say who is __________ wisest man __________ all.

① of　② in　③ the
④ very　⑤ one

36 다음 문장의 밑줄 친 부분 중 어법상 어색한 것은?

- 그것은 유럽에서 가장 높은 건물 중 하나이다.
  = ① It is ② one of ③ highest ④ buildings ⑤ in Europe.

37 다음 대화의 빈칸에 들어갈 알맞은 말은?

A: We don't have enough time.
B: Let's take a taxi. It must be __________ than a bus.

① the fastest　② faster　③ fast
④ fastest　　　⑤ more fast

38 우리말과 같은 뜻이 되도록 주어진 단어를 바르게 배열하여 문장을 완성하세요.

- 그녀는 예전보다 더 커 보인다.
  = She __________________________.
  (than, taller, before, looks)

39 다음 문장의 빈칸에 들어갈 수 없는 것은?

This truck is __________ better than that one.

① very　② much　③ even
④ far　⑤ a lot

40 괄호 안에 주어진 단어를 알맞게 배열하여 문장을 완성하세요.

- The Rocky Mountains are __________
  __________________________.
  (than, beautiful, I, more, expected)

41 다음 대화의 빈칸에 들어갈 단어끼리 알맞게 짝지어진 것은?

A: I like this shirt, but it is too __________ for me. Do you have it in a larger size?
B: I'm very sorry, but it is the __________ one in our store.

① smallest – largest
② smaller – to large
③ small – to large
④ small – largest
⑤ to small – largest

42 다음 중 그 의미가 나머지 넷과 다른 하나는?

① Sue is the tallest girl in the class.
② Sue is taller than any other girl in the class.
③ No other girl in the class is taller than Sue.
④ No other girl in the class is as tall as Sue.
⑤ Sue is one of the tallest girls in the class.

43 빈칸을 채워 주어진 문장과 같은 의미의 문장을 완성하세요.

(1) Taking a bus is more eco-friendly than driving a car.
 = Driving a car __________ __________ __________ taking a bus.

(2) They tried to make the second movie in the series as exciting as possible.
 = They tried to make the second movie in the series __________ __________ __________ __________ .

44 다음 중 어법상 어색한 것은?

① The students were so calmer today.
② The woman is far taller than her brothers.
③ Bob is much heavier than Jenny.
④ This statue is a lot higher than that statue.
⑤ Heesun is even more beautiful than her friends.

다음을 읽고 물음에 답하시오.

(A) <u>Insects are one of the most fascinating creature on earth.</u> More than 800,000 species are known to exist. Despite their somewhat frightening appearance, many insects are beneficial to humans. In fact, (B) <u>some products that we use in our daily life is made by insects.</u>
First, (C) <u>silk is a valuable product that has been around for over 5,000 years.</u> It is used for all sorts of clothing. Silk is made from cocoons of silkworms. (D) <u>Beeswax is other thing made by insects.</u> It is a natural wax produced by honey bees. This wax is used to make lotions, ointments, and even candles. Lastly, red dyes are produced by insects called cochineals.
People tend to dislike insects, but (E) <u>they aren't as scary as they seem.</u> Actually, we use products made by them every day without even knowing it.

*cochineal: 코치닐 연지벌레 (멕시코와 같은 중미 지방에서 선인장에 기생하는 벌레로, 그 암컷을 말려 붉은빛 안료나 물감을 만듦.)

45 밑줄 친 (A)~(E) 중 어법에 맞는 문장끼리 짝지어진 것은?

① (A), (C)
② (B), (D)
③ (B), (E)
④ (C), (D)
⑤ (C), (E)

46 다음 문장의 <u>틀린</u> 부분을 <u>모두</u> 찾아 문장을 바르게 고쳐 쓰세요. (단, 최상급을 사용하세요.)

> It is one of the most simplest way to
> succeed in your life.

➡ _______________________________

____

47 그림을 보고 괄호 안의 말을 이용하여 주어진 우리말을 as 원급 비교구문의 문장으로 쓰세요.

> • 그 케이크는 내 여동생의 얼굴만큼 크다.

➡ _______________________________

____

(sister, face, big)

48 다음 대화의 (A), (B)에 알맞은 말을 골라 쓰세요.

> *Mira*: What's wrong, Dan? You look (A) paler /better than usual.
>
> *Dan* : I caught a cold, so I haven't been eating well.
>
> *Mira*: I see. Are you okay now?
>
> *Dan* : Yes, thank you. By the way, you look (B) more and more beautiful /beautifuller and beautifuller . What's your secret?
>
> *Mira*: I've started eating more fruit and vegetables.

(A) __________ (B) _______________

49 다음 표를 보고 괄호 안의 조건에 맞게 두 스마트폰을 비교하는 긍정문을 쓰세요. (단, 비교급 강조 표현을 함께 쓰세요.)

Smartphone	Price	Weight
Optimum 6	$360	200g
Galas	$900	130g

(1) Optimum 6 is _______________

_______________________. (Price)

(2) Galas is _______________

_______________________. (Weight)

50 다음 중 어법상 올바른 것을 <u>모두</u> 고르세요.

① Teresa weighs 60kg. Terry weighs 60kg. Terry is as heavier as Teresa.

② I got two presents from my friends. My sister got three presents. She got more presents than I did.

③ Samuel was happy when he ate two pieces of pizza. He was happier when he ate four pieces of pizza. More he ate, happier he became.

④ Susie runs 1km every day. Simon runs 2km every day. I run 3km every day. No one runs farther than me every day.

⑤ My brother is very diligent. My parents are diligent. I'm not so diligent than they are.

CHAPTER 14
관계사

PSS 1 관계대명사

관계대명사는 앞에 오는 선행사를 수식하며, 「접속사＋대명사」의 역할을 한다.

선행사 ＼ 격	주격	소유격	목적격
사람	who	whose	who(m)
사물, 동물	which	whose	which
사물, 동물, 사람	that	–	that
사물 (선행사 포함)	what	–	what

PSS 1-1 who

who는 선행사가 사람일 때 쓴다.

1. **주격 who** – 관계대명사가 이끄는 절 안에서 주어의 역할을 한다.

> She is **my friend**. ✛ **She** helps me a lot.
>
> She is **my friend who** helps me a lot.
>
> 그녀는 나를 많이 도와주는 친구이다.

> *cf.* 주격 관계대명사가 쓰인 관계대명사절의 동사의 수는 관계대명사의 선행사에 따라 결정된다.
>
> I remember **the boys who were** kind to me.
>
> 나는 나에게 친절했던 그 소년들을 기억한다.

2. **소유격 whose** – 관계대명사가 이끄는 절 안에서 관계대명사 바로 뒤에 나오는 명사를 꾸며주는 역할을 한다.

> I saw a man. **His** hair was red. 나는 한 남자를 보았다. 그의 머리는 빨간색이었다.
>
> ➡ I saw a man **whose hair** was red. 나는 머리가 빨간색이었던 한 남자를 보았다.

3. **목적격 who(m)** – 관계대명사가 이끄는 절 안에서 목적어의 역할을 한다. 구어체에서는 whom 대신 who를 쓰기도 한다.

> They are the students. Mr. Smith taught **them**. 그들은 학생들이다. Smith 씨는 그들을 가르쳤다.
>
> ➡ They are the students **who(m)** Mr. Smith taught. 그들은 Smith 씨가 가르쳤던 학생들이다.

PRACTICE 1

다음 문장의 빈칸에 who, whose, whom 중 알맞은 것을 쓰세요.

1 Do you know the people? They live near the school.

➡ Do you know the people ___________ live near the school?

2 A boy is standing there. His name is Charlie.

➡ A boy ___________ name is Charlie is standing there.

3 The woman left for India. I wanted to meet her.

➡ The woman ___________ I wanted to meet left for India.

4 The man looks so sad. His dog is sick.

➡ The man ___________ dog is sick looks so sad.

5 I met the old lady. She used to walk around the park.

➡ I met the old lady ___________ used to walk around the park.

6 Do you remember the boy? I met him at church.

➡ Do you remember the boy ___________ I met at church?

7 There are a few children. They are playing baseball.

➡ There are a few children ___________ are playing baseball.

8 My grandparents live in Incheon. I visit them once a month.

➡ My grandparents ___________ I visit once a month live in Incheon.

9 His sister is beautiful. Her nose is sharp.

➡ His sister ___________ nose is sharp is beautiful.

10 The boy always tells lies. I don't like him.

➡ The boy ___________ I don't like always tells lies.

PRACTICE 2 [1-10]

괄호 안에 주어진 단어 중 알맞은 것을 고르세요.

1 I had dinner with the boy who (is, are) my student.

2 The girl who (was, were) hurt in the accident is my neighbor.

3 My friend whose eyes (is, are) very big left Korea.

4 I want to talk to the people who (loves, love) cooking.

5 My sister whose dream (is, are) to be a doctor studies hard.

6 The man whose books (is, are) popular is a great writer.

7 I like the singer who (sings, sing) very well.

8 I met the girl whose brothers (is, are) my friends.

9 I have three brothers whose favorite sport (is, are) basketball.

10 The boys who (is, are) best friends are jogging together.

PSS 1-2 which

which는 선행사가 사물이나 동물일 때 쓴다.

1. **주격 which**

    This is a book. **It** is about nature. 이것은 책이다. 그것은 자연에 관한 것이다.
    ➡ This is a book **which** is about nature. 이것은 자연에 관한 책이다.

2. **소유격 whose**

    This is a book. **Its** cover is red. 이것은 책이다. 그것의 표지는 빨갛다.
    ➡ This is a book **whose** cover is red. 이것은 표지가 빨간 책이다.

3. **목적격 which**

    This is a book. Minho bought **it**. 이것은 책이다. 민호가 그것을 샀다.
    ➡ This is a book **which** Minho bought. 이것은 민호가 산 책이다.

정답 p.82

PRACTICE 3

which나 whose를 이용하여 두 문장을 한 문장으로 연결하세요.

1 I took some pictures. Jason liked them.
   ➡ I took some pictures which Jason liked.

2 There is a tree. My family planted it.
   ➡

3 I have a dog. Its name is Happy.
   ➡

4 The dolls are my sister's. They are on the sofa.
   ➡

5 This is the room. Its walls are blue.
   ➡

6 Heejun is reading the book. You gave him the book.

➡ ____

7 The flowers are beautiful. He brought them.

➡ ____

8 He made the movie. It became famous.

➡ ____

9 This is the computer. Its keyboard is broken.

➡ ____

10 You should take the magazine. It is on my desk.

➡ ____

정답 p.82

PRACTICE 4

괄호 안에 주어진 단어 중 알맞은 것을 고르세요.

1 The boxes which (is, are) on the table are mine.

2 We are looking for the parents whose children (is, are) here.

3 My mother loves movies which (have, has) happy endings.

4 Jim is wearing the shoes which (is, are) too big for him.

5 We helped the travellers whose bags (was, were) too heavy.

6 I'll buy a table whose legs (doesn't, don't) break easily.

7 She has a lot of homework which (takes, take) many hours.

8 They have a small garden which (looks, look) beautiful.

9 Cathy entered the room whose windows (was, were) closed.

10 Give me the book whose cover (is, are) hard.

PSS 1-3 **that**

1. that은 who와 which의 주격, 목적격을 대신할 수 있다.

I talked to the people **that** live there. 나는 거기에 사는 사람들에게 말했다.

= I talked to the people **who** live there.

Jinsu has some photos **that** I took. 진수는 내가 찍었던 몇 장의 사진을 갖고 있다.

= Jinsu has some photos **which** I took.

2. 선행사에 다음이 포함되어 있을 경우에는 주로 that을 쓴다.

형용사의 최상급	Sora is **the most beautiful** woman **that** I've ever seen. 소라는 지금껏 내가 봤던 가장 아름다운 여자이다.
서수	I'm **the first** student **that** heard the news. 나는 그 소식을 들은 첫 번째 학생이다.
all, much, little, no	These are **all that** I can do for you. 이것들이 내가 널 위해 할 수 있는 전부이다. There isn't **much** information **that** you can get. 네가 얻을 수 있는 정보가 많지 않다.
something, anything	You can eat **anything that** is on the table. 너는 테이블 위에 있는 것은 무엇이든지 먹을 수 있다.

cf. 선행사가 「사람＋and＋사물[동물]」일 경우에는 주로 that을 쓴다.
This is a story about **a woman and her dog that** lived in a cave.
이것은 동굴에 살았던 한 여성과 그녀의 개에 관한 이야기이다.

정답 p.82

PRACTICE 5

괄호 안에 주어진 관계대명사 중 알맞은 것을 <u>모두</u> 고르세요.

1 The man (whom, which, that) I talked to was very nice.

2 This is the most interesting book (who, whom, that) I've ever read.

3 There is little food (who, whose, that) I can eat.

4 He wanted to meet the people (who, whom, that) work for this company.

5 This is the first movie (whom, who, that) Mr. Smith has made.

6 The car and the driver (whose, that, who) fell into the river were rescued.

7 Mt. Halla is the highest mountain (whom, who, that) we've ever been to.

8 Mom didn't like those cats (whom, which, that) I brought home.

9 I saw something (who, whose, that) was very shocking.

10 Let me introduce my friend (who, whose, that) name is Sunho.

정답 p.82

PRACTICE 6

다음 문장의 밑줄 친 부분을 바르게 고쳐 쓰세요.

1 Is there anything <u>who</u> you'd like to say?　　　　　　　　　　　　

2   Look at the man <u>who he is</u> wearing jeans.

3   A student <u>which</u> spoke English well helped me.

4   It is the most surprising news <u>who</u> I've heard.

5   These are the glasses <u>whom</u> I wear.

6   I called my friend <u>whom</u> likes watching movies.

7   This is my new friend whom <u>I met her</u> at the party.

8   I said something <u>whom</u> made him angry.

9   We gave him the toys <u>that they were</u> made in China.

10   He was the first man <u>which</u> used the machine.

11   Jeff is the tallest boy <u>whose</u> I've ever met.

12   This is my sister <u>whom</u> birthday was a week ago.

13   I saw a boy whose jeans <u>was</u> too long for him.

14   I went to the mountain <u>who</u> was covered with snow.

15   She liked the doll which <u>she got it</u> from her mom.

PSS 1-4 what

what은 선행사를 자체에 포함하는 관계대명사이므로 선행사가 따로 있지 않고, the thing(s) which[that]로 바꿔 쓸 수 있다.

> That is **what** James said. 그것이 James가 말했던 것이다.
> = That is **the thing which[that]** James said.

> **What** I really want to be is a judge. 내가 정말로 되고 싶은 것은 판사이다.
> = **The thing which[that]** I really want to be is a judge.

정답 p.83

PRACTICE 7 [1-12]

괄호 안에 주어진 관계대명사 중 알맞은 것을 고르세요.

1   I can't believe (what, which) Tom said.

2   I gave Nick a watch (what, which) he liked very much.

3   This is (what, which) we were looking for.

4   Today's meeting was (what, which) I've been waiting for.

5 Here is the fish (what, which) you should take care of.

6 The 9 o'clock news is (what, which) I usually watch.

7 Taking pictures is (what, which) he does in his free time.

8 That's not (what, which) I meant.

9 Mr. Hong suggested an idea (what, which) sounded wonderful.

10 Think about (what, which) you should do first.

11 (What, Which) she said made me laugh.

12 He packed the clothes (what, which) he would need for the winter.

PSS 1-5 관계대명사의 생략

1. **목적격 관계대명사 whom, which, that은 생략 가능하다.**

   This is the boy **(whom)** I found at the hotel. 이 아이가 내가 호텔에서 찾은 소년이다.
   This is the building **(which)** I built. 이것이 내가 지은 건물이다.
   Everything **(that)** she told you is true. 그녀가 당신에게 이야기했던 모든 것은 사실이다.

2. **주격 관계대명사 뒤에 be동사가 있고 그 뒤에 분사나 형용사구가 올 때, 「관계대명사+be동사」는 생략할 수 있다.**

   The girl **(who is)** standing over there is my sister. 저쪽에 서 있는 소녀가 나의 누나이다.
   The car **(which is)** parked here is my father's. 여기에 주차된 차는 나의 아버지의 것이다.

정답 p.83

PRACTICE 8

다음 문장에서 생략해도 되는 부분이 있으면 그 부분에 괄호 표시하세요.

1 Try this cake which I've just baked.

2 The girl whom I met yesterday was John's sister.

3 My cousin who loves camping will join our trip.

4 Look at those birds which are flying in the sky.

5 I'm worried about the exam which follows the holiday.

6 We spent all the money that Jenny saved for the vacation.

7 I recommend the pants that have pockets.

8 The lady paid for the window which was broken by her kid.

PRACTICE 9

다음 문장의 빈칸에 관계대명사를 활용하여 알맞은 말을 쓰세요.

1 The man _____who[that]_____ _____is_____ planting trees now is my dad.

2 I love the songs ______________ ______________ popular during the '90s.

3 The shoes ______________ ______________ washed clean looked like new ones.

4 I called those people ______________ ______________ waiting there for tickets.

5 The water ______________ ______________ boiling on the stove is for tea.

6 We like to see the stars ______________ ______________ shining brightly.

7 The president ______________ ______________ known as a gentleman before disappointed us.

8 There are lots of students ______________ ______________ studying in the classroom.

9 The house ______________ ______________ located on top of the hill is my uncle's.

10 You will find a man ______________ ______________ making cotton candies for children.

PSS 1-6 계속적 용법

선행사에 대해 부가적인 설명을 덧붙일 때는 관계대명사 앞에 ,(comma)를 쓰며 순차적으로 해석한다.

I made a new friend**, who** is from China.

나는 새 친구를 사귀었는데, 그 아이는 중국 출신이다.

= I made a new friend**, and she** is from China.

She is wearing a watch**, which** was a gift from her mother.

그녀는 시계를 차고 있는데, 그것은 그녀의 어머니에게 받은 선물이었다.

= She is wearing a watch**, and it** was a gift from her mother.

cf. 계속적 용법으로 쓰인 관계대명사는 that으로 바꿔 쓸 수 없다.

정답 p.83

PRACTICE 10 [1-5]

관계대명사의 계속적 용법을 이용하여 두 개의 문장을 한 개의 문장으로 바꾸어 쓰세요.

1 Kevin has an uncle. He teaches English at a middle school.

➡ ____

2 She bought a blouse. It was on sale.

➡ ____

3 He was a great scientist. We all respected him.

➡ ____

4 Jenny has lost her watch. Her father bought it for her.

➡ ____

5 They climbed Mount Everest. It is the highest mountain in the world.

➡ ____

PSS 2 관계부사

PSS 2-1 관계부사의 종류

관계부사는 앞에 오는 선행사를 수식하는 절을 이끌어 접속사와 부사의 역할을 동시에 하며, 「전치사＋관계대명사」로 바꾸어 쓸 수 있다.

	선행사	관계부사	전치사＋관계대명사
장소	the place, the house, the town, the city	where	at/in/to which
시간	the time, the day, the month, the year	when	at/in/on which
이유	the reason	why	for which
방법	(the way)	how	in which

This is the city **where** I met Jim. 이곳은 내가 Jim을 만났던 도시이다.

= This is the city **in which** I met Jim.

April 15th is the day **when** I met Jim. 4월 15일은 내가 Jim을 만났던 날이다.

= April 15th is the day **on which** I met Jim.

That's the reason **why** I met Jim. 그것이 내가 Jim을 만났던 이유이다.

= That's the reason **for which** I met Jim.

That's **how** I met Jim. 그것이 내가 Jim을 만났던 방법이다.

= That's the way **in which** I met Jim.

cf. the way와 how는 함께 쓸 수 없으므로 둘 중 하나를 생략해야 한다.

That's **the way** I met Jim. (○)

That's **the way how** I met Jim. (X)

PRACTICE 11

다음 문장의 빈칸에 알맞은 관계부사를 쓰세요.

1 December 24th is the day. Hana was born then.

➡ December 24th is the day ____________ Hana was born.

2 Do you know the reason? She left so early for the reason.

➡ Do you know the reason ____________ she left so early?

3 Seoul is the city. I live there.

➡ Seoul is the city ____________ I live.

4 2022 is the year. I entered middle school then.

➡ 2022 is the year ____________ I entered middle school.

5 This is the way. We use chopsticks in the way.

➡ This is ____________ we use chopsticks.

6 This is the place. They found the lost purse here.

➡ This is the place ____________ they found the lost purse.

7 Nicole learned the way. Koreans make *gimchi* in the way.

➡ Nicole learned ____________ Koreans make *gimchi*.

8 Kevin told me the reason. He didn't come for the reason.

➡ Kevin told me the reason ____________ he didn't come.

9 He is looking for a nice hotel. He can stay there for a week.

➡ He is looking for a nice hotel ____________ he can stay for a week.

10 He teaches the way. We wash our hands in the way to fight germs.

➡ He teaches ____________ we wash our hands to fight germs.

CH
14
관계사

PSS 2-2 관계부사의 주의해야 할 용법

선행사의 생략	주로 구어체에서 굳이 나타내지 않아도 모두가 알 수 있는 일반적인 명사가 관계부사의 선행사로 올 경우 생략할 수 있다. I'll never forget **(the day) when** we first met. 난 우리가 처음 만난 날을 절대 잊지 않겠어. This is **(the place) where** I was born. 이곳은 내가 태어난 곳이다. That's **(the reason) why** we study English. 그것이 우리가 영어를 공부하는 이유이다.

<table>
<tr><td rowspan="3">관계부사의
생략</td><td>주로 구어체에서 선행사 다음에 오는 관계부사를 생략할 수 있으며, 선행사의 생략과 마찬가지로 일반적인 명사가 선행사로 올 때 생략한다.</td></tr>
</table>

주로 구어체에서 선행사 다음에 오는 관계부사를 생략할 수 있으며, 선행사의 생략과 마찬가지로 일반적인 명사가 선행사로 올 때 생략한다.

I remember **the day (when)** I graduated from high school.

나는 내가 고등학교를 졸업한 날을 기억한다.

Can you tell me **the reason (why)** he is upset?

그가 언짢은 이유를 내게 말해줄 수 있니?

cf. 관계부사 where은 place, somewhere, anywhere, everywhere, nowhere가 선행사로 올 때만 생략할 수 있으며 특정한 장소가 선행사로 올 경우에는 생략할 수 없다.

The shopping mall is **the place (where)** we used to go. (where 생략)

그 쇼핑몰은 우리가 가던 곳이다.

California is **the state where** he lives. (where 생략 X)

캘리포니아는 그가 살고 있는 주이다.

정답 p.83

PRACTICE 12

다음 문장들이 같은 뜻이 되도록 빈칸에 알맞은 단어를 쓰세요.

1 Tomorrow is the day when my friends will come.

= Tomorrow is _____the_____ _____day_____ my friends will come.

= Tomorrow is _____when_____ my friends will come.

2 That is the place where I taught kids.

= That is __________ __________ I taught kids.

= That is __________ I taught kids.

3 I don't know the reason why she canceled the meeting.

= I don't know __________ she canceled the meeting.

= I don't know __________ __________ she canceled the meeting.

4 2023 was the year when I finally achieved my lifelong dream of travelling to Spain.

= 2023 was __________ __________ I finally achieved my lifelong dream of travelling to Spain.

= 2023 was __________ I finally achieved my lifelong dream of travelling to Spain.

5 This is the way it happened.

= This is __________ it happened.

6 There should be somewhere where we can have a chat.

= There should be __________ we can have a chat.

중간·기말고사 대비문제

1 다음 중 밑줄 친 단어를 생략할 수 있는 것을 <u>모두</u> 고르면?

① I ate all the cake <u>that</u> Lily made for her friend.
② I can't see <u>that</u> small print even with my glasses on.
③ I think <u>that</u> is the biggest turtle I've ever seen.
④ Jenny is the first student <u>that</u> received an award.
⑤ My mom thinks <u>that</u> I've gained weight.

2 각 빈칸에 빠짐없이 하나씩 단어를 넣어 영작할 때, 빈칸 ⓑ, ⓔ, ⓕ에 들어갈 적절한 단어로 짝지어진 것은? (단, 축약하지 말 것)

> 그 체육관은 매일 운동하는 회원들로 가득하다.
> → The gym (ⓐ)(ⓑ)(ⓒ)
> (ⓓ)(ⓔ)(ⓕ)(ⓖ) day.

① is, of, who
② full, who, train
③ is, who, of
④ full, who, every
⑤ full, members, train

3 우리말 해석에 맞게 주어진 단어를 활용하여 빈칸을 완성하세요. (단, 필요시 어형을 변화시킬 것, 3단어)

> I can't understand _____(say, you)_____.
> (나는 네가 말한 것을 이해할 수 없다.)

➡ _______________________________

4 그림을 보고, 이 사람의 직업을 나타내는 우리말과 뜻이 같도록 관계대명사를 이용하여 알맞은 말을 쓰세요.

• 교사는 학교에서 학생들을 가르치는 사람이다.
 = A teacher is a person _____________
 _____________ _____________ at school.

5 다음 (1)~(4)의 이야기가 자연스럽도록 〈보기〉에서 알맞은 번호를 골라 빈칸에 그 번호를 쓰세요.

> 보 기
> ① who felt hungry after playing baseball
> ② which Sarah liked so much
> ③ who likes cakes and cookies
> ④ which made it possible to keep the cake cold

> (1) Sarah is a girl _____________.
> (2) One day, her mother baked a strawberry cake _____________.
> (3) Her mother put the cake in the refrigerator, _____________.
> (4) However, Sarah's youngest brother _____________ ate up the cake.
> Sarah's mother was surprised that there was no cake left in the refrigerator.

6 다음 밑줄 친 관계대명사 중 쓰임이 <u>다른</u> 하나는?

① I like the dress <u>that</u> Anna is wearing.
② This is the story <u>which</u> my father wrote.
③ This is the table <u>that</u> John made.
④ Here are some of the techniques <u>which</u> they use.
⑤ This is the girl <u>that</u> uses magic.

7 다음 영단어의 뜻풀이에서 밑줄 친 부분 중 생략이 가능한 것은?

①	method	n. the way in <u>which</u> something is done or achieved
②	purpose	n. the reason for <u>which</u> something is done or created
③	innovation	n. new ideas or methods <u>that</u> bring significant change or improvement
④	friendship	n. a bond <u>that</u> is formed between individuals based on mutual affection or trust
⑤	goal	n. an objective <u>that</u> someone aims to achieve

8 다음 빈칸에 들어갈 관계대명사로 알맞은 것은?

I like story books __________ have many interesting stories.

① what　　② whose　　③ who
④ whom　　⑤ which

9 다음 중 어법상 <u>어색한</u> 것을 <u>모두</u> 고르세요.

① The girl who has a pony tail is my sister.
② People who exercise regularly are healthy.
③ Look at the police officer, that caught the thief.
④ The shoes which he is wearing are new.
⑤ The book which cover is green was written by him.

10 다음 ⓐ～ⓔ 중, 어법상 <u>틀린</u> 것을 있는 대로 고른 것은?

ⓐ It's the house which they have lived for a long time.
ⓑ I didn't know the reason why he left me.
ⓒ This is the way she cuts the cost of living.
ⓓ He was the first player whom scored a goal in the match.
ⓔ She likes the cats, that are living next door.

① ⓐ, ⓑ　　② ⓑ, ⓒ　　③ ⓐ, ⓑ, ⓒ
④ ⓐ, ⓓ, ⓔ　　⑤ ⓐ, ⓒ, ⓓ, ⓔ

11 다음 두 문장의 뜻이 같다고 할 때 빈칸에 알맞은 단어는?

• He had two daughters, who became famous actresses.
= He had two daughters, __________ they became famous actresses.

① but　　② or　　③ so
④ and　　⑤ that

12 우리말을 어법상 바르게 영작한 것은?

① 그녀는 내가 어울리고 싶은 학교에서 가장 인기 있는 학생이다.
→ She is the most popular student in school that I would like to hang out.

② 내가 무척 보고 싶어 했던 그 영화는 결말이 뻔하다.
→ The movie that I was eager to watch have an obvious ending.

③ 수지는 그녀의 부모님을 존경하는데, 그들은 항상 가족을 최우선으로 여기신다.
→ Susie looks up to her parents, who always puts family first.

④ 내 아들이 정말로 가고 싶어 하는 놀이공원은 보수 작업을 위해서 문을 닫았다.
→ The amusement park which my son really wants to go to is closed for repair work.

⑤ 그 출판사는 원래 다음 달로 예정되었던 출시일을 앞당겼다.
→ The publisher moved up the release date which it was originally scheduled for next month.

13 다음 중 어법상 옳은 문장의 개수로 알맞은 것은?

ⓐ I often visit the elderly who lives alone.
ⓑ She painted a picture of peasants who were working.
ⓒ He played two songs that sounded similar.
ⓓ They liked watching the ballerinas who were moving.
ⓔ I know the boys who standing over there.

① 1개　　② 2개　　③ 3개
④ 4개　　⑤ 5개

14 Which is the correct pair for the blanks?

• She painted a man __________ was sitting on the bench.
• Ted has an alarm clock __________ goes off at seven o'clock.

① who – that　　② that – who
③ who – what　　④ that – what
⑤ which – that

15 다음 중 밑줄 친 부분을 생략할 수 있는 문장은 모두 몇 개인가?

ⓐ Sara is the girl who Mr. Kim is shaking hands with.
ⓑ Mike is my friend that works in New York.
ⓒ He told me that he had something important to discuss.
ⓓ My dog likes any person that gives him a treat.
ⓔ London is one of the places that I've never been to.

① 1개　　② 2개　　③ 3개
④ 4개　　⑤ 5개

16 Which one is used in the same way as the underlined what in the box?

Soccer is what I like to do.

① They showed you what to do.
② I don't know what to say.
③ What did you do last night?
④ What he said to me was unbelievable.
⑤ I thought about what kind of leader I was.

17 다음 주어진 두 문장을 한 문장으로 바르게 바꾸어 쓴 것은?

> She made spaghetti sauce with the tomatoes. She grew the tomatoes.

① She made spaghetti sauce she grew the tomatoes.
② She made spaghetti sauce with the tomatoes whom she grew.
③ She made spaghetti sauce with the tomatoes she grew.
④ She grew the tomatoes whose she made spaghetti sauce.
⑤ She grew the tomatoes that made spaghetti sauce with the tomatoes.

18 다음 우리말과 같은 뜻이 되도록 괄호 안에 주어진 말을 알맞게 배열하세요.

> • 소방대원은 불을 끄고 사람들을 구출해내는 사람이다.
>
> = ________________________
>
> ________________________ .
>
> (puts out, is, rescues, a person, a firefighter, people, who, and, fires)

19 다음 중 밑줄 친 부분의 쓰임이 <u>다른</u> 하나는?

① Everything <u>that</u> I told him was true.
② How did Andy know <u>that</u> I was smiling?
③ They show <u>that</u> these people are very rich.
④ The clean sheep knew <u>that</u> the other sheep was dirty.
⑤ He didn't inform us <u>that</u> he had already booked the tickets.

20 다음 중 두 문장을 올바르게 연결한 것은?

① He is my student. He is from America.
➡ He is my student who is from America.
② This is Kelly's sister. She is a singer.
➡ This is Kelly's sister whose is a singer.
③ This is the camera. I'm looking for it.
➡ This is the camera whose I'm looking for.
④ Jack has a girlfriend. Her job is a teacher.
➡ Jack has a girlfriend who job is a teacher.
⑤ Mr. Lee is a painter. He drew this picture.
➡ Mr. Lee is a painter whom drew this picture.

21 다음 빈칸에 들어갈 알맞은 단어는?

> A: What's the reason __________ we can't buy that car?
> B: Because it is very expensive and we don't have enough money.

① why   ② what   ③ when
④ how   ⑤ which

22 다음 중 밑줄 친 who[Who]의 쓰임이 같은 것끼리 바르게 짝지어진 것은?

> ⓐ He is the teacher <u>who</u> taught us music.
> ⓑ She is the police officer <u>who</u> brought me here.
> ⓒ Do you know <u>who</u> that girl is?
> ⓓ <u>Who</u> borrowed your umbrella?
> ⓔ There are children <u>who</u> can't focus in class.
> ⓕ Tell me <u>who</u> you are, right now!

① ⓐ, ⓒ   ② ⓐ, ⓓ   ③ ⓑ, ⓔ
④ ⓒ, ⓔ   ⑤ ⓔ, ⓕ

23 주어진 문장의 밑줄 친 that과 쓰임이 같은 것은?

> I like books that have beautiful pictures.

① Who is that girl?
② I think that she is Chinese.
③ That is my sister.
④ She is so kind that everyone likes her.
⑤ I know some girls that sing very well.

24 다음 중 밑줄 친 곳의 표현이 바른 것은?

① She likes peaches that are soft.
② He is the one who play the piano.
③ An elephant has a nose that act like a hand.
④ There is an old lady who tell stories to the kids.
⑤ Sam is looking for a shirt which have blue stripes.

25 다음 빈칸 (A)~(C)에 들어갈 말을 순서대로 배열한 것은?

> Yesterday, I saw a documentary ___(A)___ was about a man ___(B)___ tried to live without doing any harm to the environment. After watching it, I decided to start my own project ___(C)___ I named "Project Green Kid." First, I decided to take a shower every other day, instead of every day.

	(A)		(B)		(C)
①	what	–	who	–	which
②	that	–	who	–	which
③	which	–	which	–	that
④	who	–	which	–	that
⑤	that	–	who	–	who

26 다음 두 문장을 관계대명사를 사용하여 한 문장으로 쓰세요. (단, 10단어로 쓸 것.)

> I saw the house. Its roof was covered with snow.

➡ ________________________________

____

27 다음 주어진 문장의 밑줄 친 What과 쓰임이 다른 것은?

> What Samantha bought at the market was cheap looking.

① This is what I want.
② Ron asked me what the problem was.
③ The girl only eats what she likes.
④ He accepted what she offered.
⑤ Thomas listened to what his teacher explained.

28 다음 중 밑줄 친 부분을 생략할 수 있는 것을 모두 고르세요.

① Tell me how you made a lot of money.
② He danced with the woman who wore a blue jacket.
③ The man who is baking an apple pie in the kitchen is my uncle.
④ I know the city that the first Olympic Games were held in.
⑤ He couldn't understand what his sister said.

29 다음 중 어법상 자연스러운 문장은?

① The dog which has big ears are very cute.
② Can you return the book who you borrowed from me?
③ The man I met was Jimin's father.
④ I like the girl whom is wearing glasses.
⑤ Nobody knows who are they.

30 우리말 해석에 맞게 주어진 단어를 활용하여 빈칸을 완성하세요.

> We should respect ______(live, others)______ .
> (우리는 다른 사람들이 살아가는 방식을 존중해야
> 한다.)

➡ ___________________________________

31 다음 글에서 어법상 틀린 곳을 한 군데 찾아 바르게 고치세요.

> Helen Keller was the first deaf blind person
> to earn a BA degree, that was born in
> Alabama on June 27, 1880. At the age
> of 19 months, an illness left her both
> deaf and blind. However, she was able to
> communicate with people and became an
> author, political activist, and lecturer.

___________ ➡ ___________

32 다음 빈칸 (A)～(D)의 어디에도 들어갈 수 없는 말은?

> • Look at the dog ______(A)______ is walking
>   down the street.
> • The Nile, ______(B)______ is the longest river
>   in the world, is in Egypt.
> • Mr. Smith was a teacher ______(C)______
>   received the Teacher of the Year award in
>   2023.
> • ______(D)______ he wanted was to play
>   basketball after school.

① which   ② who   ③ that
④ how   ⑤ what

33 다음 각 우리말과 같은 뜻이 되도록 조건에 맞게 문장을 완성하세요.

> 조 건
> • 반드시 관계대명사를 포함시킬 것.
> • that은 사용할 수 없음.
> • 주어진 칸 수에 맞게 단어를 쓸 것.

(1) 놀이터에서 놀고 있는 그 소년은 매우 잘생겨 보인다.
➡ The boy __________ __________
__________ in the playground looks very
handsome.

(2) 이게 내가 어제 Harry한테서 빌린 그 만화책이야.
➡ This is the comic book __________

__________ __________ __________
Harry yesterday.

34 주어진 두 문장을 관계대명사를 사용하여 한 문장으로 연결하세요.

(1) I know a girl. She can speak Spanish very well.

➡ ______________________________

____

(2) The book is easy to read. I bought it last night.

➡ ______________________________

____

(3) Look at the house. Its garden is filled with beautiful flowers.

➡ ______________________________

____

35 다음 조건에 맞게 그림을 묘사하는 문장을 한 개 쓰세요.

조 건

- There is ~ 구문을 사용할 것.
- A, B, C에서 각각 한 단어씩 골라 사용할 것.
- 관계대명사 who나 which를 반드시 포함할 것.
- 동사의 현재 진행형을 사용할 것.

A	cat	boy	girl
B	watch	paint	eat
C	TV	fish	a picture

➡ ______________________________

____

36 다음 중 어법상 어색한 문장은?

① The lady who was sitting on the chair looked ill.

② This is the restaurant where I saw on TV.

③ A planet is a large round object which moves around the Sun.

④ A bat is an animal which lives in a cave.

⑤ I have a nephew who lives in Busan.

37 다음 밑줄 친 부분을 생략할 수 없는 것은?

① This is the essay which my father wrote.

② I like the glasses that my dad is wearing.

③ The man who is working in the garden is my uncle.

④ She loves the house that her grandfather built.

⑤ Some advertisers use tricks that are performed by magicians.

38 다음 문장의 빈칸에 공통으로 들어갈 단어로 알맞은 것은?

- Send me the money __________ you saved to buy a computer.
- She is the smartest girl __________ has won many awards for her achievement.
- Please tell him __________ I am Sam.

① that ② how ③ who

④ what ⑤ which

39 다음의 두 문장을 관계대명사를 이용하여 한 문장으로 쓰세요.

> These are the books. My uncle bought them for me.

➡ _______________________________________

____

40 다음 보고서의 밑줄 친 우리말 (A)와 (B)를 괄호 안의 말을 이용하여 조건에 맞게 영어로 쓰세요.

Report on Green Project

Name: Gina Soros
Date: July 31st
Place: Knoxville Park
What I did: I cleaned Knoxville Park with my classmates. A lot of children came there for a picnic. (A) <u>우리는 그들에게 공원에서 그들이 해서는 안 되는 것을 말했다.</u> For example, no dumping garbage, no walking on the grass. (B) <u>그들은 우리가 말한 것을 주의 깊게 들었다.</u> We thanked them for doing so. We finished cleaning the park at 5 in the afternoon.
How I felt: I was very happy to see the clean park.

조 건 | • 두 문장 모두 what을 사용할 것.

(A) _______________________________________

(shouldn't do, in the park)

(B) _______________________________________

(carefully)

41 다음 글의 ⓐ~ⓒ에 들어갈 알맞은 말로 바르게 짝지어진 것은?

Minimalist Life

Do you want to focus on yourself and yourself alone? Then why don't you try living a minimalist life? Many people these days pursue a minimalist lifestyle ⓐ ___________ stress and prioritize their mental well-being. So, what is a minimalist life? It's a lifestyle ⓑ ___________ you pursue simplicity and cut down on unessential items. Time, money, and energy can be saved by practicing a minimalist lifestyle. Then, how do you live a minimalist life? The easiest way is to get rid of useless things. One less thing to care for is one less stress. Another way is to digitize your movies, books, and subscriptions. When you have fewer belongings, you can feel more organized and comfortable. So, give it a go! Live as ⓒ ___________ as you can and focus more on your inner self.

	ⓐ		ⓑ		ⓒ
①	to reduce	–	where	–	simply
②	to reduce	–	what	–	simply
③	reduce	–	where	–	simple
④	to reduce	–	where	–	simple
⑤	reduce	–	what	–	simple

CHAPTER 15
접속사

PSS 1 등위접속사 and, but, or

and	~와, 그리고, ~하고 나서	**앞뒤의 내용이 대등하거나 비슷한 것을 연결한다.** Linda **and** Paul went to the movies. Linda와 Paul은 영화를 보러 갔다. ***cf.*** 접속사의 앞뒤 절의 주어가 같을 때는 접속사 뒤의 주어를 생략할 수 있다. **I** went back home **and (I)** studied for the exam. 나는 집으로 돌아가서 시험 공부를 했다.
but	하지만, 그러나	**앞뒤의 내용이 반대되는 것을 연결한다.** I was very sick **but** (I) didn't go to the doctor. 나는 매우 아팠지만 의사에게 가지 않았다. ***cf.*** not A but B 'A가 아니라 B' My garden is **not** large **but** beautiful. 나의 정원은 크지는 않지만 아름답다.
or	또는, 아니면	**둘이나 둘 이상의 대상 중에서 선택을 할 때 쓴다.** Have you been to New York **or** Chicago? 뉴욕이나 시카고에 가본 적이 있니? ***cf.*** 세 개 이상의 단어가 나열될 때는 마지막 단어 앞에 접속사를 쓴다. Have you been to New York, Chicago, **or** Los Angeles? 뉴욕, 시카고 또는 로스앤젤레스에 가본 적이 있니?

정답 p.87

PRACTICE 1

괄호 안에 주어진 접속사 중 알맞은 것을 고르세요.

1   I met Jinsu (and, but, or) Minho on the street yesterday.

2   Where is he going, to school (and, but, or) home?

3   You made the mistake. It is not I (and, but, or) you who are to blame.

4   Who's your brother, Tim, John, (and, but, or) Ryan?

5   They left Seoul (and, but, or) arrived in Daejeon 2 hours later.

6 Which do you like better, pizza (and, but, or) spaghetti?

7 Eric bought a bottle of milk (and, but, or) a piece of cake.

8 I like music (and, but, or) my brother doesn't.

9 The students entered the classroom (and, but, or) started to clean up.

10 Did you meet Mrs. Park (and, but, or) did you talk to her on the phone?

PSS 2 명령문 + and/or

명령문+and	~해라, 그러면	Wake up now, **and** you'll catch the bus. 지금 일어나라, 그러면 너는 그 버스를 탈 거야. = If you wake up now, you'll catch the bus. 만약 네가 지금 일어난다면, 너는 그 버스를 탈 거야.
명령문+or	~해라, 그렇지 않으면	Wake up now, **or** you'll miss the bus. 지금 일어나라, 그렇지 않으면 너는 그 버스를 놓칠 거야. = If you don't wake up now, you'll miss the bus. 만약 네가 지금 일어나지 않는다면, 너는 그 버스를 놓칠 거야.

정답 p.87

PRACTICE 2 [1-10]

두 문장이 같은 뜻이 되도록 빈칸에 and나 or 중 알맞은 것을 쓰세요.

1 If you exercise regularly, you'll be healthy.

= Exercise regularly, _____________ you'll be healthy.

2 If you don't take the subway, you'll be late.

= Take the subway, _____________ you'll be late.

3 If you plan ahead, you'll avoid last-minute stress.

= Plan ahead, _____________ you'll avoid last-minute stress.

4 If you don't study hard, you can't pass the exam.

= Study hard, _____________ you can't pass the exam.

5 If you don't go there, she will be disappointed.

= Go there, _____________ she will be disappointed.

6 If you are kind to others, they'll be nice to you.

= Be kind to others, _____________ they'll be nice to you.

7 If you don't write it down, you'll forget it soon.

= Write it down, ___________ you'll forget it soon.

8 If you are honest with her, she'll forgive you.

= Be honest with her, ___________ she'll forgive you.

9 If you don't clean the room now, Mom will get angry.

= Clean the room now, ___________ Mom will get angry.

10 If you get up earlier, you can have breakfast.

= Get up earlier, ___________ you can have breakfast.

PSS 3 상관접속사

1. 「both A and B」 'A와 B 둘 다'

   Both Jim and Sue like mathematics. Jim과 Sue는 둘 다 수학을 좋아한다.

   cf. 「both A and B」는 항상 복수 동사를 쓴다.

2. 「not only A but also B」 'A뿐만 아니라 B도' = 「B as well as A」

   Jim is good at **not only singing but also studying**. Jim은 노래뿐만 아니라 공부도 잘한다.
   = Jim is good at **studying as well as singing**.

   cf. 「not only A but also B」와 「B as well as A」 뒤에 오는 동사는 B의 수에 일치시킨다.
   Not only Jim but also **his friends are** playing basketball.
   Jim뿐만 아니라 그의 친구들도 농구를 하고 있는 중이다.
   Jim as well as his friends **is** playing basketball.

3. 「either A or B」 'A와 B 중 어느 하나'

   Either Jim or Sue likes mathematics.
   Jim과 Sue 중 어느 한 명은 수학을 좋아한다.

   cf. 「either A or B」 뒤에 오는 동사는 동사에 더 가까이 있는 B의 수에 일치시킨다.
   Either she or I **have** to take this bag. 그녀와 나 중 어느 한 명은 이 가방을 가져가야 한다.

4. 「neither A nor B」 'A도 B도 ~ 아닌'

   Neither Jim nor Sue likes mathematics.
   Jim도 Sue도 수학을 좋아하지 않는다.

   cf. 「neither A nor B」 뒤에 오는 동사는 동사에 더 가까이 있는 B의 수에 일치시킨다.
   Neither she nor I **have** to take this bag. 그녀도 나도 이 가방을 가져가야 할 필요가 없다.

PRACTICE 3

다음 문장의 빈칸에 알맞은 접속사를 쓰세요.(한 칸에 2개 이상의 단어가 들어갈 수도 있음.)

1 Jina has gone to China. Minsu has gone to China, too.

➡ ___________ Jina ___________ Minsu have gone to China.

2 Alice is going to study science. Or she is going to study English.

➡ Alice is going to study ___________ science ___________ English.

3 Paul doesn't play baseball. He doesn't play basketball, either.

➡ Paul plays ___________ baseball ___________ basketball.

4 The students are excited about the field trip. The teacher is, too.

➡ ___________ the students ___________ the teacher is excited about the field trip.

5 Jennie is running a marathon. Kate is running a marathon, too.

➡ ___________ Jennie ___________ Kate are running a marathon.

6 Not only students but also teachers were happy with the event.

➡ Teachers ___________ students were happy with the event.

7 She must be at home now. Or she must be at school now.

➡ She must be ___________ at home ___________ at school now.

8 Tim is sleeping on the couch. His dog is sleeping on the couch, too.

➡ ___________ Tim ___________ his dog are sleeping on the couch.

9 We didn't go into the room. We didn't leave the building, either.

➡ We ___________ went into the room ___________ left the building.

10 Chris is blonde. I am blonde, too.

➡ ___________ Chris ___________ I am blonde.

PSS 4 because, so

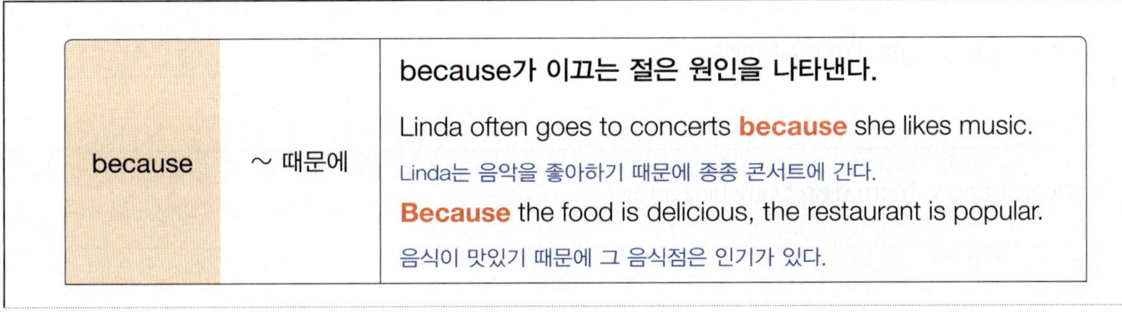

because	~ 때문에	**because가 이끄는 절은 원인을 나타낸다.** Linda often goes to concerts **because** she likes music. Linda는 음악을 좋아하기 때문에 종종 콘서트에 간다. **Because** the food is delicious, the restaurant is popular. 음식이 맛있기 때문에 그 음식점은 인기가 있다.

because	~ 때문에	***cf.*** because of는 전치사이기 때문에 뒤에 명사 상당어구가 온다. The restaurant is popular **because of the food**. 그 음식점은 음식 때문에 인기가 있다.
so	그래서	**so가 이끄는 절은 결과를 나타낸다.** Linda likes music, **so** she often goes to concerts. Linda는 음악을 좋아해서 종종 콘서트에 간다. The food is delicious, **so** the restaurant is popular. 음식이 맛있어서 그 음식점은 인기가 있다.

cf. as나 since도 이유를 나타내는 접속사로 쓰인다.

He couldn't arrive on time **as** he missed the bus.

그는 버스를 놓쳤기 때문에 제시간에 도착할 수 없었다.

Since the weather will be fine tomorrow, we will go on a picnic.

내일 날씨가 좋을 것이기 때문에 우리는 소풍을 갈 것이다.

정답 p.87

PRACTICE 4

〈보기〉와 같이 because나 so를 이용하여 두 문장을 한 문장으로 연결하세요.

보 기	I was very happy. I got a lot of birthday presents.
	➡ I was very happy because I got a lot of birthday presents.
	➡ I got a lot of birthday presents, so I was very happy.

1 We are excited. We are going to interview a popular singer.

➡ ____

➡ ____

2 Martin couldn't call you. He was very busy this week.

➡ ____

➡ ____

3 Jiyoon has a lot of friends. She is very nice.

➡ ____

➡ ____

4 I can't study tonight. I'm really sick.

➡ ____

➡ ____

5 Seho got angry. Mom didn't buy him a toy.

➡ ____

➡ ____

PRACTICE 5

다음 문장의 빈칸에 because나 because of 중 알맞은 것을 쓰세요.

1 I was very tired today ________________ I didn't get enough sleep last night.

2 The traffic was terrible ________________ the heavy snow.

3 I like John ________________ his kindness.

4 Minho had a big lunch ________________ he was very hungry.

5 Sena wants to be a teacher ________________ she loves children.

6 They bought these flowers ________________ the color.

PSS 5 if

부사절을 이끄는 if	~한다면	**If** you read the book, you can do your homework. 네가 그 책을 읽는다면, 너는 숙제를 할 수 있다. **If** you do **not** read the book, you can't do your homework. 네가 그 책을 읽지 않는다면, 너는 숙제를 할 수 없다. = **Unless** you read the book, you can't do your homework. ***cf.*** 「if ~ not」은 unless로 바꾸어 쓸 수 있다.
명사절을 이끄는 if ~ (or not)	~인지 (아닌지)	I don't know **if** she works there **(or not)**. 나는 그녀가 거기에서 일하는지 (아닌지) 알지 못한다. = I don't know **whether** she works there **(or not)**. ***cf.*** 「if ~ (or not)」는 '~인지 아닌지'의 명사절 접속사로 쓰일 경우, 목적어 자리만 가능하며, 「whether ~ (or not)」으로 바꾸어 쓸 수 있다.

PRACTICE 6 [1-10]

주어진 문장과 의미가 같도록 unless를 이용하여 다시 쓰세요.

1 I'll do the laundry if it doesn't rain.

= ____

2 Let's watch a movie together if you aren't busy.

= ____

3 I can help you if it doesn't take too long.

= ____

4 He will be in trouble if the train doesn't arrive on time.

= ____

5 She can finish the work if she doesn't go home early.

= ____

6 They will forgive you if you don't lie to them.

= ____

7 You'll miss the last bus if you don't hurry.

= ____

8 I'll buy this shirt if I don't change my mind.

= ____

9 We can go swimming if the pool isn't closed.

= ____

10 You can just walk if it's not too far from here.

= ____

정답 p.88

PRACTICE 7

다음 문장을 밑줄 친 부분에 유의하여 바르게 해석하세요.

1 <u>Unless</u> something unexpected happens, I'll see you tomorrow.

➡ _______________________________________, 난 내일 너를 만날 것이다.

2 It's unclear <u>whether</u> there is any damage.

➡ _______________________________________ 불확실하다.

3 Let me know <u>if</u> he bothers you again.

➡ _______________________________________ 내게 알려줘.

4 It's doubtful <u>whether</u> there'll be any seats left.

➡ _______________________________________ 의심스럽다.

5 Choose <u>if</u> you will take that advice or not.

➡ _______________________________________ 선택해라.

6 <u>If</u> you mix blue and yellow, you get green.

➡ _______________________________________, 초록색이 나온다.

PSS 6 so that ~, so ~ that …

so that ~	~하기 위해서, ~할 수 있도록	**목적을 나타낼 때 쓴다.** I studied hard **so that** I could enter the university. 나는 그 대학교에 들어가기 위해서 열심히 공부했다. = I studied hard **(in order) to** enter the university. = I studied hard **(so as) to** enter the university.
so+형용사/부사 +that …	너무 ~해서 …한	**결과를 나타낼 때 쓴다.** The book was **so boring that** I couldn't finish it. 그 책은 아주 지루해서 나는 그것을 다 읽을 수가 없었다. = The book was **too boring** for me **to** finish.

정답 p.88

PRACTICE 8 [1-10]

〈보기〉와 같이 주어진 문장과 의미가 같도록 빈칸에 알맞은 문장을 쓰세요. (단, 밑줄 친 부분에 절이 포함되어 있으면 구로, 구가 포함되어 있으면 절로 바꾸어 쓸 것)

보 기   Jiyoung saved her money in order to travel to Europe.

➡ *Jiyoung saved her money so that she could travel to Europe.*

1   I hurried in the morning so as to catch the train.

➡ ____

2   We were too tired to go to the party.

➡ ____

3   They practiced hard in order to win the game.

➡ ____

4   The coffee was so hot that she couldn't drink it.

➡ ____

5   I was too busy to answer the phone.

➡ ____

6   I drink a cup of coffee every morning so that I can stay awake.

➡ ____

7   The table was too heavy for me to move.

➡ ____

CH 15 접속사

8 The questions are <u>so difficult that</u> I can't answer them.

➡ ____

9 Animals live in a pack <u>so as to</u> reduce the danger of attack.

➡ ____

10 Mike took a taxi <u>so that</u> he could arrive there in time.

➡ ____

PSS 7 명사절을 이끄는 that

주어	~라는 것은	that절이 주어 역할을 할 때는 주로 문장의 맨 앞에 가주어 it을 쓰고 진주어인 that절은 뒤로 보낸다. **That she has a twin sister** is interesting. 그녀에게 쌍둥이 여동생이 있다는 것은 흥미롭다. = **It**'s interesting **that she has a twin sister**. 가주어 진주어
목적어	~라는 것을	목적어 역할을 하는 명사절을 이끄는 that은 생략할 수 있다. Some people think **(that) I'm very polite**. 어떤 사람들은 내가 매우 예의 바르다고 생각한다.
보어	~라는 것인	The problem is **that you didn't give it back to me**. 문제는 네가 내게 그것을 돌려주지 않았다는 것이다.

정답 p.88

PRACTICE 9

〈보기〉와 같이 주어진 문장을 바꾸어 쓰세요. (필요시 괄호 안의 어구를 활용할 것.)

보 기	I can't see Jenny for a while. It is sad. ➡ <u>It is sad that I can't see Jenny for a while.</u>

1 He lied to me. It is disappointing.

➡ ____

2 We are going to Jejudo. It is exciting.

➡ _______________________________________

3 They didn't come. It is strange.

➡ _______________________________________

4 The story had an unhappy ending. It is a pity.

➡ _______________________________________

5 Giho plays the piano well. It is true.

➡ _______________________________________

6 Yumi is Sujin's sister. (I know)

➡ _______________________________________

7 She was going to cry. (I thought)

➡ _______________________________________

8 Her son is diligent. (I believe)

➡ _______________________________________

9 You were having dinner at that restaurant. (I thought)

➡ _______________________________________

10 You gave Mike a lot of books. (I knew)

➡ _______________________________________

11 She doesn't like her new job. That is the fact.

➡ _______________________________________

12 We can't wait any longer. That is the point.

➡ _______________________________________

13 Minho broke the window. That is the truth.

➡ _______________________________________

14 Tom and Kate got married. That was the big news.

➡ _______________________________________

15 He didn't know how to drive. That was the problem.

➡ _______________________________________

CH
15
접속사

PSS 8 시간을 나타내는 접속사

when	~할 때	**When** I was a child, my family lived in Busan. 내가 어린아이였을 때, 나의 가족은 부산에서 살았다.
as	~하고 있을 때, ~하면서	Ann sometimes listens to music **as** she studies. Ann은 공부를 하면서 때때로 음악을 듣는다. *cf.* as는 '~대로', '~함에 따라' 또는 '~ 때문에'라는 뜻의 접속사로도 쓰인다. She did **as** I did. 그녀는 내가 하는 대로 했다. **As** Jack is honest, everybody trusts him. Jack은 정직하기 때문에, 모든 사람이 그를 신뢰한다.
before	~하기 전에	He reviews his notes **before** he takes a test. 그는 시험을 보기 전에 그의 노트들을 복습한다.
after	~한 후에	Let's go for a walk **after** you finish your dinner. 네가 저녁을 다 먹은 후에 산책 가자.
until	~할 때까지	My sister didn't go to bed **until** I got home. 나의 누나는 내가 집에 도착할 때까지 잠자리에 들지 않았다.
while	~하는 동안	**While** I was waiting for the bus, I read a book. 나는 버스를 기다리는 동안 책을 읽었다.
as soon as	~하자마자	He got a job **as soon as** he finished school. 그는 학교를 마치자마자 취업을 했다.

cf. 시간을 나타내는 접속사가 쓰인 부사절에서는 현재시제가 미래시제를 대신한다.

I'll leave for Busan **as soon as** I **finish** the project.

나는 그 프로젝트를 끝내자마자 부산으로 떠날 것이다.

I'll leave for Busan as soon as I <u>will finish</u> the project. (X)

정답 p.88

PRACTICE 10

괄호 안에 주어진 접속사 중 알맞은 것을 고르세요.

1 Did Cathy go out (as soon as, while) I was washing the dishes?

2 Susan had dinner (after, until) she finished her homework.

3 What do you usually do (before, when) you have free time?

4 The food should be ready (before, after) the customers arrive.

5 He met his teacher (as, until) he walked down the street.

6 She read a storybook for her child (while, until) he fell asleep.

7 He brushes his teeth (as soon as, until) he gets up.

8 Robert entered the room (while, after) he opened the door.

9 Somebody called me (before, while) I was taking a shower.

10 I'll keep trying (until, as) my dreams come true.

PSS 9 even though, although, though

even though	비록 ~일지라도, ~에도 불구하고	It was raining, **but** I went shopping. 비가 내리고 있었지만 나는 쇼핑하러 갔다. ➡ **Even though** it was raining, I went shopping. ➡ **Although** it was raining, I went shopping. ➡ **Though** it was raining, I went shopping. 비가 내리고 있었음에도 불구하고, 나는 쇼핑하러 갔다.
although		
though		

cf. in spite of와 despite는 '비록 ~일지라도, ~에도 불구하고'라는 의미이지만 전치사이므로, 그 뒤
에 절이 아니라 명사 상당어구가 옴에 유의한다.

In spite of the bad weather, we went on a picnic. 나쁜 날씨에도 불구하고, 우리는 소풍을 갔다.

Despite her great success, she wasn't satisfied.

그녀의 위대한 성공에도 불구하고, 그녀는 만족하지 않았다.

정답 p.89

PRACTICE 11 [1-5]

다음 우리말 해석에 맞게 괄호 안의 말을 바르게 배열하세요. (단, 부사절이 문장 맨 앞에 오게 쓸 것)

1 비록 영어는 어려울지라도 난 그것을 배우는 걸 좋아한다.

(like, even though, difficult, it, learning, is, English, I)

➡ ____________________________________

2 Andy는 규칙적으로 먹지 않음에도 불구하고, 그는 꽤 건강하다.

(healthy, is, eat, Andy, regularly, quite, he, though, doesn't)

➡ ____________________________________

3 해가 비치고 있었음에도 불구하고, 별로 따뜻하지는 않았다.

(wasn't, the sun, warm, it, although, shining, very, was)

➡ ____________________________________

4 그 두 장의 사진이 동일하진 않지만 비슷하다.
(similar, aren't, they, although, identical, the two pictures, are)

➡ ____

5 Paul은 가장 경험이 적음에도 불구하고, 그는 최고의 선생님이다.
(the best, experience, he's, Paul, teacher, the least, though, has)

➡ ____

PSS 10 접속부사

for example	예를 들면	Mina does a lot of things for her family. **For example**, she helps her mom cook. 미나는 그녀의 가족을 위해 많은 것을 한다. 예를 들어, 그녀는 그녀의 엄마가 요리하는 것을 돕는다.
however	그러나	Everyone agreed with Mark. **However**, I had a different idea. 모든 사람들이 Mark의 의견에 찬성했다. 그러나 나는 다른 생각을 가지고 있었다.
therefore	그러므로	I have an English quiz tomorrow, but I haven't studied. **Therefore**, I have to study hard tonight. 나는 내일 영어 쪽지시험을 보지만 공부를 하지 않았다. 그러므로 나는 오늘 밤에 열심히 공부해야 한다.
in addition, besides	게다가	I like the restaurant. The food is very delicious. **In addition[Besides]**, the service is very good. 나는 그 식당을 좋아한다. 음식이 매우 맛있다. 게다가 서비스도 매우 좋다. *cf.* in addition과 in addition to의 쓰임을 헷갈리기 쉬운데, in addition to 다음에는 명사 상당어구가 오며 '~일 뿐 아니라, ~에 더하여'로 해석된다. I can speak Spanish **in addition to** English. 나는 영어뿐만 아니라 스페인어를 말할 수 있다. *cf.* besides는 접속부사 말고도 전치사로도 쓰이는데 그때는 '~ 외에'라는 뜻을 갖는다. What other sports do you like **besides** soccer? 너는 축구 외에 무슨 다른 스포츠를 좋아하니?

<table>
<tr><td>finally</td><td>결국</td><td>Sena was interested in law. **Finally**, she became a lawyer.
세나는 법에 관심이 있었다. 결국 그녀는 변호사가 되었다.</td></tr>
</table>

정답 p.89

PRACTICE 12

〈보기〉에서 알맞은 말을 골라 빈칸에 쓰세요.

보 기	for example however therefore in addition finally

1   Our team has prepared very hard for this project. We have worked until late at night for two weeks. _________________, we have finished it successfully.

2   Junsu's parents didn't want him to be an actor. _________________, he became a famous actor.

3   He won the gold medal. _________________, he set a new world record.

4   You can protect the environment in your daily life. _________________, you can take a bicycle instead of a car.

5   Rachel was absent yesterday. _________________, she didn't hear about the festival.

6   There are several big holidays in Korea. _________________, Chuseok and New Year's Day are two big holidays.

7   I was caught in a traffic jam. _________________, I could get to work on time.

8   All of the workers will have a vacation for the next two weeks. _________________, the office will be empty.

9   I can't go out with you because I have to clean the house. _________________, I have to do the science homework.

10   I sent Ms. Lee an e-mail hours ago and I waited for her answer. _________________, I got a short reply now.

1 다음 빈칸에 들어갈 말이 바르게 짝지어진 것은?

> • The teacher used simple words __________ the students could understand easily.
> • He took a deep breath __________ calm down.

① in order to　　– so that
② so that　　– in order to
③ so that　　– so as that
④ in order that　– so that
⑤ in order to　　– so as that

2 다음 중 두 문장의 의미가 같지 <u>않은</u> 것을 <u>모두</u> 고르세요.

① He didn't go out because of the bad weather.
　= He didn't go out because the weather was bad.
② He runs so fast that I can't catch him.
　= He runs fast in order not to catch him.
③ Get up right now, or you'll be late for work.
　= If you get up right now, you'll be late for work.
④ The meal was not only delicious but also nutritious.
　= The meal was nutritious as well as delicious.
⑤ If you aren't sure, don't use them.
　= Unless you are sure, don't use them.

3 주어진 우리말과 같은 뜻이 되도록 빈칸에 알맞은 표현을 쓰세요.

> 많은 책을 읽어라, 그러면 너는 더 현명해질 것이다.

➡ __________ __________ __________, __________ __________ __________ be wiser.

4 다음 빈칸에 들어갈 말로 알맞은 것을 <u>모두</u> 고르세요.

> He was disappointed __________ he didn't get any Christmas cards.

① because　　② because of　　③ so
④ but　　⑤ as

5 우리말과 같은 뜻이 되도록 주어진 단어를 포함하여 8단어로 영작하세요.

> 지금 출발해라, 그렇지 않으면 너는 학교에 늦을 것이다.

➡ ________________________________
________________________________ (leave)

6 밑줄 친 부분을 생략할 수 <u>없는</u> 것은?

① Yuna told me <u>that</u> she would leave for Russia soon.
② Do you know <u>that</u> pretty girl carrying a red bag?
③ He got the concert ticket <u>that</u> he wanted so badly.
④ We all know <u>that</u> Jina is in love with Bill.
⑤ She said <u>that</u> she needed some time to think alone.

7 주어진 표현 중 내용과 가장 어울리는 것을 골라 〈보기〉처럼 because를 사용해 문장을 완성하세요. (필요할 경우 동사의 시제를 바꾸세요.)

> 보 기
>
> People think that I'm satisfied _because I don't complain._

> • be too cold   • have a new car
> • tell me to do that   • live in London

➡ We didn't stay outside long ______________

______________________________ .

8 〈보기〉에서 문장의 밑줄 친 부분을 바르게 고친 것을 모두 고르면?

> 보 기
>
> ⓐ Ronald <u>not</u> listens to K-pop but also enjoys Korean dramas.
>   ➡ not → only
> ⓑ Neither Jackson <u>or</u> Eric is good at science.
>   ➡ or → nor
> ⓒ Seulgi as well as I <u>play</u> the violin in the school orchestra.
>   ➡ play → plays
> ⓓ Not only my sister but also my parents <u>likes</u> to go hiking on weekends.
>   ➡ likes → like
> ⓔ Jina's cousins as well as Jina <u>are</u> planning to travel to Paris.
>   ➡ are → is

① ⓐ, ⓑ   ② ⓑ, ⓒ   ③ ⓐ, ⓒ, ⓔ
④ ⓑ, ⓒ, ⓓ   ⑤ ⓑ, ⓓ, ⓔ

9 다음 우리말과 같은 뜻이 되도록 빈칸에 들어갈 알맞은 한 단어를 쓰세요.

> • 비록 그가 시각장애인이긴 했지만, 그는 그의 꿈을 절대 포기하지 않았다.
> = ______________ he was blind, he never gave up his dream.

10 다음 빈칸에 들어갈 단어로 가장 적절한 것은?

> ______________ he was riding the roller coaster, we took some pictures.

① And   ② But   ③ While
④ So   ⑤ Finally

11 다음 중 밑줄 친 **that**의 쓰임이 <u>다른</u> 하나는?

① Sumi gave him the book <u>that</u> he wanted to borrow.
② The problem was <u>that</u> the library was noisy.
③ Are you sure <u>that</u> he wants to go there?
④ We know <u>that</u> fast food is not good for us.
⑤ She feels <u>that</u> she is very lucky.

12 다음의 빈칸에 들어갈 알맞은 말은?

> ______________ you have an open mind, you'll make a lot of friends.

① That   ② Though   ③ If
④ But   ⑤ Because of

13 다음 중 밑줄 친 If[if]의 뜻이 나머지 넷과 다른 것은?

① Give her this flower if you see her.
② He will tell you the truth if you ask him.
③ I wonder if I should wear a coat or not.
④ If you leave your name, we'll call you as soon as possible.
⑤ If you sit down for a few moments, I'll tell him you're here.

14 다음 빈칸에 알맞은 단어가 바르게 연결된 것은?

- They missed the train ___________ they got stuck in traffic.
- ___________ you go to bed early in the evening, it'll be easy to get up in the morning.

① because – Although ② so – If
③ but – Unless ④ because – If
⑤ so – Unless

15 주어진 문장과 같은 뜻이 되도록 문장을 바꾸어 쓰세요. (단, as well as 표현을 활용할 것.)

A good sleep is important for not only adults but also kids.

= ___________________________________

____

16 우리말과 같은 뜻이 되도록 빈칸에 알맞은 단어를 쓰세요.

- 그녀의 가족은 런던과 뉴욕 두 곳 모두에서 살았습니다.
  = Her family has lived in ___________ London ___________ New York.

17 다음 빈칸에 들어갈 가장 알맞은 단어는?

- My father read the newspaper. And then he had breakfast.
  = ___________ my father read the newspaper, he had breakfast.

① As ② When ③ Before
④ Because ⑤ After

18 같은 의미의 문장으로 바르게 짝지어진 것을 모두 고른 것은?

ⓐ
- I'm so tired that I can't stay awake anymore.
- I'm too tired to stay awake anymore.

ⓑ
- The rooms are large enough to take three beds.
- The rooms are so large that they can take three beds.

ⓒ
- The crack on the wall was too tiny for the architect to find.
- The crack on the wall was so tiny that the architect couldn't find.

ⓓ
- The weather was too bad for the school to hold the field day.
- Because the weather was too bad, the school couldn't hold the field day.

ⓔ
- It was so foggy that Dad couldn't see the lanes on the road.
- It was foggy but it wasn't that Dad couldn't see the lanes on the road.

① ⓐ ② ⓐⓓ ③ ⓐⓑⓓ
④ ⓑⓒⓔ ⑤ ⓒⓓⓔ

19 다음 두 문장이 같은 뜻이 되도록 빈칸에 알맞은 단어를 쓰세요.

> • At the age of 7, he learned to ride a bike.
> = ___________ he was 7, he learned to ride a bike.

20 다음 빈칸에 알맞은 말끼리 바르게 짝지어진 것은?

> • Everyone likes her ___________ she is kind.
> = Everyone likes her ___________ her kindness.

① because － because
② because － because of
③ because of － because of
④ because of － because
⑤ as － because

21 다음 글의 빈칸에 들어갈 말로 알맞은 것은?

> Sumi, Junho and I were talking about the math quiz. Sumi and Junho said it was very easy compared to the last quiz. ___________, I couldn't agree with them. It was very difficult for me.

① And ② However ③ Or
④ For example ⑤ Because

22 다음 문장의 빈칸에 들어갈 알맞은 단어는?

> ___________ most of his friends like western food, Jack likes Korean food better than any other food.

① So ② Although ③ Because
④ Since ⑤ But

23 〈보기〉의 우리말에 맞도록 괄호 안의 표현에 한 단어를 추가하여 (가)에 들어갈 영어 문장을 쓰세요.

> 보 기
> 셋째 돼지의 집은 너무 튼튼해서 내가 그것을 부술 수 없어.
> (destroy, sturdy, the third pig's house, can't, is, it, I, that)

(가) ___________

____

24 다음 밑줄 친 When[when]의 쓰임이 나머지 넷과 다른 하나는?

① When I was young, I lived in Mexico.
② When I saw my daughter, she smiled at me.
③ Bring your lunch when we go on a picnic.
④ He asked me when I could return the book.
⑤ Call me when you are free.

25 다음 빈칸에 들어갈 가장 알맞은 단어는?

I want to have many chances to watch new movies, ___________ I'm going to join the movie club.

① though ② while ③ so
④ but ⑤ however

26 다음 문장에서 that이 들어가야 할 곳은?

An interesting ① fact ② about eating with hands ③ is ④ they use only the right hand ⑤ when they eat.

27 다음 문장의 밑줄 친 As와 같은 의미로 쓰인 것은?

As I was passing by Bill's house, I saw his sister.

① They were used as money.
② Jenny is as tall as Alex.
③ She got prettier as she grew older.
④ As I was talking with Minsu, someone called.
⑤ As he missed the train, he couldn't be there on time.

28 다음 빈칸에 들어갈 말로 알맞은 것은?

I left work early ___________ I could attend my daughter's school event.

① but ② while ③ besides
④ so that ⑤ instead of

29 다음 빈칸에 들어갈 말로 알맞게 짝지어진 것은?

Mr. Kim is a very good person. He likes to help people. _________, when he sees the elderly carrying heavy bags, he goes to them and asks _________ they need any help.

① Even though – if
② However – even though
③ For example – though
④ However – so
⑤ For example – if

30 다음 중 빈칸 ⓐ와 같은 단어가 들어갈 문장은?

I couldn't go to the concert ___ ⓐ ___ I had to help my mom.

① I am too tired ___________ do the laundry.
② I can go to the party, ___________ I'm very happy.
③ ___________ I was young, I used to visit my grandparents every summer.
④ I had a stomachache ___________ I ate a lot yesterday.
⑤ Say "thank you," ___________ people won't know you appreciate it.

31 주어진 문장의 밑줄 친 when의 쓰임과 같은 것은?

> Make sure to close the window <u>when</u> it rains.

① I don't know <u>when</u> the show begins.
② I remember the day <u>when</u> we became best friends.
③ <u>When</u> to leave is very important.
④ <u>When</u> she came back home, she looked tired.
⑤ Can you tell me <u>when</u> we should meet?

32 다음 글의 (A)~(C)에 들어갈 말로 적절한 것은?

> Barry didn't feel well when he got up this morning, ____(A)____ he went to work anyway. He had to attend an important meeting in the morning. Luckily, the meeting was cancelled and he could relax a little. ____(B)____, he still couldn't concentrate on his work. ____(C)____, his boss got angry at him because of some errors in the report written by him.

	(A)	(B)	(C)
①	or	– However	– In addition
②	but	– However	– In addition
③	or	– However	– Besides
④	since	– As a result	– But
⑤	but	– As a result	– Therefore

33 다음 밑줄 친 부분과 바꾸어 쓸 수 있는 것은?

> Mark didn't give up and kept running for two hours. <u>In the end</u>, he won second place in the marathon.

① At most
② At least
③ Finally
④ However
⑤ Sometimes

34 다음 중 빈칸에 들어가지 <u>않는</u> 단어는?

> a. __________ I was tired, I went to bed early last night.
> b. Eat breakfast, __________ you can't focus on your study.
> c. Preheat the oven __________ you put the potatoes in it.
> d. I don't know __________ I should go there or not.

① if[If]
② or[Or]
③ but[But]
④ because[Because]
⑤ before[Before]

35 우리말 해석에 맞게 주어진 말을 활용하여 빈칸을 완성하세요.

> The problem is ____(throw away, tend, the trash, that)____ on the street.
> (문제는 사람들이 거리에 쓰레기를 버리는 경향이 있다는 것이다.)

➡ _______________________________________

36 다음 문장의 빈칸에 들어갈 말로 알맞은 것은?

> Robert is very healthy and has a very good
> memory __________ his old age.

① although　　② because of　③ despite
④ after　　　　⑤ so

37 다음 빈칸에 들어갈 말로 알맞은 것은?

> After I __________ my homework, I'll go out
> to play soccer.

① finished　　　　② will finish
③ finishes　　　　④ had finished
⑤ finish

38 다음 중 밑줄 친 단어의 문법적 쓰임이 서로 같은 것끼리 짝지은 것은?

① • Who do you think will win the singing
　　contest?
　• By joining a club, you can meet people
　　who share your interests.
② • As she tasted the tea, she put on a smile.
　• As a famous movie star, he has lots of fans.
③ • To live a happy life, you must learn to love
　　yourself.
　• Did you really make this sweater yourself?
④ • I think that she's a very talented writer.
　• Dad often tells us that he wants to live in a
　　country town.
⑤ • Sara enjoys watching the stars from time to
　　time.
　• Watching her walk away, the boy stood
　　there for a while.

39 다음 두 문장의 뜻이 같도록 빈칸에 들어갈 단어로 알맞은 것은?

> • I went home because it grew darker.
> 　= It grew darker, __________ I went
> 　　home.

① but　　　　② because　　③ for
④ so　　　　　⑤ though

40 다음 글의 빈칸에 들어갈 알맞은 단어는?

> I have a friend whose name is Sora. I like
> her very much. She studies really hard. She
> won first prize in the English contest for
> students in my school. __________, she's
> very polite and honest.

① Besides　　② However　　③ Although
④ Instead　　　⑤ Therefore

41 다음 빈칸에 들어갈 알맞은 말은?

> My friend John has a lot of clothes, ________
> __________________. He always buys
> his clothes at garage sales.

① and he spends much money on clothes
② or he doesn't spend much money on clothes
③ but he spends much money on clothes
④ but he doesn't spend much money on
　clothes
⑤ but he spends many money on clothes

42 다음 밑줄 친 if와 바꿔 쓸 수 있는 것은?

> I asked her if she had done it all by herself or if someone had helped her.

① unless ② as ③ because
④ for ⑤ whether

43 다음 중 어법상 옳은 문장을 고르세요.

① Both you and him live in Canada.
② Both my mom and dad was busy harvesting rice.
③ Guests should choose either to eat or not eat breakfast.
④ Neither he nor I am excited about our school festival.
⑤ My friend seemed neither surprised or worried.

44 다음 주어진 문장을 괄호 안의 표현을 활용해 같은 의미의 문장으로 바꿔 쓰세요.

> • Water is not only the most common substance on Earth but also one of the most unusual things.
>
> ➡ ________________________
>   ________________________
>   ________________________
>
>   (as well as)

45 다음 글에서 밑줄 친 표현과 바꾸어 쓸 수 있는 것은?

> Did you know that more than a hundred thousand pets are abandoned each year? These animals are rescued by animal shelters. But the number of homeless pets is <u>so large that the shelters cannot house</u> them all. For this reason, there is a campaign called "Adopt a Friend," which encourages people to adopt a pet from one of the shelters. So instead of buying a pet, why don't you adopt a friend?

① so that the shelters cannot house
② too large for the shelters to house
③ large enough for the shelters to house
④ large for the shelters in order to house
⑤ so large because the shelters cannot house

46 다음 두 문장을 한 문장으로 알맞게 바꾸어 쓴 것은?

> I'm hungry. I can eat a whole pizza by myself.

① I'm hungry so that I can't eat a whole pizza by myself.
② I'm so hungry that I can't eat a whole pizza by myself.
③ I'm so hungry that I can eat a whole pizza by myself.
④ I'm hungry so that I could eat a whole pizza by myself.
⑤ I'm so hungry that I couldn't eat a whole pizza by myself.

47 빈칸 (A)~(C)에 들어갈 말로 가장 적절한 것은?

> She suddenly realized that her phone was missing. She looked around with a confused expression. She asked me ______(A)______ I had seen her phone. I answered ______(B)______ I had not. ______(C)______ she lost it at home or outside was still unclear.

	(A)		(B)		(C)
①	if	–	whether	–	How
②	as if	–	whether	–	Whether
③	if	–	that	–	How
④	if	–	that	–	Whether
⑤	as if	–	that	–	Whether

48 밑줄 친 ⓐ를 〈보기〉의 단어를 한 번씩 활용하여 완성하세요.

> 보 기 | clean, before, that, room, come

> • Make sure ⓐ 손님이 오기 전에 너는 네 방을 청소하도록.
> ➡ Make sure ① ______ you ② ______
> your ③ ______ ④ ______ guests
> ⑤ ______.

49 주어진 문장의 밑줄 친 <u>as</u>와 같은 의미로 쓰인 것을 <u>모두</u> 고르세요.

> We couldn't go to the concert <u>as</u> tickets were sold out.

① <u>As</u> she isn't honest, she won't tell the truth.
② When I was in high school, I started working <u>as</u> a babysitter for my neighbors.
③ On October 31st, American children dress up <u>as</u> ghosts and monsters.
④ <u>As</u> he got up late, he was late for school.
⑤ My puppy barked <u>as</u> it came into the room.

50 다음 두 문장을 한 문장으로 만들 때 빈칸에 들어갈 단어끼리 알맞게 짝지어진 것은?

> • Semin can't speak Chinese. Juyoung can't speak Chinese, either.
> ➡ ______ Semin ______ Juyoung can speak Chinese.

① Between – and
② Both – and
③ Either – or
④ Neither – or
⑤ Neither – nor

51 주어진 단어들만을 모두 사용하여, 다음을 바르게 영작하세요.

> 조 건 |
> • 필요하다면 주어진 단어의 형태를 바꾸세요.

> 내일 비가 오면, 나는 집에 머무를 것이다.
> (at / home / if / it / rain / stay / tomorrow / will)

➡ I ________________________________.

52 우리말 문장을 영어로 바꿀 때 옳지 <u>않은</u> 것은?

① 3월 17일에 그 조약이 체결된 곳은 바로 이 도시에서였다.
→ It was in this city that the treaty was signed on March 17th.

② 이런 종류의 참사가 다시 발생하지 않도록 조치가 취해져야 한다.
→ Steps must be taken so that this kind of disaster never happens again.

③ 그 변호사는 그가 그의 마음을 바꾸도록 설득하지 못했다.
→ The lawyer failed to persuade him to change his mind.

④ 조종사들이 가능한 최고의 훈련을 받는 것은 필수적이다.
› It is essential what pilots should be given the best possible training.

⑤ 비록 당신이 식물들에 물을 주어도, 충분한 햇빛을 받지 않으면, 그것들은 자라지 않을 것이다.
→ Although you water the plants, they won't grow if they don't get enough sunlight.

53 다음 빈칸에 들어갈 수 있는 것을 <u>모두</u> 고르세요.

> _________________ has to go to China for a business trip.

① Either she or I
② Both Mary and Ron
③ Neither she nor you
④ Either Jake or Tim
⑤ Jim as well as I

54 주어진 문장과 의미가 같은 것은?

> This English book was so difficult that I couldn't read it.

① This English book was not difficult to read to me.
② This English book was difficult enough for me to read it.
③ This English book was so difficult to me read.
④ This English book was too difficult for me to read.
⑤ This English book was too difficult for me to have read.

55 다음 빈칸에 들어갈 알맞은 말은?

> _________________, it wasn't very warm.

① Because the sun was shining
② Since the sun was shining
③ Although the sun was shining
④ If the sun shines
⑤ As soon as the sun was shining

56 다음 빈칸에 들어갈 표현으로 적절한 것은?

> The old lady's name is Kim Younghee. _________ she is 70 years old, she is very healthy.

① But　　　② In spite of　　③ Or
④ If　　　⑤ Even though

57

그림을 보고, 〈보기〉의 말을 사용하여 조건에 맞게 각각의 문장을 완성하세요.

(1)

(2)

조 건

• 「so ~ that …」 구문을 사용할 것.
• 〈보기〉의 말을 중복하여 쓸 수 있음.

보 기   good / bad / can / couldn't /
the weather / I / go on a picnic

(1) Yesterday, ___________________________

_________________________________ .

(2) Today, ___________________________

_________________________________ .

58

다음 문장에서 <u>틀린</u> 부분을 한 군데 찾아 바르게 고치세요.

The school closed early because the snowstorm.

_________________ ➡ _________________

59

다음 빈칸에 알맞은 말끼리 순서대로 짝지어진 것은?

Pets can make us happy and keeping pets can teach us many things. Even small pets, ___________, need a lot of care. It takes both a huge amount of money and time to keep them. You should think carefully ___________ you adopt a pet.

① but   – because
② however – before
③ because – before
④ however – after
⑤ but   – if

60

다음 빈칸에 들어갈 단어로 가장 알맞은 것은?

Helen Keller was born in 1880. She was a healthy little baby ___________ she was eighteen months old. Then, she became very sick. When she got better, she couldn't see or hear anything at all.

① but   ② until   ③ after
④ because   ⑤ so

61

다음 빈칸에 들어갈 말로 알맞은 말은?

Seho: When I go to bed, I put my smartphone far away where I can't reach it. I used to stay up very late because of the smartphone. It made me sleepy in school ___________ I studied. So, I put it far away from my bed, and now I get to sleep earlier. It's making a difference, and now I can study with a clear head.

① and   ② because   ③ so   ④ when   ⑤ but

CHAPTER 16
전치사

PSS 1 시간을 나타내는 전치사

PSS 1 - 1 at, on, in Ⅰ

at		구체적인 시각 앞에 온다. I usually get up **at 7 o'clock**. 나는 대개 7시에 일어난다. The movie starts **at 4:50**. 그 영화는 4시 50분에 시작한다.
on		날짜나 요일 앞에 온다. My brother was born **on June 25th, 2022**. 내 남동생은 2022년 6월 25일에 태어났다. Mark and Shelly arrived here **on Monday**. Mark와 Shelly는 월요일에 이곳에 도착했다. We visit our grandparents **on Saturdays**. 우리는 토요일마다 조부모님을 방문한다.
in		연도, 월, 계절과 같은 비교적 긴 시간 앞에 온다. My family moved to Tokyo **in 2023**. 우리 가족은 2023년에 도쿄로 이사했다. My parents married **in May**. 나의 부모님은 5월에 결혼하셨다. I like to go skating **in winter**. 나는 겨울에 스케이트 타러 가는 것을 좋아한다.

정답 p.93

PRACTICE 1

괄호 안에 주어진 전치사 중 알맞은 것을 고르세요.

1 Jenny is leaving for Busan (at, on, in) Sunday.

2 I'm going to meet Ted (at, on, in) 2 p.m.

3 My younger sister was born (at, on, in) 2021.

4 Let's go shopping (at, on, in) Friday.

5 I plan to visit England (at, on, in) summer.

6 The class will begin (at, on, in) half past three.

7 We usually have dinner (at, on, in) 6:30.

8 Jack bought a new car (at, on, in) December.

9 They will take the exam (at, on, in) November 8th.

10 The piano lesson starts (at, on, in) noon.

11 I'll go to his concert (at, on, in) the 3rd of February.

12 The first modern Olympic Games were held (at, on, in) 1896.

13 Mom buys the weekly magazine (at, on, in) Wednesdays.

14 This email was sent (at, on, in) 9 in the morning.

15 I traveled in Alaska (at, on, in) June, 2023.

PSS 1-2 at, on, in Ⅱ

다음은 시간을 나타내는 전치사 at, on, in과 함께 쓰이는 명사(구)이다.

> at night   at lunchtime   at Christmas   at present   at sunset

Jenny doesn't drink even water **at night**. Jenny는 밤에는 물조차 마시지 않는다.
What are you going to do **at Christmas**? 넌 크리스마스 시즌에 뭘 할 거니?
Let's play tennis **at lunchtime**. 점심시간에 테니스 치자.

> on Christmas Day   on New Year's Eve   on Tuesday evening
> on Sunday night   on my birthday

My family went to a nice restaurant **on New Year's Eve**.
우리 가족은 새해 전날 밤에 근사한 식당에 갔다.
Did you meet Mr. Park **on Friday night**? 너는 금요일 밤에 박 선생님을 만났니?
What did you get **on your birthday**? 너는 네 생일에 무엇을 받았니?

> in the morning   in the 21st century   in the 1990s
> in the past   in the future

I wash my hair **in the evening**. 나는 저녁에 머리를 감는다.
Can you imagine living **in the 19th century**? 너는 19세기에 사는 것을 상상할 수 있니?
She dreams of holding her own art exhibition **in the future**.
그녀는 미래에 그녀 자신의 미술 전시회를 개최하는 것을 꿈꾼다.

cf. every, this, last, next 등이 붙어 시간을 나타내는 부사구를 이룰 때는 그 앞에 at, on, in을 쓰지 않는다.
Bob goes to the mountains **every Sunday**. Bob은 일요일마다 산에 간다.
Can I visit your office **this evening**? 오늘 저녁에 네 사무실을 방문해도 될까?
I studied for the exam **last night**. 나는 어젯밤에 시험 공부를 했다.

PRACTICE 2

괄호 안에 주어진 전치사 중 알맞은 것을 고르세요.

1 We gave presents to each other (at, on, in) Christmas Day.

2 I like watching TV (at, on, in) night.

3 There weren't many cars (at, on, in) the past.

4 Julia sent me a lovely card (at, on, in) my birthday.

5 We had lunch with Mr. Lee (at, on, in) noon.

6 Suji usually takes a jog (at, on, in) the morning.

7 I'll call you (at, on, in) lunchtime.

8 Can you come to my house (at, on, in) Monday afternoon?

9 She wrote several bestselling novels (at, on, in) the 21st century.

10 Are you planning to go to church (at, on, in) New Year's Eve?

PRACTICE 3

다음 문장의 빈칸에 at, on, in 중 알맞은 전치사를 쓰세요. 필요하지 않은 곳에는 ×표 하세요.

1 ① Where were you ___________ April?
② Where were you ___________ April 27th?

2 ① I go to the library ___________ Thursdays.
② I go to the library ___________ every Thursday.

3 ① They will meet ___________ noon.
② They will meet ___________ the afternoon.

4 ① Changho writes a diary ___________ night.
② Changho wrote a diary ___________ last night.

5 ① My family gets together ___________ Christmas.
② My family gets together ___________ Christmas Day.

6 ① What do you usually do ___________ the evening?
② What are you going to do ___________ this evening?

7 ① Have you been to the restaurant ___________ night?
② Have you been to the restaurant ___________ Friday night?

8 ① I took a math exam ___________ Tuesday.
② I'll take a math exam ___________ next Tuesday.

9 ① Mom was very busy ____________ the morning.

   ② Mom was very busy ____________ Sunday morning.

10 ① My school begins ____________ September 1st.

   ② My school begins ____________ September.

PSS 1-3 from, since

from	~부터	동작이나 사건이 시작되는 시점을 나타낸다. I will live in Paris **from** March. 나는 3월부터 파리에 살 것이다. ***cf.*** 「from ~ to …」 '~부터 …까지' I lived in Paris **from** 2023 **to** 2024. 나는 2023년부터 2024년까지 파리에 살았다.
since	~ 이래로	주로 완료시제와 함께 쓰이며, 과거에 시작된 사건이 현재에도 영향을 끼치고 있음을 나타낸다. I **have lived** in Paris **since** 2023. 나는 2023년 이래로 파리에서 살아왔다.

정답 p.94

PRACTICE 4

다음 문장의 빈칸에 from이나 since 중 알맞은 전치사를 쓰세요.

1 Miyoung has played the piano ____________ 2021.

2 I will learn Chinese ____________ next year.

3 Jane worked for that company ____________ January to September.

4 It has been cold ____________ yesterday.

5 This program was on TV ____________ 2022 to 2023.

6 My brother has been sick ____________ last weekend.

7 We will get up earlier ____________ tomorrow.

8 Mike has stayed at my house ____________ Monday.

9 Julie and I have been friends ____________ last year.

10 They have a class ____________ one o'clock.

PSS 1-4 by, until

		동작이나 상태가 완료되는 시점을 나타낼 때 쓴다.
by		The rain will stop **by** Tuesday. 비가 화요일까지는 그칠 것이다. I will turn off the TV **by** 3 o'clock. 나는 3시까지는 TV를 끌 것이다.
until	~까지	동작이나 상태가 한 시점까지 계속되는 것을 나타낼 때 쓴다. The rain won't stop **until** Tuesday. 비는 화요일까지 그치지 않을 것이다. (화요일까지 그치지 않고 계속 내린다는 의미) I will watch TV **until** 3 o'clock. 나는 3시까지 TV를 볼 것이다. (3시까지 TV를 계속해서 볼 것이라는 의미)

정답 p.94

PRACTICE 5

괄호 안에 주어진 전치사 중 알맞은 것을 고르세요.

1 I'm going to stay at the hotel (by, until) next Friday.

2 I have to finish my homework (by, until) tomorrow.

3 Heejin kept surfing the Internet (by, until) midnight.

4 Let me know the result (by, until) the weekend.

5 The students have to stay at school (by, until) 3:30.

6 You should return the car (by, until) this Wednesday.

7 Robert will be back (by, until) April.

8 We have to drive (by, until) the night.

PRACTICE 6

〈보기〉에서 알맞은 전치사를 골라 빈칸에 쓰세요.

보 기	at on in from since by until

1 The news starts ___________ eight o'clock.

2 I will study harder ___________ today!

3 We have to decide it ___________ next Monday.

4 The package will be delivered to you ___________ the 3rd of November.

5 I stayed in bed ___________ late in the morning.

6 Minsu has kept an English diary ___________ last summer.

7 My family moved to Seoul ___________ 2022.

8 I usually watch TV ___________ Sunday night.

9 She must come back from Japan ___________ next month.

10 My cousins will visit us ___________ Christmas.

11 I haven't seen Samuel ___________ the day he left this town.

12 You should wait for the result ___________ next week.

13 Mrs. Song likes to drink coffee ___________ the morning.

14 We played baseball ___________ two thirty to five.

15 I got those shoes ___________ my birthday.

PSS 1-5 before, after

before	~ 전에	She can answer the phone **before** 4 o'clock. 그녀는 4시 이전에 전화를 받을 수 있다. I'm not going to watch TV **before** finishing my homework. (= before I finish my homework) 나는 숙제를 끝내기 전에 TV를 보지 않을 것이다.
after	~ 후에	She can't answer the phone **after** 4 o'clock. 그녀는 4시 이후에 전화를 받을 수 없다. I'm going to watch TV **after** finishing my homework. (= after I finish my homework) 나는 숙제를 끝낸 후에 TV를 볼 것이다.

PRACTICE 7

다음은 유미가 지난 토요일에 한 일입니다. 빈칸에 before나 after 중 알맞은 전치사를 쓰세요.

Yumi's schedule

08:00 - woke up
09:00 - had breakfast
10:00 - did the laundry
11:00 - read the history book
13:00 - had lunch
14:00 - went to the movies
16:00 - went to the library
18:00 - went to a Chinese restaurant for dinner
19:30 - got home
22:00 - went to bed

1   Yumi woke up ___________ 7:00 a.m.

2   Yumi had breakfast ___________ 10:00 a.m.

3   Yumi did the laundry ___________ breakfast.

4   Yumi read the history book ___________ lunch.

5   Yumi went to the movies ___________ lunch.

6   Yumi went to the library ___________ 5:00 p.m.

7   Yumi got home ___________ dinner.

8   Yumi went to bed ___________ 9:00 p.m.

PRACTICE **8**

〈보기〉와 같이 문장을 바꿔 쓰세요.

보 기   I cleaned my room, and I studied science.

➡ After <u>cleaning my room, I studied science.</u>

1   He turned off the light, and he went out.

➡ Before ____ .

2   Jessica and Inho saw a movie, and they had dinner.

➡ After ____ .

3   Mom looked at the oranges carefully, and she bought them.

➡ Before ____ .

4   I decided what to do, and I told him about it.

➡ After ____ .

5   Nick usually prays, and he eats food.

➡ Before ____ .

6   We read the book, and we discussed it together.

➡ After ____ .

PSS 1-6   for, during

for	~ 동안	for 다음에는 시간의 길이를 나타내는 명사(구)가 온다. Alex has to stay in hospital **for two months**. Alex는 두 달 동안 입원해 있어야 한다. It rained **for a while**. 잠시 동안 비가 내렸다.
during		during 다음에는 특정 기간을 나타내는 명사(구)가 온다. Alex has to stay in hospital **during the summer vacation**. Alex는 여름방학 동안 입원해 있어야 한다. It rained **during the night**. 밤새 비가 내렸다.
cf. **while**		while은 접속사이므로, while 다음에는 '주어+동사'가 옴에 주의한다. Someone knocked on the door **while I was** asleep. 내가 잠들어 있는 동안 누군가 문을 두드렸다.

CH **16** 전치사

PRACTICE 9

다음 문장의 빈칸에 for나 during 중 알맞은 전치사를 쓰세요.

1 ① I was standing __________ almost two hours.

   ② I was standing __________ the concert.

2 ① Betty felt sleepy __________ the class.

   ② Betty felt sleepy __________ a while.

3 ① Minju will stay in London __________ the summer.

   ② Minju will stay in London __________ two months.

4 ① I turned off my cell phone __________ three hours.

   ② I turned off my cell phone __________ the movie.

5 ① Junho studied very hard __________ a week.

   ② Junho studied very hard __________ the week.

6 ① We talked about the exam __________ about thirty minutes.

   ② We talked about the exam __________ lunch.

7 ① Many soldiers fought __________ the war.

   ② Many soldiers fought __________ ten months.

8 ① I've been reading the book __________ the afternoon.

   ② I've been reading the book __________ some hours.

9 ① Sally went to the beach __________ two weeks.

   ② Sally went to the beach __________ the holiday.

10 ① My mom cooked and cleaned __________ many hours.

   ② My mom cooked and cleaned __________ the day.

PRACTICE 10

〈보기〉에서 알맞은 전치사를 골라 빈칸에 쓰세요.

보 기	before after for during

1 He became very tired when he got home __________ walking around the city.

2 The player moved very fast __________ the game.

3 I have taken tennis lessons __________ two years.

4 Let's clean the house __________ going out.

5 I asked the price __________ paying the money.

6 Charlie was talking to her __________ over an hour.

7 Somebody entered the room ____________ knocking on the door loudly.

8 ____________ going to bed, I took a shower.

9 My family doesn't talk a lot ____________ meals.

10 Andy has taught us English ____________ six months.

PSS 2 장소, 방향을 나타내는 전치사

PSS 2-1 at, in, on I

at	~에	**특정한 한 지점을 나타내거나 비교적 좁은 장소 앞에 쓰인다.** I was sitting **at** the table. 나는 탁자에 앉아 있었다. Jack was waiting for me **at** the bus stop. Jack은 버스 정류장에서 나를 기다리고 있었다.
in	~ (안)에	**공간 안에 속해 있는 느낌을 나타내거나 비교적 넓은 장소 앞에 쓰인다.** He took off his shoes **in** the room. 그는 방에서 신발을 벗었다. There are two birds **in** the cage. 새장 안에 새가 두 마리 있다.
on	~ (위)에	**표면에 접촉해 있는 것을 나타낸다.** A book lies **on** the desk. 책이 책상 위에 놓여 있다. I found some coins **on** the floor. 나는 바닥에서 동전 몇 개를 찾았다.

정답 p.94

PRACTICE 11 [1-9]

그림을 보고, 빈칸에 at, in, on 중 알맞은 전치사를 쓰세요.

1 There is a picture ____________ the door.

2 Flowers are ____________ the vase.

3 I met my friend Steve ____________ the bus stop.

4 The books are ___________ the desk.

5 My brother is standing ___________ the door.

6 I left my umbrella ___________ the restaurant, and I had to go back to get it.

7 There is a boat ___________ the lake.

8 She was sitting ___________ the window reading a book.

9 There are books ___________ the bag.

PSS 2-2 at, in, on Ⅱ

다음은 장소를 나타내는 전치사 at, in, on과 함께 쓰이는 명사(구)이다.

at home	at school	at work
at an airport	at the bottom	at a meeting
at a garage sale	at a contest	at a party
at a gym	at my grandparents' house	

Where is Junho now? – He's **at work**. 준호는 지금 어디에 있니? – 그는 직장에 있어.

There is the answer **at the bottom of** the paper. 종이 아래쪽에 답이 있다.

I met Yumi **at the party** last Saturday. 나는 지난 토요일 파티에서 유미를 만났다.

in bed	in hospital	in prison	in a mirror
in a car	in a taxi	in the middle	in a picture
in the sky	in a book	in a dictionary	

We went to the museum **in a car**. 우리는 차를 타고 박물관에 갔다.

Shelly had a car accident yesterday. She's **in hospital** now.

Mark is sitting **in the middle** of the classroom. Mark는 교실의 중앙에 앉아 있다.

on a bus	on a subway	on a train	on a plane
on a boat	on a street	on a road	on an island
on a farm	on the first floor	on one's[the] way home	

We went to Japan **on a boat**. 우리는 배를 타고 일본에 갔다.

There are so many cars **on the road**. 도로 위에는 아주 많은 차들이 있다.

The room is **on the second floor**. 그 방은 2층에 있다.

I met my uncle **on my way home**. 나는 집에 가는 길에 나의 삼촌을 만났다.

정답 p.94

PRACTICE 12

다음 빈칸에 at, in, on 중 알맞은 전치사를 쓰세요.

1 Why don't you look up the words ___________ the dictionary?

2 Namsik goes to school ___________ a bus.

3 Mrs. Lee's idea was welcomed ___________ the meeting.

4 I worked ___________ the farm during my vacation.

5 Alex has been sick ___________ bed since yesterday.

6 How many classes do you have ___________ school?

7 He got so excited while traveling ___________ a plane.

8 Hurry up! You should be ___________ the airport in an hour.

9 The car broke down ___________ the middle of the street.

10 How did you get to the city, ___________ a train or ___________ a car?

11 I think I read the story ___________ a book.

12 I want to stay ___________ home today.

13 My grandparents live ___________ an island.

14 I saw my old friend ___________ the street yesterday.

15 I left my phone charger ___________ my friend's house after the sleepover.

PSS 2-3 above, below, over, under

above	(〜보다) 위에	The clock is **above** the TV. 시계는 TV 위에 있다. The TV is **below** the clock. TV는 시계 아래에 있다.	
below	(〜보다) 아래에		
over	(뒤덮듯이) 〜 바로 위에	Look at the birds **over** the tree. 나무 위에 있는 새들을 보아라. There is a dog **under** the tree. 나무 아래에 개 한 마리가 있다.	
under	〜 아래에		

정답 p.95

PRACTICE 13

그림을 보고, 괄호 안에 주어진 전치사 중 알맞은 것을 고르세요.

1   There is a bridge (over, under) the river.

2   A few birds are flying (above, below) the people.

3   Two people are walking (above, below) the birds.

4   There is a small village (over, under) the mountain.

5   Some white clouds are (above, below) the mountain.

6   The sun is shining (over, under) the mountain.

7   Fish are swimming (above, below) the bridge.

8   We can see some flowers (over, under) the tree.

up	~ 위로	Minji and I walked **up** the mountain. 민지와 나는 산 위로 걸어 올라갔다.
down	~ 아래로	Minji and I walked **down** the mountain. 민지와 나는 산 아래로 걸어 내려갔다.
into	~ 안으로	Three students came **into** the classroom. 세 명의 학생들이 교실 안으로 들어왔다.
out of	~ 밖으로	Three students got **out of** the classroom. 세 명의 학생들이 교실 밖으로 나왔다.

PRACTICE 14

정답 p.95

그림을 보고, 〈보기〉에서 알맞은 전치사를 골라 빈칸에 쓰세요.

| 보 기 | up | down | into | out of |

1 A man is going ___________ the stairs.

2 Sejin is climbing ___________ the hill.

3 A few people were coming ___________ the building.

4 Mom was cooking when I walked ___________ the kitchen.

5 I had to go ___________ the ladder to reach the shelf.

6 Bob took a cat ___________ the box.

7 She helped her grandmother to get ___________ a car.

8 It was easy to row a boat ___________ the river.

CH
16
전치사

PRACTICE 15

그림을 보고, 괄호 안에 주어진 전치사 중 알맞은 것을 고르세요.

1 The girl is looking (into, out of) the window.

The dog is coming (up, down) the hill.

2 The sofa lies (above, below) the window.

The window is (above, below) the sofa.

3 My brother went (up, down) the tree to get the kite.

I was waiting (over, under) the tree.

4 The player served the ball (over, under) the net.

The ball is now (into, out of) the court.

5 A boy came (into, out of) the room.

He found a picture (above, below) the desk.

6 The rabbit was running (up, down) the mountain.

It has just jumped (over, under) the rock.

7 Sumi went (into, out of) the bed.

Her dog was lying (above, under) the bed.

8 I walked (up, down) the street.

I saw a man standing (above, below) the streetlight.

across	~을 가로질러	I walked **across** the road. 나는 도로를 가로질러 걸었다.
along	~을 따라	I walked **along** the river. 나는 강을 따라 걸었다.
through	~을 통과하여	I walked **through** the forest. 나는 숲을 통과하여 걸었다.
around	~ 주위에(를)	I walked **around** the school. 나는 학교 주위를 걸었다.

정답 p.95

PRACTICE 16

그림을 보고, 〈보기〉에서 알맞은 전치사를 골라 빈칸에 쓰세요.

| 보 기 | across | along | through | around |

1 Jim walked ___________ the street.

2 Many cars are moving ___________ the road.

3 I often take walks ___________ the park with my parents.

4 Dad likes driving ___________ the town.

5 A cool wind entered the room ___________ the window.

6 I tried to swim ___________ the river.

7 The postbox is just ___________ the corner.

8 She was walking ___________ the street.

PSS 2-6 by, in front of, behind

by	~ 옆에	Peter is sitting **by** Jane. Peter는 Jane 옆에 앉아 있다. = Peter is sitting **beside** Jane. = Peter is sitting **next to** Jane.
in front of	~ 앞에	Nami is sitting **in front of** Peter. 나미는 Peter 앞에 앉아 있다.
behind	~ 뒤에	John is sitting **behind** Jane. John은 Jane 뒤에 앉아 있다.

정답 p.95

PRACTICE 17

그림을 보고, 〈보기〉에서 알맞은 전치사를 골라 빈칸에 쓰세요.

1 	2 	3 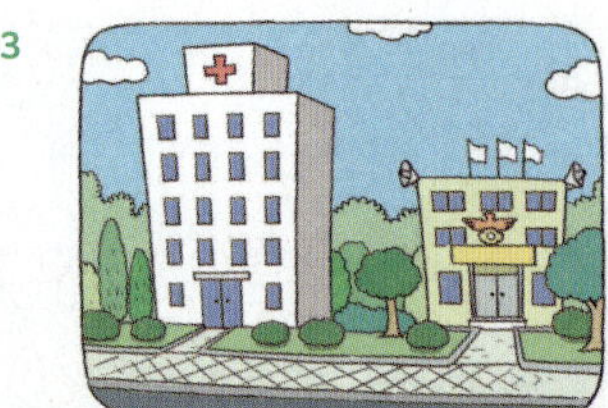
4 	5  	6 
7 	8 	9 

보 기	by in front of behind

1 The tree is ____________ the rock.

2 I'm waiting for my friend ____________ the school.

3 The police station is ____________ the hospital.

4 There are four more people ____________ me.

5 The girl ____________ Paul is Lisa.

6   I have been to the mountain ___________ these houses.

7   I saw some foreigners taking photos ___________ the stone pagoda.

8   The children are hiding ___________ the curtain.

9   I left my glasses ___________ the book.

정답 p.95

PRACTICE 18

그림을 보고, 괄호 안에 주어진 전치사 중 알맞은 것을 고르세요.

1   There is a tree (in front of, behind) the school.
    A girl is walking (across, along) the street.

2   A man is running (through, around) the park.
    A dog is running (in front of, behind) him.

3   The post office is (behind, by) the bank.
    The drug store is (across, around) the corner.

4   Some people walk (across, along) the river.
    Other people walk (across, under) the bridge.

5   My family was driving (by, through) the town.
    There was a truck (behind, around) our car.

6   Sally is standing (by, behind) me.
    Peter and Julie are standing (in front of, behind) Sally and me.

7   My parents and I were sitting (through, around) the table.
    Someone knocked on the door (in front of, behind) Mom.

8   I was standing (by, behind) the tree.
    Jenny came to me (across, along) the street.

PSS 2-7 between, among

between	(둘) 사이에	I was lying **between** the two of them. 나는 그들 둘 사이에 누워 있었다. ***cf.*** between은 「between A and B」의 형태로도 쓰인다. I was lying **between** Mom **and** Dad. 나는 엄마와 아빠 사이에 누워 있었다.	
among	(셋 이상의) 사이에	I was lying **among** my four brothers. 나는 나의 네 명의 형제들 사이에 누워 있었다.	

정답 p.95

PRACTICE 19

괄호 안에 주어진 전치사 중 알맞은 것을 고르세요.

1   Cathy is the girl sitting (between, among) Mark and Sam.

2   Bill has a good reputation (between, among) his fellows.

3   How many girls do you know (between, among) those five?

4   You have to choose (between, among) the two colors.

5   It was difficult to find Yujin (between, among) thousands of children.

6   There's a soccer game (between, among) Korea and Taiwan today.

7   The time difference (between, among) the two countries is an hour.

8   The computer game is very popular (between, among) my classmates.

9   There is a bench (between, among) the river and the road.

10 I lost my wallet (between, among) the crowd at the festival.

11 There is a black rabbit (between, among) the white rabbits.

12 She is standing (between, among) the bus stop and the tree.

PSS 2-8 to, for

to	∼로, ∼에	**go, come, return** 동사와 함께 도착지를 나타낼 때 쓰인다. I **went to** the hospital to visit my uncle. 나는 나의 삼촌을 방문하기 위해 병원에 갔다. Smith **came to** Korea three months ago. Smith는 3개월 전에 한국에 왔다. She **returned to** China in 2024. 그녀는 2024년에 중국으로 돌아갔다.
for	∼로, ∼을 향하여	**leave, start** 동사와 함께 방향을 나타낼 때 쓰인다. Linda **left for** Los Angeles yesterday. Linda는 어제 로스앤젤레스로 떠났다. My family is going to **start for** Busan. 우리 가족은 부산을 향해 출발할 것이다.

cf. to와 for는 4형식 문장을 3형식 문장으로 전환할 때 간접목적어 앞에 놓여 '∼에게, ∼께'로 해석된다.

My brother gave Mom a bunch of roses. 나의 남동생은 엄마께 장미꽃 한 다발을 드렸다.
➡ My brother gave a bunch of roses **to** Mom.

She bought her father a necktie. 그녀는 그녀의 아버지께 넥타이를 사드렸다.
➡ She bought a necktie **for** her father.

정답 p.95

PRACTICE 20

다음 문장의 빈칸에 to와 for 중 알맞은 전치사를 쓰세요.

1 We're going ___________ Madrid next month.

2 Seho started ___________ school ten minutes ago.

3 They came ___________ my house to see me.

4 Jina will return ___________ Seoul in a week.

5 The train is leaving ___________ Daegu in a few minutes.

6 I returned ___________ the bookstore and bought the book.

7 You'd better start ___________ the airport now to be on board in time.

8 She went ___________ the gym to meet Chris.

9 Jaehui made bibimbap ___________ Sarah yesterday.

10 Eddie made a call ___________ his grandmother.

CH
16
전
치
사

PSS 3 그 밖의 전치사

PSS 3 - 1 with, about, like

with	~와 함께	I live **with** my grandparents. 나는 나의 조부모님과 함께 산다.
	~의 몸에 지니고	You'd better take an umbrella **with** you. 넌 우산을 가져가는 것이 좋을 거야.
	~을 가지고 있는	The dog **with** a long tail is Max. 긴 꼬리를 가진 개가 Max야.
	~을 사용하여, ~으로	What did you make **with** snow? 넌 눈으로 무엇을 만들었니?
about	~에 대해 (= on)	We were talking **about** having a party. 우리는 파티를 여는 것에 대해 이야기하고 있었다.
like	~와 같은 (= such as)	I love Italian food **like** spaghetti and pizza. 나는 스파게티와 피자 같은 이탈리아 음식을 대단히 좋아한다.
	~처럼	Alex and Matthew look **like** brothers. Alex와 Matthew는 형제처럼 보인다.

cf. without '(사람, 물건, 경험 등이) 없이'
Can you see well **without** your glasses? 넌 네 안경 없이 잘 볼 수 있니?

정답 p.95

PRACTICE 21

괄호 안에 주어진 전치사 중 알맞은 것을 고르세요.

1 The book is (with, about) Korean history.

2 Tony enjoys sports (about, like) baseball and basketball.

3 I'd like to take a trip (about, with) my friends.

4 Did you hear the news (about, like) the traffic accident last night?

5 Do you know the boy (like, with) glasses over there?

6 What's your opinion (with, about) Sora's birthday present?

7 She made a cake (with, about) sugar, butter and flour.

8 My sister sings very well (about, like) a singer.

9 We found the place (without, like) difficulty.

10 Yunju and Sunhee look (like, with) twins.

정답 p.95

PRACTICE 22

우리말 해석과 일치하도록 〈보기〉에서 알맞은 전치사를 골라 빈칸에 쓰세요.

보 기	between among to for with about like without

1 Let's go ____________ the park after school. (방과 후에 공원에 가자.)

2 When do you plan to start ____________ Daejeon? (너는 대전으로 언제 출발할 계획이니?)

3 You can't make an omelet ____________ eggs. (너는 계란 없이 오믈렛을 만들 수 없다.)

4 I saw a movie ____________ World War II on TV.
(나는 TV에서 2차 세계대전에 대한 영화를 봤다.)

5 A squirrel was making rustling noises ____________ the leaves.
(다람쥐 한 마리가 나뭇잎들 사이에서 바스락 거리는 소리를 내고 있었다.)

6 The patient ____________ the disease has to take medicine twice a day.
(그 병을 가진 환자는 하루에 두 번 약을 복용해야 한다.)

7 People say that I look ____________ my father. (사람들은 내가 나의 아빠를 닮았다고 말한다.)

8 I can't decide which to eat ____________ pizza and steak.
(나는 피자와 스테이크 중에 어느 것을 먹을지 정할 수 없다.)

PSS 3-2 by, as, in

by	~를 타고	I went to Chicago **by** plane. 나는 비행기를 타고 시카고에 갔다. ***cf.*** by 뒤에 교통수단이 올 때는 관사를 쓰지 않는다.
	〈방법〉 ~로	Mike and I keep in touch **by** email. Mike와 나는 이메일로 계속 연락한다.
	~에 의해	This novel was written **by** James Joyce. 이 소설은 James Joyce에 의해 쓰여졌다.
	〈정도〉 ~로, ~만큼	My team lost the game **by** 3 to 1. 나의 팀은 3대 1로 경기에 졌다.

by	～함으로써, ～하며	What can you make **by** using the paper? 그 종이를 사용함으로써 너는 무엇을 만들 수 있니?
as	～로서, ～처럼	I used to use this bowl **as** a cup. 나는 이 사발을 컵으로 이용하곤 했다.
in	～을 입고 있는	Look at the woman **in** red. 빨간 옷을 입고 있는 여자를 보아라.
	〈크기〉 ～로	Cut the bread **in** half. 빵을 반으로 잘라라.
	〈방법〉 ～로	They spoke **in** English during the meeting. 그들은 회의 동안 영어로 말했다.

정답 p.95

PRACTICE 23

〈보기〉에서 알맞은 전치사를 골라 빈칸에 쓰세요.

보 기	by	as	in

1   Luke works ___________ a manager in the restaurant.

2   This famous play was written ___________ Shakespeare.

3   Mom sliced the bread ___________ three pieces.

4   She tries to lose weight ___________ swimming every morning.

5   My brother is taller than I am ___________ three centimeters.

6   We think of her ___________ the best teacher in Korea.

7   I sketched the picture ___________ pencil first.

8   It is pleasant to travel ___________ train.

9   Ten men ___________ black are standing in front of the building.

10   You can learn how to communicate with other people ___________ working together.

11   You have to speak ___________ Korean during this class.

12   Could you send it to me ___________ fax?

13   The island was discovered ___________ an English explorer, James Cook.

14   The couch can also be used ___________ an extra bed.

1. **full of** '〜로 가득한' = filled with

    This garden is **full of** beautiful flowers. 이 정원은 아름다운 꽃들로 가득하다.

2. **built of** '〜로 지어진'

    This house is **built of** brick. 이 집은 벽돌로 지어졌다.

3. **made of** '〜로 만들어진'

    The chair is **made of** wood. 그 의자는 나무로 만들어졌다.

    cf. 화학적 변화를 거쳐 만들어질 때는 made from을 쓴다.

4. **upset about** '〜에 대해 화난, 기분이 나쁜'

    I'm **upset about** your sister. 나는 너의 언니에 대해 기분이 나쁘다.

5. **good at** '〜을 잘하는'

    Jina is **good at** playing the flute. 지나는 플룻 연주를 잘한다.

6. **poor at** '〜에 서툰'

    I'm **poor at** mathematics. 나는 수학에 서툴다.

7. **proud of** '〜을 자랑스러워하는'

    Kevin is **proud of** his son. Kevin은 그의 아들을 자랑스러워한다.

8. **famous for** '〜로 유명한'

    Sumi is **famous for** her paintings. 수미는 그녀의 그림들로 유명하다.

9. **interested in** '〜에 흥미가 있는, 관심이 있는'

    My father is **interested in** classical music. 나의 아버지는 클래식 음악에 관심이 있으시다.

10. **afraid of** '〜을 두려워하는'

    John is **afraid of** birds. John은 새를 두려워한다.

11. **tired of** '〜에 싫증난, 〜이 지겨운'

    I'm **tired of** eating at the same restaurant every day. 난 매일 똑같은 식당에서 밥 먹는 게 지겨워.

12. **similar to** '〜와 비슷한'

    This question is **similar to** that question. 이 문제는 그 문제와 유사하다.

PRACTICE 24

괄호 안에 주어진 전치사 중 알맞은 것을 고르세요.

1 James is very good (at, in) many kinds of sports.

2 I'm proud (of, at) my family and country.

3 Are you interested (at, in) romantic movies?

4 Most books are made (of, in) paper.

5 Your teacher is upset (from, about) your rude manners.

6 Her eyes were full (of, with) tears.

7 Tim is poor (at, in) music and art.

8 All of the children were afraid (of, at) ghosts.

9 This building is built (of, in) stones.

10 Mr. Park is famous (of, for) his TV show.

11 I'm tired (from, of) cold weather, heavy coats, and boots.

12 He thought that Korean culture was similar (of, to) Canadian culture.

PSS 3-4 동사와 함께 쓰이는 전치사

1. **belong to** '~에 속하다, ~의 소유물이다'

    The huge house **belongs to** the famous actor. 그 거대한 집은 유명한 배우의 소유이다.

2. **look for** '~을 찾다'

    I'm **looking for** my brown bag. 나는 내 갈색 가방을 찾고 있다.

3. **die of** '~로 죽다'

    My grandfather **died of** cancer. 나의 할아버지는 암으로 돌아가셨다.

4. **consist of** '~로 구성되어 있다'

    The test **consists of** speaking and listening. 그 시험은 말하기와 듣기로 구성되어 있다.

5. **wait for** '~을 기다리다'

    The lady is **waiting for** the bus for 30 minutes. 그 숙녀는 30분 동안 버스를 기다리고 있다.

6. listen to '~을 듣다'

The children love to **listen to** bedtime stories before sleeping.

아이들은 자기 전 잠자리 동화 듣기를 아주 좋아한다.

7. thank … for '(…에게) ~을 감사하다'

Thank you **for** your quick response. 당신의 빠른 답변에 감사드립니다.

8. believe in '~을 믿다'

I **believe in** God. 나는 신을 믿는다.

9. care about '~에 대해 신경 쓰다, 관심을 가지다'

Doctors **care about** their patients. 의사들은 자신의 환자들에 대해 신경을 쓴다.

10. laugh at '~을 보고 웃다, 비웃다'

They **laughed at** Tom's stupid question. 그들은 Tom의 어리석은 질문을 비웃었다.

11. run into[across] '~와 우연히 마주치다'

I **ran into** your brother today. 나는 오늘 너희 오빠와 우연히 마주쳤다.

12. take pride in '~에 자부심을 가지다'

They **take pride in** their school. 그들은 그들의 학교에 자부심을 가진다.

정답 p.96

PRACTICE 25 [1-17]

다음 문장의 빈칸에 알맞은 전치사를 쓰세요.

1 The team consists ___________ doctors and nurses.

2 My sister is looking ___________ a new job.

3 Jake enjoys listening ___________ rap music.

4 The concert hall was full ___________ people.

5 I've always been interested ___________ cooking.

6 Does this bag belong ___________ you?

7 Mr. White is proud ___________ his students' hard work and dedication.

8 We were waiting ___________ the teacher in the classroom.

9 Everybody is afraid ___________ death.

CH
16
전
치
사

10 Brazil and Columbia are famous ___________ their coffee.

11 My grandmother died ___________ old age.

12 People laughed ___________ the clown's walking.

13 Thank you all ___________ coming tonight.

14 A few people believe ___________ UFOs.

15 She doesn't care ___________ the prize. It's not important to her.

16 She ran ___________ an old friend at the party.

17 The Korean team took pride ___________ winning the game against the Brazilian team.

정답 p.96

PRACTICE 26

괄호 안에 주어진 전치사 중 알맞은 것을 고르세요.

1 I stayed at Jinho's house (for, during) five days.

2 Thank you (to, for) inviting me to dinner.

3 I like the pretty table cloth (on, above) that table.

4 I wrote my name (down, below) my father's.

5 I'm going to a concert (at, in) Christmas.

6 Mike is poor (in, at) looking after babies.

7 There is a carpet (on, in) the floor.

8 Are you good (at, of) singing?

9 Jinyoung is not interested (in, at) making things.

10 There's a mirror (as, above) the TV.

11 People feel more tired (in, on) Mondays.

12 I'll return (to, for) my house at about 8:30.

13 Jack is proud (of, with) his height.

14 She was beautiful (in, of) white.

15 I usually go swimming (from, since) 7 to 8.

16 Mr. Smith came to Korea (at, in) 2023.

17 I've waited (for, on) his reply since last year.

18 We need to think (with, about) moving to another city.

19 My family consists (of, with) Dad, Mom, my brother, and me.

20 Mom and I planted pretty flowers (around, above) our garden.

21 I read the newspaper (at, in) the evening.

22 I haven't seen Helen (for, during) 3 months.

23 I don't know how to say this (by, in) English.

24 Do you know what happened (between, among) Nancy and Carrie?

25 This baby looks (like, with) an angel.

26 Ann put some books (down, under) the desk.

27 Go and wash your hands first (before, after) eating lunch.

28 These jeans belong (to, for) my sister.

29 We visited our grandparents (in, during) the holiday.

30 We climbed (up, down) the hill to go higher.

31 He should have finished writing it (by, until) now.

32 They ran (down, under) the stairs to get the door.

33 Many children are dying (in, of) hunger in Africa.

34 What are you going to do (by, with) the money?

35 My cats are sleeping (in, at) the living room.

36 (Under, After) getting dressed, I went out in a hurry.

37 Birds are flying high (in, at) the sky.

38 The students were standing (through, along) the white line.

39 Wine is made (in, from) grapes.

40 I can stay in Tokyo (by, until) next week.

41 They went to Australia (on, by) a plane.

42 We can save some time if we go there (in, on) a taxi.

43 Yumi has wanted to learn Chinese (from, since) last year.

44 This river flows (out of, through) the city.

45 I saw Sangho going (in, into) the building.

46 The Korean team won the game (by, in) 2 to 1.

47 My heart became full (of, with) joy.

48 Let's get (into, out of) the classroom and have some fresh air.

49 I wanted to see the actor's face (behind, in front of) the mask.

50 When do you leave (for, to) New York?

1 다음 빈칸에 들어갈 단어로 알맞은 것은?

> The annual flower festival is celebrated in Amsterdam __________ April 30th.

① to　　② of　　③ on
④ in　　⑤ at

2 다음 빈칸에 들어갈 단어로 알맞은 것은?

> Fill out the application and sign your name __________ the bottom.

① of　　② in　　③ by
④ at　　⑤ into

3 다음 우리말을 영어로 옮길 때 빈칸에 알맞은 세 단어를 쓰세요. (단, 전치사 to를 반드시 포함시킬 것.)

> • 그녀의 생각은 내 생각과 꽤 비슷하다.
> = Her idea is quite __________
> __________ __________ .

4 빈칸에 공통으로 들어갈 말로 알맞은 것은?

> • I can trust you __________ you always tell the truth.
> • She's been off work __________ Tuesday.

① because　　② for　　③ as
④ since　　⑤ during

5 다음 빈칸에 공통으로 들어갈 알맞은 단어는?

> • Put some water __________ the bowl.
> • My family is going to move __________ a new house next month.

① of　　② about　　③ on
④ for　　⑤ into

6 주어진 우리말과 같은 뜻이 되도록 괄호 안의 말을 바르게 배열하세요.

> • 그녀는 은행에 가는 길에 그녀의 선생님과 우연히 마주쳤다.
> = She __________
> __________ the bank.
> (her way, across, on, ran, her teacher, to)

7 다음 대화의 빈칸에 들어갈 단어끼리 알맞게 짝지어진 것은?

> A: Do you know __________ we can't meet Mr. Kim anymore?
> B: That's because he died __________ cancer last month.

① what – at　　② what – of
③ why – of　　④ why – by
⑤ by　 – in

8 ⓐ～ⓒ에 들어갈 단어끼리 알맞게 짝지어진 것은?

Two years ago, I visited Mexico with my family. ⓐ (With / At) that time, people were celebrating the Day of the Dead, a Mexican holiday. ⓑ (In / On) this holiday, Mexicans remember and honor their deceased loved ones. It's not a gloomy occasion, but rather it is a colorful holiday. People usually visit cemeteries and decorate the graves. Also, they make *ofrendas*, elaborately decorated altars, ⓒ (with / in) their homes to welcome the spirits.

*deceased: 사망한 **elaborately: 정교하게 ***altar: 제단

	ⓐ		ⓑ		ⓒ
①	With	–	In	–	with
②	At	–	On	–	in
③	At	–	In	–	with
④	With	–	On	–	with
⑤	At	–	In	–	in

9 다음 ⓐ～ⓔ의 밑줄 친 부분 중 어법상 틀린 것을 있는 대로 고른 것은?

ⓐ She speaks English <u>in</u> her first language.
ⓑ We should protect wild animals <u>as</u> tigers and bears.
ⓒ I'm going to travel <u>around</u> the countryside.
ⓓ We are looking <u>for</u> a used car.
ⓔ The contest was held <u>on</u> April 7th.

① ⓐ, ⓑ   ② ⓑ, ⓒ   ③ ⓐ, ⓑ, ⓒ
④ ⓐ, ⓓ, ⓔ   ⑤ ⓑ, ⓒ, ⓓ, ⓔ

10 다음 우리말과 일치하도록 빈칸에 알맞은 표현을 쓰세요.

• 내 목걸이는 파란 유리구슬로 만들어져 있다.
  = My necklace __________ __________ blue glass beads.

11 ⓐ～ⓔ 중 밑줄 친 전치사의 쓰임이 틀린 것을 있는 대로 고른 것은?

보 기
ⓐ We waited for you <u>for</u> two hours.
ⓑ I usually go <u>to</u> school on foot.
ⓒ I will call you <u>at</u> Monday morning.
ⓓ The children are playing <u>in</u> the playground.
ⓔ He was upset <u>for</u> the mistake he made in the exam.

① ⓐ, ⓒ   ② ⓒ, ⓔ   ③ ⓑ, ⓒ
④ ⓑ, ⓔ   ⑤ ⓒ, ⓓ, ⓔ

12 빈칸에 공통으로 들어갈 알맞은 단어를 쓰세요.

• I'll let you know __________ email.
• The other team was losing __________ one run.
• The great film was directed __________ Woody Allen.

➡ __________________________

13 각 빈칸에 들어갈 알맞은 전치사를 쓰세요.

• Sora is going to leave Seoul __________ Jejudo.
• She has gone __________ Jejudo.

14 우리말 문장을 영어로 바꿀 때 옳지 <u>않은</u> 것은?

① 내가 그녀를 위해 많은 것을 했다는 사실에도 불구하고 그녀는 날 돕는 걸 거절했다.
→ She refused to help me despite the fact that I've done many things for her.

② 그 학교는 아이들이 자신만의 속도에 맞춰 배우도록 해야 한다고 믿는다.
→ The school believes in letting children learn at their own pace.

③ 그 좁은 도로들은 휴일 (나들이) 차량들로 붐볐다.
→ The narrow roads were crowded with holiday traffic.

④ 판매의 감소는 신차에 대한 세금 감면이 종료된 것과 관련이 있다.
→ The drop in sales is related to the end of a tax break on new cars.

⑤ 그 뷔페는 여러가지 다양한 스페인 요리로 구성되어 있다.
→ The buffet consists with several different Spanish dishes.

15 다음 빈칸에 알맞은 단어끼리 바르게 짝지어진 것은?

> • I prefer milk __________ coffee.
> • I am sure she's __________ the airport now.

① than – to
② to – with
③ in – to
④ to – at
⑤ by – at

16 다음 빈칸에 들어갈 알맞은 단어를 〈보기〉에서 찾아 한 번씩 쓰세요.

> 보 기 | during   for   while

(1) We stayed at Jack's home __________ two weeks.
(2) He hurt his arm __________ he was playing basketball.
(3) I told my friends what I did __________ my trip to New York.

17 다음 빈칸에 알맞은 단어끼리 바르게 짝지어진 것은?

> • He took me __________ a nice restaurant.
> • My teacher asked us __________ our vacation plans.

① to – about
② to – of
③ about – to
④ on – about
⑤ in – to

18 주어진 우리말과 같은 뜻이 되도록 빈칸에 알맞은 단어를 쓰세요.

> • 그녀는 자신의 개를 도왔던 그 사람처럼 배려심 있는 수의사가 되는 것을 꿈꾼다.
> = She dreams of becoming a caring veterinarian __________ the one who helped her dog.

19 다음 빈칸에 공통으로 들어갈 단어는?

- We went there __________ a car.
- He helped me keep a diary __________ English.

① for   ② in   ③ by
④ on   ⑤ to

20 다음 중 밑줄 친 부분의 쓰임이 <u>어색한</u> 것은?

① Many people go to the beach <u>in</u> summer.
② I talked to Mr. Lee <u>of</u> the phone for an hour.
③ I didn't see your name <u>on</u> the list.
④ Why don't we take a taxi instead <u>of</u> a bus?
⑤ You should take off your shoes <u>in</u> the classroom.

21 주어진 문장의 밑줄 친 since와 의미가 같은 것을 <u>모두</u> 고르세요.

They have been friends <u>since</u> kindergarten.

① We thought that we'd stop by and see him <u>since</u> we were in the area.
② You don't have to go to see her <u>since</u> she's OK.
③ Irene has been working in a bank <u>since</u> leaving school.
④ I haven't eaten anything <u>since</u> breakfast.
⑤ I'm not worried anymore <u>since</u> you're here for me.

22 다음 대화의 빈칸에 들어갈 단어로 알맞은 것은?

A: Have you ever read the book, *Pride and Prejudice*?
B: No, I haven't. What is the book __________?

① of   ② by   ③ from
④ in   ⑤ about

23 ⓐ~ⓔ 중 어법상 맞는 것을 <u>있는 대로</u> 고른 것은?

ⓐ We walked through the forest to reach the village.
ⓑ The dog jumped on the river to catch the ball.
ⓒ Cut the sandwich in half so we can share it.
ⓓ My brother was born in July 5, 2010.
ⓔ She is good at play the piano.

① ⓐ, ⓑ   ② ⓐ   ③ ⓐ, ⓒ
④ ⓑ, ⓔ   ⑤ ⓐ, ⓑ, ⓓ

24 다음 글에서 틀린 문장을 <u>2개</u> 찾아 그 기호를 쓰고 완전한 문장으로 다시 쓰세요.

How to Get Along with Your Classmates

ⓐ <u>Don't wait until they will speak to you.</u>
ⓑ <u>Speak to them first.</u>
ⓒ <u>Help them ahead before they ask for help.</u>
ⓓ <u>Listen at what they say.</u>
ⓔ <u>If they need your advice, try to give it to them.</u>

(1) ______________________________

(2) ______________________________

25 다음 빈칸에 공통으로 들어갈 단어는?

- The telephone was invented __________ Alexander Graham Bell.
- Is it possible to deliver this package __________ tomorrow?
- He greeted us __________ shaking hands.

① by　　　② from　　　③ for
④ at　　　⑤ to

26 주어진 우리말과 같은 뜻이 되도록 빈칸에 알맞은 단어를 쓰세요.

- 만약 네가 네 자신을 믿는다면, 넌 그것을 해낼 수 있을 것이다.
  = If you __________ __________ __________, you'll be able to make it.

27 각 빈칸에 들어갈 알맞은 전치사를 〈보기〉에서 골라 한 번씩 쓰세요.

보 기 | on　in　after　with

(1) I left the books __________ the table.

(2) I'll go to the dentist __________ school.

(3) Is anything wrong __________ your computer?

(4) I practiced pronouncing difficult words __________ English with a language partner.

28 다음 글의 맥락상 (a)~(e) 어디에도 들어갈 수 없는 것은?

Meet Tom. He is an energetic boy who loves exploring nature. On weekends, he wakes up (a) __________ 7:00 and packs his small backpack. He goes hiking (b) __________ his father in the nearby hills. They enjoy walking (c) __________ the river, listening to birds singing. (d) __________ their break, they usually eat sandwiches and drink juice together. When they get home, Tom likes to write about his adventure (e) __________ his diary before going to bed.

① below　　　② along　　　③ during
④ at　　　⑤ with

29 다음 빈칸에 공통으로 들어갈 말은?

Andrew: What are you reading now?
Carroll : I'm reading *Animal Farm* written by George Orwell.
Andrew: *Animal Farm*? I also __________ reading anti-utopian novels.
Carroll : What does anti-utopian mean?
Andrew: It is the opposite of the word utopian which means "of a perfect or ideal existence." Books __________ *1984* and *Animal Farm* are anti-utopian novels.

*anti-utopian novel: 반이상향 소설

① enjoy　　　② like　　　③ into
④ around　　　⑤ without

30 다음 중 어법상 올바른 문장은?

① I like this restaurant because its delicious food and good service.
② Let's make it on 6 o'clock in front of the department store.
③ My friend James lives at Canada.
④ Why don't we go to the stadium on Saturday afternoon?
⑤ We enjoyed to dance with them.

31 다음 빈칸에 공통으로 들어갈 단어는?

- The woman __________ curly hair is my aunt.
- I walked to school __________ my friend, Jina.

① in
② by
③ on
④ out
⑤ with

32 다음 빈칸 (A)~(E)에 들어갈 수 <u>없는</u> 전치사는?

- It is similar _____(A)_____ the Korean holiday Chuseok.
- Did your classmates laugh _____(B)_____ you?
- Take pride _____(C)_____ your health and your figure.
- This book consists _____(D)_____ 12 chapters.
- I'm good _____(E)_____ reading my friends' palms.

① for
② to
③ in
④ of
⑤ at

33 다음 빈칸에 들어갈 단어끼리 알맞게 짝지어진 것은?

- Junho usually spends __________ thirty minutes to forty minutes surfing the Internet.
- His backpack was full __________ camping gear for the weekend trip.

① from – of
② from – in
③ from – with
④ in – of
⑤ in – on

34 밑줄 친 (A)~(C)에 들어갈 말이 알맞게 짝지어진 것은?

To whom it may concern,

   I am a resident of Golden Bridge Apartment. I have recently realized that our playground is filled _____(A)_____ unrepaired equipment. The swings are broken and some of the bolts on the slides seem missing. I want you to pay attention _____(B)_____ the terrible condition of the playground. Since the playground equipment is dangerous to the children playing there, it is _____(C)_____ great importance to have it repaired. Thank you for reading this.

Yours sincerely,
Dorothy Gibson

	(A)	(B)	(C)
①	over	to	for
②	with	for	to
③	of	with	to
④	with	to	of
⑤	over	with	of

35 다음 빈칸에 들어갈 전치사를 순서대로 바르게 나열한 것은?

> • __________ first he was afraid of water, but now he is a good swimmer.
> • When Junho arrived at his house, his parents were waiting __________ him anxiously.
> • __________ my surprise, I won first prize in the English speech contest.

① For – at – To
② At – to – For
③ To – for – At
④ For – to – At
⑤ At – for – To

36 다음 빈칸에 알맞은 단어끼리 바르게 짝지어진 것은?

> • The airplane started __________ Japan.
> • Thank you __________ helping me solve the problem.

① to – to
② for – for
③ to – into
④ for – into
⑤ to – for

37 다음 중 ⓐ에 들어갈 전치사와 동일한 전치사가 들어갈 수 있는 것을 <u>모두</u> 고르세요.

> My family was in Canada ⓐ __________ the summer.

① There is a secret __________ Tom and Jane.
② He is standing __________ the window.
③ We met a lot of people __________ the trip.
④ They waited for him __________ an hour.
⑤ Please be quiet __________ the meeting.

38 다음 빈칸에 들어갈 단어끼리 바르게 짝지어진 것은?

> • She got good grades in most __________ her subjects.
> • When he was young, he was interested __________ invention.

① in – of
② at – in
③ of – in
④ of – to
⑤ in – from

39 다음 우리말과 같은 뜻이 되도록 빈칸에 들어갈 알맞은 단어는?

> • 1번부터 시작할까?
>   = Shall we start __________ number 1?

① to
② in
③ of
④ for
⑤ with

40 다음 빈칸 (A)~(E)에 들어갈 수 <u>없는</u> 전치사는?

> • Water consists __________ (A) __________ hydrogen and oxygen.
> • The gallery is famous __________ (B) __________ its collection.
> • She doesn't care __________ (C) __________ what others think.
> • The statue is made __________ (D) __________ marble.
> • The library belongs __________ (E) __________ the city council.

① to
② from
③ of
④ for
⑤ about

41 다음 지도에서 건물 위치를 설명한 문장으로 알맞은 것은?

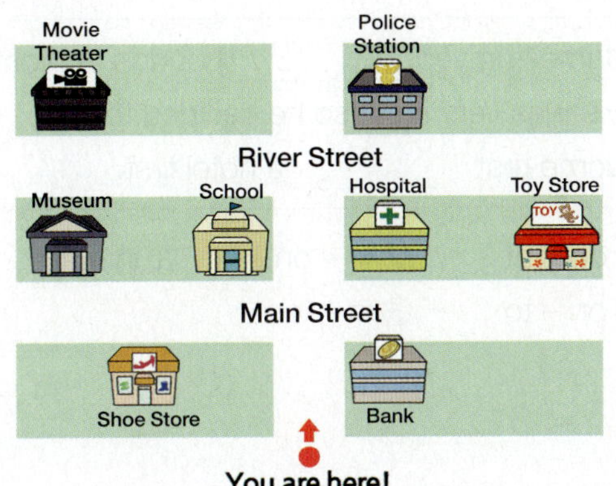

① The museum is next to the bank.
② The police station is across from the shoe store.
③ You have to go straight two blocks and turn right to find the movie theater.
④ Go straight one block and turn left. You will see the school on your right.
⑤ Go straight one block and turn right, then you can see the hospital on your right.

42 〈보기〉의 밑줄 친 like와 쓰임이 같은 것의 개수는?

보 기

The box is filled with old things like toys and coins.

ⓐ They like to collect comic books.
ⓑ I grew vegetables like potatoes and tomatoes.
ⓒ My sister sings very well like a singer.
ⓓ Do you also like drawing cartoons?
ⓔ She seems to like watching movies.

① 1개   ② 2개   ③ 3개   ④ 4개   ⑤ 5개

43 다음 빈칸에 공통으로 들어갈 알맞은 단어는?

• From now __________, I'm going to ride my bike for an hour every day.
• My family went out for dinner __________ Sunday evening.

① on   ② to   ③ in
④ of   ⑤ with

44 우리말과 같은 뜻이 되도록 할 때 빈칸에 들어갈 단어로 알맞은 것은?

• 그는 항상 일요일마다 정오까지 잠을 잔다.
  = He always sleeps __________ noon on Sundays.

① until   ② on   ③ to
④ from   ⑤ at

45 다음 빈칸에 알맞은 전치사를 순서대로 바르게 나열한 것은?

• The man __________ the brown bag is my dad.
• The thieves came into the room __________ the window.
• The house doesn't belong __________ me anymore.

① with – into   – about
② with – through – to
③ with – through – for
④ as   – into   – of
⑤ as   – through – to

46 괄호 안의 말을 알맞게 배열하여 문장을 완성할 때, <u>일곱 번째</u>에 오는 단어를 쓰세요.

> • Teresa는 1시간 동안 그녀의 친구를 기다렸기 때문에 화가 났다.
> = Teresa got angry (for / friend / she / her / because / for / waited / an hour).

➡ ______________________________

47 다음 빈칸에 공통으로 들어갈 알맞은 단어는?

> • You must come back home __________ 6:00.
> • I want to build a house __________ the river.

① for
② on
③ at
④ until
⑤ by

48 주어진 문장의 밑줄 친 <u>for</u>와 의미가 같은 것은?

> She was standing beside the window <u>for</u> a while.

① My uncle bought a new bike <u>for</u> me.
② This shirt is a little big <u>for</u> you.
③ Many students brought many things <u>for</u> the garage sale.
④ I went there <u>for</u> my swimming lesson.
⑤ She swam in the pool <u>for</u> three hours.

49 다음 빈칸에 알맞은 단어끼리 바르게 짝지어진 것은?

> James arrived __________ London at night. He was very tired, so he decided to get some rest __________ a hotel first.

① on – at
② in – on
③ in – at
④ on – to
⑤ in – to

50 다음 빈칸에 공통으로 들어갈 알맞은 단어는?

> • He has to hurry up to get to work __________ time.
> • He always goes to work __________ foot.

① as
② on
③ with
④ in
⑤ by

51 다음 빈칸에 알맞은 전치사끼리 바르게 짝지어진 것은?

> I teach math __________ a girls' middle school in Gwangju. Yesterday was my birthday. When I went __________ the classroom, all the students sang a song for me.

① on – at
② on – into
③ at – for
④ at – into
⑤ by – at

52 우리말과 같은 뜻이 되도록 빈칸에 알맞은 단어를 쓰세요.

> • 그는 호주머니에서 그 돈을 꺼냈다.
> = He took the money __________
> __________ his pocket.

53 다음 빈칸에 알맞은 단어끼리 바르게 짝지어진 것은?

> *Laura*: Ted, have you seen my passport?
> *Ted* : No. Didn't you put it __________
>   your bag?
> *Laura*: I can't find it there.
> *Ted* : Have you checked __________ the
>   bed?
> *Laura*: No. Oh, there it is!

① at – on ② in – under
③ on – at ④ in – of
⑤ at – down

54 다음 중 어법상 **틀린** 문장의 개수를 고르세요.

> ⓐ I went shopping with my mom at Sunday.
> ⓑ We went there by car. ⓒ There were a lot
> of goods on sale in the market. ⓓ My mom
> bought a cute bag for me. ⓔ It is made
> by cotton. ⓕ My mom also bought a bag
> which is similar to mine.

① 1개 ② 2개 ③ 3개 ④ 4개 ⑤ 5개

55 다음의 밑줄 친 in과 같은 뜻으로 쓰인 것은?

> In the picture, my cousin David was smiling
> in his new blue shirt.

① There are cookies in his bag.
② You look very nice in your new skirt.
③ My brother gets up early in the morning.
④ In winter, I go snowboarding with my family.
⑤ Is there a computer in your room?

56 다음 중 짝지어진 두 문장의 의미가 **다른** 것을 **모두** 고르세요.

① The box was too heavy for me to carry.
  = The box was heavy enough for me to carry.
② At the age of 10, I could run faster than now.
  = When I was 10, I was able to run faster
   than now.
③ There used to be a department store here.
  = There was a department store here in the
   past, but there isn't now.
④ The jar was filled with apple jam.
  = There was a little apple jam left in the jar.
⑤ I'm proud of constructing the building all by
 myself.
  = I take pride in constructing the building all
   by myself.

57 다음 빈칸에 공통으로 알맞은 단어를 쓰세요.

> • You should bring the book __________
> you.
> • I like playing __________ my dogs.

➡ __________

58 다음 대화의 우리말 (A)를 조건에 맞게 영작하세요.

> *W:* Justin, do you recall who that girl in the blue shirt is?
> *M:* Sure, she's Ari. We ate lunch with her last week. Don't you remember?
> *W:* I do. It's just that (A) <u>나는 이름들을 기억하는 것을 매우 못해.</u>
> *M:* Oh, I see. Well, try connecting someone's name with their character. That might help.

조 건

- 6단어, 현재시제로 쓸 것
- very, poor를 쓸 것

➡ ______________________________

59 그림을 보고, 각 문장의 밑줄 친 부분을 바르게 고쳐 문장을 다시 쓰세요.

(1) The bear is <u>over</u> the ball.

➡ ______________________________

(2) The elephant is <u>in front of</u> the box.

➡ ______________________________

(3) The tiger is <u>next to</u> the chair.

➡ ______________________________

60 다음 빈칸에 공통으로 들어갈 알맞은 단어는?

> The bicycle was invented __________ a toy for the rich. Then, it became a means of transportation. Next, it became a toy again. Now, the bicycle is popular all over the world __________ a means of transportation once more.

① so   ② to   ③ as
④ of   ⑤ by

61 다음 빈칸에 들어갈 알맞은 단어는?

> Friends should be there for each other not only in good times but also in bad times. When one friend is __________ trouble, the other friends should be ready to help him or her.

① in   ② on   ③ for
④ with   ⑤ over

62 다음 두 문장의 뜻이 같도록 빈칸에 들어갈 알맞은 단어는?

> - Koreans are proud of their traditional clothing, Hanbok.
>   = Koreans take pride __________ their traditional clothing, Hanbok.

① at   ② on   ③ of
④ with   ⑤ in

63 다음 우리말 해석과 일치하도록 빈칸에 알맞은 말을 쓰세요.

A: Who does this jacket __________ __________?
(이 재킷은 누구 것인가요?)
B: It is __________ __________ mine, but not mine.
(제 것과 비슷하지만 제 것은 아니에요.)

64 다음 글의 빈칸 (A)~(C)에 들어갈 알맞은 말은?

Hi, my name is Mohamed Rahman. I live in Bangladesh. Last year, I could not go to school for weeks because of the flood. I was very sad. ______(A)______, things are different this year. Today was my first day on a school boat. ______(B)______ going to school, the school came to me! My little sister and I went outside and waited with our friends. When the boat came, we all got excited. I love my school boat. I'm very happy to go ______(C)______ school and study now. I want to teach children like me on a school boat in the future.

	(A)		(B)		(C)
①	And	–	Instead	–	to
②	However	–	Instead of	–	by
③	However	–	Instead of	–	to
④	However	–	Instead	–	to
⑤	And	–	Instead	–	by

65 다음 대화의 밑줄 친 부분과 바꿔 쓸 수 있는 것은?

Kim : Hey, what's wrong? You look depressed.
Tony : I'm worried about my essay.
Kim : When is your essay due?
Tony : Next Friday, but I haven't started writing it yet.
Kim : Don't worry. I think I can help you.
Tony : Really? How can I ever thank you?

① By when should your essay be handed in?
② By when should you start your essay?
③ When can I write your essay?
④ By when should I help you write your essay?
⑤ Why don't I write the essay for you?

66 다음 그림에 맞게 괄호 안의 말을 바르게 배열하세요.

➡ ________________________________

____

(two, glasses, wearing, sat, between, on the subway, a woman, men)

67 다음 대화 중 밑줄 친 부분의 쓰임이 <u>어색한</u> 것은?

① A: How did you come into the house?

   B: <u>Through</u> the window.

② A: Why did you run <u>out of</u> the room so suddenly?

   B: I felt the house shaking.

③ A: Did you find your father?

   B: There were a lot of people in the park. It was impossible to find him <u>between</u> them.

④ A: What are you going to do during your summer vacation?

   B: I'll go camping <u>with</u> my family for two weeks.

⑤ A: I have played the piano <u>since</u> I was five years old.

   B: Wow, you have played the piano for 10 years!

68 다음 중 빈칸에 들어갈 말이 빈칸 ⓐ에 알맞은 말과 <u>다른</u> 것은?

> *Ms. Kim* : Good morning, Dahye. Are you going to school?
> *Dahye* : Yes, I am.
> *Ms. Kim* : How do you go to school?
> *Dahye* : I usually go there ⓐ __________ bus.

① I will turn off the TV __________ 6 o'clock.

② This poem was written __________ my father.

③ I sent you the memo __________ e-mail.

④ He goes to the cinema __________ foot.

⑤ They can learn responsibility __________ doing their homework.

69 다음 중 빈칸에 들어갈 말이 나머지 넷과 <u>다른</u> 하나는?

① I didn't know that his brother was __________ prison at that time.

② I met her __________ a big party last week and we became friends.

③ Her necklace looks so expensive that I can't believe she bought it __________ a garage sale.

④ Do you think you can meet me __________ the airport tomorrow before you take your flight?

⑤ My passport will expire __________ the end of this year.

70 다음 중 짝지어진 두 문장의 뜻이 서로 같지 <u>않</u>은 것은?

① My mother uses this bottle as a vase.

   = This bottle is used as a vase by my mother.

② I think she went to Daegu by plane.

   = I think she took a plane when she went to Daegu.

③ He seems to be in love with that girl in a blue skirt.

   = It seems like he's in love with that girl whose skirt is blue.

④ Jerry's basketball team lost the game by 45:30 score.

   = Jerry's basketball team didn't win the game and the score was 45 to 30.

⑤ It's amazing to see Chloe make such a beautiful candle by using only one hand.

   = It's amazing to see Chloe make such a beautiful candle as one hand.

CHAPTER 17
일치 · 도치 · 화법 & 속담

PSS 1 시제의 일치

PSS 1-1 시제 일치의 원칙

1. 주절의 동사가 현재시제인 경우 종속절의 동사는 의미에 따라 어떠한 시제든지 쓸 수 있다.

They **believe** that she **does** her best to overcome her fear.

그들은 그녀가 그녀의 두려움을 극복하는 데 최선을 다한다고 믿는다.

They **believe** that she **did** her best to overcome her fear.

그들은 그녀가 그녀의 두려움을 극복하는 데 최선을 다했다고 믿는다.

They **believe** that she **will do** her best to overcome her fear.

그들은 그녀가 그녀의 두려움을 극복하는 데 최선을 다할 것이라고 믿는다.

2. 주절의 동사가 과거시제인 경우 종속절의 동사는 의미에 따라 과거나 과거완료를 써야 한다.

He **knew** that I **made** a big mistake.

그는 내가 큰 실수를 한 것을 알았다.

He **knew** that I **would make** a big mistake.

그는 내가 큰 실수를 할 것이라는 것을 알았다.

He **knew** that I **had made** a big mistake.

그는 내가 큰 실수를 했었다는 것을 알았다.

cf. 과거완료 시제는 과거의 어느 시점에서 일어난 일보다 더 이전에 있었던 일을 나타낸다.

정답 p.100

PRACTICE 1

다음 문장의 시제를 바꿀 때 빈칸에 알맞은 말을 써서 문장을 완성하세요.

1 I wonder why our homeroom teacher is angry with us.

➡ I wondered why ____.

2 His school nurse told him that he would get better.

➡ His school nurse tells him that ________________________________.

3 The taxi driver tells us that there are many fancy restaurants on this street.

➡ The taxi driver told us that ____________________________________.

4 Everyone said that the Korean team would win the game.

➡ ________________________________ that the Korean team will win the game.

5 We are afraid that my son may be late for school on the first day.

➡ We were afraid that ____.

PSS 1-2 시제 일치의 예외

1. **현재의 습관, 사실, 격언, 진리는 항상 현재시제로 쓴다.**

   Sally said that she always **starts** her day with a cup of coffee.

   Sally는 그녀가 항상 커피 한 잔으로 그녀의 하루를 시작한다고 말했다.

   I learned that oil **is** lighter than water.

   나는 기름이 물보다 가볍다는 것을 배웠다.

   He taught us that the sun **rises** in the east and **sets** in the west.

   그는 해가 동쪽에서 뜨고 서쪽에서 진다는 것을 우리에게 가르쳤다.

   Mom used to tell me that practice **makes** perfect.

   엄마는 연습이 완벽을 만든다고 나에게 말씀하시곤 하셨다.

I learned that oil **is** lighter than water.

2. **역사적 사실은 항상 과거시제로 쓴다.**

   Dad told me that the Korean War **began** in 1950 and **ended** in 1953.

   아빠는 내게 한국 전쟁이 1950년에 시작되었고 1953년에 끝났다고 말씀하셨다.

정답 p.100

PRACTICE 2

다음 문장의 시제를 바꿀 때 빈칸에 알맞은 말을 써서 문장을 완성하세요.

1 Our history teacher teaches us that Columbus discovered America in 1492.

   ➡ Our history teacher taught us that ______________________________________.

2 My best friend, Jack, says that he always goes to school on foot.

   ➡ My best friend, Jack, said that ______________________________________.

3 My mom tells my father that the trains leave every 20 minutes.

   ➡ My mom told my father that ______________________________________.

4 You learn that water boils at 100℃ and freezes at 0℃.

   ➡ You learned that ______________________________________.

5 We hear that nothing is impossible to a willing heart.

   ➡ We heard that ______________________________________.

6 My little brother knows that one and one makes two.

   ➡ My little brother knew that ______________________________________.

PSS 2 도치

주어와 (조)동사의 어순이 서로 바뀌는 현상을 도치라고 한다. 강조하려는 어구를 문장의 맨 앞으로 가져올 때 도치가 일어난다.

1. 의문문에서의 도치

의문문에서는 해당 문장이 평서문이 아님을 나타내기 위해 주어와 (조)동사가 도치된다.

You can drive a car. ➡ **Can you** drive a car? 너는 운전을 할 수 있니?

한편, 의문사가 있는 의문문에서는 의문사가 강조되기 때문에 문장 맨 앞으로 나오고, 주어와 (조)동사가 도치된다.

What did you do last night? 너는 어젯밤에 무엇을 했니?

cf. 「How come+주어+동사 ~ ?」 : How come은 Why와 같이 '왜?'라는 의미로 의문문에서 사용된다. 하지만 의문문임에도 How come 뒤에서 주어와 동사의 순서가 바뀌지 않고 평서 문과 같이 「주어+동사」의 어순을 유지함을 주의해야 한다.

How come **you missed** the train? (O) 왜 너는 기차를 놓쳤니?

How come **did you miss** the train? (X)

2. There/Here + 동사 + 주어

There **is a bank** across the street.　　　　Here **come the students**.

길 건너에 은행이 있다.　　　　(여기에) 학생들이 온다.

cf. 주어가 대명사일 경우에는 주어와 동사의 순서가 바뀌지 않는다.

Here **they come**.　　　(여기에) 그들이 온다.

3. 장소나 방향을 나타내는 부사(구)의 도치 – 부사구 + 동사 + 주어

A man stood in front of the door.

➡ In front of the door **stood a man**. 문 앞에 한 남자가 서 있었다.

cf. 주어가 대명사일 경우에는 주어와 동사의 순서가 바뀌지 않는다.

She sat on the bench.

➡ On the bench, **she sat**. 벤치에 그녀가 앉았다.

4. 부정어(구)의 도치 – 부정어 + 조동사 + 주어 + 동사

I never saw such a pretty cat.

➡ **Never did I see** such a pretty cat. 나는 그렇게 예쁜 고양이는 보지 못했다.

Rarely has a debate attracted so much media attention.

토론이 그렇게 많은 언론의 관심을 끈 경우는 드물다.

Little did I think that I would succeed. 내가 성공할 것이라고 전혀 생각하지 않았다.

PRACTICE 3

괄호 안의 말을 바르게 배열하여 문장을 완성하세요.

1 ____ you ordered, sir.
　　　　(are, the pepperoni pizzas, here)

2 ____ that is bound for Busan.
　　　　(the last train, there, goes)

3 ____ standing in a long line, waiting for the tram to arrive.
　　　　(they, here, are)

4 ____ and I didn't?
　　　　(you, got invited, how come)

5 ____ in the past few years.
　　　　(been, there, several, snowstorms, have)

6 If she spent five years in China, ____ so bad?
　　　　　　　　　　(her Chinese, how come, is)

7 ____ to New York, Chicago or Los Angeles?
　　　　(been, you, have)

8 ____ in front of the hospital an hour ago?
　　　　(see, did, who, you)

PRACTICE 4

주어진 문장을 밑줄 친 부분을 강조하는 도치구문으로 바꿔 쓰세요.

1 The sun is still shining <u>behind the clouds</u>.
➡ ____

2 He <u>never</u> attended the meeting.
➡ ____

3 Charlie understood <u>little</u> about the situation.
➡ ____

4 A beautiful tree was <u>on the hill</u>.
➡ ____

5 I have <u>never</u> seen such a disaster.
➡ ____

CH
17
일치
도치
화법
&
속담

PSS 3 평서문의 화법 전환

화법이란 다른 사람의 말을 전달하는 방법이다.

직접 화법: 누군가의 말을 큰 따옴표(" ")를 사용해 직접적으로 전달하는 방법

간접 화법: 누군가의 말을 전달하는 사람의 입장으로 바꿔서 간접적으로 전달하는 방법

| 직접 화법 |
He **said**, "**I can't** believe the truth **now**."

그는 "나는 지금 그 사실을 믿을 수 없어."라고 말했다.

| 간접 화법 |
He ① **said** ② (that) ③ **he** ④ **couldn't** believe the truth ⑤ **then**.

그는 그때 그 사실을 믿을 수 없다고 말했다.

***간접화법으로 전환하는 방법**

① say는 그대로, say to는 tell로 전달 동사를 바꾼다.

② 콤마(,)와 큰 따옴표(" ")를 빼고 두 절을 that을 이용하여 연결시킨다. 이때 that은 생략 가능하다.

③ that절의 인칭 대명사는 전달하는 사람의 입장으로 바꾼다.

④ that절의 시제는 전달 동사의 시제에 따라 일치시킨다.

전달 동사가 현재시제일 때는 종속절의 시제에 변화가 없지만, 과거일 때는 시제 일치의 원칙에 따라 시제를 바꾼다.

⑤ 지시 대명사나 부사(구)는 전달하는 사람의 입장으로 바꾼다.

this[these] → that[those]	here → there	now → then
ago → before	today → that day	
yesterday → the previous day[the day before]		
tomorrow → the next day[the following day]		
last night → the previous night[the night before]		

Tom **said**, "**I'll** go to Jeju Island **tomorrow**."

Tom은 "나는 내일 제주도에 갈 거야."라고 말했다.

➡ Tom **said** (that) **he would** go to Jeju Island **the next day**.

Tom은 다음날 제주도에 갈 거라고 말했다.

Mike **said to** me, "**I am** really interested in music."

Mike는 나에게 "나는 정말 음악에 흥미가 있어."라고 말했다.

➡ Mike **told** me (that) **he was** really interested in music.

Mike는 나에게 자신이 정말 음악에 흥미가 있다고 말했다.

PRACTICE 5

〈보기〉와 같이 주어진 문장을 간접 화법으로 바꿀 때, 빈칸에 알맞은 말을 쓰세요.

> 보 기   He said to me, "I'm very grateful for your help."
> ➡ He told me that ___he was___ very grateful for ___my___ help.

1 My brother said, "I know how to play this game."
➡ My brother said that _________________________ how to play __________ game.

2 Jenny said, "My mom may not be at home now."
➡ Jenny said that __________ mom _________________________ at home __________ .

3 My friend said to me, "I'm going to learn Taekwondo."
➡ My friend __________ me that he _________________________ Taekwondo.

4 Mom said to us, "It is too cold for you to play baseball outside today."
➡ Mom __________ us that it __________ too cold for us to play baseball outside __________ .

5 Tom said, "I will meet her tomorrow."
➡ Tom said that _________________________ meet her _________________________ .

PRACTICE 6

〈보기〉와 같이 간접 화법은 직접 화법으로, 직접 화법은 간접 화법으로 바꾸세요.

> 보 기   He said, "I will go to America."
> ➡ He said that he would go to America.
>
> The student told his teacher that he studied Chinese every weekend.
> ➡ The student said to his teacher, "I study Chinese every weekend."

1 My younger brother said that the computer game was too difficult for him to play.
➡ ____

2 The man said to her, "It will take about two hours from now."
➡ ____

3 The boy said, "I don't want to eat these carrots."
➡ ____

4 The chairman told the members that the money was raised by donations.
➡ ____

5 Father said, "It will be nice to visit here again next summer."
➡ ____

PSS 4 의문문의 화법 전환

1. 의문사가 있는 의문문의 화법 전환

He **said to** me, "What is your favorite sport?"

그는 나에게 "네가 좋아하는 스포츠가 뭐니?"라고 말했다.

He ① **asked** me ② **what** ③ **my favorite sport was**.

그는 나에게 내가 좋아하는 스포츠가 무엇인지 물었다.

① say나 say to를 ask로 바꾼다.
② 콤마(,)와 큰 따옴표(" "), 물음표(?)를 빼고 의문사로 두 절을 연결한다.
③ 인칭 대명사와 시제를 적절하게 바꾸고, 어순을 「주어＋동사」로 변경한다. 단, 의문사가 주어인 경우에는 「의문사＋동사」의 어순을 그대로 유지한다.

He said to me, "What do you mean?"

그는 나에게 "무슨 뜻이야?"라고 말했다.

➡ He **asked** me **what I meant**.

그는 나에게 무슨 뜻이냐고 물었다.

Mina said, "Who can make me a dress?"

미나는 "누가 나에게 드레스를 만들어 줄 수 있을까?"라고 말했다.

➡ Mina **asked who could make her** a dress.

미나는 누가 그녀에게 드레스를 만들어 줄 수 있는지 물었다.

2. 의문사가 없는 의문문의 화법 전환

He **said**, "Are you ready to order?"

그는 "주문할 준비가 되셨나요?"라고 말했다.

He ① **asked** ② **if[whether]** ③ **I was** ready to order.

그는 내가 주문할 준비가 됐는지 물었다.

① say나 say to를 ask로 바꾼다.
② 콤마(,)와 큰 따옴표(" "), 물음표(?)를 빼고 if나 whether로 두 절을 연결한다.
③ 인칭 대명사와 시제를 적절하게 바꾸고, 어순을 「주어＋동사」로 변경한다.

She said, "Is he good at playing baseball?"

그녀는 "그는 야구를 잘 하니?"라고 말했다.

➡ She **asked if[whether] he was** good at playing baseball.

그녀는 그가 야구를 잘 하는지 물었다.

The man said to me, "Have you ever been to Hong Kong?"

그 남자는 나에게 "홍콩에 가본 적 있어요?"라고 말했다.

➡ The man **asked** me **if[whether] I had ever been** to Hong Kong.

그 남자는 나에게 홍콩에 가본 적이 있는지 물었다.

정답 p.101

PRACTICE 7

〈보기〉와 같이 주어진 문장을 간접 화법으로 바꾸세요.

보 기   He said to me, "How often do you visit my blog?"

➡ He asked me how often I visited his blog.

The man said to me, "Do you enjoy working out?"

➡ The man asked me if[whether] I enjoyed working out.

1 Kevin said to her, "May I use your dictionary?"

➡ ____

2 Mom said, "Who's calling?"

➡ ____

3 The teacher said to us, "What are your hopes for this year?"

➡ ____

4 He said to Jane, "When do you usually watch TV?"

➡ ____

5 He said to me, "Are you for or against dieting?"

➡ ____

6 Andy said to me, "Do you know how to make a movie clip on your phone?"

➡ ____

7 The man said to her, "Can you say that again?"

➡ ____

8 The gentleman said to the boy, "What makes you think so?"

➡ ____

9 I said to James, "Can you lend me your bike?"

➡ ____

10 Bob said, "Where can I get the ticket?"

➡ ____

PSS 5 명령문의 화법 전환

She **said to** her son, "Clean your room."

그녀는 그녀의 아들에게 "너의 방을 치워라."라고 말했다.

She ① **told** her son ② **to clean** ③ **his room**.

그녀는 그녀의 아들에게 그의 방을 치우라고 말했다.

① 전달 동사는 명령문의 어조에 따라 tell, ask, advise, order 등으로 바꾼다.

명령	tell, order, command
충고	advise
부탁 (주로 please가 있는 문장)	ask, beg

② 명령문의 동사원형을 to부정사로 바꾼다. (부정 명령문의 경우 Don't나 Never를 없애고, 동사원형을 not to부정사로 바꾼다.)

My teacher said to me, "Stop copying paintings."

나의 선생님은 나에게 "그림 베끼는 것을 그만 둬."라고 말씀하셨다.

➡ My teacher **told** me **to stop** copying paintings.

나의 선생님은 나에게 그림 베끼는 것을 그만두라고 말씀하셨다.

He said to me, "Don't stand in the middle."

그는 나에게 "중간에 서지 말아라."라고 말했다.

➡ He **ordered** me **not to stand** in the middle. 그는 나에게 중간에 서지 말라고 명령했다.

③ 명령문의 인칭대명사와 시제를 전달하는 사람의 입장으로 적절히 바꾼다.

정답 p.101

PRACTICE 8

〈보기〉와 같이 주어진 문장을 괄호 안의 단어를 이용하여 간접 화법으로 바꾸세요.

보 기

He said to me, "Watch out while you are swimming." (advise)

➡ He advised me to watch out while I was swimming.

The father said to his son, "Don't go near the fire." (tell)

➡ The father told his son not to go near the fire.

1 She said to her neighbor, "Look on the bright side." (advise)

➡ ____

2 Tom said to me, "Bring me a chair." (tell)

➡ ____

3 Jim said to me, "Tell me when her birthday is." (tell)

➡ ____

4 The teacher said to us, "Do not use a cell phone in class." (order)

➡ ____

5 Mom said to me, "Pass me the salt, please." (ask)

➡ ____

6 The doctor said to me, "Don't eat too much junk food." (advise)

➡ ____

7 Mom said to me, "Finish your homework by 7 p.m." (order)

➡ ____

8 Mr. Anderson said to us, "Don't be late." (tell)

➡ ____

PSS 6 속담

1. **Time is money.**
   시간이 돈이다.

2. **Haste makes waste.**
   서두름이 낭비를 만든다. (급히 서두르면 일을 망친다.)

3. **Like father, like son.**
   그 아버지에 그 아들. (부전자전)

4. **Better late than never.**
   늦는 것이 안 하는 것보다 낫다.

5. **A watched pot never boils.**
   지켜보는 냄비는 끓지 않는다.

6. **After a storm comes a calm.**
   폭풍 후에 평온함이 온다. (비 온 뒤에 땅이 굳어진다.)

7. **Blood is thicker than water.**
   피는 물보다 진하다.

Time is money.

A watched pot never boils.

8. Strike while the iron is hot.

쇠가 달았을 때 두드려라. (쇠뿔도 단김에 빼라.)

9. He laughs best who laughs last.

최후에 웃는 사람이 승자다.

10. The foot of the candle is dark.

등잔 밑이 어둡다.

Strike while the iron is hot.

11. A rolling stone gathers no moss.

구르는 돌에는 이끼가 끼지 않는다.

(① 자주 옮겨 다니는 사람은 모으는 것이 없다.

② 부지런한 사람은 침체되지 않는다.)

12. Actions speak louder than words.

말보다 행동이다. (말보다 행동이 더 설득력 있다.)

13. Every cloud has a silver lining.

모든 구름의 뒤편은 은빛으로 빛난다. (괴로움 뒤에는 기쁨이 있다.)

14. A friend in need is a friend indeed.

어려울 때 돕는 친구가 참된 친구다.

15. The pen is mightier than the sword.

펜은 칼보다 더 강하다.

16. Out of the frying pan into the fire.

튀김 팬에서 불 속으로. (갈수록 태산이다.)

17. Where there is a will, there is a way.

뜻이 있는 곳에 길이 있다.

The pen is mightier than the sword.

18. A bird in the hand is worth two in the bush.

제 손 안의 한 마리 새는 숲 속의 두 마리보다 낫다.

19. Don't count your chickens before they are hatched.

부화하기도 전에 병아리 수를 세지 마라. (김칫국부터 마시지 마라.)

20. Time flies like an arrow.

시간은 화살처럼 빨리 간다.

A bird in the hand is worth two in the bush.

21. Many hands make light work.

많은 사람들이 함께하면 일이 더 쉬워진다. (백짓장도 맞들면 낫다.)

PRACTICE 9

다음 우리말에 맞게 빈칸에 알맞은 말을 쓰세요.

1 펜은 칼보다 더 강하다.
➡ The pen is ___________________________ the sword.

2 비 온 뒤에 땅이 굳어진다.
➡ After a storm ___________________________ .

3 쇠뿔도 단김에 빼라.
➡ ___________________________ while the iron is ___________________________ .

4 튀김 팬에서 불 속으로. (갈수록 태산이다.)
➡ ___________________________ the frying pan ___________________________ the fire.

5 어려울 때 돕는 친구가 참된 친구다.
➡ A friend ___________________________ is a friend ___________________________ .

6 피는 물보다 진하다.
➡ Blood is ___________________________ water.

7 말보다 행동이다.
➡ Actions ___________________________ than words.

8 지켜보는 냄비는 끓지 않는다.
➡ ___________________________ never boils.

9 뜻이 있는 곳에 길이 있다.
➡ Where there is ___________________________ , there is ___________________________ .

10 구르는 돌에는 이끼가 끼지 않는다.
➡ A rolling stone ___________________________ .

11 제 손 안의 한 마리 새는 숲 속의 두 마리보다 낫다.
➡ A bird in the hand ___________________________ two in the bush.

12 늦는 것이 안 하는 것보다 낫다.
➡ ___________________________ than ___________________________ .

13 서두름이 낭비를 만든다. (급히 서두르면 일을 망친다.)
➡ ___________________________ makes ___________________________ .

14 최후에 웃는 사람이 승자다.
➡ He laughs best ___________________________ .

15 부화하기도 전에 병아리 수를 세지 마라. (김칫국부터 마시지 마라.)
➡ Don't count your chickens ___________________________ .

1 다음 문장들 중 어법상 <u>옳은</u> 것의 개수는?

> ⓐ We saw something interesting at the festival.
> ⓑ He sat a new rule for the team last week.
> ⓒ This singer is enough famous to be on TV every day.
> ⓓ He drives more carefully than he does last year.
> ⓔ She ended up missing the last train.

① 1개   ② 2개   ③ 3개   ④ 4개   ⑤ 5개

2 다음 문장을 간접 화법으로 바꿀 때 빈칸에 들어갈 말로 알맞은 것은?

> My friend said to me, "What do you want to do this weekend?"
> ➡ My friend asked me __________ to do that weekend.

① what you want   ② whether I wanted
③ what I do want   ④ what I wanted
⑤ whether I want

3 다음 문장의 화법을 올바르게 전환한 것은?

> Jack said, "I will keep my mouth closed."

① Jack said that I will keep my mouth closed.
② Jack said that he will keep his mouth closed.
③ Jack told he would keep his mouth closed.
④ Jack told that he kept his mouth closed.
⑤ Jack said that he would keep his mouth closed.

4 다음 문장 중 어법상 <u>어색한</u> 것을 <u>두 개</u> 고르세요.

① How come did you visit his house?
② On the desk lay today's newspaper.
③ Hardly I met a kind person like him.
④ Under the table he is with his son.
⑤ Never has she seen such a gentle boy.

5 다음 빈칸에 알맞은 말끼리 바르게 짝지은 것은?

> The general said to his soldiers, "Charge!"
> ➡ The general __________ his soldiers __________ charge.

① said to – to   ② said – to
③ told – not to   ④ advised – to
⑤ ordered – to

6 다음을 간접 화법으로 바꿀 때, 빈칸에 알맞은 말끼리 바르게 짝지은 것은?

> Mom said, "I'm writing invitation cards to my guests."
> ➡ Mom said that she __________ invitation cards to __________.

① writing – her guests
② wrote – her guests
③ was writing – my guests
④ wrote – my guests
⑤ was writing – her guests

7 다음 대화의 빈칸에 알맞은 속담은?

> A: What are you doing now?
> B: I'm collecting data for my report.
> A: Do you need my help? I think it will take a long time.
> B: No thanks. I don't want to take up your time.
> A: ___________________________
> You can save time with my help. Let's do it together.

① Many hands make light work.
② After a storm comes a calm.
③ Every cloud has a silver lining.
④ Blood is thicker than water.
⑤ The foot of the candle is dark.

8 다음 글의 내용과 어울리는 속담은?

> There once was a goose that always wanted to fly. So he practiced hard, always thinking he could fly someday. His friends thought he was a fool. But he didn't mind and kept trying to fly every day. One day, the goose stood on the roof. He jumped from the roof and began to fly high in the sky. His friends just looked at him with envious eyes.

① Time flies like an arrow.
② Like father, like son.
③ Where there is a will, there is a way.
④ The foot of the candle is dark.
⑤ The pen is mightier than the sword.

9 다음을 간접 화법으로 바꿀 때 빈칸에 들어갈 알맞은 말을 쓰세요.

> He said to me, "How do you know the guy?"
> ➡ He asked me how ________________.

10 다음 〈보기〉를 참고하여, 다음 문장을 완성하세요.

> 보 기
> He seldom realizes that he is happy.
> ➡ Seldom _does he realize that he is happy._

(1) I never saw a boring movie like this.
  ➡ Never _____________________.

(2) A pretty girl stood in front of the door.
  ➡ In front of the door ____________.

(3) He could hardly ride his bike.
  ➡ Hardly _____________________.

11 다음 중 어법상 옳은 것을 고르세요.

① One of the most popular restaurants are here.
② Neither the car nor the bike are available for rent today.
③ Never have we experienced such extreme weather.
④ Every student need to bring their own lunch.
⑤ How come is the store closed today?

12 다음 문장을 간접 화법으로 올바르게 전환한 것은?

> I said to the woman, "May I visit here with my family?"

① I said the woman if may I visit here with my family.
② I told the woman if may I visit there with my family.
③ I asked the woman whether I might visit there with my family.
④ I asked the woman whether I may visit there with my family.
⑤ I asked the woman if I might visit here with my family.

13 다음 글의 내용과 어울리는 속담은?

> A college student named Emily thought riding a bicycle on a busy road was very dangerous. Sometimes cars came close to hitting her when she was riding her bike on the road. She really wanted to ride her bike safely. So, she made a device that produced a laser image in front of her bicycle. Its purpose was to alert drivers that a passing bicycle was nearby. She hoped that the device would reduce bicycle accidents on the road.

① Step by step one goes a long way.
② Necessity is the mother of invention.
③ Out of the frying pan into the fire.
④ A friend in need is a friend indeed.
⑤ A bird in the hand is worth two in the bush.

14 다음을 간접 화법으로 바꿀 때 빈칸에 알맞은 말을 쓰세요.

> Mom said to me, "Don't stay up too late for your exam."

➡ Mom told me __________ __________ __________ __________ too late for __________ exam.

15 다음 대화의 밑줄 친 부분 중 어법상 어색한 것을 모두 고르세요.

> *Father*: You're still playing that computer game! Didn't you hear ① <u>what</u> I said to you?
>
> *Son* : I did. I know you told me ② <u>to not</u> spend too much time on it.
>
> *Father*: Then stop playing it and let's go outside ③ <u>to play</u> basketball together.
>
> *Son* : No, the reporter on the news said ④ <u>that</u> it would rain.
>
> *Father*: I thought he said it ⑤ <u>will</u> be only cloudy. I'll check it out.

16 대화 (A)를 읽고, 대화 (B)를 완성하세요.

(A) **At school**

Thomas: What are you going to do during summer vacation?

Esther : I will go fishing with my father. How about you?

Thomas: I will go to Canada, where my uncle lives.

(B) **At Esther's home**

Esther : Mom, Thomas asked me ________(1)________ to do during summer vacation.

Mom : What did you say?

Esther : I said I would go fishing with my father. He said that ________(2)________, where his uncle lives.

Mom : That sounds nice.

(1) ____________ ____________ ____________ ____________

(2) ____________ ____________ ____________ ____________

____

17 〈보기〉와 같이 문장을 전환하세요.

보 기

Father said to me, "Get out of my car."

➡ Father ordered me to get out of his car.

Deborah said to Davis, "Please buy this necklace for me."

➡ ____________

____

18 다음 글의 밑줄 친 우리말을 영어로 바르게 옮긴 것은?

We have to hand in our homework by tomorrow. Yesterday, I finished my homework and was about to go shopping with my mother. Just then, my friend Michael called me. He said that he couldn't do his homework because he had to take care of his younger brothers. 그는 내게 자기 숙제 하는 걸 도와달라고 부탁했다. I decided to help him instead of going shopping.

① He asked me help him do his homework.

② He asks me to help him do his homework.

③ He asked me to help him do his homework.

④ He would ask me help him do his homework.

⑤ He asks me help him do his homework.

19 다음 빈칸에 들어갈 알맞은 말은?

I can't believe ten years have passed since I saw Tim at the meeting. Like they say, ____________.

It is as if we had just seen each other yesterday. For ten years, I have always tried to love and respect him.

① a friend in need is a friend indeed

② time flies like an arrow

③ strike while the iron is hot

④ a rolling stone gathers no moss

⑤ every cloud has a silver lining

20 Choose all that are grammatically correct.

> (a) Rarely does Wendy offer to help.
> (b) In the parking lot were various cars.
> (c) There is a lot of people in the train.
> (d) Under the bridge does the stream flow.
> (e) Here is the most exciting part of the book.

① (a), (b), (c)　　② (a), (b), (e)　　③ (a), (c), (d)
④ (b), (c), (d)　　⑤ (c), (d), (e)

21 다음 문장을 직접 화법으로 바꿀 때 빈칸에 알맞은 말을 쓰세요.

(1) He told me to cheer up.
　➡ He ____________ ____________ me, "Cheer
　　up."

(2) Sally told me not to read her diary.
　➡ Sally ____________ ____________ me,
　　" ____________ read my diary."

(3) The cashier asked me if I had ever tried their
　　new smoothie flavor.
　➡ The cashier ____________ ____________ me,
　　" ____________ you ever tasted our new
　　smoothie flavor?"

22 다음 우리말 해석을 괄호 안의 말을 이용하여 영어로 쓰세요.

> Jane은 그에게 그가 충분한 돈을 가지고 있는지
> 물어보았다.

➡ ____
____ (ask)

23 다음 영어 속담의 우리말 의미가 <u>잘못된</u> 것은?

① Haste makes waste. (급히 서두르면 일을 망친
　다.)
② Strike while the iron is hot. (쇠뿔도 단김에 빼
　라.)
③ A friend in need is a friend indeed. (어려울 때
　돕는 친구가 참된 친구다.)
④ Every cloud has a silver lining. (모든 사물은 이
　면을 가지고 있다.)
⑤ Don't count your chickens before they are
　hatched. (김칫국부터 마시지 마라.)

24 주어진 문장을 밑줄 친 부분을 강조하는 도치 구문으로 바꿔 쓰세요.

> He has <u>never</u> had any training on the cello.

➡ ____
____

25 주어진 문장을 도치 구문으로 바꿔 쓴 것 중 어법상 <u>어색한</u> 것을 고르세요.

① She seldom drinks coffee at night.
　→ Seldom does she drink coffee at night.
② The man stood in front of the mirror.
　→ In front of the mirror stood the man.
③ I little imagined he would say such a thing.
　→ Little I did imagine he would say such a
　　thing.
④ We lived in the town called Kendal.
　→ In the town called Kendal we lived.
⑤ They have never seen such a beautiful
　picture.
　→ Never have they seen such a beautiful
　　picture.

<h1 style="text-align:center">중학영문법 3800제 2학년 교과서 활용 진도표</h1>

🐙 동아 윤정미

과	교과서 문법 내용	CH	PSS
1	수여동사	1	2-4
	both A and B	15	3
2	have to	3	4-1
	to부정사의 부사적 용법	7	3
3	수동태	4	2, 4
	목적격 보어로 쓰이는 to부정사	1	2-5
		7	1-3
4	관계대명사 주격	14	1-1~1-3
	조건을 나타내는 if	12	
		15	5
5	관계대명사 목적격	14	1-1~1-3
	Call A B	1	2-5
6	지각동사	1	2-6
	so ~ that	15	6
7	현재완료	2	5-1~5-5
	가주어 it	6	2-3
8	간접의문문	1	1-6~1-7
	because of / because	15	4

🐙 동아 이병민

과	교과서 문법 내용	CH	PSS
1	to부정사의 형용사적 용법	7	2
	명령문, and / or ~	15	2
2	현재완료	2	5-1~5-5
	목적격 보어로 쓰이는 to부정사	1	2-5
		7	1-3
3	수동태	4	2, 4
	조건을 나타내는 if	12	1
		15	5
4	관계대명사 주격	14	1-1~1-3
	최상급	13	4-1
5	가주어 it	6	2-3
	지각동사	1	2-6
6	원급 비교 as ~ as	13	2-1
	양보를 나타내는 접속사	15	9
7	so ~ that	15	6
	관계대명사 목적격	14	1-1~1-3
8	-thing+형용사	10	2
	관계부사	14	2-1

🐙 미래엔 최연희

과	교과서 문법 내용	CH	PSS
1	관계대명사 주격	14	1-1~1-3
	시간을 나타내는 접속사	15	8
2	현재완료	2	5-1~5-2
	each	6	4-4
3	to부정사의 형용사적 용법	7	2
	가주어 it	6	2-3
4	관계대명사 목적격	14	1-1~1-3
	so ~ that	15	6
5	조건을 나타내는 if	12	1
		15	5
	원급 비교 as ~ as	13	2-1
6	수동태의 시제	4	4
	-thing + 형용사	10	2
7	5형식	1	2-5
	사역동사	1	2-6
8	지각동사	1	2-6
	목적격 보어로 쓰이는 to부정사	1	2-5
		7	1-3

🐙 능률 김성곤

과	교과서 문법 내용	CH	PSS
1	주어로 쓰이는 동명사	8	1
	지각동사	1	2-6
2	관계대명사 주격	14	1-1~1-3
	빈도부사	11	2-1
3	현재완료	2	5-1~5-5
	so ~ that	15	6
4	수동태	4	2
	비교급 강조	13	3-2
5	관계대명사 목적격	14	1-1~1-3
	감정을 나타내는 분사	9	4
6	가주어 it	6	2-3
	간접의문문	1	1-6~1-7
7	목적격 보어로 쓰이는 to부정사	1	2-5
		7	1-3
	조건을 나타내는 if	12	1
		15	5

🐙 비상 김진완

과	교과서 문법 내용	CH	PSS
1	동명사	8	1~2-1
	5형식	1	2-5
2	조건을 나타내는 if	12	1
		15	5
	목적격 보어로 쓰이는 to부정사	1	2-5
		7	1-3
3	수동태	4	2, 4
	to부정사의 형용사적 용법	7	2
4	관계대명사 주격	14	1-1~1-3
	지각동사	1	2-6
5	현재완료	2	5-1~5-2
	관계대명사 목적격	14	1-1~1-3
6	가주어 it	6	2-3
	원급 비교 as ~ as	13	2-1
7	사역동사	1	2-6
	간접의문문	1	1-6
8	so ~ that	15	6
	명사를 수식하는 분사	9	2-1

🐙 YBM 박준언

과	교과서 문법 내용	CH	PSS
1	to부정사의 형용사적 용법	7	2
	명사절을 이끄는 접속사 that	15	7
2	의문사 + to부정사	7	1-4
	원급 비교 as ~ as	13	2-1
3	사역동사	1	2-6
	조건을 나타내는 if	12	1
		15	5
4	관계대명사 주격	14	1-1~1-3
	-thing + 형용사	10	2
special 1	간접의문문	1	1-6~1-7
	최상급	13	4-1
5	수동태	4	2, 4
	so ~ that	15	6
6	가주어 it	6	2-3
	not only ~ but also	15	3
7	목적격 보어로 쓰이는 to부정사	1	2-5
		7	1-3
	관계대명사 목적격	14	1-1~1-3
8	현재완료	2	5-1~5-5
	조동사 may	3	4-8
special 2	지각동사	1	2-6
	too ~ to	7	5

중학영문법 3800제 2학년 교과서 활용 진도표

🐙 YBM 송미정

과	교과서 문법 내용	CH	PSS
1	최상급	13	4-1
	to부정사의 부사적 용법	7	3
2	to부정사의 형용사적 용법	7	2
	사역동사 make	1	2-6
3	의문사 + to부정사	7	1-4
	관계대명사 who	14	1-1
4	현재완료	2	5-1~5-5
	조건을 나타내는 if	12	1
		15	5
5	부가의문문	1	1-3~1-4
	수동태	4	2, 4
6	so ~ that	15	6
	관계대명사 목적격	14	1-1~1-3
7	지각동사	1	2-6
	가주어 it	6	2-3
8	목적격 보어로 쓰이는 to부정사	1	2-5
		7	1-3
	명사를 수식하는 분사	9	2-1
9	관계부사	14	2-1
	간접의문문	1	1-6~1-7

🐙 지학사 민찬규

과	교과서 문법 내용	CH	PSS
1	부정대명사	6	4-1~4-3
	조건을 나타내는 if	12	1
		15	5
2	의문사 + to부정사	7	1-4
	관계대명사 주격	14	1-1~1-3
3	관계대명사 목적격	14	1-1~1-3
	목적격 보어로 쓰이는 to부정사	1	2-5
		7	1-3
4	-thing + 형용사	10	2
	현재완료	2	5-1~5-5
5	수동태	4	2, 4
	조동사가 있는 수동태	4	5
6	so ~ that	15	6
	원급 비교 as ~ as	13	2-1
7	가주어 it	6	2-3
	how come	17	2
8	사역동사	1	2-6
	양보를 나타내는 접속사	15	9

🐙 능률 양현권

과	교과서 문법 내용	CH	PSS
1	의문형용사	6	5-2
	재귀대명사	6	1-3
2	수동태	4	2, 4
	not only ~ but also	15	3
3	가주어 it	6	2-3
	형용사 + enough	11	1-3
4	현재완료	2	5-1~5-2
	so that ~	15	6
5	관계대명사 who	14	1-1
	had better	3	4-6
6	간접의문문	1	1-6
	Here he comes	17	2
7	to부정사의 형용사적 용법	7	2
	must	3	4-2
8	목적격 보어로 쓰이는 to부정사	1	2-5
		7	1-3
	a few	10	5-3

🐙 금성 최인철

과	교과서 문법 내용	CH	PSS
1	조건을 나타내는 if	12	1
		15	5
	부가의문문	1	1-3~1-4
2	의문사 + to부정사	7	1-4
	so that ~	15	6
3	to부정사의 형용사적 용법	7	2
	동사를 강조하는 do	3	4-5
4	간접의문문	1	1-6
	수동태	4	2, 4
5	enough to	7	5
	현재완료	2	5-1~5-5
6	관계대명사 주격	14	1-1~1-3
	가주어 it	6	2-3
7	관계대명사 목적격	14	1-1~1-3, 1-5
	관계대명사 what	14	1-4
8	too ~ to	7	5
	가정법 과거	12	2

🐙 천재 이재영

과	교과서 문법 내용	CH	PSS
1	관계대명사 주격	14	1-1~1-3
	조건을 나타내는 if	12	1
		15	5
2	관계대명사 목적격	14	1-1~1-3
	의문사 + to부정사	7	1-4
3	가주어 it	6	2-3
	to부정사의 형용사적 용법	7	2
4	수동태	4	2, 4
	원급 비교 as ~ as	13	2-1
5	목적격 보어로 쓰이는 to부정사	1	2-5
		7	1-3
	before / after	15	8
6	사역동사	1	2-6
	too ~ to	7	5
7	현재완료	2	5-1~5-5
	명사를 수식하는 분사	9	2-1
8	최상급	13	4-1
	간접의문문	1	1-6

🐙 천재 정사열

과	교과서 문법 내용	CH	PSS
1	to부정사의 형용사적 용법	7	2
	명사절을 이끄는 접속사 that	15	7
2	조건을 나타내는 if	12	1
		15	5
	지각동사	1	2-6
3	현재완료	2	5-1~5-2
	양보를 나타내는 접속사	15	9
4	관계대명사 who	14	1-1
	관계대명사의 생략	14	1-5
5	의문사 + to부정사	7	1-4
	5형식	1	2-5
6	a few / a little	10	5-3
	수동태	4	2, 4
7	명사를 수식하는 분사	9	2-1
	가주어 it	6	2-3
8	so ~ that	15	6
	사역동사	1	2-6

2026 새 교과서에 맞춘 16차 개정판

중학영문법 3800제 2학년

정답과 해설

MOTHERTONGUE
마더텅출판사
since1999.4.1.

🗂 학습 추가 자료

중학영문법 3800제 학습에 필요한 추가 자료(단어장, mp3, 해석자료, 정답과 해설)를
마더텅 홈페이지 교재자료실에서 무료로 다운받을 수 있습니다.

book.toptutor.co.kr

구하기 어려운 교재는
마더텅 모바일(인터넷)을 이용하세요.
즉시 배송해 드립니다.

💻 이용방법

마더텅 홈페이지 **www.toptutor.co.kr** 접속 → 상단 메뉴 중 [학습자료실] 선택

→ 자료 유형 `정답표/정오표/MP3/교재관련 자료` 선택

→ 학년 `중등` , 시리즈 `영문법` , 과목 `영어` 선택

→ 교재 선택에서 `중학영문법 3800제 2학년` 찾아 선택 → 원하는 자료 다운로드

마더텅은 1999년 창업 이래 **2025년까지 3,642만 부의 교재를 판매했습니다.** 2025년 판매량은 322만 부로 자사 교재의 품질은 학원 강의와 온/오프라인 서점 판매량으로 검증받았습니다. [마더텅 수능기출문제집 시리즈]는 친절하고 자세한 해설로 수험생님들의 전폭적인 지지를 받으며 누적 판매 950만 부, 2025년 한 해에만 95만 부가 판매된 베스트셀러입니다. 또한 [중학영문법 3800제]는 2007년부터 2025년까지 19년 동안 중학 영문법 부문 판매 1위를 지키며 명실공히 대한민국 최고의 영문법 교재로 자리매김했습니다. 그리고 2018년 출간된 [뿌리깊은 초등국어 독해력 시리즈]는 2025년까지 323만부가 판매되면서 초등 국어 부문 판매 1위를 차지하였습니다.(교보문고/YES24 판매량 기준, EBS 제외) 이처럼 마더텅은 초·중·고 학습 참고서를 대표하는 대한민국 제일의 교육 브랜드로 자리잡게 되었습니다. 이와 같은 성원에 감사드리며, 앞으로도 효율적인 학습에 보탬이 되는 교재로 보답하겠습니다.

마더텅 학습 교재 이벤트에 참여해 주세요. 참여해 주신 분께 선물을 드립니다.

이벤트 1 1분 간단 교재 사용 후기 이벤트

마더텅은 고객님의 소중한 의견을 반영하여 보다 좋은 책을 만들고자 합니다.
교재 구매 후, <교재 사용 후기 이벤트>에 **참여해 주신 모든 분께는** 감사의 마음을 담아
`네이버페이 포인트 1천 원` 을 보내 드립니다. 지금 바로 QR 코드를 스캔해 소중한 의견을 보내 주세요!

이벤트 2 중학영문법3800제 인증샷 이벤트

필수 태그 #마더텅 #중학영문법3800제

SNS에 <중학영문법3800제> 인증샷을 올려 주시면 **참여해 주신 모든 분께** 감사의 마음을 담아
`네이버페이 포인트 2천 원` 을 보내 드립니다. 지금 바로 QR 코드를 스캔해 작성한 게시물의 URL을 입력해 주세요!

이벤트 3 마더텅 우편 이벤트

본 교재의 Ch 7의 중간·기말고사 대비문제 페이지를 오려서 마더텅으로 보내 주세요!
추첨을 통해 소정의 상품을 보내 드립니다.

참여 방법 Ch 7 중간·기말고사 대비문제(p.193~202) **풀이 및 채점 완료**
　　　　　 → 해당 페이지를 모두 오려서 마더텅에 발송(우편, 택배 등) → QR 코드를 스캔하고 발송 인증

주소 (08501) 서울특별시 금천구 가마산로 96, 대륭테크노타운 8차 708호, 마더텅 이벤트 담당자 앞 / 010-6640-1064

※ 이벤트 기간: 2026년 12월 31일까지 (*해당 이벤트는 당사 사정에 따라 조기 종료될 수 있습니다.) ※ 자세한 사항은 해당 QR 코드를 스캔하거나 홈페이지 이벤트 공지 글을 참고해 주세요. ※ 당사 사정에 따라 이벤트의 내용이나 상품이 변경될 수 있으며 변경 시 홈페이지에 공지합니다. ※ 만 14세 미만은 부모님께서 신청해 주셔야 합니다. ※ 상품은 이벤트 참여일로부터 4~5일(영업일 기준) 내에 발송됩니다. (단, 이벤트 3은 예외) ※ 동일 교재로 세 가지 이벤트 모두 참여 가능합니다. (단, 같은 이벤트 중복 참여는 불가합니다.)

정답 및 해설
Problem Solving Skill

CHAPTER 1 문장의 기초
Introduction to Sentences

PRACTICE 1

1 Can she get there on time?
2 Aren't those gloves yours?
3 Doesn't he go to church on Sundays?
4 Is your mom angry at you?
5 Was David drawing a picture?
6 Can this be true?
7 Do your classmates study hard?
8 Didn't your brother win the race?
9 Will the bus arrive at 8 p.m.?
10 Does the dog like to play outside?

> **1, 6, 9** 조동사 can, will이 포함된 문장을 의문문으로 바꿀 때 조동사를 문장 맨 앞으로 옮겨서 「조동사+주어+동사원형~?」의 형태로 만든다.
> **2, 4, 5** be동사가 있는 문장을 의문문으로 바꿀 때 be동사(와 부정어)를 문장 맨 앞으로 옮겨서 「Be동사(+부정어)+주어~?」의 형태로 만든다.
> **3, 8** 부정어를 포함한 일반동사가 있는 문장을 의문문으로 바꿀 때 「do[does / did]+부정어」를 문장 맨 앞으로 옮겨서 「Do[Does / Did]+부정어+주어+동사원형~?」의 형태로 만든다.
> **7, 10** 일반동사의 긍정형이 사용된 문장을 의문문으로 바꿀 때 do를 주어의 인칭과 동사의 시제에 맞게 사용하여 「Do[Does / Did]+주어+동사원형~?」의 형태로 만든다.

PRACTICE 2

1 Yes, he does.
2 No, they don't.
3 Yes, I did.
4 No, he wasn't.
5 Yes, I was.
6 Yes, they can.
7 Yes, he does.
8 No, she isn't.

> **2, 3, 5, 7, 8** 부정어가 포함된 동사로 시작하는 의문문에 대한 대답은 질문과 상관없이 대답의 내용이 긍정적이면 yes, 부정적이면 no로 표현한다. 그러나 yes/no에 대한 우리말 해석은 반대로 됨에 유의해야 한다.
> **2** B: 네, 그들은 가지고 있지 않습니다.
> **3** B: 아니오, 저는 (바깥이 춥다고) 느꼈습니다.
> **5** B: 아니오, 저는 배가 고팠습니다.
> **7** B: 아니오, 그는 열심히 공부합니다.
> **8** B: 네, Linda는 (스포츠를) 잘 하지 못합니다.

PRACTICE 3

1 Who did you meet at the restaurant?
2 Why is Kelly so busy today?
3 What did he say to you?
4 Where did you find the key?
5 When will he return from the trip?
6 How do you go to school every day?
7 How is everything with you?

PRACTICE 4

2 When is
3 How was
4 Where did
5 Why were[What made]
6 Who is
7 What did
8 Where do
9 When did
10 Why did[What made]

PRACTICE 5

1 are you
2 isn't it
3 did she
4 doesn't it
5 couldn't he
6 wasn't it
7 do they
8 weren't they
9 are they
10 will she
11 doesn't she
12 didn't he

> **1, 3, 7, 9, 10** 부정문의 부가 의문문은 조동사, be동사, do동사의 긍정형으로 만든다. 7, 9번의 경우 주어에 those, these가 포함되어 있으므로 인칭대명사는 they가 적절하다.
> **2, 5, 6, 8** 긍정문의 부가 의문문은 조동사, be동사의 부정형으로 만든다. 8번의 주어 the children은 복수형이므로 인칭대명사는 they가 적절하다.
> **4, 11, 12** 일반동사의 긍정형이 사용된 문장의 부가 의문문은 do를 주어의 인칭과 동사의 시제에 맞게 사용하여 「doesn't/didn't+인칭대명사?」의 형태로 만든다.

PRACTICE 6

1 will you
2 don't I
3 isn't it
4 shall we
5 didn't he
6 were they
7 shall we
8 am I not[aren't I]
9 will you[won't you]
10 can they

> **1** 부정명령문의 부가 의문문은 'will you?'만 사용한다. 명령문은 주어 you가 생략된 것으로 간주하기 때문에 부가 의문문의 주어는 항상 you이다.
> **4, 7** 'Let's~'로 시작하는 문장의 부가 의문문은 'shall we?'를 사용한다.
> **9** 긍정명령문의 부가 의문문은 어조에 따라서 명령조일 때는 'will you?', 정중하게 말할 때는 'won't you?'를 쓴다.
> 오늘 밤 내게 전화해 줘, 알겠니? - 명령
> 오늘 밤 내게 전화해 줘, 그렇게 해 주지 않을래? - 권유

PRACTICE 7

1 Steak
2 soccer
3 a skirt
4 noodles
5 My mother
6 by train

PRACTICE 8

1 what that means
2 if[whether] it is important
3 how I can get to your school
4 who broke the window
5 if[whether] you passed the exam
6 if[whether] you love Mike
7 if[whether] she can swim
8 if[whether] they were playing soccer
9 where she lives
10 if[whether] Max bought a new car
11 how much this book costs

> **1, 3, 9, 11** 의문사가 있는 의문문을 간접 의문문으로 바꿀 때는
> 「의문사+주어+동사~」순이 된다. 의문문 구조를 만드는 데 사용되
> 었던 do동사를 없애면서 시제와 수를 일반동사에 적용하면 된다.
> 11번의 경우 how와 much를 하나의 묶음으로 간주한다.
> **2, 5, 6, 7, 8, 10** 의문사가 없는 의문문을 간접 의문문으로 바꿀
> 때, 의문문의 내용은 if나 whether이 이끄는 명사절의 일부가 되면
> 서 「if[whether]+주어+동사」 구조로 쓰인다. 5번, 8번, 10번의 경
> 우 문장의 시제가 과거, 과거 진행임을 주의한다.
> **4** 의문사 who가 간접 의문문의 주어로 쓰였기 때문에 직접 의문문
> 의 어순을 그대로 사용한다.

PRACTICE 9

1 What do you think he is making?
2 Do you know when he arrived?
3 Who do you believe is right?
4 Why do you think we should learn English?
5 I don't know if[whether] Susan has feelings for me.
6 When do you believe he will come?
7 What do you guess will happen next?
8 Can you tell me if[whether] there are bookstores near here?
9 How do you think we can solve this problem?
10 Can you guess which one I chose?
11 Where do you believe you lost it?
12 Why do you suppose he is so upset?

> **1, 3, 4, 6, 7, 9, 11, 12** 간접 의문문이 포함된 문장에서 think,
> believe, suppose, guess와 같이 생각이나 추측을 나타내는 동사
> 가 주절에 있을 때는 간접 의문문의 의문사가 문장 맨 앞에 위치한다.
> **2** 의문사가 있는 의문문을 간접 의문문으로 바꿀 때 「의문사+주어
> +동사」 구조로 쓴다.
> **5, 8** 의문사가 없는 의문문을 간접 의문문으로 바꿀 때
> 「if[whether]+주어+동사」 구조로 쓴다.
> **10** 「Can you guess?」의 경우 의문사가 문두로 나가지 않는다.

PRACTICE 10

1 How patient you are!
2 How hot and humid it is!
3 What a smart student she is!
4 What an excellent painting that is!
5 How angry they were!
6 How exciting this journey is!
7 What terrible players they were!
8 What a friendly teacher she is!
9 How polite he was!
10 What beautiful songs these are!

> **7, 10** What 감탄문의 복수형도 사용 가능하다.
> 「What+형용사+복수명사+복수대명사+복수동사」

PRACTICE 11

1 ①, ②, ③, ⑧		**2** ①, ②, ⑧, ⑧	
3 ①, ②, ④, ⑤		**4** ①, ②, ⑥, ⑧	
5 ①, ②, ③, ⑦		**6** ①, ②, ⑧	
7 ①, ②, ⑥		**8** ①, ②, ④, ⑤	
9 ①, ②, ③, ⑧		**10** ①, ②, ③, ⑦	
11 ①, ②, ⑥, ⑧		**12** ①, ②, ⑧	
13 ①, ②, ③, ⑦		**14** ①, ②, ④, ⑤	
15 ①, ②, ③, ⑧		**16** ①, ②, ⑧, ⑧	
17 ①, ②, ④, ⑤		**18** ①, ②, ⑥, ⑧	

> 보기의 ①~⑦에 해당하는 주어, 동사, 목적어(간접 목적어, 직접 목
> 적어), 보어(주격 보어, 목적격 보어)는 문장을 구성하는 필수 구성
> 요소이다. 문장의 형식은 위와 같은 문장 성분을 통해 구별할 수 있
> 다.
> ⑧부사는 필수 문장성분이 아니며 동사, 형용사, 부사, 문장 전체를
> 수식하는 역할을 한다. 부사구는 2단어 이상의 묶음이 부사 역할을
> 하는 것을 가리킨다.
> 1형식: 주어+동사 → **2, 6, 12, 16**번 문제
> 2형식: 주어+동사+주격 보어 → **4, 7, 11, 18**번 문제
> 3형식: 주어+동사+목적어 → **1, 9, 15**번 문제
> 4형식: 주어+동사+간접 목적어+직접 목적어
> → **3, 8, 14, 17**번 문제
> 5형식: 주어+동사+목적어+목적격 보어 → **5, 10, 13**번 문제

PRACTICE 12

1 late		**2** healthy	
3 cold		**4** popular	
5 bored		**6** quiet	
7 tired		**8** black	

1 be late for: ~에 늦다
2 stay healthy: 건강을 유지하다
3 turn cold: (날씨가) 추워지다.
4 become popular: 인기를 얻게 되다
5 feel bored: 지루함을 느끼다
6 keep quiet: 조용히 하다
7 get tired: 피곤하다
8 grow black: 어두워지다

PRACTICE 13

1 happy		**2** terrible
3 nicely		**4** look like
5 well		**6** salty
7 good		**8** sad
9 easily		**10** sweet
11 strange		**12** sounds like
13 feels		**14** beautifully

1, 8, 11 '~해 보이다'라는 의미의 동사 look, appear, seem이 사용되어 보어 자리에 형용사가 온다.
2, 6, 7, 10, 13 감각동사(feel, taste, sound, smell)가 사용되어 보어 자리에 형용사가 온다.
3 동사 treat이 '대하다, 다루다'라는 의미로 쓰일 때 어떤 태도로 대하는지 부사를 이용하여 설명할 수 있다. (treat nicely: 잘 대접하다)
4, 12 동사 다음에 명사가 와야 하기 때문에 형용사만을 보어로 가지는 look과 sounds는 정답이 될 수 없다.
　4 look like+명사: (명사)처럼 보이다.
　12 sound like+명사: (명사)하게 들리다.
5, 9, 14 이미 완벽한 문장이므로 동사가 어떻게 수행되는지 꾸며주는 부사가 들어가는 것이 적절하다.

PRACTICE 14

1 My uncle lent me the bike.
2 Mark will buy me a pretty doll.
　[Will Mark buy me a pretty doll?]
3 She told me a surprising story.
4 I'll give you a birthday gift.
5 They got us some food.
6 Father made us wooden toys.
7 I asked him the price of the house.
8 Why don't you show me the picture?
9 Mother cooked them a nice dinner.
10 We sent our teacher a thank-you note.

PRACTICE 15

1 I cooked some soup for my son.
2 My teacher asked a difficult question of me.
3 Jinho bought a present for her.
4 She sent a poem to her friend.
5 I wrote an email to my cousin.
6 They showed their car to me.
7 My friend made a pencil case for me.
8 Mr. Smith teaches English to us.
9 Can you get a Coke for me?
10 I didn't lend my bicycle to her.

1, 3, 7, 9 cook, buy, make, get은 4형식에서 3형식으로 전환 시 전치사 for를 사용한다.
2 ask는 4형식에서 3형식으로 전환 시 전치사 of를 사용한다.
4, 5, 6, 8, 10 send, write, show, teach, lend는 4형식에서 3형식으로 전환 시 전치사 to를 사용한다.

PRACTICE 16

1 angry		**2** sour
3 to come		**4** to leave
5 to clean		**6** heavy
7 to rest		**8** quiet
9 to have		**10** more attractive
11 to use		

1, 2, 6, 8, 10 make, turn, find, keep은 목적격 보어 자리에 명사나 형용사가 온다. 10번의 경우 부사가 아닌 형용사의 비교급이 오는 것이 적절하다.
3, 4, 5, 7, 9, 11 ask, want, tell, advise, get, allow는 목적격 보어로 to부정사가 온다.

PRACTICE 17

1 baking	**2** go	**3** sing
4 stay	**5** to consider	**6** laugh
7 shouting	**8** remember	**9** to marry
10 come	**11** to pose	**12** to choose
13 touching	**14** to study	**15** plant
16 carrying	**17** to tell	

1, 7, 13, 16 지각동사의 목적격 보어로 현재 분사가 사용되어 진행 중인 상황이나 행동을 강조할 수 있다.
2, 4, 6, 10 사역동사 let, have, make의 목적격 보어 자리에는 동사원형이 온다.
3, 15 지각동사의 목적격 보어로 동사원형이 온다.
5, 9, 11, 12, 14, 17 tell, want, get, allow, advise, ask는 사역동사나 지각동사가 아니고 to부정사를 목적격 보어로 가지는 동사들이다.
8 준사역동사 help의 목적격 보어 자리에는 동사원형 또는 to부정사가 올 수 있다.

중간·기말고사 대비문제 정답 본문 _ p.24

1 ④   2 ④   3 ②   4 ③   5 ④   6 ①   7 ①
8 ④,⑤   9 ①   10 How old do you think I am?
11 ②   12 ④   13 ④   14 ④   15 The movie
[film] made her laugh and cry.   16 ③   17 ③
18 I wonder if[whether] she was practicing
English.   19 The teacher made students clean
the classroom.   20 ③   21 ②   22 ④   23 ③
24 ⑤   25 ②   26 ③   27 ③   28 ④   29 ④
30 ③,⑤   31 ③   32 will[won't] you
33 (1) What do you think our problem is
(2) Who do you suppose baked this cake
34 ①   35 ④   36 ②   37 ⑤   38 ③   39 ④
40 ⑤   41 (1) Why did he choose to come
back? (2) What did she say?   42 (1) [3행] who
→ what (2) [8행] to do → do   43 ⑤   44 ④
45 ②   46 ①   47 ①,⑤   48 How nice her
new house is!   49 ③   50 ②   51 ③   52 ③
53 how many letters Hangeul has   54 ③
55 ④   56 had   57 ③   58 (1) healthy (2) cute
59 ⓐ how fresh the morning air was
ⓑ what an amazing view we saw from the top
60 make someone feel good   61 ⑤   62 ①
63 ③   64 Amy sent me a book. / Amy sent a
book to me.   65 ④   66 Do you know what
prize he won last year?   67 ⓑ angry, ⓒ
cheerful

중간·기말고사 대비문제 해설

1 • '누가'라는 주어의 역할을 하므로 who가 의문사로
  온다.
  • 의문사가 없는 간접의문문은 의문사 자리에 대신
    if[whether](~인지)를 쓴다.

2 ④ 부정어(Aren't)로 시작하는 의문문에 대한 대답은
  질문과 상관없이 대답의 내용이 긍정이면 Yes, 부
  정이면 No로 답한다. B가 많이 보고 싶었다고 말하
  는 긍정의 내용이므로 No가 아닌 Yes가 적절하다.

3 ② 일반동사가 긍정형인 문장의 부가의문문은 「do
  동사의 부정 축약형＋인칭대명사」의 형태로 쓴
  다. 이때, 동사가 lost이므로 과거시제이기 때문에
  doesn't가 아닌 didn't를 써야 한다.

① be동사가 긍정형인 문장의 부가의문문은 「be동사
  의 부정 축약형＋인칭대명사」의 형태로 쓴다.
③ 일반동사가 부정형인 문장의 부가의문문은 「do동
  사의 긍정형＋인칭대명사」의 형태로 쓴다.
④ 명령문의 부가의문문은 '명령문, will you?'의 형태
  로 쓴다. 어조에 따라 '명령문, won't you?'로 쓰는
  것도 가능하다.
⑤ 조동사가 부정형인 문장의 부가의문문은 「조동사
  의 긍정형＋인칭대명사」의 형태로 쓴다.

4 ⓐ make＋목적어＋동사원형(목적격 보어)
    (feeling → feel)
  ⓑ 형용사가 보어 역할 (nicely → nice)
  ⓓ make＋목적어＋형용사(목적격 보어)
    (uncomfortably → uncomfortable)

5 ④번은 '그것을 가지고 무엇을 하고 싶나요?'라는 뜻으
  로, 상대방의 의견을 묻는 나머지 보기와 다른 의미
  이다.
  ① 그것에 대한 여러분의 의견은 무엇입니까?
  ② 여러분의 관점들을 듣고 싶습니다.
  ③ 그것에 대한 생각이 있으신가요?
  ⑤ 그것에 대해 어떻게 생각하십니까?
  리더: 집중해 주세요. 이번 주의 학급 토론을 시작하겠
    습니다. 주제는 "학교는 학생들을 위해 온라인 책을
    제공하도록 요구되어야 하는가?"입니다. 그것에 대
    한 여러분의 의견은 무엇입니까?
  학생 1: 저는 완전히 동의합니다. 우리가 종이 책을 살
    때, 우리는 항상 그것을 들고 다녀야 합니다. 온라인
    책의 경우에는, 그런 짐이 없습니다.
  학생 2: 저는 다르게 생각합니다. 우리가 노트북이나 태
    블릿PC로 온라인 책을 읽을 때, 그것은 시간이 지남
    에 따라 우리의 시력을 해할 수 있습니다.
  리더: 알겠습니다. 온라인 책들이 장점과 단점을 가지고
    있기 때문에, 여러분 둘은 다른 의견을 가지는군요.

6 「make＋목적어＋동사원형」

7 주어진 문장과 ①은 '~하는 것'이라는 뜻의 관계대명
  사로 쓰였고, ②③④는 의문사, ⑤는 의문형용사로 쓰
  였다.
  ① 선행사를 포함하는 관계대명사 what은 앞에 선행
    사가 없고, 뒤에 불완전한 절이 따라온다.
  ②③ 의문사가 있는 간접의문문은 '의문사+주어+동
    사'의 어순을 따른다.
  ④ 간접의문문에서 의문사가 주어로 쓰인 경우에는
    직접의문문의 어순을 그대로 쓴다. She asked

me what happened to James.에서 의문사 what을 관계대명사로 대체해 She asked me the thing which[that] happened to James. 로 쓰는 것도 어법상으로는 가능하다. 하지만 'ask+사람+the thing+관계대명사절'은 일반적으로 잘 쓰지 않는 표현이다. ask는 목적어로 간접의문문을 자주 쓰는 동사로, 따라오는 what은 의문사로 쓰였다고 보는 것이 자연스럽다.

⑤ 의문형용사 what이 명사 color를 수식하고 있다.

주어진 문장 그 가게는 내가 필요한 것을 가지고 있지 않다.

① 난 이미 Jessie가 말한 것을 알고 있었다.

② 그녀의 이름이 무엇인지 내게 말해줘.

③ 난 그 답이 무엇인지 궁금하다.

④ 그녀는 나에게 James에게 무슨 일이 일어났는지 물었다.

⑤ 그녀의 가방이 무슨 색상인지 너는 알고 있니?

8 ① 주어인 a spider가 3인칭 단수이므로 do가 아니라 3인칭 단수 형태인 does를 써야 한다.

② 주어인 your favorite singer가 3인칭 단수이므로 be동사도 3인칭 단수인 is를 써야 한다.

③ 의문사가 있는 일반동사의 의문문의 경우 「의문사+do+주어+동사원형」의 어순으로 만든다. 이때, 과거시제라면 do를 did로 쓰고, 주어 뒤에 나오는 일반동사는 원형으로 써야한다. 따라서 came은 come으로 고쳐 써야 한다.

9 감탄문은 'What+(a/an)+형용사+명사+(주어+동사)!'의 어순으로 만든다. 주어인 그들이 복수이므로 (a/an)은 쓰지 않으며, 친절한 사람들이라는 뜻의 nice people을 What 뒤에 써준다. 주어는 그들이므로, 이어서 they are을 써준다. 이때, 감탄하는 대상이 명사인 '친절한 사람들'이므로 How를 쓰지 않는다.

10 간접 의문문이 포함된 문장에서 생각·추측을 나타내는 동사(think)가 주절에 있을 때 간접의문문의 의문사가 문장 맨 앞에 위치한다. 따라서 '의문사+do you think+주어+동사?'의 어순으로 써준다.

11 (a) 지각동사 heard는 목적격 보어로 동사원형 또는 -ing형을 쓸 수 있다.

(c) 감탄문은 'What+(a/an)+형용사+명사+(주어+동사)!'의 어순으로 쓴다. students가 복수형이므로 a/an은 쓰지 않고, 뒤의 주어+동사도 이에 맞춰 they have become으로 쓴 것은 어법상 옳다.

(e) 접시들이 '깨진' 것이므로 과거분사 broken의 수식을 받는 것은 적절하다.

(b) 이야기는 Mark에 의해 '쓰인' 것이므로 과거분사 written의 수식을 받는 것이 적절하다. (writing → written)

(d) 지각동사 saw는 목적격 보어로 동사원형 또는 -ing형을 쓴다. (to cheat → cheat[cheating])

(f) 주어 The soup를 받아주는 문장의 본동사 is가 이미 있으므로 smell delicious는 The soup의 수식어가 되어야 한다. 이때 현재분사 smelling을 사용하여 수식할 수 있다. (smell → smelling)

12 사역동사 let, make는 목적격 보어로 동사원형을 쓴다.

ⓑ let her to eat → let her eat

ⓓ make her to stop → make her stop

13 간접의문문에서 의문사 뒤의 어순은 「의문사+주어+동사」이다.

14 ④ 동사가 지각동사인 heard이므로 목적격 보어로 동사원형 또는 -ing형이 와야 한다. (fell → fall 또는 falling)

15 「make+목적어+동사원형」 '~이 …하게 만들다'

16 「How+부사[형용사]+주어+동사!」

17 ③ seem은 2형식에서 쓰이는 동사로 보어의 자리에 형용사가 온다. 만약 명사를 쓰고 싶을 때는 'seem like+명사'의 형태로 쓰면 된다. 이 경우 형용사가 보어의 자리에 있으므로 'seem+형용사'로 써준다.

18 의문사가 없는 간접의문문의 어순은 「주절+if [whether]+주어+동사」이다.

19 사역동사 make는 목적격 보어로 동사가 올 경우, 동사원형이 온다. 따라서 목적격 보어로 clean의 동사원형을 써준다. 시제는 과거시제이므로 make의 과거형인 made로 바꾸어 써야 한다.

20 ③ 공원에 가는 방법을 묻는 의문문이다.

①②④⑤ 'Let's ~', 'Shall we ~?', 'How about -ing?', 'Why don't we ~?'는 모두 권유나 제안을 하는 청유문에 쓰이는 표현들이다.

21 ⓑ a piece of는 셀 수 없는 명사의 단위를 나타내는 표현으로 명사 앞에 온다. advise는 '조언하다'라는 의미의 동사이며, '조언'이라는 의미의 명사 형태 advice를 사용하는 것이 옳다. (advise → advice)

22 「call+목적어+목적격 보어」

23 부가의문문이 'did you?'이므로 앞 문장은 You didn't ~ 로 시작해야 한다. 뒤따라오는 A의 말로 보아 문맥상 ③이 와야 한다.

24 동사 sell은 간접목적어 앞에 전치사 to를 쓰는 동사이다. I <u>sold</u> my car <u>to</u> Lisa for $800.

25 ① 현재완료 'have p.p.'는 have가 조동사 역할을 하는 것으로 본다. 조동사가 긍정형인 문장의 부가의문문은 '조동사의 부정 축약형+인칭대명사'의 형태로 쓴다. (have → haven't)

③ taste는 감각을 나타내는 동사로 동사의 보어의 자리에 형용사가 온다. (bitterly → bitter)

④ 4형식 문장은 '동사+간접목적어+직접목적어'의 어순으로 써준다. 이 경우, 간접목적어인 his mom이 직접목적어인 flowers 보다 앞에 나왔으므로 4형식이다. 따라서 전치사 to는 쓰지 않는다. (to 삭제)

⑤ help는 준사역동사로 목적격 보어로 동사원형이나 to부정사가 온다.
(to finishing → finish 또는 to finish)

26 ③ 질문이 현재시제이므로 답변도 현재 시제로 해야 한다. 따라서 과거시제인 didn't는 알맞지 않다.

27 A의 마지막 말로 보아 빈칸에는 사실에 대한 확신을 묻는 표현이 와야 한다.
③ Are you all right? 너 괜찮니?

28 ⓓ 동사 make는 목적격 보어로 명사 혹은 형용사를 취할 수 있다. 따라서 부사 joyfully를 형용사 joyful로 바꾸어야 한다.

29 look은 '~해 보이다'라는 뜻으로 보어 자리에 형용사가 온다.

30 「help+목적어+동사원형[to부정사]」

31 ③ want는 목적어로 to부정사를 쓰는 동사이다.
(learning → to learn)

32 명령문의 부가의문문은 will you? 또는 won't you?이다.

33 간접의문문이 think, suppose 등의 동사의 목적어로 쓰일 때는 의문사가 문장 맨 앞에 위치한다.

34 「feel+형용사」 '~한 느낌이 들다'

35 모두 명령문이므로 부가의문문은 will you? 또는 won't you?가 올 수 있다. 선택지에는 will만 있으므로 ④가 정답이다.

36 ⓑ 간접의문문은 「의문사+주어+동사」의 어순을 가진다.

ⓒ 간접의문문이 and로 연결되며 의문사 이하가 I last saw her으로 같은 내용이므로 두번째 간접의문문에서는 의문사 이하를 생략할 수 있다.

ⓖ 간접의문문은 「의문사+주어+동사」의 어순을 가진다.

ⓐ 간접의문문은 「의문사+주어+동사」의 어순을 가진다.
(you want what time → what time you want)

ⓓ 간접의문문이 포함된 문장에서 주절의 동사가 think와 같이 생각이나 추측을 나타낼 때는 간접의문문의 의문사가 문장 맨 앞에 위치한다. (Do you think what time → What time do you think)

ⓔ 간접의문문은 「의문사+주어+동사」의 어순을 가진다. (what is the key message of this book → what the key message of this book is)

ⓕ 간접의문문에 의문사가 없는 경우 if[whether]+주어+동사의 형태를 가진다. (that → if[whether])

ⓐ 너는 나에게 몇 시에 저녁을 먹고 싶은지 말해줄 수 있니?

ⓑ 나는 새 식당에서의 서비스가 어떤지 모른다.

ⓒ 그 탐정은 나에게 내가 언제 그리고 어디서 그녀를 마지막으로 봤는지 물었다.

ⓓ 너는 우리가 몇 시에 놀이공원을 떠날 것이라고 생각하니?

ⓔ 나는 이 책의 핵심 메시지가 무엇인지 알고 싶다.

ⓕ 나는 네가 그 영화 속 등장인물에 공감하는지 궁금하다.

ⓖ 너는 이 웹사이트를 이용함으로써 누가 주소지에 살고 있는지를 찾아낼 수 있다.

37 ⑤ 의문문에 답할 때는 의문문에 쓰인 동사와 같은 동사를 쓴다. 5번의 질문에서는 Is로 물었으므로, 대답 또한 is를 써야 한다. 따라서 올바른 대답은 No, he isn't이다. (doesn't → isn't)

38 (c) 일반동사가 사용된 의문문의 과거형「Did+주어+동사원형~?」의 형태로 쓴다. (worked → work)

(d) 일반동사가 부정형인 문장의 부가의문문은「do동사의 긍정형+인칭대명사」의 형태로 쓴다. 문장의 시제에 맞게 과거형인 did를 쓰는 것이 적절하다. (were you → did you)

A: 집에 돌아온 걸 환영해. 과학 캠프는 어땠어?

B: 정말 좋았어요! 저는 정말 재미있게 놀았어요.

A: 네가 가장 좋아했던 건 뭐였니?

B: 전 물로켓 만드는 게 가장 좋았어요.

A: 굉장하구나! 너의 것은 잘 작동했니?

B: 네, 그건 정말 하늘 높이 (올라) 갔어요.

A: 멋지다! 너 혼자 만든 건 아니지, 그렇지?

B: 네, 거기서 만난 몇몇 친구들과 같이 작업했어요.

A: 좋네. 번호는 주고받았어?

B: 그럼요! 그들을 빨리 다시 보고 싶어요!

39 「see+목적어+현재분사/동사원형」

40 ⑤ sound는 감각동사이므로 동사의 보어로 형용사가 온다. nicely는 부사이므로, 형용사 형태인 nice로

고쳐주어야 한다. (nicely → nice)

41 (1) 간접의문문을 직접의문문으로 되돌릴 때는 동사 (chose)의 과거 시제에 유의해 did he choose로 써야 한다.

(2) 주절의 동사로 guess가 쓰여 의문사가 문장 맨 앞으로 이동한 문장이다. 의문사로 시작하는 의문문으로 되돌릴 때는 동사(said)의 과거 시제에 유의해 did she say로 써야 한다.

42 (1) 위에서 셋째 줄의 'Do you know <u>who</u> you want to do in the future?'는 문맥상, '너는 미래에 네가 무엇을 하기를 원하는지 아니?'라는 뜻이 되어야 하므로 who를 what으로 고쳐야 한다.

(2) 밑에서 셋째 줄의 'Don't let them <u>to do</u> that.' 에서 사역동사 let의 목적격 보어는 동사원형이 되어야 하므로 to do를 do로 고쳐야 한다.

43 질문에 부정어가 포함된 동사가 있을 때, 대답에 not 이 포함되면 No, ~.로 대답한다.

44 •「hear + 목적어 + 현재분사/동사원형」
•「let + 목적어 + 동사원형」

45 (A) 감각동사 smell은 형용사를 보어로 취한다.
smell good: 좋은 냄새가 나다
(B) 동사 want는 to부정사를 목적격 보어로 취한다.
(C) 일반동사 긍정문의 부가의문문은 조동사 do의 부정 축약형을 쓴다.

46 「want + 목적어 + to부정사」

47 heard는 지각동사이다. 지각동사는 목적격 보어로 동사원형이나 -ing형을 쓴다. 따라서 빈칸에는 crying 혹은 cry가 들어가야 한다.

48 「How + 형용사 + 주어 + 동사!」

49 ① be동사 부정문의 부가의문문은 be동사의 긍정형으로 만든다. (isn't she → is she)
② 조동사 긍정문의 부가의문문은 조동사의 부정형으로 만든다. 현재완료시제에서는 have/has가 조동사의 역할을 한다. (didn't he → hasn't he)
④ 'Let's ~'로 시작하는 문장의 부가의문문은 shall we?를 사용한다. (will you → shall we)
⑤ 조동사 긍정문의 부가의문문은 조동사의 부정형으로 만든다. (can you → can't you)

50 「get + 직접목적어 + for + 간접목적어」

51 「look + 형용사」 '~해 보이다'

52 Let's ~, shall we?

53 「주절 + 의문사 + 주어 + 동사 ~」

54 ③ stay + 주격보어(형용사): '~한 상태를 유지하다'

① 'go + 형용사'는 '~하게 되다'라는 뜻이다.
(sourly → sour)
② 주어가 복수 명사이므로 동사도 복수형태인 grow가 와야 한다. (grows → grow)
④ 작년에 있었던 일로, 시제가 과거이므로 동사도 과거형인 became을 써야 한다.
(becomes → became)
⑤ 동사 stay는 2형식 문장에서 동사의 보어 자리에 형용사가 온다. 따라서 openness의 형용사 형태인 open이 와야 한다. (openness → open)

55 A: 넌 팝과 재즈 중에서 어느 것을 더 좋아하니?
B: 난 재즈를 더 좋아해.

56 • have a good time: 좋은 시간을 보내다
• 사역동사 <u>have</u> + 목적어 + 동사원형: 목적어가 ~하게 하다
• <u>have</u> a nice dinner: 근사한 저녁 식사를 하다
첫 번째 문장과 세 번째 문장에서 과거를 나타내는 표현(yesterday / last night)이 쓰였으므로 빈칸에는 have의 과거형 had가 들어가야 한다.

57 ③ came → come/coming
지각동사의 목적격 보어 자리에는 동사원형 또는 분사가 온다.

58 (1) 동사 make는 형용사를 목적격 보어로 취한다.
(2) 동사 find는 형용사를 목적격 보어로 취한다.

59 ⓐ How + 형용사 + 주어 + 동사
ⓑ What + a[an] + 형용사 + 명사 + 주어 + 동사

60 「make + 목적어 + 동사원형」

61 ⑤ advise는 to부정사를 목적격 보어로 취하는 동사이다. (go → to go)
① 동사 show를 3형식으로 쓸 경우 간접목적어 앞에 전치사 to를 쓴다.
② 감탄문으로 'What(+a[an]) + 형용사 + 명사 + 주어 + 동사!' 어순을 따른다.
③ 접속사 if가 명사절 접속사로 '~인지 (아닌지)'의 의미로 쓰이는 경우, 미래시제를 나타낼 때 조동사 will을 써야 한다. 시간과 조건의 부사절에서 접속사 if가 쓰일 경우에는 현재시제가 미래시제를 대신한다.
④ 'be interested in: ~에 관심이 있다.'는 표현이 쓰였으며, 2형식 동사 become이 be동사 자리에 올 수 있다.

62 •「find + 직접목적어 + for + 간접목적어」
•「ask + 직접목적어 + of + 간접목적어」

63 ③ 4형식 문장을 3형식으로 전환할 때는 '동사＋직접
목적어＋전치사＋간접목적어'의 어순으로 써준다.
동사 ask는 4형식을 3형식으로 전환할 때 전치사
of를 사용한다. (to → of)

64 4형식 문장은 '동사＋간접목적어＋직접목적어'의 어
순으로 쓴다. 동사는 '보냈다'라는 뜻의 sent를 써준
다. 간접 목적어는 '나'라는 뜻의 1인칭 단수 목적격 대
명사인 me, 직접 목적어는 책 한 권이므로 'a book'
을 써준다. 4형식 문장을 3형식으로 전환할 때는 '동
사＋직접목적어＋전치사＋간접목적어'의 어순으로 써
준다. send는 4형식을 3형식으로 전환할 때, 전치사
로 to를 쓴다. 따라서 me 앞에는 to를 붙여준다.

65 (A)와 ④의 found는 목적격 보어를 필요로 하는 5형
식 동사 find의 과거형이고, ①②③⑤의 found는 목
적어만을 취하는 3형식 동사 find의 과거형이다.

66 의문사가 들어간 간접의문문의 어순은 「의문사＋주어
＋동사」이다. 이때 시제가 과거이므로 과거동사를 써
야 한다.

67 ⓑ 동사 seem은 주격보어 자리에 오는 형용사와 함
께 쓰여 '~처럼 보이다'라는 뜻을 나타낸다.
ⓒ 동사 find는 형용사를 목적격 보어로 가지며 '~를
…라고 생각하다, 알게 되다'로 해석한다.

CHAPTER	**2**	시제 Tense	본문 _ p.36

PRACTICE 1

1 departs		**2** rewards	
3 bites		**4** answers	
5 uses		**6** sings	
7 breathes		**8** opens	
9 destroys		**10** closes	
11 changes		**12** proves	
13 makes		**14** cries	
15 draws		**16** reduces	
17 tells		**18** misses	
19 mixes		**20** complains	
21 leaves		**22** raises	
23 shoots		**24** lifts	
25 likes		**26** bears	
27 takes		**28** elects	
29 recycles		**30** recommends	
31 stops		**32** wants	
33 exchanges		**34** interviews	
35 allows		**36** keeps	
37 marries		**38** prays	
39 acts		**40** enjoys	
41 rescues		**42** starts	
43 vows		**44** mentions	
45 imagines		**46** brings	
47 does		**48** leads	
49 finds		**50** fights	

51 wraps	**52** flows
53 argues	**54** travels
55 produces	**56** seems
57 serves	**58** gives
59 follows	**60** finishes
61 adds	**62** borrows
63 copies	**64** discovers
65 admires	**66** sinks
67 understands	**68** worries
69 remembers	**70** quits
71 stretches	**72** knocks
73 hopes	**74** wakes
75 reports	**76** introduces
77 appears	**78** saves
79 supposes	**80** agrees
81 beats	**82** hatches
83 becomes	**84** describes
85 wonders	**86** tries

PRACTICE 2

1 s	**2** z	**3** z	**4** z	**5** z
6 s	**7** s	**8** z	**9** iz	**10** z
11 s	**12** z	**13** z	**14** iz	**15** z
16 z	**17** s	**18** z	**19** iz	**20** s
21 z	**22** iz	**23** z	**24** iz	**25** s
26 z	**27** s	**28** s	**29** iz	**30** z

31 iz	**32** s	**33** iz	**34** s	**35** z
36 s	**37** z	**38** iz	**39** s	**40** iz
41 s	**42** iz	**43** s	**44** z	**45** s

PRACTICE 3

2 plays **3** sleeps **4** is

5 moves **6** go

> **1, 4** 현재의 사실이나 상태를 나타낼 때 현재시제를 쓴다.
> **2, 3, 6** 현재의 습관이나 반복적인 동작을 나타낼 때 현재시제를 쓴다.
> **5** 불변의 진리나 격언, 과학적 사실을 나타낼 때 현재시제를 쓴다.

PRACTICE 4

2 arrives **3** have **4** leaves

5 comes **6** blames **7** hears

8 visits **9** studies **10** gets

11 reaches **12** departs **13** finishes

> **1, 5** 눈앞에서 진행되고 있는 일을 나타낼 때 현재 시제를 쓴다.
> **2, 4, 11** 왕래발착동사가 미래를 나타내는 부사구와 함께 쓰일 때 현재시제로 미래를 나타낼 수 있다.
> **3, 7, 10, 12, 13** 시간과 조건의 부사절에서는 현재시제로 미래를 나타낸다.
> **6** 격언이나 속담을 나타낼 때 현재시제를 쓴다.
> *A bad workman always blames his tools.: 서투른 일꾼이 연장 탓한다. (속담)
> **8, 9** 현재의 습관이나 반복적인 동작을 나타낼 때 현재시제를 쓴다.

PRACTICE 5

2 was **3** are **4** were **5** are **6** is

7 is **8** were **9** was **10** was

PRACTICE 6

1 were, was **2** Was, wasn't **3** Is, is

4 was, was **5** is, is

> **1** 질문의 시제가 과거이므로 기준 시점에 해당하는 when 뒤의 빈칸과 답변 모두 과거시제가 되어야 알맞다.
> **2** 답변 뒤에 덧붙인 문장이 과거시제이므로 질문과 답변 모두 과거시제가 되어야 알맞다.
> **3** 답변 뒤에 덧붙인 문장이 현재시제이므로 질문과 답변 모두 현재시제가 되어야 알맞다.
> **4** 과거 시점을 나타내는 부사구 last week가 있으므로 과거시제로 질문하고 답변해야 알맞다.
> **5** 현재 시점을 나타내는 부사구 these days가 있으므로 현재시제로 질문하고 답변해야 알맞다.

PRACTICE 7

1 stayed **2** ripped

3 smelled **4** caused

5 worried **6** destroyed

7 died **8** bowed

9 preferred **10** applied

11 judged **12** wasted

13 controlled **14** played

15 watched **16** delayed

17 invited **18** hurried

19 copied **20** hoped

21 shopped **22** expected

23 disappeared **24** observed

25 studied **26** fixed

27 chatted **28** carried

29 smiled **30** jogged

31 popped **32** noticed

33 danced **34** tried

35 stopped **36** rushed

37 enjoyed **38** married

39 planned **40** waited

41 replied **42** practiced

43 picked **44** dropped

45 agreed **46** decided

47 fried **48** grabbed

49 clapped **50** cleaned

51 saved **52** cried

53 wrapped **54** dried

PRACTICE 8

1 d	**2** d	**3** id	**4** t	**5** d
6 d	**7** id	**8** d	**9** t	**10** t
11 id	**12** t	**13** d	**14** d	**15** t
16 id	**17** d	**18** t	**19** d	**20** id
21 t	**22** id	**23** id	**24** d	**25** t
26 d	**27** id	**28** d	**29** t	**30** id
31 t	**32** d	**33** d	**34** d	**35** id
36 t	**37** d	**38** t	**39** id	**40** d
41 t	**42** id	**43** t	**44** d	**45** id

PRACTICE 9

1 chose – chosen **2** laid – laid

3 met – met **4** fell – fallen

Ch
2
시
제

5 rang – rung	**6** ran – run
7 spent – spent	**8** took – taken
9 gave – given	**10** kept – kept
11 heard – heard	**12** sat – sat
13 bore – borne/born	**14** taught – taught
15 sang – sung	**16** cost – cost
17 thought – thought	**18** flew – flown
19 wore – worn	**20** hurt – hurt
21 read – read	**22** told – told
23 made – made	**24** fought – fought
25 saw – seen	**26** went – gone
27 brought – brought	**28** paid – paid
29 drew – drawn	**30** found – found
31 hit – hit	**32** bought – bought
33 spoke – spoken	**34** began – begun
35 understood – understood	
36 lay – lain	**37** stole – stolen
38 put – put	**39** held – held
40 sank – sunk	**41** woke – woken
42 wrote – written	
43 overcame – overcome	
44 led – led	**45** knew – known
46 left – left	**47** set – set
48 rose – risen	**49** swept – swept
50 smelled/smelt – smelled/smelt	
51 ate – eaten	**52** forgot – forgotten
53 had – had	**54** became – become
55 slept – slept	**56** let – let
57 spread – spread	
58 dreamed/dreamt – dreamed/dreamt	
59 sent – sent	**60** beat – beaten
61 stood – stood	**62** drank – drunk
63 came – come	**64** said – said
65 felt – felt	**66** meant – meant
67 grew – grown	**68** built – built
69 cut – cut	**70** swam – swum
71 threw – thrown	**72** was, were – been
73 lost – lost	**74** blew – blown
75 drove – driven	**76** did – done
77 hid – hidden	**78** got – got(ten)
79 won – won	**80** rode – ridden
81 sold – sold	**82** shut – shut

PRACTICE 10

1 sent	**2** was	**3** play
4 didn't eat	**5** woke	**6** didn't hear
7 broke	**8** hit	**9** fell
10 didn't play	**11** closes	**12** lay
13 read	**14** brought	**15** saw
16 forgot	**17** drew	**18** came
19 didn't give	**20** leaves	**21** drove
22 shut	**23** sang	

> **1, 2, 6, 14, 15, 17, 18** last week, in 2018, last night, yesterday, last month, three years ago, in 2023 같은 과거를 나타내는 부사구가 있으므로 과거시제가 알맞다.
> **3** 현재를 나타내는 부사구 these days가 있으므로 현재시제가 알맞다.
> **4, 5, 7, 8, 9, 12, 16, 19, 21, 22** 접속사로 연결된 문장의 시제가 과거이므로 두 절의 시제를 과거 시제로 일치시킨다.
> **10, 13** 시간부사절(when ~/after ~)로 제시한 기준 시점이 과거이므로 주절의 시제 역시 과거가 알맞다.
> **11** on weekdays(평일에)로 보아 반복적인 동작을 나타내고 있으므로 현재시제가 알맞다.
> **20** 왕래발착동사 leave와 미래를 나타내는 부사구 tomorrow morning이 함께 왔으므로 현재시제로 미래를 나타낼 수 있다.
> **23** 과거의 특정 상황에서 일어난 일을 설명하고 있으므로 과거 시제가 알맞다.

PRACTICE 11

1 will	**2** Are	**3** go	**4** are
5 going	**6** will join	**7** going	**8** will
9 am	**10** will		

PRACTICE 12

2 Are, going to buy	**3** is going to give
4 are going to study	**5** is going to rain
6 is going to paint	

PRACTICE 13

1 planting	**2** taking
3 getting	**4** playing
5 smiling	**6** bowing
7 becoming	**8** seeing
9 losing	**10** breathing
11 standing	**12** opening
13 arguing	**14** tumbling
15 worrying	**16** biting
17 teaching	**18** wrapping

19	swimming	20	copying
21	singing	22	baking
23	dying	24	returning
25	planning	26	operating
27	serving	28	joining
29	carrying	30	climbing
31	going	32	setting
33	studying	34	cleaning
35	dating	36	encouraging
37	pulling	38	burning
39	using	40	staying
41	coming	42	acting
43	winning	44	producing
45	celebrating	46	writing
47	denying	48	repeating
49	entering	50	eating
51	making	52	hitting
53	running	54	marrying
55	shining	56	beating
57	enjoying	58	causing
59	moving	60	solving
61	facing	62	destroying
63	fighting	64	rolling
65	washing	66	saying
67	stopping	68	shaking
69	introducing	70	happening
71	flying	72	holding
73	saving	74	sharing
75	visiting	76	putting
77	lying	78	talking
79	riding	80	collecting
81	dreaming	82	controlling
83	trying	84	driving
85	hurting	86	filling
87	paying	88	wearing
89	agreeing	90	cheating
91	cutting	92	selling
93	forming	94	fixing
95	removing	96	turning
97	mentioning	98	increasing
99	waiting	100	picking

PRACTICE 14

2	is baking	3	were arguing
4	was riding	5	is sleeping
6	is removing	7	are, leaving
8	is cooking	9	were, doing
10	are playing	11	am not working
12	was standing	13	was having
14	is not using	15	am making

2, 5, 6, 8, 15 be+-ing가 현재진행시제를 나타낸다.
1, 3, 4, 9, 12, 13 be동사의 과거형+-ing는 과거진행시제로, 과거의 한 시점에 진행되고 있던 동작을 나타낸다.
7, 10, 11, 14 이미 계획된 일에 대한 가까운 미래를 표현할 때는 현재진행시제가 미래를 대신할 수 있다.

PRACTICE 15

2	was having[eating]	3	was walking
4	was cleaning	5	was talking
6	was reading		

PRACTICE 16

2	have passed		
3	Have, thought, haven't		
4	haven't touched	5	have hatched
6	has lost	7	Have, visited, have
8	have got(ten)	9	have set
10	have bought	11	has been
12	haven't learned	13	Have, been, haven't
14	has become	15	has changed
16	haven't eaten		

1 hear of: ~에 대해 듣다
2 pass away: 사망하다, 돌아가시다
3 think about: ~에 대해 생각하다
5 hatch: 부화하다, 부화되다
6 lose one's job: 실직하다
7 visit+장소 명사: ~를 방문하다
9 set up: 준비하다, 설치하다
10 buy+사람+A: ~에게 A를 사주다
13 have been to+장소: ~에 가본 적이 있다

PRACTICE 17

2	My father has gone, 결과
3	I have already done, 완료
4	She has stayed in Korea, 계속
5	He has been to India, 경험
6	They have just finished, 완료

7 Brian has just walked, 완료

8 I have never owned, 경험

9 I have played the guitar, 계속

10 He has broken, 결과

> **2** has gone은 '가버려서 지금 여기 없다'는 의미로 현재완료의 용법 중 '결과'에 해당한다.
> **3, 6, 7** already(이미)와 just(방금)는 현재완료의 '완료' 용법에서 자주 쓰이는 부사이다.
> **4** for two years(2년 동안)로 지속 기간을 나타내고 있으므로 현재완료의 용법 중 '계속'에 해당한다.
> **5** 'have been to+장소'는 '~에 가본 적이 있다'는 말로 현재완료의 '경험' 용법이다.
> **8** never는 현재완료의 '경험' 용법에서 자주 쓰이는 부사이다.
> **9** 'since I was ten'이 '10살 때부터 계속'이라는 의미를 가지므로 현재완료의 '계속' 용법이다.
> **10** has broken은 '부러트렸다 (여전히 부러진 상태이다)'는 의미로 현재완료의 용법 중 '결과'에 해당한다.

PRACTICE **18**

1 for **2** for **3** since **4** for
5 since **6** for **7** since **8** since
9 for **10** since

> **1, 2, 4, 6, 9** 빈칸 뒤에 기간 표현이 왔으므로 '~ 동안'이라는 뜻으로 어떤 일이 지속된 시간의 길이를 나타내는 for가 알맞다.
> **3, 5, 7, 8, 10** 빈칸 뒤에 특정 시점 표현이 왔으므로 '~ 이후로'의 뜻으로 사건이 시작된 시점을 나타내는 since가 알맞다.

PRACTICE **19**

1 Jack has been here for four days.

2 I have taught students for fifteen years.

3 Liz has studied Japanese for two years.

4 My mom has had the house since last year.

5 Kate has dated Dave since last April.

6 Mark has played tennis since 2023.

> **1, 2, 3** 현재완료시제(주어+have+과거분사) 뒤에 'for+기간'을 쓰면 어떤 일이 일어나 지속된 시간을 나타내어 '~ 동안 …해왔다'라는 의미가 된다.
> **4, 5, 6** 현재완료시제(주어+have+과거분사) 뒤에 'since+시점'을 쓰면 어떤 일이 시작된 시점을 나타내어 '~ 이후로 …해왔다'라는 의미가 된다.

PRACTICE **20**

1 saw **2** have never read
3 haven't talked **4** got
5 snowed **6** have never driven
7 have just finished **8** cleaned
9 haven't eaten **10** walked

> **1, 5, 8** 과거의 특정한 때를 나타내는 부사(구)(last night, this morning, yesterday)가 있으므로 과거시제가 알맞다.
> **2, 6** 과거에서부터 지금까지의 경험을 말할 때 현재완료시제를 써서 '~한 적이 있다'라고 표현할 수 있다. never를 넣으면 '~한 적이 없다'라는 뜻이 되며, before(전에, 예전에)는 현재완료의 경험 용법에서 자주 쓰이는 부사이다.
> **3** '최근에 언니와 얘기하지 않았다'는 것은 과거에 시작되어 현재까지 계속되는 상태를 묘사하고 있으므로 현재완료시제가 알맞다.
> **4, 10** 과거에 종료된 동작이나 상태를 나타내고 있으므로 과거시제가 알맞다.
> **7** '막 ~했다'라고 표현할 때는 현재완료시제를 사용한다. 완료 용법에 해당하며 just, now, already 같은 부사가 자주 함께 쓰인다.
> **9** 과거의 특정 시점 이후로(since this morning) 계속 지속된 동작이나 상태를 나타내므로 현재완료시제가 알맞다.

PRACTICE **21**

1 had **2** 잘못된 곳 없음
3 rained **4** 잘못된 곳 없음
5 was **6** bought
7 잘못된 곳 없음 **8** finished
9 잘못된 곳 없음 **10** got

> **1, 3, 6, 8, 10** 과거의 특정한 때를 나타내는 부사(구)(yesterday, last night, last year, two hours ago, last month)가 있으므로 현재완료가 아닌 단순 과거시제가 되어야 한다.
> **5** 유미가 광주에서 태어난 것은 과거에 종료된 일이므로 과거시제가 되어야 한다.
> be born in: ~에서 태어나다

PRACTICE **22**

2 I have solved ten problems so far.

3 Have they worked here since 2020?

4 The train left the station five minutes ago.

5 How did you earn so much last year?

6 Eva hasn't[has not] seen her sister for a long time.

> **2, 6** 지속 기간을 나타내는 표현(so far, for a long time)이 있으므로 '~ 동안 계속되다'라는 의미가 되도록 현재완료시제가 되어야 한다.
> **3** since를 써서 어떤 일이 시작된 시점을 나타내고 있으므로 '~ 이후로 계속되다'라는 의미가 되도록 현재완료시제가 되어야 한다.
> **4, 5** 과거의 특정한 때를 나타내는 표현(five minutes ago, last year)에 어울리는 과거시제가 알맞다.

PRACTICE **23**

1 have been studying **2** have been playing
3 has, been sleeping **4** has been working
5 Have, been reading **6** has been repairing
7 have been waiting **8** has been talking
9 Has, been baking **10** has been watching

4 work for: ~을 위해[~에서] 일하다
7 wait for: ~을 기다리다
8 talk to: ~에게 이야기하다

PRACTICE 24

2 Seyeon has been using her laptop for two hours.

3 Two people have been playing tennis since 4 o'clock.

4 Mike has been making lunch since noon.

5 Jisu and I have been building a sand castle for an hour.

6 It has been raining since this morning.

2, 5 시간의 길이를 나타내는 표현(two hours, an hour)이 명시되어 있으므로, '~동안 계속되다'라는 의미를 가진 for를 사용하는 것이 적절하다.
3, 4, 6 시점을 나타내는 표현(4 o'clock, noon, this morning)이 주어졌으므로, '~이후로 계속되다'라는 의미의 since를 사용하는 것이 적절하다.

🖊 중간·기말고사 대비문제 정답   본문 _ p.63

1 ②   2 ②   3 ③   4 ③   5 ⑤   6 ①

7 have lived in   8 ②   9 ⑤   10 ②   11 ④

12 ④   13 ①   14 ⓐ Did you finish packing your bag yesterday?   15 ②   16 ②   17 ②

18 is washing the[a] car   19 finished, went

20 ④,⑤   21 make → made   22 They have served free meals for two years.   23 ②

24 ②,⑤   25 ③   26 ⑤   27 I have learned Japanese since last summer.   28 ①,③

29 ⑤   30 ④   31 ④   32 ③   33 ②

34 ⓓ I have not[haven't] been there for two months.   35 ④   36 ②   37 ①   38 ②

39 ②   40 has been snowing   41 (1) broken (2) spread (3) to drive (4) forgotten (5) won

42 ③   43 (1) have visited Brazil once (2) have not[haven't] won a prize in the piano competition (3) has read *Anna Karenina*, has not[hasn't] read *Anna Karenina*[it]   44 ①

45 am, have been, will, will, will

중간·기말고사 대비문제 해설

1   ② will take → take

시간이나 조건의 부사절에서는 미래 시제 대신 현재 시제가 쓰인다.

2   ⓑ 지난달부터 현재까지 계속 지속된 사건에 대해 말할 때는 현재완료를 사용한다. 현재완료는 'have/has + 과거분사'로 나타낸다. (had → have)

ⓒ 의문문에 대한 답을 할 때는 의문문에 쓰인 동사에 맞춰 답을 한다. 질문에서 doesn't로 물었으므로, 긍정의 답변은 does로 한다. (is → does)

ⓐ 「There is ~」는 '~가 있다'라는 뜻으로 동사의 수를 뒤에 나오는 명사에 일치시킨다. 단수 명사 a dog이 쓰였으므로, 동사 또한 단수 동사인 is를 쓴다. There's는 There is의 축약형이다.

ⓓ 현재의 습관이나 반복적인 동작을 나타낼 때는 현재시제를 쓴다. 주어 he는 3인칭 단수이므로, 동사 또한 3인칭 단수 현재형으로 만들기 위해 '-s'를 붙인다.

ⓔ 현재진행시제는 말하고 있는 시점에 진행되고 있는 동작을 나타낼 때 쓰인다. 3인칭 단수 명사 the dog이 주어이므로 'is + -ing'의 형태로 쓴다.

3   ③ 경험 ① 결과 ② 완료 ④⑤ 계속

4   ③ 사건이 시작된 시점은 since와 함께 쓴다. (for → since)

5   ⑤ speak - spoke - spoken

6   ① 왕래발착동사 현재형이 미래시제를 뜻할 수 있으므로 올바르다.

② 과거를 나타내는 부사 yesterday가 쓰였으므로 과거시제를 사용한다. (studies → studied)

③ 미래를 나타내는 부사구 next Sunday가 쓰였으므로 미래시제를 사용한다. (was playing → will[am going to] play)

④ 주어 your parents가 복수이므로 be동사도 수를 일치시킨다. (Was → Were)

⑤ 주어 You는 2인칭이므로 부정문을 만들 때 don't을 사용한다. (doesn't → don't)

7   과거에 발생한 동작이나 상태가 현재까지 이어질 때는 「have/has + 과거분사」의 현재완료로 표현한다.

8   break-broke-broken / steal-stole-stolen (broke → broken, stole → stolen)

9   대화의 read는 과거분사 형태로 [red]로 발음된다.

⑤ 주절 시제가 과거형이므로 종속절 동사 read[red]도 과거시제여야 한다.

① to+동사원형이므로 [ri:d]로 발음된다.

② 조동사 could+동사원형이므로 [ri:d]로 발음된다.

③ 조동사 will+동사원형이므로 [riːd]로 발음된다.

④ to+동사원형이므로 [riːd]로 발음된다.

10 ⓐ 현재완료는 「have+과거분사」로 쓴다.

(trying → tried)

ⓒ 과거의 특정한 때를 나타내는 부사구 last year이 쓰였으므로 과거시제로 쓴다.

(have tried → tried)

ⓓ ever since로 과거에 시작되어 현재까지 계속되는 상태임을 알 수 있다. 따라서 현재완료시제를 사용한다. (was → has been)

11 각각 경험, 완료를 나타내는 현재완료가 필요하다.

12 과거의 특정한 때를 나타내는 부사구(in 2020, last week)가 쓰였으므로 과거시제로 쓴다.

ⓐ have met → met   ⓒ swum → swam

13 ① 계속 ②④⑤ 경험 ③ 결과

14 A의 질문에 B가 'Yes, I did.'로 답했고, yesterday는 과거의 특정한 때이므로 과거시제를 써야 한다.

15 주절(he will take care of it)의 내용으로 보아 시간이나 조건의 부사절에 현재시제가 와야 하고, something은 단수 취급한다.

16 주어진 문장은 '너는 이 도시의 노란 새에 대해 들어본 적 있니?'라는 뜻으로, 현재완료의 경험 용법이 사용되었다. ever는 주로 의문문에서 '지금까지, 여태껏'이라는 의미로 사용되는 부사이고 have와 과거분사 사이에 위치한다.

② have never seen은 '한 번도 본 적이 없다'는 의미로, '절대/한 번도 …않다'라는 뜻의 부사 never와 현재완료가 함께 쓰여 경험을 나타낸다.

① 밑줄 친 부분은 '살아 왔다'라는 의미로 해석할 수 있다. for은 사건이 일어나 지속된 시간의 길이를 나타내는 전치사로, 현재완료의 계속 용법과 함께 쓰인다.

③ just는 완료 용법과 함께 쓰여, 주로 have와 과거분사 사이에 위치한다. has just broken은 '방금 깨뜨렸다'라는 의미로, 이미 완료된 일을 나타냄을 알 수 있다.

④ have gone은 '가버렸다'라는 뜻으로, 이미 이 곳을 떠났다는 결과를 나타낸다.

⑤ have stayed는 '머물러 왔다'라는 의미로, '~이후로'의 뜻을 나타내는 since와 함께 쓰여 머무르는 행동이 계속됨을 나타낸다.

17 ② lie(누워 있다) - lay - lain (lied → lay)

18 현재에 진행 중인 동작을 물었으므로 현재진행형으로

대답한다.

19 • 완료를 나타내는 현재완료시제
• 과거의 특정한 때를 나타내는 과거시제

20 「on+요일s」, 「every+요일」 '~요일마다'

21 make - made - made

22 2년 전부터 무료 식사를 제공하기 시작해 현재까지 계속 제공하고 있으므로 현재완료시제와 for(~동안)가 쓰인다.

23 ② ever은 '지금까지, 여태껏'이라는 의미로, 현재완료의 경험 용법과 자주 쓰인다.

24 ① the kitchen → a room

③ was taking a shower → was making spaghetti

④ (Alex 기준) was having dinner with her family → was playing the cello 또는 (Samantha 기준) was listening to pop music → was playing a computer game

25 have been (to) '~에 갔었다'

26 미래를 나타내는 부사구(next Monday)가 있으므로 is going to 또는 will이 들어간다.

27 since는 현재완료 시제와 자주 쓰인다. '~이후로'의 뜻으로 사건이 시작된 시점을 나타낼 때 쓴다.

28 '절대 잃어버린 적이 없다'는 현재완료의 경험을 나타내는 용법이다. never은 현재완료의 경험 용법에서 해 본 적이 없었다는 의미를 나타낸다.

① '전에 읽은 적이 있다'는 의미로, 현재완료의 경험 용법이다. before는 경험 용법에서 자주 쓰이는 단어이다.

③ '두 번 만난 적이 있다'라는 경험을 나타내는 용법이다. twice와 같은 배수사는 경험 용법에서 쓰여, 경험의 횟수를 나타낸다.

② '벌써 했다'라는 의미로, 현재완료의 완료 용법이다. already는 '이미'라는 뜻으로 완료 용법에서 자주 쓰인다.

④ '세차했다'라는 뜻으로, 이미 세차했다는 완료된 사건에 대해 이야기하므로, 현재완료의 완료 용법이다. just는 현재완료의 완료 용법에서 자주 쓰인다.

⑤ '살아왔다'는 의미로, 계속되고 있는 사건에 대해 이야기하므로, 현재완료의 계속 용법이다. for은 현재완료의 계속 용법에서 사건이 일어나 지속된 시간의 길이를 나타낸다.

29 그녀가 20분 전부터 지금까지 계속 버스를 기다리고 있다는 것을 표현하기 위해 현재완료 진행시제(have/has+been+-ing)를 써야 한다. 주어 She에 동사의

수를 일치시킨다.

② 사건이 일어나 지속된 시간을 나타내기 위해서는 시간의 길이를 나타내는 단어 앞에 for을 쓰고 ago 는 삭제해야 한다.

30 ④ 현재완료는 「have+과거분사」로 쓴다. (stole → stolen)

31 ⓑ last year은 과거의 특정한 때를 나타내는 부사구로, 과거시제와 함께 쓰여야 한다. (has visited → visited)

ⓓ in 2018은 과거의 특정한 때를 나타낸다. 따라서 과거시제와 함께 쓰여야 한다. (has lived → lived)

ⓐ ever은 '지금까지, 여태껏'이라는 의미로, 현재완료의 경험 용법과 자주 쓰인다.

ⓒ yesterday는 과거의 특정한 때를 나타내는 부사이므로, 과거시제와 함께 쓰여야 한다.

ⓔ six months ago는 과거의 특정한 때를 나타낸다. 따라서 과거시제와 함께 쓰이는 것이 적절하다.

32 문장이 대등한 내용을 연결하는 and로 연결되어 있기 때문에 (가)에 들어갈 동사는 have started와 시제를 일치시켜야 한다. 현재완료 진행 시제이면서 능동의 의미를 나타내는 ③ have been practicing이 오는 것이 적합하다. ②는 현재완료 시제이지만 수동태이기 때문에 의미상 적절하지 않다.

나는 외국어를 배우는 최고의 방법은 그것에 지속적으로 노출되는 것이라고 믿는다. 그래서 나는 내 자신을 가능한 많이 영어에 노출하기로 결정했다. 나는 영어를 듣는 것에 적응하도록 영어 TV 방송을 보기 시작해왔고, 그리고 나는 나의 언어 교환 파트너들과 정기적으로 영어로 말하는 것을 연습해 오고 있는 중이다.

33 ⓐ 능동의 의미를 지닌 현재완료(has struggled)나 현재완료진행(has been struggling)이 적절하다.

ⓒ The use에 수일치 시켜서 has로 고친다.

ⓔ already는 긍정문과 놀람을 나타내는 의문문에 쓴다.

ⓕ 과거를 나타내는 부사구 four days ago가 있으므로 과거시제 met이 적절하다.

34 현재완료 부정문은 「have/has not+과거분사」이다. 두 달 동안 그곳에 가본 적이 없다는 뜻이므로 since(~이후로)가 아닌 for(~동안)가 와야 한다.

35 과거의 특정한 때를 나타내는 부사구가 있으면 과거시제로 쓴다.

① have gone → went

② have you taught → did you teach

③ has met → met

⑤ have been → were

36 ②「be going to+장소」'~로 가고 있다'

37 for(~동안)는 사건이 일어나 지속된 시간의 길이를 나타낸다.

38 (A) 과거에 진행되던 동작이므로 과거진행형을 쓴다.

(B) 명백한 과거를 나타내는 부사구(last week)는 과거시제와 함께 쓰인다.

(C) 현재완료 진행시제는 계속을 의미하므로 '~이후로'의 since가 적합하다.

39 ② Has he ~?에 대한 답은 Yes, he has. 또는 No, he hasn't.가 되어야 한다.

40 오후 두 시부터 눈이 내리기 시작해 현재까지 계속 내리는 중이므로 현재완료 진행시제로 표현한다.

41 (1) 지각동사 saw의 목적어인 the window는 깨어지는 것이므로 과거분사 broken이 와야 한다. (break-broke-broken)

(2) 현재완료 시제이므로 과거분사(spread)를 써야 한다. (spread-spread-spread)

(3) 동사 allowed는 to 부정사를 목적격 보어로 쓰므로 to drive가 와야 한다.

(4) 현재완료 시제이므로 과거분사(forgotten)를 써야 한다. (forget-forgot-forgotten)

(5) 현재완료 시제이므로 과거분사(won)를 써야 한다. (win-won-won)

42 (A) 앞에 현재완료 동사(has made)가 술어로 나오고, 뒤에 과거시제 동사(was)가 나와 '어린 시절 이후로 엄마가 계속 타르트를 만들어주셨다'는 의미를 이루므로 since가 적절하다.

(B) 앞에 현재완료의 have('ve)가 나오므로, (B)에는 과거분사인 eaten이 적절하다.

43 현재완료의 문장은 「have/has+과거분사」로 쓴다. 주어가 복수형이면 have, 3인칭 단수형이면 has를 사용하며, 부정문은 「have/has not+과거분사」로 쓴다.

44 빈칸 앞에 No가 있으므로 빈칸에는 해운대에 가본 적이 없다는 내용이 와야 한다.

45 예정된 계획을 나타내는 be going to, 과거에 시작된 동작이 현재까지 계속되는 현재완료진행 have been+-ing, 미래에 대한 의지를 나타내는 will이 필요하다.

PRACTICE 1

1 ①	2 ②	3 ①	4 ②	5 ②
6 ①	7 ③	8 ③	9 ①	10 ②
11 ③	12 ②	13 ③	14 ②	15 ②

1, 2, 3, 5, 6, 7, 8, 10, 11, 12, 13 조동사 뒤에는 동사원형이 와야 한다.
4, 15 주어가 3인칭 단수면 동사도 3인칭 단수 동사가 온다.
9 two weeks ago라는 명백한 과거를 나타내는 시간부사구가 있으므로 과거 시제를 써야 한다.
14 강조의 does 뒤에는 동사원형을 써야 한다.

PRACTICE 2

2   I cannot[can't] wait to meet them.
3   You may not play the computer game now.
4   You must not[mustn't] break your promise.
5   You had better not['d better not] go on a diet.
6   It might not[mightn't] be safe to do so.
7   I could not[couldn't] get to the office early.
8   You had better not['d better not] bring your kids.
9   I will not[won't] bring it to you.
10   You should not[shouldn't] hang it on the wall.
11   I did not use to[didn't use to/used not to] play the guitar.
12   She could not[couldn't] finish the work on time.
13   I do not[don't] clean my room every Saturday.
14   They should not[shouldn't] wear their hats.
15   You must not[mustn't] cross the street now.

5, 8 had better의 부정형은 had better 뒤에 not을 붙인다.
11 used to의 부정형은 didn't use to 또는 used not to라고 쓴다. 후자는 격식체에서 주로 사용한다.

PRACTICE 3

2   Will Dave play basketball?
3   Should Jihye take the first train?
4   Can he drive a car?
5   Should I give him my notebook?
6   Will he teach English at a middle school?
7   Can Mike speak five languages?
8   Will she take art classes in Italy?

9   Can I order some food?
10   Can they make Chinese dishes?

1~10 조동사로 시작하는 의문문은 「조동사+주어+동사원형 ~?」의 어순으로 쓴다.

PRACTICE 4

1 have	2 must	3 must
4 have	5 have	6 must
7 have	8 must	9 had
10 has		

1 'to+동사원형'과 함께 '~해야 한다'는 의무를 나타내는 have가 알맞다. Did로 시작되는 의문문이므로 과거동사 had는 올 수 없다.
2, 3, 6, 8 바로 뒤의 동사원형과 함께 '~해야 한다'라는 의무를 나타내야 하므로 조동사 must가 알맞다.
4 'to+동사원형'과 함께 '~해야 한다'는 의무를 나타내야 하고, 현재를 나타내는 부사(now)가 있으므로 have가 알맞다.
5, 7 조동사 will과 must가 나란히 올 수 없다. 'to+동사원형'과 함께 사용되면서 must처럼 의무를 나타내는 have가 알맞다.
9 과거를 나타내는 부사구 last night이 있으므로 '~해야 했다'라는 의미로 과거의 의무를 나타내는 had to의 had가 알맞다.
10 'to+동사원형'과 함께 '~해야 한다'는 의무를 나타내야 하고, 주어가 3인칭 단수이므로 has가 알맞다.

PRACTICE 5

1 have to[will have to]	2 had to
3 have to[will have to]	4 have to
5 has to[will have to]	6 had to
7 has to[will have to]	8 has to[will have to]
9 had to	10 have to[will have to]

1, 3, 10 의미상 현재 또는 미래의 의무를 나타내는 표현이 적합하므로 have to 또는 will have to가 알맞다.
2, 6, 9 기준 시점이 과거인 경우(when she was young)이거나 과거를 나타내는 부사구(last Friday, yesterday)가 있으므로 '~해야 했다'라는 의미로 과거의 의무를 나타내는 had to가 알맞다.
4 현재를 나타내는 부사 now가 있으므로 현재의 의무를 나타내는 have to가 알맞다.
5, 7, 8 의미상 현재 또는 미래의 의무를 나타내는 표현이 적합한데, 주어가 3인칭 단수이므로 has to 또는 will have to가 알맞다.

PRACTICE 6

1 must	2 can't	3 must	4 must
5 can't	6 can't	7 must	8 can't
9 must	10 can't		

PRACTICE 7

1 must not   **2** don't have to
3 don't have to   **4** must not
5 don't have to   **6** must not

PRACTICE 8

2 were able to   **3** am able to
4 wasn't able to   **5** Aren't, able to
6 won't be able to[isn't able to]
7 was able to   **8** weren't able to
9 will be able to[are able to]
10 is able to

PRACTICE 9

2 추측   **3** 능력   **4** 능력
5 추측   **6** 요청   **7** 능력
8 요청   **9** 허가   **10** 능력
11 허가   **12** 허가

PRACTICE 10

1 Do   **2** does   **3** does   **4** did
5 does   **6** Do   **7** does   **8** do
9 don't   **10** did

PRACTICE 11

1 must be
2 doesn't have to[doesn't need to/need not] give
3 will have to take
4 does like
5 can't[cannot] fail

PRACTICE 12

1 You should not talk to your parents like that.
2 Should I go there again?
3 We should be polite to our teachers.
4 Jenny should not forget the truth.
5 I should apologize to her.

1, 4 should not+동사원형: ~해서는 안 된다
2 Should I+동사원형 ~?: 제가 ~해야 하나요?
3, 5 should+동사원형: ~해야 한다

PRACTICE 13

2 He'd better get　　3 We'd better go
4 You'd better study　　5 You'd better not drive

1~5 조동사 had better는 일상 대화에서 보통 축약형「'd better」로 사용된다. 부정형은「'd better not」으로 '~하지 않는 편이 낫다'는 뜻이다

PRACTICE 14

1 Would　　2 Will　　3 Would
4 Can　　5 Would　　6 Can
7 Will　　8 Would　　9 Could
10 Do　　11 Would　　12 Could
13 Will　　14 Would　　15 Will

1, 11, 14 상대에게 음식 등을 권할 때「Would you like+명사?」로 표현할 수 있다.
2, 7, 13, 15 Will/Would you ~?는 '~해주시겠습니까?'라는 뜻으로, 상대에게 요청/부탁을 할 때 쓰는 표현이다.
3, 5, 8 Would you like to+동사원형 ~?는 '~하시겠습니까?'라는 뜻으로, 상대에게 무언가를 제안할 때 쓰는 표현이다.
4, 6, 12 Can/Could I ~?는 '제가 ~해도 되겠습니까?'라는 뜻으로, 상대에게 허락을 구할 때 쓰는 표현이다.
9 Could you ~?는 '~해주시겠습니까?'라는 뜻으로, 상대에게 요청/부탁을 할 때 쓰는 표현이다.
10 '당신의 새 차가 마음에 드나요?'라고 묻는 일반동사의 의문문이므로 Do가 알맞다.

PRACTICE 15

2 may feel　　3 may not know
4 may come　　5 may not want
6 may work

2, 4, 6 조동사 may는 '~일지도 모른다, 아마 ~일 것이다'라는 뜻으로 약한 추측을 나타낼 때 쓴다.
3 민수가 나의 이름을 부르지 않는 이유로는 '네 이름을 알지 못할 수도 있다.'가 적절하므로 부정형(may not know)으로 쓴다.
5 Tom이 전화를 받지 않는 이유로 '누구와도 대화하기를 원하지 않을 수도 있어.'가 적절하므로 부정형(may not want)으로 쓴다.

PRACTICE 16

1 May　　2 might　　3 Will
4 did　　5 must not　　6 Can

7 have to　　8 Would　　9 be able to
10 May　　11 Would

1, 10 상대방에게 허락을 구하는 상황이므로 '~해도 될까요?'라는 뜻의 May I ~? 구문이 알맞다.
2 'Jane이 아플지도 모른다'라는 뜻이 되도록 약한 추측을 나타낼 때 쓰는 조동사 might가 알맞다.
3 상대방에게 부탁하는 상황이므로 '~해주시겠어요?'라는 의미로 쓰는 Will you ~? 구문이 알맞다.
4 동사를 강조하기 위해 do를 쓸 수 있는데, 여기서는 주어가 He이므로 did가 알맞다. 이때 원래의 동사는 원형으로 써야 한다.
5 허락을 구하는 말에 거절하는 상황이므로 '~하면 안 된다'는 뜻의 must not이 알맞다.
6 상대에게 부탁하는 상황이므로 '~해주시겠습니까?'라는 뜻으로 쓰이는 Can you ~? 구문이 알맞다.
7 시험에 대비해 열심히 공부해야 한다는 내용이므로 '~해야 한다'는 의미로 의무를 나타낼 때 쓰는 have to가 알맞다.
8, 11 '~하시겠어요?'라고 상대방에게 무언가를 제안하거나 권하는 상황이므로 Would you like (to) ~? 구문이 알맞다.
9 '~할 수 있을 것이다'라는 미래의 능력을 나타낼 때는 will과 can을 함께 사용할 수 없으므로 can을 대신하여 will be able to를 쓴다.

PRACTICE 17

2 used to have　　3 used to own
4 used to[would] play　　5 used to[would] ride
6 used to live

1, 2, 3, 6 과거의 상태에 대해 '과거에는 ~한 상태였지만 지금은 아니다'라고 할 때는 used to를 쓴다. 이 경우에는 과거의 행위에 대한 것이 아니므로 would를 쓰지 않는다.
4, 5 과거에 반복적으로 일어났으나 지금은 더 이상 이뤄지지 않는 행위를 나타내고 있으므로 '~하곤 했다'의 의미의 used to나 would를 쓴다.

PRACTICE 18

1 am used to doing yoga
2 were used to plant
3 used to go to bed
4 were used to carry
5 is not[isn't] used to driving
6 are used to volunteering
7 is used to make chocolate
8 used to be chubby
9 is used to waking up
10 used to be afraid of

1, 5, 6, 9 '~하는 데 익숙하다'는「be used to+ -ing」로 나타낸다.
2, 4, 7 '~하는 데 사용되다'는「be used to+동사원형」으로 나타낸다.
3, 8, 10 '~하곤 했다'는「used to+동사원형」으로 나타낸다.

📑 중간·기말고사 대비문제 **정답** 본문 _ p.89

1 ④ **2** ② **3** ③ **4** ⑤ **5** ④ **6** ① **7** ①,⑤
8 ④ **9** ① **10** ② **11** ⑤ **12** ④ **13** There must be another way to solve this problem.
14 ④ **15** ④ **16** ② **17** I used to work at a restaurant near my house **18** ③ **19** ⑤
20 ⑤ **21** ④ **22** (1) You had better[You'd better] take some medicine. (2) You had better[You'd better] go to bed earlier. (3) She had better[She'd better] check the Lost and Found. **23** ⑤ **24** You had better not go out tonight. **25** ④ **26** ② **27** ②,③ **28** ②
29 Could you give[hand/pass] me the tape?
30 ③ **31** ①,③ **32** ③ **33** (1) was not able to (2) were able to **34** will be able to
35 should not turn right

중간·기말고사 대비문제 **해설**

1 ④ 'Shouldn't you~?'는 '너 ~해야 하지 않아?'라는 의미의 질문이므로 대답은 you가 아닌 I로 해야 한다. 여기서 should는 의무를 나타낸다.
①② could/can과 may는 허가의 의미를 가지며 의문문으로 써서 허락을 구하는 질문(~해도 될까요?)을 만들 수 있다. 이때 대답은 긍정(해도 된다)과 부정(하면 안 된다)의 두 가지가 나올 수 있다.
⑤ can은 '~해 주시겠어요?'라는 요청의 의미를 지니며 Can you give me a hand?는 '도와주시겠어요?'라는 의미이다.

2 '~해 주시겠어요?'라는 표현은 Would[Will] you~?로 쓴다. lend는 '(~을) 빌려주다'라는 뜻이고, borrow는 '(~을) 빌리다'라는 뜻이다.

3 ③ '~임에 틀림없다' ①②④⑤ '~해야 한다'

4 ⑤ 미래에 일어날 동작을 예측하는 것이므로, 미래시제를 쓰는 것이 알맞다.
① 「Here is/are ~」은 뒤에 나오는 명사에 수를 일치시킨다. Donna's plan이 단수 명사구이므로, 동사 또한 단수 동사 is로 써야 한다. (are → is)
② 등위 접속사 and로 인해, 밑줄 친 부분은 vacuum과 병렬구조를 이루고 있다. vacuum은 조동사 다음에 와서 동사원형 형태이므로, wipe도 동사원형이 되어야 한다. (wipes → wipe)

③ want는 목적격 보어로 to부정사를 쓰는 동사이다. (spending → to spend)
④ if처럼 조건을 나타내는 접속사가 쓰인 조건의 부사절에서는 현재시제로 미래를 나타낸다. (will be → is)

5 ⓐ used to는 '~하곤 했다'는 의미의 조동사로, 뒤에 동사원형을 쓴다. (living → live)
ⓑ actress를 설명해주는 관계대명사절에서, 주격 관계대명사는 생략할 수 없다. 선행사가 사람이기 때문에, 주격 관계대명사인 who를 써야 한다. (was → who was)
ⓓ 조동사는 현재시제의 3인칭 단수형으로 쓰지 않는다. (musts → must)
ⓖ want는 to부정사를 목적격 보어로 쓰는 동사이다. (attend → to attend)
ⓒ 의문사가 없는 간접의문문은 「if + 주어 + 동사」의 어순으로 쓴다.
ⓔ 현재의 사실이나 상태를 나타내므로, 현재시제로 써주어야 하고, 주어 Penny가 3인칭 단수이므로 동사에 -s를 붙여야 한다.
ⓕ stop은 동명사를 목적어로 쓰는 동사이다.

6 문맥상 can의 과거형 could가 알맞다.

7 ② '주말마다 축구를 하곤 했다'는 뜻이므로 「used to + 동사원형」으로 나타낸다. (playing →play)
③ '고기를 먹곤 했다'는 뜻이므로 「used to + 동사원형」으로 나타낸다. (is used to → used to)
④ '그리는(칠하는) 데 사용되다'라는 뜻이므로 「be used to + 동사원형」으로 나타낸다. (painting → paint)

8 「used to + 동사원형」 (과거에) ~하곤 했다'

9 ① must의 부정형은 must not으로 쓴다. (doesn't must → must not)

10 ② 일반동사 do ①③④⑤ 동사를 강조하는 역할의 do

11 ⑤ knows → know

12 종속절(because ~)의 내용으로 보아 should not이 적절하다.

13 '~가 있다'라는 의미를 가진 「There is/are ~」를 활용한다. '~임에 틀림없다'는 강한 추측은 조동사 must를 활용해 나타낸다. '해결할 다른 방법'이라는 부분은 to부정사의 형용사적 용법을 사용해 명사(another way)를 뒤에서 수식해준다.

14 close, need, enjoy는 모두 동사이다. 동사의 의문문과 부정문에 쓰이며, 동사를 강조하는 역할을 하는 조

동사는 do이다.

15 제주도에 이미 가본 적이 있는 A가 거기서 할 수 있는 활동을 추천하는 상황이므로 shouldn't(~하지 않는 게 좋다)가 아닌 should(~하는 게 좋다)를 사용하여 추천, 제안을 나타내는 것이 적절하다.

16 ② 동사를 강조하는 do　①⑤ 일반동사 do
③ 동사의 반복을 피하는 대동사 do
④ 의문문에 쓰이는 do

17 현재는 더 이상 하지 않는 과거의 동작이나 상태는 used to로 나타낸다.

18 ③ had better는 '~하는 게 낫다'라는 의미의 조동사이고, would like to는 '~하고 싶다'라는 뜻이므로 서로 바꿔 쓸 수 없다.
① don't have to는 불필요의 의미를 나타내며 need not으로 바꿔 쓸 수 있다.
② 과거의 습관적인 행위(~하곤 했다)를 나타내는 used to는 would로 바꿔 쓸 수 있다.
④ 능력/가능을 의미하는 can은 be able to로 바꿔 쓸 수 있다.
⑤ 'Would you~?'가 '~해 주시겠습니까?'라는 요청의 의미로 쓰였을 때 'Could you~?'로 바꿔 쓸 수 있다.

19 대화의 내용에 따르면 해당 좌석은 몸이 불편한 분들을 위한 것이므로 빈칸에는 '우리는 여기에 앉으면 안 된다.'는 금지의 내용이 들어가야 한다. ⑤ don't have to는 불필요를 의미하므로 빈칸에 들어가기에 적절하지 않다.

20 ⓐⓑⓒⓓ 규칙에 대하여 설명하므로 '~해야 한다'라는 의무나 당위를 나타내는 조동사 must나 should가 들어가야 한다.
ⓔ 규칙을 어기면 일어날 일에 대해서 설명하므로 미래의 일에 대한 가능성이나 추측을 나타내는 조동사 can[could], may[might], will[would]이 들어가야 한다.

21 앞에 나온 cries의 반복을 피하기 위한 대동사로 do의 3인칭 단수형인 does가 적절하다.

22 「had better+동사원형」'~하는 게 낫다'

23 ⑤ why don't you + 동사원형?: ~ 하는 게 어때?
will be able to + 동사원형: ~ 할 수 있을 것이다.
① like는 to부정사 또는 동명사를 목적어로 취한다.
(read → to read[reading])
② would like to + 동사원형: ~하고 싶다
(having → have)
③ 조동사 might 뒤에는 동사원형이 와야 한다.

(looks → look)
④ 등위접속사 and가 where절에 있는 두 개의 동사, talk와 watch를 연결하고 있다. talk 앞에 조동사 can이 있으므로 watch 앞에도 조동사 can이 생략된 것으로 보는 것이 적절하다. 따라서 watching을 watch로 고쳐야 한다.
(watching → watch)

24 had better의 부정문은 「had better not+동사원형」의 어순으로 쓴다.

25 호텔 안에 반려동물을 데려오는 것이 허가되지 않은 것이므로 불필요(don't have to: ~할 필요 없다)를 나타내는 대답은 적절하지 못하다.

26 동사구의 반복을 피하는 대동사 did

27 긍정이면 Yes, you may.로, 부정이면 No, you may not[must not, can't].로 대답한다.

28 would like to = want to '~하고 싶어하다, ~하기를 원하다'

29 4형식 형태에 맞춰 '간접목적어(사람)+직접목적어(사물)' 어순으로 써야 한다. 테이프를 건네 줄 수 있는지 Could를 사용해 묻는 상황이므로 Could you give me the tape?로 작성하는 것이 적절하다.

Emma는 교실 벽에 큰 포스터를 걸려고 애쓰고 있다. 그녀는 두 손으로 포스터를 붙잡고 있어서 테이프가 (손에) 닿지 않는다. 그녀는 누군가가 그녀에게 그것을 건네주길 원한다. 그때 그녀의 반 친구 Carl이 들어와서 "내가 도와줄까?"라고 말한다.

30 because가 이끄는 절의 주어인 I 뒤에 am이 있으므로 be able to의 형태가 되어야 한다.

31 '옷을 고르는 것을 도와주시겠어요?'라고 물었으므로 ① '너는 그녀를 위한 드레스를 살 거야.', ③ '너는 Priya를 너의 파티에 초대하는 것이 낫겠어.'는 대답으로 적절하지 않다.

32 had better은 뒤에 동사원형이 온다. 부정형은 had better not으로 쓴다.
ⓐ I'd not better → I'd better not
ⓒ to answer → answer
ⓓ to bring → bring

33 be able to는 '~할 수 있다'라는 뜻이며, 이때 be는 주어의 인칭과 수, 시제에 따라 변한다. 부정문은 be동사 뒤에 not을 써서 표현한다.

34 '능력'을 뜻하는 조동사 can의 미래형은 will be able to로 쓴다.

35 우회전을 하지 말라는 표지판이므로, should not으로 금지를 나타낸다.

PRACTICE 1

2	read	**3**	stolen	**4**	sung
5	made	**6**	broken	**7**	caught
8	taught	**9**	written	**10**	spoken
11	grown	**12**	fed	**13**	taken
14	kept				

PRACTICE 2

2 I am loved by my friends.

3 The Mona Lisa was painted by Leonardo da Vinci.

4 Plastic bottles are recycled by them.

5 Those black pants were bought by me.

6 Those cookies were made by my mom.

7 A lot of books are read by him.

8 All the classmates were invited to the party by Jason.

9 Thieves are caught by the police.

10 The news was reported by Harry.

11 Stamps and coins are collected by Mrs. Lopez.

12 Two black bears were killed by the hunter.

13 The bus was stopped by the police officer.

14 The meeting was held by Mr. Kim.

15 The rules of the meeting were changed by the president.

> **2~15** 능동태 문장의 목적어를 수동태 문장의 주어로 하고, 능동태 문장의 동사를 「be동사+과거분사」의 형태로 바꾼 다음, 능동태 문장의 주어를 「by+목적격」으로 바꾼다.

PRACTICE 3

2 The cookies weren't made by my mother.

3 English isn't spoken by some people in Japan.

4 Was he grounded for a week?

5 Was that book written by him?

6 Shakespeare didn't write that play.

7 The elderly aren't respected by some students.

8 Is Frank loved by his classmates?

9 Yuri didn't pay the bill.

10 Was the stray cat fed by Jake?

> **2, 3, 7** 수동태의 부정문은 「주어+be동사+not+과거분사+by+목적격」의 어순으로 쓴다.
> **4, 5, 8, 10** 수동태의 의문문은 「be동사+주어+과거분사+by+목적격?」의 어순으로 쓴다.
> **6, 9** 수동태 부정문을 능동태로 전환하면 「be동사+not+과거분사」 부분이 「don't/doesn't/didn't+동사원형」이 된다.
> **9** pay the bill: 요금을 지불하다, 대금을 치르다

PRACTICE 4

2 The magazine will be delivered by the man.

3 The room will be cleaned later (by somebody).

4 A new restaurant has been built by Roger.

5 More trees will be cut down in the future (by people).

6 His lies have been believed (by everyone).

7 Movies or TV programs are made by directors.

8 The car was fixed this morning by Tom.

9 This building has been built for three years by the people.

10 The money will be used to buy a new game character by him.

> **2, 3, 5, 10** 미래시제의 수동태에서는 동사가 「will be+과거분사」의 형태이다.
> **4, 6, 9** 현재완료시제의 수동태에서는 동사가 「have/has been+과거분사」의 형태이다.
> **7** 현재시제의 수동태에서는 동사가 「am/are/is+과거분사」의 형태이다.
> **8** 과거시제의 수동태에서는 동사가 「was/were+과거분사」의 형태이다.

PRACTICE 5

1	was invented	**2**	was moved
3	will be done	**4**	was painted
5	has been polluted		

> **1** 과거의 특정 연도(1879)가 있으므로 과거시제 수동태가 알맞다.
> **2, 4** 과거를 나타내는 부사(구) yesterday, last week가 있으므로 과거시제 수동태가 알맞다.
> **3** 미래를 나타내는 부사구 next Friday가 있으므로 미래시제 수동태가 알맞다.
> **5** '~ 이후로'라는 의미의 「since+시점」 표현이 있으므로 현재완료시제 수동태가 알맞다.

PRACTICE 6

2 It may be done tomorrow by Tony.

3 The problem must be solved by him.

4 The rules for this game should be obeyed by them.

5 The plans for the summer might be changed by us.

6 Dinner couldn't[could not] be prepared last night by me.

7 A computer must be used for this task by Suji.

8 They should not[shouldn't] be put here by us.

9 The promise may not be kept by Tom.

10 The view could be seen very well by the people.

> **2~10** 조동사가 있는 문장을 수동태로 바꿀 때는 「주어+조동사 +be동사원형+과거분사+by+목적격」 순으로 쓴다.

PRACTICE 7

1 should be washed **2** can be saved

3 will be cooked **4** must be painted

5 will be loved

> 각 문장을 능동태로 표현하면 다음과 같다.
> **1** You should wash your clothes soon.
> **2** You can save a lot of resources.
> **3** Paul will cook them.
> **4** You must paint this house by tomorrow.
> **5** I will love my dog forever.

PRACTICE 8

1 A new bag was bought for the boy by Mr. Kim.

2 My brother was made angry by me.

3 He was elected the president by them.

4 Bob was shown their pictures by them.
  Their pictures were shown to Bob by them.

5 I was given lovely flowers by Nick.
  Lovely flowers were given to me by Nick.

6 The place was kept clean by Jenny.

7 The fish was named "Wish" by my daughter.

8 The restaurant is called George's (by people).

9 Spaghetti was cooked for me yesterday by my mom.

10 I was lent 5,000 won yesterday by Minho.

5,000 won was lent to me yesterday by Minho.

> **1, 9** buy, cook은 직접목적어만을 수동태의 주어로 하는 동사들이다. 직접목적어가 수동태의 주어가 될 때는 간접목적어 앞에 전치사 for이 온다.
>
> **4, 5, 10** 4형식 문장이므로 간접목적어와 직접목적어 둘 다 수동태의 주어가 될 수 있지만, 직접목적어가 수동태의 주어가 될 때는 간접목적어 앞에 to, for, of와 같은 전치사가 온다.
>
> **2, 3, 6, 7, 8** 5형식 문장을 수동태 문장으로 바꿀 때, 목적격 보어가 명사나 형용사인 경우에는 「be동사+과거분사」 뒤에 목적격 보어를 이어서 쓴다.
>
> **1** buy A B: A에게 B를 사주다 (4형식)
> = B be bought for A
> **2** make A B: A를 B하게 만들다 (5형식)
> = A be made B
> **3** elect A B: A를 B로 선출하다 (5형식)
> = A be elected B
> **4** show A B: A에게 B를 보여주다 (4형식)
> = A be shown B
> = B be shown to A
> **5** give A B: A에게 B를 주다 (4형식)
> = A be given B
> = B be given to A
> **6** keep A B: A를 B한 상태로 유지하다 (5형식)
> = A be kept B
> **7** name A B: A를 B라고 이름을 짓다 (5형식)
> = A be named B
> **8** call A B: A를 B로 부르다 (5형식)
> = A be called B
> **9** cook A B: A에게 B를 요리해주다 (4형식)
> = B be cooked for A
> **10** lend A B: A에게 B를 빌려주다 (4형식)
> = A be lent B
> = B be lent to A

PRACTICE 9

1 with **2** in **3** about

4 to **5** with[about] **6** about

7 from **8** with **9** at

10 with **11** from **12** for

PRACTICE 10

1 The president was welcomed by the crowd.

2 The work could be finished easily by me.

3 Science will be taught by Mr. Song.

4 The movie was watched by millions of people.

5 The living room and the bathroom are cleaned by my kids.

6 The party has been postponed by Susan.

7 We were given some information by John.
  Some information was given to us by John.

8 A pretty skirt was bought for me by my grandmother.

9 I am called Jen by Alex.

10 I was asked some difficult questions by my son. Some difficult questions were asked of me by my son.

11 The photocopier can be fixed by Mike.

12 This wall wasn't painted by Cathy.

13 Bill must be invited to the show by you.

14 We were made bored by his story.

15 I was paid 30,000 won by Seho. 30,000 won was paid to me by Seho.

16 The Internet can be used for our homework by us.

17 His cat was named Rachael by him.

18 Sandwiches were made for me by him.

1, 4 과거시제의 수동태는 「주어+was/were+과거분사+by+목적격」 순으로 쓴다.

2, 3, 11, 13, 16 조동사가 있는 수동태는 「주어+조동사+be동사 원형+과거분사+by+목적격」 순으로 쓴다.

5 현재시제의 수동태는 「주어+am/are/is+과거분사+by+목적격」 순으로 쓴다. 주어의 the living room과 the bathroom이 접속사 and로 연결되어 복수 취급한다.

6 현재완료시제의 수동태는 「주어+have/has been+과거분사 +by+목적격」 순으로 쓴다.

7, 10, 15 4형식 문장의 수동태는 능동태의 간접목적어나 직접목적어가 주어가 되는데, 직접목적어가 주어가 될 때는 간접목적어 앞에 to, for, of 같은 전치사가 온다.

8, 18 buy와 make는 목적어가 2개인 4형식 문장을 만드는 동사지만, 사람(간접목적어)이 주어인 수동태 문장은 의미상 어색하기 때문에 쓰이지 않는다. 따라서 수동태의 주어로 직접목적어만 허용된다.

9, 14, 17 목적격 보어가 명사나 형용사인 5형식 문장의 수동태는 「be동사+과거분사」 뒤에 목적격 보어를 이어서 쓴다.

12 과거시제 수동태의 부정문은 「주어+was/were+not+과거분사+by+목적격」 순으로 쓴다.

📝 중간·기말고사 대비문제 정답 본문 _ p.108

1 ③ **2** ③ **3** ②,⑤ **4** ④ **5** ③ **6** ①

7 Rice noodles were cooked for his friends by him. **8** ③ **9** ⑤ **10** ④ **11** of **12** ②

13 was constructed, is held **14** ④ **15** was covered with **16** ② **17** ②,④ **18** ②

19 (1) A lot of time will be given to you by me. [You will be given a lot of time by me.] (2) My car has been stolen (by someone).

(3) The mystery can be explained by them.

20 ④ **21** ⑤ **22** ②,⑤ **23** ⑤ **24** (A) was stolen (B) were saved **25** ② **26** made of **27** ④ **28** ⑤ **29** ② **30** ② **31** All the plants have been watered by us. **32** This cup is filled with water. **33** ④ **34** It was fought between North Korea and South Korea **35** ② **36** ④ **37** was kept clean by her **38** ⑤ **39** were killed **40** ⓐ are known ⓑ are trained ⓒ happiness **41** (1) with (2) of (3) about **42** will be saved by this medicine

중간·기말고사 대비문제 해설

1 ③ → Our grandmother has the red car. '가지다, 소유하다'라는 뜻의 have는 수동태 문장으로 만들 수 없다.

2 수동태는 「be동사 + 과거분사」로 쓴다. (b) sing → sung   (c) cook → cooked (f) broke → broken   (i) eat → eaten (j) 주어(The test papers)가 복수형이므로 동사 또한 이에 맞춰 are을 써야 한다. (is → are)

3 수동태는 「be동사+과거분사」로 쓴다. ② teached → taught   ⑤ wrote → written

4 be interested in '~에 흥미가 있다'

5 ① 수동태는 「be동사+과거분사」의 형태이다. (was catch → was caught) ② 도둑이 훔친 것이므로 능동태를 쓴다. (was stolen → stole) ④ 경찰이 본 것이므로 능동태를 쓴다. (was seen → saw) ⑤ 수동태는 「be동사+과거분사」의 형태이다. (was arrest → was arrested)

6 ② 조동사가 포함된 수동태는 「조동사+be동사+과거분사」로 쓴다. (prepared → be prepared) ③ 수동태는 「be동사+과거분사」로 쓴다. (made → are[were] made) ④ 주어 This novel이 단수이므로 be동사는 was로 쓴다. (were written → was written) ⑤ 'by Ms. Pierce(Pierce 선생님에 의해서)'의 표현으로 보아 주어인 They는 가르침을 받아온 것이므로 현재완료 수동태 표현으로 고쳐야 한다. (have taught → have been taught)

7 4형식 동사 cook은 직접목적어를 주어로 삼아 수동태로 쓸 때 「직접목적어+be cooked+for+간접목적어」의 형태로 쓴다.

8 ③ 주어가 3인칭 단수(My friend)인데 동사 read에 -s가 없으므로 read가 과거시제로 쓰였음을 알 수 있다. 따라서 수동태로 전환한 문장 또한 과거시제여야 한다. (is read → was read)

9 ⓐ '가방이 금화로 가득 차 있다'는 의미이므로 빈칸에는 '~로 가득 찬'을 의미하는 'be filled with'가 들어가야 한다. (be filled with = be full of)
ⓑ '~이래로'를 의미하는 since는 현재완료시제와 주로 쓰여 특정 시점 이후로 계속되었음을 나타내므로 has been built가 적절하다.
ⓒ 주어(The result of the game)가 사람이 아니기 때문에 '만족감을 느꼈다'는 의미의 'was satisfied'는 적절하지 않다. '경기의 결과가 학생들을 만족시켰다.'는 뜻이므로 satisfied가 들어가야 한다.

10 (D) be interested in '~에 흥미가 있다'
(learning → in learning)
(A) -thing로 끝나는 대명사는 형용사가 뒤에서 수식한다.
(B) try+동명사는 '(시험 삼아) ~ 해보다'라는 뜻이다. try의 목적어로 부정사가 올 경우 '~하려고 노력하다, 애쓰다'라는 뜻이 된다.
(C) start는 동명사와 부정사를 모두 목적어로 가질 수 있다.
(E) 간접의문문의 어순은 「의문사+주어+ 동사」로 나타낸다.

11 4형식 문장의 직접목적어가 수동태의 주어가 될 때는 간접목적어 앞에 전치사를 쓴다. 동사 ask의 간접목적어 앞에는 전치사 of가 온다.

12 수동태의 시제가 과거이므로 능동태도 과거시제가 되어야 한다.

13 • '건설되었다'는 과거시제 수동태이므로 was constructed가 적절하다.
• 월드컵이 4년마다 개최되는 것은 반복되는 사실이므로 현재시제 수동태를 써서 is held가 적절하다.

14 ⓓ 현재완료시제의 수동태는 「have+been+과거분사」로 쓴다.
(have being washed → have been washed)
ⓔ 수동태는 「be동사+과거분사」로 쓴다. choose의 과거분사는 chosen이다. (chose → chosen)

15 be covered with '~로 덮여 있다'

16 (A) be동사가 포함된 문장의 부정문은 be동사 뒤에 not을 사용하여 쓴다.
(B) be동사가 포함된 문장의 의문문은 「Be동사+주어 ~?」의 형태로 쓴다.

17 ①③⑤ 타동사 resemble, 자동사 disappear, 타동사 suit 등은 수동태 문장으로 만들 수 없다.

18 수동태의 부정문은 「주어+be동사+not+과거분사」의 어순이므로 ②는 The school was not built in 2011.이 되어야 한다.

19 (1), (3) 「조동사+(not)+be+과거분사」
(2) 「have[has]+been+과거분사」
행위 주체가 someone, anyone 등일 때 'by+목적격'은 생략이 가능하다.

20 ④ → Spaghetti with cream sauce was made for him by his wife.
4형식 동사 make는 직접목적어만을 수동태의 주어로 취한다.

21 ⑥ 방이 매일 아침 청소가 되어지는 것이므로 수동대를 사용해야 한다. (cleaning → cleaned)

22 ① 집이 지어진 것이므로 수동태를 사용해야 한다. (built → was built)
③ 수동태는 「be동사+과거분사」로 쓴다. (calls → is called)
④ 과거 시제를 써서 질문했으므로 대답도 과거 시제로 해야 한다. (is caught → was caught)

23 ⑤ 동사 buy는 간접목적어가 주어로 나올 수 없는 동사로 직접목적어인 a toy car가 주어로 나온 문장으로 적절하다.
① 불규칙 동사 cut은 원형, 과거형, 과거분사형이 같다. (cutted → cut)
② 5형식의 수동태 문장으로 시제가 과거이므로 is가 아닌 was가 적절하다. (is → was)
③ '발견하다'의 의미를 지닌 동사 find의 과거분사는 found이다. '설립하다'의 의미를 지닌 found의 과거분사가 founded이다. (founded → found)
④ 4형식 문장의 직접목적어가 주어로 온 수동태 문장이다. 동사 make는 간접목적어 앞에 전치사 for를 쓴다. (to → for)

24 (A) steal-stole-stolen   (B) save-saved-saved

25 ② 주어 The cookies가 복수이므로 be동사는 were을 사용한다. (was baked → were baked)

26 be made of '~로 만들어지다'(물리적 변화)

27 ④ 5형식 문장을 수동태로 전환할 때 목적격 보어는 「be동사＋과거분사」 뒤에 그대로 쓴다. (be happy → happy)

28 ⑤ 4형식 문장을 3형식으로 고칠 때, buy는 전치사 for을 수반하는 동사이다. (to her → for her)

29 ② 능동태의 시제가 과거이므로 수동태도 과거로 쓴다. (is sent her → was sent to her)

30 바르게 배열하면 The preparation should be completed by next Friday.가 된다.

31 주어가 3인칭 복수인 현재완료시제의 수동태이므로 「have＋been＋과거분사」의 형태가 되어야 한다.

32 be filled with '~로 가득 차 있다'

33 행위의 주체가 일반인이거나 굳이 말하지 않아도 알 수 있는 경우에는 「by＋목적격」을 생략할 수 있다.

34 우리말 해석이 과거시제이고, 대명사 it이 지칭하는 것이 Korean War이므로 be동사는 3인칭 단수 was를 사용한다.

35 ⓑ 문장의 주어가 The most tragic one으로 단수이기 때문에 was를 쓰는 것이 적절하다. (were → was)

한국은 고대 이래로 수많은 전쟁을 겪어왔다. 그것들 중 가장 비극적인 것은 한국 전쟁이었다. 그것은 일본의 식민 지배가 끝나고 얼마 지나지 않은 1950년부터 1953년까지 북한과 남한 간에 싸워졌다.

그 전쟁은 1950년 6월 25일 북한이 남한을 침략했을 때 시작됐다. 남한은 눈 깜짝할 사이에 부산으로 밀려났다. 그러다 남한이 패배할 지경에 처하자, UN군이 파견되었다. 1951년에 그들은 성공적으로 북한을 물리쳐 38도 선 근처의 위치로 돌려보냈다. 그 전쟁은 2년간 더 계속됐다. 그러고 나서 그것은 북한과 남한을 영구적으로 분리하는 한반도 비무장 지대(DMZ)를 만든 휴전 협정과 함께 끝났다.

36 ④ be satisfied with '~에 만족하다' (to → with)

37 5형식 문장의 목적격 보어인 clean은 수동태로 전환될 때 「be동사＋과거분사」 뒤에 이어서 쓴다.

38 ⑤ 집이 칠해지는 것이므로 수동태를 사용해야 한다. (painting → painted)

39 주어가 3인칭 복수이고 과거의 역사적 사실을 나타내는 과거시제의 수동태이므로 「were＋과거분사」의 형태가 되어야 한다.

40 ⓐ 개들이 '충성스럽고 친근한 동반자'로 알려지는 것이므로 동사를 수동태 형태로 써야 한다. be known for: ~로 알려지다 (are known)

ⓑ 몇몇 개들이 훈련되어지는 것이므로 동사를 수동태 형태로 써야 한다. 주어가 Some dogs로 복수이므로 are을 쓰는 것이 적절하다. (are trained)

ⓒ 동사 bring의 목적어가 들어가는 자리로, 접속사 and의 앞에 명사 joy가 있으므로 동일하게 명사형으로 바꾸어 쓰는 것이 적절하다. (happiness)

개들은 많은 사람들이 사랑하는 멋진 반려동물들이다. 개들은 충성스럽고 친근한 동반자로 알려져 있다. 그들은 (장난감을) 물어오는 놀이, 산책 가기, 그리고 그들의 주인들과 껴안기를 좋아한다. 몇몇 개들은 맹인을 위한 안내견들이나 환자들의 기운을 북돋기 위해 병원을 방문하는 치료견들과 같이 사람들을 돕기 위해 훈련되어진다. 개를 돌보는 것은 그들을 먹이고, 물을 주고, 그들이 아플 때 그들을 수의사에게 데려가는 것을 포함한다. 개들은 사람들의 삶에 많은 즐거움과 행복을 가져다주고 그들은 종종 가족의 일부로 생각된다.

41 (1) be covered with '~로 덮여 있다'

(2) be made of '~로 만들어지다' (물리적 변화)

(3) be worried about '~에 대해 걱정하다'

42 수동태의 미래형은 「will be＋과거분사」로 쓴다.

CHAPTER **5** **명사와 관사**
Nouns and Articles

PRACTICE 1

1 eggs	**2** watches	**11** photos	**12** geese
3 horses	**4** pens	**13** roofs	**14** teeth
5 shoes	**6** glasses	**15** tomatoes	**16** fish/fishes
7 books	**8** dishes	**17** knives	**18** clocks
9 churches	**10** classmates	**19** calves	**20** yourselves
11 bottles	**12** classes	**21** mosquito(e)s	**22** radios
13 girls	**14** cameras	**23** wives	**24** memos
15 buses	**16** months	**25** leaves	**26** deer
17 beaches	**18** boxes	**27** heroes	**28** neighbors
19 neighbors	**20** brushes	**29** blouses	**30** safes
21 houses	**22** places	**31** shelves	**32** feet
23 customs	**24** friends	**33** kangaroos	**34** thieves
25 foxes	**26** matches	**35** studios	**36** chiefs
27 sandwiches	**28** wishes	**37** women	**38** zoos
29 bicycles	**30** animals	**39** pianos	**40** emergencies

16 fish의 일반적인 복수형은 fish로, 물고기 여러 마리를 의미하고, fishes는 여러 종류의 물고기를 가리킬 경우에 쓴다.

PRACTICE 2

1 ladies	**2** stories		
3 keys	**4** parties		
5 diaries	**6** songs		
7 couches	**8** monkeys		
9 babies	**10** activities		
11 cities	**12** donkeys		
13 students	**14** cultures		
15 days	**16** families		
17 boys	**18** habits		
19 ways	**20** factories		
21 hobbies	**22** ferries		
23 candies	**24** computers		
25 benches	**26** countries		
27 memories	**28** doctors		
29 pennies	**30** communities		

PRACTICE 3

1 videos	**2** children
3 wolves	**4** beliefs
5 lives	**6** oxen
7 potatoes	**8** mice
9 sheep	**10** men

PRACTICE 4

1 ○	**2** 앞에 a나 an을 쓰지 않음.
3 ○	**4** ○
5 앞에 a나 an을 쓰지 않음.	**6** ○
7 ○	**8** 앞에 a나 an을 쓰지 않음.
9 ○	**10** ○
11 앞에 a나 an을 쓰지 않음.	**12** ○
13 ○	**14** 앞에 a나 an을 쓰지 않음.
15 ○	

PRACTICE 5

1 books	**2** scientist	**3** dogs
4 hospital	**5** teams	**6** people
7 calendar	**8** was, were	**9** friends
10 are	**11** girl	**12** class
13 families	**14** is, are	**15** building

※ 8번의 family, 14번의 team은 집합체를 하나의 단위로 보아 단수 취급하거나 개별 구성원에 중점을 두어 복수 취급할 수 있음.

(밑줄: 정답의 근거)
1 Lisa bought <u>two</u> **books** for me.
2 The **scientist** <u>was</u> happy to solve the problem.
3 I think your **dogs** <u>are</u> all very cute.
4 There <u>is</u> <u>a</u> **hospital** around the corner.
5 <u>Five</u> **teams** will take part in the contest.
6 They invited more than <u>a hundred</u> **people** to their wedding.
7 I need <u>a</u> **calendar** in my room.
8 My <u>family</u> **was/were** very glad to meet Mr. Park.
9 I met <u>three</u> **friends** of Minsu's yesterday.
10 There **are** eleven <u>classes</u> in my year at school.
11 The brave **girl** never <u>cries</u> in front of others.
12 The **class** <u>is</u> going to go on a picnic.
13 <u>Many</u> **families** in America <u>have</u> pets.
14 My <u>team</u> **is/are** ready to start the game.
15 We found <u>a</u> new **building** in our town.

PRACTICE 6

2	follows	3	countries	4	a car
5	are	6	Leaves[The leaves]		
7	are	8	a[the] bag		
9	a[the] restaurant			10	was

2, 5 2번의 경우 the class를 a unit이라는 하나의 단위로 보았기 때문에 단수 동사 follows가 적절하며, 5번의 경우 the class를 they로 지칭하며 개별 구성원에 중점을 두었기 때문에 복수 동사 are이 알맞다.
3 country는 셀 수 있는 명사이므로 many의 수식을 받으려면 복수형이 되어야 한다.
4, 8, 9 car, bag, restaurant은 셀 수 있는 명사이므로 단수형으로 쓰려면 앞에 관사가 와야 한다.
6 leaf는 셀 수 있는 명사이므로 단수형 또는 복수형으로 모두 쓸 수 있는데, fall이 복수 동사이므로 복수 명사 Leaves[The leaves]로 써야 한다.
7 teeth는 tooth의 복수형이므로 동사가 복수형 are가 되어야 한다.
10 주어가 단수 명사인 the book이므로 단수 동사 was가 알맞다.

PRACTICE 7

1	water	2	Saturday	3	a computer
4	beauty	5	New York	6	happiness
7	air	8	dogs	9	Death
10	A family	11	September	12	salt
13	Christmas	14	paper	15	advice

1, 7, 12, 14 일정한 형태가 없는 물질을 나타내는 물질명사는 a/an의 수식을 받을 수 없으며 복수형으로 쓰지 않는다.
2, 5, 11, 13 사람, 장소, 요일 등을 나타내는 고유명사는 a/an의 수식을 받을 수 없으며 복수형으로 쓰지 않는다.
3, 8 셀 수 있는 명사는 관사와 함께 단수형으로 쓰거나 관사가 없을 때는 반드시 복수형으로 써야 한다.

4, 6, 9, 15 눈에 보이지 않는 개념을 나타내는 추상명사는 a/an의 수식을 받을 수 없으며 복수형으로 쓰지 않는다.
10 집합명사 family는 셀 수 있는 명사이므로 단수 형태로 쓰려면 앞에 관사가 있어야 한다.

PRACTICE 8

1	information	2	juice	3	Seoul
4	happiness	5	Jane	6	time
7	families	8	class	9	questions
10	apples				

1, 2, 4, 6 추상명사(information, happiness, time)와 물질명사(juice)는 셀 수 없는 명사로, 양을 나타낼 때는 much, (a) little, some, any, no, all, lots of, a lot of 같은 형용사와 함께 쓰인다.
  1 lots of information: 많은 정보
  2 there is little juice: 주스가 거의 없다
  6 take a lot of time: 시간이 많이 걸리다
3, 5 고유명사는 관사 없이 쓰며, 첫 글자는 항상 대문자다.
7 집합명사 family는 셀 수 있는 명사이므로 복수 형태로 those의 수식을 받을 수 있다.
8 each는 셀 수 있는 명사 class의 단수형 앞에 와서 '각 학급'이라는 뜻으로 쓰인다.
9, 10 셀 수 있는 명사의 복수형은 수사, many, a lot of, lots of, (a) few 등의 다양한 수량 형용사와 함께 쓸 수 있다.

PRACTICE 9

1	a piece[sheet] of	2	three slices[pieces] of
3	four glasses of		
4	ten spoonfuls[teaspoonfuls] of		
5	five pounds of	6	a piece[slice] of
7	three cups of	8	a bottle of
9	six bars of	10	two slices[pieces] of

PRACTICE 10

2 loaf of bread
3 piece of advice
4 glasses[cups/bottles] of water
5 pieces of furniture
6 pieces[slices/loaves] of bread
7 cup of tea
8 spoonfuls[teaspoonfuls] of salt
9 pounds of meat
10 glass[bottle] of wine

PRACTICE 11

1	was	**2**	is
3	socks	**4**	is
5	glasses, them	**6**	five-story
7	is	**8**	those scissors
9	two-hour	**10**	pairs, shoes
11	three-month-old	**12**	pants
13	ten-dollar	**14**	makes
15	gloves		

> **1, 2, 4, 7, 14** the news(뉴스, 소식), customs(세관), politics(정치학), economics(경제학), mathematics(수학)와 같은 명사들은 형태는 복수형으로 보이지만 단수 취급한다.
> **3, 5, 8, 10, 12, 15** 한 쌍을 이루어 사용되는 명사는 복수형으로 쓰고 복수 취급한다.
> **6, 9, 11, 13** 「수사+명사」가 뒤에 이어지는 명사를 수식하는 형용사처럼 쓰일 때는 수사 다음의 명사를 복수형으로 쓰지 않는다.

PRACTICE 12

2	Mr. Kim's friend	**3**	Mr. Kim's wife
4	Mr. Kim's son	**5**	Mr. Kim's niece

PRACTICE 13

2 my dog's tail
3 the exit of the building
4 the owner of this car
5 today's TV programs
6 the bottom of the bottle
7 my students' report cards
8 Mr. Brown's blanket
9 the result of the test
10 my sisters' clothes

> **2, 7, 8, 10** 사람이나 동물을 나타내는 명사는 '(s)를 이용하여 소유격을 만든다.
> **3, 4, 6, 9** 무생물의 소유격은 주로 of를 이용한다.
> **5** 시간을 나타내는 명사는 '(s)를 이용하여 소유격을 만든다.

PRACTICE 14

1	that	**2**	,	**3**	that
4	,	**5**	of	**6**	of
7	that	**8**	of	**9**	that
10	,				

> **1, 3, 7, 9** 명사구와 문장이 동격을 이루고 있으므로 동격의 접속사 that을 이용한다.
> **1** the fact = The Earth moves around the Sun 지구가 태양 주위를 돈다는 사실
> **3** a dream = He wants to be a famous actor 그가 유명한 배우가 되기를 원한다는 꿈
> **7** our opinion = He should attend the meeting 그가 회의에 참석해야 한다는 우리의 의견
> **9** the rumor = She stole the money 그녀가 돈을 훔쳤다는 소문
> **2, 4, 10** 두 명사(구)가 같은 대상을 가리킬 때는 콤마(,)를 이용해 동격을 나타낸다.
> **2** Tom = the man in a blue shirt 푸른색 셔츠를 입은 남자 Tom
> **4** My mom = a great cook 훌륭한 요리사인 나의 엄마
> **10** Ms. Scott = the ballet teacher 발레 선생님 Scott 씨
> **5, 6, 8** 명사와 동명사구가 서로 동격일 때는 of를 이용한다.
> **5** The news = her coming to Seoul 그녀가 서울에 온다는 소식
> **6** the idea = moving to Chicago 시카고로 이사한다는 생각
> **8** hope = winning the game 경기에서 이긴다는 희망

PRACTICE 15

1	×	**2**	×	**3**	○	**4**	○
5	×	**6**	○	**7**	○	**8**	×
9	×	**10**	×				

> **1, 5, 10** that이 관계대명사로 쓰였다.
> **1** the song <u>that</u> is easy to sing: 부르기 쉬운 노래 (주격 관계대명사)
> **5** a book <u>that</u> I borrowed from my friend: 친구에게 빌린 책 (목적격 관계대명사)
> **10** the one <u>that</u> I love most: 내가 가장 사랑하는 사람 (목적격 관계대명사)
> **2** of가 소유격(~의)을 나타내는 전치사로 쓰였다.
> the picture <u>of</u> my little dog: 내 작은 강아지의 사진
> **3, 7** that이 동격의 접속사로 쓰였다.
> **3** the surprising news = we would go to an amusement park: 우리가 놀이공원에 갈 거라는 놀라운 소식
> **7** the advice = I should drink more water: 내가 물을 더 많이 마셔야 한다는 충고
> **4** of가 동격을 나타내는 전치사로 쓰였다.
> the fact = his not coming to the class: 그가 수업에 오지 않을 거라는 사실
> **6** 콤마(,)를 이용해 두 명사(구)가 동격임을 나타내고 있다. (David = my boss)
> **8** 콤마(,)가 A, B and C 구조로 세 개의 명사(Mary, Kate, Tom)를 나열하는 데 쓰였다.
> **9** that이 명사절(목적어 역할)을 이끄는 접속사로 쓰였다.

PRACTICE 16

1	an	**2**	a	**3**	an	**4**	a
5	An	**6**	an	**7**	a	**8**	a
9	a	**10**	an	**11**	an	**12**	a

Ch 5 명사와 관사

13 an   **14** a   **15** a

> **1, 11, 13** 첫소리가 모음으로 발음되는 명사의 단수형 앞에는 an 을 쓴다.
> **2, 9, 12, 15** 명사 앞의 형용사의 첫소리가 자음으로 발음되면 a를 쓴다.
> **3, 5, 6, 10** 명사 앞의 형용사의 첫소리가 모음으로 발음되면 an을 쓴다.
> **4, 7, 8, 14** 첫소리가 자음으로 발음되는 명사의 단수형 앞에는 a 를 쓴다.

PRACTICE 17

1 an egg   **2** a house
3 a tree   **4** a baby
5 a glass   **6** A police officer
7 an elephant **8** a monitor

PRACTICE 18

1 ③   **2** ①   **3** ④   **4** ⑥
5 ②   **6** ①   **7** ⑤   **8** ⑤
9 ②   **10** ⑥ **11** ④ **12** ③

PRACTICE 19

1 the   **2** the   **3** a   **4** The
5 the   **6** a   **7** the **8** The
9 a   **10** a   **11** the **12** The
13 the **14** a, The **15** The, the

> **1, 5** 유일한 것을 나타낼 때 the를 쓴다.
> **1** the Earth, **5** the Moon
> **2, 7, 15** 듣는 사람이 무엇을 가리키는지 알 수 있을 때 the를 쓴다.
> **3, 9** one(하나의)의 의미일 때 a/an을 쓴다.
> **3** a jacket: 재킷 하나
> **9** a glass of water: 물 한 잔
> **4, 8, 13** 앞에 나온 명사가 반복될 때 the를 쓴다.
> **4** John and Mary's baby → the baby
> **8** a pen → the pen
> **13** a skirt → the skirt
> **6** some(약간의, 어느 정도)의 의미일 때 a/an을 쓴다.
> a while ago: 조금 전에
> **10** per(~당, ~마다)의 의미일 때 a/an을 쓴다.
> two long vacations a year: 1년마다 두 번의 긴 휴가
> **11, 12** 명사 뒤에 명사를 수식하는 구나 절이 있을 때 the를 쓴다.
> **11** the concert that you told me about:
> 네가 나에게 말했던 그 콘서트
> **12** the book on my desk: 책상 위에 있는 그 책
> **14** 앞의 restaurant는 '어떤 식당(a certain restaurant)'을 의미하고, 뒤의 restaurant는 앞에서 언급한 '그 식당'을 의미하므로 각각 a restaurant와 the restaurant가 되어야 알맞다.

PRACTICE 20

1 the   **2** the, the   **3** a   **4** the
5 The   **6** an   **7** the **8** the
9 a   **10** the **11** A

> **1, 2, 4, 5, 10** 서수, 최상급, only, very, same 앞에는 the를 쓴다.
> **3, 6** one(하나의)의 의미일 때는 a/an을 쓴다.
> **7** 듣는 사람이 무엇을 가리키는지 알 수 있을 때 the를 쓴다.
> **8** 악기 이름 앞에는 the를 쓴다.
> **9, 11** a certain(어떤)의 의미일 때는 a/an을 쓴다.

PRACTICE 21

1 the poor   **2** the face
3 the Pacific   **4** a week
5 the Netherlands **6** The rich
7 ○   **8** a post office
9 ○   **10** ○
11 the Thames   **12** *The New York Times*
13 ○   **14** the back
15 ○

> **1, 6, 9** 「the+형용사」를 써서 '~한 사람들'이라고 표현한다.
> **1** the poor: 가난한 사람들
> **6** the rich: 부유한 사람들
> **9** the young: 젊은 사람들
> **2, 7, 14** 어떤 동작을 가하는 신체의 일부를 나타내는 단어 앞에는 the를 쓴다.
> **2** hit in the face: 얼굴을 때리다
> **7** by the hand: 손을 잡고
> **14** push+사람+on the back: ~의 등을 밀다
> **3, 5, 11, 12, 15** 특정 고유명사 앞에는 the를 쓴다.
> **3** the Pacific, **5** the Netherlands, **11** the Thames, **12** *The New York Times*, **15** the Alps
> **4** per(~당, ~마다)의 의미일 때 a/an을 쓴다.
> once a week: 일주일에 한 번
> **8** 맥락상 처음 언급된 정해지지 않은 단수명사에 대해 묻고 있으므로 a/an을 쓴다.
> **10** some(약간의, 어느 정도)의 의미일 때 a/an을 쓴다.
> for a while: 잠시 후에
> **13** one(하나의)의 의미일 때 a/an을 쓴다.
> a newspaper: 신문 한 부

PRACTICE 22

The, The, The, the, the, a

> The old want to live a comfortable life.
> → the+형용사(~한 사람들)
> *The Korean Times* reported ~.
> → the+특정 고유명사

The Philippines is one of <u>the most popular</u> countries for them to live in.
→ the+특정 고유명사 / the+최상급
It is in <u>the Pacific Ocean</u>.
→ the+특정 고유명사
My family visits the country about once <u>a year</u>.
→ per(~당, ~마다)를 의미하는 a/an

PRACTICE 23

1 bus   **2** ○   **3** ○
4 lunch   **5** Math   **6** ○
7 TV   **8** ○   **9** ○
10 school   **11** listening to music
12 a doctor

1 「by+교통수단」일 때는 교통수단에 해당하는 명사 앞에 관사를 쓰지 않는다.
2 운동 경기를 나타내는 명사 앞에는 관사를 쓰지 않는다.
3 가족 구성원을 나타내는 명사 앞에는 관사를 쓰지 않는다.
4 식사를 나타내는 명사 앞에는 관사를 쓰지 않는다.
5 과목을 나타내는 명사 앞에는 관사를 쓰지 않는다.
6, 10 장소, 기구를 나타내는 명사가 본래의 목적으로 쓰일 때는 앞에 관사를 쓰지 않는다.
7, 11 listen to music과 watch TV는 관용적으로 관사 없이 쓴다.
8 home이 '자기 집, 고향'의 뜻으로 쓰이면 보통 관사 없이 쓴다.
9 인명 앞에서 칭호로 사용되는 명사 앞에는 관사를 쓰지 않는다.
12 doctor는 자음으로 시작하는 명사이므로 관사 an이 아닌 a를 쓴다.

PRACTICE 24

1 ×   **2** the   **3** the
4 ×   **5** the   **6** an
7 the   **8** ×   **9** a
10 the   **11** ×   **12** the
13 a   **14** ×   **15** A
16 ×   **17** the[a], the[a]
18 the   **19** a   **20** The
21 the   **22** a, a   **23** ×, ×
24 ×   **25** ×   **26** ×
27 ×   **28** The, an   **29** The
30 ×   **31** the   **32** the
33 ×   **34** The

1, 16 식사를 나타내는 명사 앞에는 관사를 쓰지 않는다.
2, 18 악기 이름 앞에는 the를 쓴다.
3, 7, 12, 32 서수, only, very 앞에는 the를 쓴다.
4, 30 운동 경기를 나타내는 명사 앞에는 관사를 쓰지 않는다.
5 어떤 동작을 가하는 신체의 일부를 나타내는 단어 앞에는 the를 쓴다.

6 one(하나의)의 의미일 때 a/an을 쓴다.
8, 27 listen to music과 watch TV는 관용적으로 관사 없이 쓴다.
9, 22 per(~당, ~마다)의 의미일 때 a/an을 쓴다.
10, 29 「the+형용사/분사」를 써서 '~한 사람들'이라고 표현한다.
11, 24, 33 장소, 기구를 나타내는 명사가 본래의 목적으로 쓰일 때는 앞에 관사를 쓰지 않는다.
13, 19 some(약간의, 어느 정도)의 의미일 때 a/an을 쓴다.
14 가족 구성원을 나타내는 명사 앞에는 관사를 쓰지 않는다.
15 a certain(어떤)의 의미일 때는 a/an을 쓴다.
17 어떤 종류의 전체를 나타내는 보통 명사를 대표 단수로 표현할 때 a/an이나 the를 쓴다.
20 유일한 것을 나타낼 때 the를 쓴다.
21, 34 명사 뒤에 명사를 수식하는 구나 절이 있을 때 the를 쓴다.
23 「by+교통수단」일 때는 교통수단에 해당하는 명사 앞에 관사를 쓰지 않는다.
25 관직, 신분을 나타내는 명사 앞에는 관사를 쓰지 않는다.
26 과목을 나타내는 명사 앞에는 관사를 쓰지 않는다.
28 명사 뒤에 명사를 수식하는 구나 절이 있을 때 the를 쓰므로 the children이 알맞고, a/an에 the same(같은, 동일한)의 의미가 있으므로 of an age는 '나이가 같은'이라는 뜻으로 쓰인다.
31 특정 고유명사 앞에는 the를 쓴다.

📑 중간·기말고사 대비문제 정답   본문 _ p.140

1 ②   **2** ④   **3** ②,③   **4** a cup of coffee, four slices[pieces] of cake   **5** ①   **6** ③   **7** ④
8 five pairs of socks   **9** ③   **10** ④   **11** ③
12 ②   **13** ②   **14** ②   **15** ②,⑤   **16** (1) a bowl of rice (2) two bottles of water (3) three pairs of shoes (4) a glass of orange juice   **17** ①
18 ②   **19** ①   **20** ③   **21** that he won a marathon   **22** ③   **23** ⑤   **24** ⑤   **25** ⑤
26 ①,③   **27** ③   **28** ①   **29** (1) (A) → breakfast (2) (D) → pairs   **30** ⓐ slices ⓑ bars ⓒ loaves ⓓ bottle ⓔ pieces ⓕ bars

중간·기말고사 대비문제 해설

1 ① piano - pianos   ③ wolf - wolves
   ④ tooth - teeth   ⑤ beauty - beauties

2 furniture(집합적 물질명사: 유사한 사물들의 집합체이지만 양으로 나타내는 물질 명사의 성격을 갖는 명사)와 cheese, coffee, cereal(물질명사)은 셀 수 없는 명사로, 수를 나타내는 경우 단위 명사를 이용한다.
① five pieces of furniture
② two slices of cheese
③ three cups of coffee

⑤ two bowls of cereal

3 물질명사는 셀 수 없으며 수를 나타내야 할 때는 단위 명사를 사용한다.
① piece → pieces, breads → bread
④ two salt → two (tea)spoonfuls of salt
⑤ five meat → five pounds[pieces] of meat

4 a cup of '한 잔의 ~'
four slices[pieces] of '네 조각의 ~'

5 ② mouse의 복수형 - mice
③ bench의 복수형 - benches
④ bird의 복수형 - birds
⑤ fox의 복수형 - foxes

6 ③ some juices → some juice
물질명사인 juice는 복수형으로 쓰일 수 없다.

7 서수, same, 악기의 이름 앞에는 정관사 the를 쓴다.
ⓑ first → the first   ⓓ same → the same
ⓔ piano → the piano

8 한 쌍을 이루어야 하나의 물건으로 제 기능을 하는 명사는 복수형으로 쓰고 복수 취급한다.

9 • a glass of '한 잔의 ~'
• 무생물의 소유격은 주로 전치사 of를 사용한다.
• 명사 a plan과 동명사구 studying for the test를 동격으로 연결하는 of

10 ⓐ some은 '몇몇의, 약간의'라는 뜻으로 뒤에 셀 수 있는 명사가 올 경우 복수형으로 써야 한다.
(apple → apples)
ⓑ 유일한 것을 나타낼 때는 정관사 the를 쓴다.
(Moon → The Moon, Earth → the Earth)
ⓔ 명사 뒤에 명사를 수식하는 구가 있을 때 정관사 the를 쓴다. (capital → the capital)

11 셀 수 없는 물질명사는 단수형으로 쓴다.
① milks → milk
② meats → meat
④ sugares → sugar
⑤ 고치지 않은 형태가 어법상 옳다.

12 ② child의 복수형은 childrens가 아니라 children이다. (childrens → children)

13 ① student가 셀 수 있는 명사이고, 단수형이므로 부정관사 a나 정관사 the를 써야 한다.
(student → a[the] student)
③ second와 같은 서수의 앞에는 정관사 the를 써야 한다. (a second → the second)
④ math teacher는 셀 수 있는 명사이고, 단수형

이므로 부정관사 a나 정관사 the를 써야 한다.
(math teacher → a[the] math teacher)
⑤ '~해 보이다'는 뜻의 look은 주격 보어로 형용사를 쓴다. 부정관사 a는 명사의 앞에만 쓰이므로 삭제해야 한다. (a very → very)

14 ② a lot of는 '많은'이라는 뜻으로 명사 앞에 온다. 따라서 밑줄 친 부분에는 명사가 들어가야 한다. noisy는 '시끄러운'이라는 형용사이며, '소리, 소음'이라는 뜻의 명사 noise를 쓴다. 참고로 'make a lot of noise'는 '시끄럽게 하다'라는 뜻이다. (noisy → noise)
① 정황상 무엇을 가리키는지 알 수 있으므로 정관사 the를 쓴다.
③ 동사 were playing을 꾸며주고 있으므로 부사인 loudly의 쓰임은 적절하다.
④ games는 셀 수 있는 명사이고, '게임들'이라는 뜻이므로 '-s'를 붙여 복수형으로 만든다.
⑤ 앞에서 언급한 the students를 의미하므로, 대명사 them의 쓰임은 적절하다.

15 식사를 나타내는 명사 앞, 장소를 나타내는 명사가 본래의 목적으로 쓰일 때, 과목을 나타내는 명사 앞에는 관사를 쓰지 않는다.
① the lunch → lunch
③ to the school → to school
④ the economics → economics

16 (1) a bowl of '한 그릇의 ~'
(2) two bottles of '두 병의~'
(3) three pairs of '세 켤레의~'
(4) a glass of '한 잔의 ~'

17 ① 사람을 나타내는 명사는 's를 사용하여 소유격을 만든다. (bag of Jenny's → Jenny's bag)

18 ② 「수사＋명사」가 뒤에 이어지는 명사를 수식하는 형용사처럼 쓰일 때는 수사 다음의 명사를 복수형으로 쓰지 않는다. (40-years-old → 40-year-old)
① 주어가 he로 3인칭 단수이며 현재 시제이므로 동사에 -s를 붙인 3인칭 단수 현재형(needs)으로 쓰는 것이 적절하다.
③ 등위접속사 and가 문장의 동사인 comes와 밑줄 친 부분을 병렬구조로 이어주고 있다. 주어 His 40-year-old mom은 3인칭 단수이고 현재 시제이므로, comes와 마찬가지로 -s를 붙인 3인칭 단수 현재형(brings)으로 써야 한다.
④ every는 뒤에 단수 명사를 쓰고, 단수 취급한다.

⑤ 등위접속사 and가 문장의 동사인 is와 밑줄 친 부분을 병렬구조로 이어주고 있다. 주어는 every student in his class로, every+단수 명사는 단수 취급한다. 따라서 3인칭 단수 현재형인 helps로 쓰는 것이 적절하다.

19 ① 컵은 셀 수 있는 명사이므로 여러 개 있을 때는 복수형으로 쓴다. (two cup → two cups)

20 many 뒤에는 명사의 복수형이 와야 하므로, 단·복수의 형태가 같은 sheep이 가능하다.

21 the news와 he won a marathon은 that으로 연결되는 동격 관계이다.

22 ③ per(~당, ~마다)
① 대표 단수　　　　　　② one(하나)
④ the same(같은)　　⑤ a certain(어떤)

23 ⑤ 유일한 것을 나타내는 명사 앞에는 the를 쓴다.

24 ⑤ 어떤 동작을 가하는 신체의 일부를 나타내는 단어 앞에 the를 쓴다. (in an eye → in the eye)

25 ⑤ a bread → a loaf of bread
물질명사는 단위명사를 이용하여 수를 나타낸다.

26 furniture(가구)와 information(정보)은 셀 수 없는 명사이다. 셀 수 없는 명사는 many와 함께 쓸 수 없다.

27 ③ 동격
① 지시대명사　　　　　　② 지시형용사
④ 명사절을 이끄는 접속사　⑤ 관계대명사

28 ① the+형용사는 '~한 사람들'이라는 뜻을 나타낸다.
(a → the)

29 (A) 식사명 앞에는 관사를 쓰지 않는다.
(D) 앞에 복수인 two가 나오므로 pair는 pairs로 고쳐야 한다.

30 ⓐ three slices '세 장'
ⓑ two bars '두 개'
ⓒ three loaves '세 덩어리'
ⓓ a bottle '한 병'
ⓔ four pieces '네 장'
ⓕ three bars '세 개'

Ch
5
명사와 관사

PRACTICE 1

1 him	**2** We	**3** You
4 me	**5** they	**6** us
7 her	**8** it	**9** them
10 She		

> **1, 6, 7, 9** 동사의 목적어 자리이므로 목적격이 알맞다.
> **2, 3, 10** 문장의 주어 자리이므로 주격이 알맞다.
> **4** 전치사 다음에는 대명사의 목적격이 들어가는 것이 적절하다.
> **5** 의문문에서는 주어-(조)동사 도치가 일어나기 때문에 조동사 Did 다음에 주격인 they가 나오는 것이 적절하다.
> **8** 앞에 나온 This book을 가리키므로 단수인 it이 적절하다.

PRACTICE 2

2 his, his	**3** their, theirs
4 my, mine	**5** your, yours
6 our, ours	

PRACTICE 3

1 He	**2** my, her	**3** They
4 us	**5** hers	**6** his
7 ours	**8** him	**9** your
10 its		

> **1, 3** 문장의 주어 자리이므로 주격 대명사가 들어가는 것이 알맞다.
> **2** 명사 friend를 앞에서 수식할 수 있는 소유격이 적절하다. / like 의 목적어 자리이므로 her이 알맞다.
> **4, 8** 수여동사 bring과 tell의 간접 목적어 자리이므로 목적격 대명사가 들어가야 한다.
> **5, 7** 소유격인 her과 our는 꾸며줄 명사 없이 혼자 쓰일 수 없으므로 소유대명사를 사용하는 것이 적절하다.
> **6, 9, 10** 명사의 앞에서 명사를 꾸며줄 수 있는 소유격이 들어가야 한다.

PRACTICE 4

1 himself, 강조	**2** herself, 재귀
3 myself, 강조	**4** yourself, 재귀
5 itself, 재귀	**6** ourselves, 재귀
7 himself, 재귀	**8** themselves, 재귀

> **2** by oneself: 혼자
> **5** 'repeat itself'는 '같은 방식으로 계속 반복되다'는 의미의 관용적 표현이다. repeat은 타동사로 쓰였기 때문에 itself는 생략할 수 없다.
> **6** for oneself: 혼자 힘으로
> **8** make oneself at home: 느긋하게 쉬다, 자기 집에 있는 것처럼 편하게 지내다

PRACTICE 5

1 me	**2** himself	**3** them
4 us	**5** herself	**6** you
7 itself	**8** myself	**9** myself
10 her		

> **1, 3, 4, 6, 10** 행동의 주체와 대상이 같지 않으므로 재귀대명사를 사용할 수 없다.
> **8, 9** 행동의 주체와 대상이 같으므로 재귀대명사를 사용할 수 있다.
> **2, 5, 7** by oneself: 혼자서, 스스로

PRACTICE 6

1 비	**2** 비	**3** 대
4 비	**5** 비	**6** 대
7 비	**8** 대	

> **1** 명암을 가리키는 비인칭주어다.
> **2, 4** 날씨를 가리키는 비인칭주어다.
> **3** 앞선 문장의 the cat을 가리키는 대명사다.
> **5** 거리를 가리키는 비인칭주어다.
> **6** 앞선 문장의 autumn을 가리키는 대명사다.
> **7** 시간을 가리키는 비인칭주어다.
> **8** 문장 내에 언급되지는 않았지만 it이 가리키는 특정 사안이 있음을 알 수 있다. 따라서 it은 대명사로 쓰였다.

PRACTICE 7

1 You seemed to be very confident when you made the speech.

2 It seems that my sister has a plan to stay at Sumi's for a while.

3 She seems to be nervous about her job interview.

4 It seemed that you were satisfied with your test result.

5 He seems to know what he is doing now.

PRACTICE 8

1 It was Minji's brother that I saw at the theater yesterday.

2 It was a week ago that I met Sumin at the amusement park.

3 It was my uncle that was seriously injured in the car accident.

4 It is at the bus stop that I'm going to meet the children this Sunday.

5 It was at five that we were supposed to meet in front of the statue.

PRACTICE 9

1 It is important to recycle the bottles.

2 It is very exciting to read science fiction.

3 I thought it strange that you said so.

4 It is disappointing that you lied again.

5 I found it difficult to memorize new words every day.

6 It made me happy that our team won the game.

7 It is important to play for the team.

8 It is amazing that he can keep cool in a crisis.

> **1, 2, 7** to부정사 주어가 길 때는 문장의 맨 뒤로 보내고 이를 대신하여 주어 자리에 가주어 it이 온다.
> **3** 'that you said so'가 진목적어인 문장이나. 목석어로 쓰인 명사절이 길 때는 그 자리에 it을 쓰고 명사절을 문장의 맨 뒤로 보낸다.
> **4, 6, 8** that이 이끄는 명사절이 진주어인 문장이다. 주어로 쓰인 명사절이 길 때는 그 자리에 it을 쓰고 that절을 문장의 맨 뒤로 보낸다.
> **5** 진목적어인 to부정사구의 길이가 길 경우, 목적어 자리에 it을 쓰고 to부정사구를 문장의 맨 뒤로 보낸다.

PRACTICE 10

1 Is this **2** That car

3 These girls **4** this

5 those buildings **6** That

7 These books **8** Those

PRACTICE 11

1 that **2** those, those

3 those **4** that

5 those **6** Those

7 that **8** those

9 those **10** that

> **1** 단수명사 population의 반복을 피하기 위해서 that을 사용한다.
> **2, 6, 9** '~한 사람들'이라는 의미를 가진 those가 적절하다.
> **3** 복수명사 shoes를 대신하기 위해 those를 사용한다.
> **4** 단수명사 classroom의 반복을 피하기 위해 that을 사용한다.
> **5** 복수명사 buildings를 대신하기 위해 those를 사용한다.
> **7** 단수명사 the price의 반복을 피하기 위해 that을 사용한다.
> **8** 복수명사 the employees의 반복을 피하기 위해 those를 사용한다.
> **10** 단수명사 vacation의 반복을 피하기 위해 that을 사용한다.

PRACTICE 12

1 it **2** ones **3** one

4 them **5** One **6** one

7 it **8** them **9** one

10 ones **11** them **12** One

13 them **14** it **15** ones

16 ones **17** it

> **1, 7, 14, 17** 앞서 언급한 바로 그 명사를 지칭해야 하기 때문에 대명사 it이 적절하다.
> **2, 16** 같은 종류이지만, 다른 속성(색상, 사이즈)을 가진 대상들을 가리키기 위해 ones를 사용한다.
> **3** 앞서 언급한 a small balloon과 같은 종류이지만, 다른 속성(big)을 가진 대상을 가리키기 위해 one을 사용한다.
> **4, 8, 11, 13** 앞서 언급한 바로 그 명사를 지칭한다. 복수형 명사이므로 대명사 them이 적절하다.
> **5, 12** 일반적인 사람들을 가리킬 때는 one을 사용한다.
> **6** an eraser라고 했으므로 명확한 대상이 정해지지 않은 지우개를 언급하였고, 대상이 다르면서 종류는 같은 명사에 대해 반복을 피하기 위해 one을 사용한다.
> **9** 앞서 언급한 a nice bicycle과 같은 종류이지만 다른 대상을 가리키기 위해 one을 사용한다.
> **10, 15** 특정한 대상을 짚어 질문하였지만 대답에서 그것과 같은 종류의 다른 개체를 지칭하고 있기 때문에 부정대명사를 사용해야 하고, 그 대상이 복수이므로 ones가 적절하다.

PRACTICE 13

1 another **2** The other

3 another **4** other

5 others **6** the other

7 the others **8** The others

9 others **10** other

11 other **12** another

13 others **14** the other

15 another **16** others

1, 15 other은 명사 앞에서 꾸며주는 식으로만 사용 가능하기 때문에 '또 다른 하나'를 가리키는 another이 적절하다.
2, 6 전체 범위가 두 가지로 명시된 경우, 무작위로 고른 첫 번째 것은 one, 남은 하나는 the other이라고 쓴다.
3, 12 뒤에 따라오는 단수 명사를 수식할 수 있는 another가 적절하다.
4, 10, 11 뒤에 따라오는 복수 명사를 수식할 수 있는 other이 적절하다.
5, 9, 13, 16 앞서 전체 범위가 몇 명인지 언급되지 않았고, 문맥상 불특정 다수(다른 사람들)를 가리키므로 others가 적절하다.
7 복수형 동사 are와 수를 일치시키려면 the others가 적절하다.
8 앞서 병의 전체 개수가 4개라고 언급되었으므로 색상이 붉은 색인 두 개의 병을 제외한 나머지가 특정되었다. 따라서 '나머지 것들'을 가리키는 the others가 적절하다.
14 길의 반대편을 말할 때 'the other side'를 사용하는 것이 적절하다.

1 each of+관사/소유격+복수명사는 단수 취급하여 단수 동사와 함께 쓰인다.
2 every+단수명사는 단수 취급한다.
3, 5 each+단수명사는 단수 취급한다.
4 every Sunday: 매 일요일마다
6 every가 not과 함께 쓰여 '모든 책들이 다 ~한 것은 아니다'라는 부분 부정을 나타낸다.

PRACTICE 16

1 You should read all the books in this room.

2 Ms. Ford gave me all of those dishes for my birthday present.

3 She is going to tell you all of the information.

4 I will invite both boys to my performance.

5 Both of the tests were very difficult for me.

6 He didn't follow both of the rules.

7 She ate the rest of the cake on the table.

8 The rest of you may go home now.

9 The rest of the crew were rescued from the burning ship.

10 All of the participants looked tired when the bell rang.

11 Not all people are happy with the changes.

PRACTICE 14

1 the other		**2** others	
3 the others		**4** the other	
5 One, the other		**6** Some, the others	
7 Another, The other		**8** others	
9 One, the other		**10** others	
11 One, the other		**12** Some, others	
13 One, another		**14** One, the other	
15 Some, the others			

1, 5, 9, 14 전체 범위가 두 가지로 명시된 경우, 두 개 중 무작위로 먼저 고른 하나를 one, 나머지 하나를 the other이라고 한다.
2, 8, 10, 12 전체 개수가 불특정한 경우, 그 중 일부를 가리킬 때 some, 다른 일부를 언급할 때 others라고 한다.
3, 6, 15 전체 개수가 명시된 경우, 그 중 무작위의 일부를 가리킬 때 some, 그 외 나머지를 언급할 때 the others라고 한다.
4, 7, 11, 13 전체 개수가 3개일 때 처음 고른 하나는 one, 남은 두 개 중 하나를 another, 나머지 하나를 the other이라고 한다.

PRACTICE 17

1 student		**2** the taxis	
3 kids		**4** night	
5 Does		**6** was	
7 morning		**8** the restaurants	
9 those words		**10** parent	
11 are		**12** has	
13 have to		**14** is	
15 The rest of		**16** are	
17 ways		**18** was	
19 minute		**20** are	

PRACTICE 15

1 Each of the flowers has a different color.

2 Mr. Kim called every student last night.

3 Each table is covered with green cloth.

4 I used to go to my grandmother's house every Sunday.

5 Each player is wearing red pants.

6 Not every book in this room is about politics.

1, 4, 7, 10, 19 every/each는 단수 명사만을 꾸밀 수 있다.
2 all of the+복수 명사는 복수형 동사와 함께 쓰인다.
3, 8, 16, 17 both와 both of는 복수 명사 및 복수 동사와 사용된다.
5 each+단수 명사(girl)는 단수형 동사와 함께 쓰인다.
6, 18 all of와 셀 수 없는 명사가 함께 쓰일 경우 동사는 단수형으로 사용한다.
9, 12 each of는 복수 명사와 함께 쓰이며, 동사는 단수형으로 사용한다.
11 all the+복수 명사(guests)는 복수 취급하므로 are과 함께 쓰는 것이 적절하다.

13 the rest of와 복수 명사가 함께 쓰일 경우 동사는 복수형으로 사용한다.
14, 15 the rest of와 셀 수 없는 명사가 함께 쓰일 경우 동사는 단수형으로 사용한다.
20 the rest가 단독으로 쓰일 경우 '나머지 것들(모자)'이라는 의미를 나타낸다. 복수형 동사와 함께 사용한다.

PRACTICE 18

1 Someone [Somebody]

2 someone [somebody]

3 ○ **4** something

5 ○ **6** anything

7 Anyone [Anybody] **8** ○

9 anything **10** Something

11 Someone [Somebody]

12 ○

1, 2, 11 anyone[anybody]은 보통 부정문이나 의문문에 쓰이고, 긍정문에 쓰인 경우는 '어떠한 ~라도'의 뜻으로 쓰인다. '누군가'라는 뜻으로 긍정문에서 쓰인 경우, someone[somebody]가 적절하다.
3 anything은 긍정문에서 '어떠한 ~라도'라는 의미로 쓰이므로 적절하다.
4 anything이 긍정문에 쓰일 경우는 '어떠한 ~라도'의 뜻이다. 긍정문에서 '(어떤) 것'이라는 의미는 something이 적절하다.
5 anyone은 의문문에서 '누군가'라는 의미로 쓰이므로 적절하다.
6, 9 something은 부정문에 쓰이지 않는다. 이 문장에서는 '아무 것'이라는 의미로 쓰여야 하므로 anything이 적절하다.
7 Someone은 긍정문에서 '누군가'라는 의미로 쓰인다. 긍정문에서 '어떤 사람이라도'라는 의미로 쓰여야 하므로 Anyone[Anybody]이 적절하다.
8 something은 긍정의 대답을 예상하는 의문문에 쓰이므로 적절하다.
10 Anything이 긍정문에 쓰일 경우는 '어떠한 ~라도'의 뜻이다. 이 문장에서는 '무슨 일'이라는 의미의 단어가 쓰여야 하므로 Something이 적절하다.
12 anything은 의문문에서 '무언가'라는 의미로 쓰이므로 적절하다.

PRACTICE 19

1 Who **2** Whose **3** whom

4 Who **5** whom **6** Whose

7 Who **8** Whose **9** Whose

10 whom

1, 4, 7 문장의 주어가 없기 때문에 주격 의문대명사 who가 오는 것이 적절하다.
2, 6, 9 명사를 앞에서 꾸며줄 수 있어야 하기 때문에 소유격 의문형용사 whose가 오는 것이 적절하다.
3, 5, 10 전치사(to, for, with)의 목적어 역할을 하는 목적격 의문대명사 whom을 사용하는 것이 적절하다.
8 사물에 대해 물어보고 있으므로 who는 적절하지 않고, 뒤에 따라오는 명사가 없으므로 whose가 소유격 의문대명사(누구의 것)로 사용되었다.

PRACTICE 20

1 What **2** Which **3** Whom

4 What **5** What **6** Which

7 Whose **8** Which **9** Which

10 What

1 사람의 직업을 물어볼 때 what을 사용한다.
2 선택지가 주어진 상황에서 질문하므로 which를 사용한다.
3 구동사 talk to의 목적어가 없으므로 목적격 의문대명사 whom으로 질문하는 것이 적절하다.
4 선택의 범위가 주어지지 않은 상황에서 사물에 대해 질문하므로 what을 사용한다. 여기서 what은 kind를 꾸며주는 의문형용사로 쓰여 '어떤 종류'라는 의미를 나타낸다.
5, 10 선택의 범위가 주어지지 않은 상황에서 사람이 아닌 것에 대해 질문하므로 what을 사용한다.
6 선택의 범위가 주어진 상황에서 질문하고 있기 때문에 which가 적절하다. which는 사람을 가리킬 때도 사용 가능하다.
7 선택의 범위가 주어지지 않았기 때문에 which로 질문할 수 없다. '누구의 것'을 의미하는 의문대명사 whose를 사용하는 것이 적절하다.
8 사과와 오렌지 중 어느 것이 더 저렴한지 묻고 있기 때문에 선택의 범위가 정해져 있다. 따라서 which로 질문하는 것이 적절하다.
9 선택의 범위가 part1, 2로 정해져 있으므로 which를 사용한다. 여기서 which는 part를 앞에서 수식하는 의문형용사로 쓰였으며 '어느 파트'라는 의미를 나타낸다.

PRACTICE 21

1 Which seat do you want?

2 What classes do you have tomorrow?

3 Which food does Cathy like?

4 What countries does he want to visit?

5 Which wallpaper is good for your room?

중간·기말고사 대비문제 정답 본문 _ p.169

1 ③　**2** ④　**3** ②　**4** ③　**5** ①　**6** ②　**7** ④

8 ①　**9** (1) has → have　(2) her → hers

10 every[each] summer　**11** ④　**12** ①　**13** ①

14 ②　**15** ⑤　**16** ①　**17** ④　**18** ③　**19** ③

20 ⑤　**21** ③　**22** ④　**23** ③　**24** ④　**25** ②

26 other　**27** ③　**28** ①,④,⑤　**29** ②　**30** ⑤

31 ②　**32** ②　**33** the winter　**34** ⑤　**35** ③

36 (1) those　(2) this　(3) These　(4) that　**37** ⑤

38 Everyone seems to be thinking the same thing now.　**39** myself　**40** The queen used to look at herself in the mirror.　**41** ①　**42** ④

43 ③　**44** It is not easy to decide which club I should join.　**45** ④　**46** ②　**47** (1) Which (2) What (3) Whose

중간·기말고사 대비문제 해설

1 (A) 물질명사인 water는 단수형으로 쓴다.

(B) 주어는 앞서 언급된 '바다'를 가리키고, 3인칭 단수 현재형 동사(plays)를 사용하였으므로 주어도 3인칭 단수인 It을 써야 한다.

(C) 문맥상 '그것의 건강(its health)'이라는 뜻이 오는 것이 자연스러우므로 소유격 대명사 its를 써야 한다. it's는 it is 또는 it has의 축약형이다.

바다는 지구의 표면의 많은 부분을 덮는 거대한 수역이다. 그것은 작은 생선부터 거대한 고래까지 수많은 생명체의 집이다. 바다는 돌고래, 상어, 그리고 바다거북을 포함하는 많은 동물들에게 음식과 서식지를 제공한다. 그것은 또한 지구의 기후와 날씨 패턴을 조절하는 데 결정적인 역할을 한다. 불행하게도, 바다는 오염, 과도한 어획, 그리고 기후 변화와 같은 많은 어려움을 마주하고 있다. 이러한 위협들은 해양 생명체와 생태계를 해치고 있다. 모든 사람이 바다를 지키기 위한 행동을 취하고 미래 세대를 위해 그것의 건강을 지키는 것이 중요하다.

2 주어진 문장의 밑줄 친 himself는 재귀용법으로 쓰였다.

④ 재귀 용법 ①②③⑤ 강조 용법

3 주어진 문장의 밑줄 친 it은 비인칭주어로 쓰였다.

② 비인칭주어 it ①③④⑤ 인칭대명사 it

4 ③ 'Each of + 복수명사'가 주어일 경우 단수 동사를

써야 하므로 어법에 알맞은 문장이다.

① be known for: ~로[때문에] 유명하다 / be known as: ~로서 알려져 있다

문장의 의미상 be known for로 쓰는 것이 적절하다. (as → for)

② 「It ~ that」 강조구문에서 강조하고자 하는 말을 It is와 that 사이에 쓴다. 한국어 문장에서 Laura를 강조하고 있으나 영어 문장에서는 the difficult puzzle을 강조하고 있기 때문에 의미를 바르게 전달하려면 It is와 that 사이에 Laura가 들어가는 것이 적절하다. (It is the difficult puzzle that Laura solved. → It is Laura that solved the difficult puzzle.)

④ it's는 it is 혹은 it has를 줄여서 쓴 것이다. 소유격인 '그것의'라는 의미로 쓰려면 its로 써야 한다. (it's → its)

⑤ 'the rest of + 복수 명사'가 주어일 때 동사는 복수형을 쓴다. (is → are)

5 ① 강조 용법의 재귀대명사는 생략이 가능하다.

②③④⑤ 전치사의 목적어로 쓰인 재귀대명사는 생략할 수 없다.

6 any는 부정문에 쓰여 '아무(것)도'의 의미를 가진다. 따라서 <보기>의 문장은 '그녀는 남자 형제가 아무도 없다.'라는 의미이다.

① have → has

③ doesn't has no → doesn't have / has no

④ doesn't no have → doesn't have any

⑤ has not → has no / doesn't have

7 ④ Each of + 복수 명사는 단수 취급한다.

(have → has)

8 by oneself '혼자서, 홀로'

9 (1) Laura and I는 복수형 주어이므로 has를 have로 바꾼다.

(2) 문맥상 '저 빨간 것은 그녀의 것이다'라는 뜻이 되어야 하므로 her를 hers로 바꾼다.

10 every[each] 뒤에 시간 관련 명사가 오면 '매 ~, ~마다'의 의미가 된다.

11 저기 있는 저 그림들을 봐. 저것들은 내 그림들이야.

12 ① '그것'이라는 뜻의 인칭대명사로 쓰였다. 그것은 정말 맵니?

② 요일을 나타내는 비인칭주어 it이다.

③ 날씨를 나타내는 비인칭주어 it이다.

④⑤ 시간을 나타내는 비인칭주어 it이다.

13 ⓐ 내 고양이가 잃어버린 그 장난감을 찾은 것이므로 앞서 언급한 것을 가리키는 it을 쓰는 것이 적절하다.
ⓑ 장난감을 의미하지만 앞 문장에서 언급한 고양이가 망가뜨린 장난감이 아닌 불특정한 장난감 하나를 가리키는 것이므로 one을 쓰는 것이 적절하다.
ⓒ 고양이에게 또 하나의 장난감을 사주는 것이 좋겠다는 의미이므로 another를 쓰는 것이 적절하다.

14 의문대명사가 전치사 뒤에 오면 목적격으로 쓴다.

15 ⑤ 주어와 목적어의 대상이 you로 같으므로, 목적어의 자리에는 재귀대명사(yourself)를 쓰는 것이 알맞다.
① his는 이미 그 자체로 소유격 대명사이므로, '(어퍼스트로피)를 이용하여 소유격을 만들어줄 필요가 없다. (his' → his)
② 문장의 주어와 목적어의 대상이 astronauts로 같으므로 재귀대명사를 쓰는 것이 알맞다. 그러나 astronauts는 복수형이므로, 재귀대명사 또한 3인칭 복수형인 themselves가 되어야 한다. (himself → themselves)
③ 밑줄 친 부분은 문장의 주어 자리이므로 주격 인칭대명사가 나와야 한다. her의 주격은 she이다. (her → she)
④ 주어와 목적어의 대상이 각각 All the teachers와 her로 다르므로 재귀대명사를 쓰지 않는다. 밑줄 친 부분은 목적어 자리이므로 3인칭 단수 여성의 목적격 대명사인 her로 고쳐야 한다. (herself → her)

16 지금 '다른 할 일'이 있다는 것을 나타내야 하므로, 긍정문에 쓰이는 something이 들어간다.

17 one ~, another …, and the other –
'(셋 중에) 하나는 ~, 다른 하나는 …, 나머지 하나는 –'

18 긍정문에서 '누군가'라는 뜻을 나타내는 대명사는 someone이다. anyone이 긍정문에 쓰이면 '누구라도, 어떤 사람이라도'라는 뜻인데 여기서는 맥락상 적절하지 않다.

19 • 선택의 범위가 주어질 때는 which를 쓴다.
• What do you think of ~?
'~에 대해 어떻게 생각하니?'

20 주어진 문장의 밑줄 친 It은 가주어로 쓰였다.
⑤ 가주어 it   ①②④ 비인칭 주어 it
③ 인칭대명사 it

21 one ~ the other …
'(둘 중에) 하나는 ~, 다른 하나는 …'

22 ④ 관계대명사   ①②③⑤ 의문대명사

23 ③ this of → that of

24 (A) (B) 전체 개수가 불특정한 경우, 그 중 일부를 가리킬 때 some, 다른 일부를 언급할 때 others라고 한다.
(C) '또 다른 하나'를 가리키는 another이 적절하며 이때 other은 명사를 수식하는 형태로만 사용할 수 있기 때문에 빈칸에 들어갈 수 없다.

25 (A),② 지시대명사, ① 주격 관계대명사, ③ 동격의 접속사, ④ 지시형용사, ⑤ It~that 강조구문의 that
(A) 그것은 훌륭한 계획처럼 들린다.
① 어제 온 택배는 어디에 있니?
② 너는 어느 것을 가질래, 이것 아니면 저것?
③ 난 Mike가 날 좋아하는 것 같은 느낌이 든다.
④ 저기에 있는 저 여자를 봐.
⑤ 내 인생을 바꾼 것은 바로 그 책이다.

26 • each other '서로'
• on the other hand '반면에'

27 ① 날짜를 나타내는 비인칭주어 it
② 인칭대명사 it
④ 거리를 나타내는 비인칭주어 it
⑤ It ~ that 강조구문

28 주어진 문장의 밑줄 친 It은 가주어로 쓰였다.
②③ 가주어 it
① 인칭대명사 it
④ 날씨를 나타내는 비인칭주어 it
⑤ 시간을 나타내는 비인칭주어 it

29 every는 뒤에 단수 명사와 단수 동사를 취한다.

30 ⑤ '유일한'의 의미를 지닌 형용사 one
①②③④ 명사의 반복을 피하기 위한 부정대명사 one

31 ② 학생들이 10명이라고 명시되어 있다. 특정한 수의 사람들 중에서 나머지를 얘기할 때는, the others를 쓴다. (others → the others)
① 앞에 나온 car와 종류는 같지만, 다른 대상이므로 명사의 반복을 피하기 위해 one을 쓰는 것이 적절하다.
③ 'a lot of entertainers'로 불특정한 수의 사람들을 말하고 있으므로, 그 중 몇몇은 some, 다른 사람들은 others로 쓴다.
④ 세 개의 대상 중에 제일 처음 언급하는 것은 one, 다른 하나는 another, 나머지 하나는 the other로 쓴다.
⑤ 나는 이것이 맘에 들지 않으니 또 하나의 다른 것을

보여달라는 내용이 되어야 한다. 따라서 another
의 쓰임은 적절하다.

32 some ~ others …
'(불특정한 수의 사람들 중에서) 몇몇은 ~ 다른 사람들
은 …'

33 that은 앞에 나온 명사의 반복을 피하기 위해 쓰였다.

34 ⑤「all of + 셀 수 없는 명사 + 단수 동사」
(were → was)

35 앞에 나온 명사가 복수형일 때, 그 반복을 피하기 위해
쓰는 부정대명사는 ones이다.

36 (1) those days '그 당시, 그 때'
(2) this Friday '이번 금요일'
(3) these '이것들'
(4) that은 앞에 나온 the population의 반복을 피하
기 위해 쓰였다.

37 • He burned <u>himself</u>.
• My little sister can't look after <u>herself</u>.
• They set up their tents by <u>themselves</u>.
• You should be proud of <u>yourself</u>.

38 It seems that 주어 + 동사
= 주어 seem(s) to 동사원형

39 • by oneself '혼자서'

• burn oneself '불에 데다'
• enjoy oneself '즐거운 시간을 보내다'

40 문장의 주어와 목적어의 대상이 같으므로 재귀대명사
를 쓴다.

41 ⓐ one ~, the other… '(둘 중에) 하나는 ~, 나머지
하나는 …'
ⓑ 앞에 나온 some books를 대신하는 대명사는
them이다.
ⓒ another + 단수명사 '또 다른 ~'

42 「whose + 명사」 '누구의 ~'

43 「be able to + 동사원형」 '~할 수 있다'
by oneself '혼자서, 홀로'

44 가주어 it을 가장 앞에 놓고, 진주어인 to부정사구는
문장 뒤로 보낸다.

45 글의 ⓐ rest와 ④는 '나머지'라는 의미이다.
① 쉬다 ② 휴식 ③ 받치다, 기대다 ⑤ 그대로 있다

46 those는 뒤에 who가 와서 '~한 사람들'의 의미로 쓰
인다.

47 (1) 어느 재킷이 더 싸니?
(2) Paul에게 무슨 일이 일어났니?
(3) 난 그 얘기가 마음에 들어. 그건 누구의 아이디어야?

| CHAPTER **7** | **부정사** Infinitives | 본문 _ p.178 |

PRACTICE 1

2 It is important to read a lot of books.
3 To go to a concert is exciting.
4 It was not easy to make my dream come true.
5 It is a lot of fun to visit foreign countries.
6 To watch English TV programs is helpful.
7 It is not good to spend so much time playing
computer games.

> **1, 3, 6** to부정사가 이끄는 구가 문장 내에서 주어 자리에 위치하
> 며, 단수 취급한다.
> **2, 4, 5, 7** '가주어(It) ~ 진주어(to부정사)' 구문이 쓰인 문장이다.

PRACTICE 2

1 to be a famous singer
2 to see things clearly
3 to take care of patients
4 to watch movies
5 to go to Europe
6 to jog every day

> **1~6** 명사처럼 쓰이는 to부정사가 문장 내에서 보어 역할을 할 때,
> '~하는 것이다'로 해석한다.

PRACTICE 3

2 to meet **3** to keep
4 not to fail **5** to apologize
6 to eat **7** not to have
8 to swim **9** to see
10 not to talk **11** to take

12 not to forget   **13** to visit

14 to study   **15** not to spend

> **1** lose weight: 체중을 감량하다
> **3** keep a diary: 일기를 쓰다
> **4, 7, 10, 12, 15** to부정사의 부정형은 「not to+동사원형」으로 쓴다.
> **4** fail the exam: 시험에 떨어지다
> **11** take a shower: 샤워하다
> **13** refuse: 거절하다

PRACTICE 4

2 Becky to open the door

3 Becky to meet his parents

4 Becky to come to his place

5 Becky to clean the room

6 Tony to repair her car

7 Tony to go out to play

8 Becky to shut the door

9 Becky not to touch anything

10 Tony to say sorry to his brother first

> **1~10** tell, ask, would like, expect, want, allow, order, warn, advise와 같은 동사는 목적격 보어로 to부정사를 가진다.

PRACTICE 5

2 how to solve   **3** how to help

4 what to wear   **5** how to use

6 what to say   **7** how to grow

8 what to buy

> **4, 6, 8** 문장 내에 wear, say, buy의 목적어가 없으므로 '무엇을 ~ 할지'라는 의미를 가진 what+to부정사가 적절하다.

PRACTICE 6

1 no one to understand him

2 something to eat

3 no money to give him

4 to start the meeting

5 something cold to drink

6 a friend to play with

7 a lot of things to buy

8 enough time to think

9 the best way to get there

10 a nice house to live in

> **6, 10** to부정사가 수식하는 명사가 전치사의 목적어일 경우 꼭 전치사를 써야 한다.

PRACTICE 7

1 deal with   **2** ○

3 rely on   **4** wait for

5 ○   **6** complain about

PRACTICE 8

1 to say hello to me

2 to check her email

3 to protect your eyes

4 to take care of the sick

5 to buy a present for his mom

6 to ask about the test

7 to pass the exam

8 to stay healthy and slim

PRACTICE 9

1 Hana went to the library in order to study for the final exam.

2 I called Minho so as to ask him if he could go shopping with me.

3 Mom stopped the car so as to pick up Kelly.

4 Tony opened the door in order to watch the birds in the tree.

5 I turned on the computer in order to send an email.

6 Jenny bought some vegetables so as to make a salad.

PRACTICE 10

1 for   **2** for   **3** to   **4** to

5 for   **6** to   **7** to   **8** for

9 to   **10** for

> **1** thank+사람+for+명사/동명사: ~에 대해 …에게 고마워하다
> **2** keep[save] money for a rainy day: 어려울 때에 대비해 돈을 모아두다
> **3, 4, 6, 7, 9** 빈칸 다음에 원형부정사가 나오는데 목적/의도를 설명할 수 있도록 연결하려면 to가 들어가야 한다.
> **5, 8, 10** 빈칸 다음에 명사가 나오는데 목적/의도를 설명할 수 있도록 연결하려면 전치사 for가 들어가야 한다.
> **5** for some cookies: 쿠키를 좀 사기 위해서
> **8** for lunch: 점심식사를 하기 위해서
> **10** for carbonara pasta: 카르보나라 파스타를 만들기 위해서

Ch **7** 부정사

PRACTICE 11

1 I was really excited to go back to my hometown.

2 I was surprised to see Nancy on the street.

3 I was so happy to get a new computer.

4 Jason was stupid to show the answer to his classmate.

5 I was glad to introduce my family to you.

6 Sora was lucky to pass such a difficult test.

> 1, 2, 3, 5 to부정사가 형용사 중 감정을 나타내는 excited, surprised, happy, glad를 수식하여 감정의 원인을 나타낸다.
> 4, 6 to부정사가 형용사 stupid, lucky를 수식하여 판단의 근거를 나타낸다.

PRACTICE 12

1 소라는 수진이를 다시 보게 되어 기뻤다.

2 내 딸은 자라서 경찰관이 되었다.

3 그 강은 수영하기에 매우 위험하다.

4 그녀를 매일 기다리다니 그는 그녀를 많이 좋아하는 게 틀림없다.

5 나는 역에 도착했지만 내 기차가 이미 떠난 것을 알게 되었을 뿐이었다.

PRACTICE 13

1	for	2	for	3	to	4	of
5	for	6	of	7	to	8	of
9	for	10	of	11	of	12	for

> 1, 2, 5, 9, 12 to부정사의 행위의 주체가 되는 의미상의 주어 앞에 위치하기에는 for이 적절하다.
> 3 to부정사의 명사적 용법으로, to부정사는 진주어, it은 가주어가 된다.
> 7 형용사를 수식하여 '~하기에'라는 의미를 나타내는 to부정사의 부사적 용법이 오는 것이 적절하다.
> 4, 6, 8, 10, 11 사람의 성격을 묘사하는 형용사를 꾸며줄 때 의미상의 주어를 「of+목적격」으로 나타낸다.

PRACTICE 14

2 The book was so interesting that I could read it twice.

3 I studied very hard (in order/so as) to be the top student.

4 The curry was so spicy that I couldn't eat it.

5 The dress was so expensive that she couldn't buy it.

6 Mina went to Canada (in order/so as) to study English.

7 The movie was so scary that children couldn't watch it.

8 The blue shirt is so big that I can't wear it.

9 The stadium was so big that ten thousand people could fit into it.

10 The box is so light that I can carry it.

> 1, 4, 5, 7, 8 「so+형용사+that+주어+can't[couldn't]~」는 「too+형용사+for+의미상의 주어+to부정사」로 바꾸어 쓸 수 있다.
> 2, 9, 10 「so+형용사+that+주어+can[could]~」는 「형용사+enough+for+의미상의 주어+to부정사」로 바꾸어 쓸 수 있다.
> 3, 6 「so that+주어+can[could]」는 「(in order/so as) to부정사」로 바꾸어 쓸 수 있다.

PRACTICE 15

1	wear	2	shake[shaking]
3	carry[to carry]	4	ring[ringing]
5	do	6	feel
7	enter[entering]	8	find[to find]
9	plant[planting]	10	practice

> 1, 5, 6, 10 사역동사의 목적격 보어 역할은 원형부정사만 가능하다.
> 2, 4, 7, 9 지각동사의 목적격 보어 자리에는 원형부정사를 사용하고, 동작이 진행 중임을 강조할 때 현재분사도 가능하다.
> 3, 8 준사역동사 help의 목적격 보어 자리에는 원형부정사와 to부정사 모두 사용 가능하다.

PRACTICE 16

2 clean the room first

3 play[playing] the guitar

4 use her laptop

5 study English for the test

6 the table move[moving]

📝 중간·기말고사 대비문제 정답 본문 _ p.193

1 ② 2 ③,⑤ 3 ⑤ 4 ③ 5 ©, The question was too difficult to answer. 6 ⑤ 7 to buy

8 ③ 9 too boring to watch until the end

10 ⑤ 11 ⑤ 12 ③ 13 ② 14 ④ 15 ④

16 ⑤ 17 ④ 18 ② 19 ②,⑤ 20 ⑤ 21 ④

22 ⑤　**23** ⑤　**24** It is useful to learn a second language.　**25** ③　**26** to say how many people use it　**27** (1) looking, to study with (2) to participate in　**28** ②　**29** ③　**30** ⑤　**31** ⓐ,ⓒ/(목적을 나타내는) 부사적 용법　**32** what to do　**33** ③,⑤　**34** ①　**35** ⑤　**36** ②　**37** ⑤　**38** ①,③　**39** ⑤　**40** The water was so dirty that I could not drink it.　**41** asked Minji not to miss her piano lesson　**42** ③　**43** ran fast enough to catch him　**44** It is important to remember your friend's birthday.　**45** ⑤　**46** to learn how to make a cake　**47** ⑤　**48** ①　**49** ④　**50** ⑤　**51** (A) I drank coffee (in order/so as) to stay awake.　(B) And I also skipped meals (in order/so as) to study more.　**52** ③　**53** ①　**54** (1) how to play the cello　(2) what to wear　**55** of, to help, go up the stairs　**56** ⑤　**57** (1) He was too sleepy to stay up late. (2) He was so sleepy that he couldn't stay up late.

중간·기말고사 대비문제 해설

1　주어진 문장은 '외국인과 대화하기 위해서'라는 뜻으로, 목적을 나타내는 to부정사의 부사적 용법이다.
　② '공부하기 위해서'라는 목적을 나타내는 to부정사의 부사적 용법이다.
　①③ to부정사의 명사적 용법으로 문장 내에서 목적어로 쓰이고 있다.
　④ 앞에 나오는 명사 something을 수식하는 to부정사의 형용사적 용법이다.
　⑤ to부정사의 명사적 용법으로, to부정사가 주어의 역할을 하고 있다. 이때 진주어인 to부정사는 뒤로 보내고, 주어의 자리에 가주어인 it을 써주었다.

2　③⑤ 앞에 나온 명사를 수식하는 to부정사의 형용사적 용법이다.
　①② 문장 내에서 주어 역할을 하는 to부정사의 명사적 용법이다.
　④ 감정의 원인을 나타내는 to부정사의 부사적 용법이다.

3　It takes 사람＋시간＋to부정사
　＝ It takes 시간＋for 사람＋to부정사
　It takes me an hour to go to school by bus.

4　빈칸에 들어갈 말은 necessary for me to study이

다. to부정사의 의미상 주어는 「for＋목적격」으로 표현한다.

5　ⓒ to부정사의 목적어가 주어와 일치하는 경우 to부정사 뒤에는 목적어를 쓰지 않는다. (it 삭제)
　ⓐ to부정사가 수식하는 명사 emails가 전치사 to의 목적어이므로 전치사를 포함하여 to reply to로 쓴 것은 적절하다.
　ⓑ 목적어 her computer가 고쳐지는 것이므로 목적격 보어 자리에 과거분사 fixed를 쓴다.
　ⓓ 사역동사 made는 목적격 보어 자리에 동사원형을 쓴다.
　ⓔ 목적어 his car가 세차되는 것이므로 목적격 보어 자리에 과거분사 washed를 쓴다.
　ⓕ 지각동사 noticed의 목적격 보어로 ~ing을 쓸 수 있다.

6　주어진 문장의 밑줄 친 to protect는 명사구 an easy way를 수식하는 to부정사의 형용사적 용법으로 쓰였다.
　⑤ 명사 a pet을 수식하는 to부정사의 형용사적 용법이다.
　① to부정사의 명사적 용법으로, 문장에서 주격 보어로 쓰였다.
　② '바닥을 닦기 위해서'라는 목적을 나타내는 to부정사의 부사적 용법이다.
　③ surprised라는 형용사를 수식하여 감정의 원인을 나타내는 to부정사의 부사적 용법이다.
　④ 동사 decide의 목적어로 쓰인 to부정사의 명사적 용법이다.

7　'~하기 위해서'라는 뜻을 가진 to부정사의 부사적 용법이 필요하다.

8　「what to＋동사원형」'무엇을 ~할지'

9　「too＋형용사＋to부정사」'…하기에 너무 -한'

10　⑤ '바람이 우리가 밖에 놀러 가기에 충분히 강하게 불었다'는 의미이다.
　①②③④ '바람이 너무 강해서 우리는 밖에 놀러 갈 수 없었다'는 의미이다.

11　⑤ 사역동사 make는 목적격 보어로 동사원형이 온다. (thinking → think)

12　ⓒ 동사 decide는 to부정사를 목적어로 한다. (meeting → to meet)
　ⓔ 사역동사 make는 원형부정사를 목적격 보어로 쓴다. (to take → take)
　ⓕ 동사 want는 목적격 보어로 to부정사를 쓴다.

(bring → to bring)

13 to부정사의 의미상의 주어는 'for+목적격'으로 나타낸다. to부정사가 사람의 성격을 묘사하는 형용사를 꾸며줄 때는 'of+목적격'으로 쓴다.
② of ①③④⑤ for

14 감정을 나타내는 형용사 뒤에 오는 to부정사는 그 감정을 느끼는 원인이 된다.

15 ⓑ '영어를 공부하기 위해서'라는 목적을 나타내는 to부정사의 부사적 용법이다.
ⓔ '시험을 통과하기 위해서'라는 목적을 나타내는 to부정사의 부사적 용법이다.
ⓐ to부정사의 명사적 용법으로, 문장의 진주어 역할을 하고 있다. 이때 to부정사구는 문장의 뒤로 보내고, 주어 자리에는 가주어 it을 써주었다.
ⓒ agree의 목적어로 쓰인 to부정사의 명사적 용법이다.
ⓓ 명사 the fastest way를 수식해주는 to부정사의 형용사적 용법이다.

16 ⑤ to부정사는 to+동사원형의 형태로 만든다. 이 경우, 문장의 주어로 쓰인 to부정사이므로, to study로 써주는 것이 맞다. (studying → study)
① something과 같이 -thing 형태의 대명사는 형용사가 뒤에서 수식한다. 따라서 고치지 않은 형태가 맞다.
② 등위 접속사 and가 있으므로 밑줄 친 자리는 to see 혹은 see와 병렬구조를 이루고 있다. 따라서 to부정사나 동사원형으로 써주는 것이 맞다. (heard → (to) hear)
③ 동사 tell은 목적격 보어로 to부정사를 쓴다. (coming → to come)
④ stop은 동명사만을 목적어로 쓰는 동사이지만, 목적을 나타내는 부사적 용법의 to부정사가 함께 쓰이기도 한다. 여기에서는 '점심을 사는 것을 멈추다'가 아니라 '점심을 사기 위해'라는 목적을 나타내는 to부정사로 쓰는 것이 적절하다.

17 ⓐ 지각동사 hear는 목적격 보어로 동사원형 또는 현재분사가 온다. (talk or talking)
ⓑ need는 to 부정사를 목적어로 취하는 동사이다. (to listen)
ⓒ 목적을 나타내야 하므로(그가 말하는 것을 이해하기 위해서는) to 부정사의 부사적 용법을 쓰는 것이 적절하다. (to understand)

18 명사 some books를 수식해주는 to부정사의 형용사적 용법이다.
② 명사구 a list of tasks을 수식해주는 to부정사의 형용사적 용법이다.
①④ 동사 wish와 would love의 목적어로 쓰인 to부정사의 명사적 용법이다.
③ '그를 만나기 위해서'라는 목적을 나타내는 to부정사의 부사적 용법이다.
⑤ to부정사의 명사적 용법으로, 문장의 진주어로 쓰였다. 이때, to부정사는 문장의 뒤로 보내고 주어의 자리에 가주어 it을 써주었다.

19 ② '방문할 장소들'이라는 뜻으로, places를 수식하기 위해서는 to부정사가 필요하다. (visit → to visit)
⑤ '노래를 잘하기 위해'라는 목적을 나타내주어야 하므로, to부정사의 부사적 용법을 활용해야 한다. (sing → to sing)
① want는 목적격 보어로 to부정사를 쓰는 동사이다.
③④ plan과 would like은 목적어로 to부정사를 쓰는 동사이다.

20 ⑤ 할머니께 컴퓨터를 사용하는 방법을 알려드렸다는 뜻이므로 의문사 how를 사용한다. (what → how)

21 (A), (B), (C), (E) how
(D) What

22 대화에서 밑줄 친 부분, ⑤ 형용사적 용법
①② 명사적 용법
③④ 부사적 용법

23 주어진 문장의 밑줄 친 It은 가주어이다.
⑤ 가주어 it
①④ 비인칭주어 it
②③ 인칭대명사 it

24 「It(가주어) ~ to부정사(진주어)」 구문

25 ③ something과 같은 -thing 형태의 대명사 뒤에 이를 수식하는 형용사가 나오면 to부정사는 형용사 뒤에 위치한다. (to eat cold → cold to eat)

26 「to+동사원형」이 문장의 뒤에서 구를 이끌어 진주어 역할을 한다.

27 (1) 진행중인 동작을 나타내므로 현재진행형 동사 looking을 쓰고, 명사 a partner를 수식하는 형용사적 용법의 to부정사를 쓴다.
(2) 주어 My wish의 보어가 필요하므로 명사적 용법의 to부정사를 쓴다. participate in은 '~에 참여하다'라는 뜻이다.

28 to부정사의 의미상의 주어는 'for+목적격'으로 쓴다. to부정사가 사람의 성격을 묘사하는 형용사를 꾸며줄

때는 'of+목적격'으로 쓴다.

② of ①③④⑤ for

29 ③ allow는 목적격 보어로 to부정사를 쓴다.

(go → to go)

① tell은 목적격 보어로 to부정사를 쓰는 동사이다.

② 사역동사 make는 목적격 보어로 원형부정사를 쓴다.

④ 준사역동사 help는 목적격 보어로 to부정사 또는 원형부정사를 쓴다.

⑤ 지각동사 see는 목적격 보어로 원형부정사나 현재분사를 쓴다.

30 「dying+to부정사」 '몹시 ~하고 싶어하는'

31 〈보기〉의 밑줄 친 부분 to catch는 '~을 타기 위하여'라는 뜻으로 to부정사의 목적을 나타내는 부사적 용법으로 쓰였다.

ⓐ to ask: 구하기 위하여(목적을 나타내는 부사적 용법)

ⓒ To make: 만들기 위하여(목적을 나타내는 부사적 용법)

ⓑ to do: 하는 것을(문장에서 목적어의 역할을 하는 명사적 용법)

ⓔ to recommend: 추천 할(명사 books를 수식하는 형용사적 용법)

ⓓ to know: 알기를(문장에서 목적어의 역할을 하는 명사적 용법)

제목: 책 추천

Dewey 선생님께

저는 선생님의 영어 수업의 학생들 중 한명인 Paul이에요. 저는 선생님께 조언을 구하기 위해 이메일을 쓰고 있어요. 저는 많은 독서를 하는 것을 계획하고 있어요. 좋은 책들의 목록을 만들기 위해, 약간의 책을 추천해주실 수 있을까요? 저는 선생님이 추천 할 많은 흥미로운 책을 생각할 수 있다고 확신해요. 저는 선생님의 십대 시절동안 어떤 책들이 선생님에게 영감을 주었는지 알기를 원해요.

시간 내주셔서 감사합니다.

Paul 드림

32 「what to+동사원형」 '무엇을 ~할지'

33 ③ 주어 역할을 하고 있는 자리이므로 to부정사의 명사적 용법 또는 동명사를 쓸 수 있다.

⑤ start는 목적어로 to부정사나 동명사를 쓴다.

① advise는 목적격 보어로 to부정사를 쓴다.

② 준사역동사 help는 목적격 보어로 to부정사 또는

원형부정사를 쓴다.

④ to부정사가 sorry라는 형용사를 수식하여 감정의 원인을 나타내는 부사적 용법으로 쓰였다.

34 주어진 문장의 to부정사구는 명사구 a special way를 수식하는 형용사적 용법으로 쓰였다. '요리하는 (특별한 방법)'으로 해석한다.

① 명사구 a lot을 수식해주는 형용사적 용법이다. '배울 (많은 것)'로 해석한다.

② 동사 promise의 목적어로 쓰였으며, 명사적 용법이다.

③ '졸업하기 위해'라는 목적을 나타내는 to부정사의 부사적 용법이다.

④ '건강하게 유지하기 위해'라는 목적을 나타내는 부사적 용법이다.

⑤ '수영하기 위해'라는 목적을 나타내는 부사적 용법이다.

35 「too+형용사+to부정사」=「so+형용사+that+주어+cannot」 '너무 ~해서 …하지 못하다'

36 ② 'It's time ~'은 '~할 시간이다'의 뜻으로, time 뒤에 동사가 올 때는 to부정사의 형태로 쓴다.

(for → to)

37 가주어로 it, 진주어로 to부정사를 쓴다. 사람의 성격을 나타내는 형용사인 generous(관대한)를 썼기 때문에 의미상의 주어는 to부정사 앞에 「of+목적격」 형태로 쓴다.

38 (A) agree의 목적어로 쓰인 to부정사의 명사적 용법이다.

(B) '사진을 찍기 위해'라는 목적을 나타내는 to부정사의 부사적 용법이다.

(C) '물리학자가 되기 위해'라는 목적을 나타내는 to부정사의 부사적 용법이다.

(D) 명사 person을 수식해주는 to부정사의 형용사적 용법이다.

(E) decide의 목적어로 쓰인 to부정사의 명사적 용법이다.

39 ① 그녀가 거기서 무엇을 하고 있냐는 뜻이 적절하므로 진행형으로 써야 한다. 진행형은 「be+-ing」의 형태로 쓴다. (do → doing)

② 과거를 나타내는 부사구 last night이 쓰였으므로 과거시제로 써야 한다. (studies → studied)

③ 수사+명사가 형용사처럼 명사를 수식할 때는 명사를 복수형으로 쓰지 않는다.

(30-years-old → 30-year-old)

Ch **7** 부정사

④ need는 to부정사를 목적어로 쓰는 동사이다. to부정사는 to+동사원형으로 쓴다.
(to helps → to help)

40 「so+형용사+that+주어+can't」 '너무 ~해서 …할 수 없다'

41 5형식 동사 ask는 to부정사를 목적격 보어로 취한다. 이때 빈칸에는 '하지 말아야' 하는 내용에 대한 요청을 나타내야 하므로 「not+to부정사」를 이용하여(not to miss) 답안을 작성한다. 대명사 your는 목적어에 맞게 her로 바꾼다.

42 ③ 동사 refuse는 목적어로 to부정사를 쓴다.
(taking → to take)
① smell과 같은 감각동사는 보어 자리에 형용사가 온다.
② '~만큼 …한'이라는 뜻의 원급 비교는 「as+원급+as」의 어순으로 쓴다.
④ try는 to부정사와 동명사 모두 목적어로 쓸 수 있지만, 여기서는 '책을 읽기 위해 노력하다'라는 의미로 쓰였으므로 to부정사로 써야 한다. try의 목적어로 동명사가 올 경우, '(시험 삼아) ~ 해보다'라는 뜻이 된다.
⑤ told는 목적격 보어로 to부정사를 받는 동사이다.

43 「so+형용사/부사+that+주어+can(could)」
=「형용사/부사+enough+to부정사」'매우 ~해서 …할 수 있다'='…하기에 충분히 ~하다'

44 to부정사를 진주어로, 본래의 주어 자리에 it을 가주어로 쓴 문장이 필요하다.

45 ⑤ to부정사의 의미상의 주어는 'for+목적격'으로 쓴다. 사람의 성격을 묘사하는 형용사가 쓰였을 때는 'of+목적격'으로 쓴다. impossible은 성격을 묘사하는 형용사가 아니므로 for가 적절하다.
(of → for)

46 want의 목적어로 to부정사(to learn)가 쓰였으며, learn은 'how to+동사원형'을 목적어로 가진다.

47 promise 뒤에 동사가 목적어로 올 때는 「to+동사원형」의 형태로 쓴다.

48 (A) 현재완료 동사와 빈도부사를 함께 쓸 경우 「have+빈도부사+과거분사」의 어순으로 쓴다.
(B) decide는 목적어로 to부정사를 취하는 동사다.
(C) 그녀는 내 선물을 받아서 기쁜 것이므로 감정의 이유를 나타내는 부사적 용법의 to부정사를 쓰는 것이 적절하다.

49 ④ make의 목적격 보어는 동사원형으로 쓴다.

①②③⑤ 목적격 보어로 to부정사의 형태를 갖는 동사들이다.

50 ⑤ 감정의 원인을 나타내는 부사적 용법
①②③④ 목적을 나타내는 부사적 용법

51 in order to = so as to = to부정사의 부사적 용법 중 '목적'

52 ⓒ '너무 ~해서 …할 수 있(었)다'는 뜻인 「so+형용사/부사+that+주어+can/could」는 '…할 정도로 충분히 ~한'의 뜻을 갖는 「형용사/부사+enough+to부정사」와 바꾸어 쓸 수 있다. 「too+형용사/부사+to부정사」는 '~하기에는 너무 …한'이라는 의미이다. (too hard to win→ hard enough to win)
ⓐ 동명사와 to부정사는 모두 주어에 대한 설명을 보충하는 보어의 역할로 쓰일 수 있다. 이때의 to부정사는 명사적 용법이다.
ⓑ 「의문사+to부정사」는 「의문사+주어+should+동사원형」으로 바꾸어 쓸 수 있다.
ⓓ happy와 같이 감정을 나타내는 형용사를 수식하는 to부정사는 '~해서, ~하게 되어'의 뜻으로 감정의 원인을 나타내기 때문에 이유, 원인을 나타내는 접속사 because절로 바꾸어 쓸 수 있다.
ⓔ 준사역동사 help는 목적격 보어로 원형부정사와 to부정사를 모두 쓸 수 있다.

53 The doctor <u>advised her not to eat</u> sugary foods.
advise는 목적격 보어로 to부정사를 취하는 동사이며, to부정사의 부정형은 'not+to+동사원형'이다.

54 (1)「how+to부정사」'~하는 법'
(2)「what+to부정사」'무엇을 ~할지'

55 to부정사가 사람의 성격을 나타내는 형용사를 꾸며줄 때에는 의미상의 주어를 「of+목적격」으로 나타내고, help의 목적격 보어로는 원형부정사 또는 to부정사를 쓴다. 여기서는 빈칸의 수에 맞추려면 원형부정사가 와야 한다.

56 ⓐ want는 목적격 보어로 to부정사를 쓰는 동사이다.
ⓑ order는 목적격 보어로 to부정사를 쓰는 동사이다. 낯선 사람들에게 말을 걸지 말라고 했으므로, to부정사의 부정형을 써준다. to부정사의 부정형은 「not to+동사원형」의 어순으로 쓴다.

57 「too+형용사+to부정사」=「so+형용사+that+주어+couldn't」'너무 ~해서 …할 수 없었다'

PRACTICE 1

1 Working seven days a week is exhausting.

2 Her job is designing shoes.

3 Taking a shower makes you feel refreshed.

4 Learning English takes a lot of time and effort.

5 My hobby is taking photos outside.

6 Your mistake was speaking too fast.

> 동명사는 「동사원형+-ing」의 형태로 '~하는 것'이라고 해석하며 문장 내에서 주어, 보어, 목적어의 역할을 할 수 있다.
>
> **1** 일주일에 7일을 일하는 것: Working seven days a week (주어)
> **2** 신발을 디자인하는 것: designing shoes (주격 보어)
> **3** 샤워를 하는 것: Taking a shower (주어)
> **4** 영어를 배우는 것: Learning English (주어)
> **5** 야외에서 사진을 찍는 것: taking photos outside (주격 보어)
> **6** 너무 빠르게 말한 것: speaking too fast (주격 보어)

PRACTICE 2

1 Practicing the violin

2 Being honest

3 travel(l)ing around the world

4 Making new friends

5 teaching English to kids

6 Living in the countryside

> **1, 2, 4, 6** to부정사 주어가 문장 맨 뒤로 가고 가주어 it이 그 자리를 대신하는 문장이다. 진주어인 to부정사의 to를 뗀 후 -ing를 붙여 동명사로 바꾸고 원래 자리인 맨 앞으로 오게 한다.
> **3, 5** 보어로 쓰인 to부정사구를 동명사구로 바꾼다.

PRACTICE 3

1 working **2** to watch **3** talking

4 having **5** to send **6** cooking

7 working **8** to go **9** writing

10 to see

> **1, 3, 4, 6, 7** finish, stop, put off, enjoy, quit은 동명사를 목적어로 가지는 동사이다.
>   **3** stop+동명사 ~하는 것을 멈추다
>   stop+to부정사 ~하기 위해 멈추다 (부사적 용법)
> **2, 5, 8, 10** decide, promise, plan, hope는 to부정사를 목적어로 가지는 동사이다.
> **9** keep+-ing: 계속 ~하다

PRACTICE 4

2 not having **3** not going

4 not eating **5** staying

> **1** doesn't mind: 신경 쓰지 않다, 괜찮다
> **3** Tony: You didn't go to the library, did you?
>   너는 도서관에 가지 않았어, 그렇지?
>   Becky: Yes, I did!
>   아니야, 나 갔었어!
> Tony는 Becky가 도서관에 가지 않은 것으로 생각하고 질문했지만, Becky는 갔었다고 말하며 Tony의 질문에 부인했다. 따라서 Becky는 '도서관에 안 갔다는 것(not going)을 부인했다.'가 맞다. 여기서 부정 의문문의 대답으로 쓰인 yes는 '아니오'로 해석하고, I did는 긍정으로 해석한다.

PRACTICE 5

1 to eat, eating **2** wasting

3 reading **4** to move

5 to paint, painting **6** to snow, snowing

7 to be **8** to go, going

9 to drink **10** playing

11 making **12** to spend, spending

13 to throw, throwing **14** to get

15 to run, running

> **1, 5, 6, 8, 12, 13, 15** 동사 like, love, begin, intend, hate, continue, start는 동명사와 to부정사를 모두 목적어로 취하고, 그 중 어느 것을 목적어로 취하든지 뜻이 달라지지 않는 동사들이다.
> **2, 3, 10, 11** 동사 quit, finish, practice, dislike는 동명사만을 목적어로 가지는 동사이다.
> **4, 7, 9, 14** 동사 decide, refuse, would like, wish는 to부정사만을 목적어로 가지는 동사이다.

PRACTICE 6

1 to find **2** talking

3 buying **4** not travel(l)ing

5 to set **6** opening

7 adding **8** to fill

9 telling **10** seeing

11 not to spend **12** meeting

13 not to be **14** cleaning

15 to visit

1 tried to find: 찾으려고 노력했다
2 stopped talking: 말하기를 멈췄다
3 regret buying: 구매한 것을 후회하다 (일어난 일)
4 suggest not travel(l)ing: 여행하지 말 것을 제안하다
5 forgot to set: (알람을) 맞추는 것을 잊었다 (일어나지 않은 일)
6 mind opening: 여는 것을 꺼리다
7 try adding: 추가하는 것을 시도해봐라
8 stopped to fill up: 채우기 위해서 멈췄다 (목적을 나타내는 부사구로 쓰인 to부정사)
9 dislike telling lies: 거짓말하는 것을 싫어하다
10 won't forget seeing: 본 것을 잊지 않을 것이다 (일어난 일)
11 decide not to spend: (여름휴가를 제주도에서) 보내지 않기로 결정하다
12 remember meeting: 만난 것을 기억하다 (일어난 일)
13 promised not to be late: 늦지 않기로 약속했다
14 finish cleaning: 청소하는 것을 끝내다
15 have forgotten to visit: 방문할 것을 잊었다 (일어나지 않은 일)

1, 10, 13 go+-ing: ~하러 가다
2, 9, 12 spend+시간/돈+-ing: ~하느라 시간/돈을 쓰다
3 need+to be p.p./-ing: ~될/할 필요가 있다
4 How[What] about -ing?/What do you say to+-ing?: ~하는 것 어때?
5 be busy+-ing: ~하느라 바쁘다
6 It's no use+-ing: ~해도 소용없다
7 can't help+-ing: ~하지 않을 수 없다
8, 14 have trouble[difficulty/a hard time]+-ing: ~하는 데에 어려움을 겪다
11 There is no+-ing = It is impossible to부정사: ~할 수 없다
15 be worth+-ing: ~할 만한 가치가 있다

PRACTICE 7

1	in playing	2	about[of] moving
3	like having	4	about taking
5	about[of] going	6	of watching
7	for cleaning	8	at singing
9	about fixing	10	about visiting
11	for being	12	to having
13	from coming	14	hearing
15	to living		

PRACTICE 8

1 go skating
2 spent, buying
3 fixing[to be fixed]
4 How[What] about taking,
What do you say to taking
5 busy studying
6 no use trying
7 couldn't help laughing
8 having trouble[difficulty/a hard time] getting
9 spent, thinking
10 go skiing
11 There is no defeating [It is impossible to defeat]
12 spends, reading
13 went camping
14 had trouble[difficulty/a hard time] understanding
15 is worth visiting

중간·기말고사 대비문제 정답 본문 _ p.213

1 ④ 2 ④ 3 ① 4 ③ 5 ④ 6 (1) I really dislike being interrupted by people. (2) Don't forget to feed our dog after school tomorrow.
7 ③ 8 ⑤ 9 to give, washing, planting, doing 10 ③ 11 ③ 12 ④ 13 ③ 14 ②
15 Exercise → Exercising [To exercise] 16 ③
17 ③ 18 ② 19 ③ 20 ① 21 They are having difficulty solving this problem. 22 ③
23 ① 24 ⑤ 25 take → taking
26 (A) cheating (B) to take 27 ①,④
28 Getting[Waking] up early 29 (1) ⓐ, to give → giving (2) ⓒ, to wash → washing 30 ②
31 ③ 32 using smartphones in the classroom
33 ④ 34 ② 35 ③ 36 (1) is → are (2) to talk → talking (3) theirs → them 37 ② 38 forget to plan to study for the exam next time
39 ③,④ 40 ③ 41 ③,④ 42 (1) eight glasses water → eight glasses of water
(2) to do → doing 43 ⑤

중간·기말고사 대비문제 해설

1 (A) 우유는 치즈를 만드는 데 사용된다는 뜻이므로 「be used to + 동사원형」을 사용하여 나타낸다. (making → make)
(B) cannot[couldn't] help+-ing는 '~하지 않을 수 없(었)다'는 뜻의 관용표현이다. (to buy → buying)
(D) prevent A from -ing는 'A가 ~하는 것을 못하게 하다'는 뜻의 관용표현이다.

(to cross → from crossing)

(E) be responsible for -ing는 '~에 책임이 있다'는 뜻의 관용표현이다. 전치사의 목적어로 동사가 올 때는 동명사의 형태로 쓴다.

(prepare → preparing)

2 ⓑ quit은 동명사를 목적어로 취하는 동사이다.

ⓒ forget -ing: (과거에) ~했던 것을 잊다

ⓔ be busy -ing: ~하느라 바쁘다

ⓐ 누군가가 정원에 물을 주는 것이므로 동사를 수동태의 형태로 써야 한다. (watering → watered)

ⓓ remember + to부정사: ~할 것을 기억하다 (bringing → to bring)

3 ① 진행의 의미를 나타내는 현재분사이다.

②③④⑤ 문장에서 보어의 역할을 하는 동명사이다. 해석은 '~하는 것'으로 한다.

4 ③ 너 함께 일출 봤던 것을 기억하니?

「remember+동명사」 '(과거에) 했던 일을 기억하다'

「remember+to부정사」 '(미래에) 할 일을 기억하다'

5 그녀가 그녀의 과제를 제출했던 것을 기억한다는 의미이므로 'remember -ing: (과거에) ~했던 것을 기억하다'의 형태가 되어야 한다.

6 (1) dislike는 동명사만을 목적어로 취하는 동사다.

(2) 「forget+to부정사」 '(미래에) 할 일을 잊다'

cf. 「forget+동명사」 '(과거에) 했던 일을 잊어버리다'

7 (B) taking → to take

(E) study → studying

8 look forward to+-ing '~을 고대하다'

9 동사 promise의 목적어로는 to부정사가 오고, 전치사의 목적어로는 동명사가 온다.

10 (A) 「be busy+-ing」 '~하느라 바쁘다'

(B) 「keep+-ing」 '~을 계속하다'

(C) 「wish+to부정사」 '~하기를 원하다, 바라다'

11 ③ deny는 동명사를 목적어로 쓰는 동사이다.

① feel like은 '~하고 싶다'는 뜻으로 뒤에 동명사가 온다. (feel like to talk → feel like talking)

② decide는 to부정사를 목적어로 쓰는 동사이다. (decided taking → decided to take)

④ mind는 동명사를 목적어로 쓰는 동사이다. (mind to hold → mind holding)

⑤ agree는 to부정사를 목적어로 쓰는 동사이다. (agreed changing → agreed to change)

12 ④ 「What do you say to+동명사 ~?」

'~하는 게 어때?' (to go → to going)

13 ⓐ agree는 to부정사를 목적어로 취하는 동사이다. (to meet)

ⓑ mind는 동명사를 목적어로 취하는 동사이다. (helping)

ⓒ forget이 to부정사를 목적어로 취하는 경우, 아직 일어나지 않은 일에 대해 '~할[하는] 것을 잊다'는 의미로 쓰인다. (to set)

14 「try+to부정사」 '~하려고 노력하다, 애쓰다'

cf. try+-ing '(시험삼아) ~해보다'

15 문장의 주어로는 동명사(Exercising)나 to부정사(To exercise)가 온다.

16 ⓐ 「be worried about -ing」 '~에 대해 걱정하다'

ⓑ to부정사의 부사적 용법(목적)

ⓒ 「explain A to B」 'B에게 A를 설명하다'

17 ③ 현재분사   ①②④⑤ 동명사

18 문맥상 미래의 행동에 관해 말하는 것이므로 「remember+to부정사」(미래에 할 일을 기억하다)인 ②가 맞다.

19 ③ practice+-ing '~을 연습하다' (to play → playing)

20 「remember+to부정사」 '~할 것을 기억하다'

cf. remember+-ing '~한 것을 기억하다'

21 「have difficulty+동명사」 '~하는 데 어려움을 겪다'

22 • 「like+-ing/to부정사」 '~을 좋아하다'

• be interested in+-ing '~에 관심 있다'

23 ⓐ 「How about+-ing」는 '~하는 게 어때?'라는 관용어구이며 여기서 -ing는 '~하는 것'을 의미하는 동명사이다.

ⓑ be동사와 함께 쓰여 진행시제를 나타내는 현재분사이다.

ⓒ 주격 보어 역할로 쓰인 동명사이다. '~하는 것'으로 해석한다.

ⓓ hear과 같은 지각동사의 목적격 보어로는 동사원형이나 진행의 의미를 강조하는 현재분사를 쓸 수 있다.

ⓔ 명사(baby)의 앞에서 명사의 동작이나 상태를 수식해주는 현재분사이다. (The sleeping baby: 자고 있는 아기)

ⓕ 전치사의 다음에 나왔으므로 명사 역할을 하는 동명사이다.

24 ⑤ ⓐ 과거진행시제(he was doing his homework)를 나타내는 현재분사이다. (해석: 나는 그가 숙제

를 하고 있었다는 것을 알아채지 못했다.)

ⓑ 전치사의 목적어로 쓰인 동명사이다. 'be tired of'는 '~에 지겨워하다'는 뜻의 관용표현이다. (해석: 나는 너의 질문들에 대답하는 것이 지겹다.)

① 문장의 주어로 쓰인 동명사이다.

　　ⓐ Taking a nap: 낮잠을 자는 것

　　ⓑ Eating vegetables: 채소를 먹는 것

② 명사를 수식하는 현재분사이다.

　　ⓐ the boring news: 지루한 뉴스

　　ⓑ The girl sleeping on the couch: 소파에서 자고 있는 소녀

③ 타동사(enjoy/finish)의 목적어로 쓰인 동명사이다.

　　ⓐ Tom은 바다에서 수영하는 것을 즐긴다.

　　ⓑ 너는 언제 보고서 쓰는 것을 끝마쳤니?

④ 주격 보어로 쓰인 동명사이다.

　　ⓐ 나의 직업은 중학생들에게 영어를 가르치는 것이다.

　　ⓑ 나의 이번 여름 방학 계획은 캐나다를 가는 것이다.

25 think of + -ing '~하는 것에 대해 생각하다'

26 (A) deny + -ing '~을 부인하다'

(B) afford + to부정사 '~할 여유가 되다'

27 ⓐ 5년 전부터 현재까지 쭉 운동을 해오고 있었다는 의미이기 때문에 현재완료 진행 형태로 쓰는 것이 적절하다.

ⓓ keep + ~ing: 계속해서 ~하다

ⓑ 횟수를 나타내는 two가 명사 time 앞에 있기 때문에 복수형인 times로 쓰는 것이 적절하다.

(time → times)

ⓒ mind는 동명사를 목적어로 취하는 동사이므로 telling의 형태로 쓰는 것이 적절하다.

(tell → telling)

ⓔ 문장의 일부로 간접의문문이 사용되는 경우에는 「의문사 + 주어 + 동사」의 어순을 가진다. 따라서 do를 삭제해야 한다.

28 '일찍 일어나다'라는 표현은 'get[wake] up early'이다. 문장의 주어로는 동명사나 to부정사가 올 수 있는데 세 단어로 써야 하므로 답은 'Getting[Waking] up early'가 된다.

29 ⓐ mind는 동명사를 목적어로 취한다.

ⓒ finish는 동명사를 목적어로 취하는 동사다.

30 ② like는 to부정사와 동명사 모두를 목적어로 가질 수 있으며 의미가 달라지지 않는 동사이다. 따라서 (나)에 riding이 들어가는 것은 적절하다.

① want는 to부정사만을 목적어로 가지는 동사다. (가)에는 to go가 들어가야 한다.

③ would like는 to부정사와 함께 쓰여 '~하고 싶다'라는 뜻을 나타낸다. (다)에는 to drink가 들어가야 한다.

④ 주어 자리에는 동사원형이 들어갈 수 없다. (라)에는 동명사 Yelling 또는 to부정사 To yell이 적합하다.

⑤ be used to는 to 다음에 동사원형이 올 경우 '~하는 데에 사용되다'라는 뜻을 나타내고, 동명사가 와서 'be used to -ing'가 될 경우 '~하는 데에 익숙하다'라는 뜻을 나타낸다. 여기서는 '그는 많은 사람들 앞에서 공연하는 데에 익숙하지 않다.'라는 의미가 적절하므로 (마)에는 동명사 performing이 들어가야 한다.

31 ③의 decide는 to부정사를 목적어로 취하는 동사이고 나머지 동사는 동명사를 목적어로 취하는 동사이다.

32 The topic was <u>using smartphones in the classroom</u>.

주제는 교실에서 스마트폰을 사용하는 것이었다.

33 전치사의 목적어로는 동명사가 온다.

34 「There is no + 동명사」

= 「It is impossible + to부정사」 '~할 수 없다'

35 (A) 「stop + 동명사」 '~하는 것을 그만두다'

(B) 「감정의 형용사 + to부정사」 '~하니 (기분이) …하다'

(C) keep + -ing '~을 계속하다'

36 (1) 첫 번째 줄: 「there is + 단수명사」, 「there are + 복수명사」 (is → are)

(2) 밑에서 네 번째 줄: enjoy는 동명사를 목적어로 취한다. (to talk → talking)

(3) 마지막 줄: 전치사 뒤에는 목적격이 온다.

(theirs → them)

37 ⓑ '~하는 데 익숙하다'는 「be used to + -ing」로 나타낸다. (walk → walking)

ⓐ 전치사의 목적어로 쓰인 동명사로 적절하다.

ⓒ other은 명사 앞에서 수식하는 역할을 할 수 있다.

ⓓ 사역동사 make는 목적격 보어로 동사원형 feel을 가질 수 있다.

ⓔ stay는 주격 보어 자리에 형용사나 명사가 올 수 있다.

38 「Don't forget＋to부정사」 '~할 것을 잊지 말아라'
「plan＋to부정사」 '~할 계획을 세우다'

39 「begin＋-ing/to부정사」 '~을 시작하다'

40 ③ imagine은 동명사를 목적어로 쓰는 동사이다.
(to meet → meeting)
① suggest는 동명사를 목적어로 쓰는 동사이다.
② hate는 동명사와 to부정사 모두 목적어로 쓰고, 그 중 어느 것을 목적어로 써도 뜻이 달라지지 않는다.
④ to fix가 '(내 컴퓨터를) 고치기 위해서'라는 목적을 나타내는 to부정사의 부사적 용법으로 쓰였다.
⑤ refuse는 to부정사를 목적어로 쓰는 동사이다.

41 ① 「expect＋목적어＋to부정사」 '목적어가 ~하기를

기대하다' (doing → to do)
② 「decide＋to부정사」 '~하기로 결심하다'
(support → to support)
⑤ 「dislike＋동명사」 '~하기를 싫어하다'
(to work → working)

42 (1) 두 번째 줄: 물질명사의 수를 나타내는 단위명사의 뒤에는 of가 와야 한다.
(eight glasses water → eight glasses of water)
(2) 밑에서 두 번째 줄: enjoy는 동명사를 목적어로 취한다. (to do → doing)

43 if 조건절에서는 일어나지 않은 일이더라도 현재 시제를 쓴다. '~하는 데 시간을 쓰다'는 「spend time ＋~ing」로 나타낸다.

CHAPTER **9**	분사 Participles	본문 _ p.222

PRACTICE 1

1	repaired	**2**	surprising
3	sleeping	**4**	depressing
5	boiled	**6**	eating
7	given	**8**	invited
9	taken	**10**	amazing
11	used	**12**	rising

1 has just repaired: '막, 방금'이라는 의미의 부사 just와 함께 쓰여 현재완료시제의 완료를 나타낸다.

2 some surprising news: 현재분사 surprising이 명사 news를 꾸며서 능동(놀라게 하는)의 의미를 나타낸다.

3 the sleeping puppy: 현재분사 sleeping이 명사 puppy를 꾸며서 진행(자고 있는)의 의미를 나타낸다.

4 depressing: 현재분사 depressing이 문장 내에서 주격 보어로 사용되어 능동(우울하게 하는)의 의미를 나타낸다.

5 boiled eggs: 과거분사 boiled가 명사 eggs를 앞에서 수식하여 완료(삶아진)의 의미를 나타낸다.

6 were eating: 현재분사 eating이 were과 함께 쓰여 과거진행 시제를 나타낸다. 여기서 과거분사가 사용될 경우 수동태(They were eaten: 그들은 먹혔다)가 되어 의미상 적절하지 않다.

7 given name: 과거분사 given이 명사를 앞에서 수식하여 수동 (주어진)의 의미를 나타낸다. given name은 first name과 같은 뜻으로, 성을 제외한 이름을 가리킨다.

8 was invited: 과거분사 invited가 과거시제 be동사와 함께 쓰여 과거 수동태(초대되었다)를 나타낸다. 내가 아닌 그의 생일파티이기 때문에 초대를 받는 수동의 의미가 적절하다.

9 were taken: 과거분사 taken이 과거시제 be동사와 함께 쓰여 과거 수동태(찍혔다)를 나타낸다. 사진이 주어이므로 능동보다는 수동태 사용이 적절하다.

10 amazing: 현재분사 amazing이 the story를 보충 설명하는 주격 보어로 쓰여 능동(놀라게 하는)의 의미를 나타낸다.

11 a used car: 과거분사 used가 car를 앞에서 수식하여 수동 및 완료(사용된)의 의미를 나타낸다.

12 a rising sun: 현재분사 rising이 sun을 앞에서 수식하여 진행 (뜨고 있는)의 의미를 나타낸다.

PRACTICE 2

2	barking	**3**	broken
4	painted	**5**	Used
6	shocking	**7**	written
8	talking	**9**	interesting
10	burned[burnt]		

2 dogs <u>barking at people</u>: 사람을 향해 짖고 있는 개들(진행)
3 the <u>broken</u> glasses: 깨진 안경(수동, 완료)
4 the wall <u>painted in red</u>: 빨간색으로 칠해진 벽(수동)
5 <u>Used</u> cars: 사용된(중고의) 차(수동, 완료)
6 a <u>shocking</u> accident: 충격적인 사고(능동)
7 a book <u>written by James Joyce</u>: James Joyce에 의해 쓰여진 책(수동)
8 That boy <u>talking with the old lady</u>: 노부인과 대화 중인 저 소년(진행)
9 some <u>interesting</u> questions: 몇 가지 흥미로운 질문들(능동)
10 A <u>burned[burnt]</u> child: 화상을 입은 아이(수동)

PRACTICE 3

1 lost wallet

2 dancing students

3 fallen on the ground

4 reading a book

5 burned cookies

6 filled with tears

7 exercising in the gym

8 covered with snow

9 shining sun

10 singing on the stage

PRACTICE 4

2 cooking, 목적격 보어

3 fixed, 목적격 보어

4 depressed, 주격 보어

5 waiting, 목적격 보어

6 dancing, 명사 수식

7 excited, 주격 보어

8 running, 목적격 보어

9 taken, 명사 수식

10 cleaned, 목적격 보어

11 smiling, 주격 보어

12 listening, 주격 보어

13 interesting, 명사 수식

14 baked, 명사 수식

15 walking, 목적격 보어

16 touched, 목적격 보어

2, 5, 8, 15 목적격 보어로 현재분사를 사용하여 목적어가 하고 있는 행위를 서술한다. 지각동사의 목적격 보어로 현재분사가 사용될 경우 진행의 의미를 강조할 수 있다.
3, 10, 16 목적격 보어로 과거분사를 사용하여 목적어가 당하는 행위나 상태를 서술한다. '(목적어가)~되는 것을'로 해석한다.
4, 7 주격 보어로 과거분사를 사용하여 주어가 느끼는 감정을 서술한다.
　4 depressed: 우울한
　7 excited: 신이 난, 들뜬
6, 14 구를 이루는 분사는 명사 뒤에서 명사를 꾸며줄 수 있다.
9, 13 분사가 단독으로 쓰일 때는 명사 앞에서 명사를 꾸며줄 수 있다.
11, 12 be 동사와 함께 현재분사를 사용하여 주어가 하는 행위가 진행 중임을 나타낸다.

PRACTICE 5

1 A		**2** B		**3** B	
4 A		**5** B		**6** A	
7 B		**8** A		**9** A	
10 B					

[보기]
A. are <u>playing</u> soccer: 축구를 하는 중이다. (현재분사)
B. <u>running</u> shoes: 달리기용 신발 (동명사)

1, 4 be 동사와 함께 쓰여 진행 시제를 나타내는 현재분사이다.
2, 5, 10 용도를 나타내는 동명사다. '~을 하기 위한', '~로 쓰는'이라고 해석할 수 있다.
3, 7 주격 보어로 쓰인 동명사이다. '~하는 것'으로 해석한다.
6, 8 명사를 꾸며주는 형용사 역할의 현재분사이다. 앞에 정관사나 소유격이 온다.
　6 the boring class: 지루한 수업
　8 her smiling face: 그녀의 웃는 얼굴
9 현재분사가 주어의 내용을 보충 설명하는 주격 보어로 쓰였다.

PRACTICE 6

1 boring, bored

2 depressed, depressing

3 confused, confusing

4 disappointing, disappointed

5 moved, moving

6 worrying, worried

7 surprised, surprising

8 satisfied, satisfying

9 tiring, tired

10 puzzling, puzzled

11 excited, exciting

12 shocked, shocking

13 amazing, amazed

14 pleased, pleasing

15 embarrassing, embarrassed

> **1~15** 수식을 받거나 서술되는 대상이 사람일 때, 보어로 과거분사를 사용하여 '~된', '~감정을 느끼는'이라는 의미를 나타낸다.
> 한편, 수식을 받거나 서술되는 대상이 사람이 아닐 때, 보어로 현재분사를 사용하여 사물의 성질을 나타낼 수 있고, '~하게 하는'이라고 해석한다.

PRACTICE 7

bored, interesting, disappointed, tiring, exciting, satisfied

> I started to feel <u>bored</u>: 주어가 사람이고, 주어의 감정/상태를 나타내므로 과거분사를 사용한다.
> something <u>interesting</u>: something을 수식하여 능동(~하게 하는)의 의미를 나타낸다. -thing 형태의 대명사는 뒤에서만 수식해 줄 수 있다.
> You won't be <u>disappointed</u> : 주어가 사람이고, 주어의 감정을 나타내므로 과거분사를 사용한다.
> <u>It(가주어)</u> was a little <u>tiring</u> to go there by bus(진주어): 사람이 아닌 주어의 성질을 나타낼 때 현재분사를 사용하여 '피곤한', '피곤하게 하는' 등의 의미를 나타낼 수 있다.
> the concert was very <u>exciting</u> : 사람이 아닌 주어의 주격 보어로 현재분사를 사용한다.
> Both of us … were <u>satisfied</u>: 사람인 주어의 감정을 나타내기 위해 과거분사를 사용하여 '만족스러운'의 의미를 나타낸다.

PRACTICE 8

2 Studying hard

3 Cooking in the kitchen

4 Meeting Hana at the bookstore

5 Taking a walk

6 arriving in Busan at 11:10

7 Listening to pop music

8 Pushing a boy by mistake

9 Planning to stay at home

10 Knowing him well

PRACTICE 9

1 with my sister following me

2 with his lamp turned on

3 with the trash cleaned up

4 with our legs tied

5 with his friends dancing

6 with my alarm clock ringing

> [보기]
> … and he was crossing his legs. (사람 주어, 능동)
> = … with <u>his legs crossed</u>. (with+신체일부+과거분사)
>
> **1, 5** 접속사 다음에 나오는 주어가 사람이고, 주어가 직접 행위를 하는 내용이기 때문에 「with+명사+현재분사」로 나타낼 수 있다.
> **2, 3, 4** 접속사 and 다음의 주어가 사물/신체 일부이고, 주어가 동사의 행위를 당하는 내용이기 때문에 「with+명사+과거분사」로 나타낼 수 있다.
> **6** 접속사 while 다음에 나오는 주어가 사물(my alarm clock)이지만, 동사가 능동태이기 때문에 「with+명사+현재분사」로 나타낼 수 있다.

📑 중간·기말고사 대비문제 정답 본문 _ p.233

1 ④ **2** ⓑ, taken ⓓ, mentioned **3** ④ **4** ③

5 ③ **6** ①,② **7** ③ **8** ② **9** ② **10** ④ **11** ③

12 ② **13** ③ **14** ③ **15** ③ **16** ②,④ **17** ①

18 ① **19** wearing **20** ④ **21** ②

22 After we finished the work **23** The woman waving to my father is my mother. **24** ④

25 with his eyes closed **26** ③ **27** ⑤ **28** ①

29 surprised, broken **30** ③ **31** ④

32 ④,⑤ **33** ③ **34** ① **35** ②

36 (1) (A), building, built (2) (D), excited, exciting

37 Because[As/Since] I missed the bus

38 ⑤ **39** ① **40** ④ **41** ② **42** ②

중간·기말고사 대비문제 해설

1 interesting '흥미로운'

2 ⓑ taking → taken
수동태 문장이므로 과거분사를 쓴다.
ⓓ mentioning → mentioned
목적어와 목적격 보어가 수동 관계이므로 과거분사를 쓴다.

3 ④ 현재분사   ①②③⑤ 동명사

4 ③ satisfying → satisfied

5 목적어와 목적격 보어가 수동의 관계이므로 과거분사가 필요하다.

6 밑줄 친 부분은 전치사 다음에 쓰였기 때문에 동명사이다.
① 명사 'the girl'을 수식하는 현재분사이다. (the girl dancing on the stage: 무대 위에서 춤추고 있는 소녀)

Ch
9
분
사

② be동사와 함께 쓰여 진행시제를 나타내는 현재분사이다.

③ 「give up -ing」는 '-하는 것을 포기하다'라는 의미이며 여기서 -ing는 '~하는 것'을 나타내는 동명사이다.

④ waiting room은 '대기실'이라는 뜻으로, 여기서 waiting이 명사의 용도(대기용)를 나타내므로 동명사다.

⑤ 문장의 주어로 쓰인 동명사이다. (Keeping your body warm: 네 몸을 따뜻하게 유지하는 것)

7 (A) 「need+-ing」는 '~되어야 할 필요가 있다'의 뜻이다. need가 목적어로 동명사를 취하는 경우 현재분사가 수동의 의미를 나타낸다. need ironing = need to be ironed

(B) 「with+명사+분사」는 '~이(가) …한 채로'의 뜻이다. 'arms'와 'outstretch'가 수동의 관계이므로 분사 자리에 과거분사를 쓰는 것이 적절하다.

(C) 이야기가 감동을 느끼게 하는 주체이기 때문에 현재분사를 쓰는 것이 적절하다.

(D) suffer from~은 '~로 고통을 겪다'라는 뜻을 갖는다. 따라서 현재분사 suffering을 쓰는 것이 적절하다.

(E) 가이드라인은 제공되는 것이므로 수동의 의미를 가진 과거분사를 쓰는 것이 적절하다.

8 접속사(while)와 부사절의 주어(he)를 빼고 부사절의 동사(cleaned)를 -ing형으로 바꾸어 분사구문을 만들 수 있다.

9 ② 'me'가 피곤한 감정을 느끼는 대상이므로 과거분사를 써야 한다.

① 'Ben's grades'가 실망스러운 감정을 느끼게 하는 것이므로 현재분사를 쓰는 것이 맞다.

③ 'I'가 충격을 받는 대상이므로 과거분사를 써야 한다.

④ 영화가 감정을 일으키는 주체이므로 현재분사를 써야 한다.

⑤ 'her room'은 청소가 되는 대상이므로 과거분사를 써야 한다.

10 ⓐ ⓒ ('~한 감정을 느끼는'의 의미로 분사를 사용할 때는) 과거분사(overwhelmed, pleased)를 쓰는 것이 적절하다.

cf. be pleased with '~에 기뻐하다, 좋아하다'

ⓑ 동사 offered를 수식하는 부사 kindly가 들어가야 한다.

ⓓ he 이하는 the excellent service를 수식하는 관계대명사절로, 문장의 시제가 과거이므로 동사의 과거형(provided)을 쓰는 것이 적절하다.

11 worried '걱정스러운'
-ed '~한 감정을 느끼는'

12 ② 현재분사　①③④⑤ 동명사

13 목적어(Jane)와 목적격 보어(lie)가 능동의 관계일 때는 현재분사를 쓴다.

14 ⓒ 영화가 감동을 느끼게 하는 것이므로 '감동적인'이라는 뜻의 현재분사 moving을 쓴다.
(move → moving)

ⓔ 자동사 fall '(어떤 상태에) 빠지다' 뒤에는 서술적 용법의 형용사 asleep이 온다.
(sleeping → asleep)

15 ⓒ A and B 형태의 주어는 복수 취급한다.
(attracts → attract)

ⓔ promote는 등위접속사 and에 의해 to preserve와 병렬 연결되어 있으므로 형태를 일치시켜야 한다. (promoting → (to) promote)

ⓐ 「one of the+최상급+복수 명사」 '가장 ~한 것 중의 하나'

ⓑ The cave ~ 절의 결과를 나타내는 분사구문 형태의 making의 사용은 적절하다.

ⓓ 동굴의 일부 구역이 제한되어 있다는 수동의 의미이므로 수동태 형태의 「be+p.p.(are restricted)」의 사용은 어법상 옳다.

제주도에 있는 만장굴은 세계에서 가장 긴 용암 동굴 중 하나이다. 그것은 그것의 독특한 용암 지형과 안정적인 온도로 유명하다. 그 동굴은 연중 약 11도의 온도를 유지하여, 심지어 여름에도 그것을 탐험하기에 쾌적하다. 그것의 생태학적 가치와 지형적 특성은 연구자들과 관광객 모두를 끌어들인다. 동굴의 몇몇 구역들은 민감한 지역에의 피해를 보호하기 위해 제한되어 있다. 그것의 자연적인 아름다움을 보존하고 지속 가능한 관광을 촉진하기 위해 노력이 계속되고 있다.

16 ② '이미 사용된 종이를 재활용해야 한다'는 뜻이므로 수동과 완료의 의미를 가진 과거분사를 써야 한다.
(using → used)

④ 'the book'이 혼란스러운 감정을 느끼게 하는 것이므로 현재분사를 써야 한다.
(confused → confusing)

① 'people'이 흥분을 느끼는 대상이므로 과거분사를 써야 한다.

③ 'this book'은 Thomas Hardy에 의해 쓰여진 것이므로, 수동의 의미를 가진 과거분사를 써야 한다.

⑤ 'The flowers'는 물 주기(water)라는 행위의 대상이므로 수동의 의미를 가진 과거분사를 써야 한다.

17 surprised '놀란' - surprising '놀라운'

18 ① 'Her speech'가 충격적인 감정을 느끼게 하는 것이므로 현재분사를 써야 한다. (shocked → shocking)

② 'I'가 흥분을 느끼는 대상이므로 과거분사를 써야 한다.

③ 'person'이 놀라운 감정을 느끼게 하는 것이므로 현재분사를 써야 한다.

④ 'I'가 피곤한 감정을 느끼는 것이므로 과거분사를 써야 한다.

⑤ 'Drinking a lot of water'는 문장에서 주어의 역할을 하는 동명사로 쓰였다.

19 빈칸부터 muffler까지는 That woman을 수식하는 분사구이다. 여자가 파란 머플러를 착용하고 있는 능동의 상태이기 때문에 현재분사를 쓰는 것이 적절하다. (wearing)

Pete: 어이, Kate. 저 쪽을 봐!

Kate: 사람들이 아주 많다. 무슨 소란이지?

Pete: 그들이 무언가를 촬영하고 있는 것처럼 보여.

Kate: 우와! 나는 예전에 촬영이 진행중인 것을 본 적이 없어.

Pete: 한 번 보자! 유명한 배우들이 준비중일지도 몰라.

Kate: 우와! 파란 머플러를 착용하고 있는 저 여자는 아름다워.

Pete: 세상에! 사람은 이가은이야! 나는 그녀의 엄청난 팬이야! 우리가 여기 있다니 정말 운이 좋다!

20 (A) 'a lot of animals'가 기다리는 행위의 주체이므로 능동의 의미를 나타내는 현재분사를 써야 한다. (waited → waiting)

(C) forget은 to부정사를 목적어로 쓰면 '~할 것을 잊다(일어나지 않은 일)'라는 뜻이고 동명사를 목적어로 쓸 경우 '~한 것을 잊다(이미 일어난 일)'를 의미한다. 여기에서는 '밥 먹이는 것을 잊었다'는 뜻이므로 to부정사를 쓰는 것이 맞다. (feeding → to feed)

(B) 「take (good) care of」 '~를 (잘) 돌보다'

(D) 「be filled with」 '~로 가득 차 있다'

(E) 「think of」 '~을 생각하다, 머리에 떠올리다'

21 ① 운동이 피곤함을 느끼게 하는 것이므로 현재분사 tiring을 쓴다. (tired → tiring)

③ 우리가 충격을 받은 것이므로 과거분사 shocked를 쓴다. (shocking → shocked)

④ 다큐멘터리가 흥미진진한 것이므로 현재분사 fascinating을 쓴다. (fascinated → fascinating)

⑤ 그녀가 실망을 느끼는 것이므로 과거분사를 써야 한다. (disappointing → disappointed)

22 문맥에 맞는 접속사(after)와 주어(we)를 더하고 분사 형태인 동사를 주절의 동사와 시제가 일치하도록 하여(finished) 부사절로 만들 수 있다.

23 현재분사가 뒤의 다른 어구들과 함께 명사를 수식할 때는 명사 뒤에 놓는다.

24 ④ surprised '놀란' → surprising '놀라운'

25 '~을 …한 채로'라는 뜻의 「with+명사+분사」를 이용하여 쓴다. 이때, 'his eyes'와 'close'가 수동의 관계이므로 과거분사를 사용한다.

26 (A) 'a concert'가 열리는 대상이므로 수동의 의미를 가진 과거분사 held를 쓴다.

(D) 'used to'는 '~하곤 했다'는 뜻의 조동사이므로, 뒤에 동사원형을 쓴다.

(B) '누구의 콘서트'인지 묻는 것이므로 소유격 의문형용사 whose를 써야 한다. whom은 목적격 의문대명사이다. (whom → whose)

(C) 'I'가 놀라운 감정을 느끼는 대상이므로 과거분사 surprised를 써야 한다. surprising은 '놀라게 하는'의 의미이다. (surprising → surprised)

(E) 진주어를 뒤로 보내고 가주어 it을 주어의 자리에 쓴 형태이다. 의미상의 주어로 「for+목적격(me)」이 쓰인 것으로 보아서 진주어가 to부정사구가 되는 것이 적절함을 알 수 있다.
(understand → to understand)

27 ⓔ 등위접속사 and로 fell down과 병렬구조를 이루고 있다. fell down이 과거시제 동사이므로 break도 과거시제로 써야 한다. (broken → broke)

ⓐ Jay가 3인칭 단수이므로, 동사도 3인칭 단수 현재형의 'plays'를 쓴다.

ⓑ 「with+명사+분사」는 '~을 …한 채로'라는 뜻으로, 'her arms'와 'fold'가 수동의 관계이므로 과거분사를 쓴다.

ⓒ books는 셀 수 있는 명사이므로, 셀 수 있는 명사를 수식하는 a few를 쓴다.

ⓓ 'She'가 흥분을 느끼는 대상이므로 과거분사의 형

28 '~하고 있는'의 뜻일 때는 현재분사를 쓴다.

29 • 주어(We)가 '놀란' 감정을 느끼는 것이므로 과거분사 surprised가 적절하다.
 • 꽃병이 깨진 것이므로 수동, 완료를 나타내는 과거분사 broken이 적절하다.

30 ③ 현재분사　①②④⑤ 동명사

31 ⓒ 'The man'이 입고 있는 주체이므로 현재 분사(wearing)를 쓴다. 이때, 분사가 구를 이루어 명사를 수식하므로 명사의 뒤에서 수식한다.
 ⓓ 'the guys'가 말을 하고 있는 주체이므로 현재 분사(talking)를 쓴다.
 ⓕ 'the crowd'가 흥분을 느끼는 대상이므로 과거분사(excited)를 쓴다.
 ⓐ the boy가 돌보는 행위(look after)의 주체이므로 현재분사를 써야 한다. (Looked → Looking)
 ⓑ 「with + 명사 + 분사」는 '~을 …한 채로'라는 뜻으로, 'her legs'와 'cross'가 수동의 관계이므로 과거분사를 쓴다. (crossing → crossed)
 ⓔ 'The door'가 페인트칠 되는 대상이므로 수동의 의미를 가진 과거분사를 쓴다.
 (painting → painted)

32 ⑤ '~하면서'라는 뜻의 동시동작은 접속사 while을 사용하여 나타낼 수 있다. 주어는 Sally이므로 반복을 피하기 위해 대명사 she를 쓴다. 보고 있었던 것이므로 과거진행형을 사용한다.
 ④ ⑤번의 문장에서 접속사와 부사절의 주어를 지우고, 동사를 현재분사로 바꾸어 동시동작을 나타내는 분사구문을 만들 수 있다. 이때 looking이 이미 진행의 의미를 담고 있으므로 being은 쓰지 않는다.

33 (A) 주어 it은 영화를 가리키는 인칭대명사이며 감정을 불러일으키는 것이므로 현재분사가 알맞다.
 (B) 주어 it은 Sophie가 적극적인 모습으로 영화에 나왔다는 것을 나타내며, 감정을 느끼게 하지 않았다는 문장이므로 현재분사가 알맞다.

34 ⓐ 오두막은 '버려진' 것이므로 수동의 의미를 나타내는 과거분사 abandoned의 수식을 받는 것이 적절하다.
 ⓑ 그들이 놀라운 감정을 느끼는 대상이므로 과거분사 amazed를 쓴다.
 ⓒ 부사절의 동사 make를 -ing형으로 바꾸어 결과를 나타내는 분사구문으로 쓰는 것이 적절하다.
 등산객들은 숲 속에 버려진 오두막까지 산길을 따라갔

다. 그들은 폭풍우 이후에 달라진 풍경에 놀랐다. 흩어진 나뭇가지들이 길을 덮고 있어, 그들이 걷는 것을 더 힘들게 만들었다.

35 (a) 그 그림들은 내 여동생에 의해 '그려진' 것이므로 과거분사 painted의 사용은 어법상 옳다.
 (c) 부사절의 동사 hear를 -ing 형태로 바꾸어 연속동작을 나타내는 분사구문을 쓴 것은 적절하다.
 (e) 숙제가 '끝난' 대상이므로 과거분사 finished의 사용은 적절하다.
 (g) 학생들은 '공부하는' 주체이므로 현재분사 studying의 사용은 어법상 옳다.
 (b) 주격 관계대명사 뒤에는 동사가 와야 하므로 is wearing을 사용해 주어를 수식하는 것이 올바르다. 또는 관계대명사를 삭제하고 현재분사 wearing이 주어를 수식하는 것이 적절하다. (who wearing → who is wearing / wearing)
 (d) a friend를 선행사로 하는 주격 관계대명사이므로 which 대신 who를 쓴다. (which → who)
 (f) 맥락상 유명한 사원이 위치한 도시라는 의미이므로 where절 내에서 주어는 the famous temple이, 동사는 수동태 형태의 is located가 되어야 한다. (located the famous temple → the famous temple is located)
 (h) 문장의 본동사가 없으므로 that it을 삭제하고 sleeps를 본동사로 한다. (that it 삭제)

36 (1) '눈으로 지어진 집'이라는 수동의 의미이므로 과거분사가 되어야 한다.
 (2) '~한 감정을 느끼게 하는' 것이므로 현재분사가 되어야 한다.

37 원인을 나타내는 접속사 Because[As/Since]와 주어 I를 넣는다. 동사의 시제는 주절과 동일하게 과거시제(missed)로 쓴다.

38 ⓑⓔ 동명사
 ⓐⓒⓓ 현재분사

39 '~을 …한 채로'라는 뜻의 「with + 명사 + 분사」를 이용하여 쓴다. 이때, 'his eyes'와 'close'가 수동의 관계이므로 과거분사를 사용한다.

40 ⓐ 한 문장 내에서 접속사 없이 두 개의 동사가 나올 수 없다. leaned와 chat의 주체가 모두 She이므로 chat을 현재분사 chatting으로 바꾸어 동시동작(친구와 이야기하면서)을 나타낼 수 있다.
 (chat → chatting)
 ⓓ 주어인 we가 보고 있는 주체이므로 현재분사를 쓴다. (watched → watching)

ⓔ 「look at + 목적어 + 현재분사」 (sang → singing)
ⓑ by + -ing: ~함으로써
ⓒ 'the man'이 줍고 있는 주체이므로 능동의 의미를 가진 현재분사(picking)로 쓴다.

41 주어진 분사구문이 '그는 부지런히 공부했음에도 시험을 통과하는데 여전히 분투했다.'라는 내용이므로, 이를 부사절로 바꿀 때는 양보를 나타내는 접속사 Though(~이지만)를 쓰는 것이 적절하다.

42 move는 '이동하다, 이사하다'와 '감동시키다'라는 뜻의 동사이고, move의 과거분사 moved는 '감동한'이라는 뜻의 형용사로 문장의 주격 보어 역할을 할 수 있다.

CHAPTER 10 형용사
Adjectives

본문 _ p.242

PRACTICE 1

2 Ms. Song is a famous doctor.
3 Mary is wearing a beautiful necklace.
4 I'd like to have hot coffee.
5 Paul watched an exciting movie yesterday.
6 Look at the small bird over there.
7 Inho used to live in a large apartment.
8 Could you pass me the blue ball?
9 Put them on the plastic table.
10 I drank Irish tea last night.

형용사는 명사의 앞에서 명사를 수식한다. 첫소리가 모음으로 시작하는 형용사가 셀 수 있는 단수 명사를 수식할 경우, 명사의 발음과는 상관없이 형용사 앞에 관사 an이 온다.

1 an old car: 오래된 자동차
2 a famous doctor: 유명한 의사
3 a beautiful necklace: 아름다운 목걸이
4 hot coffee: 뜨거운 커피
5 an exciting movie: 흥미진진한 영화
6 the small bird: 작은 새
7 a large apartment: 넓은 아파트
8 the blue ball: 파란색 공
9 the plastic table: 플라스틱 탁자
10 Irish tea: 아일랜드 차

PRACTICE 2

1 woman is intelligent
2 movie was impressive
3 house is empty
4 computer is broken
5 student is diligent
6 artists are famous

PRACTICE 3

1 asleep **2** sleeping **3** like
4 live **5** alike **6** alive
7 glad **8** cheerful **9** scared
10 afraid

1, 5, 6, 7 주격 보어 자리이므로 서술적 용법으로 쓸 수 있는 형용사가 알맞다.
2, 4, 8, 9 명사 앞에서 명사를 수식하는 자리이므로 한정적 용법으로 쓰일 수 있는 형용사가 알맞다.
3 like는 명사나 대명사 앞에서 '~와 유사한'이라는 의미의 전치사로 쓰인다. What's she like?는 '그녀는 어떤 사람이니?'라는 의미이다.
10 be afraid of: ~를 두려워하다 (=be scared of)

PRACTICE 4

1 eat something spicy
2 anybody familiar to you
3 someone diligent for the job
4 need anything else
5 something hot to drink[to drink something hot]
6 met anyone friendly
7 calls somebody close to her
8 buy anything expensive yesterday
9 have nothing new
10 seen nobody famous

Ch 10 형용사

1~10 -thing, -one, -body로 끝나는 대명사는 형용사가 뒤에서 수식한다.

1 something spicy: 매콤한 것
2 anybody familiar to you: 너에게 친숙한 누구라도
familiar to: ~에게 익숙한
3 someone diligent: 부지런한 누군가
4 anything else: 그밖에 또 다른 것
5 something hot: 뜨거운 것
6 anyone friendly: 다정한 누군가
7 somebody close to her: 그녀와 가까운 누군가
close to: ~와 가까운 (사이인)
8 anything expensive: 비싼 것
9 nothing new: 새로운 것이 없는
10 nobody famous: 유명한 사람이 없는

PRACTICE 5

1 The rich have their own problems.
2 He did a lot of good things for the poor.
3 These days the blind keep dogs to help themselves.
4 There are some special schools for the deaf.
5 Mr. Park encourages the young to be brave.
6 I took care of the sick in the hospital yesterday.

1~6 「the+형용사」는 '~한 사람들'의 뜻으로, 복수 명사처럼 쓰인다.

1 rich people = the rich: 부유한 사람들
2 poor people = the poor: 가난한 사람들
3 blind people = the blind: 시각 장애인들
4 deaf people = the deaf: 청각 장애인들
5 young people = the young: 젊은 사람들
encourage+사람+to+동사원형: ~를 …하도록 북돋우다, 격려하다
6 sick people = the sick: 아픈 사람들

PRACTICE 6

1 have   **2** the   **3** rich
4 learn   **5** was   **6** need

1, 4, 6 주어 자리의 「the+형용사」는 '~한 사람들'이라는 뜻으로, 복수 명사처럼 쓰이므로 복수 동사가 알맞다.
2, 3 복수 동사가 왔으므로 '~한 사람들'이라는 복수의 의미를 가진 「the+형용사」 형태가 주어 자리에 와야 한다.
5 문장의 주어는 the elderly가 아니라 the hospital(노인들을 위한 병원)이므로 단수 동사 was가 알맞다.

PRACTICE 7

1 한국어   **2** 미국인, 미국의
3 폴란드 사람들   **4** 프랑스의
5 독일어   **6** 덴마크의
7 일본의   **8** 중국어
9 캐나다의   **10** 스페인어

1 learn Korean: 한국어를 배우다
2 Sarah is an American.: Sarah는 미국인이다.
American food: 미국의 음식
3 The Polish: 폴란드 사람들
'the+국가명의 형용사'는 '국민 전체'를 의미한다.
4 French women: 프랑스의(프랑스 국적의) 여자
5 study German: 독일어를 공부하다
6 Danish dairy products: 덴마크의 낙농제품
7 Japanese food: 일본의 음식
8 Chinese is hard to learn.: 중국어는 배우기 어렵다.
9 Canadian culture: 캐나다의 문화
10 Spanish is the language~: 스페인어는 ~한 언어다

PRACTICE 8

1 big white
2 all four Korean
3 large green
4 seven small metal
5 those nice blue
6 the beautiful red
7 my young French
8 the first two
9 comfortable wooden
10 half a million[a half million]
11 both these beautiful
12 all her three

1~12 2개 이상의 형용사가 함께 쓰일 때는 '서수 → 기수 → 성질 → 크기 → 신구 → 색깔 → 국적 → 재료' 순으로 쓰고, 형용사 앞에 다른 수식어가 올 때는 'all/both/double/half → 정관사/지시형용사/소유격 → 형용사' 순으로 쓴다.

PRACTICE 9

2 both the pretty
3 her nice new
4 this small
5 those three high
6 the exciting American
7 the ugly black plastic

8 all these lovely

9 My wise older

10 that big white

11 its nice Chinese

12 the fifth happy English

13 all her three pink

14 four healthy young

15 two fresh red

PRACTICE 10

1	many	**2**	much
3	many	**4**	much
5	many	**6**	much
7	Many	**8**	many
9	many	**10**	much

> **1, 3, 5, 7, 8, 9** 셀 수 있는 명사의 복수형 앞이므로 many가 알맞다.
> **2, 4, 6, 10** 셀 수 없는 명사 앞이므로 much가 알맞다.

PRACTICE 11

1 Does Minho have many friends?

2 Does it take much time to get there on foot?

3 Are there many flowers in the vase?

4 Many drivers drive very fast.

5 Should I give the plants much water?

6 Many students stayed in the classroom after school.

7 I don't have much homework today.

8 Did they spend much money on this house?

9 We didn't have much fun.

10 Did you borrow many books from the library?

> **1, 3, 4, 6, 10** 셀 수 있는 명사의 복수형 앞이므로 many로 바꾸어 쓸 수 있다.
> **2, 5, 7, 8, 9** 셀 수 없는 명사 앞이므로 much로 바꾸어 쓸 수 있다.

PRACTICE 12

1	few	**2**	little
3	little	**4**	few
5	few	**6**	little
7	few	**8**	little
9	little	**10**	few

> **1, 4, 5, 7, 10** 빈칸 뒤에 셀 수 있는 명사의 복수형을 썼으므로 few가 알맞다.
> **2, 3, 6, 8, 9** 빈칸 뒤에 셀 수 없는 명사를 썼으므로 little이 알맞다.

PRACTICE 13

1	a few	**2**	a little
3	A few	**4**	a little
5	a little	**6**	a few
7	a little	**8**	a few
9	a little	**10**	a few

> **1, 3, 6, 8, 10** 빈칸 뒤에 셀 수 있는 명사의 복수형을 썼으므로 a few가 알맞다.
> **2, 4, 5, 7, 9** 빈칸 뒤에 셀 수 없는 명사를 썼으므로 a little이 알맞다.

PRACTICE 14

1	much	**2**	a few
3	a little	**4**	many
5	few	**6**	little
7	a few	**8**	little
9	many	**10**	a little
11	much	**12**	Few

> **1, 11** many는 '많은'이라는 의미로 셀 수 있는 명사의 수를 나타내는데, hope와 traffic은 셀 수 없는 명사이므로 much로 고치는 것이 알맞다.
> **2, 7** a little은 '약간의'라는 의미로 셀 수 없는 명사의 양을 나타내는데, days와 times는 셀 수 있는 명사의 복수형이므로 a few로 고치는 것이 알맞다. 7번의 times는 '시간'의 뜻으로 쓰일 때는 셀 수 없는 명사이지만, 여기서처럼 횟수를 나타낼 때는 셀 수 있는 명사로 취급한다.
> **3, 10** a few는 '조금의, 몇 개의'라는 의미로 셀 수 있는 명사의 수를 나타내는데, money와 meat는 셀 수 없는 명사이므로 a little이 알맞다.
> **4, 9** much는 '많은'이라는 의미로 셀 수 없는 명사의 양을 나타내는데, hours와 restaurants는 셀 수 있는 명사의 복수형이므로 many로 고치는 것이 알맞다.
> **5, 12** little은 '거의 없는'이라는 의미로 셀 수 없는 명사의 양을 나타내는데, teeth와 members는 셀 수 있는 명사의 복수형이므로 few로 고치는 것이 알맞다.
> **6, 8** few는 '거의 없는'이라는 의미로 셀 수 있는 명사의 수를 나타내는데, ice와 light는 셀 수 없는 명사이므로 little로 고치는 것이 알맞다.

PRACTICE 15

1	some	**2**	any
3	some	**4**	any

5	Any	**6**	some
7	any	**8**	some
9	any	**10**	any

> **1, 8** 일반적으로 긍정문에서 '얼마간의, 약간의'라는 뜻으로 쓰이며, 셀 수 있는 명사나 셀 수 없는 명사 모두와 함께 쓸 수 있는 some이 알맞다.
> **2, 7, 10** 일반적으로 부정문에서 '조금도 ~ (아니다)'라는 의미로 쓰이는 any가 알맞다.
> **3, 6** '~하시겠어요?' 또는 '~할 수 있을까요?'라는 의미의 권유나 요구를 나타내는 의문문에서 쓰이는 some이 알맞다.
> **4** 어떠한 질문이라도 있는지 묻는 것이므로 any를 쓴다.
> **5** 긍정문에서 '어떠한 ~라도'의 뜻으로 쓰이는 any가 알맞다.
> **9** 조건을 나타내는 if절에서는 any를 쓴다.

PRACTICE 16

2	any food	**3**	some people
4	any problems	**5**	some medicine
6	any place	**7**	some flowers
8	any[some] friends	**9**	any time
10	some cake	**11**	some money

> **1** some homework: 약간의 숙제 → some이 셀 수 없는 명사를 수식할 때
> **2** I don't have any food: 음식이 전혀 없다 → any가 부정문에서 사용될 때
> **3** some people: 몇몇 사람들 → some이 셀 수 있는 명사를 수식할 때
> **4** if you have any problems: 너에게 무슨 문제라도 있으면 → any가 조건을 나타내는 if절에서 사용될 때
> **5** some medicine: 약간의 약 → some이 셀 수 없는 명사를 수식할 때
> **6** We can go to any place: 우리는 어떤 장소라도 갈 수 있다 → any가 긍정문에서 사용될 때
> **7** some flowers: 약간의 꽃 → some이 셀 수 있는 명사를 수식할 때
> **8** Do you have any[some] friends?: 친구가 좀 있니? → 의문문에서는 any를 쓰는 것이 일반적이지만 긍정의 대답을 예상하고 질문하는 경우에는 some을 쓰기도 한다.
> **9** I don't have any time: 시간이 전혀 없다 → any가 부정문에서 사용될 때
> **10** Would you like some cake?: 케이크 좀 드시겠어요? → some이 권유를 나타내는 의문문에서 사용될 때
> **11** Would you mind lending me some money?: 나에게 돈 좀 빌려주시겠어요? → some이 요구를 나타내는 의문문에서 사용될 때
> *mind -ing: ~하는 것을 꺼리다

PRACTICE 17

1 a third[one-third]

2 two-fifths

3 two and seven-elevenths

4 five-sixths

5 a half[one-half]

6 nine-thirteenths

7 a quarter[one-quarter]

8 four and three-sevenths

9 three point one four

10 five point five six

11 sixteen point two nine

12 fifty point one five

13 a[one] hundred (and) twenty-seven point nine three

14 six hundred (and) twelve point four nine

15 two thousand one hundred (and) five point eight nine

PRACTICE 18

1 eighteen twenty-six

2 nineteen eighty-three

3 two thousand (and) four

4 two thousand (and) twenty[twenty twenty]

5 May (the) first[the first of May]

6 July (the) twelfth[the twelfth of July]

7 February (the) eighteenth
[the eighteenth of February]

8 November (the) twenty-fourth
[the twenty-fourth of November]

9 April (the) twenty-third[the twenty-third of April]

10 December (the) ninth[the ninth of December]

PRACTICE 19

1	once	**2**	three times
3	six times	**4**	four times
5	five times	**6**	twice
7	ten times	**8**	once
9	three times	**10**	eight times

> **1** only once: 딱 한 번
> **2, 4, 7** 기수+times+as+형용사+as: ~보다 (몇) 배 ⋯한
> **3, 10** 기수+times+a+day/week/month/year: 하루/일주일/한 달/일 년에 (몇) 번
> **5, 9** 기수+times+형용사 비교급+than: ~보다 (몇) 배 ⋯한
> **6** twice = two times
> **8** once a day/week/month/year: 하루/일주일/한 달/일 년에 한 번

📝 중간·기말고사 대비문제 정답 본문 _ p.258

1 ③　**2** ⑤　**3** ②　**4** ④　**5** health → healthy
6 ②　**7** Do you have something delicious to eat?　**8** ④　**9** ④　**10** ②　**11** twice a week
12 three times as many words as an average person　**13** There is little food left (in it [in the refrigerator]).　**14** ④　**15** ⑤　**16** ④　**17** much, lots of, plenty of (3개 중 2개를 골라 썼으면 정답으로 인정)　**18** (D) Japanese, (E) many
19 ①　**20** ⑤　**21** ②,④　**22** ④　**23** ①,④
24 ②,④　**25** ③　**26** ⑤　**27** old have
28 something special for you　**29** ②　**30** ④
31 ④　**32** (1) some → any (2) few → little
33 ②　**34** ②　**35** ③　**36** ②　**37** ③,⑤　**38** ②

중간·기말고사 대비문제 해설

1 (A) 한국인들　(B) 영국　(C) 영국의

2 ⑤ 한 단어인 명사 thing은 형용사가 앞에서 수식한다. (things sweet → sweet things)
① -thing으로 끝나는 대명사는 형용사가 뒤에서 수식한다.
② '버스에 남겨진'이란 뜻이므로, 수동과 완료의 의미를 가진 과거분사 left를 사용하여 anyone을 뒤에서 수식한다.
③ 분수를 표현할 때는, 분자는 기수로 분모는 서수로 쓰고 분자가 2 이상이면 분모에 '-s'를 붙인다.
④ 「배수사+as 원급 as」 '배수사만큼 ~한'

3 anything은 꾸미는 말이 뒤에 나오는 부정대명사이므로, 주어진 문장을 영작하면 is there anything interesting on the board?이다. 따라서 네 번째로 나오는 단어는 interesting이다.

4 형용사는 '성질-크기-신구-색깔-국적-재료'의 순으로 쓴다.

5 '몇몇 사람들은 많은 돈을 갖는 것보다 건강한 것이 더 중요하다고 생각한다.'는 의미로 명사 health를 형용사 healthy로 고쳐야 한다.

6 minutes는 셀 수 있는 명사이므로 a few를 쓴다.

7 대명사 something을 형용사 delicious가 뒤에서 수식한다.

8 ④ How often은 횟수나 빈도를 물어보는 표현이므로 배수사를 활용해 횟수로 대답해야 한다.

9 ⓐ years는 셀 수 있는 명사의 복수형이므로, a few를 사용하여 수식한다.
ⓑ soup는 셀 수 없는 명사이므로, a little을 사용하여 수식한다. (a few → a little)
ⓒ hot sauce는 셀 수 없는 명사이므로, a little을 사용하여 수식한다.
ⓓ students는 셀 수 있는 명사의 복수형이므로, few를 사용하여 수식한다.
ⓔ sugar는 셀 수 없는 명사이므로 little을 사용하여 수식한다.

10 • 「a few+셀 수 있는 명사의 복수형」'몇 개의'
• 「many+셀 수 있는 명사의 복수형」'많은'
• 「much+셀 수 없는 명사」'많은'
• 「a little+셀 수 없는 명사」'약간의'

11 배수사로 횟수를 표현한다.

12 「배수사+as+형용사(+명사)+as+비교대상」'~보다 몇 배 더 …한'

13 이 대화에서 food는 셀 수 없는 명사로 쓰였기 때문에 '거의 없는'이라는 뜻의 little이 수식한다. 주어가 셀 수 없는 명사이므로 be동사는 3인칭 단수형인 is를 쓴다.

14 ④ 명사 앞에 오는 수식어의 어순은 all+소유격이다. (her all → all her)

15 ⑤ 긍정문에서는 some을 쓴다. 긍정문에서 any가 쓰이면 '어떠한 ~라도'라는 뜻이지만 여기에서는 적절하지 않다. (any → some)

16 ⓑ 빈칸은 주어 You를 설명하는 보어가 들어갈 자리로, 상태를 나타내는 be동사가 쓰였으므로 서술적 용법의 형용사 confident를 쓰는 것이 적절하다. 명사 confidence를 쓸 경우 You가 자신감이 되므로 문맥상 맞지 않다.
(confidence → confident)
ⓐ prevent / 「in order to+동사원형」 '~하기 위해서'
ⓒ graduation / graduation ceremony '졸업식'
ⓓ properly / can't walk properly '제대로 걸을 수 없다'
ⓔ crowded / be crowded with '~로 붐비다'

17 이 문장에서 paper는 셀 수 없는 명사로 쓰였다. 따라서 밑줄 친 a lot of와 동일하게 '많은'의 뜻으로 셀 수 없는 명사와 함께 쓰일 수 있는 표현은 much, lots of, plenty of이다.

18 (A) 경험을 묻는 현재완료시제가 쓰였다. 해석은 '본

적 있니?'로 한다.

(B) '그것의'라는 뜻의 3인칭 단수 소유격으로, 소유격＋명사의 형태로 나타낸다.

(C) a doctor를 선행사로 하는 주격 관계대명사이므로 who를 쓴다.

(D) '일본의'라는 뜻의 형용사는 Japan에 -ese를 붙여 만든다. (Japan → Japanese)

(E) people은 셀 수 있는 명사의 복수형이므로 many를 사용하여 수식한다. (much → many)

19 (A) 「look＋형용사」 '~하게 보이다'

(B) anything은 형용사가 뒤에서 수식한다.

20 보기의 문장은 '많은 손들이 가벼운 일을 만든다(여럿이 협력하여 함께 일하는 것이 일을 더 쉽게 만든다).'라는 뜻으로 light는 '가벼운'이라는 뜻의 형용사로 쓰여 명사 work를 수식하고 있다.

ⓓ 나의 아들은 약간 가벼운 집안일을 하기 시작했다. (형. 가벼운)

ⓕ 의사가 나에게 정기적인 가벼운 운동을 하라고 조언했다. (형. 가벼운)

ⓐ Kevin은 부엌의 전등을 켜둔 채로 두었다. (명. 전등)

ⓑ 미소가 그의 얼굴 전체를 밝게 한다. (동. 밝게 하다)

ⓒ 우리의 가이드는 길을 밝혀 주기 위해 양초를 썼다. (동. 밝혀 주다)

ⓔ 그 창문은 신선한 공기와 빛이 방 안으로 들어오게 했다. (명. 빛)

21 (B) 사역동사 make는 동사원형을 목적격 보어로 취한다. (to attend → attend)

(D) a little은 셀 수 없는 명사와 함께 쓰이는데, expressions는 셀 수 있는 명사이므로 a few를 쓰는 것이 적절하다. (a little → a few)

(A) 명사 purposes를 수식하는 형용사 various의 쓰임은 적절하다.

(C) to부정사가 문장에서 보어로 사용된 경우이다.

(E) 불특정한 다른 문화를 지칭하므로 other을 쓰는 것이 적절하다.

다른 문화에서 온 사람들은 다양한 목적들로 함께 한다. 예를 들어, 당신의 직업이 당신을 외국인 고객과의 회의에 참석하게 만들 수 있다. 혹은 당신은 당신이 전혀 말하지 못하는 언어를 쓰는 나라로 여행할 수도 있다. 당신이 할 수 있는 첫 번째는 작은 노력을 하는 것이다. 당신은 "감사합니다.", 그리고 "만나서 반갑습니다."와 같은 약간의 기초적인 표현들을 배울 수 있다. 그것은 다른 문화들에 대한 당신의 존중을 보여주는 좋

은 방법이다.

22 (D) 'a number of'는 '많은'이라는 뜻으로 셀 수 있는 명사의 복수형 앞에 온다. many와도 바꾸어 쓸 수 있다. stress는 셀 수 없는 명사이므로 a lot of나 much를 사용해야 한다. (a number of → a lot of[much])

(A) some은 긍정의 대답을 예상하는 의문문에 쓰일 수 있다.

(B) weight는 셀 수 없는 명사이므로 much가 수식한다.

(C) something과 같이 -thing으로 끝나는 대명사는 형용사가 뒤에서 수식한다.

(E) dislike는 동명사를 목적어로 쓰는 동사이다.

23 ① a few '약간의, 조금의' (a few → few)

④ A number of '많은' (A number of → A few)

24 ① 분수를 읽을 때는 분자는 기수로, 분모는 서수로 읽고, 분자가 2 이상이면 분모에 '-s'를 붙여 읽는다. (three-fifth → three-fifths)

③ 날짜는 서수를 이용하여 표현한다. (the fifteen of May → the fifteenth of May [May (the) fifteenth]

⑤ 연도는 두 자리씩 끊어 읽는다. (one thousand nine hundred and seventy four → nineteen seventy-four)

25 명사 앞에 오는 형용사의 어순은 all/both＋지시형용사/소유격＋성질＋크기＋신구＋색깔＋재료 순으로 쓴다.

① a white small → a small white

② My all → All my

④ These both → Both these

⑤ a wooden new → a new wooden

26 (e) little은 '거의 없는'이라는 의미로 셀 수 없는 명사의 양을 나타내는데 사용되는 수량형용사다. few는 셀 수 있는 명사 앞에 사용된다. (few → little)

(a) care for은 '~을 (잘) 돌보다'라는 의미로 Green Garden이 학생들에 의해 잘 '돌보아지는' 것이므로 수동태 형태의 is cared for의 사용은 적절하다.

(b) 전치사 for은 시간의 길이를 나타내는 명사구와 함께 쓰인다.

(c) 문장의 주어와 목적어가 같으므로 재귀대명사의 사용은 어법상 옳다.

(d) to부정사의 명사적 용법으로 문장 내에서 주어로

쓰였다.

우리 학교 뒤의 새로운 Green Garden은 학생들에 의해 잘 관리되고 있습니다. 매일 아침, 자동 스프링클러가 10분 동안 식물에게 물을 줍니다. 원예 동아리 학생들은 그들이 흙을 건강하게 유지하는 것에 대해 스스로 자랑스럽게 여깁니다. 지난주, 도시의 재활용 팀에서 정원으로 신선한 비료가 배달되었습니다. 점심 식사를 위한 신선한 채소를 재배하는 것이 저희의 장기 목표입니다. 안타깝게도 장마 기간동안에는 햇빛이 거의 없습니다.

27 '~한 사람들'을 뜻하는 「the + 형용사」는 복수 취급한다.

28 something은 형용사가 뒤에서 수식한다.

29 ⓐ 부사는 목적격 보어로 쓸 수 없다. (sadly → sad)
ⓒ something은 형용사가 뒤에서 꾸며주는 대명사다. (warm something → something warm)
ⓓ 명사를 꾸미는 형용사가 2개 이상일 때 크기 다음에 색깔을 나타내는 형용사가 와야 한다.
(white big → big white)

30 ④ 부정문에서는 some이 아닌 any가 쓰인다.

31 ④ 「the + 나라 이름 형용사」는 '그 나라 국민 전체'를 나타낸다.

32 (1) 부정문에서는 some 대신 any를 써야 한다.
(2) 이 문장에서 time은 셀 수 없는 명사로 쓰였기 때문에 few가 아닌 little이 와야 한다.

33 a number of '많은', 뒤의 명사가 셀 수 있는 명사 (monkeys)이므로 many가 적절하다.

34 ⓑ a little과 a few는 모두 '약간의, 몇몇의'라는 뜻을 가지고 있지만, a little은 셀 수 없는 명사와, a few는 셀 수 있는 명사와 함께 사용된다. 뒤에 셀 수 있는 명사의 복수형인 seconds가 오므로 a few를 쓰는 것이 적절하다. (a little → a few)
숏폼(짧은 형식) 콘텐츠가 최근 유행하고 있다. 그 이름이 암시하듯이, 그것은 빠르게 소비되도록 설계되어진 모든 형식의 매체를 가리킨다. 그것은 몇 초에서 몇 분까지 짧아질 수 있다. 그것은 소셜 미디어 플랫폼의 성장에 따라 점점 더 두드러지고 있다. 그러면, 어떻게 숏폼 콘텐츠가 인기 있게 된 걸까? 요즘, 사람들은 더 쉽게 주의가 산만해진다. 그래서, 짧고 매우 강한 자극을

주는 콘텐츠가 소비자들의 주의를 끌기가 더 쉽다. 그러나, 숏폼 콘텐츠는 당신이 비판적으로 생각하는 것을 막을 수 있으므로 그것을 너무 많이 소비하지 않도록 주의하라.

35 ③ 형용사는 '성질-크기-신구-색깔-국적-재료'의 순으로 쓰기 때문에, beautiful(성질)이 silk(재료)보다 앞에 와야 한다. (a silk beautiful scarf → a beautiful silk scarf)
① 「수사 + 명사」가 뒤에 이어지는 명사를 수식하는 형용사처럼 쓰일 때는 수사 다음의 명사를 복수형으로 쓰지 않는다.
② 셀 수 없는 명사 advice의 앞이므로 an이 아닌 셀 수 없는 명사와 함께 쓰일 수 있는 표현 a piece of를 쓴 것은 적절하다.
④ 명사 person을 꾸며주는 역할을 하고 있으므로 부사 interestingly가 아닌 형용사 interesting의 사용이 어법상 맞다.
⑤ 감각동사 looked는 보어 자리에 형용사가 온다. 따라서 부사 happily가 아닌 형용사 happy로 고쳐 쓴 것은 적절하다.

36 c. 연도는 두 자리씩 끊어 읽는 것이 원칙이므로 16과 89로 나눠 읽어야 한다. (one six hundred eighty-nine → sixteen eighty-nine)
d. 분자는 기수로, 분모는 서수로 읽는다. 이때 분자가 2 이상이면 분모에 '-s'를 붙인다. 따라서 분자 1은 one 또는 an으로 분모 8은 eighth로 읽는다. (an eighths → one eighth 또는 an eighth)
e. 소수점까지는 기수로, 소수점은 point로, 소수점 이하는 한 자리씩 읽어야 한다. (one five point seven six → fifteen point seven six)

37 ③ something은 형용사가 뒤에서 수식한다.
(good something → something good)
⑤ 「the+형용사」는 복수 명사처럼 쓰이므로 복수 동사 were을 써야 한다.

38 첫번째 문장에서의 any는 한정사로 부정문에서 무엇의 양이나 수를 가리킨다. 두 번째 문장에서의 any는 부사로 '조금도 ~ 아니다'의 의미이고 부정문에서 형용사나 부사를 강조한다.

Ch
10
형용사

 CHAPTER **11** 부사 Adverbs

PRACTICE 1

1 widely	**2** sincerely	**3** happily
4 politely	**5** slowly	**6** slightly
7 finally	**8** easily	**9** luckily
10 quietly	**11** carefully	**12** certainly
13 suddenly	**14** sadly	**15** busily
16 beautifully	**17** really	**18** angrily
19 quickly	**20** softly	

PRACTICE 2

1 visibly	**2** simply	**3** dully
4 truly	**5** loudly	**6** gently
7 nicely	**8** seriously	**9** heavily
10 clearly	**11** safely	**12** fully
13 prettily	**14** anxiously	**15** mainly
16 foolishly	**17** terribly	**18** reasonably
19 comfortably	**20** rudely	**21** personally
22 possibly	**23** probably	**24** casually
25 rarely	**26** responsibly	**27** properly
28 sensitively		

PRACTICE 3

1 A	**2** B	**3** B	**4** A	**5** B
6 A	**7** B	**8** A	**9** B	**10** B
11 A	**12** A	**13** A	**14** B	

[보기]
My good friend, John, speaks Korean well.
　　　형용사　　　　　　　　부사

1, 4, 6, 11, 12, 13 밑줄 친 부분이 명사를 수식하는 한정적 용법의 형용사로 쓰였다.
2, 3, 5, 7, 9, 10 밑줄 친 부분이 동사를 수식하는 부사로 쓰였다.
8 밑줄 친 부분이 서술적 용법의 형용사로 쓰였다.
14 밑줄 친 부분이 형용사를 수식하는 부사로 쓰였다.

1 We walked for a long time. (긴 시간)
2 I have to go to school quite early tomorrow. (일찍 가다)
3 The cold weather will last long. (오래 지속되다)
4 My mom doesn't like fast food. (빠른 음식: 패스트푸드)
5 I'm sorry to call you so late. (늦게 전화하다)
6 I usually catch a cold in early spring. (이른 봄)
7 Alex tried hard to lose weight. (열심히 노력하다)
8 Don't be late next time. (늦다)
9 Sumin came out of the room last. (마지막으로 나오다)
10 She walked fast to be on time. (빠르게 걷다)
11 It was the last train for Seoul. (마지막 열차)
12 There aren't enough chairs for everyone. (충분한 의자)
13 I hit my head on the hard floor. (딱딱한 바닥)
14 Is the water warm enough for you? (충분히 따뜻한)

PRACTICE 4

1 late	**2** carefully	**3** ○
4 last	**5** ○	**6** politely
7 ○	**8** fast	**9** hard
10 ○	**11** easily	**12** sadly
13 suddenly	**14** ○	**15** certainly
16 ○	**17** mainly	**18** quietly

1 늦게 도착하다 (arrive lately → arrive late)
*lately: 최근에 / late: 늦게
2 그것에 대해 신중하게 생각하다 (think about it careful → think about it carefully)
3 나는 그곳에 오래 머무르지 않았다.
long(오래, 오랫동안)은 동사 stay를 수식하는 부사로 알맞게 쓰였다.
4 마지막으로 도착하다 (arrive lastly → arrive last)
*lastly: ㉮ (무엇을 열거하면서 마지막 요소 앞에서)끝으로 / last: ㉮ 마지막에
5 그는 (말이) 빠른 연설가다. (=그는 빠르게 말하는 사람이다.)
speaker(연설가, 말하는 사람)라는 명사를 앞에서 수식하고 있으므로 여기서 fast는 형용사로 쓰였다.
6 공손하게 말하다 (talk polite → talk politely)
7 나는 아침 일찍 아침밥을 먹는다.
early(일찍)는 동사 have를 수식하는 부사로 알맞게 쓰였다.
8 너무 빨리 달리다 (run so fastly → run so fast)
fast는 형용사와 부사로 모두 사용될 수 있으며 fastly라는 단어는 없다.
9 열심히 연습했다 (practiced hardly → practiced hard)
*hardly: 거의 …않는 / hard: ㉮ 열심히
10 나는 마침내 이 책을 읽는 것을 끝냈다.
finally는 동사 finished를 수식하는 부사로 알맞게 쓰였다.
11 문제를 쉽게 해결하다 (solve the problem easy → solve the problem easily)
12 슬프게 미소 지었다 (smiled sad → smiled sadly)
smile은 완전자동사로 보이나 목적어를 가지지 않는 동사이다. 따라서 sad가 아닌 동사를 꾸며줄 수 있는 부사 sadly가 오는 것이 적절하다.
13 갑자기 나를 방문했다 (visited me sudden → visited me suddenly)
14 그들은 걱정스럽게 의사를 기다리고 있었다.
anxiously(걱정스럽게)는 동사 were waiting을 수식하는 부사로

알맞게 쓰였다.
15 분명히 솔직하다 (is certain honest → is certainly honest)
16 마지막으로 비행기에 탔다. (last ㉰ 마지막으로)
last(마지막으로)는 동사 got on을 수식하는 부사로 알맞게 쓰였다.
17 주로 동아프리카에서 발견된다 (are main found in East Africa → are mainly found in East Africa)
18 조용히 그들에게 이야기를 들려줬다 (told them the story quiet → told them the story quietly)

PRACTICE 5

1 lately
2 sweet
3 near
4 closely
5 high
6 hardly
7 gently
8 highly
9 late
10 rarely
11 beautifully
12 close
13 hard
14 Nearly
15 happy

1 최근에 아무 영화도 보지 않았다는 뜻이므로 lately가 적절하다
* late: 늦게 / lately: 최근에
2 감각동사 taste는 형용사를 보어로 취하므로 sweet이 적절하다. (taste sweet: 달콤한 맛이 나다)
3 크리스마스가 가까이 다가오고 있다는 뜻이므로 near이 적절하다.
* near: 가까이 / nearly: 거의
4 신문(the paper)을 자세히 읽었다는 뜻이므로 closely가 적절하다.
* close: 가까이 / closely: 접근하여, 면밀히
5 여름에는 기온이 높이 상승한다는 뜻이므로 high가 적절하다.
* high: 높게 / highly: 크게, 대단히
6 그녀는 회의 중에 거의 말하지 않는다는 뜻이므로 hardly가 적절하다.
* hard: 열심히 / hardly: 좀처럼 ~않는
7 Smith 부인이 내게 상냥하게 말을 걸었다는 뜻이므로 gently가 적절하다.
* gentle: 온화한 / gently: 다정하게
8 대단히 성공적인 사업이라는 뜻이므로 highly가 적절하다.
* high: 높게 / highly: 대단히, 크게
9 아버지가 집에 늦게 오셨다는 뜻이므로 late가 적절하다.
* late: 늦게 / lately: 최근에
10 그것들을 드물게 먹는다는 뜻이므로 rarely가 적절하다.
* rare: 드문, 희귀한 / rarely: 드물게, 좀처럼 ~하지 않는
11 그녀가 아름답게 노래를 불렀다는 뜻이므로 동사를 수식할 수 있는 부사 beautifully가 적절하다.
12 Jane이 나의 집에 가까이 산다는 뜻이므로 close가 적절하다.
* close to: ~에 가까이 / closely: 면밀히
13 시험공부를 열심히 했냐는 뜻이므로 hard가 적절하다.
* hard: 열심히 / hardly: 좀처럼 ~않는
14 거의 150개에 달하는 국가들이 올림픽에 참가했다는 뜻이므로 nearly가 적절하다.
* near: 가까이 / nearly: 거의
15 감각동사 look은 형용사를 보어로 취하므로 happy가 적절하다. (look happy: 행복해 보이다)

PRACTICE 6

1 ① easy ② easily
2 ① clearly ② clear
3 ① late ② late
4 ① careful ② carefully
5 ① last ② last
6 ① early ② early
7 ① lucky ② Luckily
8 ① certain ② certainly
9 ① hard ② hardly
10 ① close ② closely

1 ① an easy question: 쉬운 문제 → 형용사
② solve a question easily: 쉽게 문제를 풀다 → 부사
2 ① speak clearly: 분명하게 말하다 → 부사
② the sky is clear: 하늘이 맑다 → 형용사
3 ① have lunch late: 점심식사를 늦게 하다 → 부사
② late for school: 학교에 늦은 → 형용사
4 ① Be careful: 조심해라 → 형용사
② drive a car carefully: 차를 주의해서 운전하다 → 부사
5 ① the last chance: 마지막인 기회 → 형용사
② finish last: 마지막으로 끝내다 → 부사
6 ① wake up early: 일찍 일어나다 → 부사
② an early hour: 이른 시각 → 형용사
7 ① a lucky guy: 운 좋은 녀석 → 형용사
② Luckily, she was safe.: 다행스럽게도, 그녀는 안전했다. → 부사
8 ① certain kinds: 특정한 종류 → 형용사
② certainly win the first prize: 틀림없이 우승하다 → 부사
9 ① work so hard: 매우 열심히 일하다 → 부사
② could hardly breathe: 거의 숨을 쉴 수가 없었다 → 부사
10 ① come close to: ~에 가까이 가다 → 부사
② Read the text closely: 글을 자세히 봐라 → 부사

PRACTICE 7

1 I sometimes go to Incheon to visit my grandparents.
2 He never leaves the house without his phone.
3 Sangmin could rarely come to our club meetings.
4 I have always wanted to travel around the world.
5 We will sometimes go to the movies together.
6 They usually shake hands to greet each other.
7 I should often help my mom with the housework.
8 He is seldom excited about the trip.
9 She has never learned Chinese.
10 You don't often clean your room, do you?

Ch
11
부
사

9 still 10 still 11 already 12 still
13 already 14 yet 15 already

> 9 still 10 still 11 already 12 still
> 13 already 14 yet 15 already
>
> **1, 7, 14** 부정문에서 '아직'의 의미로 쓰이고, 주로 문장 끝에 위치하는 yet이 알맞다.
> **2, 6, 13** 긍정문에서 '이미, 벌써'의 의미로 쓰이는 already가 알맞다.
> **3, 5, 9, 10** 긍정문과 의문문에서 '여전히, 아직도'의 의미로 쓰이는 still이 알맞다.
> **4** 의문문에서 '이미, 벌써, 이제'의 뜻으로 쓰이는 yet이 알맞다.
> **8, 11, 15** 놀람을 나타내는 의문문에서 '이미, 벌써'의 의미로 쓰이는 already가 알맞다.
> **12** 부정문에서 계속되는 행위를 강조할 때 쓰이는 still이 알맞다.

PRACTICE 8

1 I usually go jogging in the morning.
2 They must sometimes listen to others.
3 We will often practice swimming.
4 Hana always smiles brightly.
5 Nick can seldom understand Korean.
6 Climbing mountains is sometimes dangerous.
7 Giho never watches comic dramas.
8 I usually take care of my younger sisters.
9 She rarely buys expensive clothes.
10 I am often depressed by bad weather.

> **1** I usually **go** jogging in the morning.
> → 보통 조깅을 한다
> **2** They **must** sometimes listen to others.
> → 때때로 들어야 한다
> **3** We **will** often practice swimming.
> → 종종 연습할 것이다
> **4** Hana always **smiles** brightly.
> → 항상 웃는다
> **5** Nick **can** seldom understand Korean.
> → 좀처럼 이해할 수 없다
> **6** Climbing mountains **is** sometimes dangerous.
> → 때때로 위험하다
> **7** Giho never **watches** comic dramas.
> → 절대 보지 않는다
> **8** I usually **take** care of my younger sisters.
> → 보통 돌본다
> **9** She rarely **buys** expensive clothes.
> → 거의 사지 않는다
> **10** I am often depressed by bad weather.
> → 종종 우울하다

PRACTICE 9

1 ① already ② yet ③ still
2 ① still ② already ③ yet
3 ① yet ② still ③ already
4 ① still ② yet ③ already
5 ① yet ② already ③ still

PRACTICE 10

1 yet 2 already 3 still 4 yet
5 still 6 already 7 yet 8 already

PRACTICE 11

1 too 2 neither 3 too 4 either
5 too 6 neither 7 either 8 too
9 either 10 neither 11 neither 12 either
13 too 14 either 15 neither

PRACTICE 12

1 ① very ② much
2 ① much ② very
3 ① very ② much
4 ① very ② much
5 ① very ② much
6 ① much ② very
7 ① very ② much
8 ① much ② very
9 ① much ② very
10 ① very ② much

PRACTICE 13

1 very 2 much 3 very 4 much
5 much 6 very 7 much 8 very
9 much 10 very 11 much 12 very

> **1, 6, 8, 12** 형용사의 원급을 수식하는 자리이므로 very가 알맞다.
> very heavy: 매우 심한
> very useful: 매우 유용한
> very good: 매우 좋은
> very large: 매우 큰
> **2, 4, 7, 11** 형용사의 비교급을 수식하는 자리이므로 much가 알맞다.
> much older: 훨씬 더 나이가 많은
> much cooler: 훨씬 더 시원한
> much cheaper: 훨씬 더 싼
> much more exciting: 훨씬 더 신나는

3, 10 부사의 원급을 수식하는 자리이므로 very가 알맞다.
listen <u>very</u> carefully: 매우 주의 깊게 듣다
try <u>very</u> hard: 아주 열심히 노력하다
5, 9 부사의 비교급을 수식하는 자리이므로 much가 알맞다.
take <u>much</u> longer: 훨씬 더 오래 걸리다
speak <u>much</u> better: 훨씬 더 잘 말하다

PRACTICE 14

1 What else can I do for you?

2 I didn't even imagine it was possible.

3 It was even sad to say goodbye to everyone.

4 Where else did you visit in London?

5 He even took some medicine to fall asleep.

6 They kept practicing soccer even when it rained heavily.

7 The child brings his toy even to the bathroom.

8 Even a small pet can give you a lot of trouble.

9 Jessica even gets angry if I don't call her often.

10 David can run faster than anyone else in his class.

11 Dad sometimes works even on Sunday.

12 You can even order a pizza on the Internet.

13 Babies need to be watched even while they are sleeping.

14 You'd better write these rules somewhere else.

15 He speaks English, Chinese, French, and even Spanish.

1, 4, 10, 14 else는 '그 밖에'라는 뜻으로 수식하고자 하는 말 뒤에 온다.
2, 3, 5, 6, 7, 8, 9, 11, 12, 13, 15 even은 '~조차(도), ~까지도' 라는 뜻으로 수식하고자 하는 말 앞에 온다.

PRACTICE 15

1 even 2 else 3 even 4 else 5 even
6 else 7 even 8 even 9 else 10 else

1 You should not <u>even</u> look: 너는 보지<u>조차</u> 말아야 한다
2 anywhere <u>else</u>: 그 밖의 다른 곳
3 couldn't <u>even</u> hold a spoon: 숟가락을 들 수 <u>조차</u> 없었다
4 anyone <u>else</u>: 그 밖의 다른 사람
5 I <u>even</u> had to dance: 나는 춤을 추는 것<u>까지도</u> 해야 했다
6 what <u>else</u>: 그 밖의 무엇
7 <u>even</u> during the vacation: 휴가 동안<u>조차</u>
8 <u>even</u> knows where my grandparents are now: 나의 조부 모님이 지금 어디에 계신지<u>조차</u> 안다
9 somewhere <u>else</u>: 그 밖의 다른 곳
10 where <u>else</u>: 그 밖의 어디

PRACTICE 16

1 them on   2 about money
3 on the light   4 it up
5 at the picture   6 in the homework
7 to an audio book   8 it off
9 the show off   10 on the chair
11 it out   12 it away
13 up the paper   14 them out
15 for it   16 about it

1, 4, 8, 11, 12, 14 목적어가 대명사일 때는 「동사+목적어+부사」 의 어순만 가능하다.
try ~ on: ~을 입어[신어]보다
give ~ up: ~을 포기하다
turn ~ off: ~을 끄다
find ~ out: ~을 발견하다
throw ~ away: ~을 버리다
check ~ out: ~을 대출하다, 확인하다
2, 5, 7, 10, 15, 16 자동사 뒤에 전치사가 올 때, 전치사의 목적어 는 반드시 전치사 뒤에 온다.
care about: ~에 대해 신경 쓰다
look at: ~을 보다
listen to: ~을 듣다
sit on: ~에 앉다
look for: ~을 찾다
talk about: ~에 대해 얘기하다
3, 6, 9, 13 목적어가 일반 명사일 때는 「동사+부사+목적어」나 「동 사+목적어+부사」의 어순 둘 다 가능하다.
turn on: ~을 켜다
hand in: ~을 제출하다
call off: ~을 취소하다
pick up: ~을 줍다, 찾아오다, (차에) 태우다

PRACTICE 17

1 out   2 away[out]   3 on
4 on   5 up   6 in
7 off   8 out   9 off
10 up

1 <u>find out</u> who the thief is: 누가 도둑인지 알아내다
2 <u>throw away[out]</u> the paper: 그 종이를 버리다
3 <u>turn</u> the TV <u>on</u>: TV를 켜다
4 <u>try</u> the blue shirt <u>on</u>: 푸른색 셔츠를 입어보다
5 <u>pick up</u> the coins: 동전들을 줍다
6 <u>hand in</u> the paper: 과제물을 제출하다
7 <u>turn</u> the light <u>off</u>: 전등을 끄다
8 <u>check out</u> the books: 책들을 대출하다
9 <u>call off</u> our plan: 우리의 계획을 취소하다
10 <u>give up</u> the soccer game: 축구 경기를 포기하다

Ch
11
부
사

PRACTICE 18

1	Where	**2**	How
3	Why	**4**	How many
5	How long	**6**	When
7	How old	**8**	How much
9	How far	**10**	Where
11	When	**12**	How
13	Why	**14**	How much
15	How often		

> **1, 10** 장소/지역을 나타내는 표현으로 답하고 있으므로 Where(어디에) 의문문이 알맞다.
> **2, 12** 어떤 곳에 가는 교통편이나 누군가를 알게 된 경위 등으로 답하고 있으므로 방법을 묻는 How(어떻게) 의문문이 알맞다.
> **3, 13** 이유를 설명할 때 쓰는 접속사인 Because(~ 때문에)로 답하고 있으므로 Why(왜) 의문문이 알맞다.
> **4** 수량으로 답하고 있으므로 How many(얼마나 많은) 의문문이 알맞다.
> **5** 소요 시간으로 답하고 있으므로 How long(얼마나 오래) 의문문이 알맞다.
> **6, 11** 특정 시점으로 답하고 있으므로 때를 묻는 When(언제) 의문문이 알맞다.
> **7** 나이로 답하고 있으므로 How old(몇 살인) 의문문이 알맞다.
> **8, 14** 가격으로 답하고 있으므로 How much(얼마인) 의문문이 알맞다.
> **9** 거리로 답하고 있으므로 How far(얼마나 멀리) 의문문이 알맞다.
> **15** 빈도/횟수로 답하고 있으므로 How often(얼마나 자주) 의문문이 알맞다.

📑 중간·기말고사 대비문제 **정답** 본문 _ p.284

1 ③ **2** ① **3** ④ **4** ⑤ **5** How **6** ③,⑤
7 ① **8** ⑤ **9** ③ **10** either **11** ①,② **12** ②
13 ② **14** ① **15** ④ **16** ③ **17** ④ **18** ②
19 ③ **20** ② **21** ⑤ **22** ①,④ **23** ④ **24** ④
25 ③ **26** ① **27** ⑤ **28** ⑤ **29** ③ **30** ③
31 (A) much[far/still/even] (B) very (C) Where (D) to **32** ② **33** ⑤ **34** ③,④ **35** ④
36 ⓒ,ⓐ,ⓑ,ⓓ **37** How can I get to the airport from here? [How can I get from here to the airport?] **38** ②,③ **39** ④

중간·기말고사 대비문제 **해설**

1 형용사 – 형용사의 관계인 ③을 제외한 나머지는 형용사 - 부사의 관계이다.

③ • She's the ⓐ <u>right</u> person for this job.
그녀는 이 일에 <u>적합한</u> 사람이다.
• I didn't feel quite ⓑ <u>right</u> today.
나는 오늘 <u>몸이 안 좋았다</u>.

① • The class suddenly became ⓐ <u>quiet</u>.
교실이 갑자기 <u>조용해졌다</u>.
• She ⓑ <u>quietly</u> went out of the door.
그녀는 <u>조용히</u> 문 밖으로 나갔다.

② • He is a ⓐ <u>careful</u> man. 그는 <u>신중한</u> 사람이다.
• She ⓑ <u>carefully</u> cut the paper.
그녀는 <u>신중하게</u> 종이를 잘랐다.

④ • They will announce their decision in the ⓐ <u>near</u> future. 그들은 그들의 결정을 <u>가까운 미래</u>에 발표할 것이다.
• He's ⓑ <u>nearly</u> as tall as his father.
그는 <u>거의</u> 그의 아버지만큼 키가 크다.

⑤ • We are ⓐ <u>late</u> for the meeting.
우리는 그 회의에 <u>늦었다</u>.
• John has been acting strange ⓑ <u>lately</u>.
John은 <u>최근에</u> 이상하게 행동해오고 있다.

2 ⓐ took out의 목적어가 대명사 them이므로 them은 took와 out 사이에 위치하고, 동사 looked와 전치사 at의 목적어는 항상 전치사 뒤에 위치하므로 looked at them이 된다.
ⓑ '최근에'라는 의미의 부사 lately
'늦게'라는 의미의 부사 late
ⓒ '높게'라는 의미의 부사 high
'매우'라는 의미의 부사 highly
ⓓ enough가 형용사로서 명사를 수식할 때는 명사의 앞에 위치한다.

3 not ~ any는 no와 같고, either는 '~또한'의 의미로 부정문에 쓰인다.

4 yet은 부정문에서 '아직'이란 뜻으로 쓰인다.

5 <u>How</u> was it? 그건 <u>어땠니</u>?
<u>How</u> could you find such a great movie?
그렇게 좋은 영화를 <u>어떻게</u> 찾을 수 있었니?

6 ③ '너는 조심스럽게 길을 건너야한다'는 뜻이므로 동사 cross를 수식하는 부사를 써야 한다.
(careful → carefully)
⑤ '나는 시험을 위해 열심히 공부했다'는 뜻이므로 '열심히'라는 뜻의 부사 hard를 써야 한다. hardly는 '거의 ~않는'이라는 뜻이다. (hardly → hard)

7 <u>Why</u> were you so sad? 넌 <u>왜</u> 그렇게 슬펐니?

8 ⓐ '그들은 아직 그것을 끝내지 못했다'라는 뜻이 되어야 하므로, 부정문에서 '아직'이라는 뜻으로 쓰이는 부사 yet을 써야 한다. (already → yet)

ⓑ either은 부정문에서 '~또한'이라는 뜻을 나타낸다. too는 긍정문에 쓰인다. (too → either)

ⓓ 사역동사 make는 목적격 보어로 동사원형을 쓴다. (stopping → stop)

ⓔ 형용사의 비교급은 much로 수식한다. very는 원급을 수식한다. (very → much)

9 (C) '나도 아니다'라는 뜻은 Me, neither.을 써서 부정문에 대한 동의를 나타낸다. too는 긍정문에 대한 동의에 쓰인다. (too → neither)

10 either는 '~또한'의 의미로 부정문에 쓰인다.

11 ① 빈도부사는 조동사의 뒤에 위치한다.
(always has → has always)

② 문장의 주어는 the journey이므로 조동사는 3인칭 단수형이 적절하다. (do → does)

12 (A) '가까이'라는 의미의 부사 close
(B) '최근에'라는 의미의 부사 lately
(C) '거의'라는 의미의 부사 nearly

13 ② 비교급을 수식할 때는 much를 사용한다. very는 원급을 수식한다. (very → much)

14 ⓑ 「so+형용사/부사+that+주어+can」 '너무 ~해서 …하다'

ⓐ everything과 같이 -thing으로 끝나는 대명사는 형용사가 뒤에서 수식한다. (necessary everything → everything necessary)

ⓒ 인식을 나타내는 동사 know는 진행형으로 쓰지 않는다. (has been knowing → has known)

ⓓ 형용사 gentle의 부사형은 gently로 쓴다.
(gentley → gently)

ⓔ 감각동사 look은 주격 보어로 형용사가 온다.
(confidently → confident)

15 ④ How come은 '왜'라는 뜻으로 why와 같은 의미이다. 보기에는 이에 적절한 답이 없다.

① How far은 '얼마나 머니?'라는 뜻으로 거리를 묻는 질문이다. 따라서 (D)가 적절한 답이다.

② How long은 '(시간이) 얼마나 걸리니?'라는 뜻으로 시간의 길이를 묻는 질문이다. 따라서 (B)가 적절한 답이다.

③ How often은 '얼마나 자주'라는 뜻으로 빈도를 묻는 질문이다. 따라서 (A)가 적절한 답이다.

⑤ How much는 가격을 묻는 표현이다. 따라서 (C)가 적절한 답이다.

16 ③ '많이' ①②④⑤ '훨씬' (비교급 강조)

17 ④ '쉽게 찾을 수 있었다'는 뜻이 되어야 하므로 동사 find를 수식할 수 있는 부사의 형태로 써야 한다. (easy → easily)

18 ② '바닥에 세게 넘어졌다'는 뜻이 되어야 하므로 '세게'라는 뜻의 부사 hard를 써야 한다. hardly는 '거의 ~않는'이라는 뜻이다. (hardly → hard)

19 ③ Me, neither. = I don't, either.

20 ⓐ 「타동사+부사」의 목적어가 대명사일 때, 목적어는 반드시 동사와 부사의 사이에 쓴다.
(take off them → take them off)

ⓔ taking off shoes는 동명사구로, 동명사구가 주어로 올 때는 단수 취급한다. (are → is)

ⓑ used to는 '~하곤 했다'는 뜻의 조동사이므로 뒤에 동사원형을 쓴다.

ⓒ 「타동사+부사」의 목적어가 명사일 때, 목적어는 부사의 뒤나 동사와 부사의 사이에 쓴다.

ⓓ even은 수식하고자 하는 말 앞에 온다. 여기에서는 '생각하기도 한다'는 뜻을 나타내고자 think 앞에 쓴다.

21 ⑤ else는 수식하고자 하는 말 뒤에 온다.
(else nothing → nothing else)

22 (B) 주어인 Hollywood가 많은 영화 팬들이 방문하는 대상이므로 수동태로 고쳐주어야 한다.
(visited → is visited)

(C) near은 형용사와 부사의 형태가 같은 단어이다. 형용사 형태의 부사에 '-ly'를 붙이면 뜻이 달라지는데 이때 nearly의 뜻은 '거의'이다. 여기서는 '거의 3백 5십만 명의 관광객'이라는 의미이므로 nearly가 맞다.

(E) want는 to부정사를 목적격 보어로 취하므로 come을 to come으로 고쳐야 한다.

23 ⓐ 문장 전체를 수식하는 부사구가 나온 경우로, '처음으로 그리고 가장 중요한 것은'이란 의미를 지니며 문장 전체를 수식한다.

ⓑ 5형식 문장으로 목적격 보어 자리에 the conversation을 설명하는 형용사가 나와야 한다. 목적격 보어 자리에 부사는 나올 수 없다.

ⓒ elder과 elderly 둘 다 형용사로 나이가 더 많다는 뜻이지만 의미 차이가 있다. elder은 상대방보다 나이가 더 많은 경우, 손위의 의미일 때 사용하며 elderly는 나이가 많은 노인들을 가리킨다.

Ch
11
부
사

24 민수가 Because로 답하고 있기 때문에 이유를 묻는 문장이 들어가야 한다.

25 ③ '책이 높게 쌓여있다'는 의미이므로 '높게'라는 뜻의 부사 high를 쓰는 것이 맞다.
① '주의 깊게, 면밀히'라는 뜻을 가진 closely로 써야 한다. close는 '가까이'라는 뜻의 부사이다.
(close → closely)
② '거의 ~않는'이라는 의미의 hardly로 써야 한다. hard는 '열심히'라는 뜻의 부사이다.
(hard → hardly)
④ '최근에'라는 뜻의 lately로 써야 한다. late는 '늦게'라는 뜻의 부사이다. (late → lately)
⑤ '가까이'라는 의미의 near로 써야 한다. nearly는 '거의'라는 뜻의 부사이다. (nearly → near)

26 빈도부사는 조동사 뒤, 일반동사 앞에 위치한다.

27 (A) '어떻게 ~하고 있니?'의 의미이므로 의문부사 how
(B) 시간, 때를 나타내는 의문부사 when
(C) 장소를 나타내는 의문부사 where

28 빈칸 뒤에 나오는 소녀의 대답으로 보아 소년이 소녀에게 도서부에 대한 느낌을 물어본 것을 알 수 있으므로, ⑤ '너는 그것에 대해 어떻게 느껴?'가 정답이다.
① 너는 얼마나 자주 책을 읽니?
② 너는 무엇을 읽고 있니?
③ 너는 어떻게 지냈어?
④ 의문대명사 What이 아닌 의문부사 How를 쓰는 것이 적절하다. 혹은 What do you like about it?과 같은 형태로 쓸 수 있다.
소년: 야, 유진아! 너는 어디에 가고 있니?
소녀: 안녕, Jun. 나는 도서부 모임에 가는 길이야.
소년: 오, 나는 네가 도서부에 들어갔는지 몰랐어.
소녀: 내가 들어간 후로 몇 주밖에 되지 않았어. 너는 내가 책벌레인 걸 알잖아.
소년: 맞아. 너는 그것에 대해 어떻게 느껴?
소녀: 그것은 정말 재미있어! 그것은 나에게 책에 대한 다양한 의견들을 들을 기회를 제공해.

29 ③ 「타동사+부사」의 목적어가 대명사일 때 목적어는 항상 타동사와 부사 사이에 온다.
(picks up him → picks him up)

30 ③ already(이미, 벌써)는 긍정문과 의문문에서 쓰인다. yet은 의문문(이미, 벌써)과 부정문(아직)에서 쓰인다. 긍정문이므로 yet을 already로 고쳐야 한다.

31 (A) 비교급을 수식하는 much[far/still/even]
(B) 원급을 수식하는 very
(C) 장소에 대한 정보를 묻는 의문사 where
(D) 동사 give는 간접목적어와 직접목적어의 순서가 바뀌면 뒤로 보내진 간접목적어 앞에 전치사 to를 쓴다.

32 ② often은 빈도부사이므로 일반동사 gets 앞에 와야 한다. (gets often → often gets)

33 ⓓ wait for는 「자동사+전치사」 형태로, 전치사의 목적어는 반드시 전치사 뒤에 온다.
(waiting me for → waiting for me)
ⓕ 「타동사+부사」의 목적어가 대명사일 때, 목적어는 반드시 동사와 부사의 사이에 온다. 즉, 「타동사+목적어+부사」의 어순만 가능하다.
(pick up me → pick me up)
ⓐⓑⓒ 「타동사+부사」의 목적어가 명사일 때, 목적어는 부사의 뒤에 오거나 동사와 부사의 사이에 온다.
ⓔ 「타동사+부사」의 목적어가 대명사일 때, 목적어는 동사와 부사의 사이에 오는 것이 맞다.

34 ③ 빈도부사는 일반동사 앞에 위치한다.
(spends usually → usually spends)
④ 주어가 3인칭 단수인 현재시제이므로 동사에 -s를 붙인다. (forget → forgets)

35 ④ 타동사+부사의 어순에서, 목적어가 대명사이면 타동사와 부사의 사이에 온다.
(set up it → set it up)

36 ① - ⓒ Jane은 이미 숙제를 했다. - 난 그녀의 어머니가 숙제하는 것을 도와줬다고 생각해.
② - ⓐ 점심 먹었니? - 당연히 먹었지. 벌써 세 시야.
③ - ⓑ 당신이 시애틀에 살던 것을 기억해요. - 전 아직 거기 살아요.
④ - ⓓ 네 숙제를 보여주겠니? - 아직 끝내지 않았어요.

37 how는 '방법'을 묻는 의문사이며, 뒤에 「조동사+주어+본동사 ~?」의 어순이 온다.

38 ② fast는 부사와 형용사의 형태가 같다.
(fastly → fast)
③ '최근에 영화를 봤었니?'라는 뜻이 되어야 하므로 '최근에'라는 뜻의 부사 lately를 써야 한다. late는 '늦게'라는 뜻이다. (late → lately)

39 (A) 동사를 꾸며주는 부사가 와야 한다.
(B) 문맥상 '열심히'의 의미이므로 hard가 와야 한다.
(C) 「look+형용사」'~하게 보이다'

CHAPTER 12 가정법
Conditionals

PRACTICE 1

1 find	**2** finish	**3** comes
4 rains	**5** meet	**6** changes
7 leaves	**8** studies	**9** hurries
10 are		

조건을 나타내는 if절의 동사는 의미가 미래더라도 현재형으로 써야 한다.

2 finish homework: 숙제를 마치다(주어가 'I'이므로 finish가 적절하다.)
3 come here: 이리로 오다(주어가 'he'이므로 comes가 적절하다.)
4 it rains: 비가 오다
5 say hello to: ~에게 안부를 전하다
6 change one's mind: 생각을 바꾸다, 마음을 고쳐먹다
7 leave for: ~을 향해 떠나다
8 study hard: 열심히 공부하다
9 catch a bus: 버스를 잡아타다

PRACTICE 2

1 knew
2 had
3 couldn't travel
4 were
5 would[could/might] get
6 would[might] invite
7 would[could] bake
8 followed
9 weren't
10 would[could] talk

가정법 과거는 '만약 ~한다면 …할 텐데'의 뜻으로 현재 사실에 반대되는 일을 가정할 때 쓰며, 「If+주어+동사의 과거형 ~, 주어+would/could/should/might+동사원형 …」으로 나타낸다.

1, 2, 4, 8, 9 가정법 과거 구문에서, if절의 동사는 과거형으로 쓴다. 단, be동사일 경우에는 인칭에 상관없이 were를 쓴다.
3, 5, 6, 7, 10 가정법 과거 구문에서, 주절의 동사는 'would/could/should/might+동사원형'으로 쓴다.

PRACTICE 3

2 If Steve knew the reason, he would be angry.
3 If this movie were fun, I wouldn't be bored.
4 If you were honest, you would have many friends.
5 If I had enough money, I could buy you a piano.
6 If you were old enough, you could understand this better.
7 If my brother were hungry, he would go out for dinner.
8 If I weren't tired, I could go swimming now.
9 If she agreed with the writer, she would like his book.
10 If I didn't have other plans, I could go shopping with you.

PRACTICE 4

1 were		**2** had
3 didn't snow		**4** could speak
5 would call		**6** could give
7 were		**8** wouldn't leave
9 could sing		**10** had

1~10 「I wish+가정법 과거」는 '~라면 좋을 텐데'의 뜻으로, 현재의 사실과 반대되거나 미래에 이룰 수 없는 일을 소망할 때 쓰며, 「I wish+주어+동사의 과거형 ~」으로 나타낸다.

PRACTICE 5

2 I wish it weren't cold here.
3 I wish I were diligent.
4 I wish I knew how to drive.
5 I wish Angela could join our club.
6 I wish there were trees around here.
7 I wish the class would finish soon.
8 I wish I could play the violin.
9 I wish Mark wouldn't move to another city.
10 I wish I were good at sports.

PRACTICE 6

1 as if you were his friend
2 as if she lived here
3 as if she were Korean
4 as if he were a king
5 as if the play were exciting
6 as if today were Saturday
7 as if he knew everybody in my family
8 as if she were very smart
9 as if you were a child
10 as if they were sick

Ch **12** 가정법

> **1~10** 「as if+가정법 과거」는 '마치 ~인 것처럼'의 뜻으로 현재의
> 사실과 반대되는 일을 나타내며, 「동사의 현재형+as if+주어+동사
> 의 과거형 ~」으로 쓴다.

PRACTICE 7

1 had finished

2 had known

3 were

4 would[might] have called

5 would[could] go

6 hadn't forgotten

7 would[could] have arrived

8 liked

9 could have prevented

10 wouldn't have felt

> **1, 2, 6** 주절이 'would/could+have+과거분사' 형태로 되어 있으
> 므로 가정법 과거완료 문장임을 알 수 있다. 따라서 if절의 동사는
> 'had+과거분사' 형태로 써야 한다.
> **3, 8** 주절이 'would+동사원형' 형태로 되어 있으므로 가정법 과거
> 문장임을 알 수 있다. 따라서 if절의 동사는 '과거형'으로 써야 한다.
> **4, 7, 9, 10** If절이 'If+주어+had+과거분사 ~'형태로 되어 있으므
> 로 가정법 과거완료 문장임을 알 수 있다. 따라서 주절은 'would/
> might/could/wouldn't+have+과거분사' 형태로 써야 한다.
> **5** If절이 'If+주어+동사의 과거형 ~'형태로 되어 있으므로 가정법
> 과거 문장임을 알 수 있다. 따라서 주절은 'would/could+동사원형'
> 형태로 써야 한다.

PRACTICE 8

2 I wish she had kept her promise.

3 I wish Jinsu had come to my house.

4 I wish I were in Europe now.

5 I wish they had finished cleaning the room.

6 I wish Mina hadn't been late for the meeting.

7 I wish my brother read books.

8 I wish she had watered the plants.

9 I wish we had visited him in the hospital.

10 I wish I hadn't studied even on holidays.

> **2, 3, 5, 6, 8, 9, 10** 과거의 사실과 반대되는 일을 소망하고 있으
> 므로 「I wish+가정법 과거완료」가 적합하다. 따라서 「I wish+주어
> +had (not)+과거분사 ~」로 표현하는 것이 알맞다.
> **4, 7** 현재의 사실과 반대되거나 이룰 수 없는 일을 소망하고 있으므
> 로 「I wish+가정법 과거」가 적합하다. 따라서 「I wish+주어+동사의
> 과거형 ~」으로 표현하는 것이 알맞다.

PRACTICE 9

1 as if she hadn't slept well last night

2 as if she were married

3 as if I had broken the glass

4 as if they had been rich in their youth

5 as if I had lost my watch

6 as if you had been right all the time

7 as if he knew those students

8 as if he were popular among his classmates

9 as if they hadn't been bored by the lecture

10 as if it had been your idea

> **1, 3, 4, 5, 6, 9, 10** '마치 ~이었던 것처럼'이라는 뜻으로 과거의
> 사실과 반대되는 일을 나타내고 있으므로 「as if+가정법 과거완료」
> 가 적합하다. 따라서 「동사의 현재형+as if+주어+had (not)+과거
> 분사 ~」로 표현하는 것이 알맞다.
> **2, 7, 8** '마치 ~인 것처럼'이라는 뜻으로 현재의 사실과 반대되는 일
> 을 나타내고 있으므로 「as if+가정법 과거」가 적합하다. 따라서 「동
> 사의 현재형+as if+주어+동사의 과거형 ~」으로 표현하는 것이 알
> 맞다.

📝 중간·기말고사 대비문제 정답 본문 _ p.301

1 ③   **2** If, won't   **3** ③   **4** ①   **5** ④   **6** ⑤
7 ③   **8** ②   **9** ②,③   **10** ③   **11** am → were
12 ③   **13** wish, had finished   **14** ④   **15** had
travel(l)ed   **16** If I were her, I would refuse the
offer.   **17** were   **18** were my close friend
19 ③   **20** he had met   **21** played, spoke
22 If I knew the password, I could log into the
website.   **23** ③   **24** ②   **25** ①

중간·기말고사 대비문제 해설

1 ③ 우리말이 조건을 나타내므로 if 조건절(If+주어+
동사의 현재형 ~, 주어+will+동사원형 ~)로 쓴다.

2 「명령문, and …」는 '~해라, 그러면 …'으로 해석하고
조건을 나타내는 if절의 문장으로 바꾸어 쓸 수 있다.

3 ③ 조건을 나타내는 if절이 미래의 일을 나타낸다 하더
라도 if절의 동사는 현재형으로 쓴다.
(will snow → snows)

4 주절의 won't로 보아, 문장의 시제가 미래임을 알 수
있다. 그러나 미래의 일을 나타낸다고 하더라도 조건
을 나타내는 if절의 동사는 항상 현재시제가 미래시제

를 대신한다. (went → goes)

5 현재 사실에 반대되는 일을 가정할 때 쓰는 가정법 과거로 바꾸어 쓸 수 있다.

6 미래의 일을 나타내는 조건절이 쓰였으므로 주절은 미래 시제를 쓴다.

7 ③ 과거의 사실에 대한 가정이므로 가정법 과거완료로 쓴다. 가정법 과거완료는 「If + 주어 + had + 과거분사, 주어 + could + have + 과거분사」의 어순으로 나타낸다. (didn't tell → hadn't told)

①④ '~라면 좋을 텐데'라는 뜻의 현재 사실의 반대를 나타내는 I wish + 가정법 과거는 「I wish + 주어 + 동사의 과거형」의 어순으로 쓴다.

② 배수사를 사용한 원급의 비교는 「배수사 + as + 원급 + as」의 어순으로 나타낸다.

⑤ 주절의 동사가 현재시제인 경우 종속절의 동사는 의미에 따라 어떠한 시제든지 쓸 수 있다.

8 ② 현재 사실과 반대되는 일을 나타내는 as if + 가정법 과거는 「동사의 현재형 + as if + 주어 + 동사의 과거형」으로 쓴다. (are → were)

9 ②③ 여기서 if는 현재나 미래에 실제로 일어날 수 있는 상황에 대한 조건을 나타낸다. 이때, 미래의 일을 나타낸다 하더라도, if절의 동사는 항상 현재형으로 쓴다.

① 현재의 사실에 반대되는 가정을 나타내는 가정법 과거는 「If + 주어 + 동사의 과거형, 주어 + might + 동사원형」의 어순으로 나타낸다. (eat → ate)

④ 현재의 사실에 반대되는 가정을 나타내는 가정법 과거는 「If + 주어 + 동사의 과거형, 주어 + might + 동사원형」의 어순으로 나타낸다.
(have caught → catch)

⑤ if가 현재나 미래에 실제로 일어날 수 있는 상황에 대한 조건을 나타낸다. may는 조동사이므로 뒤에 항상 동사원형을 쓴다. (passed → pass)

10 현재의 사실에 반대되는 가정을 나타내는 가정법 과거는 「If + 주어 + 동사의 과거형, 주어 + could + 동사원형」의 어순으로 나타낸다. if절의 be동사는 인칭에 상관없이 were를 쓴다.

11 가정법 과거의 be동사는 인칭에 관계없이 were를 쓴다.

12 ⓒ 과거 사실에 대한 가정이므로 가정법 과거완료를 써야 한다. (were not → had not been)

ⓓ now로 보아 현재 사실에 반대되는 일을 가정하는 가정법 과거임을 알 수 있다.

(could have entered → could enter)

13 과거의 사실과 반대되는 일을 소망할 때 쓰는 「I wish + 가정법 과거완료」로 바꾸어 쓸 수 있다.

14 ④ 「I wish + 가정법 과거」는 현재 사실과 반대되는 일을 소망할 때 쓴다. 중국어를 현재 모른다고 했으므로 '안다면 좋을 텐데.'라는 뜻을 나타내기 위해 knew로 써야 한다. (didn't know → knew)

15 과거의 사실과 반대되는 일을 소망할 때는 「I wish + 가정법 과거완료」 구문을 쓴다.

16 현재의 사실과 반대되는 일을 가정하고 있으므로 가정법 과거 「If + 주어 + 동사의 과거형~, 주어 + would [could/should/might] + 동사원형」을 써야 한다. 가정법 과거 문장에서 if절의 be동사는 인칭에 상관없이 were를 쓴다.

17 현재의 사실과 반대되는 일을 나타낼 때는 as if 뒤에 동사의 과거형을 쓴다. 가정법 과거의 be동사는 인칭에 관계없이 were를 쓴다.

18 Mary speaks as if she were my close friend.
Mary는 마치 그녀가 나의 친한 친구인 것처럼 말한다.

19 If I had enough money, I could buy all the items I want. 만약 내가 충분한 돈을 가지고 있다면, 내가 원하는 모든 물품들을 살 수 있을 텐데.
= Because I don't have enough money, I can't buy all the items I want. 나는 충분한 돈이 없기 때문에, 내가 원하는 모든 물품들을 살 수 없다.

20 과거의 사실과 반대되는 일을 나타낼 때는 「동사의 현재형 + as if + 주어 + had + 과거분사」를 쓴다.

21 「I wish + 가정법 과거」에서 동사는 과거형을 쓴다.

22 주어진 문장은 '내가 비밀번호를 모르기 때문에 웹사이트에 로그인 할 수 없다.'라는 뜻이다. 가정법 문장으로 바꿔 쓰면 '내가 비밀번호를 알았다면 웹사이트에 로그인 할 수 있었을 텐데.'의 의미로, 현재 사실에 반대되는 일을 가정할 때 쓰는 가정법 과거 문장으로 쓰는 것이 적절하다. 가정법 과거는 「If + 주어 + 동사의 과거형 ~, 주어 + could + 동사원형 …」의 형태로 쓴다.

23 현재 사실에 반대되는 일을 가정하는 「if + 가정법 과거」가 쓰였다.

24 조건문에서는 현재 시제가 미래 시제를 대신하며, 부정의 조건을 내걸었으므로 ②가 맞다.

25 • If I were born as the son of a king, I would be a prince. 내가 왕의 아들로 태어난다면 난 왕자가 될 텐데.
• If I knew all the answers to the test, I could

Ch 12 가정법

get a good grade. 내가 그 시험의 답을 다 알고 있다면 난 좋은 성적을 얻을 수 있을 텐데.
- If I won the lottery, I could help the poor in our neighborhood. 내가 복권에 당첨된다면 우리 동네의 가난한 사람들을 도와줄 수 있을 텐데.

- If I were a movie director, I could make movies with famous actors. 내가 영화 감독이라면 유명한 배우들과 영화를 만들 수 있을 텐데.
- If I had a driver's license, I could drive to the country to relax. 내가 운전면허를 갖고 있다면 머리를 식히러 시골로 차를 몰고 갈 수 있을 텐데.

CHAPTER **13** 비교구문
Comparisons

본문 _ p.306

PRACTICE 1

1 colder – coldest
2 younger – youngest
3 nicer – nicest
4 higher – highest
5 fresher – freshest
6 smaller – smallest
7 stranger – strangest
8 faster – fastest
9 lower – lowest
10 newer – newest
11 harder – hardest
12 closer – closest
13 longer – longest
14 slower – slowest
15 taller – tallest
16 older – oldest
17 kinder – kindest
18 warmer – warmest
19 larger – largest
20 smarter – smartest

PRACTICE 2

1 happier – happiest
2 healthier – healthiest
3 hotter – hottest
4 easier – easiest
5 heavier – heaviest

6 earlier – earliest
7 wiser – wisest
8 thinner – thinnest
9 funnier – funniest
10 prettier – prettiest
11 dirtier – dirtiest
12 luckier – luckiest
13 friendlier – friendliest
14 tastier – tastiest
15 sweeter – sweetest
16 lazier – laziest
17 noisier – noisiest
18 bigger – biggest
19 busier – busiest
20 drier – driest
21 wetter – wettest
22 uglier – ugliest
23 hungrier – hungriest
24 stricter – strictest

PRACTICE 3

1 more useful – most useful
2 more serious – most serious
3 cheaper – cheapest
4 more afraid – most afraid
5 more excited – most excited
6 harder – hardest
7 more tired – most tired

8 scarier – scariest

9 more curious – most curious

10 more popular – most popular

11 more handsome[handsomer]
    – most handsome[handsomest]

12 larger – largest

13 more slowly – most slowly

14 more famous – most famous

15 more helpful – most helpful

16 more surprised – most surprised

17 more expensive – most expensive

18 poorer – poorest

19 more boring – most boring

20 more anxious – most anxious

21 more convenient – most convenient

22 wider – widest

23 lonelier – loneliest

24 more foolish – most foolish

25 more patient – most patient

26 stronger – strongest

27 more useless – most useless

28 deeper – deepest

29 more beautiful – most beautiful

30 more creative – most creative

31 more exactly – most exactly

32 milder – mildest

33 more easily – most easily

34 more important – most important

35 more fluently – most fluently

36 greater – greatest

37 more quickly – most quickly

38 more difficult – most difficult

39 more interesting – most interesting

40 more nervous – most nervous

PRACTICE 4

1 better – best

2 later – latest

3 older – oldest

4 worse – worst

5 more – most

6 farther[further] – farthest[furthest]

7 better – best

8 fewer – fewest

9 elder – eldest

10 latter – last

11 less – least

12 worse – worst

13 further – furthest

14 more – most

PRACTICE 5

1 isn't as[so] polite as

2 isn't as[so] tall as

3 isn't as[so] cute as

4 isn't as[so] fast as

5 isn't as[so] white as

6 didn't buy as[so] many books as

7 doesn't speak English as[so] well as

8 isn't as[so] comfortable as

9 don't like basketball as[so] much as

10 isn't as[so] difficult as

> [보기] Insu studies harder than Giho.
>   (인수는 기호보다 더 열심히 공부한다.)
>   = Giho doesn't study as[so] hard as Insu.
>   (기호는 인수만큼 열심히 공부하지 않는다.)
>
> **1~10** A 비교급 than B(A가 B보다 더 ~ 하다) = B not as[so] 원급 as A(B가 A만큼 ~ 하지 않다)

PRACTICE 6

1 as old as

2 not as[so] expensive as

3 as late as

4 as many brothers as

5 not as[so] tired as

6 as long as

> **1** Tony의 나이와 Becky의 나이가 같으므로 as old as(~만큼 나이가 든)로 표현한다.
> **2** Tony의 가방이 Becky의 가방보다 싸므로 not as[so] expensive as(~만큼 비싸지 않은)로 표현한다.
> **3** Tony와 Becky가 잠자리에 든 시각이 같으므로 as late as(~만큼 늦게)로 표현한다.
> **4** Tony와 Becky 모두 남자 형제의 수가 같으므로 as many brothers as(~만큼 많은 형제들)로 표현한다.
> **5** Becky는 Tony만큼 피곤하지 않은 상태이므로 not as[so] tired as(~만큼 지치지 않은)로 표현한다.
> **6** Tony와 Becky가 숙제를 하는 데 걸린 시간이 같으므로 as long as(~만큼 오래)로 표현한다.

PRACTICE 7

1 studies as hard as she can
2 speak as clearly as possible
3 got up as early as he could
4 as high as she could
5 call me as soon as possible
6 helped us as much as possible
7 counted the number as exactly as I could
8 goes swimming as often as he can
9 make the questions as easy as possible
10 look as young as possible

PRACTICE 8

2 as loud as possible
3 as much as you can
4 as quickly as possible
5 as hard as we can
6 as fast as possible
7 as kindly as she could
8 as long as possible
9 as little as she can
10 as closely as possible
11 as many things as you can
12 as quietly as he could
13 as early as possible
14 as deep as possible

PRACTICE 9

1 more		**2** more beautiful	
3 shorter		**4** more nervous	
5 later		**6** earlier	

> **1** much(많은)의 비교급은 more이다. did는 앞에 쓰인 made를 대신하여 쓰인 대동사이다.
> **2** beautiful(아름다운)의 비교급은 more beautiful이다. 앞에 쓰인 This flower와 종류는 같지만 다른 대상을 가리키므로 부정대명사 one이 쓰였다.
> **3** short(키가 작은)의 비교급은 shorter이다.
> **4** nervous(불안한)의 비교급은 more nervous이다.
> **5** late(늦게)의 비교급은 later이다.
> **6** early(일찍)의 비교급은 earlier이다. did는 앞에 쓰인 came을 대신하여 쓰인 대동사이다.

PRACTICE 10

2 mine		**3** I am	**4** us
5 her		**6** yours	

> **1** 비교급 than 다음의 목적격 대명사(him)는 '주어+동사' 형태로 바꿔 쓸 수 있다. 앞에 쓰인 동사(studied)를 대신하여 대동사 did를 썼다. 앞의 동사가 과거 시제이므로 대동사(do)의 시제도 과거형(did)으로 썼음에 유의한다.
> **2** 비교 대상이 같은 종류이면 소유대명사로 바꿔 쓸 수 있다. (my cake → mine)
> **3** 비교급 than 다음의 목적격 대명사(me)는 '주어+동사' 형태로 바꿔 쓸 수 있다. 앞에 is(be동사의 3인칭 현재 단수형)가 쓰였으므로 than 뒤에 be 동사의 현재형 형태(am)를 써야 한다.
> **4** than 다음의 '주어+동사'는 목적격 대명사로 바꿔 쓸 수 있다. (we were → us)
> **5** than 다음의 '주어+동사'는 목적격 대명사로 바꿔 쓸 수 있다. (she can → her)
> **6** 비교의 대상이 같은 종류이면 소유대명사로 바꿔 쓸 수 있다. (your dog → yours)

PRACTICE 11

2 taller than		**3** better than	
4 more diligent than		**5** heavier than	
6 more excited, than		**7** more popular than	
8 faster than		**9** harder than	
10 more active than			

> **1** Tony가 Becky보다 나이가 많으므로 older than(~보다 나이가 많은)으로 표현한다.
> **2** Becky가 Tony보다 키가 크므로 taller than(~보다 키가 큰)으로 표현한다.
> **3** Becky가 Tony보다 기타를 더 잘 치므로 better than(~보다 더 잘)으로 표현한다.
> **4** Tony가 Becky보다 부지런하므로 more diligent than(~보다 더 부지런한)으로 표현한다.
> **5** Becky가 Tony보다 체중이 더 나가므로 heavier than(~보다 더 무거운)으로 표현한다.
> **6** Tony가 Becky보다 방학에 대한 기대감이 더 크므로 more excited than(~보다 더 들뜬)으로 표현한다.
> **7** Becky가 Tony보다 인기가 더 많으므로 more popular than(~보다 더 인기가 많은)으로 표현한다.
> **8** Tony가 Becky보다 더 빨리 달리므로 faster than(~보다 더 빠른)으로 표현한다.
> **9** Tony가 Becky보다 공부를 더 열심히 하므로 harder than(~보다 더 열심인)으로 표현한다.
> **10** Becky가 Tony보다 더 활동적이므로 more active than(~보다 더 활동적인)으로 표현한다.

PRACTICE 12

1 ○	**2** ×	**3** ×	**4** ○	**5** ○
6 ×	**7** ○	**8** ×	**9** ○	**10** ×

> **2, 6, 8** very는 '매우'의 뜻으로 원급을 강조한다. 따라서 비교급 앞에서 '훨씬'의 뜻으로 비교급을 강조하는 much, still, even, far, a lot 중 하나로 바꿔야 한다.
> **3, 10** far나 a lot은 비교급 앞에서 '훨씬'의 뜻으로 비교급을 강조하므로 원급을 강조하는 very로 바꿔야 한다.

PRACTICE 13

1 (s)till **2** (a) lot **3** (e)ven
4 (f)ar **5** (m)uch **6** (e)ven
7 (f)ar **8** (m)uch **9** (s)till
10 (a) lot

PRACTICE 14

1 isn't as[so] exciting as hiking
2 isn't as[so] expensive as that one
3 didn't meet Insu as[so] often as you did
4 isn't as[so] important as friendship
5 isn't as[so] interesting as mine
6 doesn't speak Japanese as[so] fluently as Seho
7 wasn't as[so] boring as the book itself
8 isn't as[so] dangerous as swimming in the ocean

[보기] This bed is less comfortable than that bed. (이 침대는 저 침대보다 덜 편안하다.)
= This bed isn't as[so] comfortable as that bed. (이 침대는 저 침대만큼 편안하지 않다.)

1~8 A less 원급 than B(A는 B보다 덜 ~ 하다) = A not as[so] 원급 as B(A는 B만큼 ~ 하지 않다)

PRACTICE 15

1 The more you give, the happier you feel.
2 The faster I walked, the closer the building became.
3 The more you want, the more disappointed you will be.
4 The more you get to know him, the more you will like him.
5 The longer I listened to the music, the more cheerful I became.
6 The farther he went, the smaller he looked.
7 The more you practice, the better you will play.
8 The darker it grew, the more scared we felt.
9 The longer you stay, the harder it will be to leave.
10 The colder it gets, the more hot chocolate people drink.

PRACTICE 16

1 There is nothing I do better than
2 There is nothing more difficult than
3 There is nothing he is interested in more than [There is nothing he is more interested in than]
4 There is nothing more delicious than
5 There is nothing more exciting than
6 There is nothing I worry about more than
7 There is nothing John speaks better than
8 There is nothing I like better than

PRACTICE 17

1 colder and colder
2 prettier and prettier
3 taller and taller
4 older and older
5 better and better
6 more and more tired
7 more and more popular
8 higher and higher
9 faster and faster
10 more and more expensive

2 pretty의 비교급은 prettier이다.
5 get well: (병세가) 좋아지다 / 형용사 well(건강한, 몸이 좋은)의 비교급은 better이다.
6 tired(지친, 피곤한)의 비교급은 more tired이다.
7 popular(인기 있는)의 비교급은 more popular이다.
10 expensive(비싼)의 비교급은 more expensive이다.

PRACTICE 18

1 the cheapest **2** the youngest
3 the most foolish **4** the closest
5 the strangest **6** the best
7 the most serious **8** the newest
9 the worst **10** the most convenient

최상급 표현은 범위를 한정하거나, 지금까지 해 본 경험을 나타내는 표현과 같이 쓰는 경우가 많다.

3 foolish(어리석은)의 최상급은 the most foolish이다.
6 good(잘 하는)의 최상급은 the best이다.
7 serious(심각한)의 최상급은 the most serious이다.
9 bad(불쾌한)의 최상급은 the worst이다.
10 convenient(편리한)의 최상급은 the most convenient이다.

Ch **13**
비교구문

PRACTICE 19

1	① hotter than	② the hottest
2	① taller than	② the tallest
3	① heavier than	② the heaviest
4	① higher, than	② the highest
5	① earlier than	② (the) earliest

> **1** ① 7월이 6월보다 온도가 높으므로 hotter than(~보다 더 더운)이 알맞다.
> ② 8월의 온도가 가장 높으므로 the hottest(가장 더운)가 알맞다.
> **2** ① 코끼리가 사자보다 키가 크므로 taller than(~보다 더 키가 큰)이 알맞다.
> ② 기린이 가장 키가 크므로 the tallest(가장 키가 큰)가 알맞다.
> **3** ① 지수가 미나보다 무거우므로 heavier than(~보다 더 무거운)이 알맞다.
> ② 재민이가 가장 무거우므로 the heaviest(가장 무거운)가 알맞다.
> **4** ① 진호가 미영이보다 더 높은 점수를 받았으므로 higher score than(~보다 더 점수가 높은)이 알맞다.
> ② 소정이가 가장 점수가 높으므로 the highest(가장 높은)가 알맞다.
> **5** ① Andrew가 Jean보다 더 일찍 일어나므로 earlier than(~보다 더 일찍)이 알맞다.
> ② Bill이 가장 일찍 일어나므로 (the) earliest(가장 일찍)가 알맞다.

PRACTICE 20

1 one of the longest rivers

2 one of the most famous men

3 one of the most diligent students

4 one of the highest mountains

5 one of the biggest countries

6 one of the happiest boys

7 one of the most boring movies

8 one of the kindest teachers

9 one of the most beautiful girls

10 one of the most popular restaurants

> 「one of+the+최상급」 뒤에는 반드시 복수 명사가 와서 '가장 ~한 것 중의 하나'라는 뜻을 나타낸다.
>
> **1** one of the longest rivers: 가장 긴 강 중의 하나
> **2** one of the most famous men: 가장 유명한 남자들 중의 하나
> **3** one of the most diligent students: 가장 부지런한 학생들 중의 하나
> **4** one of the highest mountains: 가장 높은 산들 중의 하나
> **5** one of the biggest countries: 가장 큰 국가들 중의 하나
> **6** one of the happiest boys: 가장 행복한 소년들 중의 하나
> **7** one of the most boring movies: 가장 지루한 영화들 중의 하나
> **8** one of the kindest teachers: 가장 친절한 교사들 중의 하나
> **9** one of the most beautiful girls: 가장 아름다운 소녀들 중의 하나
> **10** one of the most popular restaurants: 가장 인기 있는 식당들 중의 하나

PRACTICE 21

1 No (other) bag, as[so] expensive as
No (other) bag, more expensive than
more expensive than any other bag
more expensive than all the other bags

2 No (other) girl, as[so] tall as
No (other) girl, taller than
taller than any other girl
taller than all the other girls

3 No (other) singer, as[so] popular as
No (other) singer, more popular than
more popular than any other singer
more popular than all the other singers

4 No (other) question, as[so] difficult as
No (other) question, more difficult than
more difficult than any other question
more difficult than all the other questions

5 No (other) dog, as[so] cute as
No (other) dog, cuter than
cuter than any other dog
cuter than all the other dogs

6 No (other) sea, as[so] salty as
No (other) sea, saltier than
saltier than any other sea
saltier than all the other seas

📝 중간·기말고사 대비문제 **정답**   본문 _ p.327

1 ④   **2** ③   **3** ④   **4** ⑤   **5** The harder he tries, the better he can dance.   **6** The more time we spend together, the closer we become.
7 ③   **8** The more, the richer   **9** ②
10 Her iguana is not as[so] fast as mine.   **11** ④
12 ③   **13** ④   **14** as hard as he could   **15** ②,③
16 ②,③   **17** possible   **18** ②   **19** ③   **20** ②
21 farther[further]   **22** ②   **23** ②   **24** ②   **25** ④
26 not as[so] bad as others'   **27** the most handsome singer[the handsomest singer]
28 ④   **29** ②   **30** city → cities   **31** ①   **32** ⑤
33 (1) as old as (2) shorter than (3) faster than
34 ③   **35** ④   **36** ③   **37** ②

38 looks taller than before **39** ① **40** more beautiful than I expected **41** ④ **42** ⑤ **43** (1) is not as[so] eco-friendly as (2) as exciting as they could **44** ① **45** ⑤ **46** It is one of the simplest ways to succeed in your life. **47** The cake is as big as my sister's face. **48** (A) paler (B) more and more beautiful **49** (1) far/still/even/much/a lot cheaper than Galas (2) far/still/even/much/a lot lighter than Optimum 6 **50** ②,④

중간·기말고사 대비문제 **해설**

1 「비교급+than」 '~보다 …한', 「the+최상급」 '가장 ~한', 「as+원급+as」 '~만큼 …한'

2 비교급의 강조는 비교급 앞에 much, still, far, even, a lot을 쓰고, very는 원급 앞에서 원급의 의미를 강조한다.

3 This room is not so dark as that room.
이 방은 저 방만큼 어둡지 않다.
= That room is darker than this room.
　저 방은 이 방보다 더 어둡다.

4 ⑤ 비교급의 수식 '훨씬'
①②④ 수량형용사 '많은'　③ 부사 '많이'

5 「the+비교급 ~, the+비교급 …」을 활용하여 영작한다. '더 열심히'는 The harder, '더 잘'은 the better로 나타낸다.

6 「the+비교급 ~, the+비교급 …」을 활용하여 영작한다. '더 많은 시간'은 The more time, '더 가까운'은 the closer로 쓴다.

7 ③ 비교의 대상이 그의 손과 그의 형의 손이므로 than 뒤에는 his brother's hands를 써야 한다. 반복을 피하기 위해 hands는 생략 가능하다.
(his brother → his brother's (hands))

8 「the+비교급, the+비교급」 '~하면 할수록 더 …한'

9 ① ⓐ the는 정관사로, 명사의 앞에 쓰인다. 주어진 문장에는 주격 보어로 쓰인 형용사 large만 있으므로 이를 수식할 수 있는 very를 써야 한다.
(the → very)
③ ⓒ very는 형용사나 부사의 원급을 수식한다. 비교급을 수식하기 위해서는 much, still, far, even, a lot을 써야 한다.
(very → much/ still/far/even/a lot)

④ ⓓ 원급 비교는 「as+원급+as」로 쓴다.
(bigger as → big as)
⑤ ⓔ -e로 끝나는 형용사의 최상급은 -st를 붙여서 만든다. 최상급의 앞에는 정관사 the를 써야 한다. (much cutest → the cutest)

10 「not+as[so]+원급+as」 '~만큼 …하지 않은'

11 ④ 사자는 기린보다 가볍다.
(as heavy as → lighter than)

12 '(몸 상태가) 어제보다 훨씬 낫다'는 표현이 들어가야 하므로 well(건강한)의 비교급인 better를 사용하고, 비교급 앞에 '훨씬'을 나타내는 much를 써서 비교급을 강조한다. than 다음에 비교 대상(yesterday)을 쓴다.

13 「not as+원급+as」 '~만큼 …하지 않은'

14 민수는 가능한 한 세게 공을 쳤다.

15 ② 「배수사+as+원급+as」 '~배 만큼 …한' 표현이 쓰였으며 「so+원급+as~」표현은 부정문에서 쓴다. (so → as)
③ pretty의 최상급은 the prettiest로 쓴다.
(the most pretty → the prettiest)

16 ② 원급 비교는 「as+원급+as」로 쓴다.
(better → well)
③ fast는 형용사와 부사의 형태가 같다. 또한 원급 비교이므로 원급으로 써야 한다. (fastly → fast)

17 「as+원급+as possible」 '가능한 한 …하게'

18 • 「the+비교급, the+비교급」
　'~하면 할수록 더 …한'
• little - less - least

19 ⓐ 원급을 이용한 비교는 「as+원급+as」의 어순으로 나타낸다. (faster → fast)
ⓒ '가장 ~한 것 중의 하나'라는 의미는 「one of+the+최상급+복수 명사」의 어순으로 나타낸다. (animal → animals)
ⓔ '가장 ~한'의 뜻으로 쓸 때는 「the+최상급」으로 나타낸다. (a very fastest → the fastest)
ⓑ 비교급을 이용한 비교는 「비교급+than」의 어순으로 나타낸다.
ⓓ 「the+비교급, the+비교급」은 '~하면 할수록 더 …하다'라는 뜻으로 쓰인다.

20 ② Ronnie가 제일 몸무게가 많이 나가므로 형용사를 heavier로 고치거나, 주어를 제일 몸무게가 가벼운 Hannah로 써야 한다.
(Ronnie → Hannah 또는 lighter → heavier)

21 '다른 누구보다 더 멀리 뛰었다'는 뜻이 되어야 하므로
「비교급＋than」을 사용하여 써준다.
far – farther[further] – farthest[furthest]
'<거리> 먼'

22 ⓐ 원급을 이용한 비교는 「as＋원급＋as」의 어순으로
나타낸다. (smartest → smart)
ⓑ 「as＋원급＋as＋주어＋can[could]」는 '~가 할 수
있는 한 …하게'라는 뜻이다.
ⓒ 현재의 사실에 반대되는 가정을 나타내는 가정법
과거는 「If＋주어＋동사의 과거형, 주어＋would＋
동사원형」의 어순으로 나타낸다. 「형용사＋ly」 형
태의 부사 fluently(유창하게)의 비교급은 more
fluently이다.
ⓓ '~하면 할수록 더 …하다'라는 의미는 「the＋비교
급, the＋비교급」으로 나타낸다.
(The well → The better)
ⓔ '가장 ~한'라는 의미의 「the＋최상급」의 뒤에는 주
로 in, of가 이끄는 전치사구나 절이 나온다. in 뒤
에는 장소나 집단을 나타내는 단수 명사가 온다.
ⓕ 「There is nothing ~ 비교급＋than …」은 '…보
다 더 ~한 것은 없다'의 뜻으로 최상급의 의미를 나
타낸다. difficult는 2음절 이상의 형용사이므로
more을 사용해 비교급을 쓴다.
(difficulter → more difficult)
ⓖ 「No (other) ~ 비교급＋than」을 사용하여 최상급
의 의미를 나타낼 수 있다. (large → larger)
ⓗ forget은 목적어로 to부정사와 동명사 중 어느 것
을 쓰냐에 따라 뜻이 달라진다. '조부모님께 전화드
리는 것을 잊지 않았다.'는 의미이므로 to부정사를
쓴다.

23 Jiyeon is not as funny as Inho.
지연이는 인호만큼 재미있지 않다.
= Inho is funnier than Jiyeon.
인호가 지연이보다 더 재미있다.

24 ② B는 D보다 작다. (as big as → smaller than)

25 prefer = like ~ better '~을 더 좋아하다'

26 비교급이 쓰인 문장은 '~만큼 …하지 않은'이라는 뜻
의 「not as[so]＋원급＋as」으로 바꾸어 쓸 수 있다.
이때 마지막 빈칸은 명사(problems)의 반복 사용을
피하기 위해서 소유격 뒤의 명사를 생략하여 others'
로 쓴다.

27 'handsome - more handsome - most
handsome' / 'handsome – handsomer

– handsomest'

28 • 「비교급＋than」 '~보다 더 …한'
• 「the＋최상급」 '가장 ~한'

29 「비교급＋than any other＋단수 명사」는 최상급의
의미를 나타낸다.

30 「one of＋the＋최상급＋복수 명사」
'가장 ~한 것 중의 하나'

31 「not as[so]＋형용사/부사 원급＋as」
＝「less＋원급＋than」

32 ⑤ 「There is nothing ~ 비교급＋than …」은 '…보
다 더 ~한 것은 없다'의 뜻으로 최상급의 의미를 나
타낸다.
① 「as＋원급＋as＋주어＋can[could]」은 '~가
할 수 있는 한 …하게'의 뜻으로 「as＋원급＋as
possible」로 바꾸어 쓸 수 있다.
(possibly → possible)
② '~하면 할수록 더 …하다'라는 의미는 「the＋비교
급, the＋비교급」으로 나타낸다. (The least →
The less, the happiest → the happier)
③ '점점 더 ~한'이라는 의미는 「비교급＋and＋비교
급」으로 나타낸다.
(darkest and darkest → darker and darker)
④ 비교급을 강조할 때는 much, still, even, far, a
lot을 사용한다. very는 '매우'의 뜻으로 원급을 강
조한다.

33 (1) Calvin은 Brad와 나이가 같다.
(2) Jason은 Calvin보다 키가 작다.
(3) Brad는 Jason보다 빠르다.

34 (다) 「비교급＋than」 '~보다 더 …한'의 의미로, 형용
사 strong의 비교급은 stronger이다.
(가) 동사 contain을 강조하기 위한 조동사 do가 쓰
인 것으로, 주어가 셀 수 없는 명사 Green tea로
단수 취급하므로 does로 써야 한다.
(do → does)
(나) tea는 셀 수 없는 명사이므로 '많은'을 표현할 때
much를 써야 한다. (many tea → much tea)
(라) '가장 ~한 것중의 하나'를 표현할 때 「one
of＋the＋최상급＋복수명사」의 형태로 써야 하므
로 복수명사 producers를 쓰는 것이 적절하다.
(producer → producers)
(마) 주어 Many people이 복수이므로 동사는 drink
로 쓰는 것이 적절하다. (drinks → drink)
차는 세계에서 가장 인기 있는 음료 중 하나이다. 녹차

는 정말로 카페인을 함유한다. 자기 전에 너무 많은 차를 마시는 것은 잠드는 것을 어렵게 할 수 있다. 홍차는 허브차보다 더 진하다. 인도는 세계에서 가장 큰 차 생산국 중 하나이다. 많은 사람들이 매일 아침 차를 마신다.

35 • 「one of+the+최상급+복수명사」 '가장 ~한 … 중의 하나'
「in+단수 명사」 비교문에서 in은 비교 대상인 '장소, 집단' 앞에 쓰인다.
• 「the+최상급+명사+of+복수 명사」 '~중에서 가장 …한'

36 「one of+the+최상급+복수 명사」
'가장 ~한 것 중의 하나'
(highest → the highest)

37 must '~임에 틀림없다'
「비교급+than」 '~보다 더 …한'

38 look '~해 보이다'
「비교급+than」 '~보다 더 …한'

39 very는 비교급 앞에 올 수 없다.

40 록키 산맥은 내가 예상했던 것보다 더 아름답다.

41 *A*: 저는 이 셔츠가 좋은데 제게 너무 작군요. 이걸로 더 큰 사이즈 있나요?
B: 매우 죄송합니다만, 그것이 우리 가게에 있는 가장 큰 사이즈입니다.

42 ⑤ Sue는 반에서 가장 키가 큰 소녀들 중 한 명이다.
①②③④ Sue는 반에서 가장 키가 크다.

43 (1) 버스를 타는 것이 차를 운전하는 것보다 더 친환경적이라는 의미이므로 「not as[so]+원급+as」 '~만큼 …하지 않은'을 쓰는 것이 적절하다.
(2) '~가 할 수 있는 한 …하게'의 의미를 가진 「as+원급+as possible」은 「as+원급+as+주어+can[could]」와 바꾸어 쓸 수 있다. 과거시제 동사(tried)가 쓰였으므로 과거형 조동사(could)를 쓰는 것이 적절하다.

44 ① so는 비교급을 수식할 수 없다.

45 (C) 주격 관계대명사절의 동사는 선행사에 일치시킨다. 선행사가 a valuable product로 단수이므로, 동사 또한 3인칭 단수형인 has로 쓴다.
(E) '~만큼 …하지 않은'이라는 뜻은 「not as[so]+원급+as」의 어순으로 나타낼 수 있다.
(A) '가장 ~한 것 중의 하나'라는 의미는 「one of+the+최상급+복수 명사」의 어순으로 나타낸다. (creature → creatures)
(B) 주어는 some products로, 복수 명사이다. 따라서 동사도 복수형으로 쓴다. (is → are)
(D) 단수 명사 앞에는, '또 하나의, 또 다른'이라는 뜻으로 another가 쓰인다. other은 복수 명사의 앞에 쓰인다. (other → another)

46 '가장 ~한 것 중의 하나'라는 의미는 「one of+the+최상급+복수 명사」의 어순으로 나타낸다. simple의 최상급은 -st를 붙여 만들어준다.
(most simplest → simplest, way → ways)

47 「as+원급+as」 '~만큼 …한'

48 (A) 의미상 '더 상백한'이란 뜻이 어울린다.
(B) '점점 더 ~한'이라는 의미는 「비교급+and+비교급」으로 나타내고, beautiful의 비교급은 more beautiful이다.

49 (1) Optimum 6는 Galas보다 훨씬 더 싸다.
(2) Galas는 Optimum 6보다 훨씬 더 가볍다.

50 ① 몸무게가 같으므로 '~만큼 …한'의 뜻을 나타내는 원급비교를 사용한다. 원급비교는 「as+원급+as」로 쓴다. (heavier → heavy)
③ 먹을수록 더 행복하다는 뜻이므로 '~하면 할수록 더 …하다'는 뜻의 「the+비교급, the+비교급」을 사용한다.
(More → The more, happier → the happier)
⑤ 나는 형과 부모님만큼 부지런하지 않다는 뜻이므로, '~만큼 …하지 않은'이라는 뜻의 「not so+원급+as」를 사용한다. (than → as)

Ch **13** 비교구문

PRACTICE 1

1 who	**2** whose	**3** who(m)	
4 whose	**5** who	**6** who(m)	
7 who	**8** who(m)	**9** whose	
10 who(m)			

1, 5, 7 선행사가 사람이고, 관계대명사절 내에서 관계대명사가 주어 역할을 하기 때문에 주격 관계대명사 who가 적절하다.
2, 4, 9 선행사가 사람이고, 관계대명사절 내에서 관계대명사가 명사를 꾸며주는 소유격 역할을 하기 때문에 소유격 관계대명사 whose가 적절하다.
3, 6, 8, 10 선행사가 사람이고, 관계대명사절 내에서 관계대명사가 목적어 역할을 하기 때문에 목적격 관계대명사 whom 또는 who가 적절하다.

PRACTICE 2

1 is	**2** was	**3** are	**4** love	**5** is
6 are	**7** sings	**8** are	**9** is	**10** are

1, 2, 4, 7, 10 주격, 목적격 관계대명사절의 동사는 선행사의 수에 일치시킨다.
3, 5, 6, 8, 9 소유격 관계대명사절의 동사는 관계대명사 바로 뒤 수식을 받는 명사의 수에 일치시킨다.

PRACTICE 3

2 There is a tree which my family planted.

3 I have a dog whose name is Happy.

4 The dolls which are on the sofa are my sister's.

5 This is the room whose walls are blue.

6 Heejun is reading the book which you gave him.

7 The flowers which he brought are beautiful.

8 He made the movie which became famous.

9 This is the computer whose keyboard is broken.

10 You should take the magazine which is on my desk.

2, 6, 7 선행사가 사물이고, 관계대명사절 내에서 관계대명사가 목적어를 대신하므로 목적격 관계대명사 which를 사용하여 연결한다.
3, 5, 9 선행사가 사물 또는 동물이고, 관계대명사가 명사를 수식하는 소유격 역할을 하므로 소유격 관계대명사 whose를 사용하여 연결한다.
4, 8, 10 선행사가 사물이고, 관계대명사절 내에서 관계대명사가 주어 역할을 하므로 주격 관계대명사 which를 사용하여 연결한다.

PRACTICE 4

1 are	**2** are	**3** have	**4** are
5 were	**6** don't	**7** takes	**8** looks
9 were	**10** is		

1, 3, 4, 7, 8 주격 관계대명사절의 동사는 선행사의 수에 일치시킨다.
2, 5, 6, 9, 10 소유격 관계대명사가 쓰였을 경우에는 whose 뒤에 오는 명사의 수에 동사를 일치시킨다.

PRACTICE 5

1 whom, that	**2** that	**3** that
4 who, that	**5** that	**6** that
7 that	**8** which, that	**9** that
10 whose		

1 선행사가 사람이고, 관계대명사가 관계대명사절 내에서 목적어 역할을 하기 때문에 목적격 관계대명사 whom과 that을 쓸 수 있다.
2, 7 선행사에 형용사의 최상급이 포함되어 있기 때문에 목적격 관계대명사로 that이 적절하다.
3 선행사에 little이 포함되어 있기 때문에 목적격 관계대명사로 that이 적절하다.
4 선행사가 사람이고, 관계대명사가 관계대명사절 내에서 주어 역할을 하기 때문에 주격 관계대명사 who와 that을 쓸 수 있다.
5 선행사에 서수(the first)가 포함되어 있기 때문에 목적격 관계대명사 that이 적절하다.
6 선행사가 「사물+and+사람」일 경우에는 주로 관계대명사 that을 쓴다.
8 선행사가 동물이고, 관계대명사가 관계대명사절 내에서 목적어 역할을 하기 때문에 목적격 관계대명사 which와 that을 쓸 수 있다.
9 선행사가 something이기 때문에 주격 관계대명사로 that이 적절하다.
10 선행사가 사람이고, 관계대명사가 명사를 수식하는 소유격 역할을 하기 때문에 소유격 관계대명사 whose를 쓴다.

PRACTICE 6

1 that	**2** who[that] is
3 who[that]	**4** that[which]
5 which[that]	**6** who[that]
7 I met at the party	**8** that[which]
9 that[which] were	**10** that[who]
11 that[who(m)]	**12** whose
13 were	**14** which[that]
15 she got from her mom	

1 선행사가 anything이기 때문에 목적격 관계대명사로 that을 써야 한다.
2 주격 관계대명사 who가 쓰였기 때문에 관계대명사절의 주어(he)는 생략해야 한다. 주격 관계대명사 who는 that으로 바꿔 쓸 수 있다.
3 선행사(A student)가 사람이기 때문에 주격 관계대명사로 who 또는 that을 써야 한다.
4, 11 선행사에 형용사의 최상급이 포함되어 있으므로 목적격 관계대명사로 that을 써야 한다.
5 선행사(the glasses)가 사물이므로 목적격 관계대명사로 which 또는 that을 써야 한다.
6 선행사가 사람(my friend)이고 관계대명사가 관계대명사절 내에서 주어 역할을 하므로 주격 관계대명사 who 또는 that을 써야 한다.
7 목적격 관계대명사 whom이 쓰였기 때문에 관계대명사절의 목적어(her)는 생략해야 한다.
8 선행사가 something이기 때문에 주격 관계대명사로 that을 써야 한다.
9 주격 관계대명사 that이 쓰였기 때문에 관계대명사절의 주어(they)는 생략해야 한다.
10 선행사에 서수(the first)가 포함되어 있으므로 주격 관계대명사로 that을 써야 한다.
12 관계대명사가 명사를 수식하는 소유격 역할을 해야 하므로 소유격 관계대명사 whose를 써야 한다.
13 관계대명사절의 주어가 whose jeans(복수명사)이기 때문에 were이 적절하다.
14 선행사(the mountain)가 사물이기 때문에 주격 관계대명사로 which 또는 that을 써야 한다.
15 목적격 관계대명사 which가 쓰였기 때문에 관계대명사절의 목적어(it)는 생략해야 한다.

PRACTICE 7

1 what **2** which **3** what **4** what
5 which **6** what **7** what **8** what
9 which **10** what **11** What **12** which

1, 3, 4, 6, 7, 8, 10, 11 선행사가 없으므로, 선행사를 자체에 포함하는 관계대명사 what을 써야 한다.
2, 12 선행사가 사물이고, 관계대명사가 관계대명사절 내에서 목적어 역할을 하기 때문에 목적격 관계대명사 which가 적절하다.
5 선행사가 동물이고, 관계대명사가 관계대명사절 내에서 목적어 역할을 하기 때문에 목적격 관계대명사 which가 적절하다.
9 선행사가 사물이고, 관계대명사가 관계대명사절 내에서 주어 역할을 하기 때문에 주격 관계대명사 which가 적절하다.

PRACTICE 8

1 (which) **2** (whom)
3 생략해도 되는 부분 없음. **4** (which are)
5 생략해도 되는 부분 없음. **6** (that)
7 생략해도 되는 부분 없음. **8** (which was)

1, 2, 6 목적격 관계대명사 which, whom, that은 생략 가능하다.
4, 8 주격 관계대명사 뒤에 be동사가 있고 그 뒤에 분사가 올 때, 「관계대명사+be동사」는 생략할 수 있다.
3, 5, 7 who, which, that이 주격 관계대명사로 사용되었기 때문에 생략할 수 없다.

PRACTICE 9

2 which[that] were **3** which[that] were
4 who[that] were **5** which[that] is
6 which[that] are **7** who[that] was
8 who[that] are **9** which[that] is
10 who[that] is

PRACTICE 10

1 Kevin has an uncle, who teaches English at a middle school.
2 She bought a blouse, which was on sale.
3 He was a great scientist, who(m) we all respected.
4 Jenny has lost her watch, which her father bought for her.
5 They climbed Mount Everest, which is the highest mountain in the world.

1 선행사가 사람이고, 관계대명사가 주어 역할을 하기 때문에 주격 관계대명사 who를 사용하여 계속적 용법으로 두 문장을 연결할 수 있다.
2, 5 선행사가 사물이고, 관계대명사가 주어 역할을 하기 때문에 주격 관계대명사 which를 사용하여 계속적 용법으로 두 문장을 연결할 수 있다.
3 선행사가 사람이고, 관계대명사가 목적어 역할을 하기 때문에 목적격 관계대명사 who(m)을 사용하여 계속적 용법으로 두 문장을 연결할 수 있다.
4 선행사가 사물이고, 관계대명사가 목적어 역할을 하기 때문에 목적격 관계대명사 which를 사용하여 계속적 용법으로 두 문장을 연결할 수 있다.

PRACTICE 11

1 when **2** why **3** where **4** when
5 how **6** where **7** how **8** why
9 where **10** how

PRACTICE 12

2 the place, where **3** why, the reason
4 the year, when **5** how
6 somewhere

중간·기말고사 대비문제 정답　본문 _ p.347

1 ①,⑤　**2** ②　**3** what you said　**4** who[that] teaches students　**5** (1) ③ (2) ② (3) ④ (4) ①
6 ⑤　**7** ⑤　**8** ⑤　**9** ③,⑤　**10** ④　**11** ④
12 ④　**13** ③　**14** ①　**15** ③　**16** ④　**17** ③
18 A firefighter is a person who puts out fires and rescues people.　**19** ①　**20** ①　**21** ①
22 ③　**23** ⑤　**24** ①　**25** ②　**26** I saw the house whose roof was covered with snow.
27 ②　**28** ③,④　**29** ④　**30** the way others live[how others live]　**31** that → who　**32** ④
33 (1) who is playing (2) which I borrowed from　**34** (1) I know a girl who[that] can speak Spanish very well. (2) The book which[that] I bought last night is easy to read. (3) Look at the house whose garden is filled with beautiful flowers.　**35** There is a boy who is painting a picture. [There is a girl who is watching TV. / There is a cat which is eating fish.]　**36** ②
37 ③　**38** ①　**39** These are the books which[that] my uncle bought for me.
40 (A) We told them what they shouldn't do in the park. (B) They listened carefully to what we said.　**41** ①

중간·기말고사 대비문제 **해설**

1　① 목적격 관계대명사
　　⑤ 목적어 역할을 하는 명사절 접속사
　　② 지시형용사 (생략 불가)
　　③ 지시대명사 (생략 불가)
　　④ 주격 관계대명사 (생략 불가)

2　회원들이 운동을 하는 것이므로 주격 관계대명사 who를 쓰고, 선행사 members가 복수이고 매일 반복되는 일을 나타내고 있으므로 동사는 현재형 train으로 쓰는 것이 적절하다. (ⓐ is ⓑ full ⓒ of ⓓ members ⓔ who ⓕ train ⓖ every)

3　선행사를 포함하는 관계대명사 what을 이용하여 understand의 목적어 역할을 하는 절을 완성한다.

4　선행사가 사람일 때 뒤에 오는 주격 관계대명사는 who[that]이다. 선행사는 3인칭 단수이고, 시제가 현재형이므로 동사도 3인칭 단수 현재형인 teaches로

쓴다.

5　(1) 선행사가 사람이므로 주격 관계대명사 who로 시작하는 문장이 뒤따르며, 내용상 ③이 알맞다.
　　(2) 선행사가 사물(케이크)이므로 목적격 관계대명사 which로 시작하는 절이 뒤따르며, 내용상 ②가 알맞다.
　　(3) 관계대명사의 계속적 용법이 쓰여 앞 내용에 대한 부가적인 설명을 덧붙이고 있으며, 내용상 ④가 알맞다.
　　(4) 선행사가 사람이므로 주격 관계대명사 who로 시작하는 절이 뒤따르며, 내용상 ①이 알맞다.

6　⑤ 주격 관계대명사 ①②③④ 목적격 관계대명사

7　⑤ 목적격 관계대명사 that은 생략할 수 있다.
　　①② 「전치사+관계대명사」의 형태일 때 관계대명사 which는 단독으로 생략할 수 없다.
　　③④ 주격 관계대명사 that은 단독으로 생략될 수 없고, 뒤따라오는 「be동사+분사/형용사구」가 있을 때 be동사와 함께 생략할 수 있다.
　　① 방법 – 명. 어떤 것이 되거나 이루어지는 방식
　　② 목적 – 명. 어떤 것이 되거나 만들어지는 이유
　　③ 혁신 – 명. 중대한 변화나 발전을 가져오는 새로운 생각이나 방법
　　④ 우정 – 명. 상호 간의 애정과 신뢰를 바탕으로 개인들 사이에서 형성되는 유대감
　　⑤ 목표 – 명. 누군가가 달성하려고 목표하는 것

8　선행사(story books)가 사물이고 관계사절에서 주어 역할을 하므로 which가 온다.

9　③ 관계대명사 that은 계속적 용법으로 쓸 수 없다. 따라서 선행사가 사람일 때 쓰이는 주격 관계대명사 who로 바꾸어야 한다. (that → who)
　　⑤ 관계대명사절에서 명사(cover)를 앞에서 수식하는 역할을 해야 하므로 소유격 관계대명사 whose가 알맞다. (which → whose)

10　ⓐ 선행사가 장소이고, 뒤따라오는 절이 완전하므로 관계부사 where을 쓴다. (which → where)
　　ⓓ 선행사에 서수가 포함되어 있고 사람이므로 주격 관계대명사 that 또는 who를 쓸 수 있다. (whom → that[who])
　　ⓔ 관계대명사 that은 계속적 용법으로 쓸 수 없다. (that → which)

11　계속적 용법의 관계대명사는 「접속사+대명사」로 바꿔 쓸 수 있다.

12　① 관계대명사 that절이 선행사 student를 수식하고

있으므로, hang out with her에서 대명사 her이 생략된 형태가 되어야 한다.
hang out with: '~와 어울리다, 시간을 보내다'
(hang out → hang out with)

② 관계대명사 that절이 선행사 the movie를 수식하고 있으므로 단수동사 has가 적절하다.
(have → has)

③ 관계대명사 계속적 용법으로 선행사가 her parents이므로 복수동사 put을 써야 한다.
(puts → put)

⑤ 주격 관계대명사 which가 이끄는 절이 선행사 the release date를 수식하고 있는데 뒤의 절이 완전하므로 주어 it을 삭제해야 한다.
(which it was → which was)

13 ⓐ 「the+형용사」는 '~한 사람들'의 뜻으로, 복수 명사처럼 쓰인다. 따라서 관계대명사절의 동사 또한 복수로 써야 한다. (lives → live)

ⓔ 주격 관계대명사 뒤에 be동사가 있고 그 뒤에 분사가 올 때, 「관계대명사+be동사」는 생략할 수 있다. 이때 「관계대명사+be동사」는 반드시 함께 생략해야 한다. (who → who are/생략)

14 • 선행사가 사람(a man)이므로 who[that]가 온다.
• 선행사가 사물(an alarm clock)이므로 which[that]가 온다.

15 ⓐⓔ 목적격 관계대명사 who(m), that은 생략 가능하다.

ⓒ 목적어 역할을 하는 명사절 접속사 that은 생략이 가능하다.

ⓑⓓ 주격 관계대명사는 생략이 불가능하다. 주격 관계대명사 뒤에 be동사가 있고 그 뒤에 분사가 올 때, 「관계대명사+be동사」는 생략할 수 있다.

16 ④ 관계대명사 ①②③ 의문사 ⑤ 의문형용사

17 선행사(the tomatoes)가 사물이므로 목적격 관계대명사 which나 that을 사용하여 두 문장을 이어준다. 목적격 관계대명사는 생략할 수 있다.

그녀는 그녀가 기른 토마토로 스파게티 소스를 만들었다.

18 who는 주격 관계대명사로 쓰였다.

19 ① 관계대명사　　②③④⑤ 접속사

20 ① 관계대명사절 안에서 주어의 역할을 하며, 선행사가 사람이므로 주격 관계대명사 who를 적절하게 사용했다.

② 관계대명사절 안에서 주어의 역할을 하며, 선행사가 사람이므로 주격 관계대명사 who나 that을 사용한다. (whose → who/that)

③ 관계대명사절 안에서 목적어의 역할을 하며, 선행사가 사물이므로 목적격 관계대명사 which나 that을 사용한다. (whose → which/that)

④ 관계대명사절 안에서 관계대명사 바로 뒤에 나오는 명사를 꾸며주어야 하므로, 소유격 관계대명사 whose를 사용한다. (who → whose)

⑤ 관계대명사절 안에서 주어의 역할을 하며, 선행사가 사람이므로 주격 관계대명사 who나 that을 사용한다. (whom → who/that)

21 선행사(the reason)가 이유를 나타내므로 관계부사 why가 온다.

22 ⓐⓑⓔ 주격 관계대명사　　ⓒⓓⓕ 의문대명사

23 주어진 문장의 that은 관계대명사절 안에서 주어의 역할을 하고 있으므로 주격 관계대명사이다.
⑤ 관계대명사절 안에서 주어의 역할을 하는 주격 관계대명사이다.
① 멀리 떨어진 사람을 나타내는 지시형용사로서 뒤에 나오는 명사 girl을 수식하고 있다. (that girl: 저 소녀)
② 명사절을 이끄는 접속사로 쓰였다.
③ 멀리 떨어진 사람이나 사물을 가리키는 지시대명사로 쓰였다. (that: 저 사람)
④ 「so+형용사+that~」은 '너무 …해서 ~하다'라는 뜻으로, 이때의 that은 접속사이다.

24 ① 선행사가 사물일 경우 주격 관계대명사는 that을 쓸 수 있고, 관계사절의 동사는 선행사의 수에 맞추어 복수형을 쓴다.
②③④⑤ 선행사가 단수 명사이므로 주격 관계대명사절의 동사도 단수로 일치시켜야 한다.

25 (A) 선행사가 사물인 주격 관계대명사 that[which]
(B) 선행사가 사람인 주격 관계대명사 who[that]
(C) 선행사가 사물인 목적격 관계대명사 which[that]

26 선행사가 사물인 소유격 관계대명사 whose를 Its의 자리에 써서 두 문장을 이어준다.

27 ② '무엇'의 의미를 지닌 의문사
①③④⑤ 선행사를 포함하고 있는 관계대명사

28 ③ 주격 관계대명사 뒤에 be동사가 있고 그 뒤에 분사가 올 때 「관계대명사+be동사」는 생략 가능하다.
④ 전치사(in)의 목적어가 없는 구조로 that이 목적격 관계대명사로 쓰였으므로 생략 가능하다.

29 ③ The man을 수식하는 관계대명사절 who(m) I met에서 목적격 관계대명사인 who(m)은 생략 가

Ch
14
관계사

능하다.
① 주어 The dog이 단수 명사이므로, 동사 또한 단수 동사로 일치시켜야 한다. (are → is)
② 선행사 the book이 사물이므로, 관계대명사 which나 that을 써야 한다. who는 선행사가 사람일 때 쓸 수 있다. (who → which[that])
④ 선행사를 주어로 하는 관계대명사절이므로, 주격 관계대명사인 who를 쓴다. whom은 목적격 관계대명사이다. (whom → who)
⑤ 간접의문문의 어순은 「의문사＋주어＋동사」로 나타낸다. (who are they → who they are)

30 선행사 the way와 관계부사 how는 함께 쓸 수 없으므로 관계부사와 선행사 둘 중 하나는 생략해야 한다.

31 관계대명사의 계속적 용법에서는 that을 쓸 수 없다.

32 (A) 선행사가 동물이므로 주격 관계대명사 which 혹은 that을 쓴다.
(B) 선행사가 무생물(The Nile: 나일강)이므로 주격 관계대명사 which를 쓴다. 이때, 계속적 용법으로 쓰였으므로 that은 쓸 수 없다.
(C) 선행사가 사람이므로 주격 관계대명사 who 혹은 that을 쓴다.
(D) 선행사가 따로 없는 관계대명사절이므로, 선행사를 자체에 포함하는 관계대명사 What을 쓴다.

33 (1) 선행사가 사람인 The boy이므로 관계대명사는 who이며, 의미상 시제는 현재진행으로 쓴다.
(2) 선행사가 사물인 the comic book이므로 관계대명사는 which이며, 어제의 일이므로 과거시제를 쓴다.

34 (1) 선행사(a girl)가 사람이므로 주격 관계대명사 who[that]를 사용해 연결한다.
나는 스페인어를 매우 잘 말할 수 있는 한 소녀를 안다.
(2) 선행사(The book)가 사물이므로 목적격 관계대명사 which[that]를 사용해 연결한다.
내가 지난밤에 산 책은 읽기 쉽다.
(3) 선행사(the house)가 사물이고, 바로 뒤에 나오는 명사를 수식해야 하므로 소유격 관계대명사 whose를 사용해 연결한다.
정원이 아름다운 꽃으로 가득 찬 그 집을 봐.

35 선행사가 사람일 때는 주격 관계대명사 who를, 동물이거나 사물이면 which를 쓰며 현재진행형은 「be동사의 현재형＋-ing」로 나타낸다.

36 ② I saw on TV는 목적어가 없는 불완전한 절이므로, 관계부사가 아닌 목적격 관계대명사가 쓰여야 한

다. 또한 선행사가 사물(the restaurant)이므로, 관계대명사 which나 that을 쓴다.
(where → which[that])

37 ③ 주격 관계대명사는 단독으로 생략할 수 없다.

38 • 사물을 선행사로 하는 목적격 관계대명사 which나 that이 들어간다.
• 선행사에 형용사의 최상급이 포함되어 있으므로 주격 관계대명사 that이 들어간다.
• 목적어 역할을 하는 명사절을 이끄는 접속사 that ('~라는 것을')이 들어간다.

39 선행사 the books가 사물이므로 목적격 관계대명사 which나 that을 이용하여 두 문장을 연결한다.

40 (A) what they shouldn't do '그들이 해서는 안 되는 것'
(B) what we said '우리가 말한 것'

41 ⓐ 해당 문장에 본동사로 pursue가 사용됐으므로 동사 reduce가 오는 것은 부적절하며, 문맥상 '스트레스를 줄이기 위하여'라는 의미가 되도록 to부정사 형태의 'to reduce'를 쓰는 것이 적절하다.
ⓑ 빈칸 뒷부분(you pursue simplicity and cut down on unessential items)을 보면 문장구성 성분 중 빠진 것이 없으므로 관계부사 where이 오는 것이 적절하다.
ⓒ 동사 Live를 수식하는 부사 simply를 사용하는 것이 적절하다.
「as＋원급＋as＋주어＋can[could]」'~가 할 수 있는 한 …하게'

미니멀리스트 생활
당신은 당신 자신에게만 집중하고 싶은가? 그렇다면 미니멀리스트 생활을 하는 것을 시도해보는 것이 어떨까? 요즘 많은 사람들은 스트레스를 줄이고 그들의 정신적인 행복을 최우선으로 하기 위해 미니멀리스트 생활을 추구한다. 그렇다면 미니멀리스트 생활이 무엇인가? 그것은 당신이 간소함을 추구하며 필수적이지 않은 물건들을 줄이는 생활방식이다. 미니멀리스트 생활을 실행함으로써 시간, 돈, 그리고 에너지가 절약될 수 있다. 그러면, 당신은 어떻게 미니멀리스트 생활을 할 수 있을까? 가장 쉬운 방법은 불필요한 것들을 제거하는 것이다. 신경 쓸 것이 하나 적어지면 스트레스도 하나 적어진다. 또 다른 방법은 당신의 영화들, 책들, 그리고 구독들을 디지털화 하는 것이다. 당신이 더 적은 소유물을 가지고 있을 때, 당신은 더 정돈되고 편안하게 느낄 수 있다. 그러므로, 시도해 봐라! 할 수 있는 한 단순하게 살아가며 당신의 내면에 더 집중해라.

CHAPTER 15 접속사
Conjunctions

PRACTICE 1

1 and	**2** or	**3** but
4 or	**5** and	**6** or
7 and	**8** but	**9** and
10 or		

1, 5, 8 'Both A and B: A와 B 둘 다'를 주어로 쓸 때는 복수형의 동사를 쓴다.
2, 7 either A or B: A와 B 중 어느 하나
3, 9 neither A nor B: A도 B도 ~아닌
4, 10 'Not only A but also B' 뒤에 오는 동사는 B에 수일치 시킨다.
6 not only A but also B=B as well as A: A뿐만 아니라 B도

1 진수와 민호를 대등하게 연결하고 있으므로 and가 적절하다. (해석: 나는 어제 거리에서 진수와 민호를 만났다.)
2 학교 아니면 집으로 가는지 묻고 있으므로 or이 적절하다. (해석: 그는 어디로 가는 거니, 학교로 아니면 집으로?)
3 문맥상 not A but B 구문이 사용되었음을 알 수 있다. 따라서 but이 적절하다. (해석: 네가 실수했어. 비난받아야 할 사람은 내가 아니라 너야.)
4 둘 이상의 대상 중에서 선택하고 있으므로 or이 적절하다. (해석: Tim, John, 아니면 Ryan 중 누가 네 형이니?)
5 서울을 떠났고 대전에 도착했다는 대등한 내용을 연결하고 있으므로 and가 적절하다. (해석: 그들은 서울을 떠났고 2시간 후에 대전에 도착했다.)
6 둘 이상의 대상 중에서 어떤 것을 좋아하는지 묻고 있으므로 or이 적절하다. (해석: 피자와 스파게티 중 너는 어느 것을 더 좋아하니?)
7 우유 한 병과 케이크 한 조각을 대등하게 연결하고 있으므로 and가 적절하다. (해석: Eric은 우유 한 병과 케이크 한 조각을 샀다.)
8 나는 음악을 좋아하고, 나의 형은 그렇지 않다는 반대되는 내용을 연결하고 있으므로 but이 적절하다. doesn't 뒤에는 like music이 생략되어 있다. (해석: 나는 음악을 좋아하지만 내 형은 그렇지 않다.)
9 학생들이 교실에 들어갔고, 청소하기 시작했다는 대등한 내용을 연결하고 있으므로 and가 적절하다. (해석: 학생들은 교실로 들어갔고 청소하기 시작했다.)
10 박 여사를 만났는지, 아니면 전화로 얘기했는지 둘 중의 하나를 선택하도록 묻고 있으므로 or이 적절하다. (해석: 너는 박 여사를 만났니, 아니면 그녀에게 전화로 얘기했니?)

PRACTICE 2

1 and	**2** or	**3** and
4 or	**5** or	**6** and
7 or	**8** and	**9** or
10 and		

PRACTICE 3

1 Both, and	**2** either, or
3 neither, nor	**4** Not only, but also
5 Both, and	**6** as well as
7 either, or	**8** Both, and
9 neither, nor	**10** Not only, but also

PRACTICE 4

1 We are excited because we are going to interview a popular singer.
We are going to interview a popular singer, so we are excited.
2 Martin couldn't call you because he was very busy this week.
Martin was very busy this week, so he couldn't call you.
3 Jiyoon has a lot of friends because she is very nice.
Jiyoon is very nice, so she has a lot of friends.
4 I can't study tonight because I'm really sick.
I'm really sick, so I can't study tonight.
5 Seho got angry because Mom didn't buy him a toy.
Mom didn't buy Seho a toy, so he got angry.

PRACTICE 5

1 because	**2** because of
3 because of	**4** because
5 because	**6** because of

1~6 because 뒤에는 절이 오고, because of 뒤에는 명사 상당 어구가 와야 한다.

PRACTICE 6

1 I'll do the laundry unless it rains.
2 Let's watch a movie together unless you are busy.
3 I can help you unless it takes too long.
4 He will be in trouble unless the train arrives on time.

Ch
15
접속사

5 She can finish the work unless she goes home early.

6 They will forgive you unless you lie to them.

7 You'll miss the last bus unless you hurry.

8 I'll buy this shirt unless I change my mind.

9 We can go swimming unless the pool is closed.

10 You can just walk unless it's too far from here.

PRACTICE 7

1 만약 예상치 못한 일이 생기지 않는다면

2 무슨 피해가 있는지는

3 만약 그가 널 또다시 귀찮게 한다면

4 어떤 자리라도 남아있을지

5 네가 그 충고를 받아들일지 말지

6 파란색과 노란색을 섞으면

PRACTICE 8

1 I hurried in the morning so that I could catch the train.

2 We were so tired that we couldn't go to the party.

3 They practiced hard so that they could win the game.

4 The coffee was too hot for her to drink.

5 I was so busy that I couldn't answer the phone.

6 I drink a cup of coffee every morning (in order[so as]) to stay awake.

7 The table was so heavy that I couldn't move it.

8 The questions are too difficult for me to answer.

9 Animals live in a pack so that they can reduce the danger of attack.

10 Mike took a taxi (in order[so as]) to arrive there in time.

> **1, 3, 6, 9, 10** '~하기 위해서, ~할 수 있도록'이라는 의미로 목적을 나타내는 「so that~」 표현은 「(in order[so as]) to+동사원형」으로 바꿔 쓸 수 있다.
> **2, 4, 5, 7, 8** 「so+형용사/부사+that+주어+can[could] not...」 표현은 「too+형용사/부사+to+동사원형」으로 바꿔 쓸 수 있다.

PRACTICE 9

1 It is disappointing that he lied to me.

2 It is exciting that we are going to Jejudo.

3 It is strange that they didn't come.

4 It is a pity that the story had an unhappy ending.

5 It is true that Giho plays the piano well.

6 I know that Yumi is Sujin's sister.

7 I thought that she was going to cry.

8 I believe that her son is diligent.

9 I thought that you were having dinner at that restaurant.

10 I knew that you gave Mike a lot of books.

11 The fact is that she doesn't like her new job.

12 The point is that we can't wait any longer.

13 The truth is that Minho broke the window.

14 The big news was that Tom and Kate got married.

15 The problem was that he didn't know how to drive.

> **1~5** 문장 앞에 가주어 it을 쓰고 진주어인 that절을 뒤로 보내서 써야 한다.
> **6~10** 목적어 역할을 하는 명사절을 이끄는 that절 형태로 써야 한다. 이때의 that은 생략 가능하다.
> **11~15** 보어 역할을 하는 that절 형태로 써야 한다.

PRACTICE 10

1 while   **2** after   **3** when
4 before   **5** as   **6** until
7 as soon as   **8** after   **9** while
10 until

> **1** 과거 진행형(was washing the dishes) 형태가 쓰여 '내가 설거지를 하고 있었던 동안'이라는 의미가 되어야 하므로 while(~하는 동안)이 적절하다.
> **2** 숙제를 끝마친 후에 저녁을 먹었다는 의미가 되어야 하므로 after(~한 후에)가 적절하다.
> **3** 한가할 때 주로 무엇을 하는지 묻는 의미가 되어야 하므로 when(~할 때)이 적절하다.
> **4** 손님이 도착하기 전에 음식이 준비되어 있어야 한다는 의미이므로 before(~전에)가 적절하다.
> **5** 거리를 걷고 있었을 때 그의 선생님을 만났다는 의미이므로 as(~하고 있을 때)가 적절하다.
> **6** 그가 잠들 때까지 이야기책을 읽었다는 의미이므로 until(~할 때까지)이 적절하다.
> **7** 그는 일어나자마자 양치질을 한다는 의미이므로 as soon as(~하자마자)가 적절하다.
> **8** 문을 연 후에 방에 들어왔다는 의미이므로 after(~한 후에)가 적절하다.

PRACTICE 11

1 Even though English is difficult, I like learning it.
2 Though Andy doesn't eat regularly, he is quite healthy.
3 Although the sun was shining, it wasn't very warm.
4 Although the two pictures aren't identical, they are similar.
5 Though Paul has the least experience, he's the best teacher.

PRACTICE 12

1	Finally	2	However
3	In addition	4	For example
5	Therefore	6	For example
7	However	8	Therefore
9	In addition	10	Finally

1 우리 팀이 프로젝트를 매우 열심히 준비해 왔고 결국 성공적으로 그것을 마쳤다는 의미이므로 Finally(결국)가 적절하다.
2 준수의 부모님이 그가 배우가 되기를 원하지 않으셨지만 그는 유명한 배우가 되었다는 반대되는 내용이므로 However(그러나)가 적절하다.
3 그가 금메달을 땄고, 추가적으로 세계 신기록을 세웠다는 부가적 사실을 말하고 있으므로 In addition(게다가)이 적절하다.
4 일상 생활에서 환경을 보호할 수 있는 사례를 들고 있으므로 For example(예를 들면)이 적절하다.
5 어제 결석을 해서 그 결과 축제에 대한 소식을 듣지 못했다는 의미이므로 Therefore(그러므로)가 적절하다.
6 한국의 중요한 명절로 추석과 설날을 예시로 들고 있으므로 For example(예를 들면)이 적절하다.
7 교통 체증이 있었지만, 직장에 시간에 맞게 도착할 수 있었다는 의미이므로 However(그러나)가 적절하다.
8 모두 다음 2주간 휴가를 가기 때문에 그 결과 사무실이 비어 있을 것이라는 의미이므로 Therefore(그러므로)가 적절하다.
9 집을 청소해야 하고 추가적으로 과학 숙제도 해야 한다는 내용이므로 In addition(게다가)이 적절하다.
10 몇 시간 전에 이메일을 보냈고, 답신을 기다리다가 마침내 지금 짧은 답신을 받았다는 의미이므로 Finally(결국)가 적절하다.

중간·기말고사 대비문제 정답 본문 _ p.370

1 ② 2 ②,③ 3 Read many books, and you will 4 ①,⑤ 5 Leave now, or you'll be late for school. 6 ② 7 because it was[we were] too cold 8 ④ 9 Although[Though] 10 ③ 11 ① 12 ③ 13 ③ 14 ④ 15 A good sleep is important for kids as well as adults. 16 both, and 17 ⑤ 18 ③ 19 When 20 ② 21 ② 22 ② 23 The third pig's house is so sturdy that I can't destroy it. 24 ④ 25 ③ 26 ④ 27 ④ 28 ④ 29 ⑤ 30 ④ 31 ④ 32 ② 33 ③ 34 ③ 35 that people tend to throw away the trash 36 ③ 37 ⑤ 38 ④ 39 ④ 40 ① 41 ④ 42 ⑤ 43 ② 44 Water is one of the most unusual things as well as the most common substance on Earth. 45 ② 46 ③ 47 ④ 48 ① that ② clean ③ room ④ before ⑤ come 49 ①,④ 50 ⑤ 51 will stay at home if it rains tomorrow 52 ④ 53 ④,⑤ 54 ④ 55 ③ 56 ⑤ 57 (1) the weather was so bad that I couldn't go on a picnic (2) the weather is so good that I can go on a picnic 58 because → because of 59 ② 60 ② 61 ④

중간·기말고사 대비문제 해설

1 so that과 in order to는 모두 '~하기 위해서'의 뜻으로 목적을 나타내지만, so that은 접속사로 뒤에 절이 오고 in order to 뒤에는 동사원형이 온다.
2 ②「so+부사+that+주어+can't」는「too+부사+for+목적격+to부정사」로 바꾸어 쓸 수 있다. in order to는 '~하기 위해서'라는 뜻으로 목적을 나타낸다.
  = He runs too fast for me to catch.
  ③「명령문+or」은 'If you don't ~'의 뜻을 나타낸다.
  = If you don't get up right now, you'll be late for work.
3 「명령문+and」 '~해라, 그러면 …'
4 크리스마스 카드를 받지 못해 실망했다고 했으므로 원인을 나타내는 접속사가 들어가야 한다.
  ① because '~때문에' ⑤ as '~때문에'

5 「명령문＋or」 '~해라, 그렇지 않으면'

6 ② 지시형용사　　①④⑤ 명사절 접속사(목적어)
③ 목적격 관계대명사

7 <u>너무 추워서</u> 우리는 밖에 오래 있지 않았다.

8 ⓑ「neither A nor B」 'A도 B도 ~ 아닌'
ⓒ「B as well as A」 뒤에 오는 동사는 B에 수를 일치
시켜야 한다. 따라서 3인칭 단수 현재형인 plays로
고치는 것이 알맞다.
ⓓ「not only A but also B」 뒤에 오는 동사는 B에 수
를 일치시켜야 한다. 따라서 복수인 my parents
에 맞춰 복수형 동사로 고쳐야 한다.
ⓐ「not only A but also B」 'A뿐만 아니라 B도'
(not → not only)
ⓔ「B as well as A」 뒤에 오는 동사는 B의 수에 일치
시킨다. 따라서, 복수 명사인 Jina's cousins에 맞
춰 복수 동사가 나와야 한다.
(are → 고칠 필요 없음)

9 although[though] '비록 ~일지라도'

10 롤러코스터를 타는 동안 사진을 찍었다는 의미이므로
동시동작을 나타내는 접속사 while을 써야 한다.

11 ① 관계대명사　　　②③④⑤ 접속사

12 '열린 마음을 가진다면, 친구를 많이 만들 것이다.'라는
뜻이므로 조건을 나타내는 접속사 if를 써야 한다.

13 ③ 명사절 접속사 if '~인지 아닌지'
①②④⑤ 조건을 나타내는 if '~라면'
① 네가 그녀를 본다면 이 꽃을 그녀에게 줘.
② 네가 그에게 묻는다면 그는 너에게 진실을 말해줄
것이다.
③ 나는 내가 코트를 입어야 하는지 아닌지 궁금하다.
④ 당신의 이름을 남겨 주신다면, 우리는 당신께 최대
한 빨리 전화 드리겠습니다.
⑤ 네가 잠시 앉아 있다면, 나는 네가 여기 있다고 그
에게 말할 것이다.

14 • 교통체증으로 기차를 놓쳤다는 의미이므로 원인을
나타내는 접속사 because를 써야 한다.
• 저녁에 일찍 잠자리에 들면 아침에 일어나기 더 쉽
다는 의미이므로 조건을 나타내는 접속사 If를 써야
한다.

15 「not only A but also B」＝「B as well as A」
'A뿐만 아니라 B도'

16 「both A and B」 'A와 B 둘 다'

17 신문을 보고 난 후, 아침을 먹었다고 했으므로 '~한 후
에'의 의미인 after을 써야 한다.

18 ⓐ • 나는 너무 피곤해서 더 이상 깨어 있을 수 없다.
• 나는 더 깨어 있기에는 너무 피곤하다.
ⓑ • 그 방은 침대 세 개를 수용할 만큼 충분히 컸다.
• 그 방은 매우 커서 침대 세 개를 수용할 수 있다.
ⓓ • 학교가 운동회를 열기에는 날씨가 너무 나빴다.
(운동회를 열 수 없었다.)
• 날씨가 너무 나빴기 때문에, 학교가 운동회를 열
수 없었다.
ⓒ • 그 벽에 있는 금은 건축가가 찾기에 너무 작았다.
• 접속사 that절에는 불완전한 절이 올 수 없는데,
the architect couldn't find에는 목적어 the
crack이 빠져 있기 때문에 어법상 잘못된 문장
이다.
ⓔ • 안개가 너무 심해서 아빠는 도로 위의 차선을 볼
수 없었다.
• 안개가 심했지만 아빠가 도로 위의 차선을 볼 수
없을 정도는 아니었다.

19 7살 때라는 특정 시점을 말하므로 '~할 때'라는 의미
의 when을 써야 한다.

20 because 뒤에는 절이 오고, because of 뒤에는 명
사(구)가 온다.

21 수미와 준호는 시험이 더 쉬웠다고 했지만 나는 동의
하지 않는다고 했으므로 대조적인 의미의 however
을 써야 한다.

22 대부분의 친구들은 양식을 좋아하지만 Jack은 한식
을 제일 좋아한다고 했으므로 '비록 ~일지라도'의 의
미인 although를 써야 한다.

23 '너무 ~해서 …할 수 없다'라는 표현은 괄호 안에 주어
진 표현들에 so를 추가하여 「so＋형용사＋that＋주
어＋can't＋동사」 구조로 나타낼 수 있다. 이 표현은
늑대가 결국 벽돌집을 부수지 못했다는 결과를 의미
한다.

24 ④ 의문부사 when '언제'
①②③⑤ 접속사 when '~할 때'
① 내가 어렸을 때, 나는 멕시코에 살았다.
② 내가 나의 딸을 보았을 때, 그녀는 내게 미소지었다.
③ 우리가 소풍을 갈 때, 너의 점심을 가져와라.
④ 그는 내게 언제 내가 책을 돌려줄 수 있는지 물었다.
⑤ 시간이 될 때, 내게 연락해라.

25 새로운 영화를 볼 기회를 가지고 싶어서 영화 동아리
에 가입할 것이라고 했으므로 결과를 나타내는 접속
사 so를 써야 한다.

26 is(be 동사) 뒤 보어 자리에 절이 오므로, 명사절을 이

끄는 접속사 that이 필요하다.

27 주어진 문장과 ④의 밑줄 친 As는 '~할 때'를 의미하는 접속사이다.
① '~로(서)' (전치사)
② 원급 비교 표현 「as+형용사+as」에서 앞의 as는 부사, 뒤의 as는 접속사 역할을 한다.
③ '~함에 따라' (접속사)
⑤ '~때문에' (접속사)

28 ④ so that ~ '~하기 위해서'

29 • Mr. Kim이 사람들을 돕는 것을 좋아한다고 했고, 그에 대한 예시를 들고 있으므로 '예를 들어'라는 뜻의 For example을 써야 한다.
• 도움이 필요한지(아닌지) 가서 물어본다는 의미이므로 접속사 if(~인지 아닌지)가 적절하다.

30 ⓐ 콘서트에 갈 수 없는 원인이 나오므로 '~때문에'라는 의미를 가진 because가 나와야 한다.
④ 배가 아픈 원인을 나타내는 절을 이끄므로, '~때문에'라는 의미를 가진 because가 나와야 한다.
① 'too+형용사+to부정사'는 '~하기에는 너무 …한'의 의미이다.
② 파티를 가게 돼서 기쁘다는 결과를 나타내는 절을 이끄므로, '그래서'라는 의미의 so가 나와야 한다.
③ '내가 어렸을 때'라는 시간을 의미하므로, '~할 때'라는 의미의 when이 쓰인다.
⑤ "감사합니다"라고 말하지 않으면 사람들이 네가 감사하는 것을 알지 못할 것이다.라는 의미의 문장이다. '~해라, 그렇지 않으면'의 의미는 '명령문+or'을 사용해 나타낸다.

31 주어진 문장, ④ 접속사(~때)
①⑤ 의문부사(언제)
② 관계부사
③ 의문사+to부정사(언제 ~할지)
[주어진 문장] 비가 내릴 때 꼭 창문을 닫아 두어라.
① 나는 언제 공연이 시작할지 모르겠다.
② 나는 우리가 단짝 친구가 되었던 날을 기억한다.
③ 언제 떠날지가 매우 중요하다.
④ 그녀가 집에 돌아왔을 때, 그녀는 피곤해 보였다.
⑤ 우리가 언제 만나야 하는지 내게 말해 줄래?

32 (A) 아침에 일어났을 때 몸이 좋지 않았지만 출근을 했다고 했으므로, 대조적인 의미의 but을 쓴다.
(B) 회사에서 회의가 취소되어 조금 쉴 수 있었다는 내용 뒤에 일에 집중할 수 없었다는 대조적인 내용이 이어지므로 '그러나'라는 뜻의 However을 쓴다.
(C) 일에 집중할 수 없었다는 내용에 더해 상사가 보고서의 오류 때문에 화가 났다고 했으므로, '게다가'라는 뜻의 In addition을 쓴다. Besides도 같은 뜻이다.

33 in the end = finally '결국, 마침내'

34 a. 피곤했기 때문에 어젯밤 일찍 잠자리에 든 것이므로 인과를 나타내는 접속사 Because를 써야 한다.
b. 아침을 먹지 않으면 공부에 집중할 수 없다는 의미이므로 빈칸에는 접속사 or(그렇지 않으면)가 적절하다. 「명령문+or …」: ~해라 그렇지 않으면 …할 것이다.
c. 감자를 오븐 안에 넣기 전에 오븐을 예열해야 하므로, 빈칸에는 접속사 before가 들어가는 것이 적절하다.
d. 내가 그곳에 가야 하는지 아닌지 모르겠다는 의미이므로 빈칸에는 접속사 if(~인지 아닌지)가 적절하다.

35 주격 보어 자리에 that이 이끄는 명사절이 온다.

36 '~에도 불구하고'의 의미이고, 구를 이끄는 전치사 despite가 들어가야 한다. 접속사 although는 뒤에 절이 온다.

37 시간을 나타내는 접속사가 쓰인 부사절에서는 현재시제가 미래시제를 대신한다.

38 ④ 두 문장에서 모두 목적어로 쓰인 명사절을 이끄는 접속사로 쓰였다.
① • 누구인지를 묻는 의문사로 쓰였다.
• 관계대명사절에서 주어의 역할을 하고 있는 주격 관계대명사로 쓰였다.
② • 그녀는 차를 맛보면서 미소를 띠었다.
'~하고 있을 때, ~하면서'라는 뜻의 접속사로 쓰였다.
• 유명한 영화 배우로서, 그는 많은 팬을 가지고 있다.
'~로서'라는 뜻의 전치사로 쓰였다.
③ • 문장의 주어와 목적어가 같으므로 재귀대명사의 재귀 용법이 쓰였다.
• '직접'이라는 뜻을 강조해주기 위한 재귀대명사의 강조 용법으로 쓰였다.
⑤ • 동사 enjoy의 목적어로 쓰인 동명사이다.
• 분사구문으로 쓰인 현재분사이다.

39 어두워졌기 때문에 집에 갔다고 했으므로 결과를 나타내는 절을 이끄는 접속사 so를 쓴다. because는 원인을 나타내는 절을 이끈다.

40 소라는 공부를 열심히 하고 영어 대회에서 1등을 했다는 내용에, 그녀는 예의바르고 정직하다는 내용을 덧붙이고 있다. 따라서 '게다가'라는 뜻의 Besides가 들어가는 것이 알맞다.

41 John은 옷이 많지만 중고 거래로 옷을 사므로, 앞과 반대되는 내용을 나타내는 접속사 but과 함께 옷을 사는 데 돈을 많이 쓰지 않는다는 내용이 와야 한다.

42 '~인지 (아닌지)'라는 뜻의 if는 whether로 바꾸어 쓸 수 있다.

나는 그녀가 그것을 전부 다 직접 했는지, 아니면 누군가 그녀를 도와주었는지 물었다.

43 ④ 'neither A nor B' 구문이 주어로 온 것으로 B에 동사의 수를 일치시켜야 하므로 동사는 am이 적절하다.

① 주어 자리에 'both A and B' 구문이 사용된 것으로 주격으로 써야 한다. (him → he)

② 'both A and B' 구문이 주어로 사용된 경우 복수동사를 쓴다. (was → were)

③ 'either A or B' 구문이 사용된 것으로 A와 B의 형태는 같아야 한다. (not eat → not to eat)

⑤ '둘 다 ~아닌'이란 의미를 지닌 상관접속사는 'neither A nor B'로 쓴다. (or → nor)

44 not only A but also B = B as well as A

45 「so+형용사/부사+that+주어+cannot(can't)…」은 '너무 ~해서 …할 수 없는' 이라는 뜻으로, 「too+형용사/부사+to부정사」로 바꾸어 쓸 수 있다.

① so that은 '~하기 위해서'라는 뜻으로 목적을 나타낼 때 쓴다.

③ 「형용사/부사+enough+to부정사」는 '~할 정도로 충분히 …한'이라는 의미이고 「so+형용사/부사+that+주어+can」으로 바꾸어 쓸 수 있다.

④ in order to는 '~하기 위해서'라는 목적의 의미를 나타낼 때 쓴다.

⑤ because는 원인을 나타내는 접속사이다. 따라서 'Because the number of homeless pets is so large, the shelters cannot house them all.' 이라고 해주어야 본문의 문장과 같은 뜻이 된다.

46 so ~ that … '너무 ~해서 …한'

47 (A) 문장에서 목적어로 쓰인 명사절을 이끌고 있으며, '~인지 (아닌지)'의 의미이므로 접속사 if를 쓰는 것이 적절하다. as if는 '마치 ~인 것처럼'의 의미로 현재 또는 과거의 사실과 반대되는 일을 가정할 때 쓴다.

(B) 동사 answered의 목적어로 쓰인 명사절을 이끄는 접속사 that이 와야 한다.

(C) '~인지 (아닌지)'의 의미로 문장의 주어 역할을 하는 명사절을 이끌고 있으므로 접속사 Whether를 쓰는 것이 적절하다.

그녀는 갑자기 그녀의 핸드폰이 없어진 것을 깨달았다. 그녀는 혼란스러운 표정으로 주변을 둘러봤다. 그녀는 나에게 그녀의 핸드폰을 본 적 있는지 물었다. 나는 보지 못했다고 대답했다. 그녀가 그것을 집에서 잃어버린 것인지, 밖에서 잃어버린 것인지는 여전히 확실하지 않았다.

48 동사구 Make sure의 목적어로 that절이 온 상태이다. that절의 주어가 you이므로 동사는 clean으로 쓰는 것이 적절하다.

49 주어진 문장의 밑줄 친 as는 '~때문에'를 의미한다.

티켓이 매진되었기 때문에, 우리는 콘서트에 갈 수 없었다.

①④ '~ 때문에'   ② '~로(서)'

③ '~처럼'   ⑤ '~하면서'

① 그녀가 정직하지 않기 때문에, 그녀는 진실을 말하지 않을 것이다.

② 내가 고등학생이었을 때, 나는 이웃집 (아이들을 돌보는) 베이비시터로 일하기 시작했다.

③ 10월 31일에, 미국 아이들은 유령과 괴물처럼 변장을 한다.

④ 그가 늦게 일어났기 때문에, 그는 학교에 늦었다.

⑤ 내 강아지는 방에 들어오면서 짖었다.

50 「neither A nor B」 'A도 B도 ~ 아닌'

51 '만약 ~라면'의 의미를 나타내기 위해 접속사 if가 쓰였으며, 시간과 조건의 부사절에서는 현재시제가 미래시제를 대신한다.

52 ④ 우리말 뜻에 따르면, pilots (should) be given the best possible training이 문장의 주어 역할을 한다. 문장의 맨 앞에 it을 쓰고 진주어를 뒤로 보낼 때 사용하는 접속사는 명사절을 이끄는 that이다. (what → that)

53 ①④ either A or B - B에 수 일치

⑤ B as well as A - B에 수 일치

② both A and B - 복수 동사

③ neither A nor B - B에 수 일치

54 「so+형용사+that+주어+can't[couldn't]」는 「too+형용사+to부정사」로 바꾸어 쓸 수 있다.

This English book was so difficult that I

couldn't read it.

= This English book was too difficult for me to read.

① 읽기에 어렵지 않았다는 뜻으로 주어진 문장과 의미가 상반된다.

② 「형용사/부사＋enough＋to부정사」는 '~할 정도로 충분히 …한'이라는 의미이므로 주어진 문장과 의미가 상반된다.

③ 의미상의 주어를 가질 때 for me to read라고 쓴다. (to me read → for me to read)

⑤ 주어진 문장 내의 시제가 모두 일치하므로 to부정사의 시제도 주절과 동일하게 맞추어 to read라고 써야 한다. (to have read → to read)

55 해가 빛나고 있었음에도 불구하고, 아주 따뜻하지는 않았다.

56 70세임에도 매우 건강하다는 의미가 되어야 하므로 '비록 ~일지라도'의 의미인 Even though가 들어가는 것이 알맞다.

57 (1) 「so~that＋주어＋couldn't…」 '너무 ~해서 …할 수 없었다'

(2) 「so~that＋주어＋can…」 '매우 ~해서 …할 수 있다'

58 because 뒤에는 절이 오고, because of 뒤에는 명사(구)가 온다.

59 • 반려동물을 키우는 것의 장점에 대한 내용 뒤에 작은 반려동물이라도 많은 보살핌을 필요로 한다(손이 많이 간다)는 대조적인 내용이 이어지므로 '그러나'라는 뜻의 however가 들어가는 것이 알맞다.

• 반려동물을 입양하기 전에 신중하게 생각해봐야 한다는 내용이 되어야 하므로, '~전에'라는 뜻의 before를 써야 한다.

60 18개월까지는 건강한 아기였다는 내용이 되어야 하므로 '~까지'의 의미를 나타내는 until이 알맞다.

61 빈칸이 포함된 문장은 '학교에서 공부할 때 그것(스마트폰을 사용하느라 매우 늦게까지 깨어 있는 것)은 나를 졸리게 했다.'는 의미이므로 '~할 때'를 나타내는 접속사 when이 적절하다.

<table>
<tr><td>CHAPTER **16**</td><td>**전치사**
Prepositions</td><td>본문 _ p.382</td></tr>
</table>

PRACTICE 1

1 on	**2** at	**3** in	**4** on
5 in	**6** at	**7** at	**8** in
9 on	**10** at	**11** on	**12** in
13 on	**14** at	**15** in	

PRACTICE 2

1 on	**2** at	**3** in	**4** on
5 at	**6** in	**7** at	**8** on
9 in	**10** on		

PRACTICE 3

1 ① in ② on	**2** ① on ② ×
3 ① at ② in	**4** ① at ② ×
5 ① at ② on	**6** ① in ② ×
7 ① at ② on	**8** ① on ② ×
9 ① in ② on	**10** ① on ② in

1 ① in+월 ② on+날짜
2 ① on+요일 ② ×, 「every+요일」 형태의 부사구 앞에 전치사를 쓰지 않는다.
3 ① at+구체적인 시각 ② in the afternoon: 오후에
*noon: 낮 12시
4 ① at night: 밤에 ② ×, last night(어젯밤)과 같은 부사구 앞에 전치사를 쓰지 않는다.
5 ① at Christmas: 크리스마스에 ② on Christmas Day: 크리스마스 날에
6 ① in the evening: 저녁에 ② ×, this evening(오늘 저녁)과 같은 부사구 앞에 전치사를 쓰지 않는다.
7 ① at night: 밤에 ② on Friday night: 금요일 밤에
8 ① on+요일 ② ×, next Tuesday(다음 주 화요일)와 같은 부사구 앞에 전치사를 쓰지 않는다.
9 ① in the morning: 아침에 ② on Sunday morning: 일요일 아침에
10 ① on+날짜 ② in+월

Ch **16**
전치사

PRACTICE 4

1 since　**2** from　**3** from
4 since　**5** from　**6** since
7 from　**8** since　**9** since
10 from

1, 4, 6, 8, 9 현재완료 시제가 쓰여 과거에서 시작된 사건이 현재까지 계속 영향을 미치고 있다는 의미이므로 since(~이래로)가 적절하다.
2, 7, 10 동작이나 사건의 시작 시점을 나타내고 있으므로 from(~부터)이 적절하다.
3, 5 from A to B(A로부터 B까지) 구문이 쓰였다.

PRACTICE 5

1 until　**2** by
3 until　**4** by
5 until　**6** by
7 by　**8** until

1, 3, 5, 8 until: ~까지(계속), 동작이나 상태가 한 시점까지 계속된다는 의미를 강조하고 싶을 때 쓴다.
2, 4, 6, 7 by: ~까지(기한), 동작이나 상태가 완료되는 시점을 강조해서 나타내고 싶을 때 쓴다.

PRACTICE 6

1 at　**2** from
3 by　**4** on[by]
5 until　**6** since
7 in　**8** on
9 by　**10** at[on]
11 since　**12** until
13 in　**14** from
15 on

1 at+구체적인 시각
2 from: ~부터
3, 9 by: ~까지(기한), 동작이나 상태가 완료되는 시점을 강조하고 싶을 때 쓴다.
4 on+날짜
5, 12 until: ~까지(계속), 동작이나 상태가 한 시점까지 계속되는 것을 나타낼 때 쓴다.
6, 11 since: ~이래로, 주로 완료 시제와 함께 쓰인다.
7 in+연도
8 on+요일, on Sunday night: 일요일 밤에
10 at Christmas: 크리스마스 시즌에
13 in the morning: 아침에
14 from A to B: A로부터 B까지
15 on my birthday: 내 생일에

PRACTICE 7

1 after　**2** before　**3** after
4 before　**5** after　**6** before
7 after　**8** after

PRACTICE 8

1 going out, he turned off the light
2 seeing a movie, Jessica and Inho had dinner
3 buying the oranges, Mom looked at them carefully
4 deciding what to do, I told him about it
5 eating food, Nick usually prays
6 reading the book, we discussed it together

PRACTICE 9

1 ① for　② during
2 ① during　② for
3 ① during　② for
4 ① for　② during
5 ① for　② during
6 ① for　② during
7 ① during　② for
8 ① during　② for
9 ① for　② during
10 ① for　② during

PRACTICE 10

1 after　**2** during
3 for　**4** before
5 before　**6** for
7 after　**8** Before
9 during　**10** for

PRACTICE 11

1 on　**2** in　**3** at
4 on　**5** at　**6** in[at]
7 on　**8** at　**9** in

PRACTICE 12

1 in　**2** on　**3** at
4 on　**5** in　**6** at

7 on		**8** at		**9** in	
10 on, in		**11** in		**12** at	
13 on		**14** on		**15** at	

PRACTICE 13

1 over	**2** above
3 below	**4** under
5 above	**6** over
7 below	**8** under

PRACTICE 14

1 down	**2** up
3 out of	**4** into
5 up	**6** out of
7 into	**8** down

PRACTICE 15

1 out of, down	**2** below, above
3 up, under	**4** over, out of
5 into, above	**6** up, over
7 into, under	**8** down, below

PRACTICE 16

1 across	**2** along
3 through	**4** around
5 through	**6** across
7 around	**8** along

PRACTICE 17

1 behind	**2** in front of
3 by	**4** in front of
5 by	**6** behind
7 in front of	**8** behind
9 by	

PRACTICE 18

1 in front of, along	**2** through, behind
3 by, around	**4** along, across
5 through, behind	**6** by, in front of
7 around, behind	**8** by, across

PRACTICE 19

1 between	**2** among
3 among	**4** between
5 among	**6** between
7 between	**8** among
9 between	**10** among
11 among	**12** between

PRACTICE 20

1 to	**2** for	**3** to
4 to	**5** for	**6** to
7 for	**8** to	**9** for
10 to		

PRACTICE 21

1 about	**2** like
3 with	**4** about
5 with	**6** about
7 with	**8** like
9 without	**10** like

PRACTICE 22

1 to	**2** for
3 without	**4** about
5 among	**6** with
7 like	**8** between

> **1** to: '~로, ~에'란 뜻으로, go, come과 함께 도착지를 나타낸다.
> **2** for: '~로, ~을 향하여'란 뜻으로, start, leave와 함께 방향을 나타낸다.
> **3** without: ~없이
> **4** about: ~에 대하여
> **5** among: (셋 이상) ~사이에
> **6** with: ~을 가진
> **7** like: ~처럼
> **8** between: (둘) ~사이에

PRACTICE 23

1 as	**2** by	**3** in
4 by	**5** by	**6** as
7 in	**8** by	**9** in
10 by	**11** in	**12** by
13 by	**14** as	

1 식당에서 매니저로 일한다는 의미이므로 자격을 나타내는 전치사 as(~로서)가 적절하다.

2, 13 수동태 문장에서 행위자를 나타내므로 by(~에 의해)가 적절하다.

3 빵을 세 조각으로 잘랐다는 의미이므로 크기를 나타내는 in(~로)이 적절하다. in three pieces(세 조각으로)

4, 10 by ~ing: ~함으로써

5 키가 3 cm 차이가 난다는 의미이므로 정도를 나타내는 by(~만큼)가 적절하다.

6 think of A as B: A를 B라고 생각하다

7 연필로 먼저 스케치를 했다는 뜻이므로 방법을 나타내는 in(~로)이 적절하다.

8 by+교통수단

9 in: ~을 입고 있는

11 수업에서 한국어로 말해야 한다는 의미이므로 방법을 나타내는 in(~로)이 적절하다.

12 그것을 팩스로 보내줄 수 있는지 묻고 있으므로 방법을 나타내는 by(~로)가 적절하다.

14 소파는 또한 여분의 침대로도 쓰일 수 있다는 의미이므로 수단이나 도구를 나타내는 as(~로써)가 적절하다.

PRACTICE 24

1	at	**2**	of
3	in	**4**	of
5	about	**6**	of
7	at	**8**	of
9	of	**10**	for
11	of	**12**	to

PRACTICE 25

1	of	**2**	for
3	to	**4**	of
5	in	**6**	to
7	of	**8**	for
9	of	**10**	for
11	of	**12**	at
13	for	**14**	in
15	about	**16**	into[across]
17	in		

PRACTICE 26

1	for	**2**	for
3	on	**4**	below
5	at	**6**	at
7	on	**8**	at
9	in	**10**	above
11	on	**12**	to
13	of	**14**	in
15	from	**16**	in
17	for	**18**	about
19	of	**20**	around
21	in	**22**	for
23	in	**24**	between
25	like	**26**	under
27	before	**28**	to
29	during	**30**	up
31	by	**32**	down
33	of	**34**	with
35	in	**36**	After
37	in	**38**	along
39	from	**40**	until
41	on	**42**	in
43	since	**44**	through
45	into	**46**	by
47	of	**48**	out of
49	behind	**50**	for

1, 22 for+시간의 길이를 나타내는 명사구, for five days(5일 동안) for 3 months(3달 동안)

2 Thank you for ~ing: ~에 대해 감사하다, invite A to dinner (A를 저녁식사에 초대하다)

4 below: (~보다) 아래에

6 be poor at: ~을 잘 못하다, look after(~를 돌보다)

8 be good at: ~에 능숙하다

9 be interested in: ~에 관심이 있다

13 be proud of: ~을 자랑스러워하다

14 in: ~을 입고 있는, in white: 흰색 옷을 입고 있는

17 wait for: ~을 기다리다

18 think about ~ing: ~하는 것에 대해 생각하다, 고려하다

19 consist of: ~로 구성되다

25 look like: ~처럼 보이다

28 belong to: ~에 속하다

29 during+특정 기간을 나타내는 명사구, during the holiday (연휴 동안)

30 더 높이 올라가기 위해서 언덕 위로 올라갔다는 의미이므로 up이 적절하다. climb up the hill(언덕 위로 올라가다), climb down the hill(언덕 아래로 내려가다)

32 run down the stairs: 계단을 뛰어내려가다

33 die of hunger: 굶어 죽다, die의 진행형은 dying임에 유의한다.

38 stand along the white line: 흰 선을 따라 줄을 서다

39 be made from: ~로 만들어지다. 와인은 포도로 만들어진다는 의미인데, 재료의 형태를 알아볼 수 없을 때는 전치사 from을 사용한다.

41 plane 앞에 부정관사(a)가 있으므로 on을 써야 한다. 교통수단 중 plane, train, bus, boat는 전치사 on과 함께 쓴다.

42 taxi 앞에 부정관사(a)가 있으므로 in을 써야 한다. 교통수단 중 taxi, car, truck은 전치사 in과 함께 쓴다.

47 become full of: ~로 가득 차게 되다

50 동사 leave와 함께 목적지 앞에는 전치사 for를 쓴다.

중간·기말고사 대비문제 **정답**   본문 _ p.410

1 ③   **2** ④   **3** similar to mine   **4** ④   **5** ⑤
6 ran across her teacher on her way to   **7** ③
8 ②   **9** ①   **10** is made of   **11** ②   **12** by
13 for, to   **14** ⑤   **15** ④   **16** (1) for (2) while
(3) during   **17** ①   **18** like   **19** ②   **20** ②
21 ③,④   **22** ⑤   **23** ③   **24** (1) ⓐ Don't wait
until they speak to you. (2) ⓓ Listen to what
they say.   **25** ①   **26** believe in yourself
27 (1) on (2) after (3) with (4) in   **28** ①
29 ②   **30** ④   **31** ⑤   **32** ①   **33** ①   **34** ④
35 ⑤   **36** ②   **37** ③,⑤   **38** ③   **39** ⑤
40 ②   **41** ④   **42** ②   **43** ①   **44** ①   **45** ②
46 for   **47** ⑤   **48** ⑤   **49** ③   **50** ②   **51** ④
52 out of   **53** ②   **54** ②   **55** ②   **56** ①,④
57 with   **58** I'm very poor at remembering
names.   **59** (1) The bear is on the ball.
(2) The elephant is in the box. (3) The tiger is
under the chair.   **60** ③   **61** ①   **62** ⑤
63 belong to, similar to   **64** ③   **65** ①   **66** A
woman wearing glasses sat between two men
on the subway.   **67** ③   **68** ④   **69** ①   **70** ⑤

중간·기말고사 대비문제 **해설**

1 날짜나 요일 앞에는 on을 쓴다.

2 어떤 지점이나 위치를 가리킬 때는 at을 쓴다.
신청서를 작성하고 맨 아래에 서명하세요.

3 be similar to '~와 비슷하다'

4 • 접속사 since가 '~ 때문에'라는 의미로 쓰였다.
  (너는 항상 진실을 말하기 때문에 난 널 신뢰할 수
  있다)
• 전치사 since가 '~부터, ~이래로'라는 의미로 쓰였
  다. (그녀는 화요일부터 휴가 중이다.)

5 • put ~ into … '~을 …안으로 넣다'
• move into ~ '~로 이사하다'

6 run across '우연히 마주치다', on one's way to+
  명사 '~로 가는 길에'

7 • 이유를 나타내는 의문부사 why가 온다.
• die of '~로 죽다'

8 ⓐ at that time '그 당시에'
ⓑ 날짜나 요일 앞에는 전치사 on이 온다.

ⓒ 집 안에서 일어나는 일이므로 전치사 in이 적절하다.

9 ⓐ '그녀는 그녀의 모국어로 영어를 말한다.'는 의미이
  므로, '~(으)로'라는 의미를 가진 전치사 as를 쓰는
  것이 적절하다. (in → as)
ⓑ '우리는 호랑이와 곰과 같은 야생 동물을 보호해야
  한다.'는 의미이므로, '~와 같은'의 의미를 가진 전
  치사 like를 쓰는 것이 적절하다. (as → like)

10 be made of '~로 만들어지다'
cf. be made from은 화학적 변화를 거쳐 만들어질
  때 쓴다.

11 ⓒ 특정한 날의 시간대를 나타낼 때는 전치사 on을 쓴
  다. (at → on)
ⓔ upset about '~에 대해 화난, 기분이 나쁜'
  (for → about)
ⓐ 뒤에 시간을 나타내는 명사구 two hours가 있으
  므로 전치사 for를 써야 한다.
ⓑ 동사 go와 함께 도착지를 나타내는 to의 쓰임은 적
  절하다.
ⓓ the playground와 같이 비교적 넓은 장소에 속해
  있는 느낌을 나타낼 때는 전치사 in을 쓴다.

12 • by email '이메일로' – 방법을 나타내는 by
• by one run '1점 차로' – 정도를 나타내는 by
• directed by '~에 의해 연출된' – '~에 의해'라는 뜻
  의 by

13 • for는 leave 동사와 함께 방향을 나타낸다.
• to는 go 동사와 함께 도착지 앞에 쓴다.

14 ⑤ consist with은 '~와 일치하다'라는 뜻으로, '~로
  구성되어 있다'의 의미로는 consist of로 써야 한
  다. (with → of)

15 • prefer A to B 'B보다 A를 더 좋아하다'
• at the airport '공항에'

16 (1) 시간의 길이를 나타내는 명사구 앞에는 for를 쓴
  다.
(2) 빈칸 뒤에 절이 나오므로 접속사 while을 쓴다.
(3) 특정 기간을 나타내는 명사구 앞에는 during을
  쓴다.

17 • take A to B 'A를 B에 데려가다'
• about '~에 대해'

18 like '~처럼'

19 방법을 나타내는 전치사 in이 들어가야 한다.
• in a car '차를 타고'   • in English '영어로'

20 ② talk on the phone '전화로 이야기하다'
  (of → on)

21 ③④ '~이래로'   ①②⑤ '~때문에'

22 ⑤ about '~에 대한'

23 ⓐ '숲을 통과하여'라는 의미로 전치사 through를 쓴 것은 적절하다.

ⓒ '(크기) ~로'의 의미를 나타낼 때는 전치사 in을 쓴다.

ⓑ 개가 강 안으로 뛰어든 것이므로 into를 쓰는 것이 적절하다. (on → into)

ⓓ 날짜가 일 단위까지 나와있으므로 on을 쓰는 것이 적절하다. (in → on)

ⓔ 전치사 at 뒤에는 동사 play가 아닌 목적어로 쓰일 수 있는 동명사 playing이 와야 한다. (play → playing)

24 (1) ⓐ 시간과 조건을 나타내는 부사절에서는 현재시제가 미래시제를 대신한다. (will speak → speak)

(2) ⓓ listen to '~을 듣다' (at → to)

25 ① by '~에 의해', '<시간> ~까지', '~함으로써'

26 '~을 믿다'라는 의미의 구동사 'believe in'을 사용한다. 또한 주어와 목적어가 같으므로 재귀대명사 yourself를 써야 한다.

27 (1) on '~(위)에'

(2) after school '방과 후에'

(3) be wrong with '~이 잘못되다, 이상하다'

(4) in English '영어로'

28 (a) 시간을 나타낼 때는 전치사 at을 쓴다.

(b) with '~와 함께'

(c) along '~을 따라'

(d) 뒤에 특정 기간을 나타내는 명사구가 있을 때 전치사 during을 써야 한다.

(e) in '~(안)에'

29 like는 동사로 '~을 좋아하다'라는 뜻을, 전치사로는 '~ 같은'이라는 뜻을 가진다.

30 ④ Saturday afternoon과 같은 특정한 요일의 시간 앞에는 전치사 on이 쓰인다.

① 명사구의 앞에 쓰였으므로 전치사 because of를 써준다. because는 접속사이므로 뒤에 절이 와야 한다. (because → because of)

② 6 o'clock은 구체적인 시각이므로, 전치사 at을 쓴다. (on → at)

③ Canada는 비교적 넓은 장소이므로, 전치사 in을 사용한다. (at → in)

⑤ enjoy는 목적어로 동명사를 쓰는 동사이다. (to dance → dancing)

31 • with '~을 가진', '~와 함께'

32 (A) similar to '~와 비슷한'

(B) laugh at '~을 비웃다'

(C) take pride in '~에 자부심을 가지다'

(D) consist of '~로 구성되다'

(E) be good at '~을 잘하다'

33 • from A to B 'A부터 B까지'

• be full of '~로 가득차다'

34 (A) be filled with : ~로 가득하다 (= be full of)

(B) pay attention to : ~에 주의를 기울이다

(C) of+추상명사는 형용사와 같은 의미를 가진다. (of great importance = greatly important)

35 • at first '처음에는'

• wait for '~를 기다리다'

• to one's surprise '놀랍게도, 뜻밖에도'

36 • start for '~로 출발하다'

• thank A for B 'A에게 B에 대해 감사하다'

37 ⓐ③⑤ 뒤에 the summer, the trip, the meeting과 같은 특정 기간을 나타내는 명사구가 왔으므로 during을 쓴다.

① between A and B: A와 B 사이에

② stand by: ~옆에 서다

④ for + 시간: ~동안

38 • most of '대부분의'

• be interested in '~에 관심이 있다'

39 start with '~부터[로] 시작하다'

40 (A) consist of '~로 구성되어 있다'
(B) be famous for '~로 유명하다'
(C) care about '~에 대해 신경 쓰다, 관심을 가지다'
(D) be made of '~로 만들어지다'
(E) belong to '~에 속하다, ~의 소유물이다'

41 ④ '한 블록을 똑바로 걸어가서 왼쪽으로 돌아라. 오른편에 학교가 보일 것이다.'라는 뜻이다.
① next to는 '~ 옆에'라는 뜻이다. 박물관은 은행이 아니라 학교 옆에 있다. (bank → school)
② across는 '~을 가로질러'라는 의미로, across from으로 쓰면 '~의 건너편에'라는 의미이다. 경찰서는 신발 가게가 아닌, 병원의 건너편에 있다. (shoe store → hospital)
③ '영화관을 찾으려면 두 블록을 똑바로 걸어가서 오른쪽으로 돌아라.'라는 뜻이다. 영화관은 두 블록을 걸어가서 왼쪽으로 돌아야 한다.
(turn right → turn left)
⑤ '한 블록을 똑바로 걸어가서 오른쪽으로 돌아라, 그러면 오른편에 병원을 볼 수 있다.'라는 뜻이다. 한 블록을 걸어가서 오른쪽으로 돌면, 오른편이 아닌 왼편에 병원이 있다.
(on your right → on your left)

42 ⓑⓒ 전치사 '~와 같은', '~처럼'
ⓐⓓⓔ 동사 '좋아하다'

43 • from now on '지금부터'
• on Sunday evening '일요일 저녁에'

44 정오까지 잠을 자는 상태가 계속되므로 '~까지'라는 의미의 until을 써야 한다.

45 • with '~을 가지고 있는'
• through '~을 통해'
• belong to '~의 소유이다'

46 단어를 배열하면 because she waited for her friend for an hour가 된다.

47 by '<시간> ~까지', '~옆에'

48 주어진 문장, ⑤ '~동안' ①② '~에게' ③④ '~을 위해, 위한'

49 in은 비교적 넓은 장소 앞에, at은 비교적 좁은 장소 앞에 쓰인다.

50 • on time '제시간에'   • on foot '걸어서'

51 • at – 비교적 좁은 장소를 나타낼 때 쓴다.
• into '~안으로'

52 take A out of B 'B에서 A를 꺼내다'

53 in '~안에' under '~아래에'

54 ⓐ 날짜나 요일 앞에는 전치사 on을 쓰므로, Sunday 앞의 전치사 at을 on으로 고쳐야 한다.
(at → on)
ⓔ made by(~에 의해 만들어진) 뒤에는 만든 주체가 나오고, made of(~로 만들어진) 뒤에는 성분이 나온다. 따라서 made by는 made of로 고쳐야 한다. (by → of)

55 ② '~을 입고' ①⑤ '~(안)에' ③④ 시간을 나타내는 in

56 ① The box was too heavy for me to carry. = The box was so heavy that I couldn't carry it.
④ The jar was filled with apple jam. = The jar was full of apple jam.
② could는 '할 수 있다'는 의미의 'be able to'의 과거형 'was/were able to'와 바꾸어 쓸 수 있다.
③ used to는 '(과거에) ~하곤 했다'는 의미를 나타내는 조동사이다. 따라서 '과거에는 여기 백화점이 있었지만 지금은 없다.'는 의미의 문장은 적절하다.
⑤ 'be proud of'는 '~을 자랑스러워하다'라는 뜻의 관용표현이다. 'take pride in'은 '~에 자부심을 갖다'라는 뜻의 관용표현이다.

57 • with '~의 몸에 지니고'
• with '~와 함께'

58 poor at은 '~에 서툰'의 뜻을 가진다. 전치사 at 뒤에는 '기억하는 것'이라는 의미의 동명사 remembering을 쓰는 것이 적절하다.
여: Justin, 너는 파란 셔츠를 입은 저 소녀가 누구인지 기억나니?
남: 당연하지, 그녀는 Ari야. 우리는 지난주에 그녀와 점심을 먹었어. 너는 기억하지 못하니?
여: 기억해. 나는 단지 이름들을 기억하는 것을 매우 못해.
남: 오, 알겠어. 그럼, 누군가의 이름을 그들의 성격과 연관 짓는 것을 시도해봐. 그게 도움이 될 거야.

59 (1) on '~ (표면) 위에'   (2) in '~ 안에'
(3) under '~ 아래에'

60 ③ 수단, 방법을 나타내는 전치사 as(~로)

61 be in trouble '곤란한 처지에 있다'

62 be proud of = take pride in '~을 자랑스러워하다'

63 • belong to: ~의 소유이다
• be similar to: ~와 비슷하다

Ch
16

전치사

64 (A) 작년에는 홍수 때문에 학교에 갈 수 없어 슬펐지만, 올해는 다르다는 대조적인 의미이다. 따라서 '그러나'라는 의미의 접속부사 however을 쓴다.

(B) 빈칸 뒤에 동명사구 going to school이 뒤따라오므로, 동명사를 목적어로 가지는 전치사 instead of를 쓴다. 해석은 '~대신에'로 한다. instead는 부사이다.

(C) to는 go, come, return 동사와 함께 도착지를 나타낼 때 쓰인다.

65 네 에세이의 마감일이 언제니? = ① 네 에세이는 언제까지 제출되어야 하니?
due '(언제) ~하기로 되어 있는(예정된)'

66 안경을 쓴 여자가 지하철에서 두 남자 사이에 앉았다.
between '~ 사이에'

67 ③ between은 '(둘) 사이에'라는 뜻으로, 두 개의 사물 또는 사람을 나타내는 말 앞에서 쓰인다. 여기에서는 많은 사람들이 있었다고 했으므로, 셋 이상의 사물 또는 사람 사이를 나타내는 말인 among을 쓰는 것이 적절하다. (between → among)

68 ⓐ by는 교통수단을 나타내는 말과 함께 쓰여, '~를 타고'라는 뜻을 나타낸다.
④ '걸어서'라는 뜻은 전치사 on을 활용해 on foot으로 쓴다.
① by는 시간을 나타내는 말과 함께 쓰여, '~까지'를 의미하며 동작이나 상태가 완료되는 시점을 나타낸다.
② by는 수동태와 함께 쓰여 행위자를 나타내며, '~에 의해'라는 뜻을 나타낸다.
③ by는 방법을 나타내는 데 쓰이고, 해석은 '~로'로 한다.
⑤ by는 동명사와 함께 쓰여, '~함으로써, ~하며'라는 의미를 나타낸다.

69 ① prison은 in과 함께 쓰이는 명사이다.
② a party는 at과 함께 쓰이는 명사이다.
③ a garage sale은 at과 함께 쓰이는 명사구이다.
④ the airport는 at과 함께 쓰이는 명사이다.
⑤ the end of this year은 at과 함께 쓰이는 명사구이다.

70 ⑤ 'by+동명사'는 '~함으로써(수단)'라는 뜻을 나타낸다. as는 '~로서(자격)'라는 뜻이다. 따라서, '~을 사용하여, ~으로'라는 뜻으로 쓸 수 있는 전치사 with로 바꾸는 것이 적절하다. (as → with)
① 수동태 문장으로 만들 때는, 목적어를 수동태 문장의 주어로 하며, 동사는 be동사+과거분사의 형태로 바꾼다. 능동태 문장의 주어는 by+목적격으로 바꾼다.
② by는 교통수단을 나타내는 말과 함께 쓰여, '~를 타고'라는 뜻을 나타낸다. 'take+교통수단'은 '~를 타다'라는 뜻이다.
③ 'seem+to be ~'와 'It seems like+주어+동사'는 '~처럼 보인다'는 뜻으로 서로 바꾸어 쓸 수 있다. 전치사 in은 '~를 입고 있는'이라는 뜻을 나타낸다.
④ 전치사 by는 'lose/win the game by+점수'의 형태로 '~점 차로 경기에 지다/이기다'라는 뜻을 나타낸다.

CHAPTER **17** 일치·도치·화법 & 속담
Agreement·Inversion·Narration & Proverbs

본문 _ p.424

PRACTICE 1

1 our homeroom teacher was angry with us
2 he will get better
3 there were many fancy restaurants on this street
4 Everyone says
5 my son might be late for school on the first day

PRACTICE 2

1 Columbus discovered America in 1492
2 he always goes to school on foot
3 the trains leave every 20 minutes
4 water boils at 100℃ and freezes at 0℃
5 nothing is impossible to a willing heart
6 one and one makes two

PRACTICE 3

1 Here are the pepperoni pizzas
2 There goes the last train
3 Here they are
4 How come you got invited
5 There have been several snowstorms
6 how come her Chinese is
7 Have you been
8 Who did you see

PRACTICE 4

1 Behind the clouds is the sun still shining.
2 Never did he attend the meeting.
3 Little did Charlie understand about the situation.
4 On the hill was a beautiful tree.
5 Never have I seen such a disaster.

> **1, 4** 장소나 방향을 나타내는 부사구(behind the clouds, on the hill)가 맨 앞에 올 경우, 주어와 동사가 도치되어 「부사구+동사+주어」 순으로 써야 한다.
> **2, 3, 5** 부정어(never, little)가 문장 맨 앞에 올 경우, 「부정어+조동사+주어+동사」 순서로 써야 한다. 조동사 없이 일반동사가 쓰였을 경우, 조동사 do를 시제에 맞추어 쓴다.
> **3** little: 거의 ~않는

PRACTICE 5

1 he knew, that
2 her, might not be, then
3 told, was going to learn
4 told, was, that day
5 he would, the next day[the following day]

PRACTICE 6

1 My younger brother said, "The computer game is too difficult for me to play."
2 The man told her (that) it would take about two hours from then.
3 The boy said (that) he didn't want to eat those carrots.
4 The chairman said to the members, "The money is raised by donations."
5 Father said (that) it would be nice to visit there again the next[following] summer.

PRACTICE 7

1 Kevin asked her if[whether] he might use her dictionary.
2 Mom asked who was calling.
3 The teacher asked us what our hopes for that year were. [The teacher asked us what our hopes were for that year.]
4 He asked Jane when she usually watched TV.
5 He asked me if[whether] I was for or against dieting.
6 Andy asked me if[whether] I knew how to make a movie clip on my phone.
7 The man asked her if[whether] she could say that again.
8 The gentleman asked the boy what made him think so.
9 I asked James if[whether] he could lend me his bike.
10 Bob asked where he could get the ticket.

PRACTICE 8

1 She advised her neighbor to look on the bright side.
2 Tom told me to bring him a chair.
3 Jim told me to tell him when her birthday was.
4 The teacher ordered us not to use a cell phone in class.
5 Mom asked me to pass her the salt.
6 The doctor advised me not to eat too much junk food.
7 Mom ordered me to finish my homework by 7 p.m.
8 Mr. Anderson told us not to be late.

PRACTICE 9

1 mightier than		2 comes a calm	
3 Strike, hot		4 Out of, into	
5 in need, indeed		6 thicker than	
7 speak louder		8 A watched pot	
9 a will, a way		10 gathers no moss	
11 is worth		12 Better late, never	
13 Haste, waste		14 who laughs last	
15 before they are hatched			

Ch **17**
일치 · 도치 · 화법 & 속담

📑 중간·기말고사 대비문제 **정답** 본문 _ p.436

1 ② **2** ④ **3** ⑤ **4** ①,③ **5** ⑤ **6** ⑤ **7** ①

8 ③ **9** I knew the guy **10** (1) did I see a boring movie like this (2) stood a pretty girl (3) could he ride his bike **11** ③ **12** ③

13 ② **14** not to stay up, my **15** ②,⑤

16 (1) what I was going (2) he would go to Canada **17** Deborah asked Davis to buy that necklace for her. **18** ③ **19** ② **20** ②

21 (1) said to (2) said to, Don't (3) said to, Have

22 Jane asked him if[whether] he had enough money. **23** ④ **24** Never has he had any training on the cello. **25** ③

중간·기말고사 대비문제 **해설**

1 ⓐ something과 같이 -thing으로 끝나는 대명사는 형용사가 뒤에서 수식한다.
　ⓔ end up ~ing: 결국 ~하게 되다
　ⓑ '(계획을) 세우다'라는 뜻의 동사는 '앉다'의 과거형 sat이 아닌 set이고, set은 현재, 과거, 과거완료의 형태가 모두 같다. (sat → set)
　ⓒ 「형용사+enough+to부정사」 '~할 정도로 충분히 …한'이므로 형용사 famous를 enough 앞에 써야 한다. (enough famous → famous enough)
　ⓓ 대동사 do가 drives를 대신하고 있는데, 작년에 운전했을 때를 말하고 있으므로 과거형 did로 써야 한다. (does → did)

2 의문사 뒤의 어순을 「주어+동사」로 바꾸고 주어를 전달자의 입장에 맞게 I로 바꾼다. 전달 동사의 시제가 과거이므로 의문사절의 시제도 과거로 바꿔야 한다.

3 전달 동사는 said이므로 그대로 두고, 인칭대명사를 전달하는 사람의 입장에 맞게 바꾸며, 주절의 시제와 종속절의 시제를 일치시킨다.

4 ① How come은 '왜?'라는 의미로 의문문에서 사용된다. 하지만 의문문임에도 how come 뒤의 어순은 평서문과 같이 「주어+동사」로 써 준다.
　(did you visit → you visited)
　③ 부정어구가 도치될 때는 「부정어+조동사+주어+동사」의 어순으로 도치된다.
　(Hardly I met → Hardly did I meet)

5 장군이 군인들에게 명령하는 내용이므로 전달 동사로 order를 쓰고 명령문의 내용은 order의 목적격 보어이므로 to부정사로 바꾼다.

6 전달 동사의 시제가 과거이므로 현재 진행형을 과거 진행형으로 바꾸고, 인칭 대명사를 전달자의 입장에 맞게 바꿔준다.

7 시간이 많이 걸리는 일을 함께 해서 시간을 절약하자는 내용이므로 '백지장도 맞들면 낫다.'라는 뜻의 'Many hands make light work.'가 적절하다.

8 날 수 없는 거위가 끊임없는 노력과 긍정적인 생각으로 결국 날 수 있게 되었다는 내용이므로 '뜻이 있는 곳에 길이 있다.'라는 뜻의 'Where there is a will, there is a way.'가 적절하다.

9 의문사 뒤의 어순을 「주어+동사」로 바꾸고 주어를 전달자의 입장에 맞게 I로 바꾼다. 전달 동사의 시제가 과거이므로 의문사절의 시제도 과거로 바꿔야 한다.

10 (1), (3) 부정어구가 도치될 때는 「부정어+조동사+주어+동사」의 어순으로 써준다.
　(2) 장소나 방향을 나타내는 부사(구)가 도치될 때는 「부사구+동사+주어」의 어순으로 써준다.

11 ③ 부정어 도치구문의 어순: 부정어 + have[has/had] + 주어 + 과거분사
　① 문장의 주어가 인기있는 레스토랑들 중 하나를 가리키는 One이므로 동사의 단수형을 써야 한다. (are → is)
　② Neither A nor B 구문에서는 동사와 더 가깝게 위치하는 B에 따라 동사의 형태를 결정한다. 동사에 더 가까운 the bike가 단수이므로 단수 동사를 쓰는 것이 적절하다. (are → is)
　④ Every에는 단수 명사와 단수 동사가 따라온다. (need → needs)
　⑤ 이유를 묻는 How come 구문에서 어순은 「How come+주어+동사?」를 따른다.
　(is the store → the store is)

12 의문문의 전달 동사는 asked로 바꾸고, 의문사가 없기 때문에 if[whether]로 문장을 연결한다. 인칭 대명사는 전달자가 I이므로 그대로 두고, 시제는 과거시제로, 부사 here는 there로 바꾼다.

13 도로에서 자전거를 타는 것에 여러 번 위험을 느낀 Emily가 필요에 의해서 보호 장치를 발명했다는 내용이므로 '필요는 발명의 어머니이다.'라는 뜻의 'Necessity is the mother of invention.'이 적절하다.

14 부정 명령문을 직접화법에서 간접화법으로 화법 전환

할 때, 부정 명령문의 Don't를 없애고 동사원형을 not to부정사로 바꾼다. 그리고 대명사를 전달하는 사람의 입장으로 바꾸어야 하는데, 시험을 치는 사람이 나 자신이므로 your exam을 my exam으로 바꾸는 것이 적절하다.

엄마는 나에게 "너의 시험을 위해 너무 늦게까지 깨어 있지 말렴."이라고 말했다.

→ 엄마가 나에게 내 시험을 위해 너무 늦게까지 깨어 있지 말라고 말했다.

15 ② to부정사의 부정형은 「not to + 동사원형」의 어순으로 쓴다. (to not → not to)

⑤ 주절의 동사가 said로 과거시제이므로, 종속절의 시제도 과거나 과거완료를 써야 한다. will의 과거형인 would로 고쳐야 한다. (will → would)

① '내가 너에게 말한 것을 듣지 못했니?'라고 묻고 있으므로 선행사를 포함한 관계대명사 what(~하는 것)의 쓰임은 적절하다.

③ '같이 농구를 하기 위해서'라는 목적을 나타내는 to부정사의 부사적 용법으로 알맞게 쓰였다.

④ 목적어 자리에 명사절을 이끄는 접속사 that이 적절하게 쓰였다.

16 (1) 의문사가 있는 의문문의 간접화법은 「주어 + ask + 목적어 + 의문사 + 주어 + 동사」로 쓴다.

(2) 평서문의 간접화법에서 간접화법 부분의 시제는 주절의 시제에 일치시킨다.

17 please가 쓰인 명령문은 간접화법으로 고칠 때 '부탁하다'의 ask를 써서 「ask + 목적어 + to부정사」로 표현한다.

18 「ask + 목적어 + to부정사」 '~에게 …해달라고 부탁하다'

19 그 모임에서 Tim을 만난 지 10년이 흘렀다는 게 믿기지 않고 어제 서로 본 것 같다고 하였으므로 '시간은 쏜살같이 지나간다.'는 의미의 'Time flies like an arrow.'가 알맞다.

20 (a) 부정어(Rarely)가 문장의 맨 앞으로 나오면, 「부정어(Rarely) + 조동사(does) + 주어(Wendy) + 동

사(offer)」의 어순으로 도치된다.

(b) 장소를 나타내는 부사구(In the parking lot)가 앞으로 나오면, 「부사구 + 동사 + 주어」의 어순으로 도치된다.

(e) Here이 문장의 앞으로 나오면, 「Here + 동사 + 주어」의 어순으로 도치된다.

(c) 주어 people이 복수명사이므로 동사도 복수인 are로 써주어야 한다. (is → are)

(d) 장소를 나타내는 부사구(Under the bridge)가 문장의 앞으로 나오면, 「부사구 + 동사 + 주어」의 어순으로 도치된다. (does the stream flow → flows the stream)

21 (1) tell을 say to로 바꾸고 시제를 과거로 일치시킨다.

(2) tell을 say to로 바꾸고 과거형으로 시제를 일치시킨 뒤 부정명령문이므로 Don't를 쓴다.

(3) ask를 say to로 바꾸어 과거시제로 일치시킨 뒤 의문사가 없는 현재완료의 의문문을 쓴다.

22 의문사가 없는 의문문에서 if[whether]는 '~인지 아닌지'의 뜻을 갖는다.

23 ④ 모든 구름의 뒷편은 은빛으로 빛난다. (괴로움 뒤에는 기쁨이 있다.)

24 부정어구가 도치될 때는 「부정어 + 조동사 + 주어 + 동사」의 어순으로 써준다.

25 ③ 부정어가 문장의 맨 앞으로 나오면, 「부정어 + 조동사 + 주어 + 동사」의 어순으로 도치된다. 동사가 과거형이므로, 과거시제를 만들어주는 조동사 did를 주어 I의 앞에 쓰고 동사는 원형으로 바꾼다.

(I did → did I)

①⑤ 부정어가 문장의 맨 앞으로 나오면, 「부정어 + 조동사 + 주어 + 동사」의 어순으로 도치된다.

②④ 장소를 나타내는 부사(구)가 문장의 맨 앞으로 나오면, 「부사구 + 동사 + 주어」의 어순으로 도치된다. 단, 주어가 대명사일 경우에는 주어와 동사의 순서가 바뀌지 않는다.

Ch **17**

일치 · 도치 · 화법 & 속담

Key expression

주요 교과서에 쓰인 260개의 의사소통 표현을 분석하여
가장 많이 쓰인 표현을 선별했습니다.
소리 내어 읽고 연습해보세요.

● 의견 묻기

Did you find the book interesting?

What do you think is the most precious thing in your life?

Which team **do you think** will win the game?

● 의무 표현하기

You're supposed to be quiet here.

You're supposed to hand in your report tomorrow.

You're supposed to clean the room now.

● 이유 말하기

I hurt my arm badly **because of** the accident.

She gets up late in the morning. **That's why** she is always late for school.

● 이해 점검하기

Are you with me?

Are you following me?

Do you know what I mean?

2026 새 교과서에 맞춘 16차 개정판

중학영문법 3800제 2학년

단어·표현 암기장

MOTHERTONGUE
마더텅출판사
since 1999.4.1.

중학영문법 3800제 단어·표현 암기장 활용법

1 중학영문법 3800제 단어·표현 암기장은 한 달 학습 계획(총 31일)으로 구성되어 있습니다.

2 오늘 외울 단어를 원어민 녹음 MP3파일을 활용하여 암기합니다.

3 세트로 구성된 Word Test를 스스로 또는 선생님과 함께 풀어 본 후 단어·표현 암기장을
확인하며 채점합니다. (정답표가 필요하신 경우 마더텅 홈페이지를 통해 다운로드 받으실 수
있습니다. www.toptutor.co.kr)

4 [오늘 외울 단어]로 제공되는 단어들은 3800제 본문에서 선정된 중학 필수 영단어입니다.
빈출 단어의 경우 반복적으로 제시하여 복습이 가능하도록 하였습니다.

5 교재와 함께 시작하여 매일의 학습 단어를 암기해 나가면, 한 달(31일)이면 3800제
주요 단어를 모두 학습할 수 있습니다.

중학영문법 3800제 2학년
단어·표현 암기장

Problem Solving Skill

MOTHERTONGUE
마더텅출판사
since 1999.4.1.

Day 01

Chapter 1 문장의 기초

PSS & PRACTICE

☐ 001 **finish** [fíniʃ]	통 끝내다, 끝나다	
☐ 002 **homework** [hóumwə̀ːrk]	명 숙제	
☐ 003 **on time**	시간에 맞게, 정각에	
☐ 004 **pass** [pæs]	통 통과하다, 지나가다	
☐ 005 **exam** [igzǽm]	명 시험	
☐ 006 **draw** [drɔː]	통 그리다, 당기다	
☐ 007 **true** [truː]	형 진실인, 사실인	
☐ 008 **classmate** [klǽsmèit]	명 동급생, 반 친구	
☐ 009 **win** [win]	통 이기다	
☐ 010 **race** [reis]	명 경주	
☐ 011 **feel** [fiːl]	통 (~하다고) 느끼다, (~한) 기분이다	
☐ 012 **during** [djúriŋ]	전 ~ 동안에	
☐ 013 **meeting** [míːtiŋ]	명 회의	
☐ 014 **be good at**	~을 잘하다	
☐ 015 **arrive** [əráiv]	통 도착하다	
☐ 016 **vacation** [veikéiʃən]	명 방학, 휴가	
☐ 017 **exercise** [éksərsàiz]	통 운동하다 / 명 운동, 연습	
☐ 018 **favorite** [féivərit]	형 가장 좋아하는	
☐ 019 **leave** [liːv]	통 떠나다	
☐ 020 **return** [ritə́ːrn]	통 돌아오다	
☐ 021 **without** [wiðáut]	전 ~ 없이	
☐ 022 **taste** [teist]	통 (~한) 맛이 나다, 맛보다	
☐ 023 **prize** [praiz]	명 상	
☐ 024 **guy** [gai]	명 사람, 녀석	
☐ 025 **enter** [éntər]	통 ~에 들어가다	
☐ 026 **take a rest**	휴식을 취하다	
☐ 027 **puppy** [pʌ́pi]	명 강아지	
☐ 028 **healthy** [hélθi]	형 건강한	
☐ 029 **go for a movie**	영화를 보러 가다	
☐ 030 **pay** [pei]	통 지불하다	
☐ 031 **cash** [kæʃ]	명 현금, 돈	
☐ 032 **credit card** [krédit kàːrd]	명 신용카드	
☐ 033 **steak** [steik]	명 스테이크	
☐ 034 **buy** [bai]	통 사다, 구입하다	
☐ 035 **noodle** [núːdl]	명 국수, 면류	

Day 02

☐ 036 **wonder** [wʌ́ndər]	동 궁금해하다, ~이 아닐까 생각하다	☐ 054 **advice** [ədváis]	명 조언, 충고	
☐ 037 **mean** [mi:n]	동 의미하다, 의도하다	☐ 055 **ask** [æsk]	동 묻다, 요청하다	
☐ 038 **important** [impɔ́:rtnt]	형 중요한	☐ 056 **question** [kwéstʃən]	명 질문, 문제	
☐ 039 **break** [breik]	동 깨뜨리다, 부수다	☐ 057 **interesting** [íntərèstiŋ]	형 흥미 있는, 재미있는	
☐ 040 **date** [deit]	동 데이트하다 명 날짜	☐ 058 **suddenly** [sʌ́dnli]	부 갑자기	
☐ 041 **yesterday** [jéstərdèi]	부 명 어제	☐ 059 **quiet** [kwaiət]	형 조용한	
☐ 042 **think** [θiŋk]	동 (~라고) 생각하다	☐ 060 **turn** [tə:rn]	동 ~로 바뀌다, 돌리다	
☐ 043 **believe** [bilí:v]	동 믿다	☐ 061 **grow** [grou]	동 ~하게 되다, 자라다	
☐ 044 **right** [rait]	형 바른, 옳은	☐ 062 **special** [spéʃəl]	형 특별한, 특수한	
☐ 045 **solve** [salv]	동 풀다, 해결하다	☐ 063 **rest** [rest]	명 휴식, 안정 동 쉬다	
☐ 046 **problem** [prábləm]	명 문제	☐ 064 **seem** [si:m]	동 ~처럼 보이다	
☐ 047 **lose** [lu:z]	동 잃다, (게임, 경기에) 지다	☐ 065 **carry** [kǽri]	동 나르다, 운반하다	
☐ 048 **creative** [kriéitiv]	형 창조적인, 독창적인	☐ 066 **appear** [əpíər]	동 ~인 듯하다, 나타나다	
☐ 049 **patient** [péiʃənt]	형 참을성 있는, 끈기 있는	☐ 067 **treat** [tri:t]	동 대우하다, 다루다	
☐ 050 **humid** [hjú:mid]	형 습기 있는	☐ 068 **sour** [sáuər]	형 신, 시큼한	
☐ 051 **terrible** [térəbl]	형 끔찍한, 서투른	☐ 069 **strange** [streindʒ]	형 이상한	
☐ 052 **friendly** [fréndli]	형 정다운, 친절한	☐ 070 **lend** [lend]	동 빌려주다	
☐ 053 **polite** [pəláit]	형 예의 바른, 공손한	☐ 071 **bring** [briŋ]	동 가져오다	

□ 072 **history** [hístəri]	명 역사	
□ 073 **surprising** [sərpráiziŋ]	형 놀라운	
□ 074 **price** [prais]	명 가격	
□ 075 **difficult** [dífikʌlt]	형 어려운, 곤란한	
□ 076 **dictionary** [díkʃənèri]	명 사전	
□ 077 **regularly** [régjələrli]	부 규칙적으로, 정기적으로	
□ 078 **temperature** [témpərətʃər]	명 온도	
□ 079 **rule** [ru:l]	명 규칙	
□ 080 **shake** [ʃeik]	동 흔들리다, 흔들다	
□ 081 **bark** [ba:rk]	동 짖다	
□ 082 **shout** [ʃaut]	동 소리치다, 외치다	
□ 083 **remember** [rimémbər]	동 기억하다	
□ 084 **consider** [kənsídər]	동 고려하다	
□ 085 **touch** [tʌtʃ]	동 건드리다, 만지다	
□ 086 **dimple** [dímpl]	명 보조개	

🧍 중간기말대비

□ 087 **prefer** [prifə́:r]	동 ~을 (더) 좋아하다	
□ 088 **laptop** [læptap]	명 휴대용 컴퓨터, 노트북 컴퓨터	

□ 089 **happen** [hǽpən]	동 (일이) 발생하다	
□ 090 **unkind** [ʌnkáind]	형 불쾌한, 불친절한	
□ 091 **awesome** [ɔ́:səm]	형 경탄할 만한	
□ 092 **famous** [féiməs]	형 유명한	
□ 093 **inventor** [invéntər]	명 발명가	
□ 094 **invent** [invént]	동 발명하다	
□ 095 **include** [inklú:d]	동 포함하다	
□ 096 **bulb** [bʌlb]	명 전구	
□ 097 **typewriter** [táipràitər]	명 타자기	
□ 098 **phonograph** [fóunəgræf]	명 축음기	
□ 099 **iron** [áiərn]	명 철, 쇠, 다리미	
□ 100 **smile at**	~에게 미소를 짓다	
□ 101 **fall on the ground**	땅에 떨어지다	
□ 102 **grade** [greid]	명 성적, 학년, 등급	
□ 103 **look like**	~처럼 보이다[생기다]	
□ 104 **upset** [ʌpsét]	형 속상한, 화가 난	
□ 105 **throw** [θrou]	동 던지다	
□ 106 **bullet** [búlit]	명 총알	

☐ 107 **sleepy** [slí:pi]	형 졸린	
☐ 108 **warm** [wɔːrm]	형 따뜻한	
☐ 109 **bitter** [bítər]	형 맛이 쓴	
☐ 110 **diligent** [dílidʒənt]	형 성실한	
☐ 111 **semester** [siméstər]	명 학기	
☐ 112 **physics** [fíziks]	명 물리학	
☐ 113 **chemistry** [kémistri]	명 화학	
☐ 114 **funny** [fʌ́ni]	형 재미있는, 우스운	
☐ 115 **lonely** [lóunli]	형 외로운	
☐ 116 **scream** [skri:m]	동 소리 지르다	
☐ 117 **delicious** [dilíʃəs]	형 맛있는	
☐ 118 **realistic** [rì(ː)əlístik]	형 현실적인	
☐ 119 **neat** [niːt]	형 정돈된	
☐ 120 **all the time**	항상	
☐ 121 **spotlessly** [spátlisli]	부 아주 깨끗하게	
☐ 122 **big hand** [big hænd]	큰 박수	
☐ 123 **cheerful** [tʃíərfəl]	형 발랄한	
☐ 124 **inside** [insáid]	전 ~의 안[속/내부]에	

☐ 125 **mine** [main]	명 광산
☐ 126 **serious** [sí(ː)əriəs]	형 심각한, 진지한

Chapter 2 시제

🚶 **PSS & PRACTICE**

☐ 127 **relax** [rilǽks]	동 휴식을 취하다, 느긋하게 쉬다
☐ 128 **copy** [kápi]	동 복사하다
☐ 129 **depart** [dipá:rt]	동 출발하다
☐ 130 **reward** [riwɔ́:rd]	동 보답하다, 보상하다
☐ 131 **bite** [bait]	동 물다
☐ 132 **breathe** [briːð]	동 숨 쉬다, 호흡하다
☐ 133 **destroy** [distrɔ́i]	동 파괴하다
☐ 134 **prove** [pruːv]	동 입증하다, 증명하다
☐ 135 **reduce** [ridúːs]	동 줄이다
☐ 136 **complain** [kəmpléin]	동 불평하다
☐ 137 **raise** [reiz]	동 올리다, 기르다
☐ 138 **shoot** [ʃuːt]	동 (총, 화살을) 쏘다
☐ 139 **lift** [lift]	동 들어 올리다
☐ 140 **bear** [bɛər]	동 (아이를) 낳다, 견디다

141 **elect** [ilékt]	통 선출하다
142 **recycle** [riːsáikl]	통 재활용하다
143 **recommend** [rèkəménd]	통 추천하다
144 **exchange** [ikstʃéindʒ]	통 교환하다
145 **interview** [íntərvjùː]	통 면접을 보다 명 면접
146 **allow** [əláu]	통 허락하다
147 **marry** [mǽri]	통 ~와 결혼하다
148 **pray** [prei]	통 기원하다, 기도하다
149 **rescue** [réskjuː]	통 구조하다, 구하다
150 **vow** [vau]	통 맹세하다
151 **mention** [ménʃən]	통 언급하다
152 **imagine** [imǽdʒin]	통 상상하다
153 **lead** [liːd]	통 인도하다, 안내하다
154 **fight** [fait]	통 싸우다
155 **wrap** [ræp]	통 싸다, 포장하다
156 **flow** [flou]	통 (액체, 기체, 전류가) 흐르다
157 **argue** [ɑ́ːrgjuː]	통 논하다, 언쟁하다
158 **produce** [prədjúːs]	통 생산하다

159 **serve** [səːrv]	통 제공하다, 차려 주다
160 **add** [æd]	통 더하다
161 **discover** [diskʌ́vər]	통 발견하다
162 **admire** [ədmáiər]	통 감탄하다, 존경하다
163 **sink** [siŋk]	통 가라앉다
164 **quit** [kwit]	통 그만두다
165 **stretch** [stretʃ]	통 늘이다, 늘어나다
166 **suppose** [səpóuz]	통 ~라고 가정하다
167 **beat** [biːt]	통 치다, 두드리다
168 **hatch** [hætʃ]	통 (알을) 까다, 부화하다
169 **describe** [diskráib]	통 묘사하다
170 **appreciate** [əpríːʃieit]	통 고마워하다
171 **close** [klouz]	통 닫다
172 **in need**	어려움에 처한
173 **pick** [pik]	통 따다, 고르다
174 **dig** [dig]	통 (땅을) 파다
175 **push** [puʃ]	통 밀다
176 **spill** [spil]	통 엎지르다, 쏟다

☐ 177 **publish** [pʌ́bliʃ] — 통 공표하다, 출판하다

☐ 178 **select** [silékt] — 통 고르다, 선택하다

☐ 179 **dictate** [díkteit] — 통 받아쓰게 하다

☐ 180 **consist** [kənsíst] — 통 ~로 이루어져 있다

☐ 181 **drop** [drɑp] — 통 떨어뜨리다, 떨어지다

☐ 182 **fix** [fiks] — 통 수리하다

☐ 183 **tease** [ti:z] — 통 괴롭히다, 놀리다

☐ 184 **rise** [raiz] — 통 (해, 달이) 뜨다, 오르다

☐ 185 **indeed** [indí:d] — 부 실로, 참으로

☐ 186 **around** [əráund] — 전 ~의 주위에

☐ 187 **blame** [bleim] — 통 비난하다

☐ 188 **tool** [tu:l] — 명 연장, 도구

☐ 189 **pull** [pul] — 통 당기다

☐ 190 **delay** [diléi] — 통 늦추다, 미루다

☐ 191 **pop** [pɑp] — 통 튀어나오다

☐ 192 **offer** [ɔ́:fər] — 통 제공하다, 제안하다

☐ 193 **rip** [rip] — 통 찢다

☐ 194 **judge** [dʒʌdʒ] — 통 재판하다, 판단하다

☐ 195 **notice** [nóutis] — 통 주의하다, 인지하다

☐ 196 **rush** [rʌʃ] — 통 돌진하다, 서두르다

☐ 197 **kick** [kik] — 통 발로 차다

☐ 198 **collect** [kəlékt] — 통 모으다, 수집하다

☐ 199 **practice** [prǽktis] — 통 연습하다, 실행하다

☐ 200 **waste** [weist] — 통 낭비하다

☐ 201 **worry** [wə́:ri] — 통 걱정하다, 걱정하게 만들다

☐ 202 **form** [fɔ:rm] — 통 형성하다

☐ 203 **disappear** [dìsəpíər] — 통 사라지다

☐ 204 **chat** [tʃæt] — 통 수다를 떨다

☐ 205 **realize** [rí:əlàiz] — 통 깨닫다

☐ 206 **bow** [bau] — 통 숙이다, 절하다

☐ 207 **reply** [riplái] — 통 대답하다 명 대답

☐ 208 **observe** [əbzə́:rv] — 통 관찰하다

☐ 209 **cause** [kɔ:z] — 통 초래하다, 야기하다

☐ 210 **operate** [ɑ́pərèit] — 통 작동하다, 수술을 하다

☐ 211 **control** [kəntróul] — 통 통제하다, 제어하다

☐ 212 **die** [dai] — 통 죽다

□ 213 **report** [ripɔ́:rt] — 图 보고하다 图 보고서

□ 214 **blow** [blou] — 图 (입으로/바람이) 불다

□ 215 **hide** [haid] — 图 숨기다

□ 216 **hold** [hould] — 图 (손에) 들다, 잡다

□ 217 **lay** [lei] — 图 놓다, (알을) 낳다

□ 218 **lie** [lai] — 图 눕다, 놓여 있다

□ 219 **steal** [sti:l] — 图 훔치다

□ 220 **overcome** [òuvərkʌ́m] — 图 극복하다

□ 221 **build** [bild] — 图 짓다, 건설하다

□ 222 **shut** [ʃʌt] — 图 닫다

□ 223 **sweep** [swi:p] — 图 (빗자루로) 쓸다, 털다

□ 224 **be born** — 태어나다

□ 225 **fall down** — 넘어지다, 떨어지다

□ 226 **speech** [spi:tʃ] — 图 말하기, 연설

□ 227 **contest** [kántest] — 图 대회, 시합

□ 228 **show** [ʃou] — 图 보여주다

□ 229 **painting** [péintiŋ] — 图 그림, 회화

□ 230 **housework** [háuswə̀:rk] — 图 집안일

□ 231 **midnight** [mídnait] — 图 한밤중, 자정

□ 232 **follow** [fálou] — 图 따라가다, 따르다

□ 233 **face** [feis] — 图 직면하다, 마주하다

□ 234 **tumble** [tʌ́mbl] — 图 넘어지다, 굴러 떨어지다

□ 235 **join** [dʒɔin] — 图 결합하다, 가입하다, 참여하다

□ 236 **encourage** [inkə́:ridʒ] — 图 격려하다, 장려하다

□ 237 **burn** [bə:rn] — 图 불에 태우다

□ 238 **act** [ækt] — 图 행동하다

□ 239 **celebrate** [séləbreit] — 图 기념하다, 축하하다

□ 240 **deny** [dinái] — 图 부인하다

□ 241 **repeat** [ripí:t] — 图 되풀이하다

□ 242 **hit** [hit] — 图 때리다, 치다

□ 243 **shine** [ʃain] — 图 빛나다

□ 244 **roll** [roul] — 图 구르다

□ 245 **share** [ʃɛər] — 图 함께 나누다, 공유하다

□ 246 **fill** [fil] — 图 채우다

□ 247 **cheat** [tʃi:t] — 图 속이다

□ 248 **remove** [rimú:v] — 图 제거하다

☐ 249 **take a shower**		샤워를 하다
☐ 250 **on one's way to**		~로 가는 도중에
☐ 251 **stand** [stænd]	동	서 있다, 일어서다
☐ 252 **actor** [ǽktər]	명	배우
☐ 253 **parent** [pέ(:)ərənt]	명	부모
☐ 254 **pass away**		사망하다
☐ 255 **hen** [hen]	명	암탉
☐ 256 **plant** [plænt]	명	식물, 초목
☐ 257 **set up**		설비하다, 설치하다
☐ 258 **several** [sévrəl]	형	몇몇의
☐ 259 **popular** [pápjulər]	형	인기 있는
☐ 260 **a lot**		훨씬, 많이
☐ 261 **fable** [féibl]	명	우화
☐ 262 **empty** [émpti]	형	비어 있는
☐ 263 **lately** [léitli]	부	요즘에, 최근에
☐ 264 **pride** [praid]	명	자부심, 자만, 긍지
☐ 265 **prejudice** [prédʒudis]	명	편견, 선입관
☐ 266 **sure** [ʃuər]	형	확신하는, 확실히 아는
☐ 267 **recently** [ríːsəntli]	부	최근에
☐ 268 **nervous** [nə́ːrvəs]	형	불안한, 신경과민의
☐ 269 **useful** [júːsfəl]	형	쓸모 있는, 유용한
☐ 270 **heavily** [hévili]	부	심하게, 대량으로, 무겁게

🏃 중간기말대비

☐ 271 **send** [send]	동	보내다
☐ 272 **spend** [spend]	동	(돈, 시간을) 쓰다
☐ 273 **hurt** [həːrt]	동	다치다, 아프다
☐ 274 **leave for**		~를 향해 떠나다
☐ 275 **flight** [flait]	명	항공편, 항공기
☐ 276 **climbing** [kláimiŋ]	명	등산, 등반
☐ 277 **theater** [θí(:)ətər]	명	극장
☐ 278 **depart from**		~에서 출발하다
☐ 279 **vase** [veis]	명	꽃병
☐ 280 **captain** [kǽptin]	명	선장
☐ 281 **wallet** [wálit]	명	지갑, (서류를 넣는 납작한) 가방
☐ 282 **keep a diary**		일기를 쓰다
☐ 283 **take a nap**		낮잠을 자다

☐ 284 **take care of**	~를 돌보다	
☐ 285 **seed** [siːd]	몧 씨앗	
☐ 286 **bud** [bʌd]	몧 싹, 꽃봉오리	
☐ 287 **mobile phone** [móubəl foun]	몧 휴대 전화기	
☐ 288 **bleed** [bliːd]	동 피를 흘리다	
☐ 289 **thief** [θiːf]	몧 도둑, 절도범	
☐ 290 **escalator** [éskəlèitər]	몧 에스컬레이터	
☐ 291 **department store** [dipάːrtmənt stɔːr]	몧 백화점	
☐ 292 **break into**	몰래 잠입하다	
☐ 293 **statue** [stǽtʃuː]	몧 조각상	
☐ 294 **liberty** [líbərti]	몧 자유	

Chapter 3 조동사

PSS & PRACTICE

☐ 295 **take off**	(옷 등을) 벗다, 벗기다
☐ 296 **go for a walk**	산책 가다
☐ 297 **give an answer**	대답하다
☐ 298 **horror** [hɔ́ːrər]	몧 공포
☐ 299 **truth** [truːθ]	몧 진실

☐ 300 **go on a diet**	다이어트를 하다
☐ 301 **safe** [seif]	형 안전한
☐ 302 **hang** [hæŋ]	동 걸다
☐ 303 **cross** [krɔːs]	동 횡단하다
☐ 304 **first** [fəːrst]	형 첫 번째의
☐ 305 **notebook** [nóutbùk]	몧 공책
☐ 306 **language** [lǽŋgwidʒ]	몧 언어
☐ 307 **find** [faind]	동 찾다
☐ 308 **exit** [égzit]	몧 출구
☐ 309 **pick up**	태우러 가다, 태우다
☐ 310 **carefully** [kɛ́ərfəli]	부 조심스럽게, 신중하게
☐ 311 **feed** [fiːd]	동 먹이를 주다
☐ 312 **walk** [wɔːk]	동 산책시키다, 걷다
☐ 313 **park** [pɑːrk]	동 주차하다
☐ 314 **elderly** [éldərli]	몧 중장년층, 어르신
☐ 315 **zoo** [zuː]	몧 동물원
☐ 316 **university** [jùːnəvə́ːrsəti]	몧 대학교
☐ 317 **dish** [diʃ]	몧 요리, 접시

Day 10

- ☐ 318 **possible** [pásəbl] — 형 가능한
- ☐ 319 **unbelievable** [ʌnbilíːvəbl] — 형 믿을 수 없는
- ☐ 320 **second** [sékənd] — 명 (시간 단위의) 초
- ☐ 321 **memory** [méməri] — 명 기억
- ☐ 322 **certain** [sə́ːrtn] — 형 확신하는, 확실한
- ☐ 323 **bright** [brait] — 형 빛나는, 밝은
- ☐ 324 **future** [fjúːtʃər] — 명 미래
- ☐ 325 **again** [əgén] — 부 이번에도, 디시 한 번
- ☐ 326 **stadium** [stéidiəm] — 명 경기장
- ☐ 327 **kind** [kaind] — 명 유형, 종류
- ☐ 328 **make a noise** — 시끄럽게 하다
- ☐ 329 **school uniform** [skuːl juːnəfɔ́ːrm] — 명 교복
- ☐ 330 **sore** [sɔːr] — 형 아픈, 쓰린
- ☐ 331 **throat** [θrout] — 명 목
- ☐ 332 **midterm** [mídtə̀ːrm] — 명 중간고사
- ☐ 333 **accident** [ǽksidənt] — 명 사고
- ☐ 334 **favor** [féivər] — 명 호의, 친절
- ☐ 335 **do someone a favor** — ~의 부탁을 들어주다

- ☐ 336 **living** [líviŋ] — 명 생계 수단, 생활
- ☐ 337 **turn down** — (소리, 온도 등을) 낮추다
- ☐ 338 **sell** [sel] — 동 팔다
- ☐ 339 **by oneself** — 혼자
- ☐ 340 **salty** [sɔ́ːlti] — 형 짠, 짭짤한

중간기말대비

- ☐ 341 **look around** — 주위를 둘러보다
- ☐ 342 **do one's best** — 최선을 다하다
- ☐ 343 **do well** — 잘하다, 성공하다
- ☐ 344 **near** [niər] — 형 가까운, 근처의
- ☐ 345 **handicapped** [hǽndikæ̀pt] — 형 장애를 가진
- ☐ 346 **koala** [kouáːlə] — 명 코알라
- ☐ 347 **get lost** — 길을 잃다
- ☐ 348 **go out** — 외출하다, 나가다
- ☐ 349 **shopper** [ʃápər] — 명 쇼핑객
- ☐ 350 **errand** [érənd] — 명 심부름
- ☐ 351 **win a prize** — 상을 받다
- ☐ 352 **competition** [kàmpitíʃən] — 명 대회, 경쟁

☐ 353 **turn right** — 우회전하다

Chapter 4 수동태

👤 **PSS & PRACTICE**

☐ 354 **catch** [kætʃ] — 동 잡다

☐ 355 **change** [tʃeindʒ] — 동 바꾸다, 변화시키다

☐ 356 **keep** [ki:p] — 동 가지다, 유지하다

☐ 357 **understand** [ʌndərstǽnd] — 동 이해하다

☐ 358 **bottle** [bátl] — 명 (물체를 담는) 병

☐ 359 **hunter** [hʌ́ntər] — 명 사냥꾼

☐ 360 **hold** [hóuld] — 동 개최하다

☐ 361 **president** [prézidənt] — 명 대통령, 회장

☐ 362 **play** [plei] — 명 연극

☐ 363 **respect** [rispékt] — 동 존경하다

☐ 364 **bill** [bil] — 명 계산서, 청구서

☐ 365 **deliver** [dilívər] — 동 배달하다

☐ 366 **magazine** [mæ̀gəzíːn] — 명 잡지

☐ 367 **cut down** — 베어내다

☐ 368 **lie** [lai] — 명 거짓말 동 거짓말하다

☐ 369 **director** [diréktər] — 명 감독

☐ 370 **forgive** [fərgív] — 동 용서하다

☐ 371 **pollute** [pəlúːt] — 동 오염시키다

☐ 372 **obey** [əbéi] — 동 복종하다, 준수하다

☐ 373 **plan** [plæn] — 명 계획

☐ 374 **prepare** [pripɛ́ər] — 동 준비하다

☐ 375 **task** [tæsk] — 명 직무, 과제

☐ 376 **view** [vjuː] — 명 경치

☐ 377 **resource** [ríːsɔːrs] — 명 자원, 물자

☐ 378 **call** [kɔːl] — 동 ~라고 부르다

☐ 379 **lovely** [lʌ́vli] — 형 사랑스러운, 아름다운

☐ 380 **tear** [tiər] — 명 눈물

☐ 381 **result** [rizʌ́lt] — 명 결과

☐ 382 **joy** [dʒɔi] — 명 기쁨

☐ 383 **word** [wəːrd] — 명 말, 단어

☐ 384 **postpone** [poustpóun] — 동 연기하다, 미루다

☐ 385 **information** [ìnfərméiʃən] — 명 정보

☐ 386 **photocopier** [fóutoukàːpiər] — 명 복사기

☐ 387 **name**
[neim]
동 ~에 이름을 지어주다

🧍 중간기말대비

☐ 388 **principal**
[prínsəpəl]
명 학장, 교장

☐ 389 **rubber**
[rʌ́bər]
명 고무

☐ 390 **release**
[rilíːs]
동 발표하다, 공개하다

☐ 391 **poem**
[póuəm]
명 시

☐ 392 **classroom**
[klǽsrù(ː)m]
명 교실

☐ 393 **ring**
[riŋ]
명 반지

☐ 394 **be held**
열리다, 개최되다

☐ 395 **experiment**
[ikspérəmənt]
명 실험 동 실험하다

☐ 396 **ruin**
[rúːin]
동 망치다

☐ 397 **neighbor**
[néibər]
명 이웃

☐ 398 **surround**
[səráund]
동 둘러싸다

☐ 399 **stamp**
[stæmp]
명 우표

☐ 400 **resemble**
[rizémbl]
동 닮다

☐ 401 **a bunch of**
다수의, 한 묶음의

☐ 402 **suit**
[sjuːt]
동 ~에게 맞다, 어울리다

☐ 403 **rob**
[rɑb]
동 도둑질하다

☐ 404 **personal**
[pə́rsənəl]
형 개인의, 개인적인

☐ 405 **mystery**
[místəri]
명 수수께끼, 불가사의

☐ 406 **canned**
[kænd]
형 통조림으로 된

☐ 407 **conference**
[kánfərəns]
명 회의, 학회

☐ 408 **firefighter**
[fáiərfàitər]
명 소방관

☐ 409 **theory**
[θí(ː)əri]
명 이론

☐ 410 **mayor**
[méiər]
명 시장, 군수

Chapter 5 명사와 관사

👤 **PSS & PRACTICE**

☐ 411 **custom**
[kʌ́stəm]
명 관습, 풍습

☐ 412 **match**
[mætʃ]
명 성냥, 경기, 시합

☐ 413 **penny**
[péni]
명 잔돈, 1페니

☐ 414 **couch**
[kautʃ]
명 긴 의자, 소파

☐ 415 **activity**
[æktívəti]
명 활동

☐ 416 **donkey**
[dɔ́ŋki]
명 당나귀

☐ 417 **culture**
[kʌ́ltʃər]
명 문화

☐ 418 **factory**
[fǽktəri]
명 공장

☐ 419 **ferry**
[féri]
명 나룻배, 여객선

☐ 420 **community** [kəmjúːnəti]	명 공동체, 지역사회
☐ 421 **hero** [híːrou]	명 영웅
☐ 422 **mosquito** [məskíːtou]	명 모기
☐ 423 **calf** [kæf]	명 송아지
☐ 424 **safe** [seif]	명 금고 형 안전한
☐ 425 **belief** [bilíːf]	명 믿음, 신조
☐ 426 **chief** [tʃiːf]	명 장(長), 상사
☐ 427 **sheep** [ʃiːp]	명 양
☐ 428 **ox** [ɑks]	명 황소
☐ 429 **emergency** [imə́ːrdʒənsi]	명 비상사태
☐ 430 **audience** [ɔ́ːdiəns]	명 청중
☐ 431 **furniture** [fə́ːrnitʃər]	명 가구
☐ 432 **knowledge** [nɑ́lidʒ]	명 지식
☐ 433 **kindness** [káindnis]	명 친절, 호의
☐ 434 **across** [əkrɔ́ːs]	전 ~을 가로질러
☐ 435 **while** [wail]	접 ~하는 동안
☐ 436 **express** [iksprés]	동 표현하다
☐ 437 **beauty** [bjúːti]	명 아름다움
☐ 438 **subject** [sʌ́bdʒikt]	명 주제
☐ 439 **support** [səpɔ́ːrt]	동 후원하다, 지탱하다
☐ 440 **take part in**	참여하다
☐ 441 **go on a trip**	여행을 가다
☐ 442 **cheerful** [tʃíərfəl]	형 쾌활한
☐ 443 **autumn** [ɔ́ːtəm]	명 가을
☐ 444 **downtown** [dàuntáun]	형 도심지의 명 도심지
☐ 445 **honesty** [ɑ́nisti]	명 정직
☐ 446 **policy** [pɑ́ləsi]	명 정책
☐ 447 **death** [déθ]	명 죽음
☐ 448 **look forward to**	~을 고대하다
☐ 449 **economics** [ìːkənɑ́miks]	명 경제학
☐ 450 **politics** [pɑ́litiks]	명 정치학, 정치
☐ 451 **customs** [kʌ́stəmz]	명 세관
☐ 452 **means** [miːnz]	명 수단, 방법
☐ 453 **earthquake** [ə́ːrθkwèik]	명 지진
☐ 454 **shocking** [ʃɑ́kiŋ]	형 충격적인
☐ 455 **tax** [tæks]	명 세금

Day 14

- ☐ 456 **goods** [gudz] — 명 상품, 물품
- ☐ 457 **foreign** [fɔ́:rən] — 형 외국의
- ☐ 458 **government** [ɡʌ́vərnmənt] — 명 정부
- ☐ 459 **interest** [íntrest] — 동 흥미를 끌다 / 명 흥미, 관심
- ☐ 460 **handmade** [hǽndméid] — 형 손으로 만든
- ☐ 461 **walk** [wɔ:k] — 명 산책
- ☐ 462 **niece** [ni:s] — 명 여자 조카
- ☐ 463 **bottom** [bátəm] — 명 바닥
- ☐ 464 **report card** [ripɔ́:rt kà:rd] — 명 성적표
- ☐ 465 **blanket** [blǽŋkit] — 명 담요
- ☐ 466 **fact** [fækt] — 명 사실
- ☐ 467 **borrow** [bárou] — 동 빌리다
- ☐ 468 **impossible** [impásəbl] — 형 불가능한
- ☐ 469 **unique** [ju:ní:k] — 형 독특한
- ☐ 470 **in a moment** — 곧, 바로
- ☐ 471 **feather** [féðər] — 명 깃털
- ☐ 472 **flock** [flɑk] — 명 떼, 무리 / 동 모이다
- ☐ 473 **whale** [hweil] — 명 고래

- ☐ 474 **capital** [kǽpitl] — 명 (국가의) 수도
- ☐ 475 **flat** [flæt] — 형 평평한
- ☐ 476 **spaceship** [spéisʃip] — 명 우주선
- ☐ 477 **psychology** [saikálədʒi] — 명 심리학, 심리
- ☐ 478 **very** [véri] — 부 매우
- ☐ 479 **row** [rou] — 명 열, 줄
- ☐ 480 **the other day** — 일전에, 며칠 전에
- ☐ 481 **stranger** [stréindʒər] — 명 낯선 사람
- ☐ 482 **sailor** [séilər] — 명 선원, 뱃사람
- ☐ 483 **carelessly** [kɛ́ərlisli] — 부 부주의하게, 무심코
- ☐ 484 **comfortable** [kʌ́mfərtəbl] — 형 편안한
- ☐ 485 **retire** [ritáiər] — 동 퇴직하다
- ☐ 486 **scenery** [sí:nəri] — 명 풍경
- ☐ 487 **professor** [prəfésər] — 명 교수
- ☐ 488 **lesson** [lésn] — 명 수업, 교훈
- ☐ 489 **tend to** — ~하는 경향이 있다

중간기말대비

- ☐ 490 **toast** [toust] — 동 (빵을) 노르스름하게 굽다

Day 15

오늘 외울 단어 **34개**

☐ 491 **piece** [pi:s] 명 조각

☐ 492 **title** [táitl] 명 제목

☐ 493 **faithful** [féiθfəl] 형 충성스러운

☐ 494 **slice** [slais] 명 (얇게 썬) 조각

☐ 495 **bowl** [boul] 명 사발, 공기

☐ 496 **loaf** [louf] 명 (빵의) 덩어리

☐ 497 **pound** [paund] 명 (중량의 단위) 파운드

☐ 498 **pork** [pɔ:rk] 명 돼지고기

☐ 499 **master** [mǽstər] 동 ~에 통달하다

☐ 500 **set foot on** ~에 발을 딛다

☐ 501 **spoonful** [spú:nfùl] 명 숟가락으로 하나

☐ 502 **honest** [ánist] 형 정직한

☐ 503 **noisy** [nɔ́izi] 형 시끄러운

☐ 504 **loudly** [láudli] 부 큰소리로, 소란스럽게

☐ 505 **fail** [feil] 동 실패하다

☐ 506 **plain** [plein] 형 있는 그대로의

☐ 507 **black pepper** [blǽk pépər] 명 (검은) 후추

☐ 508 **cucumber** [kjú:kʌmbər] 명 오이

☐ 509 **grind** [graind] 동 (잘게) 갈다

☐ 510 **stir** [stə:r] 동 젓다, 섞다

☐ 511 **season** [sí:zən] 동 양념하다

☐ 512 **refrigerate** [rifrídʒərèit] 동 냉장하다

☐ 513 **at least** 적어도

☐ 514 **marathon** [mǽrəθàn] 명 마라톤

☐ 515 **ignore** [ignɔ́:r] 동 무시하다

☐ 516 **innocent** [ínəsənt] 형 순수한, 순결한, 결백한

Chapter 6 대명사

PSS & PRACTICE

☐ 517 **lawyer** [lɔ́:jər] 명 변호사

☐ 518 **through** [θru:] 전 ~을 통하여

☐ 519 **musical instrument** [mjú:zikl ínstrəmənt] 명 악기

☐ 520 **cover** [kʌ́vər] 명 표지

☐ 521 **importance** [impɔ́:rtns] 명 중요성

☐ 522 **be proud of** ~을 자랑스러워 하다

☐ 523 **come true** 실현되다

☐ 524 **by accident** 우연히

- ☐ 525 **make oneself at home** 편하게 있다
- ☐ 526 **introduce** [ìntrədjúːs] 图 소개하다
- ☐ 527 **mirror** [mírər] 명 거울
- ☐ 528 **degree** [digríː] 명 (온도, 각도 단위) 도, 정도
- ☐ 529 **fiction** [fíkʃən] 명 소설, 허구
- ☐ 530 **disappointing** [dìsəpɔ́intiŋ] 형 실망스러운
- ☐ 531 **expensive** [ikspénsiv] 형 비싼
- ☐ 532 **smoke** [smouk] 图 흡연하디
- ☐ 533 **population** [pàpjuléiʃən] 명 인구
- ☐ 534 **succeed** [səksíːd] 图 성공하다
- ☐ 535 **employee** [implɔ́ii] 명 피고용자, 종업원
- ☐ 536 **balloon** [bəlúːn] 명 풍선
- ☐ 537 **friendship** [fréndʃip] 명 우정
- ☐ 538 **throw away** 내다 버리다
- ☐ 539 **twin** [twin] 명 쌍둥이 중 한 명 / 형 쌍둥이의
- ☐ 540 **chance** [tʃæns] 명 기회
- ☐ 541 **care** [kɛər] 图 신경 쓰다
- ☐ 542 **dozen** [dʌ́zn] 명 12개, 12개짜리 한 묶음

- ☐ 543 **cloth** [klɔːθ] 명 천, 옷감
- ☐ 544 **passenger** [pǽsəndʒər] 명 승객
- ☐ 545 **performance** [pərfɔ́ːrməns] 명 공연, 연주
- ☐ 546 **all of a sudden** 갑자기
- ☐ 547 **correctly** [kəréktli] 부 정확하게, 바르게
- ☐ 548 **wait for** ~를 기다리다
- ☐ 549 **suggestion** [sədʒéstʃən] 명 제안, 의견
- ☐ 560 **drop by** 방문하나, ~에 들르다

🧗 중간기말대비

- ☐ 551 **astronomer** [əstránəmər] 명 천문학자
- ☐ 552 **author** [ɔ́ːθər] 명 저자, 작가
- ☐ 553 **be known for** ~로 알려지다
- ☐ 554 **club** [klʌb] 명 동호회
- ☐ 555 **logo** [lɔ́(ː)gou] 명 상징, 로고
- ☐ 556 **closet** [klázit] 명 옷장
- ☐ 557 **treasure** [tréʒər] 명 보물
- ☐ 558 **example** [igzǽmpl] 명 예, 예시
- ☐ 559 **always** [ɔ́ːlweiz] 부 항상, 늘

☐ 560 **save**
[seiv]
동 구하다, 안전하게 하다

☐ 561 **for sale**
팔려고 내놓은, 판매 중인

☐ 562 **own**
[oun]
형 자기 자신의, 자기 소유의

☐ 563 **umbrella**
[ʌmbrélə]
명 우산

☐ 564 **spicy**
[spáisi]
형 양념 맛이 강한, 매콤한

☐ 565 **minute**
[mínit]
명 (시간 단위의) 분

☐ 566 **astronaut**
[ǽstrənɔ̀ːt]
명 우주비행사

☐ 567 **space**
[speis]
명 우주, 공간

☐ 568 **dentist**
[déntist]
명 치과의사

☐ 569 **lily**
[líli]
명 백합

☐ 570 **fluently**
[flúːəntli]
부 유창하게

☐ 571 **topic**
[tápik]
명 주제, 화제

☐ 572 **same**
[seim]
형 같은

☐ 573 **divide up**
분배하다, 나눠 갖다

☐ 574 **homeroom**
[hóumrù(ː)m]
명 (미국의) 교실

☐ 575 **climate**
[kláimit]
명 기후

☐ 576 **pollution**
[pəlúːʃən]
명 오염

☐ 577 **opinion**
[əpínjən]
명 의견

☐ 578 **stare at**
빤히 쳐다보다

☐ 579 **break down**
고장 나다

☐ 580 **purple**
[pə́ːrpl]
형 자주색의, 보라색의

☐ 581 **be afraid of**
〜을 두려워하다

☐ 582 **tiny**
[táini]
형 아주 작은

☐ 583 **blind**
[blaind]
명 (창문에 치는) 블라인드

☐ 584 **glove**
[glʌv]
명 장갑

☐ 585 **entertainer**
[èntərtéinər]
명 연예인

☐ 586 **look after**
〜을 맡다[돌보다]

☐ 587 **set up the tent**
텐트를 치다

☐ 588 **live with**
〜와 함께 살다

☐ 589 **boil**
[bɔil]
동 끓이다, 끓다

☐ 590 **teapot**
[tíːpàːt]
명 찻주전자

☐ 591 **burn**
[bəːrn]
동 타오르다, 타다

☐ 592 **Halloween**
[hæ̀ləwíːn]
명 할로윈

☐ 593 **used to**
〜하곤 했다

☐ 594 **comic book**
[kámik buk]
명 만화책

☐ 595 **violin**
[vàiəlín]
명 바이올린

□ 596 **decide** [disáid]	동 결심하다	□ 612 **final exam** [fáinəl igzǽm]	명 기말고사
□ 597 **matter** [mǽtər]	명 문제, 일	□ 613 **surf the Internet**	인터넷 서핑을 하다
□ 598 **jacket** [dʒǽkit]	명 재킷, 상의	□ 614 **windshield** [wíndʃìːld]	명 (자동차의) 앞 유리
□ 599 **cheap** [tʃiːp]	형 저렴한, 싼	□ 615 **nod** [nɑd]	동 (고개를) 끄덕이다

Chapter **7** 부정사

👤 **PSS & PRACTICE**

□ 600 **clearly** [klíərli]	부 또렷하게	□ 616 **lucky** [lʌ́ki]	형 운 좋은
□ 601 **jog** [dʒɑg]	동 조깅하다	□ 617 **pleased** [pliːzd]	형 기쁜
□ 602 **eyesight** [áisàit]	명 시력	□ 618 **surprised** [sərpráizd]	형 놀란
□ 603 **expect** [ikspékt]	동 기대하다, 예상하다	□ 610 **disappointed** [dìsəpɔ́intid]	형 실망한
□ 604 **refuse** [rifjúːz]	동 거절하다, 거부하다	□ 620 **essential** [isénʃl]	형 필수적인, 없어서는 안 될
□ 605 **musician** [mjuːzíʃən]	명 음악가	□ 621 **trust** [trʌst]	동 믿다, 신뢰하다
□ 606 **protect** [prətékt]	동 보호하다	□ 622 **college** [kɑ́lidʒ]	명 대학, 단과대학
□ 607 **garage sale** [gərɑ́ːdʒ seil]	명 차고에서 하는 중고품 세일	□ 623 **reach** [riːtʃ]	동 도달하다, 도착하다
□ 608 **repair** [ripέər]	동 수리하다	□ 624 **shelf** [ʃelf]	명 선반
□ 609 **explain** [ikspléin]	동 설명하다	□ 625 **attract** [ətrǽkt]	동 유인하다, 끌어당기다
□ 610 **crop** [krɑp]	명 농작물	□ 626 **butterfly** [bʌ́tərflài]	명 나비
□ 611 **enough** [inʌ́f]	형 충분한	□ 627 **generous** [dʒénərəs]	형 관대한
		□ 628 **confusing** [kənfjúːziŋ]	형 혼란시키는
		□ 629 **upstairs** [ʌ́pstέərz]	부 위층으로, 위층에(서)

□ 630 **ring** [riŋ] 통 (벨, 종이) 울리다

🧍 중간기말대비

□ 631 **library** [láibrèri] 명 도서관

□ 632 **post office** [poust ɔ́(:)fis] 명 우체국

□ 633 **pass the exam** 시험을 통과하다

□ 634 **business** [bíznis] 명 사업, 업무

□ 635 **course** [kɔːrs] 명 강의, 강좌

□ 636 **have dinner** 저녁 식사를 하다

□ 637 **get up early** 일찍 일어나다

□ 638 **table tennis** [téibl ténis] 명 탁구

□ 639 **dangerous** [déindʒərəs] 형 위험한

□ 640 **deep** [diːp] 형 깊은

□ 641 **helpful** [hélpfəl] 형 도움이 되는

□ 642 **mask** [mæsk] 명 가면, 복면

□ 643 **apologize** [əpɑ́lədʒàiz] 통 사과하다

□ 644 **proud** [praud] 형 거만한, 자랑스러워하는

□ 645 **end** [end] 통 끝나다, 끝내다

□ 646 **license** [láisəns] 명 면허증

□ 647 **saving** [séiviŋ] 명 예금, 저금, 절약

Chapter 8 동명사

🧍 PSS & PRACTICE

□ 648 **depress** [diprés] 통 우울하게 하다

□ 649 **design** [dizáin] 통 디자인하다 명 디자인

□ 650 **refresh** [rifréʃ] 통 상쾌하게 하다

□ 651 **effort** [éfərt] 명 노력

□ 652 **outside** [áutsàid] 부 밖에서, 옥외로

□ 653 **countryside** [kʌ́ntrisàid] 명 시골, 지방

□ 654 **mind** [maind] 통 신경 쓰다, 꺼려하다

□ 655 **put off** 연기하다, 미루다

□ 656 **dislike** [disláik] 통 싫어하다

□ 657 **dolphin** [dɑ́lfin] 명 돌고래

□ 658 **skip** [skip] 통 거르다, 건너뛰다

□ 659 **continue** [kəntínjuː] 통 계속하다

□ 660 **chairman** [tʃɛ́ərmən] 명 의장, 회장

□ 661 **trash** [træʃ] 명 쓰레기

□ 662 **for a while** 잠시 동안

- □ 663 **fill up** — (~로) 가득 차다, 채우다
- □ 664 **gas station** [gǽs stèiʃən] — 명 주유소
- □ 665 **in the end** — 결국에
- □ 666 **responsible** [rispánsəbl] — 형 책임이 있는
- □ 667 **care for** — ~을 돌보다
- □ 668 **prevent** [privént] — 동 막다, 방해하다
- □ 669 **illness** [ílnis] — 명 병, 질환
- □ 670 **ignorant** [ígnərənt] — 형 무식한, 무지한
- □ 671 **major** [méidʒər] — 명 전공, 전공자 / 동 전공하다
- □ 672 **laugh** [læf] — 동 (소리 내어) 웃다

중간기말대비

- □ 673 **usually** [júːʒuəli] — 부 보통, 대개
- □ 674 **interrupt** [ìntərápt] — 동 ~을 방해하다
- □ 675 **grow up** — 자라다, 성장하다
- □ 676 **plant** [plænt] — 동 (나무, 씨앗 등을) 심다
- □ 677 **recent** [ríːsnt] — 형 최근의
- □ 678 **turn on** — (전등, 기계 등을) 켜다
- □ 679 **schedule** [skédʒuːl] — 명 일정, 스케줄

- □ 680 **fall in love** — 사랑에 빠지다
- □ 681 **upgrade** [ápgrèid] — 동 (기계 등을) 개선하다
- □ 682 **postcard** [póustkàːrd] — 명 엽서
- □ 683 **difficulty** [dífikʌ̀lti] — 명 어려움, 곤경
- □ 684 **take a walk** — 산책하다
- □ 685 **dessert** [dizə́ːrt] — 명 디저트, 후식
- □ 686 **violate** [váiəlèit] — 동 위반하다, 어기다
- □ 687 **traffic** [trǽfik] — 명 교통
- □ 688 **regulation** [règjuléiʃən] — 명 규정
- □ 689 **balanced** [bǽlənst] — 형 균형 잡힌
- □ 690 **debate** [dibéit] — 명 토론, 토의
- □ 691 **pocket money** [pákit mʌ́ni] — 명 용돈
- □ 692 **package** [pǽkidʒ] — 명 소포, 포장물

Chapter 9 분사

PSS & PRACTICE

- □ 693 **fall** [fɔːl] — 동 떨어지다
- □ 694 **depressing** [diprésiŋ] — 형 우울하게 하는
- □ 695 **boiled** [bɔild] — 형 삶은, 끓은

□ 696 **be filled with** ~로 가득 차다

□ 697 **gym** [dʒim] 명 체육관

□ 698 **stage** [steidʒ] 명 무대, 단계

□ 699 **run away** 도망치다

□ 700 **frying pan** [fráiŋ pæ̀n] 명 후라이팬

□ 701 **drinking water** [dríŋkiŋ wɔ́:tər] 명 식수

□ 702 **satisfy** [sǽtisfài] 동 만족시키다

□ 703 **embarrass** [imbǽrəs] 동 당황스럽게 하다

□ 704 **move** [mu:v] 동 감동시키다

□ 705 **amaze** [əméiz] 동 놀라게 하다

□ 706 **puzzle** [pʌ́zl] 동 곤혹하게 하다, 어리둥절하게 하다

□ 707 **essay** [ései] 명 에세이, 수필

□ 708 **public** [pʌ́blik] 명 대중 형 공공의

□ 709 **festival** [féstivl] 명 축제

□ 710 **by mistake** 실수로

□ 711 **beside** [bisáid] 전 ~ 곁[옆]에

□ 712 **cross** [krɔ:s] 동 교차시키다, 건너다, 가로지르다

□ 713 **clean up** ~을 치우다, 청소하다

□ 714 **tie** [tai] 동 묶다, 매다

중간기말대비

□ 715 **excited** [iksáitid] 형 신이 난, 들뜬

□ 716 **beach** [bi:tʃ] 명 해변, 바닷가

□ 717 **shed** [ʃed] 동 (피, 눈물 등을) 흘리다

□ 718 **pot** [pɑt] 명 냄비, 솥

□ 719 **restroom** [réstrùm] 명 화장실

□ 720 **grass** [græs] 명 잔디, 풀

□ 721 **fantastic** [fæntǽstik] 형 환상적인

□ 722 **fall asleep** 잠들다

□ 723 **owner** [óunər] 명 주인, 소유주

□ 724 **after all** 결국에는

□ 725 **holiday** [hálədèi] 명 휴가, 방학

□ 726 **amusement park** [əmjú:zmənt pɑ:rk] 명 놀이공원

□ 727 **type** [taip] 명 유형, 종류

□ 728 **cartoon** [kɑːrtúːn] 명 (시사 풍자) 만화

Chapter 10 형용사

PSS & PRACTICE

☐ 729 **alive**
[əláiv]
형 살아 있는

☐ 730 **ashamed**
[əʃéimd]
형 부끄러워하는, 수치스러운

☐ 731 **necklace**
[nékləs]
명 목걸이

☐ 732 **intelligent**
[intélidʒənt]
형 지적인, 총명한

☐ 733 **impressive**
[imprésiv]
형 인상적인, 인상 깊은

☐ 734 **starfish**
[stá:rfiʃ]
명 불가사리

☐ 735 **scared**
[skɛərd]
형 겁에 질린

☐ 736 **handsome**
[hǽnsəm]
형 잘생긴

☐ 737 **familiar**
[fəmíljər]
형 잘 아는, 익숙한

☐ 738 **rich**
[ritʃ]
형 부유한, 돈 많은

☐ 739 **blind**
[blaind]
형 눈이 먼

☐ 740 **deaf**
[def]
형 귀가 먼

☐ 741 **brave**
[breiv]
형 용감한

☐ 742 **intonation**
[ìntənéiʃən]
명 억양

☐ 743 **metal**
[métl]
명 금속

☐ 744 **million**
[míljən]
형 100만의 명 100만

☐ 745 **plenty**
[plénti]
명 많음, 풍부

☐ 746 **chapter**
[tʃǽptər]
명 (책의) 장

☐ 747 **except**
[iksépt]
전 ~을 제외하고

☐ 748 **unpleasant**
[ʌnpléznt]
형 불쾌한

🏃 중간기말대비

☐ 749 **fitness center**
[fítnəs sèntər]
명 피트니스 센터, 헬스클럽

☐ 750 **trendy**
[tréndi]
형 최신 유행의

☐ 751 **refrigerator**
[rifrídʒərèitər]
명 냉장고

☐ 752 **daughter**
[dɔ́:tər]
명 딸

☐ 763 **collection**
[kəlékʃən]
명 수집품, 소장품

☐ 754 **proverb**
[právə:rb]
명 속담

☐ 755 **wrong**
[rɔ(:)ŋ]
형 틀린, 잘못된

☐ 756 **gain weight**
체중이 증가하다

☐ 757 **get stressed**
스트레스를 받다

☐ 758 **asleep**
[əslí:p]
형 잠이 든

☐ 759 **alike**
[əláik]
형 비슷한

☐ 760 **experience**
[ikspíriəns]
명 경험

☐ 761 **depressed**
[diprést]
형 우울한

Chapter 11 부사

🚶 PSS & PRACTICE

762 **sudden** [sʌ́dn]	형 갑작스러운, 뜻밖의	
763 **final** [fáinl]	형 마지막의, 결정적인	
764 **sincere** [sinsíər]	형 진실한, 진심의	
765 **slight** [slait]	형 약간의, 근소한	
766 **gentle** [dʒéntl]	형 온화한, 친절한	
767 **simple** [símpl]	형 간단한, 단순한	
768 **reasonable** [ríːznəbl]	형 합리적인, 타당한	
769 **visible** [vízəbl]	형 눈에 보이는	
770 **anxious** [ǽŋkʃəs]	형 불안해하는, 염려하는	
771 **last** [læst]	동 지속되다	
772 **closely** [klóusli]	부 주의 깊게, 면밀히	
773 **hardly** [háːrdli]	부 거의 ~ 않다	
774 **highly** [háili]	부 높이 평가하여	
775 **nearly** [níərli]	부 거의, 대략	
776 **shake hands**	악수를 하다	
777 **greet** [griːt]	동 인사하다, 환영하다	
778 **graduate** [grǽdʒuèit]	동 졸업하다	
779 **attend** [əténd]	동 참석하다, 출석하다	

780 **cool** [kuːl]	형 시원한, 서늘한	
781 **mean** [miːn]	형 짓궂은, 비열한	
782 **try on**	입어 보다	
783 **give up**	포기하다	
784 **look for**	~을 찾다	
785 **check out**	(책 등을) 대출하다	
786 **call off**	취소하다	
787 **admission** [ædmíʃən]	명 입장(료)	

🧍 **중간기말대비**

788 **slow** [slou]	형 느린, 더딘	
789 **easily** [íːzəli]	부 쉽게, 용이하게	
790 **take out**	(안에서 밖으로) 꺼내다	
791 **still** [stil]	부 여전히	
792 **deeply** [díːpli]	부 깊게	
793 **impressed** [imprést]	형 감명을 받은	
794 **such** [sətʃ]	대 앞에 이미 언급한, 그런[그러한]	
795 **intention** [inténʃən]	명 의도, 목적	
796 **alcohol** [ǽlkəhɔ̀ːl]	명 술, 알코올	

□ 797 **interview** 〔íntərvjùː〕 명 면접, 인터뷰

□ 798 **successful** 〔səksésfəl〕 형 (어떤 일에) 성공한, 성공적인

□ 799 **station** 〔stéiʃn〕 명 (기차)역, (버스) 정류장

□ 800 **firework** 〔fáiərwɛ̀ːrk〕 명 불꽃놀이, 폭죽

□ 801 **display** 〔displéi〕 명 전시, 표현

□ 802 **cherry blossom** 〔tʃéri blásəm〕 명 벚꽃

□ 803 **bloom** 〔bluːm〕 동 꽃을 피우다

□ 804 **visit** 〔vízit〕 동 방문하다, 찾아가다

□ 805 **pile** 〔pail〕 동 (물건을) 쌓다

□ 806 **bomb** 〔bɑm〕 명 폭탄

□ 807 **explode** 〔iksplóud〕 동 폭발하다

□ 808 **skin** 〔skin〕 명 피부

□ 809 **set up** 건립하다, 수립하다

□ 810 **church** 〔tʃəːrtʃ〕 명 교회

□ 811 **hard** 〔hɑːrd〕 형 열심히 하는, 단단한, 어려운

□ 812 **quickly** 〔kwíkli〕 부 빨리, 빠르게

Chapter 12 가정법

PSS & PRACTICE

□ 813 **be in danger** 위험에 처하다

□ 814 **for free** 공짜로, 무료로

□ 815 **discuss** 〔diskΛs〕 동 토론하다, 논의하다

□ 816 **cell phone** 〔sél fòun〕 명 휴대폰

□ 817 **in fact** 실은, 사실

□ 818 **give someone a ride** ~를 태워주다

□ 819 **youth** 〔juːθ〕 명 청년 시절, 젊음, 젊은이

□ 820 **lecture** 〔léktʃər〕 명 강의, 강연

중간기말대비

□ 821 **be able to** ~을 할 수 있다

□ 822 **pass the test** 시험에 통과하다

□ 823 **lose weight** 살이 빠지다

□ 824 **as if** 마치 ~인 듯이

□ 825 **fly** 〔flai〕 동 날다

□ 826 **item** 〔áitem〕 명 항목, 품목

□ 827 **invite** 〔inváit〕 동 초대하다

□ 828 **let someone know** ~에게 알리다

□ 829 **do the dishes** 설거지하다

Chapter 13 비교구문

PSS & PRACTICE

☐ 830 **thin** [θin]	형	얇은, 가는
☐ 831 **tasty** [téisti]	형	맛있는
☐ 832 **useless** [júːslis]	형	쓸모없는
☐ 833 **exactly** [igzǽktli]	부	정확히, 엄밀하게는
☐ 834 **wet** [wet]	형	젖은
☐ 835 **scary** [skέəri]	형	무서운, 두려운
☐ 836 **curious** [kjúriəs]	형	호기심이 많은, 호기심을 돋우는
☐ 837 **convenient** [kənvíːniənt]	형	편리한, 사용하기 좋은
☐ 838 **foolish** [fúːliʃ]	형	바보 같은
☐ 839 **write back to**		~에게 답장을 쓰다
☐ 840 **mild** [maild]	형	온화한, 순한, 따뜻한
☐ 841 **kindly** [káindli]	부	친절하게
☐ 842 **count** [kaunt]	동	세다, 계산하다
☐ 843 **weigh** [wei]	동	무게가 ~ 나가다
☐ 844 **per** [pəːr]	전	~마다, ~당
☐ 845 **active** [ǽktiv]	형	활동적인, 적극적인
☐ 846 **version** [vɚːrʒən]	명	개작, 각색

☐ 847 **article** [áːrtikl]	명	글, 기사
☐ 848 **boring** [bɔ́ːriŋ]	형	재미없는, 지루한
☐ 849 **invention** [invénʃən]	명	발명품, 발명
☐ 850 **transportation** [trænspɚrtéiʃn]	명	수송, 운송기관

중간기말대비

☐ 851 **product** [prádəkt]	명	생산물, 상품
☐ 852 **save** [seiv]	동	아끼다, 절약하다
☐ 853 **especially** [ispéʃəli]	부	특히
☐ 854 **elephant** [éləfənt]	명	코끼리
☐ 855 **giraffe** [dʒərǽf]	명	기린
☐ 856 **turtle** [tɚːrtl]	명	거북
☐ 857 **lifespan** [láifspæn]	명	수명
☐ 858 **height** [hait]	명	높이, 키
☐ 859 **fame** [feim]	명	명성
☐ 860 **wise** [waiz]	형	현명한
☐ 861 **pale** [peil]	형	창백한
☐ 862 **present** [préznt]	명	선물

Chapter **14** 관계사

PSS & PRACTICE

863 **sharp** [ʃɑːrp]	형 날카로운, 예리한
864 **belong to**	~에 속하다, ~의 것이다
865 **judge** [dʒʌdʒ]	명 판사
866 **suggest** [sədʒést]	동 제안하다, 추천하다
867 **pocket** [pɑ́kit]	명 주머니
868 **stove** [stouv]	명 가스레인지, 화로
869 **disappoint** [dìsəpɔ́int]	동 실망시키다
870 **on sale**	할인 중인
871 **reason** [ríːzn]	명 이유, 동기
872 **chopstick** [tʃɑ́pstìk]	명 젓가락
873 **cancel** [kǽnsəl]	동 취소하다

중간기말대비

874 **person** [pə́ːrsn]	명 사람, 개인
875 **teach** [tiːtʃ]	동 가르치다
876 **eat up**	~을 다 먹다
877 **police officer** [pəlíːs ɔ́(ː)fisər]	명 경찰관
878 **street** [striːt]	명 거리, 도로

879 **award** [əwɔ́ːrd]	동 수여하다
880 **table** [téibl]	명 탁자
881 **technique** [tekníːk]	명 기법, 기술
882 **magic** [mǽdʒik]	명 마술
883 **stone** [stoun]	명 돌, 비석
884 **tomb** [tuːm]	명 무덤
885 **site** [sait]	명 장소, 부지
886 **heritage** [héritidʒ]	명 (국가의) 유산
887 **ginseng** [dʒínseŋ]	명 인삼
888 **environment** [inváiərənmənt]	명 환경
889 **leader** [líːdər]	명 지도자
890 **put out**	(불을) 끄다
891 **do harm**	해를 끼치다
892 **painter** [péintər]	명 화가
893 **focus on**	~에 주력하다, 초점을 맞추다
894 **village** [vílidʒ]	명 마을, 촌락
895 **documentary** [dɑ̀kjəméntəri]	명 다큐멘터리, 기록물
896 **project** [prɑ́dʒekt]	명 과제, 연구

☐ 897 **bake** [beik]	동 (빵 등을) 굽다	☐ 913 **be in trouble**	곤란한 상황에 있다
☐ 898 **earn** [əːrn]	동 (돈을) 벌다, (자질이 되어 무엇을) 받다	☐ 914 **pool** [puːl]	명 수영장, 웅덩이
☐ 899 **BA degree** [biːei digríː]	명 학사 학위	☐ 915 **unhappy** [ʌnhǽpi]	형 불행한
☐ 900 **communicate** [kəmjúːnəkèit]	동 의사소통을 하다	☐ 916 **pity** [píti]	명 유감, 연민
☐ 901 **political** [pəlítikəl]	형 정치적인	☐ 917 **customer** [kʌ́stəmər]	명 손님, 고객
☐ 902 **activist** [ǽktəvist]	명 운동가, 활동가	☐ 918 **quite** [kwait]	부 아주, 꽤, 제법
☐ 903 **lecturer** [léktʃərər]	명 강연가, 강사	☐ 919 **successfully** [səksésfəli]	부 성공적으로
☐ 904 **advertiser** [ǽdvərtàizər]	명 광고인, 광고회사	☐ 920 **instead of**	~ 대신에
☐ 905 **trick** [trik]	명 속임수, 장난	☐ 921 **absent** [ǽbsnt]	형 결석의, 결근의
☐ 906 **dump** [dʌmp]	동 버리다	☐ 922 **traffic jam** [trǽfik dʒǽm]	명 교통 정체
☐ 907 **garbage** [gáːrbidʒ]	명 쓰레기		

Chapter **15** 접속사

👤 **PSS & PRACTICE**

☐ 908 **talk on the phone**	전화로 얘기하다	👤 **중간기말대비**	
☐ 909 **hurry up**	서두르다	☐ 923 **in order to**	~하기 위해
☐ 910 **tonight** [tənáit]	부 오늘밤에	☐ 924 **nutritious** [njuːtríʃəs]	형 영양가 높은
☐ 911 **heavy snow** [hévi snòu]	명 폭설	☐ 925 **ride** [raid]	동 (차량을) 타다
☐ 912 **do the laundry**	빨래를 하다	☐ 926 **roller coaster** [róulər kòustər]	명 롤러코스터
		☐ 927 **wear** [wɛər]	동 입다
		☐ 928 **breakfast** [brékfəst]	명 아침 식사
		☐ 929 **wash one's hair**	머리를 감다

☐ 930 **be compared to** — ~와 비교되다

☐ 931 **western** [wéstərn] — 형 서부의, 서쪽에 위치한

☐ 932 **pass by** — 지나다, 지나치다

☐ 933 **in addition** — 게다가

☐ 934 **luckily** [lʌ́kili] — 부 운 좋게, 다행히도

☐ 935 **concentrate** [kɑ́nsəntrèit] — 동 집중하다

☐ 936 **boss** [bɑs] — 명 상사

☐ 937 **error** [érər] — 명 오류, 실수

☐ 938 **second place** [sékənd pleis] — 명 2등, 준우승

☐ 939 **feeling** [fíːliŋ] — 명 감정, 기분

☐ 940 **eventually** [ivéntʃuəli] — 부 결국

☐ 941 **attain** [ətéin] — 동 이루다, 획득하다

☐ 942 **aim** [eim] — 명 목적, 목표

☐ 943 **order** [ɔ́ːrdər] — 동 주문하다

☐ 944 **substance** [sʌ́bstəns] — 명 물질

☐ 945 **unusual** [ʌnjúːʒuəl] — 형 특이한, 흔치 않은

☐ 946 **adopt** [ədɑ́pt] — 동 입양하다

☐ 947 **resign** [rizáin] — 동 사임하다

☐ 948 **amount** [əmáunt] — 명 양, 액수

Chapter 16 전치사

🚶 **PSS & PRACTICE**

☐ 949 **modern** [mɑ́dərn] — 형 현대적인, 현대의

☐ 950 **sunset** [sʌ́nsèt] — 명 해질녘, 일몰

☐ 951 **discovery** [diskʌ́vəri] — 명 발견, 발견물

☐ 952 **coin** [kɔin] — 명 동전, 주화

☐ 953 **floor** [flɔːr] — 명 마루, 층

☐ 954 **at work** — 일하는 중인, 직장에서

☐ 955 **prison** [prízn] — 명 감옥, 교도소

☐ 956 **middle** [mídl] — 명 중앙 / 형 한가운데의, 중앙의

☐ 957 **plane** [plein] — 명 비행기

☐ 958 **island** [áilənd] — 명 섬

☐ 959 **look up** — (사전에서) 찾아보다

☐ 960 **welcome** [wélkəm] — 동 환영하다 명 환영

☐ 961 **bridge** [bridʒ] — 명 다리

☐ 962 **get out of** — ~에서 나가다, ~에서 내리다

☐ 963 **stair** [stɛər] — 명 계단, 층계

☐ 964 **ladder**
[lǽdər]
명 사다리

☐ 965 **row**
[rou]
동 노를 젓다

☐ 966 **serve**
[səːrv]
동 공을 서브하다

☐ 967 **jump**
[dʒʌmp]
동 뛰다, 뛰어오르다

☐ 968 **rock**
[rɑk]
명 바위

☐ 969 **streetlight**
[stríːtlàit]
명 가로등

☐ 970 **forest**
[fɔ́ːrist]
명 숲

☐ 971 **postbox**
[póustbàks]
명 우체통

☐ 972 **corner**
[kɔ́ːrnər]
명 모퉁이, 구석

☐ 973 **tower**
[tauər]
명 탑

☐ 974 **time difference**
[taim dífərəns]
명 시차

☐ 975 **relationship**
[riléiʃənʃip]
명 관계

☐ 976 **start**
[stɑːrt]
동 출발하다, 떠나다

☐ 977 **be on board**
(배, 비행기 등에)
승선하다, 탑승하다

☐ 978 **flour**
[flauər]
명 밀가루

☐ 979 **traditional**
[trədíʃənl]
형 전통의, 전통적인

☐ 980 **be supposed to**
~하기로 되어 있다

☐ 981 **unlock**
[ʌnlák]
동 (자물쇠를) 열다

☐ 982 **keep in touch**
연락하다

☐ 983 **novel**
[návəl]
명 소설

☐ 984 **in half**
반으로

☐ 985 **manager**
[mǽnidʒər]
명 경영자, 관리자

☐ 986 **sketch**
[sketʃ]
동 스케치하다

☐ 987 **romantic**
[roumǽntik]
형 낭만적인

☐ 988 **manner**
[mǽnər]
명 태도, 몸가짐

☐ 989 **cancer**
[kǽnsər]
명 암

☐ 990 **response**
[rispáns]
명 응답, 반응

☐ 991 **folk music**
[fóuk mjúːzik]
명 민속 음악

☐ 992 **clown**
[klaun]
명 어릿광대

☐ 993 **hunger**
[hʌ́ŋgər]
명 굶주림, 기아

☐ 994 **dressed**
[drest]
형 옷을 입은, 치장한

☐ 995 **in a hurry**
급히, 서둘러

🏃 중간기말대비

☐ 996 **address**
[ǽdres]
명 주소

☐ 997 **stick**
[stik]
동 찌르다,
(풀 따위로) 붙이다

☐ 998 **envelope**
[énvəlòup]
명 봉투

☐ 999 **first language** [fəːrst lǽŋgwidʒ]	명 모국어
☐ 1000 **wild** [waild]	형 야생의
☐ 1001 **bead** [biːd]	명 구슬, 염주
☐ 1002 **frame** [freim]	명 액자, 틀
☐ 1003 **entrance** [éntrəns]	명 입장, 입학
☐ 1004 **federal** [fédərəl]	형 연방 정부의
☐ 1005 **patent** [pǽtnt]	명 특허권
☐ 1006 **emigration** [èməgréiʃən]	명 이민, 이주
☐ 1007 **atomic** [ətámik]	형 원자의, 원자력의
☐ 1008 **participate** [paːrtísəpèit]	동 참가하다, 참여하다
☐ 1009 **ahead** [əhéd]	부 앞으로, 앞에
☐ 1010 **anti** [ǽnti]	전 반대하는, 좋아하지 않는
☐ 1011 **utopian** [juːtóupiən]	형 유토피아적인, 이상적인
☐ 1012 **ideal** [aidí(ː)əl]	형 이상적인, 완벽한
☐ 1013 **existence** [igzístəns]	명 존재, 실재
☐ 1014 **passport** [pǽspɔːrt]	명 여권
☐ 1015 **construct** [kənstrʌ́kt]	동 건설하다
☐ 1016 **flood** [flʌd]	명 홍수

☐ 1017 **due** [djuː]	형 ~하기로 예정된

Chapter 17 일치 · 도치 · 화법&속담

👤 **PSS & PRACTICE**

☐ 1018 **grateful for**	~를 감사히 여기는
☐ 1019 **learn** [ləːrn]	동 배우다
☐ 1020 **member** [mémbər]	명 회원, 구성원
☐ 1021 **raise** [reiz]	동 모으다
☐ 1022 **donation** [dounéiʃən]	명 기부
☐ 1023 **be ready to**	~할 준비가 되다
☐ 1024 **hope** [houp]	명 희망 / 동 바라다
☐ 1025 **against** [əgénst]	전 ~에 반대하여
☐ 1026 **watch out**	주의하다, 조심하다
☐ 1027 **junk food** [dʒʌ́ŋk fùːd]	명 즉석식품, 정크푸드
☐ 1028 **haste** [heist]	명 서두름
☐ 1029 **waste** [weist]	명 낭비
☐ 1030 **command** [kəmǽnd]	동 명령하다
☐ 1031 **calm** [kaːm]	명 평온함 / 형 차분한
☐ 1032 **thick** [θik]	형 진한, 두꺼운

Day 31

☐ 1033 **strike** [straik] 동 치다, 때리다

☐ 1034 **candle** [kǽndl] 명 양초

☐ 1035 **fear** [fíər] 명 두려움, 공포

☐ 1036 **worth** [wəːrθ] 형 ~의 가치가 있는

☐ 1037 **gather** [gǽðər] 동 모이다, 모으다

☐ 1038 **moss** [mɔːs] 명 이끼

☐ 1039 **mighty** [máiti] 형 강력한

☐ 1040 **sword** [sɔːrd] 명 검, 칼

☐ 1041 **will** [wil] 명 의지

☐ 1042 **bush** [buʃ] 명 덤불

중간기말대비

☐ 1043 **wrath** [ræθ] 명 분노, 노여움

☐ 1044 **keep one's mouth closed** 비밀을 지키다

☐ 1045 **give away** 거저 주다, 수여하다

☐ 1046 **turn up** 나타나다, (소리·온도 등을) 올리다

☐ 1047 **turn away** 물리치다, 외면하다

☐ 1048 **general** [dʒénərəl] 명 장군

☐ 1049 **invitation** [ìnvitéiʃən] 명 초대, 초대장

☐ 1050 **data** [déitə] 명 자료, 정보

☐ 1051 **take up one's time** ~의 시간을 빼앗다

☐ 1052 **goose** [guːs] 명 거위

☐ 1053 **fool** [fuːl] 명 바보

☐ 1054 **roof** [ruːf] 명 지붕

☐ 1055 **envious** [énviəs] 형 부러워하는

☐ 1056 **come close to** 거의 ~하게 되다

☐ 1057 **safely** [séifli] 부 무사히

☐ 1058 **device** [diváis] 명 장치

☐ 1059 **laser** [léizər] 명 레이저

☐ 1060 **image** [ímidʒ] 명 영상, 이미지

☐ 1061 **purpose** [pə́ːrpəs] 명 목적

☐ 1062 **alert** [ələ́ːrt] 동 (위험을) 알리다, 경보를 발하다

☐ 1063 **nearby** [níərbài] 형 인근의, 가까운 곳의

☐ 1064 **lessen** [lésn] 동 줄이다

☐ 1065 **silver lining** [sílvər láiniŋ] 명 구름의 흰 가장자리, 밝은 희망

☐ 1066 **cloudy** [kláudi] 형 날이 흐린

☐ 1067 **cheer up** 격려하다, 힘을 불러일으키다

중학영문법 3800제 2학년

Word Test

Problem Solving Skill

MOTHERTONGUE
마더텅출판사
since 1999. 4. 1.

● 영어를 우리말로 쓰세요.

01	pay
02	homework
03	pass
04	be good at
05	draw
06	leave
07	meeting
08	exam
09	guy
10	vacation
11	favorite
12	during
13	prize
14	arrive
15	take a rest
16	finish
17	cash
18	buy

● 우리말을 영어로 쓰세요.

19	진실인, 사실인
20	스테이크
21	시간에 맞게, 정각에
22	건강한
23	～ 없이
24	(～하다고) 느끼다, (～한) 기분이다
25	운동하다, 운동, 연습
26	돌아오다
27	이기다
28	(～한) 맛이 나다, 맛보다
29	～에 들어가다
30	강아지
31	경주
32	영화를 보러 가다
33	신용카드
34	동급생, 반 친구
35	국수, 면류

날짜: 학급: 이름: 점수   / 36

●영어를 우리말로 쓰세요.

01 | wonder	10 | solve
02 | important	11 | polite
03 | think	12 | ask
04 | right	13 | interesting
05 | friendly	14 | turn
06 | problem	15 | special
07 | mean	16 | appear
08 | patient	17 | strange
09 | terrible	18 | bring

●우리말을 영어로 쓰세요.

19 | 창조적인, 독창적인	28 | 휴식, 안정, 쉬다
20 | 깨뜨리다, 부수다	29 | 잃다, (게임, 경기에) 지다
21 | 대우하다, 다루다	30 | 갑자기
22 | 어제	31 | 질문, 문제
23 | 믿다	32 | 조언, 충고
24 | ~처럼 보이다	33 | 조용한
25 | 데이트하다, 날짜	34 | 나르다, 운반하다
26 | 신, 시큼한	35 | ~하게 되다, 자라다
27 | 빌려주다	36 | 습기 있는

날짜: 학급: 이름: 점수: / 35

●영어를 우리말로 쓰세요.

01	inventor	10	laptop
02	surprising	11	consider
03	grade	12	bulb
04	regularly	13	typewriter
05	include	14	rule
06	bullet	15	iron
07	shake	16	unkind
08	shout	17	upset
09	throw		

●우리말을 영어로 쓰세요.

18	유명한	27	역사
19	가격	28	~처럼 보이다[생기다]
20	~에게 미소를 짓다	29	~을 (더) 좋아하다
21	온도	30	짖다
22	경탄할 만한	31	발명하다
23	기억하다	32	사전
24	어려운, 곤란한	33	(일이) 발생하다
25	보조개	34	건드리다, 만지다
26	축음기	35	땅에 떨어지다

Day 04

<table>
<tr><td>날짜:</td><td>학급:</td><td>이름:</td><td>점수　/34</td></tr>
</table>

●영어를 우리말로 쓰세요.

01 | serious

02 | all the time

03 | neat

04 | spotlessly

05 | depart

06 | lonely

07 | chemistry

08 | semester

09 | bitter

10 | inside

11 | warm

12 | diligent

13 | scream

14 | reward

15 | relax

16 | sleepy

●우리말을 영어로 쓰세요.

17 | 광산

18 | 물리학

19 | 입증하다, 증명하다

20 | 들어 올리다

21 | 줄이다

22 | 맛있는

23 | 현실적인

24 | (아이를) 낳다, 견디다

25 | 재미있는, 우스운

26 | 큰 박수

27 | 발랄한

28 | 복사하다

29 | 파괴하다

30 | (총, 화살을) 쏘다

31 | 물다

32 | 불평하다

33 | 올리다, 기르다

34 | 숨 쉬다, 호흡하다

●영어를 우리말로 쓰세요.

01	recommend	10	exchange
02	serve	11	add
03	allow	12	mention
04	vow	13	admire
05	discover	14	quit
06	imagine	15	argue
07	close	16	appreciate
08	wrap	17	lead
09	suppose	18	in need

●우리말을 영어로 쓰세요.

19	묘사하다	28	엎지르다, 쏟다
20	재활용하다	29	선출하다
21	늘이다, 늘어나다	30	(알을) 까다, 부화하다
22	~와 결혼하다	31	면접을 보다, 면접
23	(땅을) 파다	32	치다, 두드리다
24	구조하다, 구하다	33	기원하다, 기도하다
25	밀다	34	따다, 고르다
26	생산하다	35	싸우다
27	(액체, 기체, 전류가) 흐르다	36	가라앉다

Word Test 177-212 — Day 06

날짜: 학급: 이름: 점수   /36

● 영어를 우리말로 쓰세요.

01	control	10	rip
02	consist	11	rush
03	reply	12	delay
04	indeed	13	worry
05	chat	14	around
06	blame	15	realize
07	practice	16	fix
08	offer	17	cause
09	notice	18	select

● 우리말을 영어로 쓰세요.

19	공표하다, 출판하다	28	숙이다, 절하다
20	관찰하다	29	받아쓰게 하다
21	떨어뜨리다, 떨어지다	30	죽다
22	(해, 달이) 뜨다, 오르다	31	형성하다
23	발로 차다	32	당기다
24	연장, 도구	33	낭비하다
25	튀어나오다	34	재판하다, 판단하다
26	작동하다, 수술을 하다	35	모으다, 수집하다
27	사라지다	36	괴롭히다, 놀리다

날짜:　　　　학급:　　　　이름:　　　　점수　　/ 36

●영어를 우리말로 쓰세요.

01	contest	10	tumble
02	blow	11	painting
03	burn	12	report
04	lay	13	deny
05	share	14	fill
06	sweep	15	build
07	be born	16	roll
08	join	17	cheat
09	show	18	remove

●우리말을 영어로 쓰세요.

19	훔치다	28	빛나다
20	닫다	29	행동하다
21	직면하다, 마주하다	30	되풀이하다
22	극복하다	31	기념하다, 축하하다
23	따라가다, 따르다	32	때리다, 치다
24	한밤중, 자정	33	숨기다
25	집안일	34	격려하다, 장려하다
26	말하기, 연설	35	눕다, 놓여 있다
27	넘어지다, 떨어지다	36	(손에) 들다, 잡다

날짜: 학급: 이름: 점수   / 35

●영어를 우리말로 쓰세요.

01	a lot		10	recently
02	send		11	sure
03	nervous		12	climbing
04	spend		13	empty
05	prejudice		14	fable
06	flight		15	parent
07	pass away		16	several
08	stand		17	set up
09	hurt		18	leave for

●우리말을 영어로 쓰세요.

19	일기를 쓰다		28	심하게, 대량으로, 무겁게
20	~로 가는 도중에		29	낮잠을 자다
21	암탉		30	배우
22	식물, 초목		31	인기 있는
23	선장		32	꽃병
24	쓸모 있는, 유용한		33	요즘에, 최근에
25	자부심, 자만, 긍지		34	~에서 출발하다
26	극장		35	지갑, (서류를 넣는 납작한) 가방
27	샤워를 하다			

날짜:　　　　　　학급:　　　　　　이름:　　　　　　점수　　　/ 34

●영어를 우리말로 쓰세요.

01	elderly
02	feed
03	language
04	exit
05	bud
06	notebook
07	statue
08	hang
09	zoo
10	horror
11	seed
12	thief
13	give an answer
14	liberty
15	take off
16	mobile phone
17	take care of

●우리말을 영어로 쓰세요.

18	몰래 잠입하다
19	산책 가다
20	조심스럽게, 신중하게
21	태우러 가다, 태우다
22	대학교
23	찾다
24	산책시키다, 걷다
25	에스컬레이터
26	주차하다
27	횡단하다
28	첫 번째의
29	요리, 접시
30	안전한
31	백화점
32	다이어트를 하다
33	진실
34	피를 흘리다

날짜:　　　　　　학급:　　　　　　이름:　　　　　　점수　　　/ 35

● 영어를 우리말로 쓰세요.

01	unbelievable	10	bright
02	kind	11	handicapped
03	get lost	12	favor
04	possible	13	midterm
05	accident	14	shopper
06	stadium	15	school uniform
07	look around	16	throat
08	koala	17	by oneself
09	competition	18	go out

● 우리말을 영어로 쓰세요.

19	시끄럽게 하다	28	상을 받다
20	잘하다, 성공하다	29	(소리, 온도 등을) 낮추다
21	아픈, 쓰린	30	생계 수단, 생활
22	가까운, 근처의	31	(시간 단위의) 초
23	심부름	32	확신하는, 확실한
24	최선을 다하다	33	이번에도, 다시 한 번
25	미래	34	팔다
26	짠, 짭짤한	35	기억
27	~의 부탁을 들어주다		

●영어를 우리말로 쓰세요.

01	turn right		10	bottle
02	call		11	obey
03	plan		12	change
04	prepare		13	resource
05	keep		14	catch
06	joy		15	result
07	hold		16	understand
08	play		17	postpone
09	director			

●우리말을 영어로 쓰세요.

18	거짓말, 거짓말하다		27	정보
19	말, 단어		28	베어내다
20	잡지		29	용서하다
21	복사기		30	사냥꾼
22	사랑스러운, 아름다운		31	오염시키다
23	대통령, 회장		32	직무, 과제
24	존경하다		33	계산서, 청구서
25	경치		34	눈물
26	배달하다			

날짜: 학급: 이름: 점수   / 33

● 영어를 우리말로 쓰세요.

01 | canned

02 | resemble

03 | experiment

04 | rob

05 | mystery

06 | conference

07 | surround

08 | activity

09 | neighbor

10 | ferry

11 | ruin

12 | penny

13 | custom

14 | classroom

15 | firefighter

16 | poem

● 우리말을 영어로 쓰세요.

17 | 다수의, 한 묶음의

18 | ~에게 맞다, 어울리다

19 | 당나귀

20 | 문화

21 | 시장, 군수

22 | 이론

23 | 긴 의자, 소파

24 | 성냥, 경기, 시합

25 | 발표하다, 공개하다

26 | 반지

27 | 공장

28 | 고무

29 | 우표

30 | ~에 이름을 지어주다

31 | 개인의, 개인적인

32 | 열리다, 개최되다

33 | 학장, 교장

날짜:　　　학급:　　　이름:　　　점수　　/ 36

●영어를 우리말로 쓰세요.

01 | cheerful

02 | furniture

03 | policy

04 | across

05 | look forward to

06 | express

07 | sheep

08 | beauty

09 | tax

10 | take part in

11 | audience

12 | autumn

13 | knowledge

14 | death

15 | while

16 | politics

17 | shocking

18 | support

●우리말을 영어로 쓰세요.

19 | 모기

20 | 수단, 방법

21 | 공동체, 지역사회

22 | 경제학

23 | 금고, 안전한

24 | 주제

25 | 장(長), 상사

26 | 친절, 호의

27 | 비상사태

28 | 지진

29 | 영웅

30 | 세관

31 | 송아지

32 | 도심지의, 도심지

33 | 정직

34 | 여행을 가다

35 | 황소

36 | 믿음, 신조

Word Test 456 - 490

날짜:　　학급:　　이름:　　점수　　/ 35

●영어를 우리말로 쓰세요.

01 | feather

02 | toast

03 | carelessly

04 | interest

05 | walk

06 | bottom

07 | comfortable

08 | borrow

09 | tend to

10 | in a moment

11 | goods

12 | very

13 | the other day

14 | government

15 | fact

16 | scenery

17 | impossible

●우리말을 영어로 쓰세요.

18 | 외국의

19 | 평평한

20 | 고래

21 | 심리학, 심리

22 | 독특한

23 | 낯선 사람

24 | 담요

25 | 교수

26 | 퇴직하다

27 | 수업, 교훈

28 | (국가의) 수도

29 | 떼, 무리, 모이다

30 | 우주선

31 | 여자 조카

32 | 손으로 만든

33 | 성적표

34 | 열, 줄

35 | 선원, 뱃사람

날짜:	학급:	이름:	점수	/ 34

●영어를 우리말로 쓰세요.

01 | lawyer

02 | piece

03 | title

04 | innocent

05 | spoonful

06 | noisy

07 | loaf

08 | cucumber

09 | musical instrument

10 | fail

11 | slice

12 | marathon

13 | pork

14 | loudly

15 | bowl

16 | plain

17 | pound

●우리말을 영어로 쓰세요.

18 | ～을 통하여

19 | 무시하다

20 | 적어도

21 | 중요성

22 | 냉장하다

23 | 표지

24 | 젓다, 섞다

25 | 양념하다

26 | (검은) 후추

27 | 우연히

28 | ～에 발을 딛다

29 | ～을 자랑스러워하다

30 | 충성스러운

31 | ～에 통달하다

32 | 정직한

33 | 실현되다

34 | (잘게) 갈다

Day 16

날짜: 학급: 이름: 점수   / 35

●영어를 우리말로 쓰세요.

01	make oneself at home	10	suggestion
02	wait for	11	always
03	disappointing	12	treasure
04	throw away	13	be known for
05	club	14	chance
06	care	15	logo
07	all of a sudden	16	author
08	correctly	17	drop by
09	fiction		

●우리말을 영어로 쓰세요.

18	천, 옷감	27	(온도, 각도 단위) 도, 정도
19	거울	28	쌍둥이 중 한 명, 쌍둥이의
20	우정	29	12개, 12개짜리 한 묶음
21	비싼	30	소개하다
22	예, 예시	31	풍선
23	인구	32	천문학자
24	옷장	33	성공하다
25	피고용자, 종업원	34	공연, 연주
26	승객	35	흡연하다

날짜: 학급: 이름: 점수: / 36

●영어를 우리말로 쓰세요.

01	be afraid of		10	save
02	astronaut		11	pollution
03	fluently		12	minute
04	climate		13	burn
05	tiny		14	divide up
06	look after		15	homeroom
07	boil		16	for sale
08	spicy		17	own
09	same		18	dentist

●우리말을 영어로 쓰세요.

19	빤히 쳐다보다		28	우주, 공간
20	바이올린		29	장갑
21	고장 나다		30	~하곤 했다
22	할로윈		31	~와 함께 살다
23	자주색의, 보라색의		32	주제, 화제
24	연예인		33	의견
25	우산		34	텐트를 치다
26	(창문에 치는) 블라인드		35	백합
27	만화책		36	찻주전자

날짜:　　　　　　학급:　　　　　　이름:　　　　　　점수　　　/34

●영어를 우리말로 쓰세요.

01 | enough

02 | cheap

03 | confusing

04 | expect

05 | reach

06 | explain

07 | disappointed

08 | repair

09 | protect

10 | jacket

11 | pleased

12 | surprised

13 | garage sale

14 | trust

15 | refuse

16 | generous

17 | clearly

●우리말을 영어로 쓰세요.

18 | 운 좋은

19 | 시력

20 | 나비

21 | 농작물

22 | 선반

23 | 인터넷 서핑을 하다

24 | (고개를) 끄덕이다

25 | 대학, 단과대학

26 | 기말고사

27 | 음악가

28 | 위층으로, 위층에(서)

29 | 결심하다

30 | (자동차의) 앞 유리

31 | 문제, 일

32 | 필수적인, 없어서는 안 될

33 | 유인하다, 끌어당기다

34 | 조깅하다

날짜:　　　학급:　　　이름:　　　점수　　/ 33

●영어를 우리말로 쓰세요.

01	continue
02	depress
03	refresh
04	put off
05	dangerous
06	design
07	chairman
08	skip
09	saving
10	license
11	dislike
12	course
13	business
14	apologize
15	have dinner
16	pass the exam

●우리말을 영어로 쓰세요.

17	시골, 지방
18	쓰레기
19	잠시 동안
20	일찍 일어나다
21	신경 쓰다, 꺼려하다
22	돌고래
23	밖에서, 옥외로
24	가면, 복면
25	도움이 되는
26	도서관
27	노력
28	우체국
29	거만한, 자랑스러워하는
30	끝나다, 끝내다
31	깊은
32	탁구
33	(벨, 종이) 울리다

날짜:　　　　학급:　　　　이름:　　　　점수　　/ 33

●영어를 우리말로 쓰세요.

01 | debate

02 | prevent

03 | violate

04 | usually

05 | interrupt

06 | plant

07 | responsible

08 | regulation

09 | package

10 | depressing

11 | recent

12 | difficulty

13 | postcard

14 | grow up

15 | major

16 | illness

●우리말을 영어로 쓰세요.

17 | 결국에

18 | 디저트, 후식

19 | ~을 돌보다

20 | 교통

21 | 용돈

22 | (소리 내어) 웃다

23 | 삶은, 끓은

24 | 무식한, 무지한

25 | 떨어지다

26 | (전등, 기계 등을) 켜다

27 | 산책하다

28 | 주유소

29 | 균형 잡힌

30 | 일정, 스케줄

31 | (기계 등을) 개선하다

32 | 사랑에 빠지다

33 | (~로) 가득 차다, 채우다

●영어를 우리말로 쓰세요.

01	restroom		10	festival
02	cross		11	embarrass
03	shed		12	public
04	excited		13	cartoon
05	pot		14	gym
06	puzzle		15	fall asleep
07	beside		16	satisfy
08	amaze		17	fantastic
09	amusement park			

●우리말을 영어로 쓰세요.

18	결국에는		27	무대, 단계
19	식수		28	묶다, 매다
20	~을 치우다, 청소하다		29	실수로
21	해변, 바닷가		30	감동시키다
22	유형, 종류		31	후라이팬
23	에세이, 수필		32	휴가, 방학
24	도망치다		33	~로 가득 차다
25	주인, 소유주			
26	잔디, 풀			

날짜: 학급: 이름: 점수 / 33

● 영어를 우리말로 쓰세요.

01 | experience

02 | intonation

03 | collection

04 | proverb

05 | asleep

06 | rich

07 | unpleasant

08 | familiar

09 | trendy

10 | depressed

11 | brave

12 | refrigerator

13 | blind

14 | alike

15 | wrong

16 | daughter

17 | fitness center

● 우리말을 영어로 쓰세요.

18 | 부끄러워하는, 수치스러운

19 | 살아 있는

20 | 100만의, 100만

21 | 많음, 풍부

22 | 체중이 증가하다

23 | 지적인, 총명한

24 | 겁에 질린

25 | 잘생긴

26 | ~을 제외하고

27 | 귀가 먼

28 | 불가사리

29 | 스트레스를 받다

30 | 목걸이

31 | (책의) 장

32 | 금속

33 | 인상적인, 인상 깊은

날짜: 학급: 이름: 점수   / 35

● 영어를 우리말로 쓰세요.

01	shake hands		10	slow
02	sincere		11	call off
03	impressed		12	nearly
04	closely		13	take out
05	still		14	hardly
06	highly		15	deeply
07	admission		16	anxious
08	final		17	such
09	look for		18	check out

● 우리말을 영어로 쓰세요.

19	간단한, 단순한		28	인사하다, 환영하다
20	짓궂은, 비열한		29	입어 보다
21	지속되다		30	눈에 보이는
22	시원한, 서늘한		31	합리적인, 타당한
23	쉽게, 용이하게		32	갑작스러운, 뜻밖의
24	의도, 목적		33	술, 알코올
25	약간의, 근소한		34	온화한, 친절한
26	졸업하다		35	포기하다
27	참석하다, 출석하다			

날짜:　　　학급:　　　이름:　　　점수　　/ 33

●영어를 우리말로 쓰세요.

01 | be able to
02 | interview
03 | quickly
04 | set up
05 | discuss
06 | youth
07 | as if
08 | lecture
09 | fly

10 | visit
11 | item
12 | be in danger
13 | bomb
14 | cell phone
15 | successful
16 | invite
17 | station

●우리말을 영어로 쓰세요.

18 | 실은, 사실
19 | 공짜로, 무료로
20 | ~를 태워주다
21 | 열심히 하는, 단단한, 어려운
22 | 폭발하다
23 | 꽃을 피우다
24 | 전시, 표현
25 | 시험에 통과하다

26 | 교회
27 | ~에게 알리다
28 | 피부
29 | 설거지하다
30 | 살이 빠지다
31 | (물건을) 쌓다
32 | 불꽃놀이, 폭죽
33 | 벚꽃

●영어를 우리말로 쓰세요.

01	present	10	count
02	tasty	11	version
03	especially	12	mild
04	curious	13	convenient
05	transportation	14	save
06	write back to	15	exactly
07	boring	16	wise
08	kindly	17	thin
09	per		

●우리말을 영어로 쓰세요.

18	무게가 ~ 나가다	27	명성
19	무서운, 두려운	28	높이, 키
20	활동적인, 적극적인	29	쓸모없는
21	기린	30	젖은
22	거북	31	글, 기사
23	수명	32	발명품, 발명
24	창백한	33	바보 같은
25	생산물, 상품		
26	코끼리		

날짜:　　　　학급:　　　　이름:　　　　점수　　/34

●영어를 우리말로 쓰세요.

01	technique
02	cancel
03	village
04	disappoint
05	stove
06	judge
07	suggest
08	do harm
09	eat up
10	heritage
11	pocket
12	environment
13	focus on
14	site
15	sharp
16	magic
17	project

●우리말을 영어로 쓰세요.

18	~에 속하다, ~의 것이다
19	가르치다
20	거리, 도로
21	탁자
22	돌, 비석
23	(불을) 끄다
24	화가
25	젓가락
26	지도자
27	이유, 동기
28	다큐멘터리, 기록물
29	수여하다
30	경찰관
31	인삼
32	무덤
33	사람, 개인
34	할인 중인

날짜:　　　　　학급:　　　　　이름:　　　　　점수　　/ 33

● 영어를 우리말로 쓰세요.

01	advertiser	10	successfully
02	communicate	11	instead of
03	pity	12	quite
04	absent	13	pool
05	unhappy	14	earn
06	garbage	15	political
07	customer	16	activist
08	lecturer	17	dump
09	trick		

● 우리말을 영어로 쓰세요.

18	학사 학위	26	교통 정체
19	폭설	27	(차량을) 타다
20	～하기 위해	28	영양가 높은
21	입다	29	곤란한 상황에 있다
22	아침 식사	30	전화로 얘기하다
23	머리를 감다	31	오늘밤에
24	(빵 등을) 굽다	32	빨래를 하다
25	롤러코스터	33	서두르다

Word Test 930 - 963　　Day 28

날짜:　　　　학급:　　　　이름:　　　　점수　　/ 34

● 영어를 우리말로 쓰세요.

01 | amount

02 | unusual

03 | resign

04 | eventually

05 | discovery

06 | look up

07 | bridge

08 | attain

09 | western

10 | luckily

11 | concentrate

12 | adopt

13 | feeling

14 | order

15 | in addition

16 | substance

17 | be compared to

● 우리말을 영어로 쓰세요.

18 | ~에서 나가다, ~에서 내리다

19 | 계단, 층계

20 | 현대적인, 현대의

21 | 중앙, 한가운데의, 중앙의

22 | 환영하다, 환영

23 | 지나다, 지나치다

24 | 감옥, 교도소

25 | 섬

26 | 동전, 주화

27 | 목적, 목표

28 | 비행기

29 | 상사

30 | 마루, 층

31 | 2등, 준우승

32 | 일하는 중인, 직장에서

33 | 해질녘, 일몰

34 | 오류, 실수

●영어를 우리말로 쓰세요.

01 | row

02 | in a hurry

03 | corner

04 | response

05 | relationship

06 | in half

07 | flour

08 | keep in touch

09 | unlock

10 | be supposed to

11 | novel

12 | start

13 | manner

14 | tower

15 | dressed

16 | serve

17 | stick

●우리말을 영어로 쓰세요.

18 | 시차

19 | 봉투

20 | 전통의, 전통적인

21 | 굶주림, 기아

22 | 스케치하다

23 | 바위

24 | 암

25 | 숲

26 | 민속 음악

27 | 경영자, 관리자

28 | 우체통

29 | 낭만적인

30 | 가로등

31 | 어릿광대

32 | 뛰다, 뛰어오르다

33 | 사다리

34 | (배, 비행기 등에) 승선하다, 탑승하다

35 | 주소

<table>
<tr><td colspan="2">날짜:</td><td>학급:</td><td>이름:</td><td>점수</td><td>/ 34</td></tr>
</table>

●영어를 우리말로 쓰세요.

01	donation	10	entrance
02	frame	11	due
03	hope	12	bead
04	haste	13	ideal
05	patent	14	participate
06	against	15	utopian
07	raise	16	anti
08	existence	17	construct
09	emigration		

●우리말을 영어로 쓰세요.

18	명령하다	27	앞으로, 앞에
19	회원, 구성원	28	연방 정부의
20	홍수	29	~할 준비가 되다
21	낭비	30	배우다
22	평온함, 차분한	31	주의하다, 조심하다
23	진한, 두꺼운	32	모국어
24	즉석식품, 정크푸드	33	여권
25	~를 감사히 여기는	34	원자의, 원자력의
26	야생의		

날짜: 학급: 이름: 점수   / 35

●영어를 우리말로 쓰세요.

01	purpose
02	invitation
03	lessen
04	take up one's time
05	turn up
06	device
07	turn away
08	alert
09	sword
10	roof
11	give away
12	fool
13	general
14	envious
15	keep one's mouth closed
16	nearby
17	safely

●우리말을 영어로 쓰세요.

18	두려움, 공포
19	분노, 노여움
20	강력한
21	의지
22	자료, 정보
23	영상, 이미지
24	날이 흐린
25	구름의 흰 가장자리, 밝은 희망
26	～의 가치가 있는
27	레이저
28	격려하다, 힘을 불러일으키다
29	모이다, 모으다
30	양초
31	거의 ～하게 되다
32	덤불
33	이끼
34	거위
35	치다, 때리다

16차 개정판 중학영문법 3800제 2학년 학습계획표

DAY	Ch	학습내용	학습날짜		DAY	Ch	학습내용	학습날짜
DAY 1	1	PSS 1-1 ~ 1-4	월 일		DAY 31	9	PSS 1 ~ 3	월 일
DAY 2		PSS 1-5 ~ 1-8	월 일		DAY 32		PSS 4 ~ 5-2	월 일
DAY 3		PSS 2-1 ~ 2-6	월 일		DAY 33		중간·기말고사 대비문제	월 일
DAY 4		중간·기말고사 대비문제	월 일		DAY 34	10	PSS 1 ~ 4	월 일
DAY 5	2	PSS 1-1 ~ 2-4	월 일		DAY 35		PSS 5-1 ~ 5-4	월 일
DAY 6		PSS 3 ~ 4-2	월 일		DAY 36		PSS 6-1 ~ 6-3	월 일
DAY 7		PSS 5-1 ~ 5-5	월 일		DAY 37		중간·기말고사 대비문제	월 일
DAY 8		중간·기말고사 대비문제	월 일		DAY 38	11	PSS 1-1 ~ 1-4	월 일
DAY 9	3	PSS 1 ~ 4-4	월 일		DAY 39		PSS 2-1 ~ 2-7	월 일
DAY 10		PSS 4-5 ~ 4-9	월 일		DAY 40		중간·기말고사 대비문제	월 일
DAY 11		중간·기말고사 대비문제	월 일		DAY 41	12	PSS 1 ~ 2-3	월 일
DAY 12	4	PSS 1 ~ 2	월 일		DAY 42		PSS 3-1 ~ 3-3	월 일
DAY 13		PSS 3 ~ 4	월 일		DAY 43		중간·기말고사 대비문제	월 일
DAY 14		PSS 5 ~ 7	월 일		DAY 44	13	PSS 1-1 ~ 1-4	월 일
DAY 15		중간·기말고사 대비문제	월 일		DAY 45		PSS 2-1 ~ 3-6	월 일
DAY 16	5	PSS 1-1 ~ 1-3	월 일		DAY 46		PSS 4-1 ~ 4-3	월 일
DAY 17		PSS 2-1 ~ 2-7	월 일		DAY 47		중간·기말고사 대비문제	월 일
DAY 18		PSS 3-1 ~ 5	월 일		DAY 48	14	PSS 1-1 ~ 1-4	월 일
DAY 19		중간·기말고사 대비문제	월 일		DAY 49		PSS 1-5 ~ 2-2	월 일
DAY 20	6	PSS 1-1 ~ 2-3	월 일		DAY 50		중간·기말고사 대비문제	월 일
DAY 21		PSS 3-1 ~ 4-3	월 일		DAY 51	15	PSS 1 ~ 5	월 일
DAY 22		PSS 4-4 ~ 5-2	월 일		DAY 52		PSS 6 ~ 10	월 일
DAY 23		중간·기말고사 대비문제	월 일		DAY 53		중간·기말고사 대비문제	월 일
DAY 24	7	PSS 1-1 ~ 1-4	월 일		DAY 54	16	PSS 1-1 ~ 1-6	월 일
DAY 25		PSS 2 ~ 3-2	월 일		DAY 55		PSS 2-1 ~ 2-6	월 일
DAY 26		PSS 4 ~ 6	월 일		DAY 56		PSS 2-7 ~ 3-4	월 일
DAY 27		중간·기말고사 대비문제	월 일		DAY 57		중간·기말고사 대비문제	월 일
DAY 28	8	PSS 1 ~ 2-3	월 일		DAY 58	17	PSS 1-1 ~ 3	월 일
DAY 29		PSS 3 ~ 4	월 일		DAY 59		PSS 4 ~ 6	월 일
DAY 30		중간·기말고사 대비문제	월 일		DAY 60		중간·기말고사 대비문제	월 일

2026 제6기 마더텅 중학교 학습수기 공모전 안내

대상 **100** 만 원

금상 **20** 만 원

은상 **10** 만 원

 지원 자격 및 장학금

중1·중2·중3

지원 과목 국어 / 영어 중 1과목 이상 지원 가능

※여러 과목 지원 시 가산점이 부여됩니다.

성적 기준 아래 2가지 항목 중 1개 이상의 조건에 해당하면 지원 가능

① 2025년 2학기 중간·기말고사 또는 2026년 1학기 중간·기말고사 성적표

② 2025년 7월~ 2026년 6월 시행 중학생 대상 국어/영어 해당 인증시험 성적표

　책과함께 KBS한국어능력시험, J-ToKL, 전국 영어 학력경시대회, TOEIC, TOEFL, G-TELP, TOSEL

위 조건에 해당한다면

마더텅 중학 교재로 공부하면서 **느낀 점**과 **공부 방법, 학업 성취, 성적 변화** 등에 관한 자신만의 수기를 작성해서 마더텅으로 보내 주세요. 우수한 글을 보내 주신 분들께 **학습수기 공모 장학금**을 드립니다!

응모 대상　마더텅 중학 교재로 공부한 중1·중2·중3

뿌리깊은 중학국어 독해력, 중학영문법 3800제, 중학영문법 3800제 스타터, 중학영문법 3800제 중간·기말고사 대비편, 중학영문법 3800제 워크북, 중학영문법 3800제 쓰기 WRITING, 마더텅 100% 실전대비 MP3 중학영어듣기 24회 모의고사, 중학영단어 9000, 문법별/주제별로 정리한 중학 영어 독해 101 및 기타 교재 중 1권 이상 신청 가능

응모 방법

① 마더텅 홈페이지 커뮤니티 - 이벤트 게시판에 접속

② [2026 마더텅 중학교 학습수기 공모전 게시글] 클릭 후 [2026 마더텅 중학교 학습수기 공모전 첨부 파일]을 다운

③ [2026 마더텅 중학교 학습수기 공모전 지원서] 작성 후 메일(mothert.marketing@gmail.com)로 발송

접수 기한 2026년 7월 31일　**수상자 발표일** 2026년 8월 17일　**장학금 수여일** 2026년 9월 17일

※세부 일정은 당사 사정에 따라 변경될 수 있습니다.

영어의 8품사

		예문
명사	**사람, 사물, 동물의 이름**을 나타내는 말 → 주어, 목적어, 보어 예) Jane, Mr. Brown, desk, chair, computer, bag, dog, bird	This **computer** looks new. 이 컴퓨터는 새것처럼 보인다. I have a **dog**. 나는 개가 한 마리 있다.
대명사	명사를 **대신**하는 말 → 주어, 목적어, 보어 예) I, my, you, he, she, it, them, we, myself, yourself, ourselves	Look at the dog! **It** is cute. 개 좀 봐! 그것은 귀여워. I'm proud of **myself**. 나는 내 자신이 자랑스럽다.
동사	**행위, 동작, 상태를 묘사**하며 '~다'로 해석되는 말 → 서술어 - 일반동사: 주로 움직임을 나타내며 '~하다'라고 해석 　예) walk, run, eat, study, play, make, buy, love, like - be동사: 상태나 위치를 주로 묘사하며 '~이다'라고 해석 　예) am, are, is, was, were	We **eat** dinner at 7. 우리는 7시에 저녁을 먹는다. She **loves** her daughter. 그녀는 그녀의 딸을 사랑한다. I **am** an artist. 나는 예술가이다.
형용사	**명사**를 꾸미거나 보충 설명하는 말 → 수식어, 보어 **생김새, 색깔, 크기, 성격, 특징**을 묘사하는 말 예) pretty, beautiful, red, tall, big, small, nice, kind, easy, difficult	She has **big** eyes. 그녀는 큰 눈을 가지고 있다. He is a **kind** boy. 그는 친절한 소년이다. The book is **easy**. 그 책은 쉽다.
부사	**형용사, 동사, 다른 부사, 문장 전체**를 자세히 설명하여 문장의 의미를 더욱 풍부하게 하는 말 → 수식어 **시간, 장소, 정도, 빈도**를 묘사하는 말 예) now, here, very, well, always, early, really, happily, sadly	What are you doing **now**? 지금 뭐 하고 있어? Your sister is **very** pretty. 네 언니는 무척 예쁘다. We **really** enjoyed the party. 우리는 정말 그 파티를 즐겼다.
접속사	**단어와 단어, 구와 구, 절과 절**을 이어주는 말 - 등위접속사: **같은 종류**의 말을 연결 　예) and, but, or, so - 종속접속사: **명사절, 부사절, 형용사절**을 **주절**에 연결 　예) because, when, as, if	She is old **and** wise. 그녀는 나이가 있고 지혜롭다. I slept early, **because** I was tired. 나는 피곤했기 때문에 일찍 잤다.
전치사	명사 앞에서 **시간, 장소, 방향, 위치**를 나타내는 말 예) at, on, in, before, after, under, from, to, for, with, between, in front of	I sleep **at** 11 p.m. 나는 밤 11시에 잔다. Your pen is **under** the chair. 네 펜은 의자 밑에 있다. Let's meet **in front of** the building. 건물 앞에서 만나자.
감탄사	**감정**을 표현하는 말 예) Oh, Wow, Well	**Wow**, you got a new phone! 와, 너 새로운 전화기를 샀구나!

		예문
단어	의미를 지니는 **말의 최소 단위** 명사, 대명사, 동사, 형용사, 부사, 전치사, 접속사, 감탄사로 나눌 수 있음	He lied to all of us. 그는 우리 모두에게 거짓말을 했다.
구	완결된 의미를 가지고 있는 두 단어 이상의 모음으로 **주어와 동사를 포함하지 않음** - 명사구 → 주어, 목적어, 보어 - 형용사구 → 명사 수식 - 부사구 → 동사, 형용사, 다른 부사, 문장 전체 수식	There is a pencil on the desk. 책상 위에 연필이 있다. Thank you for helping me. 나를 도와주어서 고마워.
절	완결된 의미를 가지고 있는 두 단어 이상의 모음으로 **주어와 동사를 반드시 포함** - 대등절: 등위접속사로 연결된 대등한 절 - 종속절: 주절에 종속접속사로 연결되어 명사, 형용사, 부사의 역할을 함	She got very angry, but she tried not to show it. 그녀는 매우 화가 났지만, 그것을 보이려고 하지 않았다. Please let me know if he is kind. 그가 친절한지 아닌지 내게 알려 줘.
주어	동작이나 상태의 **주체**를 가리키는 말	She arrived at her office. 그녀는 그녀의 사무실에 도착했다.
동사	주어의 **동작이나 상태**를 나타내는 말	He is a nurse. 그는 간호사이다. They call her an angel. 그들은 그녀를 천사라 부른다.
목적어	동작이나 상태의 **대상**을 가리키는 말	I put this rabbit in the hat. 나는 모자에 이 토끼를 넣는다.
보어	주어나 목적어를 **보충 설명**해 주는 말	I want to become a teacher. 나는 선생님이 되고 싶다. He forced me to hurry. 그는 내가 서두르도록 강요했다.
수식어	문장의 주요 성분을 **부연 설명**하는 역할 생략해도 문법적인 오류를 일으키지 않음	You look pretty tired. 너 꽤 피곤해 보여.